STANDARD LESSON COMMENTARY 1992-93

International Sunday School Lessons

published by

STANDARD PUBLISHING

Eugene H. Wigginton, *Publisher*

Richard C. McKinley, *Director of Curriculum Development*

James I. Fehl, *Editor*

Hela M. Campbell, *Office Editor*

Fortieth Annual Volume

The STANDARD PUBLISHING Company
division of STANDEX INTERNATIONAL Corporation
8121 Hamilton Avenue, Cincinnati, Ohio 45231
Printed in U.S.A.

In This Volume

Autumn Quarter, 1992 (page 1)

Theme: Old Testament Personalities

Writers

ORRIN ROOT, Lesson Development
CHARLES R. BOATMAN, Verbal Illustrations
MIKE MCCANN, Learning by Doing
KENTON K. SMITH, Let's Talk It Over

Winter Quarter, 1992-93 (page 113)

Theme: Good News for All

Writers

JOHN W. WADE, Lesson Development
THOMAS D. THURMAN, Verbal Illustrations
ELEANOR DANIEL, Learning by Doing
JOE SUTHERLAND, Let's Talk It Over

Spring Quarter, 1993 (page 225)

Theme: Believing in Christ

Writers

S. EDWARD TESH, Lesson Development
RICHARD W. BAYNES, Verbal Illustrations
DANIEL SCHANTZ, Learning by Doing
KENTON K. SMITH, Let's Talk It Over

Summer Quarter, 1993 (page 337)

Theme: Following God's Purpose

Writers

KNOFEL STATON, Lesson Development
WOODROW PHILLIPS, Verbal Illustrations
MARK A. TAYLOR, Learning by Doing
ROBERT CHITWOOD (1-4), DAVID W. WEAD (5-8), DEBORAH SUE BRUNSMAN (9-13), Let's Talk It Over

Artists

JAMES E. SEWARD, Title Pages; NED OSTENDORF, Lesson Illustrations; ROBERT E. HUFFMAN, Maps

Cover design by Gottry Advertising & Marketing, Inc.

Index of Printed Texts, 1992-93

The printed texts for 1992-93 are arranged here in the order in which they appear in the Bible. Opposite each reference is the number of the page on which it appears in this volume.

Use Methods of Expression

WHEN WE LEARN TO DRIVE an automobile, play the piano, or make a cake, we may hear someone tell us how it is done, or we may read how it is to be done. We may even see someone else do it, but we still do not know how to drive an automobile, play the piano, or make a cake. We must do it ourselves. The more we do it, the better we do it. Practice makes perfect. This is known as learning by doing, or by participation, or as educators say it, learning by impression plus expression.

When someone tells us or shows us, we are learning by impression. When we do it, we learn by expression. Both methods are necessary. (In the preceding chapter, we considered the more common methods of teaching by impression.)

Applied to teaching in the Sunday school, the expression method means that the teacher must gain the participation of the pupil. In the pupil's mind, consciously or unconsciously, is the principle of "Use me or lose me." The teacher leads the pupil to learn by getting him to participate in the class session and then to practice in daily life the principles learned in the Bible class. The pupil learns by participating in the learning process.

Whether the aim of the lesson is for an understanding of the Bible or the application of Bible truth to life, the pupil must participate actively and know that it is for a purpose. The pupil's activity may be easily observed such as participation in a discussion. Or the activity may be largely mental, such as thinking through a proposition presented by the teacher, solving a problem, or arriving at a general conclusion.

A class is much like a fruit tree—some pupils are ripe and ready to understand what is being taught, some are nearly ripe, others are only partly ripe, and some are entirely green. The teacher cannot plan for the advanced pupil or for the entirely green pupil, but he must plan to engage the participation of everyone. The teacher will learn which methods are most effective after he studies the pupils and after he has tried several methods.

Activate Thinking

The purpose of pupil participation is the teacher's constant aim—to get the pupil to think. Merely to give the pupil something to do to occupy the time is a sinful waste of opportunity. For example, engaging the minds of an adult class by means of an interesting illustration is wasted time unless the illustration bears directly on the purpose of the lesson and will be effective in accomplishing that purpose.

When a pupil reproduces in his own mind the truth being taught, he is learning. He is not learning until he participates in this manner.

Merely pouring out knowledge is not teaching. The teacher who talks on and on, telling what he knows without arousing mental response, is wasting his time and the pupil's time. He is getting nowhere.

Nor is true learning mere memorization and repetition of the words of the teacher, of a quarterly, or, for that matter, of the Bible. Catechism may have its merits as a method of imparting truth. For children, particularly those in the elementary grades, memorization is recommended. But catechism alone is not education. It is memorization.

A pupil is sometimes said to have learned the lesson when he has committed it to memory and can repeat or recite it word for word. Education would be simple if this were true. It is not true, however; when the pupil is merely reciting, he is not participating at his most productive level.

The teacher's aim is to teach the pupil not only the words, but the thought of Scripture. In teaching the Bible, it is important to know and to remember words, but it is even more important to know and to remember the lesson thought.

Advancing in Participation

The pupil is to be encouraged to express the lesson truth in his own words. Sometimes the thought will be expressed crudely. The capable teacher will pardon the pupil's inability to express the thought acceptably while he encourages the pupil to think more accurately in order to express himself more adequately.

As the pupil advances in participation, he will give a reason for that which he believes. He will discover a truth, seek proof for that which he has discovered, voice these proofs, and thus become a stronger believer than the one who believes but does not know why or who cannot explain why. The Bible teaches that we are to find out for ourselves if these truths are so. The pupil will take a stronger hold of the truth if he can see a reason for it. In searching for proof, the pupil also encounters new knowledge on the way, just like the mountain climber who finds the landscape always widening around him. The teacher's effort to encourage the pupil to seek out proof for a truth that is taught is made effective when the learner participates by telling of the proof that he has discovered.

The participating pupil's next advancement is found in the study of the application of knowledge. Having his mind stirred by the presentation of a truth, then seeking and discovering verification of that truth, he next applies the truth to his own life. What was idle knowledge now becomes practical wisdom. The learning process is completed when this stage is reached.

Summing up this process of participation, the teacher is to:

1. Help the pupil to understand clearly the lesson aim.
2. Get him to express in his own words (or in his own thoughts) the meaning of the lesson as he understands it.
3. Aim to make the pupil an investigator, finding for himself whether a certain statement is true, and thereby being able to give a reason for his opinions.
4. Motivate the pupil to apply to his own personal life and circumstances the truth which he has heard, investigated, and proven.

Not only does participation help the pupil to learn, but it also makes the class session more interesting and vital, both to teacher and pupil. Every teacher can remember the class session in which the dismissal bell seemed to come too suddenly. Where did the time go? Everyone was so busily occupied that the time just flew. Each was so keyed up throughout the session that he was almost sitting on the edge of his seat listening and participating. But every teacher can also remember the class session which, it seemed, would never end. The pupils were restless, indifferent, and unappreciative. Illustrations fell flat. Nothing seemed to arouse interest. The class session was a dismal failure.

What made the first so interesting and the second so dull? Why was the first class so absorbing and the other so boring that both pupils and teacher thought it would never end? The answer may be given in two words—pupil participation. In the first class, the pupils were so interested that they were aroused to make them think. When a pupil does not take part, he does not think. When he does not think, he does not learn. The teacher's task is to make him learn. To do this he must make the pupil think. To make him think, he must lead him to take part.

Adapt to Pupil Interest

How does the teacher get the pupil to participate? To repeat, the successful teacher learns which methods are the most effective for his class by study, by observation, by trial and error. He then employs those methods, singly, in combination, and with adaptations to meet the particular situation.

The Sunday-school teacher cannot compel participation as can the teacher in the public school. But the public schoolteacher, if asked, will admit that compulsion is the least effective method.

Nor can the Sunday-school teacher reward the pupil for participation as the public schoolteacher does by administering grades. But, again, the public schoolteacher knows that the pupil who participates merely to gain a good grade is not learning as well as he should.

Only when the pupil's interest is engaged to the point that he willingly participates because he wants to is the learning process most effective. It is in this highest realm of interest that the Sunday-school teacher must function. His task is to so engage the pupil's interest that the pupil will voluntarily, of his own free will and because of his personal desire, take part as a learner.

Avoid Distractions

The careful teacher also will consider obstacles that interfere with pupil interest. What teacher has not attracted the attention of the pupils and rejoiced at getting the lesson off to a good start, only to have the learning situation marred by some unavoidable influence. It may be worthwhile to discuss a few of these obstacles.

1. *Disturbing noises* are all too common in the Sunday school. Not all noise can be eliminated, but much of it can by discussing the problem at the Sunday-school teachers' and officers' meeting, by a discreet use of signs and announcements, by a proper example on the part of the teachers, by installation of carpets, and by use of soundproof ceilings. Often mere recognition of the problem is the most important step toward its solution.
2. *Interruptions* by secretaries, treasurers, superintendents, or others are unnecessary except in case of dire emergency.
3. *Self-consciousness on the part of the pupil* must be taken into consideration. Often an informal, friendly attitude of the teacher will result in a more comfortable feeling by the pupil. Seating the pupils around a table or in a circle may help avoid stiff formality.
4. *Physical discomfort* interferes with interest. Overcrowding, poor arrangement of classroom, inadequate light, poor ventilation, or an unattractive classroom will make class interest difficult. Too hot, too cold, bare floors, bare walls, dingy curtains, broken chairs—these are

indicative of neglect and are found in the Sunday school far too often.

Now let us consider several ways by which the teacher may enlist the participation of adult pupils in the lesson. The teaching methods shown here are arranged alphabetically. An explanation of each and suggestions for using the method are included.

Assignment

What It Is:

The assignment method consists of the teacher asking a pupil to prepare in advance for participation in the lesson. The method is best for teenagers and adults.

How to Use It:

Plan assignments well in advance.

Make sure that the pupil's effort will contribute to the achievement of the lesson aim.

Arouse interest before the assignment is made. The teacher may say, "Next Sunday we will study about giving money for the Lord's work. What questions would you like to have answered about giving?" With encouragement, such questions as "Who is to give?" "How much?" "When?" and "Why?" are asked. The teacher makes assignments, asking pupils to find the answers and to be prepared to give them in class next Sunday. To help the pupil, the teacher can write the question on a piece of paper, listing Scripture verses for the pupil to read in order to find the answer.

Define carefully just what is to be done, making certain that the pupil knows what is expected of him.

Avoid embarrassing a pupil by insisting that he accept an assignment. He may have a good reason for not accepting. As a safeguard, it is wise to have a pupil in mind when the assignment is planned, perhaps even talking with the pupil about it beforehand.

Do not make the assignment too difficult or too simple.

See that the pupil who accepts the assignment goes through with it. Telephone to ask how he is progressing.

Many types of assignments are possible, including definitions of Scriptural words, finding an answer to a question, bringing objects or pictures or other information, doing something such as making a call or writing a letter, interviewing someone, gathering data, taking a poll, or conducting an experiment.

Be sure to call for a report on assignments.

Show sincere appreciation for completion of assignments.

Buzz Session

What It Is:

A buzz group is a small group of three to seven people who buzz (talk) for a brief time about a problem assigned to them by the teacher. They arrive at a group conclusion which is then presented to the class as a whole. This learning method is appropriate for youth and adults.

How to Use It:

Usually a buzz group is assigned to discuss some aspect of a general subject. For example, if the subject is stewardship, one group could be asked to make a list of needs for money in the local church work while other groups could list needs in other fields such as home missions, foreign missions, benevolences, colleges, and other work to which the congregation contributes.

Each pupil should know exactly what is expected of him.

A time limit of not more than ten minutes is set and strictly observed.

Be sure to allow time for each group to make its report.

Express appreciation for the work each group has done.

Keep the subjects directed toward the lesson aim.

Let each group select its own chairman who will keep the discussion on the subject and see that everyone participates.

Let each group select its own reporter who will relate the summary of the group's findings to the entire class.

Check Chart

What It Is:

A check chart is a questionnaire that may be answered by checking the answers to questions.

How to Use It:

Prepare the chart in advance. It needs to be typed and reproduced so that each pupil may have one. If it is necessary, it could be written on the chalkboard for the group to work on as a whole.

Keep the questions directed toward the purpose of the lesson.

Explain carefully what the pupils are to do and why.

Make sure that each pupil has a pencil if the check chart is for individual use. Each person will also need something to write on.

Keep the answers confidential unless pupils are told otherwise ahead of time.

Collage or Montage

What It Is:

A montage is a display of pictures arranged so as to expand a theme. The pictures usually overlap each other so that no white space is left. A collage includes other materials, thus adding a three-dimensional effect to the pictures.

How to Use It:

Pupils may make collages or montages to illustrate applications of Bible material. Provide necessary materials to complete it.

Plan enough time for pupils to make the project and then to explain it.

Debate

What It Is:

Two teams participate—the affirmative and the negative. Each debater speaks briefly. After all have spoken, one member on each side has a few minutes for rebuttal to disprove the other team's claims and to reaffirm his own.

How to Use It:

Pupils can be assigned to teams in advance in order to do research work and other preparation.

Do not take all of the class period for the debate, but allow time for a brief explanation at the opening and for comment by the other pupils at the close.

Discussion

What It Is:

Discussion is one of the most effective means of getting pupil participation. One of its chief advantages is discovering and clarifying misconceptions. It is also an effective way of determining just what each pupil needs to know to complete his understanding of a subject. It also encourages pupils to think.

How to Use It:

Discussion comes most easily when the group is seated around a table or in a circle with the teacher sitting in as part of the group.

Encourage every pupil to participate. When he does, let him know that his comments are welcome. That can be done with a smile, a nod, or a word of encouragement.

The purpose of the discussion must be made clear to all, particularly to the teacher. Everything that is said must contribute to the achievement of the purpose.

Good discussion procedure follows these six steps: (1) objectives or aims are clarified, (2) problems are analyzed, (3) facts are assembled and studied, (4) pros and cons are considered, (5) advantages and disadvantages are discussed, and (6) efforts are made to arrive at a conclusion.

Avoid arguments. If the argument is about factual information, suggest reference to the source. If the difference is in the field of opinion or interpretation, make this fact clear and invite the class to give consideration to both points of view.

Panel Discussion

What It Is:

Two or more members of the class, each fully informed and interested in one phase of a subject, discuss the subject while the other pupils listen.

How to Use It:

A panel discussion is best used in classes of teens or adults. The subject chosen should have as many phases as there are members of the panel.

The participants are to do research work, have notes in hand, and be adequately prepared to bring out all of the lesson teachings possible.

Choose pupils who can speak clearly and loudly enough to be heard by all.

Coach the participants carefully, making sure that each understands the lesson aim and that the contribution each is to make will apply definitely to the attainment of that aim.

Seat the panel where the participants can be seen and heard by everyone.

Warn the participants against merely talking with one another rather than presenting the material for which they are responsible.

Question

What It Is:

A question is an inquiry, the act of asking. It reveals knowledge and provokes thinking. The teacher needs to know how to ask questions in a way that will stimulate and guide learning. He must also know how to answer questions in a way that will aid the pupil to learn. If the pupil does not think, he does not learn.

Jesus made frequent use of the question method, and His answers to questions were invariably effective, generally leading to more thinking and often to action.

How to Use It:

Use questions for the following purposes: (1) to help the pupil understand what he knows and what he needs to know, (2) to arouse curiosity, stimulate interest, and develop purpose, (3) to direct attention to the important and away from the unimportant, (4) to lead the pupil to express his thoughts and thus help you guide his thinking, and (5) to ascertain what the pupil knows and thus decide what he needs to learn.

Plan your questions—and their correct answers—in advance. Make certain that the questions lead directly toward the achievement of the lesson aim.

Be sure that the question is complete and fully understood. Pupils are confused by questions that are incomplete or based on information that they do not have.

Answers should be complete and well-rounded, indicating that the pupil has a full understanding.

Questions should be of the kind that will create and maintain interest on the part of the entire class, not merely the more advanced pupils or the less advanced pupils.

Give the pupils plenty of time to answer. If they hesitate, perhaps the question should be reworded.

If only part of an answer is correct, accept that part with appreciation. Then proceed to clear up the rest of the answer. Do not leave any doubt as to what is the correct answer.

Encourage questions by the students. Sometimes a pupil's question may be more illuminating than the teacher's.

There are several kinds of questions: (1) factual—"In her song to Elisabeth, Mary gave several reasons why her soul magnified the Lord. What were they?" (2) interpretive—"What do you think Mary meant?" (3) application—"How do these several reasons apply to us?" (4) choice—"Which of these several reasons means most to you?" (5) reasoning —"Why?"

Study the Lord's use of questions: "For if ye love them that love you, what reward have ye?" "Is not life more than food?" Note how He led others to ask questions (Matthew 19:16-22).

How to Select the Method to Be Used

We have just examined several methods of involving adult participation in a Sunday-school class. No teacher will use all of them in one lesson—or in many lessons, for that matter. With the methods that are available for making a lesson interesting and effective (and there are still more ways of teaching, not listed here), there is no excuse for any teacher to fall into the deadly rut of monotony in lesson presentation. No teacher should ever be like the one of whom a pupil said, "I know exactly how my teacher will begin next Sunday's lesson or the lesson a month from now, what he will say about it, and how he will end it. How can a person be interested when the teacher doesn't even try to make the lesson interesting?"

Every teacher ought to become acquainted with a variety of teaching methods and use them on occasion. Here are some factors to be considered when choosing the methods to be used in a lesson.

1. *Would you like to try it?* The teacher must be enthusiastic if he wants the pupil to become enthusiastic.

2. *What is the lesson aim?* Is the method the best to accomplish that aim?

3. *What is the lesson content?* Is it a "story" lesson? A "question and answer" lesson? A "tell and explain" lesson for the lecture method? Lessons differ, and this difference often makes one method better than another.

4. *Which method will appeal most to your pupils?* You will want to introduce them to new methods from time to time. In your teaching, you will discover which of them appeals most to your pupils. Your purpose, after all, is to help the pupils to learn. Therefore, always keep them in mind.

5. *What method did you use last Sunday?* And the Sunday before? And the Sunday before that? Avoid monotony by using a variety of methods, but do not become a "methods addict," subjecting your class to something different all of the time.

6. *Do you have the time to use the method?* You have a very limited period of time during the class session. Use it to the best advantage. Do not waste precious moments with a method that takes more time than is justified.

7. *Will the method make the pupil desire to investigate?* The pupil's mentality must be stimulated, prodded, aroused to a keen interest in the truth being taught. Will the method stimulate such interest?

8. Is the method adapted to the capacities and interests of the pupils? You know the maturity of your pupils, Biblically speaking. You know their capacities and interests. Is the method under consideration one that will be on their level of interest?

Dedicated Sunday-school teachers want to lead their pupils to a deeper understanding of God's Word and to a higher level of spiritual living. They may find their teaching more effective and satisfying by gaining the participation of their pupils in the process.

This article is adapted from the book, *Teach With Success*, by Guy P. Leavitt, revised by Eleanor Daniel, ©1956 by The STANDARD PUBLISHING Company. Used by permission.

Autumn Quarter, 1992

Theme: Old Testament Personalities

Special Features

Lessons

Unit 1: God Chooses and Relates to a People

Unit 2: The People Choose a Monarchy

Unit 3: The Prophets' Roles in a Divided Kingdom

Related Resources

The following publications are suggested to provide additional help on the subjects of study presented in the Autumn Quarter. They may be purchased from your supplier. Prices are subject to change.

A Loser, A Winner, and A Wise Guy, by David McCord. This book presents lessons we can learn from Saul, David, and Solomon, the first three kings of Israel. Order #11-40084, $2.25.

Bible Time Line. A large, colorful wall chart that presents major Biblical characters and events in chronological sequence. Separate column correlates important people and events of secular history. Order #14-02628, $9.99.

Divided We Fall, by James E. Smith. A review of selected events and persons involved in the decline and fall of Israel and Judah. Order #11-40086, $2.25.

Wonders in the Midst, by Ward Patterson. This book is a stirring study of God's leading of His people from the exodus to the kingship in Israel. Order #11-40076, $2.25.

Of Highest Importance

The International Sunday School Lessons, on which the studies in this manual are based, are arranged in six-year cycles. A new cycle of lessons begins with the Autumn 1992 quarter and concludes with the Summer 1998 quarter. During these six years, studies that are considered basic for an understanding of the total Biblical message will be offered.

To provide a review of the whole Bible, the first two quarters of the cycle (Autumn 1992 and Winter 1992-93, highlighted by the color panel in the chart below) consist of surveys of the Old and New Testaments respectively. These will serve as a helpful basis for the more detailed studies that will come later.

After we have completed this review of the Bible, which essentially is the account of God's plan of redemption for humankind, we will focus our attention on Jesus, who is the center of God's redemptive acts. Our Spring 1993 study of the Gospel of John proclaims that Jesus was sent from God and declares the critical importance of believing in Him. He fulfilled the Old Testament law's demands, He paid the price for the sins of humankind, and by His resurrection He made it possible for all to have eternal life.

Having seen that God's purpose for us centers in His Son, we shall be challenged in the Summer quarter to follow that purpose. That challenge will come from the writings of Paul.

International Sunday School Lesson Cycle
September, 1992—August, 1998

YEAR	AUTUMN QUARTER (Sept., Oct., Nov.)	WINTER QUARTER (Dec., Jan., Feb.)	SPRING QUARTER (Mar., Apr., May)	SUMMER QUARTER (June, July, Aug.)
1992-1993	Old Testament Personalities (Old Testament Survey)	Good News for All (New Testament Survey)	Believing in Christ (John)	Following God's Purpose (Ephesians, Philippians, Colossians, Philemon)
1993-1994	The Story of Beginnings (Genesis)	The Story of Jesus (Luke)	Good News for God's People (Romans) Set Free by God's Grace (Galatians)	God Redeems a People (Exodus, Leviticus, Numbers, Deuteronomy)
1994-1995	From the Conquest to the Kingdom (Joshua, Judges, 1 and 2 Samuel, 1 Kings)	Jesus the Fulfillment (Matthew)	Christians Living in Community (1 and 2 Corinthians)	A Nation Turns From God (1 and 2 Kings, Amos, Hosea, Micah, Isaiah)
1995-1996	The Story of Christian Beginnings (Acts)	God's Promise of Deliverance (Isaiah) God's Love for All People (Jonah, Ruth)	Teachings of Jesus (Matthew, Mark, Luke)	A Practical Religion (James) God Is With Us (Psalms)
1996-1997	God's People Face Judgment (2 Kings, Jeremiah, Lamentations, Ezekiel, Habakkuk)	New Testament Personalities	Hope for the Future (1 and 2 Thessalonians, Revelation)	Guidance for Ministry (1 and 2 Timothy, Titus) A Call to Faithfulness (Hebrews)
1997-1998	God Leads a People Home (Major Prophets, Minor Prophets, Nehemiah)	God's People in a Troubled World (1 and 2 Peter, 1, 2, 3 John, Jude)	The Gospel of Action (Mark)	Wisdom for Living (Job, Proverbs, Ecclesiastes)

Glimpses of God's People

by Orrin Root

"OH WHY SHOULD THE SPIRIT of mortal be proud?" A poet asked that question nearly two centuries ago. Truly, the record of mankind on planet earth gives us human beings little reason for pride.

Perhaps the brightest day in history was day six. Creation was new, "and, behold, it was very good" (Genesis 1:31). Adam and Eve soon made it less good, and the long war was on between good and bad.

The advantage seemed to be with bad. Man went wrong till "every imagination of the thoughts of his heart was only evil continually" (Genesis 6:5). But one good man was left. Wonder of wonders, he brought up a good family in a world of evil. So God wiped out all the bad people with a flood, and the human race began again with Noah and his family.

The war between good and bad began again too, and again bad seemed to be winning. This time God did not destroy all the bad people. Out of an unbelieving world He chose one great man of faith to be the father of a nation dedicated to the Creator.

Through the next three months our lessons will bring us glimpses of that nation, the children of Abraham, the Hebrew nation, the nation of Israel, the Jews. We will see only glimpses, but enough of them to show the progress of the continuing battle between good and bad. The series of lessons is in three parts corresponding to the three months.

September
God Chooses and Relates to a People

Lesson 1 tells that God called Abram, and Abram believed and obeyed. His name was changed to Abraham, father of many, for God said he was to be the father of a great nation. Abram believed even though he was a hundred years old before he had a son by his proper wife. Two hundred years later there were about seventy of Abraham's descendants. Abraham's grandson, Jacob, was head of the family when it moved to Egypt. In a few more centuries it grew to number perhaps three million. Then it was time for it to leave Egypt and go back to the promised land.

Lesson 2 tells how God called Moses to lead the people from Egypt to the promised land. Moses accepted the job reluctantly, but did it well. Little cause for pride can be found in the way the people followed. Sometimes they grumbled and sometimes they rebelled, but in forty years they came to the border of the promised land.

Lesson 3 records that God chose Joshua to lead his people into the promised land after Moses died. Then, if ever, the Hebrew people had reason to be proud of their behavior. Through years of war and years of peace they served God faithfully as long as Joshua lived to lead them. But after he died the people began to drift away from God and ignore His law (Judges 17:6). So God sent a heathen tribe to overrun the land and oppress the people. Then the troubled people again turned to God with respect and obedience, and God called a leader who rallied them to defeat the oppressors and restore peace. This happened over and over in the three centuries after Joshua died.

Lesson 4 brings one example of how God rescued His people from oppression during those three centuries. God called Deborah, Deborah called Barak, Barak called ten thousand men, and God gave them a tremendous victory.

October
The People Choose a Monarchy

Lesson 5 tells us that the people of Israel decided they should have a king as other nations did. Samuel was then the leader. He and God warned that a king would not solve Israel's problems; but the people insisted, and God chose Saul to rule them for many troubled years.

Lesson 6 tells of David, the next king. He was a military genius as well as a wise statesman and a sweet singer. Skillfully he subdued the heathen tribes on every side and built a mighty empire.

Lesson 7 tells of David's son, Solomon. Inheriting an empire at peace and well managed, he brought Israel to the peak of prosperity and power. But in his later years Solomon failed to follow his own good advice. He disobeyed God, and he oppressed the people till they were ready to rebel. After his death the northern tribes did revolt. The empire then became two little nations, Israel in the north and Judah in the south.

Lesson 8 leaps over three hundred years from the time of Solomon to tell of one of the twenty monarchs who ruled in Judah. King Josiah inherited a kingdom far gone in idolatry and sin, but he vigorously restored the worship of God.

November
The Prophets' Roles in the Divided Kingdom

Lesson 9 introduces Elijah. He was a famous prophet in the northern kingdom of Israel long before Josiah ruled in the south. Among the nineteen rulers of the northern kingdom there was no reformer like Josiah in the south. But Elijah, speaking for God, did much to slow the slide into idolatry and wickedness.

Lesson 10 tells of Amos, a farmer from Judah whom God sent to preach in Israel. Boldly he denounced the sins he saw, and pleaded with the people to let justice flow as waters, and righteousness as a river.

Lesson 11 deals with Hosea, who also prophesied in the northern kingdom. His theme was the unfailing love of the Lord, even when His people had turned away from Him.

Lesson 12 turns to the southern kingdom, Judah. That country had several kings like Josiah, who earnestly tried to keep their people true to the Lord. Delivering God's word during administrations both good and bad, Micah pleaded with the people to "do justly, and to love mercy, and to walk humbly with thy God" (Micah 6:8).

Lesson 13 brings us a few words from the prophet Jeremiah. He was God's spokesman in the time when northern Israel had been destroyed and Judah was about to plunge to the same fate. Persistently he told kings and people how that fate could be averted; persistently they derided and persecuted him. So destruction came, and the people of Judah were dragged away to captivity in Babylon.

These thirteen lessons bring us to the doom of Israel and Judah, the doom foretold by many prophets. But that was not the end of the story. The prophets proclaimed also another chance for Israel. Captivity would end; God's people would be planted again in their own land; again God would be their shepherd if they would follow Him.

Best of all, the prophets sang of a virgin-born Messiah from Bethlehem, of a new era and a new covenant, of God's word going out from Jerusalem, of people of all nations flowing into God's kingdom.

We who live in Messiah's light can learn also from Israel's darkness. These lessons do not just bring us ancient history; they bring us inspired messages that were "written for our admonition" (1 Corinthians 10:11). Let's read and be admonished.

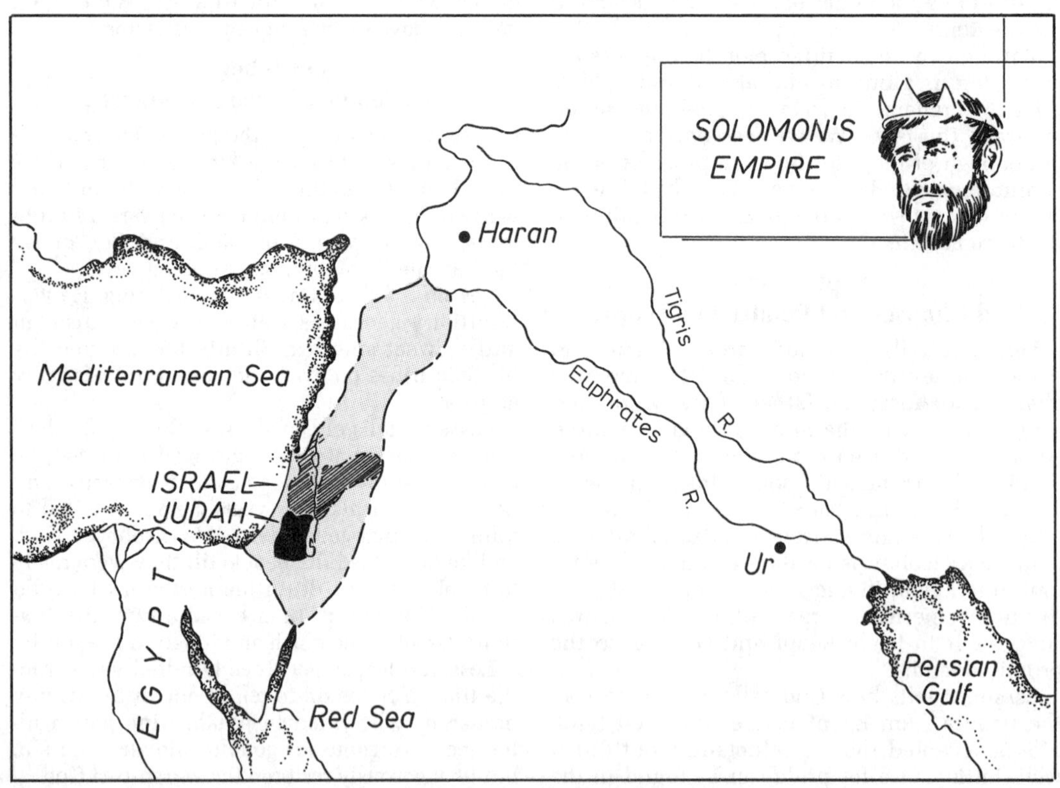

What Is Man?

by Edwin V. Hayden

I LOOKED AROUND at those mountains reaching up to the sky, and I thought, 'What an insignificant little bug is man in God's creation!'"

The deacon who taught us grade-school boys in Sunday School had just returned from a visit to the Mountain Mission School at Grundy, Virginia, where he was overawed by the tall, steep, wooded ridges of Buchanan County. The timeless quality of the mountains impressed him as much as their sheer bulk.

Among the tall ridges of Buchanan County, however, our teacher had seen evidences that human beings are not so unimportant after all. Small they may be, and short of life as compared to the ancient hills; but, for evil or for good, human beings do wield a mighty influence. The Mission School he was visiting bore testimony to that. Human wickedness in many forms played its part in breaking up homes and families, leaving children orphaned, neglected, and in need; yet human compassion, created and empowered by the Lord Jesus Christ, had arisen in the hearts of his people to meet the need at Grundy.

Men and their machines would later slash their way into those mountains, to wrest the coal from within them and to build roads for swift and easy passage over them, but these material conquests would not equal the earlier conquest of the spirit. Men and women, and not mountains, are the objects of God's deepest disappointments and His greatest triumphs.

God's Word declares that truth, even in the account of creation. Step by step, after calling into being, first light, then the land, the growing things, the fish and fowls, and the animals that inhabit the land, God saw what He had made and pronounced it good. Only after He had created man—male and female—and given them charge over all the rest of creation did God survey the whole accomplishment and call it *very* good (Genesis 1:1-31).

Shared Experience

The subsequent Biblical record, with its account of human failures in matters of obedience and responsibility, may cause one to suspect God of being like the human parent who is too quick to give an adolescent child the keys to the family car.

Parenthood, with all its vulnerability and its deep satisfactions, is in fact an experience that our Father God shares with those whom He made in His likeness and image. Announcing the punishment for the sin of the first human pair, God said to Eve, "I will greatly increase your pains in childbearing; with pain you will give birth to children. Your desire will be for your husband, and he will rule over you" (Genesis 3:16).* But there was a triumphant note in Eve's response to the first fulfillment of that prophecy: "She conceived and gave birth to Cain. She said, 'With the help of the Lord I have brought forth a man'" (Genesis 4:1).Our first mother, filled to bursting with pride in her firstborn son, was to know an equally great pain when that son became the murderer of his brother (Genesis 4:2-12). The same dramatic plot, with endless variations of intensity and detail, is played out in every household where parents care deeply about their children. Count the youthful accomplishments that bring to proud parents their highest sense of fulfillment, and then count the youthful follies that fill those same parents with despair. Eve's song, "With the help of the Lord I have brought forth a man," introduces heights and depths of triumph and tragedy that can be found nowhere else as much as in the interplay of developing personalities.

The bittersweet parental experience that began in our Father God is seen nowhere more powerfully than in Mary, the mother of Jesus. When told that she was to bear God's Son as her child, she rejoiced, "From now on all generations will call me blessed" (Luke 1:48); but after the child was born, she was warned of coming tragedy: "And a sword will pierce your own soul too" (Luke 2:35). Both predictions were to be abundantly fulfilled—and without any fault in Jesus!

Divine Disappointment

God's manifold disappointments in the human focus of His creation provide a recurrent theme throughout the Bible. Very early "God saw how corrupt the earth had become, for all the people on earth had corrupted their ways" (Genesis 6:12). So He moved to wipe out a whole generation and to start over with Noah and his family.

Centuries later Isaiah compared God's chosen nation, Israel, to a vineyard on which the owner had lavished the best possible care, but which produced no good fruit (Isaiah 5:1-7). In His own time, Jesus sounded a similar theme in His story of caretakers who were entrusted with their master's well-prepared vineyard and who scornfully refused to yield any of its fruits to the landlord (Matthew 21:33-44).

Reginald Heber (1783-1826) echoed the divine disappointment theme in his well-known "Missionary Hymn":

"What though the spicy breezes
Blow soft o'er Ceylon's isle;
Though every prospect pleases,
And only man is vile;
In vain, with lavish kindness,
The gifts of God are strown;
The heathen, in his blindness,
Bows down to wood and stone."

One can only marvel at the long-suffering of God in the face of such rejection!

Special Endowment

One of God's more notable spokesmen asks and answers the obvious question, "Why?"

"When I consider your heavens,
the work of your fingers,
the moon and the stars,
which you have set in place,
what is man that you are mindful of him,
the son of man that you care for him?
You made him a little lower than the heavenly beings
and crowned him with glory and honor.
You made him ruler over the works of your hands;
you put everything under his feet:
all flocks and herds,
and the beasts of the field,
the birds of the air,
and the fish of the sea,
all that swim in the paths of the seas.
O Lord, our Lord,
how majestic is your name in all the earth!"
(Psalm 8:3-9)

The psalmist had no telescope with which to measure the universe. Unaided contemplation of the night sky was enough to make him feel very inadequate by comparison. Astronomy is, indeed, a humbling science—even humiliating, until one realizes that a human being is the astronomer, tracing the patterns established by the Creator. For reasons sufficient to himself, God has endowed His created children with capacities far out of proportion to their size, length of days, or strength of physique. For causes beyond our comprehension, He has entrusted humankind with stewardship over His material creation—the earth and its resources, all things green and growing, and creatures great and small. Yet our worth is not within ourselves, except as God has put it there.

Humankind's track record in fulfilling this stewardship is not very impressive. Too often God's created children have forgotten how they received their capacities and so have ignored their responsibilities. Only as a person joins the psalmist in his conclusion of thankful praise to his Maker can one justify the trust with which God has invested him or her.

A glorious company of God-fearing folk have done that beautifully. Frequently they are the same persons who have dismayed their Father with the careless follies of their youth, but with His loving patience have been brought to responsible maturity. To Him no accomplishment of theirs is unknown or goes unnoticed. They encourage and sustain their kinfolk and neighbors, helping them toward the fulfilling of their own stewardship. Some of them come to public attention.

A number of the most worthy personalities are known through the pages of the Bible. For the next three months we shall give attention to some who made Old Testament history during some fifteen hundred years, from Abraham to Jeremiah. They have made repayment on God's amazing investment in His human family.

Along the way we'll encounter some of the other kind, who demonstrated a dismaying capacity for evil. The contrast between the heroes and the villains will be seen not through differences in their size, appearance, intelligence, or scientific skills, but in their relationship to God as their Heavenly Father. They came either to resemble Him through loving worship and service, or to oppose Him through proud rebellion. God's children are still His greatest treasure or His greatest despair.

---

*All Biblical quotations in this article are from the *New International Version.*

Answers to Quarterly Quiz on page 8

Lesson 1—1. Ur of the Chaldees. 2. 75, Haran. **Lesson 2**—1. holy ground. 2. false. **Lesson 3**—1. Joshua. 2. the Jordan River. **Lesson 4**—1. Deborah. 2. woman. **Lesson 5**—1. king. 2. God. **Lesson 6**—1. outward, heart. 2. 71/2 years, 33 years. **Lesson 7**—1. earth. 2. false. **Lesson 8**—1. the book of the law. 2. false. **Lesson 9**—1. Mount Carmel. 2. fire. **Lesson 10**—1. not. 2. true. **Lesson 11**—1. goodness. 2. mercy, knowledge. **Lesson 12**—1. rams, oil. 2. justly, mercy, humbly. **Lesson 13**—1. false. 2. bones

You Can Make a Difference!

by Douglas Redford

ABRAHAM LINCOLN is credited with saying, "God must love the common man; he made so many of them." The Old Testament reverberates with a theme that can be expressed in somewhat similar terms: "God must love the common man; he *used* so many of them." Let us consider how the sacred history of Israel encourages believers of the nineties to "make a difference" in their world.

A Consistent Pattern

The Old Testament emphasizes God's use of common people to accomplish His purposes. See Moses in the desert of Midian tending sheep when called to confront Pharaoh and become Israel's deliverer. Hear Gideon express his profound unworthiness to lead Israel to victory over her oppressors. Read of Israel's first two kings (Saul and David), who manifested genuine humility in accepting the position.

Later, when the kingship had become corrupt and incompetent, God raised up prophets to champion His cause. These men were characterized by a relentless dedication to God's message regardless of the consequences. Where we are provided with details surrounding a prophet's calling (as with Isaiah and Jeremiah), we cannot escape their extreme sense of unworthiness to undertake such a monumental task. James reminds us that Elijah, whose powerful words and deeds thundered against the idolatry of his day, was a person just like us (James 5:17).

The examples cited above also illustrate a prominent paradox of Scripture, one that is still true: those who see themselves least worthy of being used by God are actually in the best position of all to become His tools. It was not the educated, self-assured Moses of Exodus 2 who delivered God's people from bondage; it was the humble, sheepherding Moses of Exodus 3 who was most adequately prepared to become exactly what the Master Designer needed.

A Contemporary Perspective

The principle that God employs ordinary people to make a difference may not be all that revolutionary to most of us. Yet one cannot truly appreciate this theme before considering how other religions in the Old Testament world viewed the common man.

Because of significant archaeological finds, our understanding of pagan temples, offerings, sacrifices, and clergy has been greatly enhanced. Invariably these items describe the religion of the *king* of a particular nation and are seldom applicable to the average person's situation. It was almost unthinkable that the "man on the street" could receive a divine revelation or maintain meaningful communication with his god. In summarizing his own research, scholar Leo Oppenheim writes, "The common man . . . remains unknown, the most important unknown element in Mesopotamian religion."

This same phenomenon applies to the concept of life after death among peoples of the ancient Near East. Much is often made of the Egyptians' belief in the afterlife, reflected particularly in their burial customs. This afterlife, however, was reserved for the Pharaoh and the important members of society. By contrast, Biblical faith offers hope to *anyone* who faithfully serves the Lord, whether he is king or slave.

One can quickly discern the "great gulf" that this highlights between Old Testament religion and that of the pagan world. In ancient Israel, God used shepherds (Moses and David), a fig picker (Amos), and even individuals outside the covenant community (Ruth) to achieve His purposes. It is certainly worth noting that the first person depicted in Scripture as being "filled . . . with the Spirit" was not a priest or a prophet; he was Bezaleel, the chief craftsman of the tabernacle (Exodus 31:1-5). This may hardly seem to have been the most "spiritual" dimension of the tabernacle, but it illustrates well the fact that in God's eyes, the common man has always been "king." The ministry of Jesus communicated the same truth, for "the common people heard him gladly" (Mark 12:37).

A Current Privilege

Though we live in a time when participation in religious activities is open to all, many persons regard spiritual matters as having little practical significance. It is likely that every day we are in touch with individuals who see Christianity as having little or no bearing on the "real" concerns of life. They are "common people" who desperately need to see Christ enfleshed in the life-styles of other "common people."

Can we make a difference? The Old Testament sounds an unmistakable "Yes!" Whether we *will* make a difference is a question that only we can answer.

Quarterly Quiz

The questions on this page may be used in several ways: as a pretest at the beginning of the quarter; as a review at the end of the quarter; or as a review after each lesson. The questions are based on the Scripture text of each lesson (King James Version). ***The answers are on page 6.***

Lesson 1

1. Terah, Abram, Sarai, and Lot departed from what place to go into the land of Canaan? *Genesis 11:31*

2. Abram was (75, 99, 100) years old when he, Sarai, and Lot left ______ to go into the land of Canaan. *Genesis 12:4*

Lesson 2

1. At the burning bush, Moses was told to take off his shoes because the place where he was standing was ______ ______. *Exodus 3:5*

2. When God asked Moses to go to Pharaoh to gain Israel's release from Egypt, Moses agreed without hesitation to do so. T/F *Exodus 3:11*

Lesson 3

1. After Moses' death, whom did the Lord appoint to lead the children of Israel into the promised land? *Joshua 1:1*

2. What physical barrier had to be overcome before the children of Israel could enter the promised land? *Joshua 1:2*

Lesson 4

1. Who gave God's instructions to Barak to take ten thousand men to fight against Sisera, the captain of Jabin's army? *Judges 4:4, 6*

2. The honor for Sisera's defeat would not go to Barak, but to a ______. *Judges 4:9*

Lesson 5

1. When Samuel was old, the elders of Israel asked him to make them a ______ to judge them. *1 Samuel 8:5*

2. In making this request, the people were rejecting whom? *1 Samuel 8:7*

Lesson 6

1. God told Samuel that the Lord sees not as man sees, for man looks on the ______ appearance but the Lord looks on the ______. *1 Samuel 16:7*

2. How long was David king over Judah in Hebron, and how long was he king over all Israel and Judah in Jerusalem? *2 Samuel 5:5*

Lesson 7

1. Referring to his death, which was soon to occur, David told his son Solomon, "I go the way of all the ______ ." *1 Kings 2:1, 2*

2. Solomon asked God for an understanding heart, so that by his wisdom he could bring glory and honor to God. T/F *1 Kings 3:9*

Lesson 8

1. When the temple in Jerusalem was being repaired at the order of King Josiah, what did Hilkiah the priest find there? *2 Chronicles 34:15*

2. King Josiah was pleased with the discovery and proclaimed a feast so all Judah could celebrate. T/F *2 Chronicles 34:19, 21*

Lesson 9

1. Where did the contest between Elijah and the prophets of Baal take place? *1 Kings 18:24*

2. The prophets of Baal and Elijah each were to offer a sacrifice on different altars, and the God who answered by ______ would show himself to be the true God. *1 Kings 18:24*

Lesson 10

1. In Amos's day, the people of Israel told the prophets, "Prophesy ______." *Amos 2:12*

2. Amos stated that the children of Israel would be punished for their iniquities because of the special blessings they had received from God. T/F *Amos 3:2*

Lesson 11

1. The Lord said that His people's (mercy, goodness, obedience) was as a morning cloud, and that it vanished as the early dew. *Hosea 6:4*

2. The Lord said that He desired ______, and not sacrifice; and the ______ of God more than burnt offerings. *Hosea 6:6*

Lesson 12

1. Micah pictures a man of Judah asking if God would be pleased with thousands of ______, or ten thousands of rivers of ______. *Micah 6:7*

2. Micah said that the Lord required of man to do ______, and to love ______, and to walk ______ with his God. *Micah 6:8*

Lesson 13

1. God appointed Jeremiah a prophet by touching a hot coal to his lips. T/F *Jeremiah 1:9*

2. When Jeremiah refused to preach, God's word was in his heart as a burning fire shut up in his ______. *Jeremiah 20:9*

September 6
Lesson 1

God's Call and Promise to Abram

PRINTED TEXT: **Genesis 11:31—12:9.**

DEVOTIONAL READING: **Genesis 13:14-18.**

Genesis 11:31, 32

31 And Terah took Abram his son, and Lot the son of Haran his son's son, and Sarai his daughter-in-law, his son Abram's wife; and they went forth with them from Ur of the Chaldees, to go into the land of Canaan; and they came unto Haran, and dwelt there.
32 And the days of Terah were two hundred and five years: and Terah died in Haran.

Genesis 12:1-9

1 Now the LORD had said unto Abram, Get thee out of thy country, and from thy kindred, and from thy father's house, unto a land that I will show thee:
2 And I will make of thee a great nation, and I will bless thee, and make thy name great; and thou shalt be a blessing:
3 And I will bless them that bless thee, and curse him that curseth thee: and in thee shall all families of the earth be blessed.
4 So Abram departed, as the LORD had spoken unto him; and Lot went with him: and Abram was seventy and five years old when he departed out of Haran.
5 And Abram took Sarai his wife, and Lot his brother's son, and all their substance that they had gathered, and the souls that they had gotten in Haran; and they went forth to go into the land of Canaan; and into the land of Canaan they came.
6 And Abram passed through the land unto the place of Sichem, unto the plain of Moreh. And the Canaanite was then in the land.
7 And the LORD appeared unto Abram, and said, Unto thy seed will I give this land: and there builded he an altar unto the LORD, who appeared unto him.
8 And he removed from thence unto a mountain on the east of Bethel, and pitched his tent, having Bethel on the west, and Hai on the east: and there he builded an altar unto the LORD, and called upon the name of the LORD.
9 And Abram journeyed, going on still toward the south.

GOLDEN TEXT: Get thee out of thy country, and from thy kindred, and from thy father's house, unto a land that I will show thee: and I will make of thee a great nation, and I will bless thee, and make thy name great; and thou shalt be a blessing.
—Genesis 12:1, 2.

Old Testament Personalities

Unit 1: God Chooses and Relates to a People (Lessons 1-4)

Lesson Aims

After this lesson a student should be able to:

1. Trace Abram's journey to the places named in our text.
2. Compare his own response to God with Abram's response.

Lesson Outline

INTRODUCTION
- A. Terah
- B. Lesson Background

I. MOVING TO HARAN (Genesis 11:31, 32)
- A. The Movers (v. 31a)
- B. The Destination (v. 31b)
- C. The End of an Era (v. 32)

II. GOD'S CALL (Genesis 12:1-3)
- A. Call to Move (v. 1)
- B. Blessing for Abram—and Others (vv. 2, 3)
  A Promise Kept

III. MOVING AGAIN (Genesis 12:4-9)
- A. Obedience (vv. 4, 5)
  Grasping Opportunities
- B. Traveling and Worshiping (vv. 6-9)

CONCLUSION
- A. Abraham's Devotion
- B. Results of Devotion
- C. Prayer
- D. Thought to Remember

Display the map of Abraham's journeys (visual 1 of the packet) and trace his journeys as you proceed through this lesson. The map is shown on page 13.

Introduction

Can you imagine a city that actually worshiped *Sin*? It was ancient Ur, beside the lower Euphrates River in the country we now call Iraq.

Of course there was no English language then, and the people of Ur had no idea what the word sin would mean in that language three or four thousand years later. The chief god of their city was the moon. In the old Sumerian language his name was Nannar, but the Semites called him Sin. His shrine was seventy feet above the plain, at the peak of a stepped-back pyramid, the famous ziggurat of Ur.

A. Terah

Terah was one of the Semites who lived in Ur. Semites were descendants of Shem, Noah's son. We don't know whether Terah joined in the worship of Sin or not, but he did worship some god or gods besides the real one (Joshua 24:2). He may have had his own private god, a little image kept in his home. Such images have been found in the ruins of Ur.

Of course, the real God was not forgotten. Terah was born only about 222 years after the big flood (Genesis 11:10-24). Noah was still living (Genesis 9:28). His descendants had been scattered and no longer spoke the same language (Genesis 11:1-9), but surely all of them had heard how God had destroyed all the sinners of the world. They knew the real God even while they took up the worship of unreal ones.

B. Lesson Background

From Genesis 20:12 we see that Terah had at least two wives, not necessarily at the same time. He had three sons, Abram, Nahor, and Haran. From Genesis 11:26 we might suppose Abram was the oldest, born when Terah was seventy years old. But no; Abram is named first because he is the important one in the record that follows. In the text of this lesson we shall see that he was not born till Terah was 130 years old (Genesis 11:32; 12:4). Terah had also at least one daughter, Sarai. She became the bride of her half-brother, Abram (Genesis 20:12).

I. Moving to Haran (Genesis 11:31, 32)

No sooner do we meet Abram than we see him moving to a new home, and before we reach the end of our text we shall see him moving to another. And in his new land he was to keep on moving from place to place.

A. The Movers (v. 31a)

31a. And Terah took Abram his son, and Lot the son of Haran his son's son, and Sarai his daughter-in-law, his son Abram's wife.

Terah's son *Haran* had died (v. 28), but Haran's son *Lot* went with Terah, Abram, and Sarai.

B. The Destination (v. 31b)

31b. And they went forth with them from Ur of the Chaldees, to go into the land of Canaan; and they came unto Haran, and dwelt there.

Their destination was the *land of Canaan*, six hundred miles west across the desert, but they did not know it yet (Hebrews 11:8). Even if they had known, they would not have tried to take

How to Say It

AI. *A*-eye.
EUPHRATES. U-*fray*-teez.
HAI. *Hay*-eye.
MAMRE. *Mam*-reh.
SARAI. *Say*-rye.
SHECHEM. *Shee*-kem or *Shek*-em.
SICHEM. *Sye*-kem.
TERAH. *Tee*-ruh.

their cattle and sheep straight west across that waterless country. The usual way to Canaan was the way they went, six hundred miles up the Euphrates river toward *Haran*, and then south. We are not told why they stopped and dwelt at Haran, but it seems reasonable to suppose that was what God told them to do.

C. The End of an Era (v. 32)

32. And the days of Terah were two hundred and five years: and Terah died in Haran.

We are supposing the family was following God's leading, but still we wonder why God led them to Haran and stopped them there. Whatever may have been the reason for God's plan, the result was excellent. The plan worked.

II. God's Call (Genesis 12:1-3)

The first part of our text says nothing about God's call and leading. If we had no more information, we might think it was Terah's own idea to move from Ur to Haran. But now we are to see that there was more to the story.

A. Call to Move (v. 1)

1. Now the LORD had said unto Abram, Get thee out of thy country, and from thy kindred, and from thy father's house, unto a land that I will show thee.

In the Hebrew language, the same form of the verb can mean either *said* or *had said*. In some versions it is translated *said*, meaning God said this to Abram after Terah died in Haran. This seems reasonable, since the record of the call is placed after the record of the move to Haran and the death of Terah.

On the other hand, Stephen said God gave such a call to Abram before he moved to Haran (Acts 7:2, 3). Therefore the *King James Version* and some others translate the verb as *had said*, meaning God had said this earlier back in Ur.

Probably the Lord gave this call in Ur when it was time to leave that city, and then gave it again when it was time to move on from Haran. Note that He did not tell Abram where to go, but said, *Unto a land that I will show thee*. Abram did not know where he was going (Hebrews 11:8). First the Lord showed the way to Haran; later He showed the way to Canaan.

Abram was to be separated from his *country*, which was full of moon worshipers. He was also to leave his *kindred*, who "served other gods" as well as the real one (Joshua 24:2). He would be far from his brother Nahor, and from his uncles, aunts, cousins, nephews, and nieces. Of his *kindred*, only his wife and one nephew went with him from Haran (v. 5). Probably they, like Abram, served only one God. Of course, they would find idol worshipers in the new land too, but they would not be under pressure from idolatrous members of their own family.

B. Blessing for Abram—and Others (vv. 2, 3)

2. And I will make of thee a great nation, and I will bless thee, and make thy name great; and thou shalt be a blessing.

In ancient times a man with a big family was considered fortunate. Abram's children in future generations would become *a great nation*—an amazing promise to a childless man whose wife could not bear children (Genesis 11:30). But a larger promise was to come later. Not only one nation, but several nations were to come from this one man. With that promise he received a new name, Abraham, father of many (Genesis 17:5). Our hero is better known by that new name.

I will bless thee is a very big promise, for throughout the Old Testament we see that God's blessing brought success, prosperity, health, and happiness. *Make thy name great* means make you famous. The promise is nearly four thousand years old, and Abram's name is famous still.

Thou shalt be a blessing. Abram was not only to receive blessing from God; he was also to be a blessing to others. Chapter 14 gives an example. Abram defeated powerful invaders and recaptured property and people that were being taken away. But verse 3 points to a far greater blessing that was to come through Abram.

3. And I will bless them that bless thee, and curse him that curseth thee: and in thee shall all families of the earth be blessed.

God promised to be on Abram's side. He would favor those who would favor Abram; He would be against those who would be against Abram. The long extent of that promise is seen in the fate of whole nations who have opposed Abram's people. Nations from Assyria to Nazi

Germany have set themselves to destroy Israel; but they are gone, and Israel remains.

The last promise of this verse is greatest of all. From Abram would come a great nation, and through that nation would come the Savior of the world, Jesus. His salvation today is available *to all families of the earth*, and there is no greater blessing.

A PROMISE KEPT

What thoughts may have run through Abram's mind when God spoke His amazing promise? "It's a farfetched idea if I ever heard one!" "How could I father a great nation? I don't even have a son!" "I am a humble man; how could my life bless the whole world?"

We who live at this end of history's thread may be thankful that Abram acted upon his faith rather than upon his doubts. He did father a great nation; his name (Abraham) is honored by billions of people; his life's example has been a blessing to multitudes.

The world's population is pressing toward six billion. Of these not quite twenty million are Jews, physical descendants of Abraham through Isaac, the child of God's promise. Nearly a billion are Muslims, most of them children of Abraham through Ishmael. And two billion are nominally Christians, spiritual heirs of Abraham, the father of the faithful, as the New Testament explains God's dealings with humanity.

The blessing comes even to those who have no faith in our God: the world is a better place since God became flesh in Jesus the Christ, the one through whom the divine pledge to Abraham found ultimate fulfillment. How wondrously does God keep his promises! —C. R. B.

III. Moving Again (Genesis 12:4-9)

Abram's faith is famous, and it ought to be. By faith he became one of the great heroes of the Bible (Hebrews 11:8). Better than that, his believing was counted to him for righteousness (Genesis 15:6). Likewise we sinners of today can be "justified by faith" (Romans 5:1). We never become righteous by our efforts alone, but we receive "the righteousness which is of God by faith" (Philippians 3:9).

But Abram did more than believe. He obeyed. He went when and where God ordered (Hebrews 11:8), and so he was justified by his doing as well as by his believing (James 2:21). "Ye see then how that by works a man is justified, and not by faith only" (James 2:24). Likewise we are not justified by faith without obeying God (James 2:17).

> **VISUALS FOR THESE LESSONS**
>
> The *Adult Visuals/Learning Resources* packet contains classroom-size visuals designed for use with the lessons in the Autumn Quarter. The packet is available from your supplier. Order No. ST 192.

A. Obedience (vv. 4, 5)

4. So Abram departed, as the LORD had spoken unto him; and Lot went with him: and Abram was seventy and five years old when he departed out of Haran.

Now *Abram departed, as the Lord had spoken unto him*, and *he departed out of Haran*. This indicates that God spoke to him in Haran and told him to move on. We need not debate whether verses 1-3 refer to this speaking or to the earlier speaking in Ur. God spoke both in Ur and in Haran. The orders were substantially the same.

Abram was seventy and five years old. We who retire at sixty-five may marvel that a man of seventy-five set out boldly to begin a new life in a strange country. But Abram at seventy-five was barely middle-aged. He lived a hundred years more (Genesis 25:7).

Lot went with him. This was Abram's nephew, the son of Abram's dead brother Haran (Genesis 11:27, 28).

5. And Abram took Sarai his wife, and Lot his brother's son, and all their substance that they had gathered, and the souls that they had gotten in Haran; and they went forth to go into the land of Canaan; and into the land of Canaan they came.

Abram . . . Sarai . . . Lot. These were the principal people of the journey, but they did not go alone. *The souls that they had gotten* were slaves, and possibly some hired men. We are not told how many of them there were, but some years later there were three hundred able fighting men among them (Genesis 14:14). *Their substance* must have included flocks of sheep and herds of cattle. No doubt a long caravan of camels and donkeys carried tents and household goods, and perhaps many people were riding instead of walking. We are not told how long it took to make the four-hundred-mile trip, but *into the land of Canaan they came*.

GRASPING OPPORTUNITIES

William Safire tells of a lesson he learned as a young reporter. He was working against a deadline for the New York *Herald Tribune* when a secretary tried frantically to interrupt him. He waved her away. Later, he went down to the lobby of his building and discovered that it was filled with policemen and reporters. A jewelry store had been robbed, and he had been "scooped" by newsmen from another paper. Dejected, he sat on the steps outside. A woman asked if he needed help, and he replied, "I just want to be left alone." He later learned that the woman was Greta Garbo, the most sought-after celebrity of that era.

Safire was so focused on his immediate concerns that he missed a great opportunity for a story taking place just two floors below him. Then, when he could have made up for his mistake by interviewing Greta Garbo, he was so busy bemoaning his fate that he missed opportunity knocking a second time that day!

Too often, we are so busy with present concerns that we can't see the opportunities surrounding us. Abram was different: when an opportunity came for him to enrich his life by following God into the unknown, he wisely let go of the present so that he could firmly grasp the future God had in store for him. Because he was willing to walk with God in faith, God gave him great blessings. We may find that God still works this way! —C. R. B.

B. Traveling and Worshiping (vv. 6-9)

6. And Abram passed through the land unto the place of Sichem, unto the plain of Moreh. And the Canaanite was then in the land.

Probably the travelers came into the land of Canaan north of the sea that was later called the Sea of Galilee. Then they went southward to *Sichem* (Shechem) in the central part of Canaan. *The plain of Moreh* was in that vicinity. Some scholars think the word should be translated *oak* instead of *plain*. Others think it should be *terebinth*, a tree somewhat like an oak. The *New International Version* dodges that controversy by translating "the great tree of Moreh." Apparently the plain or the tree was well known at the time this record was written.

The land of Canaan was not empty. The people living there were called Canaanites. Both the people and the land were named for Noah's grandson Canaan (Genesis 10:1, 6).

7. And the LORD appeared unto Abram, and said, Unto thy seed will I give this land: and there builded he an altar unto the LORD, who appeared unto him.

The Lord appeared unto Abram. Was there a visible form like that of a man or an angel? Was there a mystic vision in the night? Was there a brilliant light? We are not told, but the verb *appeared* indicates there was something Abram could see. And the Lord *said*. Whether God could be heard by Abram's ears or only by his mind, Abram got the message and knew who gave it. The land of Canaan then belonged to the Canaanites (v. 6), but in the future God would give it to Abram's *seed*, his descendants. They would become a great nation (v. 2), and this country would be their homeland. Thus reminded of God's presence and care, Abram responded with worship. *There builded he an altar unto the Lord*, and no doubt he used it to offer sacrifices along with his thanksgiving and prayers.

8. And he removed from thence unto a mountain on the east of Bethel, and pitched his tent, having Bethel on the west, and Hai on the east: and there he builded an altar unto the LORD, and called upon the name of the LORD.

From Shechem, Abram moved south about twenty-five miles and set up his camp in the hill country between *Bethel* and *Hai*. Abram's grandson named the place Bethel, house of God (Genesis 28:18, 19). That name was given long after Abram was there, but before this record was written. The name *Hai* is often spelled *Ai*, without the *H*. In his new campground Abram built another altar and continued to worship.

9. And Abram journeyed, going on still toward the south.

The Lord had specifically directed Abram's moves from Ur to Haran and from Haran to Canaan. We need not suppose that He directed every move within Canaan just as specifically, though of course He may have done so. But Abram had huge numbers of cattle and sheep. When the grass was eaten in one place, another pasture had to be found. Abram's men could scout the country and find a place where the grass was plentiful. We now see Abram moving from Bethel *toward the south*. In later references we see that he ranged as far north as Bethel (Genesis 13:3) and as far south as Kadesh (Genesis 20:1). In time of famine he even went to Egypt (Genesis 12:10). He lived in tents, never building a house or a town, but it seems that he established his headquarters in the plains of Mamre near Hebron. That vicinity is mentioned often (Genesis 13:18; 14:13; 18:1). There he

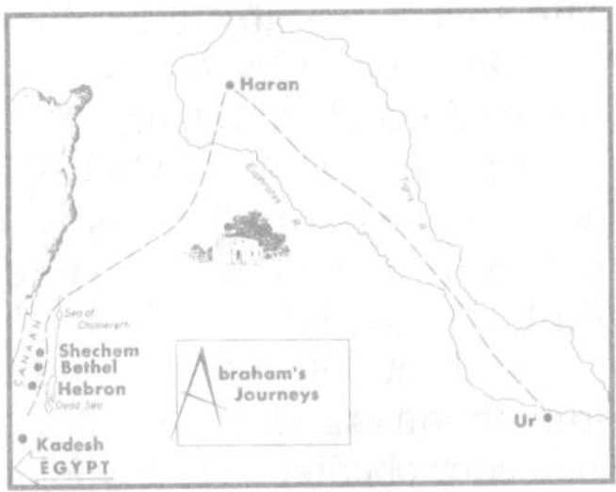

visual 1

obtained a burial place for his wife and himself (Genesis 23:19, 20; 25:8-10). With his great wealth and many followers, he could easily have built a town. He could have settled down with comforts such as those he had known in Ur when he was young. He could have taken life easy, leaving his men to drive the cattle and sheep as far as necessary to find pasture. But the writer of Hebrews finds a profound meaning in his nomadic life. Even in the promised land he did not consider himself a permanent resident. His final destination was beyond this world (Hebrews 11:9, 10, 16). The moving story of Abram may well move us to live on earth as pilgrims bound for a Heavenly land.

Conclusion

Abram was later named Abraham, father of many (Genesis 17:5). That name indicates his unique place in the Scriptures and in the world. Physically and literally he is the father of all the Jews. They are descendants of Isaac, son of Abraham and Sarah, the wife of his youth. But Abraham is also the father of many of the Arabs. Ishmael was born to Abraham and a slave girl, and his descendants ranged the wide desert east of Egypt (Genesis 25:18). Abraham's younger sons also went away to the east to populate Arabia (Genesis 25:6).

Spiritually, Abraham is the father of all the Christians (Galatians 3:6-9). Jesus rebuked Abraham's physical children because their way of living did not match Abraham's (John 8:39, 40). We spiritual children of Abraham may well consider our own lives in comparison with his.

A. Abraham's Devotion

Abraham loved God. No one can doubt that God loved Abraham, but Abraham's love for God is indicated when he is called God's friend (2 Chronicles 20:7; Isaiah 41:8). The Hebrew word for *friend* is from the verb *love*, and it is what we would call a present participle in English. It describes Abraham as God's *loving one* rather than as God's *loved one*.

The law called each of God's people to love Him completely (Deuteronomy 6:5). Our Master said that is the greatest commandment of them all (Matthew 22:34-40). How are we doing? Does our love match Abraham's?

Abraham believed God (Genesis 15:6). God doesn't speak to all of us in the same way He spoke to Abraham, but He does speak in the Bible. Do you believe all of it?

Abraham obeyed God. Even when it meant a tremendous sacrifice he obeyed (James 2:21-23). Has your obedience cost you anything lately?

Home Daily Bible Readings

Monday, Aug. 31—God's Faithfulness to Abraham (Genesis 12:10-20)

Tuesday, Sept. 1—God Blesses Abraham's Descendants (Genesis 14:13-18)

Wednesday, Sept. 2—God Promises Abraham a Son (Genesis 15:1-6)

Thursday, Sept. 3—God Promises to Deliver Abraham's People (Genesis 15:12-16a)

Friday, Sept. 4—God's Relationship With Abraham (Genesis 17:1-8)

Saturday, Sept. 5—Abraham's Relationship With God (Genesis 17:9-14)

Sunday, Sept. 6—God's Relationship With Abraham's Family (Genesis 17:15-21)

Abraham worshiped God. Our text speaks of his altars in two places. There was another at Hebron (Genesis 13:18), and probably there were others at other campgrounds. Have you been worshiping the Lord everywhere you go?

B. Results of Devotion

Abraham was blessed. God said, "I will bless thee," and He did. Abraham was rich (Genesis 13:2). He was at peace with his neighbors, and that is marvelous. He came to Canaan with a host of hungry cattle and sheep. Instead of trying to drive him out, people of the land became his allies and friends (Genesis 14:13; 21:22-24; 23:1-6). More than three thousand years have passed since Abraham died, but today he is honored by Muslims, Jews, and Christians.

Abraham was a blessing to others. One example was his rescue of the captives (Genesis 14), but no doubt there were other helpful acts to win the favor of his neighbors. Greater than all of these, of course, is the blessing to us through him. He began the nation that preserved God's Word and brought to the world God's Son with a blessing for all families of the earth.

How fortunate we are to be blessed along with Abraham! (Galatians 3:9). How wonderful it is to be "heirs of God, and joint-heirs with Christ," who is "heir of all things"! (Romans 8:17; Hebrews 1:2). Blessed as we are, how joyfully each of us ought to be a blessing to others!

C. Prayer

Make me a blessing, O Savior, I pray;
Make me a blessing to someone today.

D. Thought to Remember

"Thou shalt be a blessing."

Learning by Doing

This page contains an alternate lesson plan emphasizing learning activities. Classes desiring such student involvement will find these suggestions helpful.

Learning Goals

Seek to help your students accomplish these goals in this lesson:

1. Identify God's command and promises to Abram in Genesis 12.
2. Create a definition of faith based upon the events in Genesis 11:31—12:9.
3. Grapple with what it means to walk by faith and not by sight.

Into the Lesson

In this lesson you will be helping your class members wrestle with the relationship between faith and personal security. Faith often puts a person in a position that seems insecure. Yet one actually is very secure because of God's presence in his or her life.

Provide copies of the questions below for students. Begin the lesson by having your students discuss these questions in groups of six:

1. What are some things we look to for security in life?
2. Which of these produce true security?
3. What tends to happen to us when these "securities" are taken away from us?

Allow five or six minutes for discussion. Then lead into the Bible study by saying something like, "Today we begin a series of lessons that examines the lives of key individuals in the Old Testament. Today's lesson looks at Abram, who later was named Abraham. We'll focus on his call from God and how his faith placed him in a position that might have seemed insecure, even though he was actually quite secure."

Into the Word

Ask a volunteer to read Genesis 11:31—12:9. Then present a brief lecture on the background of this passage, using information under the Introduction heading on page 10.

Direct your students to discuss the following questions in their groups of six. These questions are in the student book.

1. What did God command Abram to do? (12:1).
2. What promises did God give Abram? (12:2, 3).
3. Imagine that you are Abram. God has just approached you with the command and promises recorded in Genesis 12:1-3. You have a decision to make. In your thinking, what are the advantages of obeying God? What are the disadvantages?
4. How did Abram demonstrate faith in God? (12:4-9).
5. What "securities" may Abram have forfeited in order to obey God's command?
6. Based on the events of Genesis 11:31—12:9 and Hebrews 11:8-10, how would you define faith?

Allow the groups fifteen to twenty minutes for discussion. Then ask each group to share their definition of faith with the class.

Into Life

Have a volunteer read 2 Corinthians 5:7. Lead your class in discussing this question: When we choose to live by faith instead of by sight, what "securities" may we need to give up?

Write the following statement on the chalkboard: Faith is the most insecure position in the world. Ask class members, "Do you agree, or disagree, with the statement?" Take a tally of those who agree and those who disagree. Ask students on each side to defend their opinion.

After discussing the statement, give each student a copy of the Biblical commands listed below. Ask students, "Which command makes you feel the most insecure?" Have them put a check mark in front of it. Here are the commands:

___ Share your faith with unbelievers (1 Peter 3:15).

___ Give financially to God in proportion to the way He has prospered you (1 Corinthians 16:2).

___ Love your enemies and do good to them (Matthew 5:44).

___ Use your spiritual gift (1 Peter 4:10).

___ Assist the lowly and needy (James 1:27).

___ Look out for the interests of others (Philippians 2:4).

___ Seek first God's kingdom and His righteousness (Matthew 6:33).

Have the students form the same groups as before. Ask them to share their answers with their group, and then to discuss the following questions:

1. Why does the command you marked cause you to feel insecure?
2. How can you (or, How do you) overcome your feelings of insecurity to go ahead and obey God?

Close with a time of silent prayer.

Let's Talk It Over

The questions on this page are designed to encourage review of the lesson Scriptures and to promote discussion of the lesson by the class. The answers provided are only discussion starters. Let your class talk it over from there.

1. God leads us, like Abraham, on a step-by-step basis. What can we do to align ourselves with this kind of leadership?

As Christians, we know that "we walk by faith, not by sight" (2 Corinthians 5:7). Still, when we commence a new spiritual duty or personal enterprise, we are inclined to want to know beforehand how it will turn out. But faith requires that we take each step and make each decision as it comes, prayerfully depending on God's guidance. In Proverbs 3:6 we are advised, "In all thy ways acknowledge him, and he shall direct thy paths." This indicates that we should bring even seemingly small decisions before the Lord for His guidance. Perhaps we can use a morning devotional time to preview the decisions we must make during the day in our work, family, social relationships, recreation, etc. and pray that God will show us the right way to go. We must also learn to pray for guidance at the actual time a decision is required of us.

2. Why is it important to examine the blending of faith and obedience in the career of Abraham?

It is significant that Paul could point to Abraham as an example of faith (Romans 4), and James could refer to him as an example of works (James 2:20-24). Here is a man who illustrates how true faith is an active force and how true obedience must spring from trust in God. We still see many instances today of defective faith and religious works. Most churches have some members who profess faith in God but do virtually nothing to demonstrate that faith. At the same time, there are people of high moral character who perform humanitarian acts but who exhibit little or no dependence on God. If the New Testament writers felt that Abraham was a person whose life exemplified the relationship of faith and works, we should give his life some emphasis in our teaching and preaching.

3. If we, like Abraham, see ourselves as strangers and pilgrims on earth, what are some examples of behavior that will differentiate us from those who are earthbound?

As those whose "citizenship is in heaven" (Philippians 3:20, *New International Version*), we will adhere to the values, customs, and practices of our true home. This will involve a refusal to conform to the ever-changing cycle of earthly fads and standards (Romans 12:1, 2). As strangers and pilgrims here, we will view material wealth as of far less importance than what the world assigns it—we will be preoccupied rather with laying up treasures in Heaven (Matthew 6:20). A Heaven-bound Christian will also deal differently with the reality of death. To the person who sees life only in terms of this world, death may seem the ultimate tragedy; but we, like Paul, can perceive even the "gain" it offers as the door to an eternal Heaven (Philippians 1:21).

4. One of Abraham's most interesting titles is "friend of God." How would it help us spiritually if we thought of ourselves as friends of God?

If our relationship to God tends to be a formal one, or even a fearful one, it may help us to gain more joy and comfort in that relationship by focusing on our friendship with God. We may find it easier to be faithful in our attendance at public worship and in our personal devotions, since a friend is someone whose company we enjoy, someone whom we think about frequently. Another aspect of friendship is that we speak well of our friends in the presence of others. When we think of God or Christ as a friend, our efforts at witnessing or personal evangelism can be a simple matter of enthusiastically introducing our earthly friends to our Heavenly best Friend.

5. Abraham was promised that he would "be a blessing." How would it help us spiritually if we were to aim at being a blessing to others?

The word blessing may may not call forth any definite pictures in our mind, so we may reword this to say, "How would it help us spiritually if we were to aim at making other people happy?" It would be quite an adventure to direct our prayers and our efforts toward bringing happiness to our family members, fellow church members, neighbors, and friends. We could make it a priority matter to say or do something encouraging, comforting, complimentary, or helpful in a practical way. This approach to life is similar to Jesus' aim "not to be ministered unto, but to minister" (Mark 10:45). So it would give us the joy of walking with Jesus, of following in His steps (1 Peter 2:21), of serving in His stead.

God's Call to Moses

September 13
Lesson 2

PRINTED TEXT: Exodus 3:1-7, 10-14.

DEVOTIONAL READING: Exodus 4:10-16.

Exodus 3:1-7, 10-14

1 Now Moses kept the flock of Jethro his father-in-law, the priest of Midian: and he led the flock to the backside of the desert, and came to the mountain of God, even to Horeb.

2 And the angel of the LORD appeared unto him in a flame of fire out of the midst of a bush: and he looked, and, behold, the bush burned with fire, and the bush was not consumed.

3 And Moses said, I will now turn aside, and see this great sight, why the bush is not burnt.

4 And when the LORD saw that he turned aside to see, God called unto him out of the midst of the bush, and said, Moses, Moses. And he said, Here am I.

5 And he said, Draw not nigh hither: put off thy shoes from off thy feet; for the place whereon thou standest is holy ground.

6 Moreover he said, I am the God of thy father, the God of Abraham, the God of Isaac, and the God of Jacob. And Moses hid his face; for he was afraid to look upon God.

7 And the LORD said, I have surely seen the affliction of my people which are in Egypt, and have heard their cry by reason of their taskmasters; for I know their sorrows.

. . . .

10 Come now therefore, and I will send thee unto Pharaoh, that thou mayest bring forth my people the children of Israel out of Egypt.

11 And Moses said unto God, Who am I, that I should go unto Pharaoh, and that I should bring forth the children of Israel out of Egypt?

12 And he said, Certainly I will be with thee; and this shall be a token unto thee, that I have sent thee: When thou hast brought forth the people out of Egypt, ye shall serve God upon this mountain.

13 And Moses said unto God, Behold, when I come unto the children of Israel, and shall say unto them, The God of your fathers hath sent me unto you; and they shall say to me, What is his name? what shall I say unto them?

14 And God said unto Moses, I AM THAT I AM: and he said, Thus shalt thou say unto the children of Israel, I AM hath sent me unto you.

GOLDEN TEXT: Come now therefore, and I will send thee unto Pharaoh, that thou mayest bring forth my people the children of Israel out of Egypt.—Exodus 3:10.

Old Testament Personalities

Unit 1: God Chooses and Relates to a People (Lessons 1-4)

Lesson Aims

After studying this lesson a student should be able to:

1. Tell how God called Moses to a special task.
2. Recall excuses Moses offered, and compare excuses that are offered today.
3. Plan to do some special Christian service this week.

Lesson Outline

INTRODUCTION
- A. Prosperity in Egypt
- B. Growing in Egypt
- C. Slavery in Egypt
- D. Lesson Background

I. A SURPRISE FOR MOSES (Exodus 3:1-5)
- A. Setting (v. 1)
- B. Angel Fire (vv. 2, 3)
- C. A Place for Reverence (vv. 4, 5)
  Awareness of the Holy

II. A MESSAGE FOR MOSES (Exodus 3:6, 7, 10)
- A. The Speaker (v. 6)
- B. The Need (v. 7)
- C. The Mission (v. 10)

III. A BACKER FOR MOSES (Exodus 3:11-14)
- A. Inadequate Messenger (v. 11)
- B. Adequate Backer (v. 12)
- C. Question of Identity (vv. 13, 14)
  What's in a Name?

CONCLUSION
- A. Who, Me?
- B. They Will Not Believe Me
- C. I Can't
- D. God Can
- E. Prayer
- F. Thought to Remember

The map of the Sinai Peninsula (visual 2 of the visuals packet) will be useful as you present this lesson on Moses. The map is shown on page 20.

Introduction

"I will make of thee a great nation." So said the Lord to Abram (Genesis 12:2). It was an amazing promise to a man seventy-five years old and childless.

When the man was ninety-nine and still childless, he was renamed Abraham, father of many (Genesis 17:5). Still the promise seemed incredible. Abraham laughed, and so did his wife (Genesis 17:15-17; 18:10-15). But when he was a hundred years old, the promised son was born to him and his wife. Abraham named his son Isaac, which comes from the Hebrew word meaning "to laugh" (Genesis 17:19; 21:1-7). Now Abraham and Sarah could laugh with pure joy.

But where was the great nation? Isaac had only two sons, and only one of them was chosen to inherit the promise (Genesis 25:20-26; 28:10-17). So in the third generation of Abraham's family, Jacob was the sole member of the great nation that was to be. But Jacob had twelve sons (Genesis 35:23-26), and it began to seem more probable that the family would become a nation.

A. Prosperity in Egypt

Jacob's favorite son was Joseph, and the father made no secret of his favoritism (Genesis 37:3, 4). Jealous brothers sold Joseph as a slave, and the buyers took him to Egypt (Genesis 37:12-36).

With special help from God, plus his own ability, industry, and good will, the slave rose to become a ruler in Egypt, second in authority only to the king. Due to God's warning and Joseph's planning, there was plenty of food in Egypt when deadly famine descended on the world (Genesis 39—41).

Like many others, Joseph's brothers went to Egypt to buy food for their families. After a time they learned that the ruler in Egypt was their brother. At his invitation they took Jacob and the entire family to Egypt to live, and Joseph provided them with the best that Egypt could supply. This good fortune continued for the remaining seventy-one years of Joseph's life, and perhaps longer (Genesis 42—50).

B. Growing in Egypt

About seventy people of Jacob's family moved to Egypt (Exodus 1:5), but the number swiftly increased (v. 7). When they left Egypt, more than six hundred thousand men were fit for military duty (Numbers 1:45, 46). If all the women, children under twenty, and old men were four times as many as the fighting men, the whole family then numbered about three million.

C. Slavery in Egypt

Sometime after Joseph died—we don't know how long—there arose a new king who didn't know Joseph (Exodus 1:8). He was alarmed when he saw how many alien Israelites were in his country. He thought they might join forces with some enemy and overthrow him (Exodus 1:10).

How could these foreigners be kept under control? The king's first plan was to make them slaves and work them to death. But the Israelites were tough; they thrived on hard work. So the king ordered the midwives to see that all the boy babies died aborning. But the midwives feared God more than they feared the king, and the babies survived. Finally the king issued a blanket order that every Israelite boy baby was to be "cast into the river" (Exodus 1:11-22).

D. Lesson Background

Moses was one of the boys born during this time. For three months his mother hid him and nourished him. But a growing boy grows harder to hide. The mother obeyed the king's order and put him in the river—but she put him in a neat little boat, and she put him near the king's daughter's swimming hole, and she put him among the papyrus reeds near the bank so he would not float down the stream (Exodus 2:1-4).

So the princess found the floating baby and was captivated. Cleverly led by his sister, she hired his mother to nurse him. She brought him up as her own son, and gave him the best education Egypt could provide. Because she drew him out of the water, she named him Drawn Out, which is *Moses* in the language of the record (Exodus 2:5-10; Acts 7:22). The Bible says no more about Moses' youth, but takes up the story when he was forty years old.

One day Moses went out among his overworked people, the Israelites or Hebrews. We are not told how often he had done this before, but this time he saw an Egyptian beating a Hebrew. Seeing no one around to watch, he killed the Egyptian and buried his body in the sand. The killing became known, and not even a prince could be allowed to kill an Egyptian for abusing a slave. To save his own life, Moses fled two hundred miles across the eastern desert to the land of Midian (Exodus 2:11-15).

One day Moses met some shepherd girls by a water hole in Midian. Bravely he helped them against unfair competition for the water, and their grateful father welcomed him to their home. The father was a priest as well as a sheepman. He had two names, Reuel and Jethro. Moses settled down with this man's family and later married one of his daughters. It seems that he lived as a contented shepherd for the next forty years (Exodus 2:16-21).

How to Say It

KETURAH. Keh-*too*-ruh.
PHARAOH. *Fair*-o or *Fay*-ro.
REUEL. *Roo*-el.
SINAI. *Sye*-nay-eye or *Sye*-nye.

I. A Surprise for Moses (Exodus 3:1-5)

Midian was one of Abraham's sons by Keturah, the wife of his old age (Genesis 25:1, 2). The people of Midian therefore were distant cousins of Moses. They were nomadic shepherds and traders, so the boundaries of their land were indefinite. They ranged widely around the eastern arm of the Red Sea and northward from it. In forty years Moses must have become very familiar with a part of that area, knowing where the few oases were and where to find the best of the poor pasture.

A. Setting (v. 1)

1. Now Moses kept the flock of Jethro his father-in-law, the priest of Midian: and he led the flock to the back side of the desert, and came to the mountain of God, even to Horeb.

The back side of the desert was the west side, the side away from Jethro's headquarters. *Horeb* is another name for Sinai. Perhaps it is called *the mountain of God* because God appeared there at this time and later, or perhaps the Midianites had given it that name because for them it had some sacred significance unknown to us.

B. Angel Fire (vv. 2, 3)

2. And the angel of the LORD appeared unto him in a flame of fire out of the midst of a bush: and he looked, and, behold, the bush burned with fire, and the bush was not consumed.

How strange to see a bush on fire in that remote spot! Moses may have lived in that land for forty years without seeing a bush ignited by lightning or in any other way. But stranger still, *the bush was not consumed.* In the flame the leaves and twigs seemed to be untouched by heat. We are told that the angel of the Lord was in the flame, but Moses didn't know that yet. He had no explanation for the unusual sight.

3. And Moses said, I will now turn aside, and see this great sight, why the bush is not burnt.

Moses was highly educated and apparently of a scientific turn of mind. He meant to investigate this unusual fire to find an explanation.

C. A Place for Reverence (vv. 4, 5)

4. And when the LORD saw that he turned aside to see, God called unto him out of the midst of the bush, and said, Moses, Moses. And he said, Here am I.

Now that He had Moses' attention, the Lord gave the man something else to wonder at: his own name called from the flame. The scientist coming to investigate must have been stopped in his tracks. Perhaps he trembled, but he bravely acknowledged that he heard the call: *Here am I.*

5. And he said, Draw not nigh hither: put off thy shoes from off thy feet; for the place whereon thou standest is holy ground.

The scientist should stay where he was. This was a place and time for reverence, not investigation. All the science of future centuries could never find a natural cause for that supernatural phenomenon. God was there, and His presence made holy all the nearby ground.

AWARENESS OF THE HOLY

As a result of the 1917 Bolshevik Revolution, the ornate, golden-domed cathedral standing in Moscow's Kremlin was made into a secular museum and concert hall. With heavy step, the Communists trampled on every aspect of religion in the life of the Russian people. Denying the existence of God, they suppressed the Christian faith of their people for seven decades.

With the coming of the "Gorbachev revolution," faith finally asserted itself over the bankrupt atheistic social system that had held sway for so long. In September, 1990, when the huge fifteenth-century cathedral in the Kremlin was reconsecrated, thousands of the faithful joined in glad celebration. The reconsecration was also a symbol: Christian faith may be declared illegal, but not eradicated.

Communist leaders long tried to ignore or deny the holy—that which the spiritual side of humanity longs for and seeks. By secularizing places that were consecrated to God, they foolishly thought they could destroy faith.

Unlike these modern atheists, Moses recognized the holy when he faced it and knew how to respond in the presence of God. Humble faith recognizes God's existence and His use of even common things to call us into His service. Where do we take off our sandals? —C. R. B.

II. A Message for Moses (Exodus 3:6, 7, 10)

The angel of the Lord appeared (v. 2), but God himself called (v. 4). Sometimes we find it hard to distinguish between the Lord and His angel. The word *angel* means a messenger. Possibly the visible flame was a messenger God used to get Moses' attention, and then God's own Spirit spoke. But we need not solve the mystery; probably we cannot. Verse 6 leaves no doubt about who spoke to Moses.

visual 2

A. The Speaker (v. 6)

6. Moreover he said, I am the God of thy father, the God of Abraham, the God of Isaac, and the God of Jacob. And Moses hid his face; for he was afraid to look upon God.

What did Moses know about God? His Egyptian schooling had taught him about the many gods of Egypt, but it seems unlikely that Abraham's God had a place in the curriculum of the national university. What did Moses know about Abraham, Isaac, and Jacob? He had been brought up as an Egyptian from the time he was weaned (Exodus 2:6-10). Had the prince of Egypt found time to sit with Hebrew sages and learn the lore of their people? Had he possibly been instructed by his own natural father? Or had Moses learned from his father-in-law? Jethro was a priest, and it seems that he served the real God. He was a descendant of Abraham. Had his people been in touch with the Hebrews so he could tell about Isaac and Jacob too? These questions have no answers, but it seems that somehow Moses had learned how Abraham had believed God and obeyed Him, how Isaac had continued in his father's faith, and perhaps even how Jacob in gratitude had vowed to give a tenth of his income to the Lord (Genesis 28:10-22). Among other things, Moses knew the God of his fathers was fearsome as well as benevolent. Moses had been eager to investigate an unusual flame; but when he knew who was there, he was *afraid to look.*

B. The Need (v. 7)

7. And the LORD said, I have surely seen the affliction of my people which are in Egypt, and have heard their cry by reason of their taskmasters; for I know their sorrows.

Moses now was about eighty years old (Exodus 7:7), and the bitter bondage of his people had begun an unknown number of years before he was born. Many Hebrews must have doubted that God knew or cared what was happening to them. Moses may have wondered too. His own feeble attempt to help his people had no result but his banishment. But God did know, and He did care. He was going to do something about it.

He was going to rescue His people from Egypt and transport them to a rich and fruitful land that was to be their own (v. 8).

C. The Mission (v. 10)

10. Come now therefore, and I will send thee unto Pharaoh, that thou mayest bring forth my people the children of Israel out of Egypt.

God was going to bring the children of Israel out of Egypt (v. 8), but so was Moses. Many of God's great works require the help of human beings. He rescues sinners from their bondage, and He transports them to glory; but He sends people like you and me to tell the good news of this rescue. If we fail to do our part, sinners remain in bondage.

III. A Backer for Moses (Exodus 3:11-14)

The Lord had come to deliver His people (v. 8), and no doubt Moses was delighted to hear it. But when the Lord said, *"I will send thee unto Pharaoh,"* that was something else. Moses was not so well pleased.

A. Inadequate Messenger (v. 11)

11. And Moses said unto God, Who am I, that I should go unto Pharaoh, and that I should bring forth the children of Israel out of Egypt?

Who am I? We can sympathize with Moses in his question. In Egypt he was a criminal marked for death (Exodus 2:15). His life would be in danger if he would so much as set foot inside the borders of Egypt. How could he be expected to stride into the throne room and demand that the king give up the big pool of cheap labor that built his cities?

B. Adequate Backer (v. 12)

12. And he said, Certainly I will be with thee; and this shall be a token unto thee, that I have sent thee: When thou hast brought forth the people out of Egypt, ye shall serve God upon this mountain.

Certainly I will be with thee. Moses was not adequate for the rescue, but God was. The king would not see Him standing by Moses; but He would be there, and the king would have evidence of His presence. After ten terrible plagues, finally the king would urge the people of Israel to get out (Exodus 7:14—12:36).

How could Moses know God was with him? God gave him *a token,* a sign. When the people finally were free from Egypt, they would pause for worship and service at that same mountain where God was speaking to Moses. Then Moses would realize that God had been with him all the way; but for the present he was asked to trust God, to believe and obey as Abraham had done. Perhaps Moses was not quite as daring as Abraham had been. The Lord consented to give other signs of His presence and power before Moses began the job (Exodus 4:1-8).

C. Question of Identity (vv. 13, 14)

13. And Moses said unto God, Behold, when I come unto the children of Israel, and shall say unto them, The God of your fathers hath sent me unto you; and they shall say to me, What is his name? what shall I say unto them?

The people of Israel had been brutally driven and overworked for more than eighty years, and perhaps more than a hundred. It was hardly possible for them to keep up an adequate program of religious teaching. The present generation had grown up with scant instruction, and in the midst of the multiple gods of Egypt. When Moses would come and say he was sent by the God of their fathers, they would want to know more about that God. Who is He? *What is his name?*

14. And God said unto Moses, I AM THAT I AM: and he said, Thus shalt thou say unto the children of Israel, I AM hath sent me unto you.

The God who sent Moses was the God who is the only God who really exists. The so-called gods of Egypt were not gods at all. God called himself *I Am;* Moses and others used a different form of the verb and called Him *He is.* That is the personal name of the one living, eternal God, the name that is His alone, not shared with any of the fictitious gods. Hebrews of later times were so impressed by the majesty of *He is* that they would not speak His name at all. He had warned them, "Thou shalt not take the name of *He is* thy God in vain, for *He is* will not hold him

Home Daily Bible Readings

Monday, Sept. 7—God Promises to Rescue the Israelites (Exodus 3:15-22)

Tuesday, Sept. 8—Moses Responds Reluctantly to God's Call (Exodus 4:1-9)

Wednesday, Sept. 9—God Recommends Aaron to Speak for Moses (Exodus 4:10-17)

Thursday, Sept. 10—Moses Accepts God's Call (Exodus 4:18-24)

Friday, Sept. 11—Aaron Accepts God's Call to Moses (Exodus 4:27-31)

Saturday, Sept. 12—Pharaoh's Heart Is Hardened Against Israel (Exodus 5:1-9)

Sunday, Sept. 13—God Reminds the Israelites of Their Covenant (Exodus 6:1-9)

guiltless that taketh his name in vain" (Exodus 20:7). To be sure they did not take that name in vain, the Jews did not use it at all. In reading the Scripture, when they came to the name *He is* they read *the Lord* instead. The English name *Jehovah* comes from a curious combination of the word that was written and the word that was read. *Jehovah* is seen in a few places in the *King James Version,* but usually that version follows the custom of the fearful Jews and substitutes *the Lord* for the sacred name *He is* or *Jehovah.* Often in the *King James Version* we see *the Lord* printed in small capital letters. That lets us know that the Hebrew at that point has God's personal name, *Jehovah* or *He is.*

WHAT'S IN A NAME?

A line from William Shakespeare's *Romeo and Juliet* has been often quoted:

What's in a name? That which we call a rose
By any other name would smell as sweet.

Perhaps, but there is more to a rose than its fragrance. Names *mean* something; they describe, define, and delineate. When we hear the word, *rose,* we think of smell (as Shakespeare did), but we also think of shape, petal formation, color, leaf structure, and even thorns!

Names are important to each of us: our own, those of others with whom our lives intertwine, as well as the identity of each of the "things" with which we must deal in life. So it was that Moses raised questions of identity when God confronted him at the burning bush.

"Who am I that I should go on this mission?" "Whom shall I say has sent me to deliver Israel?" Moses' first question raised the issue of his identity and responsibility to God and Israel. God's answer was indirect: knowing who we are is of secondary importance to knowing who God is. Knowing God puts both our place and our purpose into proper perspective. Knowing who God is determines how we will deal with others—whether we choose to destroy, ignore, or serve them. The "I AM" cares for others; those who know Him will also. —C. R. B.

Conclusion

Of course Moses did go to see Pharaoh. With the help of God and ten terrible plagues, he finally did get the people of Israel free from bondage. After leaving Egypt the Israelites did serve the Lord at the mountain of God called Horeb or Sinai. They camped there for about a year while they received God's law and built His tabernacle.

But Moses had some more protests to make before he went to Pharaoh. His excuses have a familiar sound. Have you heard some of them more recently than the fifteenth century B. C.?

A. Who, Me?

Moses said, "Who am I, that I should go unto Pharaoh?" (Exodus 3:11). It did seem strange to give that job to a condemned criminal.

On the other hand, Moses was well qualified. Brought up in the court of Pharaoh, he knew how things were done there. God knew what He was doing when He chose Moses.

"Who, me?" Is that your response when you are asked to do something you have never done?

Be an usher — Lead a Bible study
Clean up after dinner — Manage a dinner
Lead a prayer — Cheer up a patient
Help in the nursery — Mow the churchyard.
Or whatever *you* have been asked to do.

Of course it is frightening. But don't be scared out. Probably you can do the job, with a little good advice and a lot of effort.

B. They Will Not Believe Me

Most of us lack confidence in our ability to teach and lead. We may wish for a handy miracle. That would show them! Or would it? Jesus did more miracles than anybody, and still the unbelievers killed Him. If we have no miracles to support our teaching, we need to be all the more careful to pass on the teaching that was supported long ago by the miracles of Jesus and the apostles.

C. I Can't

Moses said, "I am slow of speech." So God sent a good talker to help him (Exodus 4:10-16).

Of course you don't know how to do a job you have never done. But somebody knows. If you are not qualified to take care of babies, or minister to the sick, or teach children, you can work with someone who is qualified, and soon you will be qualified too. With a willing spirit, you can get the know-how.

D. God Can

"Certainly I will be with thee." So said God to Moses (Exodus 3:12). Don't you think He will be with you too? God and you can do much more than you can.

E. Prayer

Our Father, we know You are the God who is and the God who can. Help us to find Your strength in our weakness and Your wisdom in our simplicity. Help us to trust You. Amen.

F. Thought to Remember

"He is!"

Learning by Doing

This page contains an alternate lesson plan emphasizing learning activities. Classes desiring such student involvement will find these suggestions helpful.

Learning Goals

Guide your students to:

1. Explore God's call of Moses to a mission.
2. Analyze Moses' response to God's call.
3. Compare God's call of Moses with His call of each Christian to be involved in ministry.
4. Commit themselves to be involved in ministry.

Into the Lesson

Begin by posing this situation to your class: "Imagine that only five percent of all Christians were involved in any kind of ministry in the church or in the world. What do you think would be the results?" Allow for a number of responses. Try to get your class members to be as specific as they can in their imagining.

Then pose this situation: "Imagine that ninety-five percent of all Christians were highly committed and involved in ministry in the church and in the world. What do you think would be the results? Again, allow for discussion.

Continue by asking, "What would it take to get every Christian committed to high involvement in ministry?" Let students wrestle with that one for a few minutes. Then move into the Scripture study by saying, "Getting people involved in ministry isn't a new problem. In fact, one of the key figures in the Old Testament was very resistant to become involved in God's mission for His people. Today we will study Moses and analyze his reluctance to participate in the ministry to which God called him."

Into the Word

Set the stage for today's passage by presenting a brief lecture (three to five minutes) on the background. You will find the information you need in the introduction to the commentary for this lesson, especially point D.

Ask several volunteers to read Exodus 3:1-14 and 4:1-17. Then have students form groups of six. Give each student a copy of the questions and the chart that follow. Make the chart big enough so they can write in their answers.

1. To what mission did God call Moses? (3:1-10).
2. From the record of this call (3:1-10), what do we learn about God?
3. What excuses did Moses suggest for not fulfilling this mission? How did God answer each excuse? Read the passages below and jot down your observations on the following chart:

	Moses' Excuse	God's Answer
3:11, 12		
3:13, 14		
4:1-5		
4:10-12		
4:13-17		

4. On the basis of these Scriptures,
   a. What was Moses' view of himself?
   b. What was Moses' view of God?

Allow students twenty to twenty-five minutes to complete their study. Then bring the groups together and discuss their observations.

Into Life

Point out that just as Moses was called to a mission, each Christian is called to participate in ministry for Christ. Have volunteers read the following Scriptures: 1 Peter 2:9; Matthew 28:18-20; 1 Peter 4:10; Ephesians 4:11-16. For each passage ask your class, "To what is God calling each Christian?"

Then brainstorm this question: *What are some excuses Christians might use for not being involved in ministry for Jesus?* List the class's suggestions on the chalkboard.

Have students form their small groups again. Provide each group with paper and a pencil. Have each group select one or two of the excuses listed on the chalkboard and determine how they think God might respond to the excuse. Ask each group to write down their ideas. After five to seven minutes, have each group report which excuses they selected and what they thought God's response to each might be.

At this point, help your students to personalize the lesson by asking them to close their eyes and meditate on the following questions. Read each one, and allow a brief time for students to reflect on it before you read the next one.

- Am I actively involved in ministry for Christ either in His church or in the world?
- If I am not involved, how much am I seeking to find a ministry in which to serve Christ?
- If I am involved in regular ministry, is my heart committed to doing my best? Do I participate in ministry joyfully?

Close with prayer, thanking God for the privilege of participating in His mission in the world.

Let's Talk It Over

The questions on this page are designed to encourage review of the lesson Scriptures and to promote discussion of the lesson by the class. The answers provided are only discussion starters. Let your class talk it over from there.

1. The lesson writer calls attention to Moses' "scientific turn of mind" as he viewed the burning bush. What are the limitations of a scientific approach to the miracles of the Bible?

God gave us minds that tend to be curious and inquiring, and so it is natural for us to speculate on just what was involved in Biblical miracles. In some cases the Bible tells of natural "tools" God utilized to perform His wonders. For example, in the dividing of the Red Sea (Exodus 14), "a strong wind" was the tool, while in the ten plagues in Egypt such natural phenomena as frogs, hail, and locusts were used to execute God's judgment on the Egyptians. The danger, of course, is that in speculating on the tools that were used we may lose sight of God's sovereign power that controlled them. This is exactly what has happened with some scholars who have attempted to explain the Bible's miracles on a purely naturalistic basis.

2. Like Moses, some are inclined to ask, "Who am I?" as a way of excusing themselves from a task laid before them. When is that a legitimate question, and when is it not?

If such a question arises from a genuine sense of humility, it is legitimate. In various places the Bible shows us a blend of such humility with a readiness to take on a task. David was certainly humble (see his "Who am I?" in 1 Samuel 18:18 and 2 Samuel 7:18). But he took on Goliath, and later he took on many challenges as king. Jesus said to His disciples, "Without me ye can do nothing" (John 15:5), but in the same discourse He spoke about their bringing forth fruit for God. We Christians are to be aware of our weakness, but we are also to be aware of God's power undergirding our weakness and thus making it possible to accomplish His will. So we should not say, "Who am I?" as an automatic rejection of a challenge, but only as the preface to further declaring, "God helping me, I will do it!"

3. How should we respond to God's name, "I am," revealed to Moses?

Certainly that name should fill us with awe. It sums up the mystery of God's existing from eternity to eternity. It shows that He is the source of our own existence. We should be inspired to worship when we read that great declaration of God to Moses. That name also reminds us of the exclusive nature of faith in God. He said, "I am the Lord, and there is none else" (Isaiah 45:18). We respect the right of other people to worship the god or gods of their choice, but we must assert that the God of the Bible, the "I am," the Father of Jesus Christ, is the one true, eternal God, the only God who exists. In line with that assertion we must invest our time, efforts, and financial resources to make the one God known to a world weltering in religious confusion and spiritual ignorance.

4. It is tempting to assume that if we could work miracles today, people would be more likely to accept our message of salvation through Jesus Christ. What is wrong with this assumption?

In the first place, people often show little interest in investigating the miracles already in plain view. The Bible itself, with its remarkable unity, fulfilled prophecies, life-changing truths, etc., is a continuing miracle, but many people find it easy to ignore. There is a sense in which the resurrection of Jesus Christ is a miracle ever open to human investigation. The New Testament facts and historical realities such as the Lord's Day and the Lord's Supper, which came into being in connection with the resurrection, provide much evidence to examine; but there seem to be few earnest inquirers. As in the days of Moses and Jesus, many persons today are simply too hard of heart to be impressed by past or present miracles.

5. How can we overcome our tendency to say, "I can't," too quickly to God's challenges?

It may help if we make a habit of repeating Philippians 4:13: "I can do all things through Christ which strengtheneth me." We can cultivate a positive attitude regarding the work of the church, most of which is not difficult, but does require some diligent and prayerful effort. Of course, sometimes we must say, "I can't," because we may be taking on so many jobs that we will be unable to do any of them well. Even on these occasions, however, we dare not be too hasty. It may be that the new challenge is one of such great importance that it merits relinquishing some other responsibility in order to fit it in.

God's Choice of Joshua to Succeed Moses

September 20
Lesson 3

LESSON SCRIPTURE: Joshua 1.

PRINTED TEXT: Joshua 1:1-11.

DEVOTIONAL READING: Joshua 3:1-7.

Joshua 1:1-11

1 Now after the death of Moses the servant of the LORD, it came to pass, that the LORD spake unto Joshua the son of Nun, Moses' minister, saying,

2 Moses my servant is dead; now therefore arise, go over this Jordan, thou, and all this people, unto the land which I do give to them, even to the children of Israel.

3 Every place that the sole of your foot shall tread upon, that have I given unto you, as I said unto Moses.

4 From the wilderness and this Lebanon even unto the great river, the river Euphrates, all the land of the Hittites, and unto the great sea toward the going down of the sun, shall be your coast.

5 There shall not any man be able to stand before thee all the days of thy life: as I was with Moses, so I will be with thee: I will not fail thee, nor forsake thee.

6 Be strong and of a good courage: for unto this people shalt thou divide for an inheritance the land, which I sware unto their fathers to give them.

7 Only be thou strong and very courageous, that thou mayest observe to do according to all the law, which Moses my servant commanded thee: turn not from it to the right hand or to the left, that thou mayest prosper whithersoever thou goest.

8 This book of the law shall not depart out of thy mouth; but thou shalt meditate therein day and night, that thou mayest observe to do according to all that is written therein: for then thou shalt make thy way prosperous, and then thou shalt have good success.

9 Have not I commanded thee? Be strong and of a good courage; be not afraid, neither be thou dismayed: for the LORD thy God is with thee whithersoever thou goest.

10 Then Joshua commanded the officers of the people, saying,

11 Pass through the host, and command the people, saying, Prepare you victuals; for within three days ye shall pass over this Jordan, to go in to possess the land, which the LORD your God giveth you to possess it.

GOLDEN TEXT: Be strong and of a good courage; be not afraid, neither be thou dismayed: for the LORD thy God is with thee whithersoever thou goest.
—Joshua 1: 9.

Old Testament Personalities

Unit 1: God Chooses and Relates to a People (Lessons 1-4)

Lesson Aims

After this lesson a student should be able to:

1. Tell what Joshua and Israel were to receive after crossing the Jordan.
2. Tell what they were to do to insure success.
3. List three things that God's people should be doing now.
4. Find one way to do God's will better this week.

Lesson Outline

INTRODUCTION
- A. God's Help
- B. On the Verge of Victory
- C. Lesson Background

I. MARCHING ORDERS (Joshua 1:1-4)
- A. Command (vv. 1, 2)
- B. Promise (vv. 3, 4)

II. ENCOURAGEMENT (Joshua 1:5-9)
- A. Guarantee of Victory (v. 5)
- B. Call to Courage (v. 6)
- C. How to Succeed (vv. 7, 8)
  The Secret of Success
- D. A Reason for Confidence (v. 9)
  When Courage Is Called For

III. PREPARATION (Joshua 1:10, 11)
- A. Chain of Command (v. 10)
- B. Call to Prepare (v. 11)

CONCLUSION
- A. Knowing God's Will
- B. Doing God's Will
- C. Prayer
- D. Thought to Remember

Visual 3 of the visuals packet illustrates the teaching in verse 8 and the thoughts presented in points A and B of the Conclusion section. The visual is shown on page 29.

Introduction

Can you imagine starting out on a two-hundred-mile trip across the desert with three million people? This was not a vacation trip, but a move to a new home. Can you imagine the tons of tents and beds and household goods that had to be packed on donkeys and ox carts? Can you imagine the thousands of sheep and cattle?

The trip would not be fun for the three million. But they were slaves in Egypt, and beyond the desert was freedom. More important still, God told them to go, and God promised to help them.

A. God's Help

The places mentioned below, or in the Scripture references cited, may be found on the map (visual 2 of the visuals packet) that you used in last week's lesson.

God guided the march, moving in a pillar of cloud that turned to fire for night marches (Exodus 13:21, 22). The deep waters of the Red Sea lay across the way, but God made a dry path with towering walls of water to the left and right (Exodus 14:21, 22). At an oasis the water was not fit to drink, but God told Moses how to make it good (Exodus 15:22-25). Would the people starve in the desert? No, God filled the camp with quail and gave manna from the sky (Exodus 16:1, 13-15). Was there water enough in the desert? No, but God poured out an abundant supply from dry rock (Exodus 17:1-6). Did hostile desert tribes attack the caravan with violence? Yes, but God gave victory (Exodus 17:8-13).

In the third month of their traveling the people of Israel came to Mount Sinai or Horeb, the place from which God had called Moses to lead them out of Egypt (Exodus 19:1). They stayed at Sinai about a year, and the millions of liberated slaves were shaped into a nation.

B. On the Verge of Victory

The people moved on from Sinai and after several months came to Kadesh-barnea, near the border of the promised land. It was less than two years since they had left Egypt. At the border they camped for forty days, while twelve scouts went ahead to study the lay of the land, the quality of its produce, the strength of its warriors, and the defenses of its cities (Numbers 13:1-24).

The scouts brought back good news and bad news. The land indeed was excellent, and its produce was superb. But the cities had strong walls, and the men were gigantic. Ten of the twelve scouts said it would be impossible to take that country. Joshua and Caleb dissented vigorously. With God's help, they said, the land could be taken easily. But the people accepted the report of the majority and refused to go on (Numbers 13:25—14:10).

Their punishment was to have their own way. Instead of taking over a rich and fruitful land, they must live in the desert for thirty-eight more years. In that time all the adult men would die. The teenagers and younger children would become adults, and they would take the land of promise from which their fathers had turned away (Numbers 14:26-35).

C. Lesson Background

We come now to the end of the forty years of desert life. Again the people of Israel are at the border of the promised land. This time they have circled around and approached from the east. They have conquered the heathen tribes east of the Jordan. Moses has died, and Joshua has been appointed to replace him as leader. For thirty days the people have mourned the man who has led them for forty years (Deuteronomy 34:1-8). Now it is time to go forward.

> **How to Say It**
>
> EUPHRATES. U-*fray*-teez.
> KADESH-BARNEA. *Kay*-desh-*bar*-nee-uh (strong accent on *bar*).
> SINAI. *Sye*-nay-eye or *Sye*-nye.

I. Marching Orders (Joshua 1:1-4)

There was no struggle for leadership after Moses died. Of all the men who had left Egypt as adults, only Joshua and Caleb remained alive (Numbers 26:63-65). Joshua was clearly the one to replace Moses. He had been Moses' right-hand man from the beginning (Exodus 17:8-13). God had chosen him as the next leader, and all Israel knew it (Deuteronomy 31:1-8).

A. Command (vv. 1, 2)

1. Now after the death of Moses the servant of the LORD, it came to pass, that the LORD spake unto Joshua the son of Nun, Moses' minister, saying.

Previously God had spoken face to face to Moses the servant of God (Exodus 33:11). Now *Moses' minister* or servant was promoted to the place formerly held by Moses, and *the Lord spake unto Joshua.*

2. Moses my servant is dead; now therefore arise, go over this Jordan, thou, and all this people, unto the land which I do give to them, even to the children of Israel.

Of course Joshua knew Moses was dead. The fact was mentioned now as a reason for giving the command to Joshua. No longer could he wait for Moses to lead the way. The people of Israel were camped in the plains of Moab on the east side of the Jordan. Already they had taken the land on that side. Now was the time to *go over this Jordan,* and Joshua was the man to lead.

B. Promise (vv. 3, 4)

3. Every place that the sole of your foot shall tread upon, that have I given unto you, as I said unto Moses.

Moses was dead, but the promise was no less than it had been before. The people could walk all through the length and breadth of the land of Canaan, and all of it was theirs.

4. From the wilderness and this Lebanon even unto the great river, the river Euphrates, all the land of the Hittites, and unto the great sea toward the going down of the sun, shall be your coast.

This description of the promised land does not seem quite clear to us. Perhaps it will be plainer if we imagine we are in the plains of Moab with Joshua. Away to the south is *the wilderness* where we have been wandering for forty years; that is the south border of our new land. Looking northward we can see the peaks of *this Lebanon* on the horizon, but the promised land stretches northward beyond them and touches the upper part of the *great river, the river Euphrates.* The west boundary of our promised land is *the great sea toward the going down of the sun,* the Mediterranean. The east boundary is the desert east of the plains of Moab where we are standing with Joshua.

The Hittites were descendants of Heth, son of Canaan (Genesis 10:15). Here their name seems to be used for all the people living in the land of Canaan. A more detailed list of them is found in Exodus 33:2. *Your coast* means primarily your boundary, but sometimes it means all the land within your boundaries. That seems to be the meaning here.

II. Encouragement (Joshua 1:5-9)

Thirty-eight years had passed since Israel first had come to the border of the promised land and had sent scouts into the country. Of the people now with Joshua, the older ones had been teenagers then. They could remember that ten of the twelve scouts had said Israel could not conquer that land, because its cities were fortified and its men were giants (Numbers 13:25-33). Those who had been teenagers then were in their fifties now. They would need courage if they were to invade that fearsome land and battle its giants. If Joshua was to lead them, he would need courage and determination. So the Lord was ready with an encouraging word.

A. Guarantee of Victory (v. 5)

5. There shall not any man be able to stand before thee all the days of thy life: as I was with Moses, so I will be with thee: I will not fail thee, nor forsake thee.

In the promised land the enemies were many, and they and their cities looked strong; but Joshua's unseen companion was stronger than all of them. The Lord would be with Joshua, and His presence and power guaranteed victory.

B. Call to Courage (v. 6)

6. Be strong and of a good courage: for unto this people shalt thou divide for an inheritance the land, which I sware unto their fathers to give them.

How could Joshua be afraid? The Lord promised that he would conquer the country and divide it among his people. This was no new promise. God had made it centuries earlier to the ancestors of these people—Abraham, Isaac, and Jacob (Genesis 13:14-17; 17:8; 26:4; 28:13; 35:9-12).

C. How to Succeed (vv. 7, 8)

7. Only be thou strong and very courageous, that thou mayest observe to do according to all the law, which Moses my servant commanded thee: turn not from it to the right hand or to the left, that thou mayest prosper whithersoever thou goest.

To be successful, God's people must trust and obey. Their own strength was not enough to overcome all the heathen in Canaan, but they must have confidence in God—enough confidence to go boldly forward and use what strength they had. And they must obey *all the law* that God had given to Moses and Moses had given to the people at Sinai. They must not turn away from the law in any way. Only thus could they *prosper* as they advanced into the promised land.

8. This book of the law shall not depart out of thy mouth; but thou shalt meditate therein day and night, that thou mayest observe to do according to all that is written therein: for then thou shalt make thy way prosperous, and then thou shalt have good success.

Verse 7 is repeated and emphasized. Joshua must have the law in his mouth: he must talk about it. He must have it in his mind: he must think about it *day and night.* He must obey it in his actions: he must take care to *do according to all that is written therein.* On these conditions he could be sure his way would be *prosperous* and he would have *good success.*

THE SECRET OF SUCCESS

An estimated ninety-five percent of American motel and hotel rooms have a Bible in them, most of which have been supplied by the Gideon organization.

Since 1908, when a group of Christian salesmen left the first Bibles in a Midwestern hotel, these Bibles have given solace and encouragement to travelers. As recently as 1989, however, they became the object of a campaign by atheists who wanted Bibles banned from the inns of the nation. An organization of atheists claimed that Bibles in hotel and motel rooms were an invasion of privacy for "freethinking" travelers. This is simply one more example of how our society is turning its back on its Biblical heritage.

God wanted to prevent ancient Israel from becoming a secular society, so He commanded them to live every aspect of their lives according to His law. They were to discuss it, meditate upon it, and obey it. His word was to be the center of their lives. God promised success and prosperity to them if they would heed His law.

The results are the same in every age: those who live by the Word of God will prosper spiritually—the true measurement of success—and usually in other ways, as well. —C. R. B.

D. A Reason for Confidence (v. 9)

9. Have not I commanded thee? Be strong and of a good courage; be not afraid, neither be thou dismayed: for the LORD thy God is with thee whithersoever thou goest.

God had given the order to advance and take the land of Canaan. That was reason enough to *be strong and of a good courage.* When God's people are obeying His orders there is no reason to be *afraid* of gigantic men or to be *dismayed* by strong city walls. When you do His will, *the Lord thy God is with thee whithersoever thou goest.* The enemy may be too strong for you, but it cannot stand against you and Him.

WHEN COURAGE IS CALLED FOR

Five Costa Rican fishermen set out in January, 1988, for a few days of fishing in the Pacific. They enjoyed calm seas for six days, but suddenly a storm struck their small craft. Thirty-foot waves crashing into the cabin destroyed their radio. Their fuel was soon gone, and the hull began to leak.

Two months after the boat began to drift, fresh water and food were gone. Only an occasional rain gave them water; only the intermittent catch of fish or sea turtle supplied food. The crew was finally rescued after 142 days at sea; no one had ever survived so long through such an ordeal. The five men testified that only courage and faith in God, on which that courage was based, enabled them to survive.

Joshua and his people faced strong enemies. Thirty-eight years earlier, Israel's spies had persuaded the people that invading Canaan was too perilous to attempt. Now, God called upon the descendants of that faithless generation to demonstrate the courage their parents had lacked. Almighty God would be the source of their courage, if only they were willing. The question is the same for us today as it was for them: Are we willing to trust God to carry us through life's stormiest seas and harshest battles? —C. R. B.

III. Preparation (Joshua 1:10, 11)

God's presence assures success when we are doing what He wants us to do; but it does not take the place of our own thinking, our own planning, our own effort.

A. Chain of Command (v. 10)

10. Then Joshua commanded the officers of the people, saying.

Soon after the people of Israel had left Egypt, Moses had taken the advice of his father-in-law and had organized them thoroughly (Exodus 18:24-26). Now we are looking at a time nearly forty years later. Whether the organization was exactly the same or not, there were *officers* who could pass Joshua's order on to the people and see that it was carried out.

B. Call to Prepare (v. 11)

11. Pass through the host, and command the people, saying, Prepare you victuals; for within three days ye shall pass over this Jordan, to go in to possess the land, which the LORD your God giveth you to possess it.

The command was to get ready to march. The people had been camped in one place through the month of mourning for Moses (Deuteronomy 34:8), so their possessions were no longer packed for travel.

The Passover was near (Joshua 5:10). The rainy season was ending, but the Jordan was still in flood, overflowing its banks (Joshua 3:15). It was not hard for two men to swim that swollen river, perhaps with the help of a floating log (Joshua 2:1). But millions of men, women, and children, loaded down by their goods and handicapped by their sheep and cattle—how could they hope to cross that river? The call to get ready to *pass over this Jordan* was a call to have faith. The people responded and did their packing.

Conclusion

The people of Israel took up their loads and went toward the overflowing Jordan. Priests led the way, carrying the ark of the covenant. Their feet splashed into the shallow water at the edge of the stream; and the water in front of them ran away to the south, leaving a dry stream bed for them to cross. The water flowing down from the north piled up in a heap instead of flowing past (Joshua 3:16).

visual 3

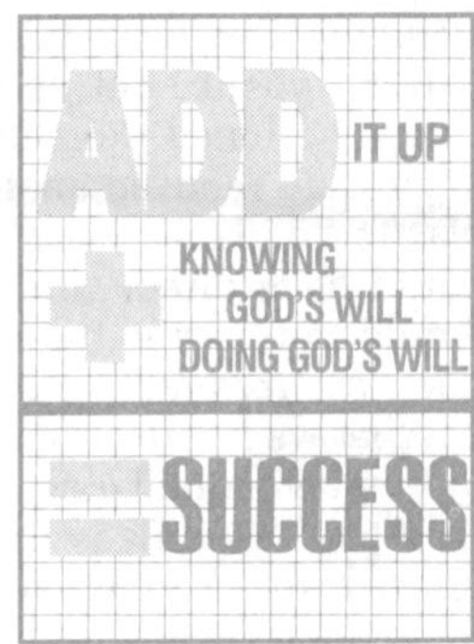

The Jordan carries a lot of water in time of flood. The heap must have grown to a mountain, but it stood firm till all the people reached the west bank. Then the mountain of water flowed on to the Dead Sea, and the river was back to its normal flood stage (Joshua 3, 4). That was a symbol and foretaste of things to come.

The people used no battering ram against the walls of Jericho. God told them to march around the city, blow the trumpets, and shout. They did as He said, and those massive walls collapsed (Joshua 6).

So Israel swept across the country, taking city after city and defeating coalitions of cities (Joshua 8—12). Only when God's orders were disobeyed did they have trouble (Joshua 7). The secret of success is to know what God wants you to do, and to do it.

A. Knowing God's Will

Which college shall I choose? Which girl shall I court? Which job shall I seek? Which house shall I buy, or will it be better to rent an apartment?

Wouldn't it be great if God would talk to us as He did to Joshua? Wouldn't we love to have all our troublesome decisions made for us? But the Lord has always reserved that kind of guidance for special occasions, and even those who were so guided had to make some decisions for themselves. Sometimes they made bad decisions.

Adam and Eve had all the instruction they needed, but they chose to ignore the instruction and get in trouble. Abraham heard God's call and answered, but he made some abominable decisions on his own. He lied about his wife (Genesis 12:10-20); he fathered a son by a slave girl (Genesis 16). Moses had special directions, but he blundered so badly that he was barred from the promised land (Numbers 20:1-12;

Deuteronomy 32:48-52; 34:1-6). Paul was an inspired apostle, but he said he sometimes did things he hated (Romans 7:15). And Paul once vigorously rebuked another apostle, saying, "He was to be blamed" (Galatians 2:11). Even if we could have direct guidance from the Lord, we would not escape the responsibility of making decisions for ourselves.

What we know of God's will is enough to provide reliable guidelines. God does not want me in a godless college unless my faith is strong enough to survive every possible attack and temptation. The Lord does not want me to share my life with a mate who does not share my love for Him. He does not want me in a job that requires lying or cheating. He does not want me to buy a house I can't pay for. You can go on and on with a list of things you know God does not want you to do, and probably you have done some of them. The fault is not in the instructions we have; it is in our failure to follow instructions.

B. Doing God's Will

Haven't we all chuckled at the old story of a farmer who declined an invitation to attend a clinic where he could learn how to farm better? He said, "I already know how to farm better than I do."

Most of us know how to follow the Lord's leading better than we do. We do well to keep on in thoughtful study of His Word. It not only helps us know more about His will, but also encourages us to do His will more completely. But as we study to learn more, let us not neglect to live by what we already know.

Don't we all know the Lord wants us to help those who are in need? Early Christians did it both as individuals and as congregations (Acts 4:34-37; Romans 15:25-27). How long has it been since you deprived yourself of anything you wanted in order to help someone whose need was greater than yours?

Don't we all know it is our job to take the gospel to all the world and every creature? (Mark 16:15). How long has it been since you personally took it to any creature? How long has it been since you made a notable sacrifice to help missionaries take it to hundreds on the other side of the world?

Don't we all know God wants His children to be peacemakers? (Matthew 5:9). What have you done with a quarrel lately: started it, ended it, or prevented it?

Don't we all know God wants us to be careful with our talk? The tongue can be "an unruly evil, full of deadly poison" (James 3:8). Has yours been a poison or an antidote?

Don't we all know God wants us to be regular churchgoers? (Hebrews 10:25). Is He satisfied with your attendance record? Are you satisfied with it?

Don't we all know God wants us to be "steadfast, unmovable, always abounding in the work of the Lord"? (1 Corinthians 15:58). Count up the hours you have given to His work in the past week. Are they abundant?

Don't stop now. Keep on till you think of something in which you personally have not been doing as well as you know how. At that point this lesson can help you—if you really want to do better.

James wrote, "Be ye doers of the word, and not hearers only, deceiving your own selves" (James 1:22). We are fooling ourselves if we think we are good Christians just because we study the Bible and confess that Jesus is the Christ, the Son of the living God. He said, "Not every one that saith unto me, Lord, Lord, shall enter into the kingdom of heaven; but he that doeth the will of my Father which is in heaven" (Matthew 7:21). How are we doing?

C. Prayer

Our Father in Heaven, how we are enriched by Your Word! It is good to read of great men of old who followed Your leading well, even though they did not follow it perfectly. We delight in feasting on the teaching of Jesus and the inspired writers of the New Testament. Give us wisdom to understand what we read, we pray; and give us strength and courage and determination to follow it. In Jesus' name, amen.

D. Thought to Remember

"Be ye doers of the word."

Home Daily Bible Readings

Monday, Sept. 14—Joshua Succeeds Moses (Joshua 1:12-18)

Tuesday, Sept. 15—Rahab Protects Joshua's Messengers (Joshua 2:1-14)

Wednesday, Sept. 16—The Israelites Follow the Ark of the Covenant (Joshua 3:1-6)

Thursday, Sept. 17—God Promises to be With Joshua (Joshua 3:7-13)

Friday, Sept. 18—Joshua Makes a Memorial of Twelve Stones (Joshua 4:1-7)

Saturday, Sept. 19—Joshua Meets a Man of God Near Jericho (Joshua 5:10-15)

Sunday, Sept. 20—Joshua's Army Brings Down the Wall of Jericho (Joshua 6:15-21)

Learning by Doing

This page contains an alternate lesson plan emphasizing learning activities. Classes desiring such student involvement will find these suggestions helpful.

Learning Goals

This lesson will help each class member:

1. Analyze God's promise of success for Joshua.
2. Determine how they can have spiritual success.
3. Commit or renew their commitment to meditate regularly on God's Word and obey it.

Into the Lesson

Lead your students in a brainstorm of this question: "If you were to ask your neighbors and friends, 'What is the secret of success in life' what do you think they would say?"

As the students call out their answers, list them on the chalkboard. Then ask, "Which answer do you think you would hear most often?" Circle the top two or three choices they suggest.

Then say, "In our study today we will explore an approach to true success that God revealed to Joshua. And we will consider how we can apply that approach in our lives."

Option

Ask for three volunteers to participate in a role play. Write the following directions on three index cards and give one to each volunteer: *You will be discussing with the other two role players what your definition of success is and how to achieve it. You will base your views upon your assigned profession. You will pretend that the following is your profession:*

On one card write, professional football player; on another write, politician; on the third write, professional rock star. (Substitute other professions, if you desire.)

Allow the role players a minute to think about their role. Then have them come to the front of the class and engage in a discussion about what success is and how to achieve it. Stop the role play when the points have been clearly made and the discussion begins to repeat itself.

Ask the class, "How would your definition of success compare with the ones expressed in the role play?" After a time of brief discussion, lead into the Bible study by saying, "Today we will explore true success and how to achieve it."

Into the Word

Prepare a two-minute lecture on the lesson background. The information you need is in the Introduction to the lesson commentary.

Ask a volunteer to read Joshua 1:1-11. Then lead your class in discussing the questions below. Be sure to provide a dictionary for question 4a.

1. What mission did God have for Joshua and the Israelites? (vv. 1, 2, 10, 11).
2. What promises did God give to Joshua? (vv. 3-9).
3. What was the key to success in accomplishing the mission? (vv. 6-9)
4. Focus on the command to meditate on the "book of the law" (God's Word) given in verse 8. Discuss:
   a. What is meditation? (Look up the word in a dictionary.)
   b. When is meditation to occur? (v. 8).
   c. What should be the goal of meditation? (v. 8).
5. What in this passage indicates that obedience doesn't happen by accident?
6. According to this passage, how would you define success?

Into Life

Provide each student with paper, pencil, and a copy of the following questions:

1. What keeps many Christians from implementing God's plan for success as explained in Joshua 1:7, 8?
2. Meditating on God's Word and carefully obeying it are critical to spiritual success. What can you do to make these central in your life? Write a plan for putting these at the core of your life (or keeping them at the core).
3. How much of this plan will you begin to implement? When will you do it?

Option

Have students form groups of six. Provide each group with several sheets of paper and several pencils. Ask the groups to prepare a brochure entitled *The Secret of True Success.* In the brochure they should define success from God's perspective and seek to apply principles from Joshua 1:1-11. They can add artwork if they desire. Allow fifteen to twenty minutes. Then ask each group to present and read their brochure for the rest of the class.

Conclude the session by asking the students to consider how they can apply this passage more consistently to their lives.

Let's Talk It Over

The questions on this page are designed to encourage review of the lesson Scriptures and to promote discussion of the lesson by the class. The answers provided are only discussion starters. Let your class talk it over from there.

1. It is interesting to observe that God promised Joshua He was giving the land of Canaan to Israel, and yet they would have to take it. What does this indicate about how we are to appropriate God's promises?

It reminds us of the ineffectiveness of "armchair religion," of the kind of Christianity that is "all talk and no action." In spite of God's promises, Israel would not have possessed the land if they had not taken action. Similarly, God's promises to us regarding evangelistic success, victories over evil, answers to prayer, etc. will come about as we respond with works of faith. In Colossians 1:28, 29 Paul gives us an example of the approach we must take when he speaks of his preaching and teaching efforts and then declares, "Whereunto I also labor, striving according to his working, which worketh in me mightily."

2. God kept urging Joshua to "be strong," and in the New Testament we also are urged to "be strong" (1 Corinthians 16:13, Ephesians 6:10). How can we accomplish this?

Such an exhortation shows up regularly in the self-help literature that is prominent in our society. The kind of positive thinking advocated in this literature is often of a humanistic nature, and Christians must be wary of it. But the New Testament gives us justification for a kind of "sanctified" positive thinking. Because of our salvation and the presence of the Holy Spirit within us, we have good reason to declare, "I am strong, and I will be strong in the Lord!" When we do that, we are not engaging in self-deception or "trying to pull ourselves up by our own bootstraps." Instead, we are expressing our confidence that the Lord has provided a boundless reservoir of strength for His people, and we are by faith drawing from that reservoir.

3. Why is the practice of meditating on God's Word one that merits emphasis today?

It is distressing to learn that many Christians do not take time for devotional reading of the Bible. And some who do set aside time for Bible reading engage in only a superficial investigation of the Word. Meditation on the Word involves the expending of time and effort in order to discern God's nature and will. It requires that we give the Bible a higher priority in our schedule, and that we curtail some activities of lesser importance so that we may have adequate time for what is of supreme importance. And more than time alone is required—somehow we must eliminate the distractions that can hinder our understanding of and personal applying of God's Word. Some Christians have found that either early morning or late evening work well for this purpose (see Psalm 119:147, 148).

4. How should we respond if God lays challenges before us that we may be inclined to regard as impossible?

The familiar chorus reminds us that "God specializes in things thought impossible." The Bible gives many examples showing that God accomplishes things that seem beyond human reach. This fact suggests that we in the church should not be too hasty to declare any task impossible. Such challenges as raising the money to construct a new building, hire a full-time youth minister, or provide living-link support for a missionary may seem out of the question for our church. But God has enabled churches like our own to accomplish such "impossible" feats, and He can do the same with us. John's question seems appropriate in this regard: "Who is he that overcometh the world, but he that believeth that Jesus is the Son of God?" (1 John 5:5).

5. We sometimes lament our inability to ascertain the will of God in a particular matter. But the lesson writer reminds us that we already know much about God's will. How can we use that knowledge in gaining guidance?

In regard to a specific decision we must reach in determining God's will, it may help us if we will make a list of Biblical principles that apply. We can begin by putting down Biblical prohibitions against lying, stealing, sexual impurity, etc., insofar as they relate to our options. We can add those Scriptural principles that are of broader interpretation: how this will affect our physical health, how it will affect our witness for Christ, whether or not it may damage someone else's faith, etc. Once we have narrowed the options to those that are Scripturally sound, we can pray more intelligently and confidently regarding which of them is best.

God's Provision of Leadership Through Deborah

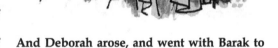

September 27
Lesson 4

LESSON SCRIPTURE: Judges 4, 5.

PRINTED TEXT: Judges 4:4-10, 14-16.

DEVOTIONAL READING: Judges 6:11-16.

Judges 4:4-10, 14-16

**4 And Deborah, a prophetess, the wife of
Lapidoth, she judged Israel at that time.
5 And she dwelt under the palm tree of
Deborah, between Ramah and Bethel in
mount Ephraim: and the children of Israel
came up to her for judgment.
6 And she sent and called Barak the son of
Abinoam out of Kedesh-naphtali, and said
unto him, Hath not the LORD God of Israel
commanded, saying, Go and draw toward
mount Tabor, and take with thee ten thousand
men of the children of Naphtali and of the
children of Zebulun?
7 And I will draw unto thee, to the river
Kishon, Sisera the captain of Jabin's army,
with his chariots and his multitude; and I will
deliver him into thine hand.
8 And Barak said unto her, If thou wilt go
with me, then I will go: but if thou wilt not go
with me, then I will not go.
9 And she said, I will surely go with thee:
notwithstanding the journey that thou takest
shall not be for thine honor; for the LORD
shall sell Sisera into the hand of a woman.
And Deborah arose, and went with Barak to
Kedesh.
10 And Barak called Zebulun and Naphtali
to Kedesh; and he went up with ten thousand
men at his feet: and Deborah went up with
him.**

. . . .

**14 And Deborah said unto Barak, Up; for
this is the day in which the LORD hath delivered Sisera into thine hand: is not the LORD
gone out before thee? So Barak went down
from mount Tabor, and ten thousand men
after him.
15 And the LORD discomfited Sisera, and all
his chariots, and all his host, with the edge of
the sword before Barak; so that Sisera lighted
down off his chariot, and fled away on his
feet.
16 But Barak pursued after the chariots, and
after the host, unto Harosheth of the Gentiles:
and all the host of Sisera fell upon the edge of
the sword; and there was not a man left.**

GOLDEN TEXT: [Deborah] sent and called Barak . . . and said unto him, Hath not the LORD God of Israel commanded, saying, Go and draw toward mount Tabor, and take with thee ten thousand men of the children of Naphtali and of the children of Zebulun?—Judges 4:6.

Old Testament Personalities

Unit 1: God Chooses and Relates to a People (Lessons 1-4)

Lesson Aims

After studying this lesson a student should be able to:

1. Retell the story of Deborah and Barak.
2. Tell why Israel was oppressed and why she was liberated.
3. Give more attention to Bible study.

Lesson Outline

INTRODUCTION
- A. Instant Prosperity
- B. Crime and Punishment
- C. Lesson Background

I. MESSAGE FROM GOD (Judges 4:4-7)
- A. The Spokesperson (vv. 4, 5)
  - *The Best Man for the Job . . .*
- B. Call for a Warrior (v. 6)
- C. Plan of Battle (v. 7)

II. DUAL LEADERSHIP (Judges 4:8-10)
- A. The Leaders (vv. 8, 9)
- B. The Army (v. 10)

III. COMBAT (Judges 4:14-16)
- A. Attack (v. 14)
  - *Divine Deliverance*
- B. Victory (vv. 15, 16)

IV. THE REST OF THE STORY
- A. A Bit of Background
- B. Deadly Refuge
- C. Epilogue

CONCLUSION
- A. The Lord Still Rules
- B. The Lord Still Speaks
- C. Prayer
- D. Thought to Remember

Using the map (visual 4 of the visuals packet), locate the places mentioned in this lesson. The map is shown on page 37.

Introduction

1. Be strong and courageous.
2. Keep God's law.

The Lord said these two things should be done to assure success when the people of Israel invaded the promised land (Joshua 1:7-9). The people met those conditions well enough to be successful in driving out or destroying the heathen in every conflict. When they had captured as much land as they could use, they divided it among their tribes and settled down to normal living (Joshua 14-21).

A. Instant Prosperity

With the land came instant prosperity. The promise of Deuteronomy 6:10-12 was fulfilled. They did not have to build houses, for they captured whole towns with the furnished homes of the former occupants. They took over vineyards and orchards mature and bearing fruit. They found grainfields ready for harvest, and stores of grain already harvested.

B. Crime and Punishment

Keeping God's law made these people winners; but when they had won, they gradually became careless about obeying God. The record mentions especially that they began to join their heathen neighbors in worshiping false gods. Feasting was prominent in such worship. Perhaps the Israelites at first meant only to enjoy a banquet, but later they were bowing to heathen gods (Judges 2:11-13). Then they began to adopt heathen moral standards. As long as their priests are well paid, heathen gods have no objection to lying, stealing, adultery, cruelty. The book of Judges does not go into details, but later prophets speak plainly about the misconduct that goes with paganism. See Amos 2:6-8, for example.

Such misconduct deserved punishment, and the Lord's way of punishing was simple. He let some of the displaced heathen invade Israel, rustling cattle and sheep and stealing the harvest of grain (Judges 2:14, 15). Sometimes He let outsiders dominate a part of Israel for years, taking tribute year after year (Judges 3:7, 8).

Reduced to poverty and hardship, the people of Israel remembered who had made them prosperous before. They turned back to the Lord and begged for His help. Then He provided a godly leader to rally them and drive out the invaders. Peace and prosperity returned. But when the leader died, soon the people drifted into paganism again; and then they were punished again (Judges 2:16-19). This cycle was repeated over and over. This week we see one time when oppressing heathen were defeated.

C. Lesson Background

After one period of increasing sin in Israel, some of the remaining Canaanites got control of the country, or at least the north part of it. King of these Canaanites was Jabin. His capital was at Hazor, a few miles north of the Sea of Chinnereth, which later was called the Sea of Galilee.

The main part of Jabin's army was stationed at Harosheth on the Kishon River. Its commander was Sisera. These pagans dominated the people of Israel for twenty years, and "mightily oppressed" them. But the suffering people again were appealing to the Lord (Judges 4:1-3). At last He moved to rescue them.

I. Message From God (Judges 4:4-7)

In past lessons we have seen that God spoke directly to Abraham, Moses, and Joshua. This time He spoke to a lady known as His prophetess, and she relayed the call to the man who would lead the army.

A. The Spokesperson (vv. 4, 5)

4. And Deborah, a prophetess, the wife of Lapidoth, she judged Israel at that time.

A prophetess, like a prophet, is one who receives communications directly from God and passes them on as He directs. Of *Lapidoth* we know only what this verse tells us. This prophetess was not a lonely old maid in a sequestered hermitage. She was a wife and mother, unless the term *mother* in Judges 5:7 means that her leadership made her a mother to the whole nation. The statement that *she judged Israel* shows that she had a powerful influence in the nation. In that time of severe oppression, she may have done much to help her people turn from heathen ways to the Lord (v. 3).

5. And she dwelt under the palm tree of Deborah, between Ramah and Bethel in mount Ephraim: and the children of Israel came up to her for judgment.

Mount Ephraim means the hill country belonging to the tribe of Ephraim rather than one single mountain. Deborah's home was in the central part of Israel, where people could come to it from any direction. There is no indication she had police to enforce her decisions or arrest wrongdoers, but *the children of Israel came up to her for judgment* because they had learned that she spoke for God and her decisions were fair and right. After years of oppression brought on by wrongdoing, the people were hungry for leadership like Deborah's.

THE BEST MAN FOR THE JOB . . .

Kenilworth-Parkside in Washington, D. C., was a public housing development that failed. Neither the bureaucracy that created it nor the residents who neglected it would acknowledge responsibility for its failure. What the residents broke, the bureaucrats refused to fix, and "the project" became unlivable.

In 1981, one of the residents, Kimi Gray—a forty-two-year-old-mother of five—decided to do something about the situation. She convinced government to let residents take control, organized a management corporation to run the project, and lobbied Congress to allow renters to buy their homes in public housing projects. After seven years of her determined effort, it was clear that Kenilworth-Parkside worked: it was clean, free of graffiti, and the businesses created by Gray's management corporation employed more than one hundred residents. Pride of ownership replaced the shame of poverty. As it has been said, sometimes "the best man for the job may be a woman!"

It was true in Israel in the time of today's lesson. Deborah was God's prophetess and leader of His people. When God needs a servant, He seems to be more interested in a person's love for Him and willingness to be used by Him than in factors by which we arbitrarily determine a person's worth and usefulness. —C. R. B.

B. Call for a Warrior (v. 6)

6. And she sent and called Barak the son of Abinoam out of Kedesh-naphtali, and said unto him, Hath not the LORD God of Israel commanded, saying, Go and draw toward mount Tabor, and take with thee ten thousand men of the children of Naphtali and of the children of Zebulun?

Barak lived in *Kedesh,* a town in the territory belonging to the tribe of *Naphtali.* This was perhaps a four-days' journey north of Deborah's place. It seems that Barak dropped whatever he was doing and came promptly when Deborah's messenger came with the call.

What Deborah said to Barak appears as a question, but that is a Hebrew way of stating a fact less abruptly and peremptorily. *Hath not the Lord commanded* means *The Lord hath commanded.* The Lord wanted Barak to raise an army of ten thousand men from his own tribe and the neigh-

How to Say It

ABINOAM. A-*bin*-o-am.
BARAK. *Bay*-ruk or *Bair*-uk.
CHINNERETH. *Kin*-e-reth or *Chin*-ne-reth.
HAROSHETH. Ha-*ro*-sheth.
HEBER. *Hee*-ber.
JAEL. *Jay*-ul.
KEDESH-NAPHTALI. *Kee*-desh-*naf*-tuh-lye.
KISHON. *Kye*-shon.
SISERA. *Sis*-er-uh or *Sis*-uh-ruh.
ZEBULUN. *Zeb*-you-lun.

boring tribe of *Zebulun,* and to lead them to *mount Tabor.* While mount Ephraim (v. 5) was a wide hilly area, Mount Tabor was a single knob overlooking the plain where the river Kishon flowed.

C. Plan of Battle (v. 7)

7. And I will draw unto thee, to the river Kishon, Sisera the captain of Jabin's army, with his chariots and his multitude; and I will deliver him into thine hand.

If Barak would take ten thousand men to Mount Tabor, the Lord would bring Jabin's army to meet them and would give the victory to Barak and his men. He would bring the army *to the river Kishon,* not to Mount Tabor. The most terrible part of the Canaanite army was its chariots, nine hundred of them made of iron (v. 3). They could not charge up the wooded slopes of Tabor, so Barak's men would be safe there till they were ready to launch their attack. *Sisera* would bring an uncounted *multitude* of foot soldiers as well as his chariots, but the Lord promised to *deliver him,* turn him and all his army over to Barak and his troops.

II. Dual Leadership (Judges 4:8-10)

Israel had been helpless before the Canaanites for twenty years. If Barak could enlist ten thousand men, they would be untrained and certainly not very well armed. They would have to face an army of unknown size, plus those fearsome chariots of iron. It took faith and courage to accept the assignment, but Barak accepted—on one condition.

A. The Leaders (vv. 8, 9)

8. And Barak said unto her, If thou wilt go with me, then I will go: but if thou wilt not go with me, then I will not go.

Some students think Barak showed a lack of faith and courage when he insisted that Deborah go with him; others think rather that he showed commendable prudence. This was the Lord's project, and Deborah was the Lord's prophetess. She could supply the Lord's direction for every step of the campaign. Suppose Barak would send messengers to every town in Zebulun and Naphtali to say, "Barak says God wants you in the army." Wouldn't men answer, "Who is Barak? How does he know what God wants?" But suppose the messengers would proclaim, "Deborah is in Kedesh! She says God wants you in the army." That would be an electrifying call. Deborah was known as God's prophetess. Men would respond to her call as Barak had done. And when the ten thousand came to Mount Tabor, wouldn't it be great to have God's spokesperson to tell them what to do next?

9. And she said, I will surely go with thee: notwithstanding the journey that thou takest shall not be for thine honor; for the LORD shall sell Sisera into the hand of a woman. And Deborah arose, and went with Barak to Kedesh.

Deborah readily consented to go with Barak. The advantages of her presence were obvious. However, she warned Barak that credit for the final victory would go to a woman, not to him. At this point we might suppose that Deborah herself would be that woman, but at the end of the story we shall find that another woman put an end to Sisera.

Some who think Barak was lacking in faith and courage think also that he was punished for that lack by being deprived of credit for that victory. That opinion is seen in the *New International Version* at this point: "But because of the way you are going about this, the honor will not be yours." If we think Barak was lacking, we may well take this as his punishment. If we do not see such a lack in him, this appears as merely a prediction of fact. Hearing it at this time would keep Barak from being disappointed later when the greatest glory would go to someone else.

And Deborah arose, and went with Barak to Kedesh to begin enlisting soldiers for the army of liberation.

B. The Army (v. 10)

10. And Barak called Zebulun and Naphtali to Kedesh; and he went up with ten thousand men at his feet: and Deborah went up with him.

It was no small task to recruit an army. We can only guess how long it took to send messengers to all the towns of *Zebulun and Naphtali.* In time ten thousand men were assembled at Kedesh, and Barak led them to the south. *At his feet* means following in his footsteps, going with him. He was taking them to Mount Tabor, *and Deborah went up with him* and the army.

III. Combat (Judges 4:14-16)

King Jabin of the Canaanites had his home at Hazor, not far from Kedesh. His people could not fail to see ten thousand men assembling at Kedesh and marching off to Tabor. It was plain that the Hebrews were planning to fight for freedom; so word was sent to Sisera, general of the Canaanite army. He and his troops were at Harosheth on the lower Kishon River, probably to guard the highway from the coast to the interior.

visual 4

With nine hundred chariots and uncounted infantrymen, Sisera moved up the river to meet the Hebrew army (vv. 12, 13).

A. Attack (v. 14)

14. And Deborah said unto Barak, Up; for this is the day in which the LORD hath delivered Sisera into thine hand: is not the LORD gone out before thee? So Barak went down from mount Tabor, and ten thousand men after him.

From Mount Tabor, Deborah and Barak could see Sisera's army, and those terrible chariots, on the low ground by the river. Now was the time to attack. Victory was sure, for the Lord had promised it. Already the Lord had gone out to the field of battle; it was time for His people to follow. So Barak and his ten thousand charged down the side of Tabor and across the plain.

DIVINE DELIVERANCE

Today's auto thieves steal cars on order from unethical repair shops that need parts for specific cars. They deliver cars to "chop shops" where they are cut up for resale as parts that cannot be easily traced. Expensive brands of cars are stolen and smuggled out of the country for sale to foreign buyers.

Now the "good guys" have a new, electronic weapon in their arsenal: a device hidden on a car can be activated by the police when the vehicle is reported stolen. The signal can be accurately traced, and the thieves unwittingly deliver themselves into the hands of the law.

The forces of Sisera were up against a force far more powerful than an electronic stolen car tracer. They were doomed to failure when they went into battle against the army of Israel, led by Deborah and Barak. Sisera opposed the plan of God for Israel. Because God was watching over Israel, He would give Sisera into their hands. God's purposes will be accomplished. We, His people, should be sure that we are living within His will, so we may prosper by His deliverance. —C. R. B.

B. Victory (vv. 15, 16)

15. And the LORD discomfited Sisera, and all his chariots, and all his host, with the edge of the sword before Barak; so that Sisera lighted down off his chariot, and fled away on his feet.

Discomfited is a very mild word to tell what the Lord did to *Sisera* and his army. The same Hebrew word is sometimes translated *destroyed* or *consumed.* To see how the Lord did it, we look at the song composed later to celebrate the victory. The Lord brought a terrific rainstorm, such a cloudburst that the mountains seemed to be melting as the water cascaded down their sides (Judges 5:4, 5). It is easy to guess additional details. The soft alluvial plain became a sea of mud. The chariots bogged down; the horses floundered in the mire. When the chariots were helpless, the footmen lost heart. And the pouring rain was full of furious Hebrews, attacking *with the edge of the sword.* The Canaanite troops broke and ran. General Sisera saw no hope of rallying them. He abandoned his useless chariot, and, veiled by the rain, he managed to make his way out of the melee and run away alone. A flash flood brought the river over its banks to sweep away the dead bodies (Judges 5:21).

16. But Barak pursued after the chariots, and after the host, unto Harosheth of the Gentiles: and all the host of Sisera fell upon the edge of the sword; and there was not a man left.

Leaderless and terrified, Sisera's men ran back down the river. Vengeful Hebrews chased them all the way to Harosheth and slaughtered every one. *There was not a man left.*

IV. The Rest of the Story

Still the victory was not quite complete. The enemy army was dead, but its general was fleeing northward as fast as his feet could carry him. He kept going till he found a friendly refuge, or so he thought.

A. A Bit of Background

The Kenites were a clan of the Midianites with whom Moses lived for forty years before God sent him to lead Israel out of Egypt. Moses' brother-in-law, Hobab, was a Kenite who went with the people of Israel to give them the benefit of his knowledge of the desert country (Numbers 10:29-32). The *King James Version* sometimes calls him Moses' father-in-law, but the Hebrew term is loosely used of any relative by marriage. Hobab's children settled in the south part of the promised land (Judges 1:16). The country there was much like their home country, Midian. In the time of Deborah and Barak, however, one of them had left the clan and lived in the north part of Israel. Probably he was still a shepherd, for he continued to live in a tent as his forefathers had done. This man's name was Heber (Judges 4:11). He was friendly with the Canaanites (v. 17), probably because he cooperated with them in some way and so escaped the oppression that burdened the people of Israel.

B. Deadly Refuge

Sisera was exhausted when his headlong flight brought him to Heber's tent. This was about forty miles from the disastrous battlefield. The fleeing man must have been on his feet all through the night and part of the preceding day.

Heber probably was out with his sheep, but his wife was at home. She gave the runaway general a cordial welcome. He was hungry and thirsty; she gave him milk to drink and cottage cheese to eat (Judges 5:24, 25). He was worn out; he lay down to sleep, and she covered him so anyone looking into the tent would see only a pile of bedding.

But when the guest was sound asleep, the hostess came stealthily with a tent peg in one hand and a hammer in the other. Uncovering his head, she drove the peg through it into the ground. "So he died" (Judges 4:17-21).

So the victory was complete; and a woman got credit for the final stroke, just as Deborah had predicted (Judges 4:9). The victory song gave high praise to "Jael the wife of Heber the Kenite" (Judges 5:24-27).

C. Epilogue

After all, there was credit enough to go around. Deborah and Barak also had a place in the song of victory (Judges 5:6-9, 12, 13). Better than that, Israel was free from the oppression that had troubled the nation for twenty years. Best of all, God's people had turned away from the greed and cruelty and crooked dealing that had brought on the oppression. Idols were forgotten, and Jehovah was worshiped. The victory song praised Him most of all (Judges 5:1-3). And Israel was at peace for forty years (v. 31).

Conclusion

Dismayed by the greed and cruelty and crooked dealing in our world today, we may be tempted to ask, "Where is the Lord now?" Of course we know the answer. God is in His Heaven as He always has been. He has not gone away; the world has gone away from Him. Israel did that again and again, and trouble resulted every time.

A. The Lord Still Rules

The Lord rules. This very morning I stepped out of my door into one of His gentle reminders that He is in charge. Severe reminders are tornadoes and earthquakes. They stop us short in our busy lives, and their devastation tells us there is a power far beyond anything we can create or control. But today I stepped out into a world shrouded in fog. The fog does no damage like that of earthquake or tornado, but it stops the planes from flying and slows the cars and buses so much that nearly everyone is late for work—and there is nothing we can do about it. The Lord rules.

If we have eyes to see and minds to think, we do not need even the gentle fog to tell us who is in charge. God gives us sunshine and rain, planting time and harvest (Acts 14:17). The Lord rules.

B. The Lord Still Speaks

Sometimes we may wish we could have a prophetess like Deborah to tell us what to do. But in fact we do have in one volume all the prophets from Abraham the friend of God to John the apostle. We do not need another guide so much as we need to know and follow the guide we have, the Holy Bible.

C. Prayer

Lord God Almighty, how gracious You have been to lay before us the inspired words of prophets and wise men through the ages! We do want to do Your will, our Father. Give us wisdom to understand and courage to obey, we pray in Jesus' name. Amen.

D. Thought to Remember

The Lord still rules.

Home Daily Bible Readings

Monday, Sept. 21—Deborah and Barak Sing Praises to God (Judges 5:1-5)
Tuesday, Sept. 22—Deborah's Rise to Leadership (Judges 5:6-10)
Wednesday, Sept. 23—Victory for Deborah and Barak (Judges 5:11-15a)
Thursday, Sept. 24—Disunity Among the Israelites (Judges 5:15b-23)
Friday, Sept. 25—The Enemy Is Defeated (Judges 5:24-51)
Saturday, Sept. 26—God Calls Gideon to Lead the Israelites (Judges 6:11-17)
Sunday, Sept. 27—God Assures Gideon of Israel's Deliverance (Judges 7:36-40)

Learning by Doing

This page contains an alternate lesson plan emphasizing learning activities. Classes desiring such student involvement will find these suggestions helpful.

Learning Goals

By the conclusion of this lesson each class member should be able to:

1. Determine how the faith of Deborah and Barak made a difference in their world.
2. Suggest ways they can make a difference in their world through their faith.

Into the Lesson

Before class look through newspapers for articles to illustrate that much in our world needs to be changed. Examples: articles dealing with crime, poverty, broken families, substance abuse, or the rise of the occult. Before students arrive, tape these articles on your classroom walls and write this question on the chalkboard: *From the news articles, what evidence do you see that our world needs to be changed?*

As students arrive, give each one a sheet of paper and a pencil. Ask them to skim several of the articles and to list their answers to the question on the chalkboard. Then have students take their seats and lead them in discussing their findings by asking, "What observations did you make about changes needed in our world?"

Lead into the Bible study by saying, "We live in a world that is broken and needs to be fixed. God has called His people to see the needs of the world and make a difference. Today we will observe two leaders in Israel whose faith made a difference in their world. And we'll consider how we can make a difference in our world."

Into the Word

Divide the students into groups of six and appoint a discussion leader for each. Provide these instructions for each group. (This activity is included in the student book.)

Read Judges 4. Then summarize each of the following sections in twelve words or less:

vv. 1-3
vv. 4-7
vv. 8-11
vv. 12-16
vv. 17-21
vv. 22-24

Provide each group with the student books or a sheet of paper and pencil for the writing of their summaries. After about fifteen minutes, call time. Then refer to each section, one at a time. Ask one of the groups to read their summary for the first section. Then ask another group to read their summary for the second section. Continue in this way until each group has opportunity to summarize a section.

Help your students analyze some lessons from this passage by leading a discussion of these two questions:

1. What do you learn about faith from Deborah and Barak?
2. How did the faith of Barak and Deborah make a difference in their world?

Option

Have your students prepare and participate in an informal debate. They are to analyze the roles played by Deborah and Barak in the deliverance of Israel.

Have the class form two groups. One group is to defend this proposition: *Barak was more instrumental than Deborah in delivering Israel.* The other group will defend this proposition: *Deborah was more instrumental than Barak in delivering Israel.* Allow the groups fifteen minutes to read Judges 4 and form their arguments. Then allow each group three minutes to present their arguments. The goal, of course, is not to win the debate, but to carefully investigate the Biblical passage.

Then lead the class in discussing the two questions listed earlier in *Into the Word.*

Into Life

Help your students apply today's passage by saying, "God uses people of faith to make a difference in the world. God used Deborah and Barak to deliver Israel from oppression. And God can use you to make a difference today. That difference may not be very noticeable to the world. You may involve yourself in only a few lives, touching them in a meaningful way for Jesus. Or your impact may be very visible, affecting many people or key situations."

Have students form the same groups of six as they did earlier and discuss the three questions below:

1. In what way(s) has God used you to make a difference in people or situations around you?
2. How can your class make a difference in your world?
3. What are some opportunities you have for making a difference in your world right now? What can you do about at least one of them?

Let's Talk It Over

The questions on this page are designed to encourage review of the lesson Scriptures and to promote discussion of the lesson by the class. The answers provided are only discussion starters. Let your class talk it over from there.

1. It is rare in the Bible to see a woman like Deborah exercising spiritual leadership outside the home. What kinds of "Deborahs" do we have providing Christian leadership today?

There is an ongoing discussion today as to what roles women may legitimately perform in the church. This Old Testament account obviously contributes little to that discussion. But it may remind us of the increasing number of women, including Christian women, who are filling public offices and thereby influencing our society. We note also that godly women are prominent in organizations that combat abortion, pornography, drug abuse, and other evils in our society. In the area of direct spiritual leadership, it is impressive to see how many women carry on ministries of writing, music, and public speaking in the cause of Christ. Also, who can begin to say how much good has been done by those "Deborahs," single women and married women alike, who labor on the mission fields?

2. In Hebrews 11:32 Barak is listed among the heroes of the faith. On the basis of what we are told in Judges 4 and 5, what can we say positively and negatively about Barak's faith?

Barak demonstrated great faith by his willingness to go up against Jabin's army, which was definitely better equipped for battle and almost certainly better trained. He did not offer excuses as to why he should not accept his responsibility. On the other hand, Barak's insistence that Deborah go with him may indicate some weakness in his faith. In Judges 6:36-40 we have the account of Gideon's fleece. Like Barak, Gideon was ready to obey the Lord, if certain conditions were fulfilled. Both of these men's responses to the Lord's commission may be open to varied interpretations, but it is clear that we must not place conditions on our response to God's commands.

3. Why should it be unimportant to us as to who gets the credit for some act of service or occasion of success in the church?

In the church, we occasionally find that some member has become offended or upset because he or she did not receive recognition for a task completed. God's Word makes it clear, of course, that our Christian work is to bring glory to God (Matthew 5:16; 1 Corinthians 10:31). Therefore, we must not perform our service for the applause of other human beings (Matthew 6:1-4). It is a part of our human nature to expect appreciation for our efforts, and we should be prompt in the church to express such appreciation to those who render faithful service. But when anyone places too high value on receiving credit for such service, that betrays the presence of an unhealthy pride and spiritual immaturity.

4. God used the elements of the weather to help the Israelites defeat Jabin's army. What can we say about how God uses weather conditions in His dealings with people today?

One reminder to us of our comparative human weakness is that we are still unable to control the weather. We are able to predict the weather with a high degree of accuracy; we also have developed flood control provisions, methods for dealing with ice and snow on roads, and other such devices to offset some of weather's unpleasant effects; but we do not control it. How God may use the weather to judge and discipline people today we can only speculate. However, when a land suffers from drought or floods or damaging winds, its people will do well to examine their lives to see if there is need for godly sorrow and renewal of faith in God.

5. Jael was regarded as a heroine for her killing of Sisera. What can we say positively and negatively about her action?

This is one of those brutal acts recorded in Judges that grates on our Christian sensibilities. If Jael had been in some way threatened by Sisera, her act could be seen as one of self-defense; but nothing in the text hints at such a threat. On the other hand, we have no reason to expect Jael to conduct herself according to Christian principles. The era in which she lived was not characterized by even a careful adherence to Old Testament principles (see Judges 17:6). If she felt it was her duty to kill Sisera, she did it in perhaps the only way open to her. She surely could not have overcome him while he was awake, and even while he was asleep, she would be unlikely to have used a conventional weapon. So she used what was familiar to her: a hammer and a tent peg.

Samuel, the Last Judge

October 4
Lesson 5

LESSON SCRIPTURE: 1 Samuel 7:15—8:22.

PRINTED TEXT: 1 Samuel 7:15—8:9, 19-22a.

DEVOTIONAL READING: 1 Samuel 8:10-18.

1 Samuel 7:15-17

15 And Samuel judged Israel all the days of his life.

16 And he went from year to year in circuit to Bethel, and Gilgal, and Mizpeh, and judged Israel in all those places.

17 And his return was to Ramah, for there was his house; and there he judged Israel; and there he built an altar unto the LORD.

1 Samuel 8:1-9, 19-22

1 And it came to pass, when Samuel was old, that he made his sons judges over Israel.

2 Now the name of his firstborn was Joel; and the name of his second, Abiah: they were judges in Beersheba.

3 And his sons walked not in his ways, but turned aside after lucre, and took bribes, and perverted judgment.

4 Then all the elders of Israel gathered themselves together, and came to Samuel unto Ramah,

5 And said unto him, Behold, thou art old, and thy sons walk not in thy ways: now make us a king to judge us like all the nations.

6 But the thing displeased Samuel, when they said, Give us a king to judge us. And Samuel prayed unto the LORD.

7 And the LORD said unto Samuel, Hearken unto the voice of the people in all that they say unto thee: for they have not rejected thee, but they have rejected me, that I should not reign over them.

8 According to all the works which they have done since the day that I brought them up out of Egypt even unto this day, wherewith they have forsaken me, and served other gods, so do they also unto thee.

9 Now therefore hearken unto their voice: howbeit yet protest solemnly unto them, and show them the manner of the king that shall reign over them.

. . . .

19 Nevertheless the people refused to obey the voice of Samuel; and they said, Nay; but we will have a king over us;

20 That we also may be like all the nations; and that our king may judge us, and go out before us, and fight our battles.

21 And Samuel heard all the words of the people, and he rehearsed them in the ears of the LORD.

22a And the LORD said to Samuel, Hearken unto their voice, and make them a king.

GOLDEN TEXT: The LORD said unto Samuel, Hearken unto the voice of the people in all that they say unto thee: for they have not rejected thee, but they have rejected me, that I should not reign over them.—1 Samuel 8:7.

Old Testament Personalities

Unit 2: The People Choose a Monarchy

(Lessons 5-8)

Lesson Aims

After this lesson a student should be able to:

1. Explain why the people of Israel wanted a king.
2. Tell what would have been better than having a king.
3. Find a way to improve his own obedience to God.

Lesson Outline

INTRODUCTION
- A. Samuel
- B. Lesson Background

I. GOOD JUDGMENT AND BAD (1 Samuel 7:15—8:3)
- A. Good Judgment (vv. 15-17)
- B. Bad Judgment (vv. 1-3)

II. CALL FOR A CHANGE (1 Samuel 8:4-9)
- A. Request to Samuel (vv. 4, 5)
- B. Appeal to God (vv. 6-9)

III. INSISTENT CALL (1 Samuel 8:19-22a)
- A. Repeated Request (vv. 19, 20)
  To Be Like Everyone Else
- B. Repeated Appeal (vv. 21, 22a)

CONCLUSION
- A. Our Problems
- B. Our Task
- C. Prayer
- D. Thought to Remember

Visual 5 of the visuals packet illustrates the thoughts in the conclusion section of this lesson. The visual is shown on page 45.

Introduction

Isn't it strange that people who have plenty keep on wanting more? Gifted with homes and vineyards and farms in the land of promise, some of the Hebrews soon resorted to greedy and dishonest ways of increasing their holdings. For the sake of pleasure, some joined in heathen feasting and worshiped heathen gods. So in time God's people became more devilish than godly. To punish them, God let a heathen tribe dominate them and take a large part of their harvest. In poverty and misery the people again worshiped God and obeyed Him, and then He gave them a leader who organized and encouraged them to drive out the heathen. Prosperity was restored.

For perhaps about three hundred years this cycle was repeated over and over: peace and prosperity, sin and idolatry, defeat and poverty, repentance and godliness, victory and prosperity again (Judges 2:16-19). Last week's lesson brought us a sample: Deborah and Barak were leaders God chose to defeat the Canaanites and let Israel enjoy the abundant produce of their land in peace (Judges 4, 5). Now this week's lesson brings us to the end of the three-hundred-year period recorded in the book of Judges.

A. Samuel

Samuel was brought up by a godly priest, and he became a godly man. But the priest's own sons were corrupt and greedy, and the nation as a whole was depraved (1 Samuel 1—3). This time the Philistines from the coastal plain (see map from last week's lesson) were the instrument God used to punish His people. They defeated Israel's forces and took control of the land (1 Samuel 4). They continued to dominate and oppress Israel for more than twenty years (1 Samuel 7:2). Meanwhile Samuel became known as God's prophet (1 Samuel 3:19, 20).

B. Lesson Background

Twenty years of robbery and oppression made the people very tired of conditions as they were, and Samuel told them how to change things. At his advice they got rid of their idols and worshiped only the Lord (1 Samuel 7:3, 4). Then Samuel called a big prayer meeting. The Philistines got word of the meeting, and to them it sounded like a rebellion against their rule. Quickly they gathered their forces and went to subdue the uprising. They might have subdued Israel if Israel had been alone. But now the Lord was with Israel. He "thundered with a great thunder on that day upon the Philistines" (v. 10). Confused and dismayed by the terrific thunderstorm, they retreated. The Israelites chased them back to their own country, striking down as many as they could catch. "So the Philistines were subdued, and they came no more into the coast of Israel" (v. 13).

I. Good Judgment and Bad (1 Samuel 7:15—8:3)

Now the people of Israel were free from oppression. The problem was to keep them from drifting again into the worship of false gods and into greedy and crooked ways of doing business. Their hero, Samuel, was the man who would be able to do it.

A. Good Judgment (vv. 15-17)

15. And Samuel judged Israel all the days of his life.

Samuel had called Israel back to the worship of the true God. He had led them in prayer for God's help. Under his leadership they had routed the Philistines and won their independence. Now they gratefully accepted his leadership in peacetime. As long as he lived he guided them in godly ways.

16. And he went from year to year in circuit to Bethel, and Gilgal, and Mizpeh, and judged Israel in all those places.

Knowing Samuel was God's spokesman (1 Samuel 3:20), the people came to him to have their disputes settled in God's way. At the same time he could instruct them in God's law so they could follow it and solve many of their own problems. So they could more easily come to him, Samuel spent time in three different cities in their turns.

17. And his return was to Ramah, for there was his house; and there he judged Israel; and there he built an altar unto the LORD.

Samuel's home town was a fourth place where he held court and made himself available for counseling. *An altar unto the Lord* made the city a place of worship as well as of legal decisions and counseling. *Ramah* means *height.* Naturally that name was given to several different places in the hill country. There were also several places called *Gilgal,* which means "circle" or "rolling," and several called *Mizpeh,* which means "watch tower" or "lookout point." Therefore we cannot be sure where the places were that are named in our text. *Bethel* was about twelve miles north of Jerusalem. Its name means "house of God."

B. Bad Judgment (vv. 1-3)

1. And it came to pass, when Samuel was old, that he made his sons judges over Israel.

Samuel had a tremendous load to carry when all Israel had no other counselor to compare with him. Physical stamina fades with age, and aging Samuel asked his sons to help him.

2. Now the name of his firstborn was Joel; and the name of his second, Abiah: they were judges in Beer-sheba.

The added judges not only relieved Samuel of part of his load, but made it easier for many of the people to reach a judge. It seems all the places of Samuel's circuit were in the central part of the country. Beer-sheba was far to the south.

3. And his sons walked not in his ways, but turned aside after lucre, and took bribes, and perverted judgment.

How to Say It

ABIAH. Uh-*bye*-uh.
BARAK. *Bay*-ruk or *Bair*-uk.
BEER-SHEBA. Be-er-*she*-buh.
PHILISTINES. Fi-*liss*-teens or *Fil*-iss-teens.
RAMAH. *Ray*-muh.
SINAI. *Sye*-nay-eye or *Sye*-nye.

What a tragedy! Placed in positions of leadership, Samuel's sons became leaders in another slide into sin, the same kind of thing that had brought disaster to Israel many times before. The Hebrew word for *lucre* means gain, especially unjust gain. Sometimes it is used of plunder taken in warfare or by robbers. By taking bribes and perverting justice, those ungodly sons of a godly father were plundering their own people as surely as the Philistine enemies had plundered them.

II. Call for a Change (1 Samuel 8:4-9)

The crookedness of those young judges was too blatant to be hidden or denied. The people were concerned. Elders among them could remember when such crooked dealing had brought them under the oppression of the Philistines. Now it was being started again, started by the very people who ought to put a stop to it. Something had to be done!

A. Request to Samuel (vv. 4, 5)

4. Then all the elders of Israel gathered themselves together, and came to Samuel unto Ramah.

No doubt the elders in dozens of towns had been discussing the matter, first in their own towns and then in consultation with those of other towns in widening circles. Finally the whole country had come to an agreement about what ought to be done. They brought their request to Samuel. He was their national hero. In time of crisis he had led them to God and to freedom. They wanted him to lead them still, but not into the power of his corrupt sons.

5. And said unto him, Behold, thou art old, and thy sons walk not in thy ways: now make us a king to judge us like all the nations.

Already Samuel's sons were beginning to undo the good their father had done. Samuel was old; he would not be with them much longer. Then the slide into disaster would be swift. We can agree with the elders that a change was needed, but not necessarily the change they had in mind. They had decided they should copy the nations around them. They should have a king to make them do right. Their present form of government worked well when Samuel was at the head of it, but it was headed for failure in the next generation. The elders' solution was to change the form of government, to get a king—but certainly not either of those sons of Samuel!

B. Appeal to God (vv. 6-9)

6. But the thing displeased Samuel, when they said, Give us a king to judge us. And Samuel prayed unto the LORD.

Samuel was *displeased.* The present form of government had been working well with him to guide it. To ask for another form of government seemed to be a repudiation of him. He had spent his life trying to help these people, and he had succeeded marvelously. Why should they ask for something different? Besides, with his own wisdom and God's help, Samuel probably knew the elders' idea would not work. It was not the form of government that had brought disaster in the past; it was the wrongdoing of the people. That was where change was needed. But wise old Samuel did not launch into an instant tirade denouncing the plan and the planners. He *prayed unto the Lord.* Wisdom greater than Samuel's was needed here. The suggested plan would not work, but something had to be done. Samuel could not live forever. What could he do in the short time he had left?

7. And the LORD said unto Samuel, Hearken unto the voice of the people in all that they say unto thee: for they have not rejected thee, but they have rejected me, that I should not reign over them.

Samuel should not feel hurt because the people seemed to be rejecting him. They were rejecting the Lord himself. He was their king. They did not need another king; they just needed to obey the one they had. He had given them laws to live by. Living by those laws had brought them peace, prosperity, and power. Breaking those laws had brought them disaster. That had been proved again and again in the centuries that Israel had lived in the promised land. Now another slide toward disaster was starting, and the fault did not lie with Samuel's sons alone. They would not make an unjust decision unless someone asked for it; they could not take a bribe unless someone gave it. The fault lay with people who did wrong.

8. According to all the works which they have done since the day that I brought them up out of Egypt even unto this day, wherewith they have forsaken me, and served other gods, so do they also unto thee.

Rejecting God was not something new. The people of Israel had been doing it ever since they had left Egypt to begin their national life. They had worshiped a golden calf at Sinai. They had balked at their first opportunity to take over the promised land. And in that land they had sunk into sin again and again. The present rejection of God and Samuel was a part of their customary pattern—and the people of Israel are not the only ones who have followed that pattern.

9. Now therefore hearken unto their voice: howbeit yet protest solemnly unto them, and show them the manner of the king that shall reign over them.

Most of us who are parents can understand what God was saying. Isn't this the way we deal with our children when they want to do something that is less than best? If what they want to do is not morally wrong or sinful, and if it is not likely to be seriously harmful, and if they stubbornly insist, we let them have their own way, make their own mistake, and suffer the consequences. But first we try to talk them out of it. We point out the unpleasant consequences that are likely to follow. So God told Samuel to let the people have their way, but to warn them that a king would bring more problems instead of solving those they already had (see verses 10-18).

III. Insistent Call (1 Samuel 8:19-22a)

The troubles we have seem especially bad because they are troubling us *now.* Sometimes we are ready to try almost anything to be rid of our present problems. So it was with the elders of Israel. They could not hope to have Samuel with them much longer. Often we hear it said that the death of a great leader leaves a vacuum, but Samuel's departure would leave something worse than a vacuum. It would leave his sons in charge, and they were greedy and without conscience. A king would be different, so they wanted a king. They brushed Samuel's warning aside.

A. Repeated Request (vv. 19, 20)

19. Nevertheless the people refused to obey the voice of Samuel; and they said, Nay; but we will have a king over us.

The people said, *Nay.* They refused to believe that a king would be as bad as Samuel said he would be. Insistently they said, *We will have a king over us.*

20. That we also may be like all the nations; and that our king may judge us, and go out before us, and fight our battles.

The elders gave three reasons for having a king:

1. All the other nations had kings. "Everybody does it." This is the frequent plea of children and adults who want to do something that is less than the best. It is a powerful reason, but not a good one. We should plan our course by God's will, not by what everybody does.

2. A king would judge them; that is, govern them. He would settle their disputes; he would tell them what to do; he would enforce the law; he would be responsible for national prosperity. Actually, each person in the nation was responsible for his own keeping of the law, and these elders talking with Samuel ought to see to it that other members of their families accepted that responsibility. How convenient it would be to turn all that responsibility over to the king! Such an attitude is seen often in a democracy, too. We elect officers for our organization or church, and then we expect them to carry the whole responsibility while we do nothing but criticize. We elect a sheriff to enforce the law, and then make his job difficult by breaking the law in small ways—and to many it is unthinkable that one of us would report a violation. Certainly nobody wants to be a tattle-tale.

3. A king would fight their battles. He would be responsible for national defense as well as law enforcement. Never again would a farmer have to step in as Barak had done to raise an army and lead untrained troops into battle. The king and his standing army would take care of all that. But where did they think the king would get his army? Where did they think he would get money for weapons and provisions? No government can relieve the individual citizen of his or her responsibility.

TO BE LIKE EVERYONE ELSE

Washington, D. C., has its "National Cathedral." Paris has the cathedral of Notre Dame. Rome has St. Peter's Basilica, long the largest church building in Christendom.

Several years ago the president of the West African nation of Ivory Coast decided that his nation should have a great cathedral, just as other countries do. So the basilica of Our Lady of Peace of Yamoussoukro was built at a cost of $200 million! And how impressive it is: the bronze cross on the dome reaches almost to five hundred feet, thirty-seven feet higher than St. Peter's! There is room within its walls for eighteen thousand worshipers.

The project may have seemed good, at first. But when it was seen that upkeep on the cathedral would be $1.5 million per year, regrets began to surface. The question arose, might the

visual 5

money have been spent more wisely on the basic needs of such a poverty-stricken nation?

All of Israel's neighbors had kings. As the Israelites looked about them, a monarchy became like a shrine of national honor where the nation could proudly worship itself. Nevertheless, the time would come when Israelites would rue the day when they had wanted a king. The kings would lead Israel into ruin. If we could see the future, we would often find that what we "need" so badly today, we really don't want at all!

—C. R. B.

B. Repeated Appeal (vv. 21, 22a)

21. And Samuel heard all the words of the people, and he rehearsed them in the ears of the LORD.

Wisely Samuel consulted the Lord at every step. Samuel himself was displeased by the elders' request (v. 6), probably because it seemed to imply criticism of him. His impulsive reaction might have been harsh and mistaken, but he waited to hear from the Lord. If we do not have the prophet's direct communication with the Lord, we need to be very careful about what we say when we are displeased. It may be better to say nothing at all till we have time to study the matter in the light of God's Word.

22a. And the LORD said to Samuel, Hearken unto their voice, and make them a king.

The Lord did not say the elders were wise in asking for a king. He did not say a king was just what they needed. The best thing to do, of course, was for each person to accept his or her responsibility and keep the law without being forced to do it. Perhaps the next best thing was for the elders to accept their responsibility and keep their own families in line. But those ways did not work, and centuries of history had proved it. Neither the people nor the elders had done what they ought to do. Under the present circumstances, the best thing to do was to let the people have their way and be ruled by a king. That way would not work either, and following centuries would prove it. Would the people ever learn that there was no way to escape their individual responsibility?

Conclusion

God chose a king for Israel, and no doubt He chose the best man in the nation for the job. The chosen one was a modest man, hard to find when the choice was announced (1 Samuel 10:17-22). He was a magnificent man, a head taller than those about him (vv. 23, 24). He was an able leader, raising an army and winning the victory (1 Samuel 11:1-11). He was a forgiving man, holding no grudge against his countrymen who opposed him (1 Samuel 10:27; 11:12, 13).

Saul's leadership was good for Israel at first, but it was bad for Saul. Success "went to his head." He became a vain man, preferring his way rather than the Lord's (1 Samuel 15). He became a jealous man, trying to kill his best supporter (1 Samuel 18:6-11). He became a futile man, a defeated man, a suicide (1 Samuel 31:1-6).

How much tragedy could have been averted if all the people had acted responsibly, if each person had just lived by God's law!

A. Our Problems

We have as many problems as Israel had—maybe more—and our solutions are as futile as Israel's were.

1. *The crime problem.* Increasing crime alarms us. Our solution is to spend more money, hire more police, establish more courts, build more jails. But there would be no problem if each person would accept his responsibility and live within the law without any compulsion.

2. *The war on drugs.* Furiously we go after the sellers and producers in our country and abroad, but the war goes on. The sellers and producers would be out of business instantly if there were no buyers. Why can't everybody act responsibly?

3. *Pornography.* Lurid literature is hard to suppress. But it would soon cease to exist if nobody would look at it.

4. *What problem troubles you?* Wouldn't it cease to exist if everybody in the country would act responsibly?

B. Our Task

There are many valiant fighters against crime, drugs, pornography, and other evils. We can be among them according to our ability, and we can support them with our money and our influence. But there is something more basic.

The Lord said, *They have rejected me, that I should not reign over them* (1 Samuel 8:7). That is the basic evil of them all; that is behind all our troubles. If all the people of the world would make God their king and obey Him faithfully, what a glorious era of peace, prosperity, and happiness we would see! What can we do to bring this about?

First, we can obey the Lord personally, individually, without any compulsion or prompting. If we do not know what He wants us to do, we can spend hours with His Word to find out. Our Sunday school and other study groups can help us. But nothing in the world will make us do God's will unless we ourselves want to do it.

Second, we can help others obey the Lord. If we really hate the evil and love the good (Amos 5:15), we can find dozens of ways to oppose the one and promote the other. But the most basic, most important, and most effective way is the way Jesus put before us. He said, "Make disciples of all nations, baptizing them in the name of the Father and of the Son and of the Holy Spirit, and teaching them to obey everything I have commanded you" (Matthew 28:19, 20, *New International Version*). This is our responsibility, yours and mine.

Is it too much for us? Of course it is. But Jesus added, "I will be with you always."

C. Prayer

How good it is to be guided by Your Word, our Father! In the books of history, we see how disastrous it is to reject You, and how beneficial it is to obey. In the teaching of Jesus and the apostles, we find clear guidance for our lives. As we apply ourselves to Bible study, may we have wisdom to know Your will, and may we dare to do it when we know it. In Jesus' name, amen.

D. Thought to Remember

Let's accept our responsibility.

Home Daily Bible Readings

Monday, Sept. 28—Samuel Prays to the Lord for Israel (1 Samuel 7:1-6)

Tuesday, Sept. 29—Israel Triumphs Over the Philistines (1 Samuel 7:7-14)

Wednesday, Sept. 30—Saul Searches for a Man of God (1 Samuel 9:5-10)

Thursday, Oct. 1—Saul Meets Samuel (1 Samuel 9:15-21)

Friday, Oct. 2—Saul Is Anointed By Samuel (1 Samuel 10:1-7)

Saturday, Oct. 3—Saul Becomes a Prophet (1 Samuel 10:9-16)

Sunday, Oct. 4—Saul Is Made King of Israel (1 Samuel 10:17-27)

Learning by Doing

This page contains an alternate lesson plan emphasizing learning activities. Classes desiring such student involvement will find these suggestions helpful.

Learning Goals

In this lesson you will seek to help your students do the following:

1. Explain why the Israelites' request for a king was wrong.
2. Suggest ways we may be tempted to reject God's authority over us.
3. Determine how to develop a submissive spirit.

Into the Lesson

Write the following question on your chalkboard before students enter the room: *In what ways do people in our nation reject God's authority in their lives?*

To begin, ask students to brainstorm the question. (Remember, in a brainstorm you do not evaluate or allow class members to evaluate any suggestion. The goal is to allow members to express as many ideas as they can think of without fear of being criticized. As students call out their answers, jot them on the chalkboard. Allow two minutes for brainstorming.

Into the Word

Present a brief lecture on the background for this lesson, using the information in the introduction of the lesson commentary. Then ask several volunteers to read 1 Samuel 7:15—8:22.

Ask class members to form groups of six to eight to discuss the questions below. Be sure to provide each group with pencil, paper, and at least one copy of the questions (the questions are in the student book). Appoint in each group a leader to direct the discussion and a person to record the group's conclusions. Allot fifteen minutes for discussion.

1. What did the people ask of Samuel? (8:5).
2. Why did they want a king? (8:3-5,19, 20).
3. What was Samuel's initial reaction to the request? (8:6).
4. What was wrong with the request? (8:7, 8).
5. In warning the people, what did Samuel say the king would do to them? (8:10-17).
6. In your opinion, why did God allow the people to have a king, even though it was wrong and the king would mistreat them?
7. What principles for Christian living do you see in this passage?

When time expires, ask the class, "What answers did your group offer for question six?" Allow for discussion. Then ask, "What conclusions did you reach for question seven?" Again, allow for responses.

Option

Begin the Bible study with a brief lecture and Scripture reading, as explained in the first paragraph of *Into the Word.* Then have class members form groups of four to six.

Tell the groups that you would like them to prepare an imaginary interview with Samuel. You will provide them with the questions, and they are to write how they think he might have responded to the questions, based upon today's Bible passage. Ask them to be prepared to present the interview to the rest of the class. They will need to select from their group someone to play the interviewer and someone to play Samuel.

Appoint a leader for each group to keep the activity moving. Provide each group with paper, pencil, and at least one copy of these questions:

1. Why do the Israelites want a king?
2. How do you feel about it? Why?
3. What do you see as the pros and cons of having a king in Israel?
4. What did God tell you to do about it? Why?

Allow the groups fifteen minutes to prepare the interview. Then ask each group to present their interview to the rest of the class. After the presentations, ask, "What principles for Christian living do you see in today's passage? Allow for discussion.

Into Life

Provide pencil, paper, and a copy of the following questions for each student.

1. The Israelites had rejected God as their authority (1 Samuel 8:7). In what ways are Christians today tempted to reject God's authority in their lives?
2. In what areas of your life do you struggle with God's authority?
3. Think about how you can bring the areas you identified into submission to God. What do you need to change about—
   a. The way you think about that area?
   b. Your attitude toward God?

Have students discuss question one in their groups. Then ask students to write their answers to questions two and three individually. Close the session with prayer.

Let's Talk It Over

The questions on this page are designed to encourage review of the lesson Scriptures and to promote discussion of the lesson by the class. The answers provided are only discussion starters. Let your class talk it over from there.

1. It seems strange that a godly man such as Samuel had such ungodly sons. How can we explain this?

We may recall that the godly kings David and Hezekiah also had offspring that were morally and spiritually corrupt. Perhaps these three men were in part responsible for their sons' behavior by letting their leadership duties crowd out the time they should have spent with their families. This possibility should spur today's spiritual leaders to self-examination. To build a church and at the same time lose one's family is a tragic combination. On the other hand, Samuel may have labored at influencing his sons toward faith and godliness, but without success. Children must decide whether or not they will trust and obey the Lord. Sometimes their choice is directly opposite to the desires and examples of their parents.

2. Feeling rejected by the people's request for a king, Samuel responded by praying to the Lord. Why is this a good example for us?

It is a human tendency for us to feel rejected when someone criticizes our work. We can react to that by wallowing in self-pity, by defending ourselves without considering the merits of the criticism, or by attacking our critic. If instead we take the matter in prayer to God, we are more likely to perceive the legitimacy of the criticism, and we can then make whatever changes need to be made. If after we pray, however, we are convinced that the criticism is unjustified, then we will be better able to deal patiently and charitably with our critic. Jesus faced the ultimate rejection when He was crucified. His prayer, "Father, forgive them; for they know not what they do" (Luke 23:34) is the greatest example of prayer in the face of rejection.

3. How can we deal with the temptation to conform to the values and behavior of non-Christian people?

We often tend to conform to the worst habits of others, and when we choose to demonstrate our individuality, we choose negative ways of doing it. Actually we should feel offended when someone pressures us to conform to a practice such as using illegal drugs or alcoholic beverages or profane language. On these occasions we should be determined to express our individuality. It is our prerogative to choose to what or to whom we will conform our behavior. As Christians we are challenged to imitate Jesus Christ (1 Peter 2:21) and exemplary Christian leaders like Paul (1 Corinthians 11:1). The New Testament also urges us to avoid a mindless conformity to the world and to seek instead a transformation of our values and behavior through God's power working in us (Romans 12:1, 2).

4. How can we overcome the tendency to leave the work of the church to the leaders?

We hire a minister and somehow expect him to keep the work of the church going without our assistance. We elect elders and deacons and perhaps unconsciously transfer to them responsibilities that we should bear. One aspect of this tendency is the way members will refer to the church as "they" are not doing enough to make the church grow; we hear suggestions that "they" ought to make improvements in the worship services or teaching programs. Therefore, one answer to the question above is simply to promote a "we" mentality in the church. It must be made clear that every member bears a measure of responsibility for the church's health. In New Testament terms, every member is expected to be a functioning part of the body of Christ.

5. Each of us is an individual with potential to effect good in our church and our society. Why is it important that we emphasize this?

We often hear statements such as, "I'm only one person—there is not much that I can do to change the world." All of us feel at times that events are moving too rapidly around us, and we are helpless to do anything about them. And yet we are aware that people with no greater physical prowess or intellectual ability or financial resources than we possess have made a positive impact on society. If there is something lacking or something wrong in our society or in our church, and we are disturbed by it, we should resolve to act to change it. And of course we are not entirely dependent on our own resources—if our enterprise is attuned to God's will, we have prayer and His Word to aid us.

David: King Over All the People

October 11
Lesson 6

LESSON SCRIPTURE: 1 Samuel 16:1-13; 2 Samuel 2:1-7; 5:1-5.

PRINTED TEXT: 1 Samuel 16:1, 6, 7, 11-13; 2 Samuel 5:1-5.

DEVOTIONAL READING: 1 Samuel 16:1-13.

1 Samuel 16:1, 6, 7, 11-13

1 And the LORD said unto Samuel, How long wilt thou mourn for Saul, seeing I have rejected him from reigning over Israel? fill thine horn with oil, and go, I will send thee to Jesse the Bethlehemite: for I have provided me a king among his sons.

. . . .

6 And it came to pass, when they were come, that he looked on Eliab, and said, Surely the LORD'S anointed is before him.

7 But the LORD said unto Samuel, Look not on his countenance, or on the height of his stature; because I have refused him: for the LORD seeth not as man seeth; for man looketh on the outward appearance, but the LORD looketh on the heart.

. . . .

11 And Samuel said unto Jesse, Are here all thy children? And he said, There remaineth yet the youngest, and, behold, he keepeth the sheep. And Samuel said unto Jesse, Send and fetch him: for we will not sit down till he come hither.

12 And he sent, and brought him in. Now he was ruddy, and withal of a beautiful countenance, and goodly to look to. And the LORD said, Arise, anoint him: for this is he.

13 Then Samuel took the horn of oil, and anointed him in the midst of his brethren: and the Spirit of the LORD came upon David from that day forward. So Samuel rose up, and went to Ramah.

2 Samuel 5:1-5

1 Then came all the tribes of Israel to David unto Hebron, and spake, saying, Behold, we are thy bone and thy flesh.

2 Also in time past, when Saul was king over us, thou wast he that leddest out and broughtest in Israel: and the LORD said to thee, Thou shalt feed my people Israel, and thou shalt be a captain over Israel.

3 So all the elders of Israel came to the king to Hebron; and king David made a league with them in Hebron before the LORD: and they anointed David king over Israel.

4 David was thirty years old when he began to reign, and he reigned forty years.

5 In Hebron he reigned over Judah seven years and six months: and in Jerusalem he reigned thirty and three years over all Israel and Judah.

GOLDEN TEXT: Then Samuel took the horn of oil, and anointed [David] . . . and the Spirit of the LORD came upon David from that day forward.—1 Samuel 16:13.

Old Testament Personalities

Unit 2: The People Choose a Monarchy

(Lessons 5-8)

Lesson Aims

After studying this lesson a student should be able to:

1. Tell how David became king of Israel.
2. Recall at least two good things David did.
3. Recall two bad things David did.
4. Be earnest in choosing the right.

Lesson Outline

INTRODUCTION
- A. Demand for Change
- B. Lesson Background

I. THE LORD'S CHOICE (1 Samuel 16:1, 6, 7, 11-13)
- A. The Order (v. 1)
  - *Living in the Past*
- B. The Way of Choosing (vv. 6, 7)
  - *A Different Perspective*
- C. The Chosen One (vv. 11-13)

II. THE PEOPLE'S CHOICE (2 Samuel 5:1, 2)
- A. Kinship (v. 1)
- B. Proved Ability (v. 2a)
- C. God's Choice (v. 2b)

III. THE NEW KING (2 Samuel 5:3-5)
- A. The Kingdom United (v. 3)
- B. The Reign of David (vv. 4, 5)

CONCLUSION
- A. Good King
- B. Bad King
- C. Real Live Kids
- D. Prayer
- E. Thought to Remember

Refer to visual 6 of the visuals packet when considering 2 Samuel 5:1, 2. The visual is shown on page 53.

Introduction

Samuel was God's prophet and Israel's judge. Under his leadership the nation renewed its allegiance to God, defeated its enemies, and became prosperous (1 Samuel 7:3-17).

A. Demand for Change

As we saw last week, Samuel was not pleased when leaders of the people came to him and asked him to appoint a king to rule them. God was not pleased either. The request showed that the people were not content to be ruled by the Lord alone. Nevertheless God told Samuel to grant the request. God himself chose the man to be king: Saul the son of Kish. Tall and handsome, Saul looked like a king. Most of the people were well pleased with the choice (1 Samuel 10:17-24). Better still, Saul led them to victory.

B. Lesson Background

Unfortunately the new king started to ignore God's directions, and so in time he lost God's support. Long before Saul died, God was moving to provide another man to take his place (1 Samuel 13:13, 14).

I. The Lord's Choice (1 Samuel 16:1, 6, 7, 11-13)

Samuel was still the Lord's spokesman. He gave God's directions to King Saul, and he told the king of God's displeasure with disobedience (1 Samuel 15). When Saul was rejected, God ordered Samuel to anoint the next king.

A. The Order (v. 1)

1. And the LORD said unto Samuel, How long wilt thou mourn for Saul, seeing I have rejected him from reigning over Israel? fill thine horn with oil, and go, I will send thee to Jesse the Bethlehemite: for I have provided me a king among his sons.

Samuel had not wanted to appoint a king; but when Saul was appointed, Samuel sincerely wished for his success and mourned over his failure (1 Samuel 15:35). But now the Lord said it was time to stop mourning and get on with plans for the future. The new king was to be one of the sons of Jesse, who lived in Bethlehem. Samuel was to go and anoint the chosen one with oil. The hollow horn of a cow was a convenient flask to carry the oil.

Samuel protested. He said King Saul would kill him if he would anoint someone else to be king. But the Lord said Saul need not know about it yet. Samuel could go to Bethlehem to offer a sacrifice, not announcing any other reason (vv. 2, 3).

Leading men of Bethlehem were alarmed when Samuel appeared. Had the prophet come to announce God's judgment against them? No, this was a peaceful visit. Samuel invited the elders to the ceremony of sacrifice, and he invited Jesse and his sons also (vv. 4, 5).

LIVING IN THE PAST

Hero Street runs for one and one-half blocks in Silvis, a town of sixty-four hundred people in northwestern Illinois. The street was given this name in 1978, because the thirty-six small homes there had produced 110 members of the United States armed services, eight of whom died in World War II and the Korean War. Silvis city officials believe that no other street in America can match Hero Street's record. Residents of Silvis are justifiably proud of their contribution to America's defense forces. Public service should be rewarded with honor.

It seems natural to look to the past. We can be so enamored with the past, however, that we lose sight of the future. Some do this by complaining about "how bad things are these days" and by reminiscing about "the good old days." Others do it by grieving the death of a friend long after grief has lost its therapeutic value.

Samuel was in the latter category, grieving King Saul's death when he should have been looking to Israel's future. It is important and right to remember the past and to honor those whose efforts and sacrifices have made our lives better. But *living* in the past is self-defeating. Our God is Lord over history—past, present, and future. We should look with faith and hope to the future He has planned. —C. R. B.

B. The Way of Choosing (vv. 6, 7)

6. And it came to pass, when they were come, that he looked on Eliab, and said, Surely the LORD's anointed is before him.

When Jesse's sons were assembled with the other guests, Samuel considered Eliab first, perhaps because he was the oldest son. He was such a fine-looking man that Samuel thought he must be the one God had chosen to be king.

7. But the LORD said unto Samuel, Look not on his countenance, or on the height of his stature; because I have refused him: for the LORD seeth not as man seeth; for man looketh on the outward appearance, but the LORD looketh on the heart.

Eliab's handsome face and tall figure were impressive, but such things are not the most important qualifications for a leader of people. The Lord has X-ray vision. He sees what is in the heart of each person. On the basis of what He saw in the hearts, the Lord passed over Eliab and chose another son of Jesse.

Obediently Samuel turned away from Eliab and considered Jesse's other sons. Six more passed before him one by one, and the Lord said no to each one (vv. 8-10).

How to Say It

ELIAB. Ee-*lye*-ab.
ISH-BOSHETH. Ish-*bo*-sheth.
JEBUSITES. *Jeb*-yuh-sites.
JOAB. *Jo*-ab.
MEPHIBOSHETH. Meh-*fib*-o-sheth.
PHILISTINES. Fi-*liss*-teens or *Fil*-iss-teens.
RAMAH. *Ray*-muh.
SHIMEI. *Shim*-e-i.

A DIFFERENT PERSPECTIVE

To most people, the world seems to keep on spinning at the same rate, year after year. When midnight comes on December 31, the next year begins whether or not we are still awake to celebrate the occasion.

Actually, it is more complicated than that. Scientists tell us the earth has been rotating ever more slowly for centuries. Since 1972, those charged with keeping our time accurately have been adding about a second per year. Hydrogen maser clocks are used to determine the need for "leap seconds." These clocks are accurate to one ten-billionth of a second.

Most of us probably would say that there is no need for such accuracy. However, it is essential to deep-space navigation. Obviously, scientists don't see things the way the rest of us do. They have reasons the rest of us know nothing of.

To Samuel, the obvious attributes to look for when choosing a leader were physical characteristics. But God warned him against this. God has a different perspective: He looks on the heart. As we choose leaders today, let us do so on the basis of spiritual qualities, and not simply on outward appearance. Leadership among God's people should be based on more than the results of a "beauty contest." —C. R. B.

C. The Chosen One (vv. 11-13)

11. And Samuel said unto Jesse, Are here all thy children? And he said, There remaineth yet the youngest, and, behold, he keepeth the sheep. And Samuel said unto Jesse, Send and fetch him: for we will not sit down till he come hither.

Samuel had come all the way from Ramah at God's command to anoint one of Jesse's sons, but now God turned down seven fine-looking young men. Samuel was puzzled. Could Jesse have any more sons? Well, yes, there was one more. Somebody had to stay with the sheep, and naturally that duty fell to the kid brother. There was nothing to do but halt the proceedings till that kid brother arrived.

12. And he sent, and brought him in. Now he was ruddy, and withal of a beautiful countenance, and goodly to look to. And the LORD said, Arise, anoint him: for this is he.

The kid brother was as handsome as the others. Some think *ruddy* means "red-haired," but a healthy outdoor complexion also can be described as ruddy. But the Lord's gaze went beyond outward appearance. Looking at the heart, He told Samuel this was the man to be king.

13. Then Samuel took the horn of oil, and anointed him in the midst of his brethren: and the Spirit of the LORD came upon David from that day forward. So Samuel rose up, and went to Ramah.

With the anointing came a special gift of *the Spirit of the Lord.* Not being told what the Spirit did, we may suppose He guided David's hand on the harp strings that banished a bad spirit (1 Samuel 16:14-23), guided the same hand as it hurled a stone at Goliath (17:49), guided David's mind in military strategy (18:5) and the administration of justice (2 Samuel 8:15), and inspired the many psalms of David. When the ceremony of anointing was over, Samuel went back home, and David went on with his work as a shepherd. But that work was interrupted in interesting ways.

Saul was troubled by an evil spirit, evidently one so discordant that he could not stand good music. Known for his skill with the harp, David was called to play for the king; and the evil spirit fled (1 Samuel 16:14-23). David then could go back to the sheep till Saul needed him again (1 Samuel 17:15).

Three of David's brothers were in the army recruited to fight invading Philistines, and David went to their camp to take them some food from home. He arrived at a time when a gigantic Philistine was challenging any man of Israel to meet him in single combat. No one in the army seemed inclined to accept the challenge, so David did. He felled the giant with a stone from his sling, then used the giant's own sword to lop off his head for a trophy (1 Samuel 17).

That ended David's work as a shepherd. He was kept in the king's service, and soon became a general of the army (1 Samuel 18:2, 5). His victories made him a popular hero. At that, Saul became insanely jealous and tried to kill his musician and general (vv. 6-11). David fled to the desert, where he was joined by other men out of favor with Saul. This band roamed the desert as long as Saul lived, while Saul's army hunted them in vain (1 Samuel 18—30).

At last Saul died in battle with his old enemies, the Philistines (1 Samuel 31). Saul's son Ish-bosheth became king, supported by Abner, general of the army. But the tribe of Judah made David their king, with his capital at Hebron. Then came the sad time of civil war and treacherous intrigue that is recorded in 2 Samuel 2—4. In the conflict David grew stronger and the house of Saul grew weaker (2 Samuel 3:1).

Weak King Ish-bosheth and his strong General Abner had a bitter quarrel. Abner then decided to abandon his king and turn the kingdom over to David (2 Samuel 3:6-21). But Joab was not pleased with that. Joab was David's nephew and chief general. Perhaps he suspected that a deal with Abner to make David king would also make Abner the commander of the army instead of Joab. Besides, Abner had killed Joab's brother in one of the battles of the civil war. So Joab killed Abner, thus both avenging his brother's death and securing his own position at the head of David's army (2 Samuel 3:22-30). Then two officers of Ish-bosheth's army took it on themselves to kill their king. They carried his head to David, expecting to win David's favor because they had killed the rival king. But David promptly executed the assassins. Our text from 2 Samuel takes up the story at that point.

II. The People's Choice (2 Samuel 5:1, 2)

Saul's best known and most admirable son was Jonathan. He and two other sons died in battle along with their father (1 Samuel 31:1-6). The son who became king seems to have been a nobody. Abner was the strong man of his kingdom; the king was a mere pawn in his hands. When both the king and Abner were dead, the tribes that had followed them had no leader.

A. Kinship (v. 1)

1. Then came all the tribes of Israel to David unto Hebron, and spake, saying, Behold, we are thy bone and thy flesh.

All the tribes means elders representing all the tribes that had followed Saul's son (v. 3). Abner had been urging them to turn to David (2 Samuel 3:17-19). Undoubtedly they had held some serious discussions among themselves. They were without a national leader, and they were not happy with the war between their tribes and the tribe of Judah that David ruled. They came to David with the thought that they were his kinsmen, his flesh and bone. All the tribes belonged to one family, the family of Jacob. His other name, Israel, was the name of the whole nation. It was not fitting for that nation to be split and hostile, the other tribes against the tribe of Judah.

B. Proved Ability (v. 2a)

2a. Also in time past, when Saul was king over us, thou wast he that leddest out and broughtest in Israel.

Back in the time when Saul's kingdom was strong, David was the one who led his troops to victory and won the acclaim of the people. His outstanding ability was known to all.

C. God's Choice (v. 2b)

2b. And the LORD said to thee, Thou shalt feed my people Israel, and thou shalt be a captain over Israel.

Many years earlier, the Lord had chosen David to be king, and had sent Samuel to anoint him. That had not been announced to the nation, of course. It would have been regarded as treason. But David's family knew about it, and so did the elders of Bethlehem. There was no longer any reason to keep the secret, and now all Israel knew David was the Lord's choice.

visual 6

III. The New King (2 Samuel 5:3-5)

So the people had three reasons for making David their king: (1) He was one of them, their bone and flesh. (2) He was capable, and he had proved it. (3) He was God's choice. These were good reasons, and the people were ready to act on them.

A. The Kingdom United (v. 3)

3. So all the elders of Israel came to the king to Hebron; and king David made a league with them in Hebron before the LORD: and they anointed David king over Israel.

A league is a covenant, an agreement, a treaty. The other tribes had been at war with David's tribe; now they formally made peace. David was to be king of them all. Other terms of the treaty are not mentioned. Probably David promised not to punish those who had been fighting against him in the civil war. His chief opponents were dead, and the rest were ready to be his loyal subjects. King and people made their promises solemnly *before the Lord: and they anointed David king over Israel.* Anointing was a part of the ancient ceremony by which one was inducted into an important office. This was David's third anointing. The first one meant God had chosen him to be king (1 Samuel 16:1-13). The second one meant the tribe of Judah had chosen him to be its king (2 Samuel 2:4). The third anointing meant that all Israel now made God's choice their choice.

B. The Reign of David (vv. 4, 5)

4. David was thirty years old when he began to reign, and he reigned forty years.

It is surprising to read that David was only *thirty years old* when he became king. A lot of excitement had been crammed into his life before that. Often we hear him called a "shepherd boy"; but as a shepherd he was a grown man, capable of hand-to-claw combat with powerful wild beasts (1 Samuel 17:34-36). For an unknown length of time he was the king's favorite musician as well as a shepherd (1 Samuel 16:14-23; 17:15). After killing the Philistine giant, David had a full-time place with Saul. He rose to a position of command in the army (1 Samuel 18:2, 5). Then the king turned against him, and for an unknown length of time he was a fugitive. All this before he was thirty years old!

5. In Hebron he reigned over Judah seven years and six months: and in Jerusalem he reigned thirty and three years over all Israel and Judah.

Now we see that David became king of Judah when he was thirty. Seven and a half years later he was king of all Israel, with his capital in Jerusalem. People of Judah had taken that city long before and had set it on fire, perhaps because they did not want to live there (Judges 1:8). The ground close to the city was not suitable for farming. The heathen Jebusites had moved in again, and continued to live there (Judges 1:21). The city was on a point of land with ravines on three sides of it. With strong walls it was easily defended. The Jebusites bragged that lame and blind men were enough to keep it safe. But David and his men succeeded in capturing it, and they made its fortifications even stronger so it would be secure against attack (2 Samuel 5:6-10).

Conclusion

Now the people of Israel were solidly behind David. Better still, "the Lord God of hosts was with him." With such support "David went on, and grew great" (2 Samuel 5:10).

A. Good King

The Philistines had been perennial enemies of Israel. Soon they came to try their strength against the new king, but in two battles they were defeated decisively (2 Samuel 5:17-25).

Chapters 8 and 10 of 2 Samuel record how David went on to build an empire. He subdued nations to the east and north and forced them to pay tribute to Israel. While extending his power abroad, David also established justice at home. His government was well organized and efficient (2 Samuel 8:15-18).

B. Bad King

Why does prosperity make good people turn bad? Why is success the enemy of righteousness? Why do people turn away from God when His blessings are most abundant?

That happened over and over in Israel before there was a king in the land. The people hoped a king would make matters better, but they found that kings are people too. Saul at the peak of his power became selfish and arrogant, and even David was not immune to such evils.

David had wives enough of his own (2 Samuel 5:13), but he stole a neighbor's wife while the neighbor was away in the army. To make matters worse, he contrived to have the husband killed in battle (2 Samuel 11). Of this sad chapter in David's life we can say nothing good except that he admitted his sin and begged to be forgiven (Psalm 51).

David was forgiven (2 Samuel 12:13), but the murdered husband was still dead. Forgiveness does not erase all the terrible results of wrong that is done. For one short time David put his own selfish desire above his love for the right. His sons followed his selfish example, and for the rest of his life pain and grief pursued him (2 Samuel 12:10-12).

David was such a good man and such a good king that we are saddened by his sin; we share the grief of his later years. But can we condemn him? The word of Jesus is appropriate here: "He that is without sin among you, let him first cast a stone" (John 8:7).

Thank God, we have a Savior. "All we like sheep have gone astray; we have turned every one to his own way; and the Lord hath laid on him the iniquity of us all" (Isaiah 53:6).

C. Real Live Kids

Prevention is better than cure. It is good to be forgiven, but it is better not to sin. Then why didn't God intervene to keep David from stealing another man's wife: He sent Nathan the prophet to condemn the sin after it was done (2 Samuel 12:1-12); why didn't He send the prophet when David began to think of sending for that woman?

That line of thought is carried a step farther in the frequent question of skeptics, "If God is so great, why didn't He create people so they would never sin?"

A Sunday-school teacher was stumped when he heard that question. But after a little thought he began to question the questioner.

"Carl, you have some fine children. You must be proud of them."

"Sure," Carl grinned.

"When they were younger, did they ever do anything wrong? Did they ever make you unhappy or angry?"

"Yes, and they still do."

"Then tell me this: before you brought those kids into the world, didn't you know they would give you trouble by doing wrong?"

"Well, sure. All kids do."

"So why did you decide to have children? Why didn't you get a bunch of marionettes—you know, puppets on strings? You'd never be upset with them. They would do and say exactly what you wanted them to."

"Nuts!" Carl flared. "I wanted real live kids."

"So did God."

God wanted real live children, not puppets on strings. So He made people with wills of their own. So He lets them make their own decisions. The wise ones decide to do right. Those who choose to do wrong have to take the consequences.

D. Prayer

Father in Heaven, it is good to be real live people. Thank You for creating us with wills and minds and emotions. Sometimes we are thoughtless people, Father. Sometimes for a moment we are even malicious and wicked, but in our hearts we do want to do what is right. We are grateful for Your Word that guides us and Your Spirit who gives us power. In Jesus' name we pray, amen.

E. Thought to Remember

The right way is the best way.

Home Daily Bible Readings

Monday, Oct. 5—David Is Called to Serve Saul (1 Samuel 16:14-23)

Tuesday, Oct. 6—David Is Anointed King of Judah (2 Samuel 2:1-7)

Wednesday, Oct. 7—David Captures Jerusalem (2 Samuel 5:6-10)

Thursday, Oct. 8—David Defeats the Philistines (2 Samuel 5:17-21)

Friday, Oct. 9—David Restores the Ark of God (2 Samuel 6:1-5)

Saturday, Oct. 10—Nathan Tells David to Build God's House (2 Samuel 7:4-17)

Sunday, Oct. 11—David Makes a Covenant With God (2 Samuel 7:18-29)

Learning by Doing

This page contains an alternate lesson plan emphasizing learning activities. Classes desiring such student involvement will find these suggestions helpful.

Learning Goals

As a result of this session each student should be able to do the following:

1. Explain why God selected David as king of Israel.
2. Identify ways in which David demonstrated that he was a man after God's own heart.
3. Suggest characteristics that reveal that a person's heart imitates God's heart.
4. Determine, from Scripture, how to develop a heart that is pleasing to God.

Into the Lesson

Begin class by having students form groups of six. Give a copy of the following questions to each group. (Prepare these copies before class or write the questions on the chalkboard for everyone to see.) Ask students to discuss the questions in their groups:

1. What have you observed during the past week that indicates that our culture is concerned about a person's physical appearance?
2. What have you observed during the past week that indicates that our culture is concerned about a person's spiritual condition?
3. Which concern is more predominant? Why do you suppose it is?

Allow six to eight minutes for discussion. Then lead into the Bible study.

Into the Word

Help your students understand the background of today's lesson by presenting a brief lecture. You will find the content of the introduction section of the lesson commentary to be valuable. Then read these passages aloud: 1 Samuel 16:1, 4-13 and 2 Samuel 5:1-5.

Lead your class in discussing these questions based upon the passages.

1. In choosing leaders, what are people most apt to be influenced by?
2. What is God's criterion for choosing leaders?
3. What was God's evaluation of David? (See Acts 13:22.)
4. For what reasons did the Israelites accept David as king? (See 2 Samuel 5:1-5.)

You need not dwell long on the questions. Just make sure your class members get the main thrust of the passages and the distinction between man's focus on appearance and God's focus on the heart.

For the next portion of the study, have students work together in the same groups they formed at the beginning of class. Write the following question and Scripture references on the chalkboard, or be sure each group has a printed copy of them.

From your assigned passage, what indicates that David had a good heart?

1 Samuel 24:1-24
1 Samuel 26:1-25
2 Samuel 1:1-4, 11, 12, 17-27
2 Samuel 9:1-13 and 2 Samuel 16:5-14

Assign one passage to each group. (The last one has two passages because they are briefer.) If your class is large, you may have more than one group studying the same passage. If your class is small, you may want to form groups of two or three to study the passages. Each group is to read its assigned passage and discuss the question.

Allow eight to ten minutes for this. Then ask each group to report their findings. Be sure students grasp these dominant themes: (1) *David had love for his enemies* (Saul in 1 Samuel 24, 26, and 2 Samuel 1; Shimei in 2 Samuel 16); and (2) *David had mercy for the helpless* (Mephibosheth in 2 Samuel 9). God's heart is characterized by love for humankind, including friends and enemies, and by mercy for the helpless. Thus a person after God's own heart would reflect these qualities, as David did.

Into Life

Use the following questions to apply today's lesson to life. Lead a discussion of questions one and two. Students are to reflect on question three personally. Allow about three minutes for them to meditate on the question and write down their thoughts. Encourage them to pray silently about their observations.

1. What would you expect to observe in a person who is after God's own heart?
2. Our hearts are to be consumed with loving God and loving others. How can we develop hearts that imitate God's heart? Consider what each verse says about developing our hearts:
Isaiah 57:15
Proverbs 4:23
Hebrews 3:7, 8
Hebrews 3:12, 13.
3. What does God see when He looks at your heart?

Let's Talk It Over

The questions on this page are designed to encourage review of the lesson Scriptures and to promote discussion of the lesson by the class. The answers provided are only discussion starters. Let your class talk it over from there.

1. "The Lord looketh on the heart." Why do we need to work at doing the same?

It seems that human beings have always been unduly swayed by the physical appearance of others. It was true of godly Samuel, and it is true of us. A physically attractive candidate for public office may win votes in spite of questionable qualifications for office. Even in the church a well-dressed, outwardly appealing person may gain support for a leadership position, although that individual may be prone to doctrinal or moral weakness. Also, physical appearance often plays too great a role in a young man's or young woman's choice of a marriage partner. Jesus' teaching regarding avoidance of harsh judgment (Matthew 7:1-5) does not forbid our being careful judges of human character. We should examine the inner qualities of others, for out of the heart "are the issues of life" (Proverbs 4:23).

2. It is interesting that in spite of the Lord's minimizing of the importance of outward appearance, David's physical attributes are approvingly described just a few verses later (1 Samuel 16:7, 12). What can we say positively in regard to physical attractiveness?

While we have few details regarding David's earlier years, it is clear that his heart was tuned to God's will from the beginning. His physical appearance may have reflected his faith and his moral purity. We have known people who at first meeting did not impress us as being particularly handsome or beautiful. However, as we came to see more of their Christian character, we were able to see signs of this in their outward appearance, and their physical attractiveness was enhanced. Examples are the sparkle in their eyes, the sincerity in their smile, the erectness of their posture, the firmness in their handshake, etc.

3. David's victory over Goliath, described in 1 Samuel 17, is one of the Bible's most familiar stories. How can we derive a practical benefit from it?

We do not battle with physical giants, but the principles involved in David's victory over Goliath apply to the kind of giants we do encounter. When we combat fear, doubt, discouragement, disappointment, failure, and the like, it is good for us to recall earlier occasions of victory the Lord has given us (1 Samuel 17:34-37). As Goliath did to David, other human beings may disparage our outward attributes, and Satan will whisper in our minds that we are "losers," but we can follow David's example in ignoring that. We thrill to David's declaration in 1 Samuel 17:45-47 that he would gain victory to the glory of God. Our key to triumph in our spiritual battles is likewise a matter of doing all to God's glory.

4. One of David's admirable characteristics was his refusal to rejoice in evil, as in the cases of Abner's and Ish-bosheth's murders. What are some similar circumstances in which we may be tempted to rejoice in evil?

From time to time we hear the news of the assassination of a cruel dictator, or we may learn of the violent death of a notorious criminal. We may take a measure of satisfaction over these in the sense that that confirm the Biblical principle that human beings reap what they sow (Galatians 6:7, 8). But the tendency to rejoice over such occurrences should be checked by the warning in Proverbs 24:17: "Rejoice not when thine enemy falleth, and let not thine heart be glad when he stumbleth." With our knowledge concerning the eternal nature of every soul, we should find it sobering to contemplate the death of anyone outside of Jesus Christ.

5. We may know of a Christian leader who, like David, has experienced a moral downfall. How can we forgive such a leader in the way God forgave David?

The record of David's penitence (2 Samuel 12) and his penitential prayer (Psalm 51) show how thoroughly the king dealt with his sin. We, therefore, may legitimately expect a fallen Christian leader to give similar evidence of a "godly sorrow [that] worketh repentance" (2 Corinthians 7:10). David's fall also reminds us of how vulnerable to temptation even the most godly person can be. So we are warned, "Wherefore let him that thinketh he standeth take heed lest he fall" (1 Corinthians 10:12). Realizing that we are vulnerable should make us thankful that we ourselves have not fallen in this manner, and help us to be understanding toward the one who has.

Solomon: Wise King

October 18
Lesson 7

LESSON SCRIPTURE: 1 Kings 1:28-37; 2:1-4; 3:3-14.

PRINTED TEXT: 1 Kings 2:1-4; 3:5-12a.

DEVOTIONAL READING: 1 Kings 1:15-30.

1 Kings 2:1-4

1 Now the days of David drew nigh that he should die; and he charged Solomon his son, saying,

2 I go the way of all the earth: be thou strong therefore, and show thyself a man;

3 And keep the charge of the LORD thy God, to walk in his ways, to keep his statutes, and his commandments, and his judgments, and his testimonies, as it is written in the law of Moses, that thou mayest prosper in all that thou doest, and whithersoever thou turnest thyself:

4 That the LORD may continue his word which he spake concerning me, saying, If thy children take heed to their way, to walk before me in truth with all their heart and with all their soul, there shall not fail thee (said he) a man on the throne of Israel.

1 Kings 3:5-12

5 In Gibeon the LORD appeared to Solomon in a dream by night: and God said, Ask what I shall give thee.

6 And Solomon said, Thou hast showed unto thy servant David my father great mercy, according as he walked before thee in truth, and in righteousness, and in uprightness of heart with thee; and thou hast kept for him this great kindness, that thou hast given him a son to sit on his throne, as it is this day.

7 And now, O LORD my God, thou hast made thy servant king instead of David my father: and I am but a little child: I know not how to go out or come in.

8 And thy servant is in the midst of thy people which thou hast chosen, a great people, that cannot be numbered nor counted for multitude.

9 Give therefore thy servant an understanding heart to judge thy people, that I may discern between good and bad: for who is able to judge this thy so great a people?

10 And the speech pleased the LORD, that Solomon had asked this thing.

11 And God said unto him, Because thou hast asked this thing, and hast not asked for thyself long life; neither hast asked riches for thyself, nor hast asked the life of thine enemies; but hast asked for thyself understanding to discern judgment;

12a Behold, I have done according to thy word: lo, I have given thee a wise and an understanding heart.

GOLDEN TEXT: Give therefore thy servant an understanding heart to judge thy people, that I may discern between good and bad: for who is able to judge this thy so great a people?—1 Kings 3:9.

Old Testament Personalities

Unit 2: The People Choose a Monarchy

(Lessons 5-8)

Lesson Aims

After this lesson a student should be able to:

1. Tell what Solomon asked of God.
2. Tell what God promised to give Solomon.
3. Tell how Solomon brought his kingdom to the brink of destruction.
4. Always remember what is the beginning of wisdom and what is the purpose of it.

Lesson Outline

INTRODUCTION
- A. David's Choice
- B. Lesson Background

I. THE OLD KING'S ADVICE (1 Kings 2:1-4)
- A. Be Strong (vv. 1, 2)
- B. Obey God (v. 3)
- C. Build for the Future (v. 4)
  From One Generation to the Next

II. THE NEW KING'S PRAYER (1 Kings 3:5-9)
- A. God's Offer (v. 5)
- B. Solomon's Appreciation (v. 6)
- C. Solomon's Modesty (vv. 7, 8)
- D. Solomon's Request (v. 9)
  The Gift of Wonder

III. THE LORD'S RESPONSE (1 Kings 3:10-12a)
- A. God's Pleasure (vv. 10, 11)
- B. God's Gift (v. 12a)

CONCLUSION
- A. Wisdom
- B. Riches and Honor
- C. Unhappy Ending
- D. The Bottom Line
- E. Prayer
- F. Thought to Remember

Visual 7 of the visuals packet illustrates the truths found in 1 Kings 2:1-4. It is shown on page 60.

Introduction

"Stolen waters are sweet." So says a smiling woman trying to entice a passerby (Proverbs 9:17). Many a farm boy has found the flavor of a stolen pear or watermelon to be especially fine. How many people indulge in alcohol or drugs or illicit sex just because it is wrong? There is a sort of delight in doing what is forbidden. It makes one feel daring and powerful.

King David's harem was full of women, but it seems that his favorite wife was the one he stole. Was that just because she was stolen? Was Bathsheba actually more attractive than the others? Or did David favor her because he knew he had wronged her as well as her husband?

A. David's Choice

Whatever the reason may have been, David promised Bathsheba that her son Solomon would be the next king (1 Kings 1:17). We are not told why Solomon was chosen rather than one of her other sons. It seems that he was chosen early and given special training as a child. He later testified that his father had taught him well (Proverbs 4:3-9).

B. Lesson Background

David was old and feeble when his son Adonijah tried to take the throne, but the king was still in charge. He frustrated the plot by having Solomon publicly anointed as king. Adonijah's followers then swiftly deserted him (1 Kings 1:32-53). Solomon then was secure on the throne while David was still living.

I. The Old King's Advice (1 Kings 2:1-4)

David lived only seventy years (2 Samuel 5:4). His body became weak and frail (1 Kings 1:1). That may have encouraged Adonijah to think he could easily seize the throne. But David's mind was alert and active. He moved swiftly to defeat Adonijah and make Solomon king.

A. Be Strong (vv. 1, 2)

1. Now the days of David drew nigh that he should die; and he charged Solomon his son, saying.

Feeble as he was, David was perceptive enough to know that his own death was near, and he was concerned enough to give the new king some parting advice.

2. I go the way of all the earth: be thou strong therefore, and show thyself a man.

The way of all the earth is the way to the grave. David was near the end of that way. Soon he would be gone, and Solomon could no longer look to him for guidance. *Be thou strong therefore.* As described in Proverbs 4:3-9, Solomon's training fitted him to be a scholar and philosopher rather than a warrior or ruler. Probably David had taught him also the elements of military strategy and of government, but now the whole weight of an empire was about to fall on Solomon. He would have to be strong and vigorous and tough as well as wise. His rebellious brother Adonijah had been put on probation (1 Kings 1:50-53). Adonijah had tried to take the throne; he might try again. For his former effort he had gained the help of Joab, tough old general of the army (1 Kings 1:7). He might do that again. And who knew what other rebels might rise up against the new king when the old king was no longer there to support him? Solomon would have to be strong.

B. Obey God (v. 3)

3. And keep the charge of the LORD thy God, to walk in his ways, to keep his statutes, and his commandments, and his judgments, and his testimonies, as it is written in the law of Moses, that thou mayest prosper in all that thou doest, and whithersoever thou turnest thyself.

To be strong is not enough. A king should also do right. Many a strong king has misused his strength in selfish, greedy, unjust, and cruel ways. Sooner or later, strength so misused proves to be self-defeating. A wise king wants to do right, and God's Word tells what is right. We need not try to define exactly the differences among the words *statutes, commandments, judgments,* and *testimonies.* All of them are included in what is *written in the law of Moses,* and a wise king of Israel obeyed all of that law. That was the right thing to do, and that was the way to *prosper* in everything he did and everywhere he went.

C. Build for the Future (v. 4)

4. That the LORD may continue his word which he spake concerning me, saying, If thy children take heed to their way, to walk before me in truth with all their heart and with all their soul, there shall not fail thee (said he) a man on the throne of Israel.

David recalled God's promise given to him years earlier. The Lord told David that his descendants and Solomon's would continue to be kings forever. This is recorded in 2 Samuel 7:12-16. No condition is recorded with the promise in those verses, but perhaps more was said than is recorded. David understood that people of his family would continue to be kings if they would obey God truly and sincerely. He told Solomon that, and Solomon remembered it (1 Kings 8:25). To build a kingdom that would last, he must live and rule as God's law directed. Unfortunately, later kings forgot that. They disobeyed God so persistently that the rule of David's family was interrupted by the captivity in Babylon. But centuries after that, Jesus was born in the family of David. "He shall reign over the house of Jacob for ever; and of his kingdom there shall be no end" (Luke 1:30-33). His kingdom includes not only the literal family of Jacob or Israel, but also all those who believe in Jesus and come into the family by their faith (Galatians 3:7-9).

How to Say It

ADONIJAH. Ad-o-*nye*-juh.
EUPHRATES. U-*fray*-teez.
GIBEON. *Gib*-e-un.
JOAB. *Jo*-ab.

FROM ONE GENERATION TO THE NEXT

The St. Louis Browns have been dead for nearly forty years but some of their fans are still alive. The Browns were an American League baseball team that left St. Louis at the end of the 1953 season, and were revived the next year as the Baltimore Orioles. The Browns' only pennant came in 1944, and they finished last or next to last twenty-two times. In eight of those seasons, they lost more than one hundred games. But their fans still love them!

The Browns' fan club of more than five hundred members works to keep the memory alive. Most of them are getting along in years; young folks aren't too interested in a team that was gone before they were born.

Being a child of God is a lot like being a baseball fan. There is a lot to get excited about. There are "statistics" to learn and "great plays" to remember. But the only "game" that is really important is the one being played today. The next generation must decide for itself whether to become a part of the fan club.

David did what he could to encourage Solomon to follow in his footsteps. He gave his son the wisdom of his own experience and repeated the promises of God. But Solomon himself had to believe and obey. He could not live by his father's memories of God. As someone has said, "God doesn't have any grandchildren."

—C. R. B.

II. The New King's Prayer (1 Kings 3:5-9)

David advised Solomon to be strong, and Solomon was. David advised the new king also to obey God, and for years he did that very well. His obedience and worship were sincere, for "Solomon loved the Lord" (1 Kings 3:3). Soon the new king called the people to a huge meeting at the ancient tabernacle, which then was at Gibeon, a few miles north of Jerusalem, and he offered a thousand burnt offerings on the altar there (1 Kings 3:4; 2 Chronicles 1:2-6).

A. God's Offer (v. 5)

5. In Gibeon the LORD appeared to Solomon in a dream by night: and God said, Ask what I shall give thee.

The Lord told Solomon to make a request, to tell what gift he would like to receive. Is this a wild tale, like that of some good fairy or genie from a lamp? No, this is not a story from someone's imagination. This is a real, factual account of what happened. We know it is real because Solomon really made a wish and it really was granted.

B. Solomon's Appreciation (v. 6)

6. And Solomon said, Thou hast showed unto thy servant David my father great mercy, according as he walked before thee in truth, and in righteousness, and in uprightness of heart with thee; and thou hast kept for him this great kindness, that thou hast given him a son to sit on his throne, as it is this day.

Instead of blurting out his wish immediately, Solomon first said a word of appreciation for all the Lord had done for David. Finally the Lord had helped David's son, the son David chose, to be firmly established in control of his father's empire. Solomon understood why the Lord had favored David so greatly. It was because David, in spite of some terrible sins, had usually been upright and good, obeying the Lord.

C. Solomon's Modesty (vv. 7, 8)

7. And now, O LORD my God, thou hast made thy servant king instead of David my father: and I am but a little child: I know not how to go out or come in.

Solomon felt that he was too young and inexperienced to be in charge of a great empire. *To go out or come in* is a Hebrew expression meaning to carry on the ordinary business of life. We are not told how old Solomon was at this time, but many students guess he was about eighteen or twenty. *A little child* does not mean Solomon was literally preadolescent; it is his own modest evaluation of his knowledge and wisdom.

8. And thy servant is in the midst of thy people which thou hast chosen, a great people, that cannot be numbered nor counted for multitude.

Solomon was young and inexperienced, and the task before him was enormous. He was concerned about the welfare of a whole nation. Sometimes the different tribes had conflicting interests, and groups within tribes also had disputes. The government must be alert to prevent the growth of idolatry and corruption. Besides the uncounted millions of God's chosen people, there were nations to the north and east and south that David had brought into his empire (2 Samuel 8:1-14). They were not happy about paying tribute to Israel. The king must be alert to keep them from revolting, or to put down revolt quickly if it started. Young Solomon was at the head of all this. What a spot for a fellow just on the threshold of manhood.

D. Solomon's Request (v. 9)

9. Give therefore thy servant an understanding heart to judge thy people, that I may discern between good and bad: for who is able to judge this thy so great a people?

An understanding heart, wisdom enough *to judge thy people,* the ability to do his job well—this was Solomon's one wish. His father had taught him well (Proverbs 4:3-9). Already he was wise enough to know what to ask. He did not ask for wisdom to take the easy way and dodge the tough choices. He did not ask for wisdom to know what was expedient or inexpedient, popular or unpopular. He wanted to *discern between good and bad.*

Who is able to judge this thy so great a people? Solomon thought no one could do it without wisdom from God, and he was right. Wisdom from God is needed in the management of a nation, and in the management of a business, a home, an individual life. Too many people are forgetting God and trying to get along with human wisdom alone. The result is seen in the abused babies, the runaway children, the broken homes, the AIDS epidemic, the multiplying lawsuits, and the failing banks. How the world would be transformed if all of us were wise enough to do what is good in the eyes of God!

THE GIFT OF WONDER

"It's amazing how much my parents learned between the time I graduated from high school and the time I graduated from college!" The ironic observation by an unknown college graduate has a ring of truth to it. Something comes over most of us during adolescence that makes

visual 7

us lose our sense of wonder; we begin to think we know everything. Decades may pass before we recover that sense of awe.

Carl Sagan says, "[Wonder] is a very powerful emotion. All children feel it. In a first-grade classroom everybody feels it; in a twelfth-grade classroom almost nobody feels it. . . . Something happens between the first and twelfth grades, and it's not just puberty." The ability to wonder, to stay open to the possibility or knowledge and wisdom that may yet become ours, is a characteristic of childhood.

Solomon was a youth when he became king, but he possessed two important qualities of a good leader: his wonder at the responsibility that had been placed upon him and the knowledge of his limitations. His prayer shows a humble spirit that characterized the early years of his reign. The fact that he did not always act wisely shows that God's gift of wonder must be constantly renewed. —C. R. B.

III. The Lord's Response (1 Kings 3:10-12a)

In our dreams we may find ourselves doing something we could not or would not do if we were awake. But Solomon's dream wish was the wish of his waking mind. The Lord accepted it as such and responded accordingly.

A. God's Pleasure (vv. 10, 11)

10. And the speech pleased the LORD, that Solomon had asked this thing.

Solomon wanted to be able to do his job well, to meet his responsibility in a worthy way, to govern God's people properly. The Lord was pleased with that.

11. And God said unto him, Because thou hast asked this thing, and hast not asked for thyself long life; neither hast asked riches for thyself, nor hast asked the life of thine enemies; but hast asked for thyself understanding to discern judgment.

Solomon could have made a selfish wish, asking for himself a long life or riches or freedom from opposition. He could have made a vengeful wish, asking God to take away the life of his enemies. But above all things, Solomon wanted to *discern judgment.* The thought may be clearer if we translate *justice* instead of *judgment.* Our human society is complex and complicated. Most people have selfish wishes, and even unselfish wishes may be in sharp conflict. Sometimes it is very hard to find what is just. Solomon wanted help in doing that, for centuries of history had proved that the welfare of his nation depended on doing right.

B. God's Gift (v. 12a)

12a. Behold, I have done according to thy word: lo, I have given thee a wise and an understanding heart.

Solomon had his wish: he was given *a wise and an understanding heart.* The rest of the verse adds that never before had there been anyone like him, and there would be no one like him in the future. Only the Son of God can surpass him (Luke 11:31). Besides, God gave Solomon what he had not asked: riches and honor unmatched among the kings of his time (v. 13). And if Solomon would be faithful in obeying God, he would have long life too (v. 14).

Conclusion

It is interesting to read on through a few more chapters of 1 Kings and see the greatness of God's gift to the king who wanted above all things the wisdom to discern justice. Wisdom was his, and riches and honor; but long life? In that we see a bit of disappointment. Perhaps he lived no more than sixty years.

A. Wisdom

Solomon asked for wisdom to rule well, and he had it. Israel reveled in peace and prosperity, and the king was so securely in charge of the empire that the many little states from the upper Euphrates River in the north to the border of Egypt in the south were subject to him. These little countries were not annexed to Israel, but they paid tribute (1 Kings 4:20, 21).

Solomon's wisdom was not confined to the field of government, however. His contributions in literature and music are notable. He produced three thousand proverbs, some of which are preserved in the book of Proverbs. His songs were a thousand and five, and even today we can read his remarkable musical drama, *The Song of Solomon,* or *The Song of Songs,* as it is titled in its first verse. Philosophers are challenged by the profound thoughts of *The Preacher,* which we usually call by its Greek name, *Ecclesiastes.* In the field of science, no treatise of Solomon has been preserved; but in his time he may have been the world's foremost authority in botany and zoology (1 Kings 4:33, 34).

B. Riches and Honor

The unasked gifts of riches and honor were as abundant as the gift of wisdom. Take gold, for example. Every year Solomon received 666 talents of it (1 Kings 10:14). A footnote in the *New International Version* interprets that as twenty-five tons. If you like mathematics you can translate that into modern money. On the day I write this, the price of gold is reported to be 365.75 United States dollars per ounce. Silver was not thought to be worth much in the days of Solomon. It was plentiful as stones in Jerusalem (vv. 21, 27).

The Phoenicians were famous seamen and traders. King Hiram of Tyre was one of them. He helped Solomon develop a fleet of merchant vessels on the Red Sea and perhaps on the Mediterranean. They brought many kinds of exotic merchandise as well as gold and silver (1 Kings 9:26-28; 10:22). Egypt was the source of chariots and horses, as well as linen. Solomon had fourteen hundred chariots and twelve thousand horsemen (10:26-29). He built fortified cities for them at strategic points to guarantee the security of his kingdom (9:17-19).

Solomon's most famous building was the gold-lined temple at Jerusalem, which took seven years to build (1 Kings 6:37, 38). But it took thirteen years to build his own palace (7:1). It had to be huge to house all the bureaucrats and dignitaries of his administration. Every day the palace menu required more than five hundred bushels of flour and meal, thirty oxen, and a hundred sheep, besides the wild game that was provided (4:22, 23).

Honor was abundant as wealth. The queen of Sheba is the most famous of Solomon's foreign visitors (1 Kings 10:1-13), but there were many others (vv. 23-25). The great empires in Egypt and Mesopotamia were not at their best then, and Solomon's Israel eclipsed them both.

C. Unhappy Ending

It is sad to note that Solomon in all his glory forgot the fundamentals. He knew wisdom begins with the fear of the Lord (Proverbs 9:10). But he was so dazzled by his own glory and so secure in his own wealth that he neglected to revere the giver of them. The Lord had told His people not to marry heathen, lest they take up heathen practices (Deuteronomy 7:1-5). But if a petty king was friendly to Solomon, marrying his daughter could cement the friendship. If the foreign king became unfriendly, his daughter in Jerusalem was a hostage to secure his respectful behavior. So Solomon filled his harem with pagan princesses. Just as the Lord had warned, he became involved in pagan worship (1 Kings 11:1-8).

Besides forgetting the beginning of wisdom, Solomon forgot the purpose of it. He asked for wisdom so he could rule God's people well. But in his latter days he cared more for the glory of his court and the strength of his military than for his people. Years earlier, Samuel had predicted that a king would become oppressive (1 Samuel 8:11-18), and Solomon fulfilled the prediction. The people were so burdened by taxes and the draft that they appealed for relief as soon as Solomon died (1 Kings 12:3, 4).

So the wisest of kings acted foolishly. Forgetting both the basis of wisdom and the purpose of it, he lost both the support of God and the good will of his people. His magnificent empire was ready to fall apart. The next king copied Solomon's folly rather than is wisdom: he promised to increase the burden on the people. Many of the people rebelled at that. The nation split in two, and the little kingdoms that had paid tribute now broke away. The golden age of Israel was ended (1 Kings 12:5-20).

Home Daily Bible Readings

Monday, Oct. 12—Solomon Receives His Inheritance (1 Kings 1:28-37)

Tuesday, Oct. 13—Solomon Is Anointed King (1 Kings 1:41-48)

Wednesday, Oct. 14—Solomon Settles a Dispute Between Two Women (1 Kings 3:16-27)

Thursday, Oct. 15—God Gives Solomon Great Wisdom (1 Kings 4:29-34)

Friday, Oct. 16—Solomon Makes a Covenant to Build God's House (1 Kings 6:1-5)

Saturday, Oct. 17—God Promises to Help Solomon Build the House (1 Kings 6:6-13)

Sunday, Oct. 18—Solomon Consecrates God's House (1 Kings 8:1-13)

D. The Bottom Line

How powerful is the lure of the world! If it trapped Solomon, all of us had better take warning. Looking back at all he had accomplished, Solomon pronounced it vanity—useless and worthless, no more than a puff of wind (Ecclesiastes 1:2). "Let us hear the conclusion of the whole matter: Fear God, and keep his commandments: for this is the whole duty of man" (12:13).

E. Prayer

All-wise Father, as we ask You for wisdom and find our wisdom growing, may we remember that wisdom is but folly if we lose our reverence for You, and wisdom is but vanity unless it is used for the good of others. Amen.

F. Thought to Remember

"Fear God, and keep his commandments."

Learning by Doing

This page contains an alternate lesson plan emphasizing learning activities. Classes desiring such student involvement will find these suggestions helpful.

Learning Goals

As a result of this lesson, students should:

1. Indicate that they recognize a need for wisdom in their lives.
2. Conclude that wisdom is more valuable than riches or worldly success.
3. Determine how to gain wisdom.

Into the Lesson

Write the following on the chalkboard before students arrive:

1. Parents need wisdom in these areas/issues:
2. Children need wisdom in these areas/issues:
3. Husbands and wives need wisdom for their marriage in these areas/issues:
4. Singles need wisdom in these areas/issues:
5. Church leaders need wisdom in these areas/issues:

Have students form groups of three and ask each group to select two of the sentences to discuss. Provide each group with paper and a pencil, and give these instructions: "Take about sixty seconds for each of the two sentences. Think of several ways you might complete the sentence; then write down your suggestions."

After two or three minutes, call time. Ask the groups to share which sentences they selected and the ideas they listed.

Lead into the Bible study by saying, "Wisdom is one of our greatest needs. The wisdom we need for dealing with life's complex situations come from God. Today we will examine how Solomon gained wisdom, and explore how we can gain godly wisdom for our lives."

Into the Word

Present a brief lecture on the background of today's passages. You will find the information you need in the introduction section of the lesson commentary.

Have students work in their groups of three to discuss the following questions. Provide copies of the student book, which contains these questions, or prepare copies of the questions beforehand and distribute them at this time.

1. Read 1 Kings 2:1-4. What were the main points of the advice David gave his son, Solomon, who would succeed him as king of Israel?
2. Read 1 Kings 3:5-14. When God invited Solomon to ask for anything, Solomon requested that he be given wisdom. What factors led Solomon to ask for that?
3. What are some other requests Solomon might have been tempted to make? Why would wisdom (discernment/understanding) have been of greater value than these?
4. What was God's response to Solomon's request?
5. According to Solomon, how valuable is wisdom? Consult his writings in these passages:
Proverbs 3:13-18
Proverbs 4:7
Proverbs 8:11
6. What do these Scriptures reveal about how to gain wisdom?
Proverbs 1:7; 9:10
Proverbs 2:1-11
Proverbs 22:17
Proverbs 14:8
Proverbs 15:31, 32
James 1:5-8

Allow groups twenty-five minutes to study the passages and discuss the questions. When the time is up, bring the groups together again as a class. Ask the groups to share their observations for question two. Then ask for their answers to question six. List their answers on the chalkboard.

Next, ask a volunteer to read James 3:13-18. Then ask, "Based on everything we have studied today, how would you define wisdom as it is used in the Bible?" Allow students to discuss this. Try to lead the class to create a definition of wisdom, and write it on the chalkboard.

Into Life

During the week before class, prepare copies of the following incomplete sentences, allowing spaces for students to write their answers. Distribute them at this time.

1. One area of my life in which I really need wisdom is—
2. I need wisdom in my life more than I need—
3. One way I will seek to increase in wisdom, based upon the Scriptures we examined in this lesson, is—
4. Complete this prayer in writing: Father, in the spirit of Your instructions in James 1:5, 6, I ask You for wisdom in my life, especially regarding—

Have students complete the sentences in writing. Then close with oral prayer.

Let's Talk It Over

The questions on this page are designed to encourage review of the lesson Scriptures and to promote discussion of the lesson by the class. The answers provided are only discussion starters. Let your class talk it over from there.

1. Solomon requested "an understanding heart" so he would be able to "discern between good and bad." Why is it appropriate for modern leaders to offer such a prayer?

Surely leaders today have at least as great a need as Solomon did to understand human needs, desires, and relationships! What a challenge in our time to be able to distinguish between what is good and bad with respect to our society's complex problems. Humanists may object, and those who insist on a strict separation of church and state may be horrified, but our times virtually cry out for leaders who are committed to prayer of the kind Solomon offered. Since all Christians are to pray "for kings, and for all that are in authority" (1 Timothy 2:2), we may well use Solomon's request as a guideline for prayers we offer on behalf of our leaders.

2. God called attention to the fact that Solomon had not asked for long life. Why is the request for long life a questionable objective of prayer?

One could say that Solomon might have been better off had his life been shorter! It was "when Solomon was old" that he drifted away from the Lord (1 Kings 11:4). That serves as a reminder of the fact that length of life on earth is of secondary consideration compared to what we do for God in the years we have. The familiar saying is appropriate here: "Only one life, 'twill soon be past; only what's done for Christ will last." It would seem that Christians have a clearer knowledge than Solomon had of the better life beyond this one. Instead of praying for a longer life here, we should be developing more of the attitude of Paul when he spoke of his willingness "to be absent from the body, and to be present with the Lord" (2 Corinthians 5:8).

3. God referred to the fact that Solomon had not asked for riches. Why is the request for wealth a questionable objective for prayer?

Following up on the answer to the preceding question, one could say that Solomon might have been better off had he not obtained so many riches. The book of Ecclesiastes demonstrates how distracting his abundance of possessions and pleasures was to him. We have no idea how riches might affect us. Perhaps we have dreamed of coming into great wealth, and we have pictured ourselves giving generously to spiritual and charitable causes. In actuality, however, the acquisition of riches might produce in us selfishness, callousness, and spiritual complacency. It is wise to remember Paul's warning: "But they that will be rich fall into temptation and a snare, and into many foolish and hurtful lusts, which drown men in destruction and perdition" (1 Timothy 6:9).

4. God was pleased because Solomon had not asked for the lives of his enemies. We might be tempted to ask for the removal of all our problems. Why is that a questionable objective for prayer?

Once again, one could say that Solomon might have been better off had he been troubled by enemies throughout his reign. We are told in 1 Kings 11:14-40 of some of Solomon's adversaries, but these may not have become serious problems until the last years of the king's reign. Our problems serve many useful purposes in our lives, such as strengthening our faith, developing our capacity for patience, producing an inclination to humility, etc. Perhaps we can say that the things that vex us are our equivalent of Paul's famous "thorn in the flesh." He prayed for its removal, but was denied that answer, and as a result he discovered the Lord's strength working through his weakness (2 Corinthians 12:7-10).

5. It is disturbing to see that Solomon turned to idolatry after beginning his reign in faith in and devotion to God. How can we avoid such a reversal in our spiritual devotion?

Solomon's downfall provides an illustration of the New Testament warning, "Be ye not unequally yoked with unbelievers" (2 Corinthians 6:14). In his case, his marriages with heathen princesses led to his worship of false gods. In our time, young men and women are frequently led away from commitment to Christ by becoming linked in marriage to an unbelieving partner. Friendships and business associations of Christians with those who do not believe in Christ have led some believers to turn away from the Lord. It is a matter of wisdom therefore, for us to exercise prayerful caution before we enter into a close relationship with any non-Christian person.

Josiah: King of Reforms

October 25
Lesson 8

LESSON SCRIPTURE: 2 Chronicles 34.

PRINTED TEXT: 2 Chronicles 34:2, 8, 14b-16a, 19, 21, 30-32.

DEVOTIONAL READING: 2 Chronicles 34:9-13.

2 Chronicles 34:2, 8, 14b-16a

2 And he did that which was right in the sight of the LORD, and walked in the ways of David his father, and declined neither to the right hand, nor to the left.

. . . .

8 Now in the eighteenth year of his reign, when he had purged the land, and the house, he sent Shaphan the son of Azaliah, and Maaseiah the governor of the city, and Joah the son of Joahaz the recorder, to repair the house of the LORD his God.

. . . .

14b Hilkiah the priest found a book of the law of the LORD given by Moses.

15 And Hilkiah answered and said to Shaphan the scribe, I have found the book of the law in the house of the LORD. And Hilkiah delivered the book to Shaphan.

16a And Shaphan carried the book to the king.

. . . .

19 And it came to pass, when the king had heard the words of the law, that he rent his clothes.

. . . .

21 Go, inquire of the LORD for me, and for them that are left in Israel and in Judah, concerning the words of the book that is found: for great is the wrath of the LORD that is poured out upon us, because our fathers have not kept the word of the LORD, to do after all that is written in this book.

. . . .

30 And the king went up into the house of the LORD, and all the men of Judah, and the inhabitants of Jerusalem, and the priests, and the Levites, and all the people, great and small: and he read in their ears all the words of the book of the covenant that was found in the house of the LORD.

31 And the king stood in his place, and made a covenant before the LORD, to walk after the LORD, and to keep his commandments, and his testimonies, and his statutes, with all his heart, and with all his soul, to perform the words of the covenant which are written in this book.

32 And he caused all that were present in Jerusalem and Benjamin to stand to it. And the inhabitants of Jerusalem did according to the covenant of God, the God of their fathers.

GOLDEN TEXT: Josiah took away all the abominations out of all the countries that pertained to the children of Israel, and made all that were present in Israel to serve, even to serve the LORD their God.—2 Chronicles 34:33.

Old Testament Personalities

Unit 2: The People Choose a Monarchy

(Lessons 5-8)

Lesson Aims

After this lesson students should be able to:

1. Tell of the good that Josiah did in Judah.
2. Tell what guide Josiah found for his people, and what guide God has given us.

Lesson Outline

INTRODUCTION
- A. Looking at Hebrew History
- B. Lesson Background

I. THE KING (2 Chronicles 34:2, 8)
- A. Doing Right (v. 2)
- B. Repairing the Temple (v. 8)
  Prepared for the Moment

II. THE BOOK (2 Chronicles 34:14b-16a, 19, 21)
- A. Discovery (vv. 14b-16a)
- B. Grief (v. 19)
  Reminders of the Past
- C. Inquiry (v. 21)

III. THE COVENANT (2 Chronicles 34:30-32)
- A. Informing the Nation (v. 30)
- B. The King's Pledge (v. 31)
- C. The People's Pledge (v. 32)

CONCLUSION
- A. The Truth of God's Word
- B. The Power of a Leader
- C. The Responsibility of Each Person
- D. Prayer
- E. Thought to Remember

Refer to visual 8 of the visuals packet as you proceed through the lesson text. The visual is shown on page 68.

Introduction

The Hebrew people have a unique place in history. God called them to be His people. He gave them special care and entrusted them with a special revelation. He also laid on them a special duty. They were to demonstrate to the rest of the world that it is good and profitable to be ruled by the Lord. When they kept God's law they did demonstrate that. When they did not keep His law, they demonstrated that disobedience is disastrous. The record of their successes and failures is written to help us obey God and be blessed (1 Corinthians 10:6-11).

A. Looking at Hebrew History

This quarter we are rapidly surveying Hebrew history as recorded in the Old Testament. To get an overview of the whole, we are focusing on a few outstanding characters.

In September we began with Abraham, father of all the Hebrews. Then we leaped over more than four hundred years to Moses, who led his people out of Egypt, and Joshua, who led them into the promised land. The book of Judges records events of about three hundred years. From that time we took but a single sample, the story of Deborah and Barak.

In October we first looked at Samuel, last of the judges, and Saul, first of the kings. Then we studied David and Solomon, the two kings who brought Israel to the peak of power and prestige. After Solomon died, the kingdom was divided. In the next three and a half centuries the north part had nineteen kings and the south part had nineteen kings and a queen. From all of these we are taking just one sample, Josiah. He is the subject of this lesson.

B. Lesson Background

Among the horrid rulers of the south kingdom, none was worse than Manasseh, Josiah's grandfather. Forsaking the Lord, Manasseh energetically promoted idolatry all over his kingdom, even in the temple. (2 Chronicles 33:1-9).

In his later years, Manasseh changed his ways and tried to undo the evil he had done (2 Chronicles 33:10-17). But when he died, his son Amon promptly reverted to the wickedness of his father's earlier years (vv. 21-23).

Evil Amon lasted only two years as king (2 Chronicles 33:21). His servants killed him in his own house, probably intending to take over the government. But the people revolted at that. They had endured the corrupt rule of Manasseh and Amon, but now they thought it was time to draw the line. By a popular uprising they killed the killers of the king and put Amon's son Josiah on the throne (vv. 24, 25).

I. The King (2 Chronicles 34:2, 8)

Josiah was only eight years old when he became king (v. 1). Surely he was not able to run the country himself, but he had good help.

A. Doing Right (v. 2)

2. And he did that which was right in the sight of the LORD, and walked in the ways of David his father, and declined neither to the right hand, nor to the left.

Whoever guided King Josiah guided him well: *he did that which was right in the sight of the Lord.* Josiah's forefather *David* had died more than three hundred years before, but he had been so just and good that his *ways* were still taken as the model to be followed. Now Josiah was following those same good ways. However, it seems that he did nothing drastic till he was about twenty years old. Then he conducted a vigorous campaign to destroy all the paraphernalia of idol worship in the whole country (vv. 3-7). This was the Lord's country. He alone should be worshiped.

B. Repairing the Temple (v. 8)

8. Now in the eighteenth year of his reign, when he had purged the land, and the house, he sent Shaphan the son of Azaliah, and Maaseiah the governor of the city, and Joah the son of Joahaz the recorder, to repair the house of the LORD his God.

This was six years after Josiah began his campaign to get rid of idolatry (v. 3). The *King James Version* indicates that the campaign now was complete. He *had purged* or cleansed both *the land, and the house,* the temple of God. The *New International Version* indicates that the campaign was still continuing; the work at the temple was the climax of it.

Josiah's father and grandfather had ruled for fifty-seven years (2 Chronicles 33:1, 21), and Josiah now was in the eighteenth year of his reign. Probably the temple had been without proper care through all of those seventy-five years. It must have needed extensive repairs. To direct that work the king appointed a commission of three important officials. *Shaphan* was the scribe (v. 15), the royal secretary. *Maaseiah* was *governor of the city,* Jerusalem. *Joah* was the keeper of government records.

PREPARED FOR THE MOMENT

In 1990 a commission formed by the American Medical Association and the National Association of State Boards of Education reported on its study of the problems of today's young people.

The findings were astonishing. Nearly one in ten teenage girls becomes pregnant each year. Thirty-nine percent of high school seniors reported they had gotten drunk in the previous two weeks. Suicide is the number two cause of death among adolescents, following alcohol-induced accidents as the leading cause. Teen-age arrests are up thirtyfold since 1950.

In other words, America's youth are living lives so marred by tragedy that they are a "generation at risk," and many will be unable to fulfill the responsibilities of adulthood. As we might have expected, the commission called for more education. The Bible would call instead for regeneration.

When Josiah was called upon to take the reigns of Israel's leadership, he had prepared himself well for the task. He had walked the "strait and narrow," doing right in the sight of God. The best preparation for fulfilling responsibility when it comes is trusting God, getting one's priorities right, and developing good, moral habits of life. —C. R. B.

How to Say It

AZALIAH. Az-uh-*lye*-uh.
BARAK. *Bay*-ruk or *Bair*-uk.
HILKIAH. Hill-*kye*-uh.
JOAHAZ. *Jo*-ah-haz.
JOSIAH. Jo-*sye*-uh.
MAASEIAH. May-uh-*see*-yuh.
SHAPHAN. *Shay*-fan.

II. The Book (2 Chronicles 34:14b-16a, 19, 21)

The three officials promptly began their project. Along with Hilkiah the high priest, they took the money that had been collected in the temple treasury and used it to hire workers and buy materials. The work force was organized with capable overseers (vv. 9-13).

A. Discovery (vv. 14b-16a)

14b. Hilkiah the priest found a book of the law of the LORD given by Moses.

The first part of the verse tells us the book was found as they were bringing out the money from the temple treasury. Perhaps some priest had hidden it in the treasury to keep it safe in the evil years of Manasseh's reign. That king and his henchmen had no regard for God's law. Perhaps they even destroyed other copies of the law, but this one was kept safe. Now, seventy-five years after Manasseh began his reign, it seems that no one even knew this book existed. The priest seems to have found it by accident. God's Word was lost in God's house! Is it lost in your house? Is its helpfulness lost, even though the book is in plain sight, because it is not used?

15. And Hilkiah answered and said to Shaphan the scribe, I have found the book of the law in the house of the LORD. And Hilkiah delivered the book to Shaphan.

Shaphan the scribe might be called the chairman of the king's commission appointed to repair the temple. At least he is named first among the members of the commission (v. 8). Quite properly the priest reported his find and gave the book to Shaphan.

16a. And Shaphan carried the book to the king.

Shaphan took the book along when he went to the king to report on the progress made in repairing the temple (vv. 16b, 17). More than that, he read the book to the king (v. 18).

B. Grief (v. 19)

19. And it came to pass, when the king had heard the words of the law, that he rent his clothes.

Tearing one's clothes was a traditional way of expressing shock, grief, horror. Josiah had been trying to do God's will without knowing anything about God's Word. Now he heard the law and saw how far he and his people were from keeping it, and he was horrified.

The king heard not only what the law commanded, but also the terrible penalties it prescribed for those who broke it. Was there any way to escape those penalties? Quickly the king appointed a prestigious committee to make an investigation (v. 20).

REMINDERS OF THE PAST

The southwestern United States is mostly desert. Many parts of the region are green with vegetation, but only because of a vast system of dams and canals that now supply water to formerly barren land. Water is captured and then pumped hundreds of miles to reservoirs near where it will be used.

California entered its fifth year of drought in 1991, with reservoir levels shrinking to dangerous levels. As they did so, mining equipment from the 1850s was uncovered, as were old bridges, railroad tunnels, and stolen cars. Whole town sites were revealed in some reservoirs. Some of these reminders of the past provoked nostalgia; some produced painful memories.

When the book of God's law was found during the temple repairs the book was a reminder of what Israel had been and an indictment of what Israel had become. Josiah's pained reaction when he heard the law read indicates the intensity of the nation's spiritual drought.

We may hide God's Word from our sight, but its truth will one day be revealed. That revelation will be painful for those who have turned away from God. For those who love God and turn penitently to Him, however, God's Word always offers hope for something better. —C. R. B.

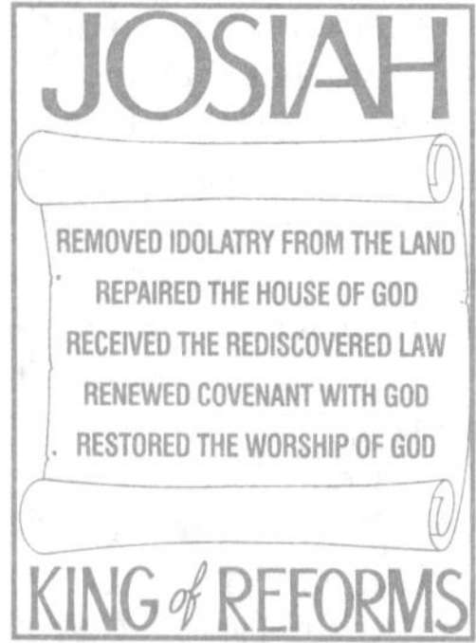
JOSIAH
REMOVED IDOLATRY FROM THE LAND
REPAIRED THE HOUSE OF GOD
RECEIVED THE REDISCOVERED LAW
RENEWED COVENANT WITH GOD
RESTORED THE WORSHIP OF GOD
KING of REFORMS

visual 8

C. Inquiry (v. 21)

21. Go, inquire of the LORD for me, and for them that are left in Israel and in Judah, concerning the words of the book that is found: for great is the wrath of the LORD that is poured out upon us, because our fathers have not kept the word of the LORD, to do after all that is written in this book.

Mention of *Israel* and *Judah* reminds us that Solomon's great country had been divided after his death. Josiah was king of Judah, the south part. About eighty years before Josiah came to the throne, the other part, called Israel, had been destroyed. Most of its people had been deported to foreign lands (2 Kings 17:1-18). Some of them however, had been *left in Israel.* Boldly Josiah had carried his campaign against idolatry into their territory (2 Chronicles 34:6). Now he inquired on behalf of that remnant of Israel as well as on behalf of Judah and himself. The book of the law spoke about the wrath of the Lord on those who broke the law. God's wrath had brought destruction to Israel already. But the remnant of Israel, and Judah, and the king himself—all these had been breaking the law too, and they were not yet destroyed. Was there any hope for them?

III. The Covenant (2 Chronicles 34:30-32)

Members of the king's committee knew where to go to inquire of the Lord. He had in Jerusalem a prophetess named Huldah. From her the committee got bad news and good news. The bad news was that the wrath of the Lord would indeed be poured out on Jerusalem and Judah. Their sin would be punished just as the law declared. The good news was that this would not happen immediately. Josiah was trying to do right, to lead the nation to worship God and obey Him. Therefore the calamity was postponed. It would not come in Josiah's lifetime.

A. Informing the Nation (v. 30)

30. And the king went up into the house of the LORD, and all the men of Judah, and the inhabitants of Jerusalem, and the priests, and the

Levites, and all the people, great and small: and he read in their ears all the words of the book of the covenant that was found in the house of the LORD.

Josiah first gathered the elders, the leading men of the nation (v. 29). Then with their help he gathered the whole nation in a huge mass meeting in the court of the temple. To the whole nation he read *all the words of the book of the covenant.* In the very beginning of Israel's national life, even before the whole law was given, the people had agreed to do whatever God commanded (Exodus 19:8). Now Josiah was about to ask the people of his time to renew the covenant by making the same promise. The first step was to let them hear the law so they would know what they were promising to do.

B. The King's Pledge (v. 31)

31. And the king stood in his place, and made a covenant before the LORD, to walk after the LORD, and to keep his commandments, and his testimonies, and his statutes, with all his heart, and with all his soul, to perform the words of the covenant which are written in this book.

The king himself led the way. Standing before the nation and *before the Lord,* he pledged himself to follow the Lord and do all that the book commanded. He promised to do it *with all his heart, and with all his soul:* that is, sincerely, willingly, earnestly, enthusiastically.

C. The People's Pledge (v. 32)

32. And he caused all that were present in Jerusalem and Benjamin to stand to it. And the inhabitants of Jerusalem did according to the covenant of God, the God of their fathers.

The south kingdom usually was known as Judah, the name of its principal tribe. Here the capital city, *Jerusalem,* stands for Judah. But the small tribe of *Benjamin* also was a part of the south kingdom. At Josiah's call, all the assembled people of the nation stood to declare that they also would obey God's law. They kept their promise too: they *did according to the covenant of God.* That lasted as long as Josiah was there to enforce the law (v. 33).

Conclusion

Josiah died about thirteen years after the covenant was renewed. Soon his son Jehoiakim became king, and the people did wrong with him as readily as they had done right with Josiah. Punishment soon began (2 Chronicles 36:5-7). Jerusalem was destroyed a little less than a quarter of a century after Josiah died, and its people were taken to Babylon (vv. 14-20).

A. The Truth of God's Word

Huldah said disaster was coming, but not in Josiah's time (2 Chronicles 34:22-28). She was sure of this, because she was God's prophetess.

We have seen the truth of God's word in every lesson of this series. God said He would make a great nation from Abraham (Genesis 12:2), and He did. God said He would rescue His people from Egypt (Exodus 3:7, 8) and He did. God said He would give the land of promise to Joshua and his people. (Joshua 1:1-5), and He did. God said He would give victory to Deborah and Barak (Judges 4:4-7), and He did. God said a king would become oppressive (1 Samuel 8:10-18), and it was true. The Lord foretold trouble and violence in David's family (2 Samuel 12:10), and trouble and violence came. The Lord promised wisdom, riches, and honor to Solomon (1 Kings 3:11-13), and Solomon had all of them.

We who treasure the Christian hope "may be greatly encouraged" by the unfailing truthfulness of God's word (Hebrews 6:18, *New International Version*). In these later days God has spoken to us in His Son, Jesus (Hebrews 1:1-4). Jesus said, "Come unto me, all ye that labor and are heavy laden, and I will give you rest" (Matthew 11:28). He will do as He said. Jesus said, "Except a man be born of water and of the Spirit, he cannot enter into the kingdom of God" (John 3:5). That is true. Jesus said, "Not every one that saith unto me, Lord, Lord, shall enter into the kingdom of heaven; but he that doeth the will of my Father which is in heaven" (Matthew 7:21). That also is true. Jesus said, "In the world ye shall have tribulation: but be of good cheer; I have overcome the world" (John 16:33). We can count on it. Jesus said He will sit on the throne of His glory, calling some blessed people to the kingdom prepared for them and consigning others to everlasting fire prepared for the devil and his angels (Matthew 25:31-46). He will do exactly that.

B. The Power of a Leader

Josiah was only twenty years old when he set out to reform his country, but he was the king. At his order his troops swept over the land to destroy every heathen altar and idol (2 Chronicles 34:3-7). The neglected temple was repaired, the neglected law was discovered, and the neglected worship of the Lord was restored. Led by Josiah, "the inhabitants of Jerusalem did according to the covenant of God . . . and all his days they departed not from following the Lord" (vv. 32, 33). So the nation was saved from destruction for a time. But when the good king died, the good nation promptly turned bad (chapter 36).

The power of a leader has been seen again and again in our lessons. Joshua led so well that "the people served the Lord all the days of Joshua, and all the days of the elders that outlived Joshua (Judges 2:7). But then came a generation of people who had never known anything but peace and prosperity, and they drifted away from God (vv. 8-13) Deborah judged the people well, and she called Barak to defeat the Canaanites and restore peace and happiness to Israel (Judges 4); "and the land had rest forty years" (5:31). But then the people reverted to evil again, and their time of rest soon ended (6:1). Samuel called a miserable nation to God and to victory and peace (1 Samuel 7:3-17), but his own sons did evil (8:1-3). Godly Solomon brought Israel to the peak of prosperity and power (1 Kings 4:20, 21). But Solomon became ungodly, and brought his great empire close to its end (1 Kings 11).

We who are leaders of various kinds—parents, teachers, employers, managers, foremen, government officials, elders in a church—we need to be aware of the power we have. If we are leaders, people are following us for better or for worse. We must be doubly careful to do that which is right in the eyes of the Lord.

You are a leader. Whether you know it or not, someone is following you. Someone is making your goodness a model for his, or someone is making your badness an excuse for his. So watch yourself!

C. The Responsibility of Each Person

If you are making someone's misdeed an excuse for yours, it is a poor excuse. If you are making someone's goodness a model for yours, there is no excuse for failing to live up to the model. The Lord gave His commandments to each person in Israel rather than to the nation as a group. In the Ten Commandments He said, "*Thou* shalt not." *Thou* is a singular pronoun, addressed to one person, each person. If the command were addressed to a group, large or small, it would be "*Ye shall not.*" God said, "*Thou* shalt love the Lord *thy* God with all *thine* heart, and with all *thy* soul, and with all *thy* might. And these words, which I command *thee* this day, shall be in *thine* heart: and *thou* shalt teach them diligently unto *thy* children" (Deuteronomy 6:5-7). Each person in Israel was responsible, personally and individually responsible, both for doing God's will and for teaching it. Anyone who failed could not put the blame on another, either his king or his neighbor.

Of course we Christians are not under the ancient law given at Mount Sinai. Jesus taught His disciples as a group: "I say unto *you*" (Matthew 5:18, 20, 22, 28, 32, 34, 39, 44). The *you* is plural. Does anyone think that makes our individual responsibility any less?

Jesus' teaching to the group was sprinkled with singular pronouns. "When *thou* doest *thine* alms, do not sound a trumpet." "When *thou* prayest, enter into *thy* closet." "When *thou* fastest, anoint *thine* head." "*Thou* hypocrite, first cast out the beam out of *thine* own eye." "Not every one that saith unto me, Lord, Lord, shall enter into the kingdom of heaven; but *he* that doeth the will of my Father." "Whosoever heareth these sayings of mine, and doeth them, I will liken *him* unto a wise man" (Matthew 6:2, 6, 17; 7:5, 21, 24).

Simon Peter said, "Repent and be baptized, *every one* of you" (Acts 2:38). *Every man* should be concerned about the good of others (1 Corinthians 10:24; Philippians 2:4). *Every man* should be swift to hear and slow to speak (James 1:19). *Every one* of us shall give account of himself to God (Romans 14:12). God judges *every man's* work (1 Peter 1:17), and Jesus will reward *every man* according to what he has done (Matthew 16:27; Revelation 22:12).

There is no way I can escape my personal responsibility, and there is no way you can escape yours.

D. Prayer

Our Father, our king, our judge, how You have blessed us by giving us Your Word to guide us! How just it is, then, to hold us responsible for what we do!. May we have courage and strength to accept our responsibility willingly and fulfill it nobly. In Jesus' name, amen.

E. Thought to Remember

No excuses.

Home Daily Bible Readings

Monday, Oct. 19—Josiah Destroys Graven Images in Judah and Jerusalem (2 Chronicles 34:3-7)

Tuesday, Oct. 20—The Lord's House Is Rebuilt (2 Chronicles 34:9-13)

Wednesday, Oct. 21—King Josiah Repents (2 Chronicles 34:17-21)

Thursday, Oct. 22—The People of Judah Are Forgiven (2 Chronicles 34:22-28)

Friday, Oct. 23—Israel Renews the Covenant With the Lord (2 Chronicles 34:29-34)

Saturday, Oct. 24—Israel Prepares for the Passover (2 Chronicles 35:1-6)

Sunday, Oct. 25—King Josiah Dies (2 Chronicles 35:20-27)

Learning by Doing

This page contains an alternate lesson plan emphasizing learning activities. Classes desiring such student involvement will find these suggestions helpful.

Learning Goals

In this lesson you will seek to lead your students to do the following:

1. Analyze Josiah's response to God's Word.
2. Explore obstacles that hinder their obedience to God's Word.
3. Commit themselves to receiving God's Word with humility and responding in obedience.

Into the Lesson

Begin the session by saying, "Mark Twain is credited with saying, 'It's not the things in the Bible I don't understand that bother me; it's the things I do understand.' " He meant that he was troubled because he didn't always do what he knew the Bible said a person should do. Then ask students, "Of the Bible truths that you understand, what most troubles you?" Have class members form groups of four to discuss that question. Allow about five minutes for discussion. Then lead into the Bible study with this transitional thought: "Although we all need to know the Bible better, Bible knowledge isn't the ultimate goal of Bible study. Rather, it is to learn how to put the Word of God into practice in our daily lives. In our lesson today we will look at the life of King Josiah—a man who wanted not only to increase his knowledge of God's Word, but was committed to obeying it."

Into the Word

Set the background for today's lesson with a brief lecture using the material in the introduction of the lesson commentary. Then ask volunteers to read 2 Chronicles 34, each reading one of these sections: vv. 1-7; vv. 8-13; vv. 14-21; vv. 22-28: vv. 29-33.

Have the class members form groups of four to six. (If they were in groups of four earlier, have them remain in the same groups.) They are to discuss the following questions, which are based on 2 Chronicles 34. The questions are included in the student book. Or you can prepare copies of the questions ahead of time to distribute to the class members.

1. From what is recorded in this chapter, how would you describe Josiah?
2. As recorded in the verses below, in what ways did Josiah please God?
   a. verses 1-7.
   b. verses 8-13.
3. According to the following verses, what was Josiah's response when the book of the law of the Lord was found?
   a. verses 14-21.
   b. verses 22-33.
4. What was God's evaluation of Josiah's response? (See verses 26, 27.)
5. What was God's promise to Josiah because of his response? (See verse 28.)

Allow groups fifteen to twenty minutes to study the passage and discuss the questions. Then bring the groups together. Help the class members summarize the passage by asking, "In your opinion, what is the most important insight in this passage?" Allow several minutes for discussion.

Then ask, "What obstacles might have discouraged Josiah from seeking God and obeying His Word?" Allow time for reflection, and then discuss the question. (Some answers that may be given are (1) it might have been unpopular with the people, (2) it might have been difficult to change the momentum of a nation that had drifted from God and His Word. Of course, these are only a few suggestions. See how many others your class can come up with.)

Into Life

In the week before class, prepare copies of the questions below. Give each student a copy of the questions at this time. Then have a volunteer read James 1:21-25. Point out that according to this passage we are to *receive* God's word with humility, and we are to *respond* to it with obedience. Lead your class in discussing questions 1-3 as a large group. Then have students individually write their answers to questions 4 and 5.

1. How can a person receive God's Word with humility?
2. What would you expect to observe in a person who receives God's Word with humility?
3. What obstacles can make it difficult for us to obey God's Word?
4. In what areas of your life are you living as a doer of God's Word?
5. What do you believe is the next step for you in becoming more obedient to God's Word? What will you do about it?

Have students gather in the groups they met with earlier and close with prayer. Encourage your students to commit themselves to becoming more obedient to God's Word.

Let's Talk It Over

The questions on this page are designed to encourage review of the lesson Scriptures and to promote discussion of the lesson by the class. The answers provided are only discussion starters. Let your class talk it over from there.

1. It is remarkable that Josiah was such a godly king, considering the exceptional wickedness of his grandfather and father. What does this say to Christians who have come out of less-than-ideal family situations?

Through the power of God, human beings can rise above their environment. Some have surmounted backgrounds of parental abuse, poverty, crime, atheistic influence, and other negative factors to become exemplary Christians. A popular view concerning a child who grows up under such unfavorable circumstances is that "he (or she) will never amount to anything." This view, however, overlooks the capacity of human beings to overcome several adversities, and it underestimates the gospel's power to transform a human character.

2. In what ways is the Bible a "lost book" today? How can we "find" it again?

Although the Bible is prominently displayed in churches and homes and is available in libraries, hospitals, and hotel and motel rooms, it is still virtually lost to the vast numbers who never read it. Even great numbers of professing Christians rarely open the Bible to read it for themselves. And it remains something of a lost book for those who do read it but have adopted the devil's clever lie that it is "impossible to understand." Furthermore, it is lost for the people who read it as a matter of habit, but fail to put its principles into practice. One key to "finding" the Bible again is for the church to emphasize programs that will encourage members to read it and personally apply its teachings to their lives. The developing of small, informal, group Bible studies is one approach that has worked in many churches.

3. How should the Bible's warnings concerning judgment on the ungodly affect us?

Have we developed a kind of hardness to these warnings, so that they no longer trouble us? Are we unmoved by a passage such as 2 Thessalonians 1:7, 8, which states that "the Lord Jesus shall be revealed from heaven with his mighty angels, in flaming fire taking vengeance on them that know not God, and that obey not the gospel of our Lord Jesus Christ"? We are not to be gripped by a tormenting fear (1 John 4:17, 18), but we should surely be stirred to more diligence in holiness as we contemplate the dangers facing the ungodly. And we should be so disturbed by the terrible fate awaiting the unsaved that we will intensify our efforts at evangelism. With Paul we must say, "Knowing therefore the terror of the Lord, we persuade men" (2 Corinthians 5:11).

4. Why is it important that Christians be encouraged to take a public stand for God?

Some persons assert that religion is a personal and private matter. Others may go so far as to suggest that our society would be better off if everyone would keep their religious views to themselves. But if we are to be "the salt of the earth" and "the light of the world," as Jesus stated in Matthew 5:13, 14, we must make it known publicly that we are committed to God, Jesus Christ, and the Bible. Certain individuals will object to this and accuse us of "trying to shove our religion down their throats." Of course, we should not attempt to force others to accept our faith or our Christian moral principles. But we must be bold in making it very clear that we are on God's side. Our witness needs to be seen in newspaper editorial pages, in letters to political officials, in petitions to television advertisers, and elsewhere.

5. We recognize the importance of responsible leadership in the church. What may be said about the need for responsible followers?

Unfortunately, leadership attributes are not restricted to wise and honest persons. An individual with wicked motives may be gifted with a commanding physical presence, a winsome personality, a persuasive tongue, and marvelous abilities for organization. Leaders like this have drawn away from a pure faith believers who were otherwise intelligent, sensible, and committed members of the church. Paul said to the Corinthians, "Be ye followers of me, even as I also am of Christ" (1 Corinthians 11:1). This is a vital factor Christians must consider before following any leader. Is this individual clearly a follower of Jesus Christ? Does this person's lifestyle and words harmonize in demonstrating genuine commitment to the Lord? These are questions Christians must ask, not in the spirit of harsh judgment, but in a careful inspection of fruits (Matthew 7:15-20).

Elijah: Prophet of Courage

November 1
Lesson 9

LESSON SCRIPTURE: 1 Kings 17:1-7; 18.

PRINTED TEXT: 1 Kings 18:17, 18, 20-24, 36-39.

DEVOTIONAL READING: 1 Kings 18:30-39.

1 Kings 18:17, 18, 20-24, 36-39

17 And it came to pass, when Ahab saw Elijah, that Ahab said unto him, Art thou he that troubleth Israel?

18 And he answered, I have not troubled Israel; but thou, and thy father's house, in that ye have forsaken the commandments of the LORD, and thou hast followed Baalim.

. . . .

20 So Ahab sent unto all the children of Israel, and gathered the prophets together unto mount Carmel.

21 And Elijah came unto all the people, and said, How long halt ye between two opinions? if the LORD be God, follow him: but if Baal, then follow him. And the people answered him not a word.

22 Then said Elijah unto the people, I, even I only, remain a prophet of the LORD; but Baal's prophets are four hundred and fifty men.

23 Let them therefore give us two bullocks; and let them choose one bullock for themselves, and cut it in pieces, and lay it on wood, and put no fire under: and I will dress the other bullock, and lay it on wood, and put no fire under:

24 And call ye on the name of your gods, and I will call on the name of the LORD: and the God that answereth by fire, let him be God. And all the people answered and said, It is well spoken.

. . . .

36 And it came to pass at the time of the offering of the evening sacrifice, that Elijah the prophet came near, and said, LORD God of Abraham, Isaac, and of Israel, let it be known this day that thou art God in Israel, and that I am thy servant, and that I have done all these things at thy word.

37 Hear me, O LORD, hear me, that this people may know that thou art the LORD God, and that thou hast turned their heart back again.

38 Then the fire of the LORD fell, and consumed the burnt sacrifice, and the wood, and the stones, and the dust, and licked up the water that was in the trench.

39 And when all the people saw it, they fell on their faces: and they said, The LORD, he is the God; the LORD, he is the God.

GOLDEN TEXT: Elijah came unto all the people, and said, How long halt ye between two opinions? if the LORD be God, follow him: but if Baal, then follow him.
—1 Kings 18:21.

Old Testament Personalities

Unit 3: The Prophets' Roles in a Divided Kingdom (Lessons 9-13)

Lesson Aims

After this lesson a student should be able to:

1. Retell the story of Elijah's challenge and contest.
2. Identify the best guide we have in distinguishing right from wrong.
3. Take a firm stand for the right.

Lesson Outline

Display visual 9 of the visuals packet and refer to it during the lesson when you deem it appropriate. The visual is shown on page 76.

Introduction

In the month of October our lessons centered on kings. We considered three kings of united Israel: Saul, David, and Solomon. Then we took one king, Josiah, as a sample of the twenty monarchs who ruled in the southern kingdom, Judah, after Solomon's empire was divided.

This month our lessons will center on prophets rather than kings, though kings still will have a prominent place. For the first lesson we drop back to a time more than two hundred years before Josiah, and perhaps about seventy years after Solomon. Now for the first time we focus on the northern part of the divided kingdom, which continued to be called Israel.

A. The Northern Kingdom

When the empire was divided, the king of the north was Jeroboam. He did not want his people to go to Jerusalem to worship with the people of the south. He was afraid united worship would result in united government and leave him without a kingdom. So he established two worship centers in his own territory, placing golden calves in them to be worshiped (1 Kings 12:26-33). Later kings of northern Israel accepted and supported that idolatry.

Perhaps the calves were supposed to represent Jehovah, the God who had rescued Israel from Egypt (1 Kings 12:28), but they were still idols. The law forbade the worship of images. No exceptions were made (Exodus 20:4-6). When idolatry begins, corruption is not far behind. Of each of the first six kings in northern Israel it is written that he did evil (1 Kings 14:7-9; 15:25, 26, 33, 34; 16:8, 9, 18, 19, 25, 30). Indeed, every king that reigned in the northern kingdom's history of two hundred plus years is characterized as being evil.

B. Ahab and the Pagan Queen

Ahab was the seventh king of northern Israel, and he was worse than those before him (1 Kings 16:30). To make matters still worse, he brought in a pagan to be his queen, and brought in her idolatry with her (1 Kings 16:31-33). An activist for her pagan religion, Queen Jezebel set about to destroy the worship of Jehovah and make her pagan religion the state religion of Israel (1 Kings 18:13).

C. Lesson Background

Elijah the prophet appeared abruptly in the midst of the growing corruption. Bluntly he announced that there would be no rain in Israel until he would say so. Then he went into hiding to save his life (1 Kings 17:1-6). For three and a

How to Say It

ASHERAH. Uh-*she*-ruh.
BAALIM. *Bay*-uh-lim.
JEROBOAM. Jair-o-*bo*-um.
JEZEBEL. *Jez*-uh-bel.
JOSIAH. Jo-*sye*-uh.
SIDON. *Sye*-dun.
SIDONIAN. Sy-*doe*-ni-un

half years there was no rain (James 5:17). There was no grain to feed Israel, neither man nor beast. King Ahab and his general manager were out searching the country for a bit of pasture to save the lives of the royal horses and mules (1 Kings 18:3-6). In that crisis, Elijah came out of hiding and went boldly to meet the king.

I. Challenge (1 Kings 18:17, 18, 20, 21)

Elijah had hidden first by a little stream near the Jordan. When months without rain had dried up that stream, he had gone north to a town near Sidon (1 Kings 17:2-16). On returning to Israel, he first met the king's manager. The manager reported to the king, who then went to meet Elijah (18:1-16).

A. Challenge to the King (vv. 17, 18)

17. And it came to pass, when Ahab saw Elijah, that Ahab said unto him, Art thou he that troubleth Israel?

The question may be translated, *Are you here, troubler of Israel?* The *New International Version* has, *Is that you, you troubler of Israel?* The king supposed Elijah had troubled Israel by pronouncing a curse that brought on the long dry spell (17:1). He was not asking whether Elijah had done that or not. Rather, his question was an expression of surprise that Elijah would dare to show his face in Israel after causing so much trouble there.

UNABLE TO COPE WITH REALITY

An occasional visitor to Florence, Italy, will rush from a church or museum in panic. Feeling disoriented and unable to cope with the surroundings, the person is experiencing a malady known as the Stendhal syndrome. The name comes from the French author Stendhal, the first person known to have experienced these sensations.

Psychiatrists say that the great beauty of the works of art in Florence has a depressing effect on some very sensitive people who are dealing with personal problems. The "ugliness" they perceive in their personal lives is in stark contrast to the beauty about them, and they are overwhelmed by it.

When Ahab faced Elijah, he knew that the prophet's faithfulness to God made his own vileness stand out in bold relief. Unable to cope with the dissonance between what he was and what he should have been as the king of Israel, he lashed out at Elijah, calling him the one who troubled Israel. He was projecting onto Elijah the judgment that he knew should be his own.

When confronted with the spiritual beauty of a life lived in God's will, are we modern Ahabs? Do we lash out against it in hopes of making our own sinfulness seem less evil? Or do we accept the challenge of turning our lives around and getting right with God? —C. R. B

18. And he answered, I have not troubled Israel; but thou, and thy father's house, in that ye have forsaken the commandments of the LORD, and thou hast followed Baalim.

Elijah promptly denied that he had caused the trouble. The drought did not come because he said it would; God sent him to say it was coming because that was true. The real cause was the king himself, along with the whole family of his father. All of them had *forsaken the commandments of the Lord.* Ahab himself, more than the rest, had *followed Baalim.* The word *Baalim* is the plural of *Baal,* which means lord or master. It is a name used for any of various imaginary gods worshiped in Canaan and elsewhere. The plural *Baalim* can mean different deities worshiped in different places, but here perhaps it means different images of one Baal. Ahab's devotion seems to have been to one Baal, the Sidonian deity brought to Israel by the pagan queen, Jezebel. Ahab joined his wife and led Israel in worship of that figment of the imagination. Baal did not share Jehovah's standards of morality and goodness, so increasing corruption and depravity went along with the worship of Baal. God had sent the long dry spell because of these evils.

Boldly the prophet was challenging the king to a contest to determine who was the real God, Jehovah or Baal. For that purpose he told the king to call all Israel to a mass meeting on Mount Carmel. Especially to be summoned were all the prophets of Jezebel's false religion (v. 19). There were four hundred and fifty prophets of Baal, plus four hundred prophets of the groves. That term *groves* in the *King James Version* follows the old Greek and Latin translations, but most scholars now agree that the Hebrew *Asherah* does not mean a grove. It is the name of an imaginary goddess supposed to be associated with the imaginary god Baal. Her symbol was a tree trunk or other pole standing upright beside Baal's altar.

B. Challenge to the People (vv. 20, 21)

20. So Ahab sent unto all the children of Israel, and gathered the prophets together unto mount Carmel.

It seems strange to see an evil king taking orders from a holy prophet, especially a prophet who had been a fugitive in hiding for years. But this king had ignored this prophet before, and there had been three dry years in a row. The king's horses and mules and people were hungry. So the king obediently called the meeting that Elijah wanted.

21. And Elijah came unto all the people, and said, How long halt ye between two opinions? if the LORD be God, follow him: but if Baal, then follow him. And the people answered him not a word.

To *halt* is to limp. The people were crippled, hobbling along between Jehovah and Baal instead of taking a firm stand for either. Elijah urged them to make up their minds, to choose one or the other and follow him. But there was no answer. From ancient tradition these people knew Jehovah had plagued Egypt with great plagues, had opened the sea for His people, had appeared in fire on Sinai. No one wanted to step out and take a stand against Jehovah. On the other hand, the queen had been busily slaughtering Jehovah's prophets. The survivors were in hiding, as Elijah had been for three years. Taking a stand for Jehovah might be dangerous to one's health. So *the people answered him not a word.*

MAKE UP YOUR MIND

Few people will ever be as famous as a garbage barge was a few years ago. The barge was filled with tons of industrial waste from New York. The disposal company that was in charge hoped to dump the material elsewhere, so it did not fill up or contaminate a Long Island landfill.

Over a two month period, the barge wandered along the Atlantic and Gulf coasts, as its owners sought to dump the material in six states and three foreign countries, one after another. It finally ended up back in New York harbor. However, even there the cargo was subjected to a court order that prevented it from being unloaded. The public began to think, "Can't the persons involved make up their minds on this?"

Elijah must have raised the same question many times as he confronted the idolatry of Israel. While claiming to be the people of God, they wandered around, spiritually "at sea," playing at worshiping God, then turning back to Baal. Finally, the time was right to clear the air once and for all. Elijah challenged Israel with the words, "Make up your minds! You have to choose between God and Baal."

visual 9

It is a choice we all must make. Some today are like Israel, vacillating between love of God and love of the world. And as with Israel, God calls upon us to make the choice—finally, irrevocably—and then to let our lives be witnesses to that choice. —C. R. B.

II. Test (1 Kings 18:22-24)

How could those limping people be induced to take a stand? To help them make up their minds, Elijah proposed a test to show who was the real God.

A. The Odds (v. 22)

22. Then said Elijah unto the people, I, even I only, remain a prophet of the LORD; but Baal's prophets are four hundred and fifty men.

It looked as if the odds were much in favor of Baal. On his side were *four hundred and fifty men,* prosperous men, men well fed and well clothed even in time of terrible famine. It was no secret that the king and queen also were on that side. On the other side was one lone man. Elijah looked like a tiny minority—but no one saw Jehovah.

B. The Preparation (v. 23)

23. Let them therefore give us two bullocks; and let them choose one bullock for themselves, and cut it in pieces, and lay it on wood, and put no fire under: and I will dress the other bullock, and lay it on wood, and put no fire under.

Elijah suggested that two bulls be prepared as burnt offerings. In such an offering the carcass was not put on the altar whole. It was skinned and cut in pieces as if for food. The pieces were arranged on a pile of wood on the altar, and burned there (Leviticus 1:3-9). Elijah proposed that Baal's prophets choose one of the bulls, prepare it in the usual way, and lay it on the wood. Elijah himself would prepare the other bull and put it on the wood, but neither he nor the other prophets would light a fire.

C. The Decisive Action (v. 24)

24. And call ye on the name of your gods, and I will call on the name of the LORD: and the God that answereth by fire, let him be God. And all the people answered and said, It is well spoken.

When the sacrifice was ready, the worshipers would ask their deity to ignite the wood and burn the offering. If one deity would do this and the other would not, that would show which one was the real God. Now at last the people responded. The plan seemed fair, and they approved it.

The same word for *God* appears three times in this verse. Once it is translated *gods,* and twice it is translated *God.* The word *elohim* is plural in form, but often used of the one God. Probably it should be translated as singular in all three appearances here. The prophets of Baal would call on their god, Baal. Elijah would call on his God, Jehovah.

III. Outcome (1 Kings 18:36-39)

Elijah let the prophets of Baal try first. Dancing about their altar, they prayed for half a day. Elijah called to them to pray louder. Perhaps their God was occupied, he said, or taking a trip, or just asleep. So Baal's men prayed louder, and cut their flesh, perhaps hoping their suffering would move Baal to do as they asked. But there was no answer (vv. 25-29).

As the time for the regular evening sacrifice came near, Elijah called the people to him. He built an altar of twelve stones to represent the twelve tribes of Israel. Around the altar he dug a trench deep enough hold about three gallons. He stacked firewood on the altar. He killed and dressed the bull, and arranged the pieces on the wood. Then he asked some of the people to drench the sacrifice and the wood with water. From some convenient source, helpful people brought water and poured it over the sacrifice till it ran down and filled the trench around the altar (vv. 30-35). Then Elijah was ready for the test.

A. Appeal (vv. 36, 37)

36. And it came to pass at the time of the offering of the evening sacrifice, that Elijah the prophet came near, and said, LORD God of Abraham, Isaac, and of Israel, let it be known this day that thou art God in Israel, and that I am thy servant, and that I have done all these things at thy word.

Elijah was doing everything properly. He had prepared the sacrifice according to the law (v. 33). This was a special sacrifice, a bull instead of a lamb, presented at the proper hour for the evening sacrifice. Elijah wanted everyone to know exactly whom he was praying to. *Lord* here represents *Jehovah,* the personal name of the real God. In addition, Elijah described Him as *God of Abraham, Isaac, and of Israel*—the God of the Hebrew people from the very beginning of their existence as a separated people, God's chosen. Then Elijah asked God to make three things known: first, that Jehovah was *God in Israel;* second, that Elijah was Jehovah's *servant;* third, that Elijah arranged this test just as Jehovah told him to do it.

37. Hear me, O LORD, hear me, that this people may know that thou art the LORD God, and that thou hast turned their heart back again.

Hear, of course, means more than hear. Elijah was asking God to hear and to respond by sending fire to burn the waiting sacrifice. He repeated the main reason for asking this: he wanted all the people of Israel to know that Jehovah was God. Further, he wanted them to realize that by this demonstration God had *turned their heart back again,* had won them away from any worship of the powerless Baal.

B. Answer (v. 38)

38. Then the fire of the LORD fell, and consumed the burnt sacrifice, and the wood, and the stones, and the dust, and licked up the water that was in the trench.

What a *fire!* In a flash it vaporized the *water* that drenched the sacrifice and wood. It burned up not only *sacrifice* and *wood,* but even the *stones* of the altar and the *dust* that had been dug out of the trench. There was this tremendous fire, and then there was nothing but the blank surface of the ground where the altar had been. This was no ordinary flash of lightning, of course. Lightning can start fires, but it does not consume stones. Besides, lightning does not strike out of a clear sky. That day the sky was so clear that a cloud the size of a man's hand was noticeable when it appeared (v. 44). This was a supernatural demonstration to let the people of Israel know that Jehovah is God—and it is one of many demonstrations that let us know the same thing.

C. Result (v. 39)

39. And when all the people saw it, they fell on their faces: and they said, The LORD, he is the God; the LORD, he is the God.

The demonstration was convincing. No longer limping, the people took a firm stand for Jehovah. Awed by what they had seen, they no longer feared the four hundred and fifty prophets of Baal, or even the king and his murderous queen. Regardless of all opposition, they knew the truth: *The Lord, he is the God!*

The next verse puts a cap on the record. Elijah enlisted the convinced people as a posse to arrest the lying prophets of Baal. They were led down to the river at the foot of Mount Carmel and put to death. That was the legal punishment for turning from Jehovah and following false gods (Deuteronomy 17:2-5). Accustomed to freedom of religion, we may think that penalty was severe. But the situation was different in Israel. Jehovah gave the law, and He was King. To rebel against Him was treason against the law and the nation, and most nations agree that death is a proper punishment for treason. All the people of the world will do well to realize that Jehovah is the king eternal, that He will finally judge every person on earth, and that the second death, the lake of fire, awaits the traitors (Revelation 20:11-15). But Jehovah is gracious, and there is pardon even for traitors. "Whosoever will" may come to the Savior and live forever (Revelation 22:17).

Conclusion

A. The Majority

In a democracy we make much of the majority. We choose our public officials and make our public laws by majority vote. We pay attention to the polls that try to tell us what most people think. Advertisers like to proclaim that their automobile, or breakfast cereal, or medicine is used by more people than any other.

Perhaps there is no better way to choose our officials, but there is a better way to know what is right. Jesus warned that the majority is headed for destruction; only a minority finds the way of life (Matthew 7:13, 14). God's Word will lead us to life, if we know it and follow it.

B. Limping

"How long go ye limping between the two sides?" (1 Kings 18:21, *American Standard Version*). Even when we want to do right, we may often be undecided. One candidate promises no new taxes, but he wants to legalize gambling. The other opposes gambling, but wants to raise our taxes. Perhaps we would like to vote against both of them, but there is no other candidate. How shall we choose?

Sometimes it is best to be undecided for a while. It is good to consider the facts before we make up our minds. But while we are wavering between two sides, we "go limping." We cannot take a firm stand and become a force for either side till we make a choice.

In some cases we can be a silent minority. For example, we can profit from a Christian film even if we would rather have a sermon. We can join in a peppy song of praise even if we prefer more dignified hymns. But if some of our brethren suggest that the resurrection of Jesus is a myth, or that Christ is not divine, or that the Bible is untrue, then it is time for us to take a stand and let our stand be known. When we know the right, do we sometimes go on limping between the two sides because we lack the courage to stand firmly for the right?

C. What's the Use?

If I am alone in my opinion, and 450 influential men are against it, why should I say anything? I'm hopelessly outnumbered.

That may be sound reasoning if only a matter of opinion divides you from the 450. If their way is good, you may choose to accept it even if your way is better. But if there is a question of basic right and wrong, and the 450 are wrong, of course you will say something.

But I am only one against 450. What's the use of saying anything? You'll never know till you try it, but here are some possibilities:

If you keep your temper and present the right plainly and reasonably, with clear evidence that it is right, maybe some of the 450 will switch sides.

If 450 are on the wrong side, perhaps two or three or ten times that number are limping between the two sides. You may help some of them to join you in the right.

Another prophet, Ezekiel, was told to sound a call that might be ignored. But even if no one would pay attention, said the Lord, "Thou hast delivered thy soul" (Ezekiel 33:1-9). So if no one will pay attention to your call to the right, you still need to sound the call for the sake of your own soul.

D. Prayer

How good it is to be guided by Your Word, our Heavenly Father. May we have the wisdom to understand it correctly, and the grace to present it in a winning way, and the power to turn many from darkness to light. In Jesus' name we pray. Amen.

E. Thought to Remember

"Stand up, stand up for Jesus."

Home Daily Bible Readings

Monday, Oct. 26—Elijah Hides By the Brook of Cherith (1 Kings 17:1-7)
Tuesday, Oct. 27—Elijah Is Fed by a Poor Widow (1 Kings 17:8-16)
Wednesday, Oct. 28—Elijah Resurrects the Widow's Son (1 Kings 17:17-24)
Thursday, Oct. 29—The Lord Sends Elijah to Ahab (1 Kings 18:7-16)
Friday, Oct. 30—Elijah Triumphs Over Ahab at Mt. Carmel (1 Kings 18:25-29)
Saturday, Oct. 31—Elijah Builds an Altar for the Lord (1 Kings 18:30-35)
Sunday, Nov. 1—The Lord Sends Rain (1 Kings 18:41-46)

Learning by Doing

This page contains an alternate lesson plan emphasizing learning activities. Classes desiring such student involvement will find these suggestions helpful.

Learning Goals

Through this session your class members will be able to:

1. Characterize Elijah as a courageous person who took a stand for God despite personal risk.
2. Determine ways they can demonstrate courage in living for Christ.

Into the Lesson

Give each student a pencil and a sheet of paper. Write the word *courage* vertically on the chalkboard as shown below, but without the other words. Students should write the word on their own papers (or locate it in their student books). Ask them to use each letter in *courage* in a word or phrase that relates to the meaning of courage. Here is an example:

Commitment
dOn't give in
Uncompromising
Risk
tAke a stand
clinG to God and His Word
sacrificE personal gain

Allow three minutes for this. Then ask several volunteers to tell what they put for C. Ask others for their ideas for O, and so on, until you complete the word *courage.*

Into the Word

Establish the background for today's text by presenting the information in the introduction section of the lesson commentary. Then ask several volunteers to read 1 Kings 18:15-39 by sections of your choosing.

Next, divide the class members into groups of six. Appoint a discussion leader for each group and give each group a copy of the following questions:

1. How would you describe Elijah in this passage? What details support this description?
2. What risks did Elijah take?
3. What excuses might Elijah have had for not facing Ahab or the prophets of Baal?
4. What were the results of Elijah's courage?
5. Based upon this passage, how would you define courage?

Allow the groups about twenty minutes for discussion. Then bring the groups together and ask for their ideas on questions 1, 3, and 5.

Option

Present the background information, and have the Scripture passage read as described above. Then form groups of six, and give one of the written assignments below to each group. Provide paper and pens and appoint a group leader. (Note: you may not have enough groups to use each assignment. Or you may need to assign the same project to more than one group.)

Group One: Your group is to write an imaginary phone conversation between two Israelites, based on the passage. One was present at Mount Carmel and saw the events. That person is explaining to the other over the phone what took place and what he or she thought of it. The other responds and asks questions. You should be prepared to have two from your group present the phone conversation to the class.

Group Two: Your group is to depict the events in today's passage through cartoons. You can use stick figures to illustrate the highlights of the contest at Mount Carmel.

Group Three: Your group is to prepare ideas for a talk-show interview with Elijah after the events in today's passage. The host will discuss with Elijah what happened on Mount Carmel, and why he approached the situation as he did. Your group is to select questions to be used and suggest ideas for the answers, based upon the passage. Select two candidates from your group to enact this interview for the class.

Allow twenty-five minutes for the groups to work. Then ask each group to present its project to the class. Following the presentations, lead the class in discussing: "Based upon this passage, how would you define courage?"

Into Life

Have students gather in their small groups again to discuss the questions below. Then ask students to pray about developing greater courage in living for Christ.

1. What situations have you faced that tested your spiritual courage?
2. What personal risks were involved in taking a stand for God in the situation(s)?
3. How did you handle the situation(s)?
4. How do you think God would have you respond in similar situations in the future?
5. What does it mean for you to be courageous in living for Christ?

Let's Talk It Over

The questions on this page are designed to encourage review of the lesson Scriptures and to promote discussion of the lesson by the class. The answers provided are only discussion starters. Let your class talk it over from there.

1. Ahab's off-target charge that Elijah was "he that troubleth Israel" may remind us of those modern-day unbelievers who attribute many of society's ills to the influence of religion. How shall we reply to this charge?

Humanists sometimes charge that the church's preaching regarding sin and God's judgment has burdened many hearers with needless guilt and fear. On the other hand, they assert that teaching people to depend on divine guidance and help through prayer hinders people from taking charge of their own lives and destinies. In truth, however, such accusers are really the ones who are troubling people's hearts and minds. When the reality of sin is denied and God's moral standards are rejected, the results are emptiness, confusion, and violence within society. When people ignore God and His commands to love their neighbors and do good to all, human compassion and kindness tend to diminish. Such self-assertion leads only to eventual self-destruction.

2. What are some examples of persons who are "limping between two sides" today?

In spite of Jesus' warning that one "cannot serve God and mammon" (Matthew 6:24), some persons seem to be trying to mix Christian faith with a devotion to the pursuit of material wealth. A modern-day Elijah might say to these, "If Jesus Christ be Lord, follow Him; but if money, then follow it!" There is an almost unrelenting quest for sexual pleasure in our society, and some of those who engage in that quest profess to be Christians. Sex is a gift that God has given us, but it is meant to serve us and not to be our master. And there are some who combine a form of Christian discipleship with a dabbling in the occult. They embrace astrology, spiritism, and the like, seemingly unaware that such practices are condemned by the Bible as belonging to Satan's realm.

3. What features of Elijah's prayer on Mount Carmel would we do well to imitate?

We do not address God in the way Elijah did. "Lord God of Abraham, Isaac, and of Israel," however, represented the most meaningful way Elijah could begin his prayer so as to draw the people's attention to the one true God. For us, the words "Our Father in Heaven, Father of our Lord and Savior Jesus Christ" hold rich meaning as a way of commencing our prayers. One of the most striking features of Elijah's prayer is the concern shown for the honor and glory of God. In this aspect, the prayer harmonizes well with Jesus' instructions to His disciples regarding their prayers (Matthew 6:9-13). Elijah also expressed concern that he would be shown to be God's servant. When we pray, the same emphasis is appropriate: that the answer we seek will glorify God and identify us as His obedient servants.

4. Why do we need to be prepared to take a stand against popular sentiments in the church?

The church is ever in danger of being infiltrated by false doctrines. Indeed, in many of today's churches the Bible is not proclaimed as the infallible word of God and Jesus is not set forth as the incarnate word of God. In other church bodies, certain practices that are contrary to Biblical teaching, such as homosexuality and abortion, are regarded as acceptable. While it may be almost unthinkable to us that such situations could develop in our church, we must nevertheless be vigilant. And we should not be hesitant to express our objections to any unscriptural teachings or practices that show up in the church.

5. Why do we need to be prepared to take a stand against popular sentiments in our society?

Moral issues are topics for discussion wherever people are together. One generally positive aspect of television is its focus on the moral controversies of our time. We may not agree with the slant given such matters by reporters and news analysts, but the information they set forth does stimulate public discussion. So we must be prepared to participate in this. One popular moral sentiment of our time is the view that sexual relations outside of marriage are acceptable. In our place of work, in social organizations to which we belong, in public gatherings we attend we are likely to have discussions with people who hold such a view. Instead of remaining silent, we ought to have sound Biblical and moral principles in mind so that we can register intelligent and forceful opposition to popular error.

Amos: Prophet of Justice

November 8
Lesson 10

LESSON SCRIPTURE: Amos 2:6—3:2.

PRINTED TEXT: Amos 2:6-12; 3:2.

DEVOTIONAL READING: Amos 2:6-16.

Amos 2:6-12

6 Thus saith the LORD; For three transgressions of Israel, and for four, I will not turn
away the punishment thereof; because they
sold the righteous for silver, and the poor for
a pair of shoes;
7 That pant after the dust of the earth on the
head of the poor, and turn aside the way of
the meek: and a man and his father will go in
unto the same maid, to profane my holy
name:
8 And they lay themselves down upon
clothes laid to pledge by every altar, and they
drink the wine of the condemned in the
house of their god.
9 Yet destroyed I the Amorite before them,
whose height was like the height of the
cedars, and he was strong as the oaks; yet I
destroyed his fruit from above, and his roots
from beneath.
10 Also I brought you up from the land of
Egypt, and led you forty years through the
wilderness, to possess the land of the Amorite.
11 And I raised up of your sons for
prophets, and of your young men for
Nazarites. Is it not even thus, O ye children of
Israel? saith the LORD.
12 But ye gave the Nazarites wine to drink;
and commanded the prophets, saying, Prophesy not.

Amos 3:2

2 You only have I known of all the families
of the earth: therefore I will punish you for all
your iniquities.

GOLDEN TEXT: Let judgment run down as waters, and righteousness as a mighty stream.—Amos 5:24.

Old Testament Personalities

Unit 3: The Prophets' Roles in a Divided Kingdom (Lessons 9-13)

Lesson Aims

After the study of this lesson a student should be able to:

1. Recall sins Amos saw in Israel and benefits Israel had received.
2. Name some sins and benefits in his or her own country.
3. Hate the evil and love the good.

Lesson Outline

INTRODUCTION
- A. A New Ruling Family
- B. Lesson Background

I. SINS OF ISRAEL (Amos 2:6-8)
- A. Too Much Sin (v. 6a)
- B. Injustice (v. 6b)
- C. Greed (v. 7a)
- D. Lust (v. 7b)
- E. Drunken Reveling (v. 8)

II. BENEFITS TO ISRAEL (Amos 2:9-12)
- A. Victory (v. 9)
- B. Rescue (v. 10)
- C. Teaching (v. 11)
- D. Ingratitude (v. 12)
  Remembering God's Goodness

III. SUMMARY (Amos 3:2)
- A. Benefits (v. 2a)
- B. Sin and Punishment (v. 2b)
  Punished by Love

CONCLUSION
- A. Not Only Israel
- B. National Benefits Today
- C. National Sins Today
- D. Hope
- E. Prayer
- F. Thought to Remember

Refer to visual 10 of the visuals packet as you consider verses 6-8 and point C of the conclusion section. The visual is shown on page 85.

Introduction

When a pagan princess of Sidon became queen of Israel, she earnestly promoted the worship of Baal instead of Jehovah. Her campaign suffered a severe setback when Jehovah first punished Israel with a three-year drought and then demonstrated His power by a spectacular fire on Mount Carmel. That convinced the people of Israel that He was the real God, as we saw in last week's lesson.

A. A New Ruling Family

The pagan queen was not convinced. She continued to promote the worship of Baal, and won for him a limited following in Israel. But when her husband Ahab was dead and her son Jehoram was ruling, there came a dramatic change. Led by an officer named Jehu, the army staged a furious rebellion. The whole wicked family of Ahab was wiped out, including the pagan queen. The worshipers of Baal were rounded up and slaughtered. Jehu was king (2 Kings 9, 10).

Unfortunately Jehu did not obey Jehovah as well as he opposed Baal. The golden calves were still worshiped at Bethel and Dan; the law of Jehovah was not enforced (2 Kings 10:29, 31). Still Jehu's family remained in power for several generations.

B. Lesson Background

We come now to the time when Jehu's great-grandson was king of Israel. This was Jeroboam II. The calf worship was still continuing, and this lesson will reveal something about other sins in the land. Still the Lord was not ready to destroy Israel. Giving the nation time to repent, He strengthened Jeroboam to enlarge the kingdom and make it prosperous—and He sent Amos the prophet to point out the national sins and sound a call to repentance.

In Israel the prophet began by talking about other countries, seven of them. He denounced their sins; he promised punishment (Amos 1:3—2:5). Then he turned his fire on Israel.

I. Sins of Israel (Amos 2:6-8)

How often the sins of other people seem more visible than our own! Probably the sins of seven nearby nations were well known among the people of Israel, but would those people acknowledge the sins of Israel?

A. Too Much Sin (v. 6a)

6a. Thus saith the LORD; For three transgressions of Israel, and for four, I will not turn away the punishment thereof.

Thus saith the Lord. Amos began the message about Israel by declaring that it was a message from the Lord, not from Amos.

For three transgressions of Israel, and for four. The same phrase is seen in the messages about other nations (1:3, 6, 9, 11, 13; 2:1, 4). The number increasing from three to four suggests that the sins of each nation were piling up till they could not be tolerated any longer. Three transgressions were bad enough; four were just too bad. Punishments had been given to Israel already, but Israel had not turned back to God with trust and obedience (Amos 4:6-11). More punishment was coming, and it would not be turned away unless Israel would repent.

B. Injustice (v. 6b)

6b. Because they sold the righteous for silver, and the poor for a pair of shoes.

Some students think this refers to injustice in the courts. *For silver* a judge could be bribed to sell out a *righteous* person and give an unjust decision against him. Or the meaning may be that a righteous person might be so poor that he could not pay his debts, and a cruel creditor would sell him into slavery for a debt as small as *a pair of shoes.*

C. Greed (v. 7a)

7a. That pant after the dust of the earth on the head of the poor, and turn aside the way of the meek.

Dust . . . on the head was a sign of deep sorrow and humiliation. The rich and powerful men of Israel are pictured as being so greedy that they panted breathlessly in their hurry to cheat a poor man out of his last penny so he would throw dust on his head in abject poverty and misery. This becomes plainer if we translate *afflicted* instead of *meek,* as the *Revised Standard Version* does. When one is afflicted by poverty, a rich creditor can smooth and straighten his way by allowing more time for payment; but the rich men of Israel preferred to bend or twist the poor man's way and make it more difficult. Thus the rich could get richer by foreclosing a mortgage and selling the debtor into slavery. The *New International Version* gives the verse a different turn by translating "trample" instead of *pant:* "trample on the heads of the poor as upon the dust of the ground."

With either translation the basic meaning is that the greedy rich people unjustly oppressed and distressed the poor to wring from them as much as they could.

D. Lust (v. 7b)

7b. And a man and his father will go in unto the same maid, to profane my holy name.

Lust for sexual pleasure accompanies greed for money. Those who rob and cheat the poor have no moral standards. Father and son use the same girl for sexual gratification. For citizens of God's chosen nation to be so depraved was an insult to His *holy name,* especially if a religious celebration degenerated into a drunken sex orgy. Such degeneracy was common in heathen worship, and sometimes it infiltrated the worship of the Hebrews.

E. Drunken Reveling (v. 8)

8. And they lay themselves down upon clothes laid to pledge by every altar, and they drink the wine of the condemned in the house of their god.

There is joy in worship, and properly so. But when people's hearts are far from the Lord, worship can be lost in sensual pleasures of eating and drinking, music and dancing, and even sexual gratification. At Sinai Aaron proclaimed "a feast to the Lord." In it "the people sat down to eat and to drink, and rose up to play." They even became naked in their play (Exodus 32:1-6, 25). It seems that Amos saw something similar going on. Amos saw people pretending to worship, but their meeting became a drunken sex orgy. No wonder Jehovah hated their feast days (Amos 5:21). *The wine of the condemned* may be another reference to the corrupt courts. One condemned, either justly or unjustly, might pay his fine in wine. Or if he paid in money, corrupt officials might use the money to buy wine for their "religious" feast. For their couches *by every altar* the joyous "worshipers" used *clothes laid to pledge.* A very poor man might pawn his outer robe to buy food for his family, hoping to earn enough that day to redeem the robe before night. According to law, the robe had to be returned in the evening whether the debt was paid or not. That same robe was the poor man's bed covering. He could not sleep comfortably without it in the chilly night (Deuteronomy 24:12, 13). It seems that some in Israel were disregarding the law and keeping the clothes for their own use.

II. Benefits to Israel (Amos 2:9-12)

Amos saw people pretending to worship God, but disregarding His law. This was inexcusable because of all that God had done for them.

How to Say It

AMORITE. *Am*-uh-rite.
ELISHA. Ee-*lye*-shuh.
JEHORAM. Jeh-*ho*-ram.
JEHU. *Jee*-hew.
JEROBOAM. Jair-o-*bo*-um.
NAZARITES. *Naz*-uh-rites.
SIDON. *Sye*-dun.

A. Victory (v. 9)

9. Yet destroyed I the Amorite before them, whose height was like the height of the cedars, and he was strong as the oaks; yet I destroyed his fruit from above, and his roots from beneath.

Amorite can be either singular or plural. As used here, it means the people who were living in the promised land when Israel arrived there. These were bigger and stronger than Israel (Deuteronomy 4:38). Our text compares them with trees: tall as *cedars* and strong as *oaks.* Still the Lord destroyed them. He did it by means of the Israelites and their swords, but it was His doing. The Israelites could not have done it without Him. Their own scouts were sure of that (Numbers 13:31). Continuing the comparison with trees, the Lord said the Amorites were destroyed thoroughly, from roots to fruits.

B. Rescue (v. 10)

10. Also I brought you up from the land of Egypt, and led you forty years through the wilderness, to possess the land of the Amorite.

Before the Lord destroyed the Amorites, He rescued the people of Israel from Egypt, where they were held in slavery. Then He led them *forty years through the wilderness.* Without His help they would not have lived *to possess the land of the Amorite.*

C. Teaching (v. 11)

11. And I raised up of your sons for prophets, and of your young men for Nazarites. Is it not even thus, O ye children of Israel? saith the LORD.

God gave His people ample opportunity to know what they ought to do. He gave them His law soon after they left Egypt, and He ordered that it be read to the nation every seven years (Deuteronomy 31:9-13). Between those readings, each adult had the duty of teaching the law to his children (Deuteronomy 6:6, 7). In addition, God selected some of the people to be *prophets.* These were teachers specially inspired to proclaim God's will. God communicated with them directly, and they passed on what He said. Note how often Amos declared that he was telling what God said (Amos 1:3, 6, 9, 11, 13, 15; 2:1, 3, 4, 6, 11, 16). Notable among the prophets of the northern kingdom were Elijah and Elisha, who spoke for God through many years. It seems that they gathered groups of students for instruction and mutual helpfulness. We read in 2 Kings 2:7, 17 of fifty of these "sons of the prophets," who apparently were part of a larger group; and there were such groups at several places (2 Kings 2:3, 5; 4:38). We do not know how many of these "sons of the prophets" became inspired prophets, but the teaching and example of the groups must have been a big influence for good. Then there were prophets like Amos with no training for the work, but with God's call and God's inspiration. There was abundant opportunity to know God's will, but many people did not want to know it.

A Nazarite was a person specially dedicated to the Lord. Marks of his dedication were that he would not drink anything intoxicating, he would not cut his hair or beard, and he would not touch a dead body (Numbers 6:1-8). We do not know how many protested against the wickedness of Israel by dedicating themselves thus, but they presented an example of goodness that many could see and follow if they chose.

Is it not even thus? Could anyone deny all the benefits God had given to Israel? In gratitude they should have responded with joyous worship and obedience.

D. Ingratitude (v. 12)

12. But ye gave the Nazarites wine to drink; and commanded the prophets, saying, Prophesy not.

The people of Israel did not appreciate the help God offered. *The Nazarites* set a fine example of devotion to the Lord. Instead of following that example, the people tempted the Nazarites to break their vow and get drunk along with the rest. *The prophets* proclaimed God's word and pointed out the wrongdoing of the people. Instead of straightening up and doing right, the people told the prophets to shut up. An example is recorded in Amos 7:10-15.

REMEMBERING GOD'S GOODNESS

A few winters ago, a retired barber in Easthampton, Massachusetts, noticed a wild goose in his yard. Something was wrong with the bird. The man examined the goose and found it to be suffering from a shattered beak. He took the injured bird into his care, named it "Broken Beak," and nursed it back to health.

When spring arrived, the goose took off on its migratory ways. But when winter came, Broken Beak returned to the man who had cared for it. It would come to him when he whistled and would eat food out of his hand.

Whereas Broken Beak remembered the man whose compassion had saved its life, Israel forgot God's mercies to her. God's people forgot that He had delivered them from Egypt and had brought them through forty years in the wilderness. They ignored the fact that God had brought low their mighty enemies. They neglected the covenant that He had made with them, and prevented others from keeping their vows to Him. They were glad to "eat from God's hand," but they turned their hearts away and refused to come back to Him.

We may recognize the sin of others when they disregard God's benevolence. But do we see our own sin as clearly? —C. R. B.

III. Summary (Amos 3:2)

Our text began with an announcement of punishment (2:6). It detailed sins that demanded punishment (vv. 6-8). Then it told of benefits that Israel enjoyed, benefits to which the people should have responded with righteousness instead of sin (vv. 9-12). Neatly the final verse of the text sums up all this in reverse order: first the benefits, then the sin and punishment.

A. Benefits (v. 2a)

2a. You only have I known of all the families of the earth.

Of course God knows all nations in the sense that He is aware of what they are doing, He lets them go their own way for a time, and He brings them low or destroys them when it suits His purpose. "The Most High ruleth in the kingdom of men, and giveth it to whomsoever he will" (Daniel 4:32). "There is no power but of God: the powers that be are ordained of God" (Romans 13:1). But God knows only Israel as His special people. Some other nations even had prophets and special revelations, but no other nation had such documents as those of the Old Testament to reveal God's call and His care, His purpose and His will.

B. Sin and Punishment (v. 2b)

2b. Therefore I will punish you for all your iniquities.

Special care and special revelation called for special attentive obedience. Israel responded with *iniquities* instead. Sin demanded punishment, and Israel's special privileges made Israel's sin more inexcusable. So the Lord said, *I will punish you.*

This was not necessarily the final word. The Lord was still calling, "Seek ye me, and ye shall live" (Amos 5:4). Israel still could change her ways, still could begin to "hate the evil, and love the good" (v. 15). But instead of hating evil, Israel hated the one who condemned evil, and she went on with her iniquities (vv. 10-12). We do not know exactly when Amos sounded this call, but perhaps it was no more than fifty years later that Israel went "into captivity beyond Damascus" (Amos 5:27; 2 Kings 17:5, 6).

visual 10

PUNISHED BY LOVE

After a Los Angeles Lakers basketball championship game in 1982, a fan who was drunk climbed up on a railing, lost his balance, and fell. He was seriously injured. He sued the arena where the game was played and was awarded $540,000! Several years later, however, the verdict was overturned by a state appeals court. The judge ruled that "there is a limit as to how far society should go . . . to protect individuals from their own stupidity, carelessness, daring or self-destructive impulses."

Sometimes, our troubles come upon us because of our own foolishness or sinfulness. It was true of Israel, as well. But the case of Israel introduces another element into the equation of human tragedy: God sometimes punishes those He loves in order to bring them to their senses and bring them back to himself.

We cannot always know whether calamity is a loving "act of God" or simply the result of our folly. When things go wrong, however, we can profit from the ordeal if, instead of blaming others, we ask ourselves such questions as these: Was this caused by my foolish or sinful behavior? How might I have avoided this? What should be my attitude about what has happened to me? What would God have me learn from this experience? —C. R. B.

Conclusion

Some teachers warn us to be careful about applying the message to Israel to our nation. They remind us that our nation is not the chosen of God, as Israel was. The reminder is true, and the warning is valid. But on the other hand, our nation is "one nation under God," and all the other nations also are under God. God's message to Israel has meaning for every nation in the world today.

A. Not Only Israel

The prophecy of Amos begins with the sin and punishment of other nations, not Israel. What is said about them sounds very much like what is said about Israel (Amos 1:1—2:8). May we not conclude that any nation with similar sins may expect similar punishment?

The Lord does rule in the kingdom of men and does give it to whomever He will (Daniel 4:32). He does put down the mighty (Luke 1:52). He does determine the times and boundaries of nations (Acts 17:26). Any nation that opposes or ignores His will can expect His wrath.

B. National Benefits Today

In most of the nations where this lesson is read in the English language, there is ample reason for gratitude to God. Those countries are independent of foreign rule. Their people enjoy a high degree of personal liberty, not being burdened either by oppressive government or by slavery or serfdom. For nearly half a century they have not been embroiled in a bloody world war. The poor are always present, as Jesus said (Matthew 26:11); but on a national scale there has been prosperity through most of that half century. And for our guidance the Word of God is readily available to all, and is proclaimed publicly in a multitude of churches. These are benefits like those Israel enjoyed when she was obedient to God (Deuteronomy 28:1-14). Do not all these benefits call for gratitude and obedience?

C. National Sins Today

You can make your own list of sins you see or read about in the newspaper. It may include some that Amos saw in Israel.

Injustice. As I write this, nearly every newspaper has something about "the savings and loan scandal." It is alleged that smooth operators have defrauded depositors of millions that must be made up by taxpayers. But it is hard to convict a wealthy wrongdoer. And if criminals are convicted, we have no room for them in our jails. Aren't you disturbed by the crimes committed by criminals on parole?

Greed. Much injustice arises from greed. Fraud and theft and violent robbery have their roots in it. My home state has a lottery. Its advertising encourages greed, urging everyone to buy a ticket in the hope of winning millions. What has become of the old-fashioned idea that a real man wants to give full value for anything he gets?

Lust. Our society seems to have given up the idea of restraining lust. We lament the many teen-age pregnancies, but our sex education seems to center on avoiding pregnancy while indulging lust. On a recent evening I watched four half-hour shows on TV. Every one dealt in some way with illicit sex, but not one suggested that it was wrong.

Drunkenness. Fifty thousand Americans die each year in traffic accidents, nearly half of which are caused by drunk driving. I have seen no statistics on the number of people who get drunk and beat their wives, lose their money, insult their friends, embarrass their children, or commit adultery. Besides all these are the many who ruin or lose their lives with illegal drugs.

D. Hope

These sins and others are as destructive as they were in the days of Amos. As in the days of Amos, the basic sin of them all is the sin of turning away from God. And the word of God through Amos is still a word to a sinful world, a sinful nation, or a sinful person: *I will punish you for all your iniquities* (Amos 3:2).

Then is there no hope? There can be hope. The call God sounded through Amos is a call to every sinner:

Seek ye me, and ye shall live (Amos 5:4). God would rather pardon than punish, but there is no pardon for those who prefer to do wrong. There is hope for any person, any nation, or a world that comes to hate the evil, and love the good (Amos 5:15). Pardon is offered through Jesus, who came to seek and save the lost (Luke 19:10). "Neither is there salvation in any other" (Acts 4:12).

E. Prayer

Our Father in Heaven, we do love the good. Led by Your Word and empowered by Your Spirit, may we rid ourselves of selfish greed and lust. Set free from these, may we love You with all our heart and soul and strength. In Jesus' name we pray, amen.

F. Thought to Remember

Hate the evil, and love the good.

Home Daily Bible Readings

Monday, Nov. 2—An Earthquake Will Be Sent to Israel (Amos 1:1-5)
Tuesday, Nov. 3—Judah and Moab Will Burn (Amos 2:1-5)
Wednesday, Nov. 4—The Lord Will Punish Israel (Amos 3:1-8)
Thursday, Nov. 5—Israel Is Unfaithful (Amos 4:1-10)
Friday, Nov. 6—Seek the Lord and Live (Amos 5:1-9)
Saturday, Nov. 7—Seek Good, Not Evil (Amos 5:10-15)
Sunday, Nov. 8—Israel's Offerings Are Rejected (Amos 5:18-24)

Learning by Doing

This page contains an alternate lesson plan emphasizing learning activities. Classes desiring such student involvement will find these suggestions helpful.

Learning Goals

In this session, lead your students to:

1. Identify and explain the sins charged against the Israelites.
2. Relate God's warnings to Israel to their nation's spiritual condition.
3. Determine how they should respond to the spiritual condition of their nation.

Into the Lesson

Attach two sheets of butcher paper to a wall in your classroom. Using a felt-tip marker, write on one of them, *Signs that our nation is turning toward God.* On the other write, *Signs that our nation is turning away from God.* Bring several felt-tip markers to class and, as students arrive, ask each to jot down on the poster one thought related to the topic.

After students have had a chance to record their observations, ask the class: "Based upon your observations, is our nation turning more toward, or away from, God?" Discuss.

Into the Word

Give each student a copy of the chart shown in the right column, but provide more space for notes than is shown here.

As you lecture on today's text, your students should take notes on each verse and record their notes in the space provided.

After the lecture, discuss these questions:

1. How could a nation that was so blessed by God turn away from Him as Israel did?
2. According to these verses, how could Israel change its destiny: Amos 5:6, 14, 15, 24?

Into Life

Help your class members to apply today's passage to our nation. Although Israel had a unique relationship with God, the laws of God regarding sin and its punishment apply to any nation. Discuss these questions:

1. In what ways has God blessed our nation?
2. How has our nation responded to God's blessings?
3. How close to God's judgment do you think our nation is? Why?
4. What will it take to get our nation right with God?
5. How can each of us make a difference for God in our nation today?

Amos 2:6-12; 3:2

Verse	Notes
6. Thus saith the Lord; For three transgressions of Israel, and for four, I will not turn away the punishment thereof.	
Because they sold the righteous for silver, and the poor for a pair of shoes.	
7. [They] pant after the dust of the earth on the head of the poor, and turn aside the way of the meek: and a man and his father will go in unto the same maid, to profane my holy name.	
8. And they lay themselves down upon clothes laid to pledge by every altar,	
and they drink the wine of the condemned in the house of their god.	
9. Yet destroyed I the Amorite before them, whose height was like the height of the cedars, and he was strong as the oaks; yet I destroyed his fruit from above, and his roots from beneath.	
10. Also I brought you up from the land of Egypt, and led you forty years through the wilderness, to possess the land of the Amorite.	
11. And I raised up of your sons for prophets, and of your young men for Nazarites. Is it not even thus, O ye children of Israel? saith the Lord.	
12. But ye gave the Nazarites wine to drink; and commanded the prophets, saying, Prophesy not.	
3:2. You only have I known of all the families of the earth: therefore I will punish you for all your iniquities.	

Let's Talk It Over

The questions on this page are designed to encourage review of the lesson Scriptures and to promote discussion of the lesson by the class. The answers provided are only discussion starters. Let your class talk it over from there.

1. God has blessed our nation with ample opportunities to learn His Word. How should we respond to this blessing?

It is inexcusable that there is so much Biblical illiteracy in our society. Concerning Scripture, our generation should be the most knowledgeable of all time. Bible translations, study books, audio and video cassette presentations, and computerized helps are among the means we possess to learn God's Word thoroughly. One appropriate response to this circumstance is gratitude. Many Bible students in past generations would have considered themselves wealthy beyond measure to have the study helps we have, so we should thank God for our riches. Another response is to take advantage of these opportunities for study. Every Christian should become thoroughly acquainted with Biblical truth.

2. In what ways do people today tell God's spokesmen to "prophesy not"?

In our time the principle of separation of church and state has been pushed to the extreme. Some critics of the church seem to believe that religion should be confined to one's personal life and should not be allowed to influence public policy. "Prophesy not," they would say to the church, "regarding governmental support of abortion or the use of tax money for pornographic art." Another way the ungodly attempt to silence God's spokesmen by the use of labels to mark them as persons not worthy of attention. For example, to call an individual a "fundamentalist" or a "right-wing religious zealot" or even a "born-again Christian" may be a way of signaling that he is not to be taken too seriously. Thus the world says, "Prophesy not if you believe that the Bible's calls to holiness and warnings of judgment apply to today."

3. With the publicity given to state-sponsored lotteries, it seems that gambling is becoming more acceptable in our society. Why should Christians avoid becoming involved in this?

As the lesson writer points out, those lotteries are successful because of their appeal to human greed. One hears of Christians who participate in them, assuring their friends that if they were to win, the church and other worthy organizations would benefit. But this leads to the ever-appropriate reminder that if all Christians were faithful stewards in providing financial support for the church, there would be funds enough to meet every need. Here again we must call to mind the various New Testament warnings about seeking riches (Matthew 6:19; 19:23, 24; Luke 12:20, 21; 1 Timothy 6:9, 10). We may assume that we could handle riches, but can we be sure that they would not pull us away from God?

4. The drinking of alcoholic beverages continues to wreak destruction on people's lives. Why do people persist in using and abusing such dangerous substances, and what can we do about it?

Over against all of the statistics and the warnings that discourage people from drinking alcohol are the clever tactics of beer and liquor advertisers. These persistently set forth the idea that if one is to be a "with-it" kind of person and is to gain the utmost zest from life, the drinking of alcoholic beverages is a must. Furthermore, the heroes and heroines in movies and television programs often portray drinking as a normal and natural way of life. While we protest to the entertainment industry and its sponsors over immoral presentations, we should also make our displeasure known regarding the way alcohol is depicted. And we should do our part to see that the statistics and warnings regarding the harmful effects of alcohol receive the broadest publicity possible.

5. How can the church develop Christians who will "hate the evil, and love the good"?

In our times the distinction between good and evil has been blurred. Some say that in terms of morality there is little that is black and white. So it is especially important that Christians "have their senses exercised to discern both good and evil" (Hebrews 5:14). The church's teaching should focus much attention on the Bible's moral absolutes, which no amount of human interpretation can change. Besides this, church members need training in moral courage. Young people and adults alike are under tremendous pressure to conform to worldly values and practices. To be able to say no and to keep on saying no to such pressures, they need the church's encouragement and support.

Hosea: Prophet of God's Love

November 15
Lesson 11

LESSON SCRIPTURE: Hosea 1:1-3; 3:1, 2; 6:4-6; 11:1-4.

PRINTED TEXT: Hosea 1:1-3; 3:1, 2; 6:4-6; 11:1-4a.

DEVOTIONAL READING: Hosea 3:1-5.

Hosea 1:1-3

1 The word of the LORD that came unto Hosea, the son of Beeri, in the days of Uzziah, Jotham, Ahaz, and Hezekiah, kings of Judah, and in the days of Jeroboam the son of Joash, king of Israel.

2 The beginning of the word of the LORD by Hosea. And the LORD said to Hosea, Go, take unto thee a wife of whoredoms and children of whoredoms: for the land hath committed great whoredom, departing from the LORD.

3 So he went and took Gomer the daughter of Diblaim; which conceived, and bare him a son.

Hosea 3:1, 2

1 Then said the LORD unto me, Go yet, love a woman beloved of her friend, yet an adulteress, according to the love of the LORD toward the children of Israel, who look to other gods, and love flagons of wine.

2 So I bought her to me for fifteen pieces of silver, and for a homer of barley, and a half homer of barley.

Hosea 6:4-6

4 O Ephraim, what shall I do unto thee? O Judah, what shall I do unto thee? for your goodness is as a morning cloud, and as the early dew it goeth away.

5 Therefore have I hewed them by the prophets; I have slain them by the words of my mouth: and thy judgments are as the light that goeth forth.

6 For I desired mercy, and not sacrifice; and the knowledge of God more than burnt offerings.

Hosea 11:1-4a

1 When Israel was a child, then I loved him, and called my son out of Egypt.

2 As they called them, so they went from them: they sacrificed unto Baalim, and burned incense to graven images.

3 I taught Ephraim also to go, taking them by their arms; but they knew not that I healed them.

4a I drew them with cords of a man, with bands of love.

GOLDEN TEXT: For I desired mercy, and not sacrifice; and the knowledge of God more than burnt offerings.—Hosea 6:6.

Old Testament Personalities

Unit 3: The Prophets' Roles in a Divided Kingdom (Lessons 9-13)

Lesson Aims

After this lesson students should be able to:

1. Tell how Hosea portrayed God's love.
2. Tell what God wants in His people, according to the text of this lesson.
3. Rejoice in God's love and care, and respond by being what God wants them to be.

Lesson Outline

Refer to visual 11 of the visuals packet when considering Hosea 11:1-4a. The visual is shown on page 94.

Introduction

In surveying the history of Israel in thirteen lessons, we have to leave some large gaps. We dip into history at widely separated points, but at enough points to show the trend of the whole history. After Abraham (lesson 1) we leaped over more than four hundred years to Moses and the beginning of Israel's life as a nation (lesson 2). After Moses and Joshua (lesson 3), we took Deborah and Barak as one example from the time of the judges, a period of about three hundred years (lesson 4). We gave three lessons to the rise of the kingdom with Saul, David, and Solomon (lessons 5-7). Then the kingdom was split. To see the trend in the southern part we leaped ahead three hundred years for a look at King Josiah (lesson 8). For lesson 9 we turned back about two hundred years from King Josiah in the southern kingdom to the prophet Elijah in the north. For lesson 10 we leaped forward a hundred years to Amos, who also prophesied in the northern kingdom. Now we come to Hosea, another prophet in the north.

I. Taking a Wife (Hosea 1:1-3)

Though our text includes only twelve verses out of Hosea's fourteen chapters, it does begin at the beginning. We learn when Hosea prophesied, and then we leap into the prophet's story in a startling way.

A. The Time (v. 1)

1. The word of the LORD that came unto Hosea, the son of Beeri, in the days of Uzziah, Jotham, Ahaz, and Hezekiah, kings of Judah, and in the days of Jeroboam the son of Joash, king of Israel.

Amos also prophesied *in the days of Jeroboam* (Amos 1:1). Hosea may have been prophesying at the same time, or he may have begun a little later. Hosea continued to prophesy longer, however. His work reached into the reign of King Hezekiah of Judah. It may have continued to the end of the northern kingdom and beyond.

B. Command (v. 2)

2. The beginning of the word of the LORD by Hosea. And the LORD said to Hosea, Go, take unto thee a wife of whoredoms and children of whoredoms: for the land hath committed great whoredom, departing from the LORD.

The Lord's first revelation to Hosea was this startling command: *Go, take unto thee a wife of whoredoms and children of whoredoms.* The word *wife* is literally *woman,* and some students think it should be so translated here. This command has been interpreted in various ways:

1. Taken literally, the command seems to be for Hosea to marry a prostitute who had children by her prostitution. It seems surprising, even shocking, that the righteous Lord would give such a command to His prophet. Therefore many students look for another explanation.

2. Some students suggest that the woman's description applied to the future, not the present. That is, Hosea was to marry a pure woman

who would later become a prostitute. Considering the possibility, we naturally wonder how Hosea could know what a woman would do in the future. But of course the order may have included more than is recorded. The Lord may even have given the name of a woman who fitted the description.

3. In a spiritual sense, all Israel was regarded as married to the Lord. To worship any other deity was spiritual adultery. Some students therefore conclude that *a woman of whoredoms* means simply *a woman who worships idols*. But would God want His prophet to take such a woman as his wife? That seems only a little less shocking than the command to marry a literal prostitute.

4. Some students think the command is explained by the last part of the verse: *For the land hath committed great whoredom, departing from the Lord.* Israel as a whole had turned away from God to worship idols: the whole country was deeply involved in spiritual prostitution. The entire nation was so adulterous that any woman of that nation could be called *a woman of whoredoms.* So some students take the command to mean simply, *Go, marry a woman of this adulterous nation.*

C. Obedience (v. 3)

3. So he went and took Gomer the daughter of Diblaim; which conceived, and bare him a son.

Hosea was married as God directed, and soon a son was born to him and his wife. Because of the problems indicated in our comments on verse 2, students focus much attention on the marriage; but verses 4-9 focus on the children of the marriage. They were given prophetic names, indicating events that were soon to come. Because the people of Israel were so disobedient, they would no longer be God's people (v. 9).

II. Buying a Slave (Hosea 3:1, 2)

God was about to disown His people (1:9), but that was not to be the end of the story. In a later time He would again claim His people and shower them with blessings (vv. 10, 11). In chapter 3 we find a striking picture of how God was going to reclaim His people.

A. The Slave (v. 1)

1. Then said the LORD unto me, Go yet, love a woman beloved of her friend, yet an adulteress, according to the love of the LORD toward the children of Israel, who look to other gods, and love flagons of wine.

Here we see another verse that has been interpreted in different ways:

1. Many students assume that the woman mentioned here is Hosea's wife, Gomer (1:3), who has left him to live in adultery with another man. The *New International Version* writes this assumption into the text: "Go, show your love to your wife again." If this is correct, Hosea's continuing love for his faithless wife presents a very apt picture of the Lord's continuing love for faithless Israel, and the last part of the verse shows that such a picture is exactly what is meant. On the other hand, the Lord's love is pictured even if the adulteress is not Gomer; and the text, translated more literally in the *King James Version,* does not say she is Gomer. If we take pride in considering anyone innocent till she is proved guilty, we can hardly find enough evidence to convict Gomer of adultery. Possibly this woman was some unnamed adulteress of whom we know no more than we learn here.

2. There is also a difference of opinion about the *friend* who loves the adulteress. The *New American Standard Bible* makes him her husband; the *New International Version* and *Revised Standard Version* make him her partner in adultery. We need not be concerned about that difference. The main point is that the woman is guilty of adultery, and the prophet is to love her anyway. Love takes various forms and is shown in various ways. The following verses reveal more about Hosea's love for this adulterous woman.

3. At the end of verse 1, some versions read "raisin cakes" instead of *flagons of wine.* With either translation, the meaning may be that the people of Israel love the sensual pleasures of feasting connected with the worship of idols.

B. The Purchase (v. 2)

2. So I bought her to me for fifteen pieces of silver, and for a homer of barley, and a half homer of barley.

This is how Hosea expressed his love for the adulteress. He *bought her.* A footnote in the *New International Version* estimates the price as six ounces of silver and ten bushels of barley. Some students think that was the price of a bride, paid either to the woman's father or to the woman herself. Other students see a different story. They think the woman, whether she was Gomer or someone else, had deserted her husband for another man; then her partner in adultery had deserted her. With no means of support, she had been forced into prostitution and finally into slavery. In love Hosea bought her to rescue her from that degradation. Verse 3 seems to fit with this thought. The woman was to wait for a long time. She was not to continue in adultery;

How to Say It

BEERI. Be-*ee*-rye.
DIBLAIM. *Dib*-lay-im or Dib-*lay*-im.
HESED (Hebrew). *hes*-ed.
HEZEKIAH. Hez-ih-*kye*-uh.
HOSEA. Ho-*zay*-uh or Ho-*zee*-uh.
JEROBOAM. Jair-o-*bo*-um.
JOASH. *Jo*-ash.
JOSIAH. Jo-*sye*-uh.
JOTHAM. *Jo*-tham..
SHESHBAZZAR. Shesh-*baz*-ar.
UZZIAH. Uh-*zye*-uh.
ZERUBBABEL. Zeh-*rub*-uh-bul.

neither was she to live with Hosea as his wife. The *King James Version* reads, "Thou shalt not be for *another* man"; but *another* is supplied by the translators. She was not to be for a man: she was to live a celibate life. Verses 4 and 5 explain the meaning of that. As the adulterous woman was cut off from all men, so idolatrous Israel was cut off both from her idols and from the Lord. For a long time she would have neither a national government nor a national religion. The last clause of verse 3 seems to say Hosea would wait for the woman, that later they would be husband and wife. Also later, people of Israel would turn again to God and to David their king. After the Assyrian captivity of Israel and the Babylonian captivity of Judah, some of the people did return to Jerusalem to reestablish their national life and national worship. They were led by Sheshbazzar, also called Zerubbabel, a man of David's line (Ezra 1). But the prophecy looks even farther into the future. It speaks of the time when many people of Israel turned to the Christ, the eternal king of David's line (Acts 2).

III. The Lord's Desire (Hosea 6:4-6)

The Lord has high standards for His people. When they fail to do as He requires, He does not lower His standards to match their actions. He lets them suffer the results of their wrongdoing, and He still calls them to live by His high standards.

A. Failure (v. 4)

4. O Ephraim, what shall I do unto thee? O Judah, what shall I do unto thee? for your goodness is as a morning cloud, and as the early dew it goeth away.

What parent has not at some time cried out in near despair, "O son, what am I going to do with you?" So the Lord in love cried out to His people. *Ephraim* was the largest tribe in Israel. Here its name stands for the whole northern kingdom. The southern kingdom, *Judah*, was not much better. Whatever *goodness* was seen in the land was like *a morning cloud*, a wisp that vanishes when the sun comes up; or like *the early dew* that evaporates and is gone.

B. Result (v. 5)

5. Therefore have I hewed them by the prophets; I have slain them by the words of my mouth: and thy judgments are as the light that goeth forth.

The wrongdoers of Israel could not say they did not know they were doing wrong. God had sent His word *by the prophets*. *Hewed* is a word used of cutting stone or wood into useful building material. God's word through the prophets was meant to shape Israel into what it ought to be. But if the people would not shape up, the prophets announced that they would be *slain* by invaders who would destroy the nation. The *judgments* of condemnation on Israel were as plain as the light of the sun.

C. What God Wants (v. 6)

6. For I desired mercy, and not sacrifice; and the knowledge of God more than burnt offerings.

Of course God did want *sacrifice* and *burnt offerings*, all of them that were prescribed in His law. But He did not want them from hypocritical worshipers, from hearts that were far from Him. *Not sacrifice* means *not only sacrifice.* The people of Hosea's time were like those of Jesus' time who paid their tithes meticulously and obeyed the law in some other easily visible ways, but neglected more important things such as justice, mercy, and faith (Matthew 23:23). What did God want from His people besides their formal worship? He wanted *mercy.* This is *hesed* in the Hebrew, and translators find it hard to represent by a single English word. The *American Standard Version* has "goodness," and a footnote suggests "kindness." In the Twenty-third Psalm and elsewhere, that version has "lovingkindness" to translate *hesed.* What the Lord wants in His people is a kindly, generous, loving attitude, an earnest desire to be helpful to others, a habit of mind that makes the other's welfare as important as one's own. As it was written in the law, "Thou shalt love thy neighbor as thyself" (Leviticus 19:18). What else does the Lord want in His people? He wants *the knowledge of God.* He wants them to know Him so well that they will love Him, and treasure His word, and obey Him with joy. As the law put that, "Thou shalt

Home Daily Bible Readings

Monday, Nov. 9—Israel Is Called a Harlot (Hosea 2:1-7)

Tuesday, Nov. 10—The Lord Will Punish Israel (Hosea 2:8-13)

Wednesday, Nov. 11—The Lord Will Make a New Covenant With Israel (Hosea 2:14-23)

Thursday, Nov. 12—The Lord Has a Controversy With Israel (Hosea 4:1-10)

Friday, Nov. 13—Israel Is Alienated From God (Hosea 5:1-7)

Saturday, Nov. 14—Israel Will Not Return to God (Hosea 7:1-10)

Sunday, Nov. 15—God Will Forgive Israel (Hosea 11:7-12)

love the Lord thy God with all thine heart, and with all thy soul, and with all thy might" (Deuteronomy 6:5; Matthew 22:34-40).

NO COMMITMENT NECESSARY

"SUPER OFFER! Any four Christian cassettes or compact discs for only $1 each. Plus this FREE BONUS 'go anywhere' tote bag!" So read the Christian record club ad in a Christian magazine. But perhaps the most telling part of the ad was the statement: "NO COMMITMENT MEMBERSHIP!"

That phrase, "no commitment membership," is a fitting description of ancient Israel's life as God's people. They were members of God's covenant nation, but they could not be troubled with commitment or loyalty to Him. The ceremonies of worship might be kept but the spirit of God's law found no place in their lives nor in their relationships with others.

We may be inclined to look back at Israel and condemn them for their lack of devotion to God. But does the record club ad suggest anything disquieting about modern Christianity? How many in the church expect to receive spiritual blessings with no commitment required of them? The blessings of the spirit don't come that way today, any more than they did in Hosea's day. They require lives given wholeheartedly to God. —C. R. B.

IV. The Lord's Love (Hosea 11:1-4a)

Why would God judge and punish His people? Because He loved them. His love was not a sickly sentiment like that of a parent who never rebukes. It was tough love, love that would punish severely, painfully. God wanted His people to know that doing wrong brought bad results. He wanted them to stop doing wrong, for their own sake as well as His.

A. Loving Call (v. 1)

1. When Israel was a child, then I loved him, and called my son out of Egypt.

Israel in Egypt was like an unborn baby: its life as a nation had not yet begun. But God recognized that unborn baby as His son. With love He called it from the place where it was in bondage, and Israel in the wilderness was a newborn nation. Such is the primary meaning of the verse. Matthew 2:13-15 reveals another meaning. The same verse foretells God's call to bring His Son Jesus out of Egypt.

B. Unloving Response (v. 2)

2. As they called them, so they went from them: they sacrificed unto Baalim, and burned incense to graven images.

To the newborn nation of Israel God gave rules to live by: the Ten Commandments of Exodus 20 and other laws recorded in Exodus, Leviticus, Numbers, and Deuteronomy. As that nation grew toward maturity, God sent prophet after prophet to them in the promised land. Prophet after prophet reminded the people of God's law, called the people to love God and obey Him as they had promised to do. But the more the prophets called, the more the people turned away from them and from the Lord and His rules. Sacrifice was an acknowledgement of God's ownership and His right to rule; but the people offered their sacrifices to *Baalim,* imaginary gods worshiped by ignorant heathen. Burning incense was a symbol of prayer going up to the Lord, but the foolish people of Israel burned incense and offered prayers to idols they carved from wood or stone or gold.

C. Loving Care (vv. 3, 4a)

3. I taught Ephraim also to go, taking them by their arms; but they knew not that I healed them.

Ephraim is Israel. Like a loving father, God held the baby nation by the arms and taught it to walk. In the desert He guided His people by a pillar of cloud and fire; at the Jordan He stopped the flow and led them across the dry river bed; in the promised land He gave them the strategy that was victorious. The Lord had the remedy for every illness or injury to a person or a nation, and these people had every opportunity to know it; but foolishly they turned away from Him and looked to dumb idols and imaginary deities.

4a. I drew them with cords of a man, with bands of love.

The Lord's loving care was designed to draw the people of Israel to Him gently and reasonably, as an intelligent person is attracted. But the people acted more like dumb animals. Stubbornly they resisted the gentle pull of love. Idol worship offered the pleasures of sin, and the people were drawn that way till God had to use the sharp goad of cruel punishment to drive them into the right way.

AS A PARENT TEACHES A CHILD

"Children don't have problems; they have parents," it is said. Emotionally immature parents can create all kinds of problems for their children. For example, the normal desire that one's child develop his or her physical and social skills can be turned into an unhealthy concern. Many of us have seen the negative results of fathers living vicariously through their sons, pressuring them to excel at sports as they themselves never did.

Other parents force their little ones toward precocious maturity by scheduling many hours per week of learning activities that result, in some cases, in intellectual burnout by the early years of grade school. Child psychologists warn of the consequences of trying to rear "superbabies." Too much pressure retards a child's development in many ways.

Our Heavenly Father doesn't pressure us, but He *does* kindly guide us (as we are able) into every opportunity for spiritual life and growth, just as He did ancient Israel. But they refused! Adults in every respect but the spiritual, they used their freedom in ways that eventually destroyed them. They turned their backs on God and showed to all generations the price to be paid for rejecting Him. Our nurturing Father will do all He can for our good, but we must learn to seize life's opportunities for growth and use them wisely. We create most of our own problems, don't we? —C. R. B.

God does not drive us
with a lash;
He draws us with
LOVE.
Grateful children
willingly respond.

visual 11

Conclusion

These lessons from the history of Israel are something more than ancient history, "for everything that was written in the past was written to teach us, so that through endurance and the encouragement of the Scriptures we might have hope" (Romans 15:4, *New International Version*). What have we been learning that provides encouragement and hope for us?

A. People Need the Lord

One thing that is very plain in these lessons is that people get in trouble when they turn away from the Lord and go their own way. Without the Lord, the people of Israel could not have escaped from Egypt, could not have survived in the wilderness, could not have taken the promised land. These lessons have shown that they turned away from the Lord time after time when they were living in the promised land, and trouble followed every time. If we learn anything from history, we learn that people left to themselves head for disaster. We find neither encouragement nor hope in that.

B. The Lord Does Help

There is another side to the story. Time after time Israel turned away from God, and disaster threatened; but many times Israel turned back to God, and disaster was averted. Hosea pictured God's love reaching out to reclaim His depraved people, but there is a greater demonstration than that. "For God so loved the world, that he gave his only begotten Son, that whosoever believeth in him should not perish, but have everlasting life" (John 3:16). In God's redeeming love there is encouragement for all of us who have faltered and failed; there is forgiveness for every sinner; there is life for every child of God. But with all the greatness of God's love and power, redemption is not automatic. We still choose to live or die. "He that believeth and is baptized shall be saved; but he that believeth not shall be damned" (Mark 16:16). Take your choice.

C. Prayer

In humility and shame, our Father, we confess that we too have turned away from You at times. All we like sheep have gone astray; we have turned every one to his own way. How gracious You are to lay on Jesus the iniquity of us all! How wonderful He is to give His life for us! In gratitude we pledge ourselves anew to follow Him, and in His name we ask Your help. Amen.

D. Thought to Remember

You choose to live or die.

Learning by Doing

This page contains an alternate lesson plan emphasizing learning activities. Classes desiring such student involvement will find these suggestions helpful.

Learning Goals

As a result of this lesson your class members will:

1. Explore the unfaithfulness of Israel to God through an overview of the book of Hosea.
2. Determine what is involved in being faithful to God.
3. Examine their own level of faithfulness to God.

Into the Lesson

Before class, write these two headings on your chalkboard: *God demonstrates His faithfulness to His people by—* and *God expects His people to demonstrate faithfulness to Him by—*. When class begins ask students to brainstorm the first heading. (Explain that in a brainstorm the goal is to get as many ideas as possible and that none of them is critiqued. Since students don't have to worry about having their suggestions evaluated, all should feel free to participate.) Jot down all suggestions on the chalkboard as they are offered.

After sufficient time has elapsed lead into the Bible study by saying, "Today we will explore the unfaithfulness of Israel to God as recorded in the book of Hosea. And we will investigate how we can firm up our faithfulness to God."

Option

Begin by asking students, "What are some examples of people who have been known for their faithfulness to each other? Let's see how many we can think of." Write all suggestions on the chalkboard. Encourage them to think of real-life examples, past or present (such as Ruth and Naomi, or David and Jonathan in the Bible) or fictitious characters (such as Batman and Robin, or the Lone Ranger and Tonto). After a number have been given, ask, "In your opinion, what are some key characteristics of faithfulness?" Allow for discussion. Then lead into the Bible study by making a comment similar to the one at the end of the first option above.

Into the Word

Tie this lesson in with the preceding lessons of this quarter by using information found in the introduction section of the lesson commentary. Then divide the students into groups of six and appoint a discussion leader for each group. Give each student a copy of the following questions. To assist in the groups' study and discussion of questions 1 and 2, provide each group with a photocopy of the lesson writer's comments under Hosea 1:2, 3, the paragraph introducing 3:1, 2, and the comments under 3:1, 2.

1. Read Hosea 1:1-3. What did God command Hosea to do? Why did God command this?
2. Read Hosea 3:1, 2. What did God command Hosea to do? What was the meaning of this?
3. Read Hosea 6:4-6. What do you see in these verses that explains why the prophets had pronounced God's judgments of condemnation on His people?
4. Throughout the book of Hosea God charges His people with unfaithfulness. According to these passages in Hosea, what are some ways they demonstrated unfaithfulness: 4:1, 2; 5:4; 7:1, 2, 13; 8:1-4; 10:4; 13:2, 6?
5. Read Hosea 11:1-4a. How had God demonstrated a fatherly love for Israel? How did Israel respond to God's love?
6. Read Hosea 14:1-4. How could Israel escape the threatened judgment of God?

Allow thirty minutes for groups to study the passages and discuss the questions. After time has expired, call for everyone's attention. Then ask the class, "Based on your study, what seems to be the main point of the book of Hosea?" Allow for discussion. Then ask, "Based on your study of Hosea, how would you describe a nation or a person who is faithful to God?" Again, allow students to discuss.

Into Life

Prepare copies of the following incomplete sentences, one for each student. Allow space for the students to write a completion to each sentence.

1. The greatest motivation for me to remain faithful to God is—
2. The greatest hindrance for me to remain faithful to God is—
3. When God looks at my life, I believe He sees faithfulness in these ways—
4. I can grow in my faithfulness to God by—

Ask students to complete the sentences as honestly as they can. Let them know that they will not be asked to share their completions with anyone. Allow three to five minutes for them to do this. Conclude the session by asking students to pray silently to God about what they wrote to complete their sentences.

Let's Talk It Over

The questions on this page are designed to encourage review of the lesson Scriptures and to promote discussion of the lesson by the class. The answers provided are only discussion starters. Let your class talk it over from there.

1. What kinds of spiritual adultery are believers sometimes guilty of today?

"Ye adulterers and adulteresses, know ye not that the friendship of the world is enmity with God? whosoever therefore will be a friend of the world is the enemy of God" (James 4:4). Spiritual adultery results from forming an unwise friendship with the world. If we accept the world's standards regarding success, pleasure, and human relationships, we are committing this kind of adultery. If we enjoy the company of worldly people more than our Christian brothers and sisters, and if we find more satisfaction in worldly activities than in Christian worship and fellowship, this may also be evidence of spiritual adultery. If we must admit that material possessions, our reputation, our love of sports or other entertainments, or our family and friends are more important to us than God, this indicates an adulterous attachment to what is temporal.

2. God continues to love even those who are unfaithful to Him. Why is this a reassuring thought?

On a human level, unfaithfulness often leads to broken relationships. For example, one serious act of unfaithfulness may destroy a marriage. Many a close friendship has been ruined because one friend betrayed the other's trust. An employee may serve his or her employer well for years and then be let go over one instance of carelessness. God's love for us, however, is not in the least fickle; He constantly offers us the opportunity to restore a broken relationship with Him. Paul wrote, "If we are faithless, he will remain faithful, for he cannot disown himself" (2 Timothy 2:13, *New International Version*). Although we may be inclined to give up on ourselves, and we may feel that other human beings have given up on us, we can be assured that God loves us, cares for us, and wants us to draw near to Him once again.

3. We can probably identify with the description of Ephraim and Judah's goodness, which was said to be "as a morning cloud." How can we develop more consistency in doing good?

We probably have nodded our heads in agreement with Paul's discussion in Romans 7:14-20 about how difficult it is to do good and how easy to do evil. But Paul used that discussion as a prelude to his marvelous description of the Holy Spirit's ministry in Romans 8. The Holy Spirit dwells within us, and if we can learn to cooperate with Him, we can experience a more consistent Christian life. We achieve such cooperation by giving the Spirit ample opportunity to speak to us through the Word. This means not only reading the Bible regularly, but reading it prayerfully, expectantly, and with a readiness to obey.

4. Hosea 6:6 speaks of God's desire that we practice mercy, goodness, and kindness. What special help do we have in understanding what is involved in this?

It is interesting to note that on at least two occasions Jesus quoted from Hosea 6:6 (see Matthew 9:13; 12:7). This reminds us that if we puzzle over what may be involved in exhibiting mercy, we turn to the Gospels and learn from Jesus' teaching and example. We are warmed by the compassion that He felt for the struggling multitudes (Matthew 9:36); we thrill to the tender words He spoke to the sorrowing (Luke 7:13) and the sinful (Luke 7:48, 50); we are amazed by His prayer for those who were responsible for His death (Luke 23:34). His example stirs us to demonstrate a similar compassion and tenderness and to direct our prayers to the healing of others.

5. God spoke of His fatherly concern for Ephraim, and of how He had been "taking them by their arms" to guide them. How is this description of God's guidance helpful to us?

This is one of those Biblical gems that we miss if we read too hurriedly. It calls to mind the picture of the small child either still struggling to master the skill of walking or tending to wander off in the wrong direction. We see the strong yet gentle father guiding those uncertain footsteps or redirecting the wanderer. We are like that small child. Some of us are young in the faith and are struggling to walk in Christ's way. Others of us are growing stronger and bolder, but we are inclined to wander off in unwise directions. How good it is to realize that our Heavenly Father desires to guide us and protect us in our walk! How important that we acknowledge our need for guidance and dependence on Him!

Micah: Prophet of Righteousness

November 22
Lesson 12

LESSON SCRIPTURE: Micah 6.

PRINTED TEXT: Micah 6:1-8.

DEVOTIONAL READING: Micah 6:9-16.

Micah 6:1-8

1 Hear ye now what the LORD saith; Arise, contend thou before the mountains, and let the hills hear thy voice.

2 Hear ye, O mountains, the LORD'S controversy, and ye strong foundations of the earth: for the LORD hath a controversy with his people, and he will plead with Israel.

3 O my people, what have I done unto thee? and wherein have I wearied thee? testify against me.

4 For I brought thee up out of the land of Egypt, and redeemed thee out of the house of servants; and I sent before thee Moses, Aaron, and Miriam.

5 O my people, remember now what Balak king of Moab consulted, and what Balaam the son of Beor answered him from Shittim unto Gilgal; that ye may know the righteousness of the LORD.

6 Wherewith shall I come before the LORD, and bow myself before the high God? shall I come before him with burnt offerings, with calves of a year old?

7 Will the LORD be pleased with thousands of rams, or with ten thousands of rivers of oil? shall I give my firstborn for my transgression, the fruit of my body for the sin of my soul?

8 He hath showed thee, O man, what is good; and what doth the LORD require of thee, but to do justly, and to love mercy, and to walk humbly with thy God?

GOLDEN TEXT: What doth the LORD require of thee, but to do justly, and to love mercy, and to walk humbly with thy God?—Micah 6:8.

Old Testament Personalities

Unit 3: The Prophets' Roles in a Divided Kingdom (Lessons 9-13)

Lesson Aims

After this lesson a student should be able to:

1. Explain why God had a controversy with Judah.
2. Point out three or four things in our country that might arouse the Lord to controversy.
3. Recall what the Lord wants from His people, as stated by Micah.

Lesson Outline

Display visual 12 of the visuals packet and let it remain before the class throughout this session. The visual is shown on page 101.

Introduction

A dozen elderly people complained that a smooth salesman persuaded them to invest their life savings, and then made off with the money.

A young man was stabbed to death in a quarrel over the price of a bit of cocaine.

Some senators are accused of unfairly favoring a businessman who made large contributions to their campaign funds. A member of a state legislature is arrested for drunk driving. A congressman is convicted of adultery with a teenage girl.

How often our newspaper reads like a passage from the prophets of ancient Judah! But today we see no headline shouting, "Hear ye now what the Lord saith!" Is that headline just what our modern world needs?

A. Two Prophets

Last week we read of Hosea, who told of God's love in a time when His beloved Israel was not responding with love for Him. Hosea gave his messages in the time of Uzziah, Jotham, Ahaz, and Hezekiah, kings of Judah (Hosea 1:1). Now we are to read of Micah, God's messenger in the days of the last three of those kings (Micah 1:1). It is evident, then, that Micah began to prophesy a little later than Hosea, and both ended their work during the reign of Hezekiah or soon after it. Hosea spoke in northern Israel and Micah in the southern kingdom of Judah; but both of them denounced the sin that was seen around them, both warned of coming punishment, and both called for people to do right and avoid punishment.

B. Lesson Background

Jotham, Ahaz, and Hezekiah ruled for a total of fifty years or more. During many of those years Micah was giving God's messages to Judah. In some parts of his book it seems that he may have been shouting protests against the godless policies of King Ahaz. That king made an alliance with pagan Assyria, and defiled God's temple with a pagan altar (2 Chronicles 28:16-25; 2 Kings 16:10-16). But when Ahaz was dead, King Hezekiah promptly began to get rid of idolatry and call his people to worship and obey the one true God (2 Chronicles 29:1-11). Micah may have been a powerful voice to help in that great reformation. He does not tell us just when his messages were given. Perhaps his book records a summary of what he said in many speeches at various times during half a century.

I. God's Controversy (Micah 6:1, 2)

Chapter 5 of Micah looks to a time that was then centuries in the future. A ruler was to come from Bethlehem to lead God's people to triumph and peace. But chapter 6 turns back sadly to Micah's own time. God's people then had turned against Him, and so He had to be against them.

A. Call to Judah (v. 1)

1. Hear ye now what the LORD saith; Arise, contend thou before the mountains, and let the hills hear thy voice.

The Lord challenged Judah to stand up and debate with Him. They had forsaken Him; they had broken the covenant they had made long before. Let them give a reason for breaking their promise! Let *the mountains* be an audience for the explanation. Changeless through the centuries, they could judge whether the people were justified in changing.

B. Call to the Mountains (v. 2)

2. Hear ye, O mountains, the LORD's controversy, and ye strong foundations of the earth: for the LORD hath a controversy with his people, and he will plead with Israel.

Having called His people to debate, the Lord called the *mountains* to listen. The *strong foundations of the earth* were unchanging; let them hear the people of Judah explain their change. Natural laws were unchanging, and moral laws were no less unchanging. Why had Judah abandoned those laws?

NO HIGHER COURT

Many young people at Christian camps have witnessed the following skit: During mail call the director is interrupted by a faculty member carrying a suitcase through the dining hall. Asked what he is doing, he replies, "I'm taking my case to court." Campers groan in unison.

A bit later, the same fellow comes through the hall carrying the suitcase and a ladder. The question comes, "What are you doing now?" He answers, "I'm taking my case to a higher court." Louder groans follow. After another brief interval, he comes back empty-handed, looking dejected. "What went wrong?" the director asks. His explanation, "I lost my case."

The silly skit directs our thoughts to a very serious truth. Micah used the language of law to describe God's disappointment with Israel: "I have a case against my people," God said. "Let Israel plead her case; let the mountains and hills and foundations of the earth hear the evidence against her." Israel had no higher court to which she could appeal. The God of the universe judges fairly and convicted Israel of her idolatry and unfaithfulness. Israel lost her case.

We too have sinned; and regardless of how loudly we may proclaim our innocence, we all stand guilty before God, our judge. There is no higher court to which we may appeal. Only God's grace can save us. —C. R. B.

How to Say It

AHAZ. *A*-haz.
AMORITES. *Am*-uh-rites.
BALAAM. *Bay*-lam.
BALAK. *Bay*-lack.
EUPHRATES. U-*fray*-teez.
HEZEKIAH. Hez-ih-*kye*-uh.
HOSEA. Ho-*zay*-uh or Ho-*zee*-uh.
JOTHAM. *Jo*-tham.
MICAH. *My*-kuh.
MOABITES. *Mo*-ub-ites.
UZZIAH. Uh-*zye*-uh.

II. What God Had Done (Micah 6:3-5)

The stage was set. The audience was in place: the mountains and hills, the strong foundations of the earth—all creation was listening. Let the debate begin!

A. What Harm Had God Done? (v. 3)

3. O my people, what have I done unto thee? and wherein have I wearied thee? testify against me.

It was not reasonable for God's people to break their promise and turn against Him unless He had wronged them in some way. What had He done? It seemed that they were tired of obeying Him. What heavy burden had He given them, what unreasonable demands had He made? Let the people *testify*.

B. What Good God Had Done (vv. 4, 5)

4. For I brought thee up out of the land of Egypt, and redeemed thee out of the house of servants; and I sent before thee Moses, Aaron, and Miriam.

God had not mistreated His people in any way. On the contrary, He had treated them very well indeed. To remind them, He mentioned a few examples. First, He brought them *up out of the land of Egypt*. That had been to them a *house of servants*: that is, a place where they had been slaves. There was no way they could win their freedom, but God set them free by His own power. Second, God had given them inspired leaders, people who had guided them by God's wisdom, not their own. Chief among those leaders was *Moses*. Then there was *Aaron*, chief priest of the newborn nation. His special field of leadership was worship. *Miriam* also was a prophet of God. If the cheerleaders are important to the team, Miriam's leadership was important to all Israel (Exodus 15:20, 21).

5. O my people, remember now what Balak king of Moab consulted, and what Balaam the son of Beor answered him from Shittim unto Gilgal; that ye may know the righteousness of the LORD.

After leaving Egypt, the people of Israel wandered in the desert forty years before they entered the promised land. Israel then approached the promised land from the east. The Moabites and Amorites lived in the country east of the Jordan River and the Dead Sea. Israel asked permission to pass peacefully through the Amorite country. Permission was refused, so the Israelites captured the Amorite territory (Numbers 21:21-35). *Balak king of Moab* was alarmed, thinking Israel might take his country by force too. The king *consulted* with his advisers and devised a plan to keep his country safe. The Moabites knew of a prophet named Balaam, who lived by the Euphrates River. They knew that events happened just as that prophet said they would. So Balak hired the prophet Balaam to say Israel would be cursed. But Balaam was really a prophet. He could not say anything contrary to God's will even if he wanted to, even if he was paid well to do it. God compelled him to say Israel would be blessed, not cursed. All this is recorded in chapters 22-24 of Numbers. It happened centuries before the time of Micah, but through Micah the Lord recalled it among the good things He had done for Israel.

In the *King James Version*, the phrase *from Shittim unto Gilgal* seems to be connected with *Balaam . . . answered;* but probably *from Shittim unto Gilgal* recalls a different thing to be remembered. The meaning seems to be this: *Remember now what Balak . . . consulted, and what Balaam . . . answered. Remember also the journey from Shittim to Gilgal.* Shittim was east of the Jordan; Gilgal was west of it. The rainy season was ending, but the flooded river was still overflowing its banks. How could Israel get across? God simply stopped the river for a while. The water rose up in a heap instead of flowing past the place of Israel's camp. When all the people had gone across the dry bed of the river, the piled-up water flowed on down to the Dead Sea (Joshua 3, 4). Truly God had done good and not harm to Israel. Through the mouth of Micah He reminded His people of some of His help so that they all might *know the righteousness of the Lord.* When He had done so much for His people, how could they be ungrateful enough to turn away from Him?

A FAILURE OF MEMORY

Stuart Haigh, a teenager from Manchester, England, has an unusual hobby: he collects aircraft identification numbers! On family vacations, Stuart may be found hanging around airports and air shows, trying to identify airplanes he has never seen before. When he sees an aircraft ID number that is new to him, he notes it in a log book.

In his first four years of logging airplane numbers, he recorded fourteen thousand different IDs. On a recent trip to the United States, he expected to identify two thousand planes, since he would be visiting airports he had not visited previously.

When you are trying to remember thousands of airplane sightings (perhaps a trivial exercise to most people), a log book is a necessity. But remembering a few very significant acts of deliverance that God had performed should not have been difficult for Israel. These were mighty acts that had formed their nation and given their people an identity that was unique in all the world. But still they forgot! They were without excuse and stood condemned.

Are we any better than they? Does Calvary mean any more to us than Sinai did to them? Do our lives ever indicate that we suffer from a failure of memory? —C. R. B.

III. What God Wants (Micah 6:6-8)

Called to debate with God (v. 1), a man of Judah could not deny what the Lord said in verses 4 and 5. No one could argue that the people had not been helped and blessed. A man might try to defend himself, however, by saying, "I pay my tithe, don't I? I make some sacrifices to the Lord as well as to other gods. What does the Lord want from me, anyway?" Such questioning is indicated in the next verse.

A. Questions (vv. 6, 7)

6. Wherewith shall I come before the LORD, and bow myself before the high God? shall I come before him with burnt offerings, with calves of a year old?

What did the Lord want from His people, for whom He had done so much? *Calves of a year old* were considered the best. They had grown to substantial size, but were still young and tender. They were costly sacrifices, for the owner had given them food and care for a year. Would the Lord be satisfied if one would offer Him the best of animals?

7. Will the LORD be pleased with thousands of rams, or with ten thousands of rivers of oil? shall I give my firstborn for my transgression, the fruit of my body for the sin of my soul?

Were yearling calves too small a sacrifice? What did the Lord want? Was He asking for *thousands,* incredible numbers, *of rams? Oil* was presented with many sacrifices. Was the Lord asking for huge quantities of it? Or was He demanding human sacrifice? Did He want a man to kill his *firstborn* son on the altar, hoping to atone for the sin of his soul by presenting the son produced from his own body? Such questioning would seem to imply that the people thought God was asking too much, that He ought to be satisfied with the ceremonial worship they were dividing between Him and pagan gods.

B. Answer (v. 8)

8. He hath showed thee, O man, what is good; and what doth the LORD require of thee, but to do justly, and to love mercy, and to walk humbly with thy God?

The offering of thousands of rams and multiplied rivers of oil could not buy the Lord's favor while His law was disregarded. The people of Judah should have known this, for God had *showed* it plainly in His law. But now through Micah He announced His requirements that were being neglected in Judah. First, He wanted His people *to do justly,* to be honest and fair in all their dealings, to put a stop to stealing and fraud, to stop bribing the judges, to end injustice. Second, He wanted them *to love mercy.* Mercy is more than justice. Justice gives what is deserved; mercy gives what is needed even if it is not deserved. And to love is more than to do. A person might do something just, or even something merciful, but do it grudgingly and with resentment. The Lord wants His people to love mercy, to be merciful willingly and gladly, to enjoy doing more than is required. Third, the Lord wants each of His people *to walk humbly with thy God.* The man of God ought to be humbly submissive, ought to obey God and do it gladly. This fits the greatest commandment of them all: "Thou shalt love the Lord thy God with all thine heart, and with all thy soul, and with all thy might" (Deuteronomy 6:5). Jesus acclaimed that commandment as first, and He called a similar command the second: "Thou shalt love thy neighbor as thyself" (Matthew 22:27-39; Leviticus 19:18). To love your neighbor as yourself is to love mercy, to find joy in giving more than is deserved.

Conclusion

What does the Lord require? Justice and mercy and humility. So there are those who say the way we live is what counts. The formal and symbolic elements of worship are not important. Going to church is not important; the Lord's Supper is not important; baptism is not important. So they say.

Is that sound reasoning? No, it is not. "Fear God, and keep his commandments: for this is the whole duty of man" (Ecclessiastes 12:13). To emphasize the importance of one or two of them is not to make the other commandments unimportant. Our whole duty includes obeying all of them.

visual 12

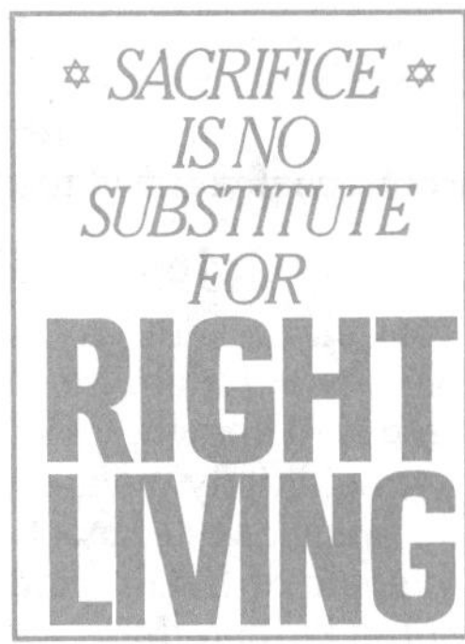
SACRIFICE
IS NO
SUBSTITUTE
FOR
RIGHT
LIVING

A. What Is Important?

Our high-school course in automobile maintenance consisted mostly of hands-on work with needy cars, but sometimes we had a written test. I remember the day when one of the questions was "What is the most important bolt and nut in an auto?" We made a variety of guesses, and waited impatiently for the next day when the teacher would give us the right answer.

When the time came, the teacher explained why he had asked that question. He wanted us to think about how a car is put together, to consider the importance of every part of engine, frame, and body. And what bolt and nut is most important? *The one that is loose.* It is important because it is loose. It needs attention; it needs to be tightened. That makes it important to the one who is taking care of that car.

God's word through Micah called attention to what was loose. The people of Judah were lax in justice and mercy toward others and in humility before God. The Lord wanted them to tighten these. That did not take any importance away from the forms of worship they were observing. The assembly, the praises and prayers, the teaching, the offerings—all were important. God's Word called for all of these too, and nothing God says is unimportant.

B. Why Are Two Things Most Important?

Jesus pointed out two things that are most important: to love God with all your being, and to love your neighbor as yourself. Why are these important? Jesus explained. These are important because the whole law depends on them (Matthew 22:40).

If you love your neighbor as yourself, you will treat him with justice and mercy. You will do this automatically, without much effort. You will not kill him, nor steal from him, nor bear false witness against him. You will not even covet what he has if you love him as yourself, because you are as happy that he has good things as you would be if you had them yourself.

C. Judah's Sins and Ours

Micah did not go into detail in telling about the sins of Judah. It was not necessary; the sins were well known, too open to be hidden. But the prophet briefly mentioned some evils. Do we see the same kinds of practices today?

People of Judah were lying awake at night to plot evil, then doing the evil in daylight (Micah 2:1). Have you recently read of a carefully planned bank robbery, or "con game," or embezzlement scheme, or a plan to cheat on someone's income tax?

They took houses and lands by violence (Micah 2:2). This does not necessarily mean by sheer brute force. It includes any unjust taking of real estate—by fraud, by unjust foreclosure, by action of crooked judges. Have any poor people been evicted unjustly in our time?

The officials of Judah were corrupt. Judges, priests, and prophets could be bought (Micah 3:9-11). Is there any corruption in our government, local or national?

Sinners of Judah were wicked at heart. They hated good and loved evil (Micah 3:2, 3). Have you ever seen a TV show that ridiculed truth and honesty and purity while exalting lying, cheating, and illicit sex?

D. Disaster

God demands that we do as He says, that we keep His commandments. Is that selfish and arrogant on His part? Not at all. He wants us to obey Him for our own good. His laws are given to help us.

We quickly learn to work in harmony with God's natural laws. Consider the law of gravity, for example. It holds our world together. It keeps us from flying off into outer space where we cannot live. But with all its benefits, gravity can kill us, too. If we blunder heedlessly over the rim of the Grand Canyon, we tumble to our death.

Likewise God's moral laws bring benefit or disaster. Doing justly and loving mercy hold humanity together in harmony. Injustice and hatred produce quarrels between neighbors and wars between nations. If we persist in ignoring God's requirements, one day we will blunder over the edge and tumble into Hell forever.

God in His mercy provides lesser disasters to wake us up before we blunder into that final disaster. Disobedient Judah was heading for national disaster, and God warned of it in the words of Micah. Jerusalem was going to be destroyed (Micah 3:12). The people would be captives in Babylon (Micah 4:10). There was still time to obey God and avert disaster; but Judah ignored the warning, and disaster came (2 Chronicles 36:11-20).

Can any nation hope to survive if it will not follow God's leading?

Home Daily Bible Readings

Monday, Nov. 16—God Will Not Forsake Israel (Micah 2:6-13)
Tuesday, Nov. 17—God's People Will Be Exalted (Micah 4:1-5)
Wednesday, Nov. 18—Israel Will Prevail Over Enemies (Micah 4:6-13)
Thursday, Nov. 19—God Will Deliver Israel (Micah 5:5-9)
Friday, Nov. 20—God Promises to Punish Israel (Micah 6:9-16)
Saturday, Nov. 21—Israel Waits for God's Compassion (Micah 7:1-7)
Sunday, Nov. 22—God Will Be Faithful to Israel (Micah 7:15-20)

E. Hope

Still there are words of hope among the dark prophecies of Micah. Though driven out and afflicted, Judah would be gathered again (Micah 4:6, 7). Better than that, people of all nations would flow into the kingdom of God, responding to His word that would go out from Jerusalem. In that kingdom will be peace and joy eternal (Micah 4:1-5). The ruler from Bethlehem will be king forever (Micah 5:2-4). His call that sounded first in Jerusalem is resounding now to the ends of the earth: "Repent, and be baptized every one of you in the name of Jesus Christ for the remission of sins, and ye shall receive the gift of the Holy Ghost" (Acts 2:38).

F. Prayer

Almighty God, how great is Your grace, how tender is Your mercy, how long and wide and deep and high is Your love! Truly all we like sheep have gone astray; we have turned every one to his own way; but You have laid on Jesus the iniquity of us all. Forgiven and made free, we pledge ourselves anew to do Your will as we see it revealed in Your Word. Help us to be faithful to this pledge, we pray in Jesus' name. Amen.

G. Thought to Remember

Trust and obey, for there's no other way
To be happy in Jesus, but to trust and obey.

Learning by Doing

This page contains an alternate lesson plan emphasizing learning activities. Classes desiring such student involvement will find these suggestions helpful.

Learning Goals

As a result of this lesson your students will:

1. Understand that one's worship of God is unacceptable to Him without the proper condition of heart and conduct of life.

2. Identify a spiritual activity in which they need to focus more upon their heart condition when they participate.

Into the Lesson

Begin the session by asking, "What are the main parts in our worship services?" As members respond, write their answers on the chalkboard. (Probably they will include the following: praying, taking the Lord's Supper, listening to the sermon, worshiping, singing hymns, giving offerings.)

After you have listed them, focus on each one separately. Ask this question for each: "What thoughts and attitudes should a worshiper have during this part of the worship service?" Allow brief discussion for each part.

After discussion, point out that in the Scripture text for this lesson, the question is raised regarding the worship of God. We shall explore the nature of worship and its relationship to our everyday lives.

Into the Word

Using the comments of explanation of the lesson text, deliver a brief lecture on Micah 6:1-8. Then divide the class into groups of six. Appoint a discussion leader for each group, and provide a pen and paper so one in each group can jot down the group's observations.

Write these two questions on the chalkboard: (1) *What does God say about spiritual activity that is not accompanied by a right heart or right conduct?* (2) *What does God expect the result of our spiritual activity to be?* Give each group a set of the following Scripture texts and have them discuss the two questions in light of them:

(1)—Micah 6:6-8; Amos 5:21-24; 1 Samuel 15:22; Psalm 51:16-19.

(2)—Micah 6:6-8; Hosea 6:6; Isaiah 1:11-17; Matthew 23:23, 24.

(3)—Micah 6:6-8; Isaiah 58:1-7; 1 Corinthians 13:1-3; Jeremiah 14:10-12.

Allow ten to twelve minutes. Then ask the groups to report briefly their observations.

Into Life

Give each student a copy of this chart, only provide more space for writing than is shown.

Spiritual Activity	Heart Response	When God Is Displeased
Prayer Matthew 6:5-8		
Giving 2 Corinthians 8:1-5; 9:7		
Singing Hymns of Worship Colossians 3:16		
Communion 1 Corinthians 11:23-32		
Reading or Hearing God's Word James 1:21-25		

Let the students work in the same groups. Assign each group one or two of the activities on the chart. They should discuss, (1) *What is the heart response God desires as one participates in this activity?* (2) *When does this activity displease God?* Students should record their group's insights. Point out that not every passage answers both questions, so they may have to apply the principles of the passage to answer a question. Allow ten minutes. Then ask groups to report their observations. Encourage students to record also the ideas suggested by other groups.

Lead the class in discussing: *How can we make sure we are participating in a spiritual activity from the heart, and not just going through the motions?* Allow for discussion.

Write these questions on the chalkboard to help students to personalize the study:

1. In which spiritual activity do you need to improve your condition of heart when you participate?

2. How can you prepare yourself to participate in this activity with your whole heart?

Encourage students to write their response on the back of their chart. Close the class session with prayer.

Let's Talk It Over

The questions on this page are designed to encourage review of the lesson Scriptures and to promote discussion of the lesson by the class. The answers provided are only discussion starters. Let your class talk it over from there.

1. Some people today, like those of Micah's time, are weary of God and believe He is too demanding. How shall we answer them?

God's demands arise out of His wisdom and His love for us. For example, He urges us to seek spiritual rather than material treasures, for He is aware of the corruption that results when people give first priority to money and possessions. He commands us to obey the laws of our land and to respect civil authority, since He knows that chaos is the result of lawlessness. He calls husbands and wives to be faithful to their spouses, for He knows how disastrous adultery can be to the home and to the nation. Those who say they are weary of such teaching are revealing their determination to live as they please. Frequently, they discover that their life-style brings them pain and frustration. When that happens, we must patiently remind them of God's truths mentioned above, with the hope that they will at last recognize that God is not the cause of their weariness, but the solution for it.

2. Micah 6:4 is one of many places in the Old Testament in which Israel's deliverance from bondage in Egypt is cited as one of God's greatest blessings to His people. In the New Testament, Jesus' death and resurrection are constantly cited as the outstanding features of the gospel. Why can such events never be cited too often?

The people of Micah's time may have disdained reference to the exodus as "past history." But God's willingness to deliver His people from Egypt was evidence of His readiness to act again and again on His people's behalf, if they would but trust and obey Him. The death and subsequent resurrection of Jesus form the basis of our salvation, and they are also a reminder of God's intention to provide a continuous supply for our spiritual needs (see Romans 8:28-39). So we should never tire of hearing "the old, old story" of how Jesus died and rose again for us.

3. Why should we learn to *love mercy*?

Mercy may be extended to others for various reasons. One may show kindness because he or she feels obligated to do so. Another may perform acts of mercy for people's applause—a practice that Jesus condemned (Matthew 6:1-4). To *love* mercy indicates that we take delight in it and that we have in view the needs of the ones to whom we minister. Jesus obviously loved mercy, for a number of times, after He had healed the sick or lame, He urged the one healed not to publicize the matter. And even though on rare occasions He did not give healing at the first request, (Matthew 15:21-28; John 4:46-54), it is clear that He took delight in ministering to human needs. If we would be like Jesus, we will extend mercy because we love to heal hurting humanity.

4. Why is it important that we learn "to walk humbly with [our] God"?

Pride is one of the great hindrances to an effective Christian life. We first must humble ourselves and admit our need of the Savior before we can receive salvation. Pride hinders us in our growth as a Christian by keeping us from asking questions about the Bible and the Christian life. In not wanting to appear ignorant, we actually remain ignorant of truth essential to our growth. Pride may hinder us in our worship of God. If we are afraid of showing any emotion, our worship may become a sterile matter. Pride hinders us in our Christian service. When we are challenged to take on a task in the church, our pride may lead us to decline because of the fear of failure. To become the kind of people God wants us to be, we must learn to walk humbly with Him.

5. The lesson writer asks, "Have you ever seen a TV show that ridiculed truth and honesty and purity while exalting lying, cheating, and illicit sex?" Is merely turning off our TV a solution to such programming? Why or why not?

Christians should certainly be wary of viewing shows that promote non-Christian values. But merely avoiding such programs is not enough. We have to be concerned with the kind of atmosphere these programs create in our society. If lying and cheating, acts of violence, and sex crimes result from such programs, then we, our families, and indeed anyone in our society may suffer as a result. So it is clear that all of us have a concern with the TV programming that is offered, and that we must make our convictions known to those who are responsible for it.

Jeremiah: Persistent Prophet

November 29
Lesson 13

LESSON SCRIPTURE: Jeremiah 1:1-10; 8:22—9:3; 20:7-13.

PRINTED TEXT: Jeremiah 1:9, 10; 20:7-11.

DEVOTIONAL READING: Jeremiah 8:18-22.

Jeremiah 1:9, 10

9 Then the LORD put forth his hand, and touched my mouth. And the LORD said unto me, Behold, I have put my words in thy mouth.

10 See, I have this day set thee over the nations and over the kingdoms, to root out, and to pull down, and to destroy, and to throw down, to build, and to plant.

Jeremiah 20:7-11

7 O LORD, thou hast deceived me, and I was deceived: thou art stronger than I, and hast prevailed: I am in derision daily, every one mocketh me.

8 For since I spake, I cried out, I cried violence and spoil; because the word of the LORD was made a reproach unto me, and a derision, daily.

9 Then I said, I will not make mention of him, nor speak any more in his name. But his word was in mine heart as a burning fire shut up in my bones, and I was weary with forbearing, and I could not stay.

10 For I heard the defaming of many, fear on every side. Report, say they, and we will report it. All my familiars watched for my halting, saying, Peradventure he will be enticed, and we shall prevail against him, and we shall take our revenge on him.

11 But the LORD is with me as a mighty terrible one: therefore my persecutors shall stumble, and they shall not prevail: they shall be greatly ashamed; for they shall not prosper: their everlasting confusion shall never be forgotten.

GOLDEN TEXT: Then I said, I will not make mention of him, nor speak any more in his name. But his word was in mine heart as a burning fire shut up in my bones, and I was weary with forbearing, and I could not stay.—Jeremiah 20:9.

Old Testament Personalities

Unit 3: The Prophets' Roles in a Divided Kingdom (Lessons 9-13)

Lesson Aims

After this lesson students should be able to:

1. Briefly tell about Jeremiah's task and troubles.
2. Mention one difficulty they have faced or are facing.
3. Be persistent in working for the Lord.

Lesson Outline

INTRODUCTION
- A. Four Prophets Plus One
- B. Bad Kings and Good
- C. Another King—Another Prophet
- D. Lesson Background

I. APPOINTMENT (Jeremiah 1:9, 10)
- A. The Lord's Message (v. 9)
- B. The Lord's Authority (v. 10)
  - *The Power of the Word*

II. TROUBLE AND PERSISTENCE (Jeremiah 20:7-9)
- A. Derision and Mockery (vv. 7, 8)
- B. Persistence (v. 9)

III. DANGER AND ASSURANCE (Jeremiah 20:10, 11)
- A. Danger (v. 10)
- B. Assurance (v. 11)

CONCLUSION
- A. Jeremiah's Persistence
- B. Christian Persistence Today
- C. Prayer
- D. Thought to Remember

Visual 13 of the visuals packet will be helpful as the thoughts in the conclusion section are presented. The visual is shown on page 109.

Introduction

How often God's people have rejected and resented God's word! It's amazing—but it's true.

In the time of Jesus, leading Jews acknowledged that their forefathers had persecuted God's messengers. Piously they said they themselves would not do such a thing, but they were doing it and would continue to do it (Matthew 23:29, 30). Jesus wept over Jerusalem, not just because it had persecuted the prophets long before, but because it would continue to persecute God's spokesmen till the city would be demolished (Matthew 23:37, 38; Luke 19:41-44).

A. Four Prophets Plus One

In our lessons for this month of November we have read of four prophets of God.

Elijah proclaimed God's word to Israel, then went into hiding to preserve his life so he could proclaim God's word again (1 Kings 17:1-6).

Amos proclaimed God's word in Israel, and the priest of Bethel told him to get out of town (Amos 7:10-13).

Through many years Hosea proclaimed God's love and begged Israel to return to the loving God (Hosea 14:1), but Israel did not return.

Micah proclaimed God's word in Judah in the time of three kings: Jotham, Ahaz, and Hezekiah (Micah 1:1). He may have helped in the great reform in the time of Hezekiah (2 Chronicles 29—31).

These lessons have not told us of Isaiah, another prophet who was giving God's word while Micah was (Isaiah 1:1). The Bible does not record the death of these two, but old tradition says Isaiah was murdered by Manasseh, the evil king who succeeded Hezekiah. Manasseh may have silenced Micah in the same way.

B. Bad Kings and Good

King Ahaz of Judah put his trust in Assyria rather than in Jehovah. He promoted idolatry in Judah (2 Kings 16). Isaiah protested in vain (Isaiah 7), and probably some of Micah's protests were made in that same time.

King Hezekiah reversed the policy of Ahaz and restored the worship of Jehovah (2 Chronicles 29—31). Isaiah gave strong support to this faithful king, and no doubt Micah helped as well.

King Manasseh ended Hezekiah's reforms and turned the nation to idolatry again (2 Chronicles 33:1-9). It is easy to believe that he killed Isaiah and Micah, for he "shed innocent blood very much, till he had filled Jerusalem from one end to another" (2 Kings 21:16).

In his later years Manasseh acknowledged Jehovah and tried to undo the harm he had done (2 Chronicles 33:10-20). But when he died, his son Amon promptly turned to idolatry and evil again (2 Chronicles 33:21-23).

When Manasseh's son was assassinated, the people of Judah rose in protest. The assassins were killed, and Amon's son Josiah became king (2 Chronicles 33:24, 25). Our present lesson takes up the story while Josiah was ruling.

C. Another King—Another Prophet

Josiah was eight years old when he became king (2 Chronicles 34:1)—hardly capable of ruling a nation. But a popular uprising made him king, and probably leaders of the uprising helped him rule till he felt old enough to take charge. In the twelfth year of his reign, when he was about twenty years old, he started a drive to get rid of idols and restore true worship and obedience to Jehovah (2 Chronicles 34:2-7).

In the following year the prophet Jeremiah was called to proclaim the word of the Lord in Judah (Jeremiah 1:1, 2).

D. Lesson Background

The Lord knows the future as well as He knows the past. He knew exactly when Josiah would begin his campaign against idols. Years before that time, the Lord designed an unborn child to be a prophet and help with the campaign. He endowed the unborn Jeremiah with the abilities he would need, and set him apart for the work of prophesying. When it was time for that work to begin, the Lord told Jeremiah that he was so designed and set apart (Jeremiah 1:4, 5).

Jeremiah protested: "Ah, Lord God! behold, I cannot speak: for I am a child" (Jeremiah 1:6). He felt that he was too young, too inexperienced, too ignorant to undertake the awesome responsibility of speaking for the Almighty. We are not told of his actual age. Perhaps he was about as old as the twenty-one-year-old king.

The Lord brushed the protest aside. Jeremiah would need no great intellect or wide experience. All he would have to do was to go where God would send him and say what God would tell him to say. What he would need was courage, for powerful men would oppose him with scowling faces. Jeremiah should not be intimidated, for the Lord would be with him and against those who would threaten him (Jeremiah 1:7, 8).

I. Appointment (Jeremiah 1:9, 10)

Often Jeremiah is called the weeping prophet because he grieved over the fate of Judah. His second book in the Bible is called Lamentations.

How to Say It

AHAZ. *A*-haz.
AMON. *A*-mun.
HEZEKIAH. Hez-ih-*kye*-uh.
HOSEA. Ho-*zay*-uh or Ho-*zee*-uh.
ISAIAH. Eye-*zay*-uh.
JEHOIAKIM. Jeh-*hoy*-uh-kim.
JOSIAH. Jo-*sye*-uh.
JOTHAM. *Jo*-tham.
MANASSEH. Muh-*nass*-uh.
MICAH. *My*-kuh.

Sometimes he is called the reluctant prophet because he protested that he was not capable. In this lesson we shall see that he thought of abandoning the work. But our lesson title calls him the persistent prophet because he went on with his work in spite of difficulty and danger. Back of his persistence was the persistence of the Lord, who ignored his protest and gave him a divine message and divine authority.

A. The Lord's Message (v. 9)

9. Then the LORD put forth his hand, and touched my mouth. And the LORD said unto me, Behold, I have put my words in thy mouth.

Did Jeremiah see the *hand*, or did he only feel its touch? He does not say; but he knew God *touched* him, and God told him what it meant. Did the Lord speak in a deep, resonant tone to Jeremiah's ears, or did He speak silently to the prophet's mind? Again we are not told; but Jeremiah got the message, and he knew who gave it. From that time on, Jeremiah would not announce his own opinions. He would deliver God's message; he would say what he was told to say.

B. The Lord's Authority (v. 10)

10. See, I have this day set thee over the nations and over the kingdoms, to root out, and to pull down, and to destroy, and to throw down, to build, and to plant.

Awesome! Jeremiah was to destroy nations, not by defeating armies and smashing fortress walls, but simply by announcing God's decree of destruction. His announcement of nations to be desolated may be found in Jeremiah 4:5-8; 27:1-10; and chapters 46 through 49. Mighty Babylon would be God's instrument of destruction, but in its time Babylon also would be destroyed (Jeremiah 50, 51).

But Jeremiah's mission was not to be entirely destructive. He was also *to build, and to plant.* God's word through Jeremiah would announce that Israel again would be planted in the homeland, and the ruined cities again would be built. His word would reach far beyond the end of captivity in Babylon to tell of a new covenant with His people, a covenant by which their sins would be forgiven and forgotten (Jeremiah 23:3-6; chapters 30, 31).

THE POWER OF THE WORD

The Pencil, a recent book by Henry Petroski, relates the interesting history of this common, yellow, wooden item most of us have used since childhood. It tells of how they came to be called "lead" pencils (even though they aren't made of lead anymore). We learn how the brand name

"Mongol" and the yellow color came about: a new supply of graphite was found in Siberia near China, and the new name and color capitalized on this association with the East, which was considered to be exotic a hundred years ago.

Many persons have replaced wooden pencils with mechanical pencils, fountain pens, ballpoint pens, felt-tip markers, typewriters, and word-processors. But regardless of the instrument used, the purpose behind all of these instruments has usually been to "write" words. Words convey ideas, and the instrument used is usually of secondary importance.

Jeremiah was the instrument God used to deliver His word of warning to Judah. But Judah was not interested in the word of God. As if Jeremiah were a cheap, expendable pencil, Judah tried to break and cast aside God's instrument. Nevertheless, God's purposes were not thwarted. Jeremiah courageously announced God's protection for the penitent and destruction to the defiant.

God's word must be given to this generation, and we are His instruments. Can He count on us?

—C. R. B.

II. Trouble and Persistence (Jeremiah 20:7-9)

Chapters 1 through 19 reveal that Jeremiah accepted the Lord's commission and faithfully proclaimed His word. Again and again he denounced the sins of Judah. Again and again he declared that such sins would surely bring disaster. Again and again sinners plotted to kill him (Jeremiah 11:18-23; 18:18). Angered by such prophecies, the manager of the temple had Jeremiah beaten and locked in the stocks where passersby would see him and jeer (Jeremiah 20:1, 2).

All this persecution indicates that we now are looking at a time when King Josiah's good influence had been taken away. That king was fatally wounded in battle with Egyptian troops who were moving north to take a share of the Assyrian Empire, which then was near its end (2 Chronicles 35:20-25).

The king of Egypt then took charge of Judah and appointed Josiah's son Jehoiakim to be its king (2 Chronicles 36:1-4). Jehoiakim was not like his father. "He did that which was evil in the sight of the Lord his God" (2 Chronicles 36:5). In his reign the Babylonians drove out the Egyptians and took charge of Judah, but they left Jehoiakim to rule and to pay tribute to Babylon (2 Kings 24:1).

Early in the reign of Jehoiakim, false prophets and priests of Judah threatened Jeremiah's life. Some government officials interceded to save him (Jeremiah 26). Probably these officials had been involved in the administration of good King Josiah. The new king, Jehoiakim, gave no support to Jeremiah. Instead, he contemptuously burned the book in which Jeremiah's prophecies were written (Jeremiah 36). Proclaiming God's word brought ridicule, danger, and pain to the prophet. Worse than that, it seemed to be doing no good. In discouragement, Jeremiah ventured another protest.

A. Derision and Mockery (vv. 7, 8)

7. O LORD, thou hast deceived me, and I was deceived: thou art stronger than I, and hast prevailed: I am in derision daily, every one mocketh me.

Surely the *American Standard Version* has a better translation here: *Thou hast persuaded me, and I was persuaded.* The Lord had not *deceived* Jeremiah. He had not said the task would be easy, or free from opposition. He had not promised that the prophet would bring the nation to repent and escape destruction. On the contrary, He had made it clear that enemies would oppose the prophet; but He had promised, "They shall not prevail against thee; for I am with thee" (Jeremiah 1:17-19). Survival was all the Lord had promised. Jeremiah had been reluctant to accept a task with no better prospects than that, but the Lord had *persuaded* him. The Lord was *stronger* than Jeremiah; Jeremiah had yielded and consented to be God's prophet (Jeremiah 1:4-8). And what did he get for his earnest work? Sneers, contempt, ridicule: *I am in derision daily, every one mocketh me.* The prophet was tired of it, and who wouldn't be?

8. For since I spake, I cried out, I cried violence and spoil; because the word of the LORD was made a reproach unto me, and a derision, daily.

Jeremiah had not soft-pedaled his message. Ever since beginning to proclaim God's word, he had been shouting it for all to hear. He had shouted of *violence and spoil.* That can be understood in two ways. First, Jeremiah had shouted that some people of Judah were violently despoiling their countrymen. With greed and injustice the rich and powerful were robbing the poor and defenseless, and the poor were robbing each other as well. Second, because the people of Judah were heartlessly despoiling each other, invaders were going to despoil the whole land just as violently and heartlessly. Both these themes are seen in Jeremiah 5, for example. Jeremiah had been shouting both these messages, and neither was acceptable to the heartless sinners of Judah. That was why those sinners were deriding him day by day.

B. Persistence (v. 9)

9. Then I said, I will not make mention of him, nor speak any more in his name. But his word was in mine heart as a burning fire shut up in my bones, and I was weary with forbearing, and I could not stay.

Jeremiah tried to quit. Speaking God's word did no good; it only brought him ridicule and abuse. So he decided not to say any more about the Lord, not to pass on His message any more. But he couldn't quit. Putting the word in Jeremiah's mouth (Jeremiah 1:9), the Lord had put it in his heart as well. When he tried to lock it up in his heart and not tell it, it was like a burning fire shut up in his bones. He could not smother that fire, and he could not keep it from breaking out in speech. He was tired of speaking God's word and being abused for it, but trying not to speak that word made him more weary still. Talking had been difficult, but silence was intolerable.

III. Danger and Assurance (Jeremiah 20:10, 11)

What a predicament! When Jeremiah spoke God's word, he was beaten and put in the stocks (Jeremiah 20:2). When he did not speak he was tormented by that intolerable burning in his bones. What could he do?

A. Danger (v. 10)

10. For I heard the defaming of many, fear on every side. Report, say they, and we will report it. All my familiars watched for my halting, saying, Peradventure he will be enticed, and we shall prevail against him, and we shall take our revenge on him.

Jeremiah could hear many people talking about him, and they were *defaming* him. *On every side* he heard threats that made him afraid. Such is the meaning of the *King James Version.* The *New International Version* has a different interpretation. It makes *fear on every side* a part of what Jeremiah heard others saying. They were accusing Jeremiah of being an alarmist, saying foreigners would invade Judah and bring fear to the people. Jeremiah had indeed said something like that (Jeremiah 6:22-26). If the people had taken it seriously and had stopped doing wrong, they could have averted the invasion and been at peace (Jeremiah 6:16). But instead of listening to the preaching and changing their ways, they wanted to silence the preacher.

People around Jeremiah were saying to him, *Report!* Go ahead and talk all you want to about how we're going to be defeated by some invader,

visual 13

JEREMIAH'S
REASONS
TO QUIT | TO KEEP ON
•BARRED FROM TEMPLE
•BEATEN
•IMPRISONED
•PUT IN CISTERN
THE LORD
JEREMIAH KEPT ON

and we will report it: we will tell the authoritiesand you will be in trouble for your subversive talk. Or perhaps they were saying to one another, *Report!* Tell about him and his unpatriotic talk. Perhaps they were saying, *Let's report it,* rather than *we will report it.* Let's tell everybody Jeremiah is preaching against our country. Or perhaps they meant *Let's report* to the authorities and get him arrested and jailed. Whatever may have been the exact meaning of *Report . . . and we will report it,* the words were hostile to the prophet. Jeremiah was being threatened.

My familiars is literally *men of my peace.* Friends who had been concerned about Jeremiah's peace and welfare had turned against him. Now they were waiting for him to stumble, to make some incautious statement that could be called subversive. They were saying, "Jeremiah is so enthusiastic about trying to reform us, so eager to tell what sinners we are, so quick to say foreigners will defeat us—maybe he can be enticed to go too far, to say something that can be used to convict him of treason. Maybe in that way we can overcome him and get our revenge. Who does he think he is, anyway?" With such an attitude all around, even among his former friends, it is no wonder Jeremiah wanted to stop his preaching. But he couldn't stop (v. 9).

B. Assurance (v. 11)

11. But the LORD is with me as a mighty terrible one: therefore my persecutors shall stumble, and they shall not prevail: they shall be greatly ashamed; for they shall not prosper: their everlasting confusion shall never be forgotten.

The Lord is with me. That was what the Lord had promised in the beginning: "Be not afraid of their faces: for I am with thee to deliver thee" (Jeremiah 1:8). The Lord is *mighty,* much stronger than the many who wanted to prevail against Jeremiah. The Lord is *terrible,* awesome. He is one to be feared. Since they did not fear Him, Jeremiah's opponents lacked the very beginning of wisdom (Proverbs 9:10). In their folly they would surely *stumble*. Being opposed to the Lord as well as Jeremiah, *they shall not prevail*. Their failure to silence the prophet might be enough to make them *greatly ashamed*, but there was much more to come. The Babylonians would come and subdue Judah as Jeremiah had predicted. Then how would those men feel who had told the prophet to shut up? But even then they would not listen to Jeremiah and submit to Babylonian rule. Repeatedly they would rebel, and finally Jerusalem would be crushed. Those who would survive the siege and battle would be dragged away to Babylon. More than ever before they would be *greatly ashamed*. To this day every Bible student knows of their shame, and *their everlasting confusion shall never be forgotten*.

Conclusion

Our lesson title calls Jeremiah a persistent prophet. The lesson tells us enough to justify that description, but there is much more. For more than forty years this prophet kept on delivering God's messages to Judah, though for more than half that time he was either ignored or derided and persecuted.

A. Jeremiah's Persistence

For about eighteen years Jeremiah and King Josiah worked together for truth and right. The the king lost his life in battle (2 Chronicles 35:20-25). The following kings gave Jeremiah no support, but he kept on with his preaching.

Jeremiah was barred from the temple so he could not talk to the assembled people. He had his prophecies of twenty years written in a book, and his secretary read them to the people in the temple (Jeremiah 36:1-10).

King Jehoiakim burned Jeremiah's book, but the prophet had it rewritten with additions (Jeremiah 36:20-32).

Falsely accused of defecting to the Babylonians, Jeremiah was put in prison. Even there he was able to reach many people with the Lord's messages, so his enemies silenced him by putting him in a cistern. There was no water in the cistern, only deep mud. A concerned slave interceded with the king and rescued the prophet. Still he persisted in giving God's messages (Jeremiah 37, 38).

The people of Judah were persistent too. They kept on in their rebellious and disobedient way till Jerusalem was destroyed as Jeremiah had predicted. Most of the people were deported to Babylon, but some peasants were left in Judah. Jeremiah stayed with them to give them guidance from the Lord (Jeremiah 39:1—40:6).

The Babylonians appointed a governor over the Jews left in Judah, but a band of rebels killed him. A little civil war followed. Fearing retaliation from Babylon, the survivors fled to Egypt. Jeremiah urged them not to go; but when they ignored his advice, he went along to give them God's word still (Jeremiah 41:1—44:30).

B. Christian Persistence Today

Have you ever heard of a Christian worker who stopped working because:

His work was not appreciated?
He was criticized unfairly?
He didn't seem to be accomplishing much?
He thought twenty years was enough?
Nobody wanted to help him?
The church got green carpet instead of red?
His classroom was crowded?
The church was always asking for money?

No doubt there have been times when you have heard other reasons no better than these. All of us can take a lesson from the persistent prophet, can't we? If his example is not enough, we can look to Jesus, "the author and finisher of our faith; who for the joy that was set before him endured the cross, despising the shame, and is set down at the right hand of the throne of God" (Hebrews 12:2).

C. Prayer

Father, You know what difficulties we face as we try to do Your work on earth. Sometimes we feel like quitting, but when we read of Your persistent prophet we are ashamed to give up. Help us to be persistent too. Amen.

D. Thought to Remember

Keep on keeping on.

Home Daily Bible Readings

Monday, Nov. 23—Jeremiah Is Called to Be a Prophet (Jeremiah 1:1-9)
Tuesday, Nov. 24—The Lord Will Fight Jeremiah's Battles (Jeremiah 1:13-19)
Wednesday, Nov. 25—Israel's Heart Is Hardened Toward God (Jeremiah 4:14-22)
Thursday, Nov. 26—God's Wrath Will Fall Upon Israel (Jeremiah 6:10-15)
Friday, Nov. 27—God Calls Israel to Repentance (Jeremiah 7:1-7)
Saturday, Nov. 28—Israel's Covenant With God Is Broken (Jeremiah 11:1-11)
Sunday, Nov. 29—God Will Free Israel From Captivity (Jeremiah 30:1-18)

Learning by Doing

This page contains an alternate lesson plan emphasizing learning activities. Classes desiring such student involvement will find these suggestions helpful.

Learning Goals

As a result of this lesson your students will:

1. Analyze Jeremiah's perseverance in the midst of severe opposition.
2. Conclude that obeying God sometimes brings opposition.
3. Persevere in their obedience to Christ despite hardships and opposition.

Into the Lesson

Before class write on the chalkboard the following verses of Scripture (both are taken from the *New International Version*):

"Be faithful, even to the point of death, and I will give you the crown of life" (Revelation 2:10);

"Therefore, my dear brothers, stand firm. Let nothing move you. Always give yourselves fully to the work of the Lord, because you know that your labor in the Lord is not in vain" (1 Corinthians 15:58).

Begin class by reading the verses aloud. Then lead a discussion by asking, "What would be the strongest discouragement to your following of Christ?" You can encourage honest interaction if you begin by sharing your own thoughts.

After several minutes of discussion ask, "What motivates you to remain faithful to God?" Again allow for discussion.

Lead into the Bible study by saying, "Most followers of God at some time become discouraged. Obeying and serving God can bring opposition and heartaches. Even the Bible mentions those who, at times, considered giving up their ministry. Today we will examine one such person—the prophet Jeremiah—to learn how we can persevere in the midst of opposition."

Into the Word

Have class members form groups of six, and give each student a copy of the following questions. As the groups discuss the questions, the students should write down their group's conclusions.

1. Read Jeremiah 1:7-10, 17-19. What did God command Jeremiah to do? (vv. 7, 10).
2. Jeremiah's mission would make him unpopular. Why should he approach his mission unafraid of his opponents? (vv. 8, 17-19).
3. Now read Jeremiah 20:1-11. What was Jeremiah's response to his opposition? (vv. 7, 8).
4. What kept Jeremiah from quitting? (v. 9).
5. What enabled Jeremiah to face opposition? (vv. 10, 11).

Allow about fifteen minutes for discussion. Then ask the groups to share their responses to questions 4 and 5. Next ask, "Which was harder for Jeremiah: to stop serving the Lord, or to keep on serving Him?" When students offer their opinions, ask them why they think so.

Have students work again in their small groups to paraphrase one of these passages: Jeremiah 1:17-19 or Jeremiah 20:9-11. They should work on the paraphrases as a group. Assign half of the groups the first passage, and the other half the second passage. Allow ten to twelve minutes for this. Then ask the groups to read their paraphrases for the rest of the class.

Option

Have students form groups of six and discuss the questions listed above. Instead of having them write the paraphrases, however, have each group examine an incident in Jeremiah's life in which he was opposed. Have groups read one of the passages listed below and summarize in twenty-five words or less what took place. They should be prepared to read their summary to the rest of the class. The passages are Jeremiah: 11:18-23; 26:7-15; 37:1-16; 38:1-13.

Allow the groups about ten minutes for their assignment. Then ask the groups to read their summaries. Afterwards, lead the class in discussing this question: "Based on our studies in Jeremiah, what principles can we identify that help us persevere in serving Christ in the face of opposition?"

Into Life

Lead a discussion of these questions:

1. Second Timothy 3:12 clearly teaches that those who strive to live a godly life in Christ will be persecuted. According to Hebrews 10:32-39, why should we persist in the midst of persecution?
2. Read Hebrews 12:1-3. How do these verses help us to persevere in the midst of opposition?
3. We have seen that Jeremiah continued to obey and serve God because God's word burned within him. He possessed a flaming passion within for God. What commitment will you make to prepare yourself to persevere when hard times come?

Let's Talk It Over

The questions on this page are designed to encourage review of the lesson Scriptures and to promote discussion of the lesson by the class. The answers provided are only discussion starters. Let your class talk it over from there.

1. Jeremiah was reluctant to undertake God's mission because of his youthfulness and inexperience. How do people today let their age affect their willingness to undertake Christian work?

Like Jeremiah, some Christians respond to a call to service by protesting that they are too young or inexperienced. Paul's exhortation to Timothy is appropriate for them: "Let no man despise thy youth; but be thou an example of the believers, in word, in conversation, in charity, in spirit, in faith, in purity" (1 Timothy 4:12). Their youthful vigor and enthusiasm and the fresh approach they bring to the task may make them more effective than someone with years of experience. At the other end of the age spectrum are those Christians who want to step aside and let the younger members take over the responsibility. But the church needs the qualities that those rich in years can offer, such as steadiness, wisdom, and expertise gained through years of Bible study, prayer, and service.

2. Jeremiah claimed that God's word "was in mine heart as a burning fire shut up in my bones," so that he had to speak it. How may Christians today have a similar experience?

Paul must have had an experience like that of Jeremiah, for he wrote, "For though I preach the gospel, I have nothing to glory of: for necessity is laid upon me; yea, woe is unto me, if I preach not the gospel!" (1 Corinthians 9:16). When Paul was in Athens we are told that "his spirit was stirred in him, when he saw the city wholly given to idolatry" (Acts 17:16). For many Christians the opportunity to see firsthand the tragic effects of people caught up in heathen worship and superstition has been the key to appreciating the gospel's superiority. And it has stirred within them a sense of urgency to proclaim the truth of Jesus Christ to people "having no hope, and without God in the world" (Ephesians 2:12). Perhaps our exposure to such great spiritual need would stir us up in like manner.

3. We may have lost some friends because of our faithfulness to Jesus Christ. How does God make up for such a loss?

Although some of Jeremiah's friends turned against him, he maintained some noteworthy friendships (see Jeremiah 36:4-8; 38:7-13). The steadfastness of these friends must have soothed the sting of losing others. When we come to Christ, some friends may reject us outright, while others may drift away from us gradually. But we gain some new friends with whom we share the love of Jesus Christ himself. Of course, even in the church our determination to follow Jesus unreservedly may cost us some friendships. But that will give us more reason to appreciate the friends who stick with us, not only when friendship is easy and when it involves some sacrifice.

4. It is tempting to take some satisfaction in the "everlasting confusion" awaiting those who oppose us in our witness for Christ. How should we respond to the fact that punishment awaits the enemies of Christ?

Jeremiah wept over the fate that was to befall his people. Centuries later Jesus also lamented over Jerusalem's approaching doom. Certainly this attitude of sadness rather than satisfaction should characterize our feelings toward the present-day enemies of the gospel. Jesus did speak in vivid terms concerning the fate of the lost (Mark 9:42-49), and so must we. Our purpose in doing so, however, must not be to give the impression that we relish the subject, but to stir up those outside of Christ to repentance and commitment to Him.

5. How may we develop the habit of persistence in our Christian work?

Occasionally preachers and teachers challenge their hearers to play the game of "what if." For example, what if Jesus had allowed discouragement over the unresponsiveness of His hearers to cause Him to give up short of the cross—how then could we be saved? What if the apostles had wearied of the constant rejections and persecutions they faced and had given up their mission of preaching—how would the message of salvation have been spread so that it would reach unto our time? We make this personal by asking, What if we give up on our Christian duty because we are busy or tired or frustrated—what will happen to the people we could have saved, the backsliders we could have reclaimed, or the other workers we could have recruited?

Winter Quarter, 1992-93

Theme: Good News for All

Special Features

Lessons

Unit 1: Coming of the Good News

Unit 2: Living the Good News

Unit 3: Sharing the Good News

Related Resources

The following publications are suggested to provide additional help on the subjects of study presented in the Winter Quarter. They may be purchased from your supplier. Prices are subject to change.

Christian Cross-Cultural Communication, by Ralph Robson and Jean Billing. Explains the nature and origins of prejudice and how to overcome it. Order #11-88551, $1.99.

Claiming God's Promises, by Alger Fitch. Among the promises discussed are forgiveness, God's presence, security, healing, and joy. Distinguishes between the promises meant for us and those that are not. Order #11-41028, $2.99.

Guidelines for Growing Christians, by LeRoy Lawson. This book offers help for improving one's attitude, relationships, and prayer life by integrating spiritual disciplines into daily life. Order #18-39950, $5.99.

Training for Service, by Orrin Root, revised by Eleanor Daniel. This survey of the Bible is a "must" for teachers. Order #18-03212, $3.99.

Quarterly Quiz

The questions on this page may be used in several ways: as a pretest at the beginning of the quarter; as a review at the end of the quarter; or as a review after each lesson. The questions are based on the Scripture text of each lesson (King James Version). ***The answers are on page 120.***

Lesson 1

1. In times past, God spoke to His people Israel through the prophets; but in these last days, by whom has He spoken? *Hebrews 1:1, 2*

2. God has blessed us, chosen us, and destined us to be His children through whom? *Ephesians 1:3-5*

Lesson 2

1. John the Baptist's father and mother were named ______ and ______, *Luke 1:5*

2. John's father was a priest. T/F *Luke 1:5*

3. Where was he and what was he doing when he learned that he and his barren wife would have a son to be named John? *Luke 1:9-11*

Lesson 3

1. Who was the Roman Caesar at the time of Jesus' birth? *Luke 2:1*

2. Who was told that he would not die till he saw the Lord's Christ? *Luke 2:25, 26*

3. What did he do when he saw Joseph and Mary with Jesus in the temple? *Luke 2:27, 28*

Lesson 4

1. When Jesus came up out of the water of the Jordan River at His baptism, what did He see the Spirit of God doing? *Matthew 3:16*

2. What event in Jesus' life occurred immediately after His baptism? *Matthew 4:1*

Lesson 5

1. What three phenomena occurred when the Holy Spirit came upon the disciples on the Day of Pentecost? *Acts 2:2-4*

2. The apostle Peter said the event of Pentecost was spoken of by what prophet? *Acts 2:16*

Lesson 6

1. God said, "Be ye holy; for I am holy." T/F *1 Peter 1:16*

2. Peter states that we were not redeemed with ______ things as silver and gold. *1 Peter 1:18*

3. "All flesh is as grass, and all the ______ of man as the flower of grass." *1 Peter 1:24*

Lesson 7

1. What charge did some in the church at Jerusalem bring against Peter when they learned he had evangelized Gentiles? *Acts 11:3*

2. What happened in the home of the Gentile Cornelius that showed that God approved Peter's actions? *Acts 11:15-17*

Lesson 8

1. To those who are saved, the preaching of the cross is what? *1 Corinthians 1:18*

2. The message that Paul preached, which centered on a crucified Christ, was a ______ to the Jews, and was considered ______ by the Greeks. *1 Corinthians 1:23*

Lesson 9

1. Paul urges all who are in Christ to work earnestly to "keep the ______ of the Spirit in the bond of ______. *Ephesians 4:3*

2. A person who is mature in Christ will not be tossed to and fro with every wind of ______. *Ephesians 4:14*

Lesson 10

1. When Jesus appeared to the apostles and those with them on resurrection evening, what did they think they had seen? *Luke 24:37*

2. The apostles were qualified to preach of Jesus' death and resurrection because they were witnesses of these things. T/F *Luke 24:46-48*

Lesson 11

1. No person will be ashamed who believes on Jesus. T/F *Romans 10:11*

2. Everyone who calls on the name of the Lord will be (satisfied, heard, saved). *Romans 10:13*

3. "______ cometh by hearing, and hearing by the ______ of God." *Romans 10:17*

Lesson 12

1. Paul said that the strong in faith ought to bear the ______ of the weak instead of pleasing themselves. *Romans 15:1*

2. Every Christian should please his ______ for his good to edification. *Romans 15:2*

Lesson 13

1. Timothy was to do his best to present himself to God as a workman who was unashamed, one who rightly divided (handled) what? *2 Timothy 2:15*

2. Everyone who names the name of Christ is to depart from what? *2 Timothy 2:19*

Surveying the New Testament

by John W. Wade

THE LESSONS OF THIS QUARTER provide an introduction to the New Testament. There are, no doubt, many different ways one could approach a study of the New Testament. One might, for example, conduct such a study by beginning with the book of Revelation. Or one could approach the subject chronologically by beginning with the life of Christ, moving to the founding of the church, looking at the growth and development of the church, and concluding with the final triumph of the church as seen in the book of Revelation.

The designers of these lessons have chosen, however, to survey the New Testament through the lens of the theme, "Good News for All." One would be hard pressed to think of a theme that better expresses the purpose of the New Testament. This little volume, consisting of twenty-seven separate segments that we call books, certainly is good news. What better news can there be than this: God sent His Son into the world to die that we might have eternal life! And it is good news for *all*! In contrast to the Old Covenant, which offered good news for the children of Israel, the New Covenant extends good news to every race, every nation, every tongue, in every clime.

Coming of the Good News

The first unit of this quarter, covering lessons one through four, deals with the prophecies concerning Christ, and His life and His ministry. Lesson one, which begins with the prologue to the epistle to the Hebrews, shows the continuity between the Old Testament and the New, but at the same time it shows a definite break between the two. Under the Old Covenant, God spoke through the prophets. Now under the New, He speaks through His Son. The other part of the lesson text, drawn from the first chapter of Ephesians, emphasizes that God's plan for human redemption originated in the mind of God even before the foundations of the world were laid. Christ's coming into the world to die for us, the establishment of the church, and the commission for Christ's followers to go into all the world with the gospel were not an afterthought on God's part but were a definite part of His plan from the beginning.

Lesson two, based on verses from the first chapter of Luke, gives us the interesting account of the confrontation of Zechariah (Zacharias) with the angel Gabriel. In his old age, Zechariah was promised a son who would come as the forerunner of the Messiah. Zechariah and his wife Elisabeth, a pious old couple, had been denied the joys of parenthood but were now to become parents. We can hardly imagine the joy that came to them. This should remind us that God sows joy all along the way when He carries out His plans.

Luke 2 provides the Scriptural basis for the third lesson, which is the Christmas lesson. The first part of the lesson deals with the familiar story of Jesus' birth in Bethlehem. The second part of the lesson tells of the visit of Mary and Joseph to the temple for the purpose of presenting Jesus to the Lord. This was done in obedience to the commandment of the law of the Lord regarding a male child that was a woman's first born. In the temple Mary and Joseph were met by Simeon, a devout man who had been promised that he would see the Messiah before he died, and they were witness to the prophetic words that he uttered.

The final lesson in this unit, drawn from Matthew 3 and 4, tells of Jesus' baptism and temptation. It sets the stage for the beginning of His public ministry. You may want to use this as an opportunity to show the importance of obeying the commands of God. Jesus made considerable effort to travel to the Jordan River, where John was baptizing, in order to be baptized. God answered His approval in a voice from Heaven. You will also want to show that the temptations that Jesus faced are typical of the temptations that all of us have to face. Emphasize His use of Scripture in blunting the blows of Satan.

Living the Good News

The second unit of the Winter Quarter logically moves from the good news to living in keeping with the good news. Lesson five tells of the coming of the Holy Spirit on the Day of Pentecost. In our present time, when there is a good deal of emphasis on the work of the Holy Spirit, this lesson should arouse considerable interest and perhaps even some controversy. Controversy can be minimized by holding to the Biblical account rather than to advancing opinions or hobbies. The important point to make is that God used special measures, including an outpouring of the Holy Spirit, at the time of the founding of the church.

"A Call to Holy Living" is the theme for lesson six. In an age that sneers at and rejects just about every Christian standard of morality, no lesson could be more needed. It is important that Christian morality not be seen as a system of rules that have to be obeyed. Rather, a holy life is one's response to God's love and holiness. Christians seek to do the will of God, not because they are compelled to do so by some legalistic system but because they want to in order to please God.

Lesson seven, based on Acts 11, points out the universality of the church. The apostle Peter was led to understand and to teach that the church of the Lord Jesus is for all people. In theory almost all Christians will accept this. The problem comes in applying this truth to life and accepting others who are different from us. This lesson challenges every follower of Christ to face up to his or her prejudices and to seek ways to overcome them.

In the Old Testament is a body of literature that we call Wisdom Literature. The book of Proverbs is an example of this. Short, pithy sayings are used to spell out rules for a life of happiness and security. These rules usually grow out of practical experience, and most persons would accept them as reasonable. But the wisdom of God in the New Testament that will be studied in lesson eight is something quite different. At the heart of this kind of wisdom is the death of Christ on the cross. The problem is that the world rejects this as foolishness. The thrust of this lesson is that God's foolishness is wiser than men's wisdom, and God's weakness is stronger than men's strength.

The theme of lesson nine is Christian unity, "One Body in Christ." Few people would deny that it was God's intention for the church to be one. When we look at Christendom today, however, we see a church that is split into hundreds of factions. Try to make the lesson emphasis a practical one. Encourage class members to find ways they can share their faith with or work with others whose understanding of Biblical teaching differs from their own.

Sharing the Good News

The third unit of this quarter deals with carrying the good news to the world. Luke's version of the Great Commission forms the basis for lesson ten. Once Jesus convinced the apostles that He had risen from the dead, He then prepared them to carry the good news to all the nations. It is quite likely that the apostles did not at first understand the full implications of the commission Jesus gave them. As God's plan began to unfold, however, they gradually came to see that the good news was for the whole world, for everyone of every nation.

Lesson eleven points out how the gospel is to be spread—namely, by proclamation. God could have used any of many methods to spread the good news. He might have used angels or numerous miraculous events. Instead He chose to use human beings, with all their weaknesses, to share the gospel with everyone who needs it. Faith comes not in some mysterious fashion, but by the hearing of the Word of God. A clear understanding of this would solve many problems in the religious world.

A concern for the weak is the theme for lesson twelve. In Romans 15, Paul spells out guidelines for relations between Christians with strong consciences and those with weak consciences. His advice is that patience, love, and forbearance should characterize Christian conduct. Encourage your students to think of ways that they can show these qualities so as to avoid friction and strife in the church.

The final lesson of the quarter deals with a subject dear to the heart of every teacher—teaching the truth. Every generation has an obligation to share the truth with the next. If it fails to do this, then the church faces a limited future. Through the Sunday school, vacation Bible school, camp, and other classes, the church is attempting to meet this responsibility. Yet we must confess that all these efforts are not getting the job done as well as we would like. Use this lesson to encourage your students to work harder at teaching in the home and in every other situation possible. We must not, we need not, surrender the field to the forces of secularism that seem intent on making Christianity irrelevant in our society.

Plainly, thirteen brief lessons are not enough time to give a complete introduction to the New Testament. Yet this survey will give your students a taste of the major themes found in it. It can whet their appetites for further study and give them a basis for study on their own.

If you are not currently using some of the creative suggestions for teaching that are found with each lesson treatment, you may want to try some of these. They will provide variety in your teaching and involve some of your students in the learning process. One suggestion is to use the quarterly quiz (see page 114). Some students, especially adults, may rebel at the idea of taking a quiz; but as long as they don't feel threatened by it they may come to appreciate this learning help. You may give the test at the beginning of the quarter or at the end of the quarter, or both, allowing them to work at home on their own.

Good News for All

by Robert C. Shannon

When my wife and I first moved to Austria to assist in taking the gospel behind the Iron Curtain, what we missed most was the news. The average American eats breakfast listening to the news, drives to work listening to the news, watches the six o'clock news before supper and the eleven o'clock news before bedtime. Our knowledge of the German language was so sketchy that we hardly had any news at all. We got used to it after a while. Then we were amused by our short-term workers, who came over to help for two or three weeks at a time. After three days without news they were having withdrawal symptoms. They were afraid the world had stopped turning and they hadn't heard about it!

Everybody is interested in the news. In the most remote village, primitive people are interested in the news. It may be only the news of what's happening in the next village, but they are interested in the news. In our modern cities, where news comes by satellite, people are fairly inundated with it.

Good News and Bad News

We hear lots of news: not much of it is good; most of it is bad. That fact has spawned a whole set of good news/bad news jokes. It is most unfortunate when those who receive regular doses of bad news from radio, television, the boss, neighbors, the children, and a husband or wife are subjected to even more bad news when they get to church. I once heard a brilliant sermon. It was a ringing castigation of sin. It was a masterful diagnosis of our human condition. Every word spoken was the truth, but there was no gospel in the sermon. If I were to suggest a different menu for that preacher he would undoubtedly say, "I must preach the gospel," meaning, "I must preach the truth." We have come to use the word *gospel* that way. We say, "What I am telling you is the gospel truth." But the word *gospel* does not mean truth; it means "good news."

A Joy to Hear

More than once, a person leaving the church building has said to me, "I enjoyed your sermon." Then, a little embarrassed, he or she would say, "I'm sorry, we're not supposed to enjoy them, are we?" But I would respond, "Yes! We *are* supposed to enjoy them." Everybody likes to hear good news. Where did the idea originate that listening to a sermon is some kind of punishment for our sins—a verbal spanking, as it were? I know that some people crave this kind of preaching. They've heard we must suffer for our sins, so they come to church, take their "spanking," and they feel better. That's a most superficial way to deal with guilt.

When I returned to preach again in the country church where I began decades before, a lady said to me, "You don't preach like you used to." She did not intend it to be a compliment. I knew exactly what she meant. She missed the harsh denunciations she had heard from me then. But I am convinced that it is far better to speak of the good that God has done, than to speak continually of the evil that we have done. Of course, the imperatives of the gospel cannot and should not be ignored, but they should rest on the declarations of the glorious things God has already done on our behalf. It has been well said that people need to know what has come into the world far more than they need to know what the world is coming to.

A woman's doctor told her there was a possibility that she had cancer. She and her husband waited anxiously for the results of all the tests. How they rejoiced when they learned that she did not have cancer after all! They went out to eat in a fine restaurant and celebrated their good news. Afterward, the husband said he would never forget that evening and the joy they felt over their good news. That is the joy of the gospel. We who were dead in sins have been made alive with Christ. (See Ephesians 2:4, 5.)

Hymn writers and gospel preachers have looked for the strongest adjectives to tell us just how good the good news is. I grew up singing,

"I stand amazed in the presence
of Jesus the Nazarene.
And wonder how he could love me,
A sinner condemned unclean."

We glory in songs like *Amazing Love* and *Amazing Grace.*

When I was a child in vacation Bible school, we always sang, "I have the joy, joy, joy, joy down in my heart." The leader would ask, "Where?" and we shouted until we were hoarse, "DOWN IN MY HEART!" What we lacked in melody we made up for in volume! We knew *where* it was, but we didn't know *what* it was! Only when the full spectrum of life has been experienced, when forgiveness and inner-healing have been realized, when the divine presence, divine comfort, and divine strength have been enjoyed can one know what that joy really is. Then we can get the joy out of our hearts and onto our faces and into our lives.

A Joy to Speak

The word *evangelism* means "to bring a message of good news." In May 1990, a bank in California mistakenly threw $42,500 into the trash. City workers sifted through two and one-half tons of garbage until they found it. Imagine the joy of the finder, when he was able to announce that the treasure had been recovered, even though he could not keep it. Then, imagine the joy of the finder if he could have kept it! Paul calls the gospel a treasure! When we've found it, it is ours to keep. But we also must give it away. And in God's gracious plan, when we do share it with others, the treasure becomes no less valuable to us. It's like seeing a rainbow. Have you ever noticed that no one can see a rainbow without pointing it out to someone else?

A man was walking down the corridor of a hospital. A total stranger grabbed him by the arm. "She's going to be all right!" he exclaimed. "She's going to be all right!"

Obviously he had just gotten some very good news and just *had* to tell somebody. Such joy is the dominant theme of many of the parables of Jesus. In one He told of a man who had lost a sheep. When he found it, he said, "Rejoice with me." In another, a woman had lost a coin. When she found it, she said, "Rejoice with me!" In yet a third, a man had lost a son. When he found him, the father gave a party. It was a dramatic way of saying, "Rejoice with me!" These parables depict Heaven's joy over one sinner who repents. But notice that God wants to share this joy with us! Anyone who has ever led someone to Christ knows that joy. There is no other joy like it. It is sharing God's joy!

In the parable of the treasure hidden in a field we read that the finder "in his joy" sells all that he has and buys the field. Here is the joy of one who finds salvation. If we help him find it, we share in *his* joy. So for every evangelist there is the opportunity to share in the joy of the one forgiven and also in the divine joy of the Forgiver.

The Gospel of Matthew says that when the women heard of the resurrection of Jesus, they experienced great joy and *ran* to report it to His disciples. The Gospel of John says that when Mary Magdalene met the risen Lord, she went and told the disciples. The Gospel of Luke says that the two men from Emmaus returned immediately to Jerusalem to tell the good news of their meeting with the resurrected Jesus. In some ancient copies of the Gospel of Mark, the end got torn off. In these copies, chapter 16 ends with verse 8. Some have even said that that is the way Mark ended his gospel and that verses 9 through 20 were added later by another hand. But that cannot be. Verse 8 reads "They said nothing to anyone, for they were afraid" (*New American Standard Bible*). That is totally contrary to what the other three Gospels say. That is totally contrary to any normal expectation. And what writer, trying to convince his readers, would end the story like that? No, we can be certain that verse 20 and not verse 8 is the true ending of the Gospel of Mark. "And they went out and preached everywhere" (*New American Standard Bible*).

Troubling Thought

So we read with joy the title of this article: "Good News for All." But one word bothers me. It's the word *All.* It bothers me because it indicts me, as in fact it indicts most of us. That disturbing word, or a synonym of it, can be found in the first book of the Old Testament and the last book of the Old Testament; in the first book of the New Testament and in the last book of the New Testament. Genesis 22:18 quotes God as saying to Abraham, "In thy seed shall all the nations of the earth be blessed." In Malachi 1:11, God says, "For, from the rising of the sun even unto the going down of the same, my name shall be great among the Gentiles; and in every place incense shall be offered unto my name, and a pure offering; for my name shall be great among the heathen, saith the Lord of hosts." In Matthew 28:19, 20 we are commissioned to "teach all nations," and Revelation 14:6 says, "And I saw another angel fly in the midst of heaven, having the everlasting gospel to preach unto them that dwell on the earth, and to every nation, and kindred, and tongue, and people."

If you believe the Bible, you believe in missions! It is just that simple and just that inescapable. If you believe the Bible, you agree with this truth expressed in the chorus: "Everybody ought to know who Jesus is." The poor person ought to know. The rich person ought to know. The educated person ought to know. The uneducated person ought to know. The cultured person ought to know. The primitive person ought to know. The Asian ought to know. The African-American ought to know. The Caucasian ought to know. The African ought to know. The South Sea Islander ought to know. Everybody ought to know who Jesus is.

We are to share the gospel, not as those reluctantly dragged to their duty, but as those joyfully sharing what they have. Let us say to everyone, "I have good news for you!"

Good News Is for Sharing

by Roy Weece

IN JANUARY OF 1982, Air Florida Flight 90 crashed into the ice-clogged Potomac River in Washington D.C. The tragedy caught the horrified attention of the entire nation, occurring as it did during the evening news time. Seventy-four passengers died, and five others were rescued by astonishing acts of bravery. One rescuer, Lenny Skutnik, plunged into the river, swam to Priscilla Tirado, and towed her back through the ice to shore. He had heard her scream, "Won't somebody please come out here and save me!" Priscilla said later, "Lenny is 'my savior'—my angel sent from Heaven."

Rightly we rush to help those in physical danger. But do we feel the same urgent motivation to rescue those in spiritual danger?

The earliest Christians were convinced that the "good news" of Christ was for sharing, and they did it each day (Acts 5:42). They wanted to claim the promise of Jesus, "Whosoever . . . shall confess me before men, him will I confess also before my Father which is in heaven" (Matthew 10:32). "Confess" means to talk to people about Jesus, to publicly admit friendship with Jesus, to acknowledge to others a relationship with Jesus. If we will do as He asks, He will do as He has promised. Psychologists estimate that each day we are given some seven hundred opportunities to say something. Talkative people utter about twelve thousand sentences every day, which averages out to about one hundred thousand words! What will you do with your opportunities?

God illustrates evangelism/sharing with familiar words to motivate us. Three of those words are *fishing, planting,* and *harvesting.*

Fishing Is Fun

This is true, whether we are fishing for fish or for people. In both types of fishing, patience is needed, bait and tactics are varied, and fishing is done where the "fish" are. Fishing for fish brings the caught from life to death, but fishing for people brings them from death to life.

Sixteen-year-old Corey expressed his joy over "fishing for souls" after my camp lesson on Personal Evangelism. He was standing on Main Street of his small town when a traveler pulled up to the curb and asked, "Do you know where Taylorville is?" "No," he responded, "but I know where Heaven is." The man gave him a hearing about the good news. Not long ago I heard Leland Duncan, campus minister at Virginia Tech, express the joy he experiences over fishing for people, though he confessed, "In my youth I was so shy that I couldn't even lead in a silent prayer!" University student Doug said, "I made a vow to talk to everyone in our dorm about Jesus." He did it as a Christian of less than one year, and you guessed it—joy! Nothing can compare!

Fishing for people can be done anytime anywhere. A Christian marine, just back from the Persian Gulf War, shared his fishing gladness when he spoke for a campus wide crusade at Oklahoma State University. While traveling from the USA by ship on his way to Saudi Arabia, he "caught" some fellow passengers for Christ and baptized them in caskets! The caskets were cargo intended for troop casualties and were a fitting instrument for "burial into Christ" (Romans 6:4). Even when he was heading into a life-threatening situation, this young marine had the joy of bringing others to new life in Christ.

Planting Is Productive

David reminds us that seed planting results in harvest time (Psalm 126). Paul repeats this truth (1 Corinthians 3:6-9). But the seed of the gospel must be planted in the "soils" of human minds.

Missouri University graduate Jim Love, a Florida high school teacher, writes of seed planting. "I took some heads of wheat to school, since my students had never seen any. My friend Ed, the French teacher, asked if he could have some for his class, so I gave him about half of them (ten to fifteen heads). On one of her visits, Ed's grandmother saw the wheat and timidly asked if she could have some, because she hadn't seen any since she and her husband had left Poland. She explained that wheat always brought back fond memories. So Ed gave her half of his supply.

"One year later Ed's grandmother proudly took him to her backyard. Using the meager heads she had been given, she had planted, harvested, and replanted until the wheat covered her garden. She told him that next year there would be enough for her to make him some bread, as she used to do for his grandfather. Then she asked where his wheat was. When he told her that it was still in the refrigerator, she said, 'Too bad. You could have had bread this year!'" Ed thought his grandmother had wanted a few heads for a memento, but she knew that memories come from the planting, growing, and harvesting. Spiritual harvesting awaits our planting of the gospel seed. This seed can't be preserved in our spiritual refrigerators.

A former acquaintance of mine had a neighbor who wasn't a Christian. For some time my acquaintance had wanted to, and knew he should, speak to his neighbor about Christ, but he delayed. Finally he could put it off no longer and he asked his neighbor to consider Jesus. The neighbor responded, "I thought you'd never ask." Who might be waiting for you to ask them about Jesus? The old question is still in order: "If you were given a $1000.00 bill for every person you won to Christ, would you work any harder?" Never! Never! We already have sufficient motivation as a result of our personal salvation and in the possible salvation of those who are lost.

Planting may not be productive, however, if we hinder the procedure. When our children were very young, we planted garden seeds to show them how plants grow. The next day when I came home from church, they sadly held out their hands containing the seeds. "They didn't come up, so we digged to see why," they explained. The same principle applies in the spiritual realm. A Christian teenager in Illinois brought her friend to an evangelistic meeting, but she whispered to her during the meeting. The friend responded, "I thought you were my best friend. You've heard this, and I never have; so please let me listen." And certainly a Christian's life-style will either help or hinder the spiritual development of those in whom the seed of the gospel has been planted.

Sometimes the production of harvest is stopped because of matters out of our control. A non-Christian journalism student met at mealtime with our family and the refugee family who was living with us at that time. She questioned all of us for her news story, and then I interviewed her briefly for Jesus. She agreed to a second interview at a later date, but she was killed in a plane crash before the set time. This tragic occurrence reminds us that we must work the works of God before the night comes "when no man can work" (John 9:4).

On one occasion I boarded the wrong plane for home, a mistake not discovered until the plane was flying in another direction! The airline lodged me in a motel, and I was escorted back to the airport early the next morning. The shuttle van had a TV, and it was news time. The driver commented apologetically, "There is no good news." I seized the planting opportunity! "I know some good news!" I exclaimed.

Every Christian has some good news. Let's plant those seeds. Let's water them with tears and the emotional zeal of Jeremiah, who cried, "Oh that my head were waters, and mine eyes a fountain of tears, that I might weep day and night for the slain of the daughter of my people!" (Jeremiah 9:1).

Harvesting Is Holy

Harvesting of souls is holy because it is commanded by God. In his book *How to Have a Soul Winning Church*, Gene Edwards writes, "Personal evangelism lies until this very hour in a must stack, labeled: 'Undiscovered Truths of the New Testament.'" Could you rediscover this "holy truth" with me? We've work to do.

In one of our student ministries (prison), we experienced a bumper crop soul harvest with eleven conversions in prison in a six-week period. As those who speak on behalf of God, we will need to pray as did the early Christians, "Lord, . . . grant unto thy servants, that with all boldness they may speak thy word" (Acts 4:29). Then let us go and speak with the conviction that the power and the presence of Christ are our constant companions (see Matthew 28:18-20).

Luis Palau of the Latin American World voiced his view of U. S. churches. "There is still a tremendously high proportion of Christians who do not witness for Christ and do not even invite their friends." Are we not convinced that soul harvesting is holy? It is the work that Christ has called us to do. Let us then do it and make a difference in our world.

Answers to Quarterly Quiz on page 114

Lesson 1—1. His Son. 2. Jesus Christ. **Lesson 2**—1. Zechariah, Elisabeth. 2. true. 3. He was in the temple to burn incense. **Lesson 3**—1. Augustus. 2. Simeon. 3. He took Jesus in his arms, and blessed God. **Lesson 4**—1. The Spirit was descending like a dove, and lighting upon Him. 2. The temptation by the devil. **Lesson 5**—1. The sound of a mighty wind, tongues of fire sat on each of them, they spoke in unlearned languages. 2. Joel. **Lesson 6**—1. true. 2. corruptible. 3. glory. **Lesson 7**—1. That he had entered the home of uncircumcised persons and had eaten with them. 2. The Holy Spirit came upon the Gentiles as on Peter and the others at Pentecost. **Lesson 8**—1. the power of God. 2. stumblingblock, foolishness. **Lesson 9**—1. unity, peace. 2. doctrine. **Lesson 10**—1. a spirit. 2. true. **Lesson 11**—1. true. 2. saved. 3. faith, word. **Lesson 12**—1. infirmities. 2. neighbor. **Lesson 13**—1. the word of truth. 2. iniquity.

December 6
Lesson 1

God's Purpose Through Love

Lesson Scripture: Hebrews 1:1-4; Ephesians 1:3-14.

Printed Text: Hebrews 1:1-4; Ephesians 1:3-14.

Devotional Reading: Ephesians 3:14-21.

Hebrews 1:1-4

1 God, who at sundry times and in divers manners spake in time past unto the fathers by the prophets,

2 Hath in these last days spoken unto us by his Son, whom he hath appointed heir of all things, by whom also he made the worlds;

3 Who being the brightness of his glory, and the express image of his person, and upholding all things by the word of his power, when he had by himself purged our sins, sat down on the right hand of the Majesty on high;

4 Being made so much better than the angels, as he hath by inheritance obtained a more excellent name than they.

Ephesians 1:3-14

3 Blessed be the God and Father of our Lord Jesus Christ, who hath blessed us with all spiritual blessings in heavenly places in Christ:

4 According as he hath chosen us in him before the foundation of the world, that we should be holy and without blame before him in love:

5 Having predestinated us unto the adoption of children by Jesus Christ to himself, according to the good pleasure of his will,

6 To the praise of the glory of his grace, wherein he hath made us accepted in the beloved:

7 In whom we have redemption through his blood, the forgiveness of sins, according to the riches of his grace;

8 Wherein he hath abounded toward us in all wisdom and prudence;

9 Having made known unto us the mystery of his will, according to his good pleasure which he hath purposed in himself:

10 That in the dispensation of the fulness of times he might gather together in one all things in Christ, both which are in heaven, and which are on earth; even in him.

11 In whom also we have obtained an inheritance, being predestinated according to the purpose of him who worketh all things after the counsel of his own will:

12 That we should be to the praise of his glory, who first trusted in Christ.

13 In whom ye also trusted, after that ye heard the word of truth, the gospel of your salvation: in whom also, after that ye believed, ye were sealed with that Holy Spirit of promise,

14 Which is the earnest of our inheritance until the redemption of the purchased possession, unto the praise of his glory.

Golden Text: God, who at sundry times and in divers manners spake in time past unto the fathers by the prophets, hath in these last days spoken unto us by his Son.—Hebrews 1:1, 2.

Good News for All

Unit 1: Coming of the Good News

(Lessons 1-4)

Lesson Aims

After this lesson a student should:

1. Understand that God has a purpose for every person.
2. Understand that Jesus Christ, God's Son, is central to that purpose.
3. Be able to suggest some specific ways that his or her life can be brought into closer conformity to the will of God.

Lesson Outline

Display visual 1 of the visuals packet throughout this session. The visual is shown on page 125.

Introduction

A. Love in Every Direction

A minister was once visiting one of his members who lived on a farm. High on the top of the barn was a weather vane with an arrow that always pointed in the direction from which the wind was blowing. Fastened to the arrow were the words, "God is love."

"Why do you have those words on the weather vane?" the minister asked. "Do you think God's love is as changeable as the wind?"

"Oh, no, I mean that God is love no matter what direction the wind blows."

That's one of the important points in today's lesson. God's love is unchangeable. He loved His people in ages past, revealing himself to them through the prophets. He loves us in this present age and has revealed that love through His Son.

B. Lesson Background

The lessons of this quarter provide a survey of the New Testament. Under the general theme, "Good News for All," they focus on the good news that Jesus Christ has come into the world to provide salvation to those who believe in Him and obey Him. The first four lessons comprise Unit 1, "Coming of the Good News." Unit 2, lessons five through nine, "Living the Good News," deals with the church and how it shares God's grace. The third unit of study "Sharing the Good News," deals with the missionary outreach of the church.

Today's lesson is based on a passage from Hebrews and one from Ephesians. Although the book of Hebrews does not indicate who its author was, it leaves little doubt regarding its destination. It seems quite obvious that it was written to Hebrew Christians who were in danger of falling back into Judaism. References in the epistle make it clear that it was written prior to the destruction of Jerusalem in A.D. 70. Today's lesson deals only with its prologue, a majestic assertion that Jesus Christ, the Son of God, is the climax of God's plan for human redemption.

The Ephesian letter clearly indicates that it was written by the apostle Paul (1:1). Later in verse 1 we read that this epistle was addressed to the "saints which are at Ephesus." Some older manuscripts, however, do not contain *at Ephesus,* which has led many to believe that these words were added later. It is generally thought that this letter to the Christians in Ephesus was intended also for those churches in Asia Minor that were near Ephesus. Most hold that Paul wrote it, along with Colossians, Philippians, and Philemon, during his first imprisonment in Rome, A. D. 61-63.

I. God's Final Revelation (Hebrews 1:1-4)

A. Messengers in the Past (v. 1)

1. God, who at sundry times and in divers manners spake in time past unto the fathers by the prophets.

Most of the other epistles in the New Testament begin by identifying the writer and the recipient. But the letter to the Hebrews does neither. In fact, it begins more like a treatise or a tract. While we never learn for certain its author,

How to Say It

EPHESUS. *Ef*-eh-sus.
MALACHI. *Mal*-uh-kye.

its destination is quickly learned. It was addressed to Jewish Christians who, in the face of persecution or for some other reasons, were being tempted to relinquish their faith in Jesus and to turn back to Judaism. The purpose of the letter was to convince them that Jesus Christ, the Son of God, was superior to all earlier revelation and that God's plan of redemption culminated in Him.

At sundry times. The Jewish people had a long history and they were proud of it, and so the writer appealed to that history. He reminded them of God's revelations, which had been given to their ancestors over many hundreds of years, even though those revelations had not come at regular intervals. In fact, God's last revelation *by the prophets* was given through Malachi in 431 B.C.

In divers manners means "in a variety of ways." Sometimes God spoke directly to a person, as with Abraham and Moses. Sometimes He revealed His will through angels, as He did to Gideon. At other times He used signs, such as the pillar of fire and the pillar of cloud. At other times His word came through dreams and visions. The prophets were a special group through whom God spoke. We are not always told how God's revelation came to them, but they spoke with a certainty that is echoed in their words, "The word of the Lord came unto me." Though they were often rejected and mistreated by their contemporaries, later generations came to hold them in high esteem.

B. The Son Has Spoken (v. 2)

2. Hath in these last days spoken unto us by his Son, whom he hath appointed heir of all things, by whom also he made the worlds.

In these last days. This refers to the Christian era, the final period in God's plan for the human race. Since this is the final age, it is reasonable to suppose that God would send His message through His most esteemed messenger. This could only be His Son, who is the *heir of all things.* We are not to understand that the Son is an heir in the normal human sense, in which the father must die before the son can receive the inheritance. Rather, it is a means of expressing the close relationship between the Father and the Son.

This close relationship is further emphasized through the Son's involvement in the creation of the physical universe. This doctrine is implied in the Genesis account of creation in the statement, "Let us make man in our image" (Genesis 1:26). It is clearly stated in the New Testament (see John 1:3; 1 Corinthians 8:6; Colossians 1:16). Who could carry a greater weight of authority than the very Creator of the universe?

C. The Son's Superiority (vv. 3, 4)

3. Who being the brightness of his glory, and the express image of his person, and upholding all things by the word of his power, when he had by himself purged our sins, sat down on the right hand of the Majesty on high.

The writer of Hebrews probes deeper into the relationship of the Father to the Son. Three aspects of this relationship are mentioned. The Son is *the brightness of his glory.* Translators struggle to find words to convey this idea to readers, and no two use the exact same language. The Son reflects or radiates the glory of the Father, indicating that they are one and yet separate and distinct.

This idea is reinforced in the expression, *the express image of his person.* Here the *New International Version* has "the exact representation of his being." The Son's oneness with the Father is confirmed in that the Son upholds *all things.* His work was not finished at creation, but He continues to work to sustain all parts of the universe.

These aspects of the Son suggest His transcendence, His remoteness from the human scene. But then the writer points out the Son's intimate involvement with man. He *purged our sins.* At this point we are not given the details about how our sins were purged. We know, however, that this could only happen because He who knew no sin became sin for us (2 Corinthians 5:21), dying for us on the cross. Once this redemptive task was completed, the Son took His place on the Heavenly throne beside the Father. This act clearly marks the Son as superior to the angels or any human messenger God chose to use in revealing himself to man.

4. Being made so much better than the angels, as he hath by inheritance obtained a more excellent name than they.

People in the ancient world accorded angels a place of high honor. Yet the Son was superior to all the angels, not just because He was obedient to the Father in going to the cross, but because He had inherited *a more excellent name,* that is, *Son.* This honor was exclusively His by right of who He was, of His divine nature, of His unique relation to the Father.

II. God's Eternal Purpose (Ephesians 1:3-14)

A. Blessed in Christ (v. 3)

3. Blessed be the God and Father of our Lord Jesus Christ, who hath blessed us with all spiritual blessings in heavenly places in Christ.

Paul begins the Ephesian letter, as he does several other of his letters, with a salutation identifying himself as the author. This letter is addressed to the "saints which are at Ephesus." We have already mentioned the opinion of many scholars that this letter may have been directed to all of the churches in Asia Minor near Ephesus, as well as to the Christians in Ephesus itself. In the Greek, this whole printed text from verse 3 to verse 14 is one long sentence. Modern translations break this up into shorter sentences to make its meaning clearer.

In verse 3 the apostle Paul begins with a doxology, that is a praise of God. In verse 2 God is referred to as "our Father." In this verse, He is called the *Father of our Lord Jesus Christ.* The fact that God is our Father and at the same time the Father of Christ indicates a kinship between ourselves and Christ. If we share the same Father, then we are in a sense brothers and sisters of Christ. At the same time, we recognize that this is a limited kinship, for He is divine and we are but human.

God has *blessed us with all spiritual blessings.* These blessings are spiritual because of their spiritual origin. Also, they are spiritual because they deal with spiritual, rather than physical, matters. God does, of course, shower many physical blessings upon us, but here Paul is concerned with spiritual blessings. Several of them are mentioned in the verses that follow. The real worth of spiritual blessings can be known only to spiritual people. As one grows spiritually, spiritual blessings become ever more meaningful. Persons with carnal minds can never begin to understand nor enjoy this kind of blessing.

In heavenly places. In the Greek, this expression is literally "in the heavenlies." Many modern translations speak of "heavenly realms," thus agreeing with the interpretation found in the *King James Version,* making it a place or location. The blessings that we have, which will come to full fruition in Heaven, are given and must be received *in Christ.*

B. Chosen in Christ (vv. 4-6)

4. According as he hath chosen us in him before the foundation of the world, that we should be holy and without blame before him in love.

He hath chosen us. Paul here allows us to catch a glimpse of the mystery that surrounds God's dealings with man. We are not to suppose that this and other brief glimpses can dissolve this mystery, for the ways of God are "past finding out." From the human point of view, man comes into Christ when he believes and is baptized. Yet on God's vaster scale, we were already chosen before the foundation of the world. Human logic insists that there is a contradiction between God's foreknowledge and human freedom, but this contradiction exists only in man's mind, not God's. By faith we believe that God has chosen the elect. By faith we also believe man is free to make moral choices and that his eternal destiny will be determined by these moral decisions.

Let us note that God's plan for human redemption was not drawn up in some haphazard, spur-of-the-moment fashion. Rather, His plan and purpose were formulated even before He laid *the foundation of the world,* and that plan centered in Christ. The remaining verses of our lesson text reveal that the blessings God planned for us, and which we in fact receive, are ours because we are united with Christ. By God's design, we are enabled to stand *holy and without blame before him* because of what Christ has done on our behalf (see verse 7).

Because our sins are forgiven in Christ, it follows that we are to live holy lives now to bring glory to God. But this is no easy task in a world that revels in sin and sneers at the very idea of holiness. Satan and his minions surround us on all sides to allure us or coerce us away from this holiness. There is no way that we can survive such opposition if we trust in our own strength alone. Yet we can find strength not only in knowing that God desires that we overcome Satan's temptations, but also in the fact that He has provided His Son as our ever-present companion to help us do so.

5. Having predestinated us unto the adoption of children by Jesus Christ to himself, according to the good pleasure of his will.

The last two words of verse 4 ("in love") seem best to go with verse 5. Even though we are alienated from God by our sinfulness, yet through His love and grace He has chosen to make us His adopted children. As His *children* we immediately begin to share in the fellowship of the divine family, and we will share in a heritage of immeasurable worth.

6. To the praise of the glory of his grace, wherein he hath made us accepted in the beloved.

God's plan for human redemption results in praise to God for His glorious grace. As parents are honored when their child does what is right and good, so our Heavenly Father is honored when we become His obedient children. By our lips also we ought to praise God, for we are made acceptable to Him not by our works, nor by our righteousness, nor by any other quality or ability of our own. We are accepted because we are *in the beloved,* God's beloved Son. We praise God for the totally unmerited favor that is ours in Christ.

C. Redeemed in Christ (vv. 7, 8)

7, 8. In whom we have redemption through his blood, the forgiveness of sins, according to the riches of his grace; wherein he hath abounded toward us in all wisdom and prudence.

Redemption suggests the idea of deliverance as the result of the payment of a ransom. In bondage to sin and death, man is completely incapable of paying the ransom to gain his release. It is as if one of our children were kidnapped and held for a trillion-dollar ransom. No matter how much we might love and wish to redeem that child, the ransom would be impossible for us to raise. Thus it is with our sins. The price for redemption is beyond our power.

Yet God has a way. In His wonderful grace, He sent His Son to shed *his blood* for our redemption price. We cannot comprehend God's grace, nor can we understand how Christ's blood can cleanse us from sin, yet we believe it is true because He has revealed it to us through the Scriptures.

Wisdom and prudence. Many Bible scholars take this to refer to the manner in which God unfolded His plan for human redemption. Others understand this to refer to the gifts of *wisdom and prudence* that allow man to appreciate God's redemptive plan.

D. United in Christ (vv. 9, 10)

9, 10. Having made known unto us the mystery of his will, according to his good pleasure which he hath purposed in himself: that in the dispensation of the fulness of times he might gather together in one all things in Christ, both which are in heaven, and which are on earth; even in him.

Mystery as used here refers to that which is beyond human comprehension until revealed. God has now revealed to us His *will,* which, Paul says, *he hath purposed in himself.* This is better rendered "in him" as it is in most modern versions, meaning Christ. *Dispensation* here refers to God's administration or plan of government of *the fulness of times,* the time of the gospel generally in which all of His plans are to be fulfilled. When God's purpose is fully realized, all things will be brought under subjection to Christ. "Every knee shall bow" to Him and "every tongue shall confess" Him in that day (Romans 14:11). (See Ephesians 1:20-23; Philippians 2:10, 11.)

THE RICHES OF GOD'S GRACE

When Heinrich Schliemann, the son of a poor German minister, was seven years old, a picture of ancient Troy going up in flames captured his imagination. Contrary to what many believed and taught, Heinrich, the man, argued that Homer's epic poems, the *Illiad* and the *Odyssey* were based on historical fact, and he set out to prove it. In 1873 he uncovered the ancient site of Troy and, along with it, some fabulous treasure. Schliemann gained fame and wealth because he dared to believe an ancient record and act upon that faith.

Paul opens his epistle to the Ephesians by speaking of the fabulous riches of God that are promised to those who believe in Jesus Christ. These include adoption into His family, redemption, forgiveness of sin, and an eternal inheritance. These blessings are promised to people previously destitute and without hope. Like Schliemann, we too must believe an ancient record—in our case, the record of Scripture—and then act upon that faith. God's great riches are waiting to be claimed. —T. T.

E. Inheritance Assured (vv. 11-14)

11, 12. In whom also we have obtained an inheritance, being predestinated according to the purpose of him who worketh all things after the counsel of his own will: that we should be to the praise of his glory, who first trusted in Christ.

Christians enjoy the blessings of forgiven sins, freedom from the bonds of darkness, and fellowship with God, Christ, and other Christians. All

God's Purpose and Love
never change...
YOU
and
both
include

visual 1

Home Daily Bible Readings

Monday, Nov. 30—A Song for a Festival (Psalm 81:1-10)

Tuesday, Dec. 1—The Work of Christ (Colossians 1:15-19)

Wednesday, Dec. 2—Prayer of Thanksgiving (Romans 1:8-15)

Thursday, Dec. 3—Called to be God's Son (1 Chronicles 17:1-14)

Friday, Dec. 4—God's Chosen Son (Psalm 2:1-7)

Saturday, Dec. 5—God Is Faithful and Gives Blessings (Hebrews 6:1-12)

Sunday, Dec. 6—Spiritual Blessings Through Christ (Ephesians 1:3-14)

these refer to what has happened in the past or is happening in the present. To these must be added the greatest of all blessings—the Heavenly *inheritance.*

13, 14. In whom ye also trusted, after that ye heard the word of truth, the gospel of your salvation: in whom also, after that ye believed, ye were sealed with that Holy Spirit of promise, which is the earnest of our inheritance until the redemption of the purchased possession, unto the praise of his glory.

The expression in verse 12 "who first trusted in Christ" refers to the Jews who were the first to become Christians. The *ye* of verse 13 refers to the Gentiles who later became believers. Once they heard and accepted the gospel, the Gentiles were *sealed with that Holy Spirit.* At baptism, believers were promised the gift of the Holy Spirit (Acts 2:38). While we do not understand the full implications of this gift, we do know that in the ancient world a seal was used to show ownership, to guarantee authenticity, or to protect a document. It is likely that the Holy Spirit acts on believers in all of these ways.

The gift of the Holy Spirit is the *earnest of our inheritance,* that is, a pledge made in advance to all, both Jew and Gentile, who believe in Christ. It is a guarantee that all of the promised blessings will be received when God has fully redeemed His purchased possession. The full consummation of that redemption will be the finest tribute to His excellence.

THE BANK OF GOD

The renowned preacher and expositor, Charles Spurgeon, published a small devotional book entitled, *A Checkbook on the Bank of Faith.* It provided a short devotional message and a promise from the Word of God for each day of the year. Spurgeon commented that each promise was as good as money in the bank to anyone who would claim it by faith. It was as simple as writing a check against God's limitless bank account!

Jesus had promised the coming of the Holy Spirit, and on the Day of Pentecost Peter told his hearers that those who repented and were baptized would receive the gift of the Holy Spirit. The Spirit's indwelling gives the believer in Christ assurance of salvation. Paul refers to the "Holy Spirit of promise, which is the earnest of our inheritance." The Spirit has been given to us as a deposit guaranteeing that we shall one day receive the full inheritance God has for us. You can count on it like money in the bank. Well, actually, it's more certain than that! —T. T.

Conclusion

A. Who's in Charge?

I have never had any fear of flying—so long as I could fly in a commercial airliner. But flying in a small private plane was different, and for years I refused to get in one of them. Then a friend of mine, a retired pilot for a major airline, offered me a ride in his small plane. I didn't hesitate a minute to accept his invitation because I knew of his record and his commitment to safety. Knowing who was in charge made a world of difference.

As we look at the world about us, one might easily get the impression that no one is in charge, that complete chaos reigns. Yet today's lesson assures us that God is in charge. Indeed, God had a plan for the universe and the beings He included in it, even before He laid its foundations.

As we have seen in this text, God's plan centered in Jesus Christ. In Him, sinful humankind can be forgiven of sin and made acceptable to God. Those who are in Christ are redeemed by His blood and have the promise of the eternal inheritance that God has prepared for His children. Praise God for His unfathomable love and grace!

B. Let Us Pray

Dear Father, we thank You that You have created the universe with a definite purpose. We give You thanks that through Your grace and the suffering of Your Son, we can be a part of that purpose. In His name we pray. Amen.

C. Thought to Remember

"God has made us for himself, and the heart of man is restless until it finds rest in Him."

—Augustine

Learning by Doing

This page contains an alternate lesson plan emphasizing learning activities. Classes desiring such student involvement will find these suggestions helpful.

Learning Goals

After examining the lesson texts, the pupil will be able to:

1. Understand the central importance of Jesus Christ to God's plan for His creation.
2. List three blessings that are ours because of Jesus Christ.
3. Suggest ways to make his or her life-style more Christlike.

Into the Lesson

Write the words of Augustine—"God has made us for himself, and the heart of man is restless until it finds rest in Him"—on small pieces of paper or small index cards. Put one word on each card and then mix them up well. Make one set of cards for each four to six persons in the class.

When the class members arrive, put them in groups of four to six. Give each group a set of cards and ask them to see if they can arrange the words into a message. Allow five to seven minutes for this activity.

After you have made sure each group has the message, tell the class that this is the theme for today's lesson.

Into the Word

Make the transition into the Bible study by presenting the material included in the "Lesson Background" section. Then ask a class member to read Hebrews 1:1-4 and another to read Ephesians 1:3-14.

Develop the Bible study by means of a discussion, using the following questions:

1. According to Ephesians 1:3, why should we praise God? (He has provided every spiritual blessing for us.)
2. What reasons for praising God do we find in Hebrews 1:1-4? (God revealed himself in various ways through the prophets; finally He sent His Son, who is the exact image of God's being, to reveal God to us; Jesus provided forgiveness of sins.)
3. According to Ephesians 1:4-10, what are the blessings that we enjoy because of the work of Jesus Christ? In Christ we are holy and without blame before God; we are adopted as God's sons; we are redeemed; God's will has been revealed to us.)
4. If in Christ we are enabled to stand holy and blameless before God, what implication does that have for our lives today? (We ought to shun evil and live holy lives now so as to bring praise and honor to God.)
5. We talk a great deal about discerning the will of God. Verses 9 and 10 tell us what it is concerning God's overall plan for His creation. How is it expressed? (His will is to bring all creation together under the headship of Christ.)
6. Verses 11 and 12 reveal more about the will of God regarding those who are in Christ. How is it defined in these verses? (They are to be for the praise of God's glory.)
7. What assurance do those who believe in Christ have that they will receive the promised inheritance? (They have the indwelling of the Holy Spirit, who is the "earnest," the down payment, to guarantee their eternal redemption.)
8. This passage from Ephesians mentions that God has blessed us with spiritual blessings. How does our possession of these blessings relate to Jesus Christ? (All of these blessings are ours because of what Christ has done for us. Through His blood we have redemption, the forgiveness of sins. Through Him we are adopted into God's family and stand spotless before God.)
9. How would you summarize the central truth of this passage from Ephesians? (God's plan for the redemption of humankind is centered in Jesus Christ. By the shedding of His blood, our sins are forgiven, we are adopted as God's children, and we will receive an eternal inheritance from Him.)

Allot twenty to thirty minutes for this section.

Into Life

Make practical application of this lesson by leading a discussion of the following question:

In light of the fact that God has chosen to save us in Christ, how can we show our gratitude to Him and bring honor to His name? (List on the chalkboard the pupils' suggestions. Then probe for specific actions relating to each item listed.) (Allot ten to fifteen minutes for this.)

Give each person a small index card with the following written on it: "My heart is restless to bring praise to God. One way I want to do that in the week to come is—." Allot two minutes for them to complete the response.

Divide the pupils into groups of three, and ask them to share their responses. Close with each group praying together, one for another.

Let's Talk It Over

The questions on this page are designed to encourage review of the lesson Scriptures and to promote discussion of the lesson by the class. The answers provided are only discussion starters. Let your class talk it over from there.

1. The letter to the Hebrews emphasizes Christ's superiority over all previous revelations and persons. In what ways is He superior?

Jesus Christ is superior in every way, but some of the more significant ways are these:

(1) His nature and being. Jesus did more than represent God or speak for God. He was and *is* God.

(2) His title. In accordance with (1), He is called "the Son of God." This title belongs to Him alone, not to any prophet, priest, king, or leader.

(3) His work. He is Creator, Sustainer, Savior, and perfect revelation. No other person could ever make these claims.

(4) His place. His rightful place is at the right hand of the Heavenly Father. That place belongs to Him alone.

2. Cite some ways God has blessed us through Jesus Christ.

Ephesians 1:3 affirms that God has blessed us with *every* spiritual blessing in Christ. All the benefits of knowing God are ours through Jesus Christ. We are blessed with the riches of His grace, redemption through His blood, the forgiveness of our sins—we have been lavishly given life. Having been adopted into His family, we are heirs of the Father, assured of the full inheritance He has promised. God has made us holy and blameless in Jesus Christ. How rich and marvelous are His blessings!

3. What are the ways God has "spoken" to humanity?

God has spoken to humanity in two ways. The first of these is *general revelation.* All creation testifies to the Creator. Through the created order He speaks of His goodness, His greatness, and His power. Nature reveals something of God's nature. But our understanding that we attain of God through general revelation is incomplete. Through *special revelation* God revealed to humankind more of His nature. He did this as He spoke directly to some (as to Moses), through angels (as with Abraham), and through dreams and visions (as to Joseph, Peter, and Paul). God spoke to His people through His prophets (oral) and His inspired authors (written). But the perfect, most complete revelation of God is seen in Jesus Christ. The Son is "the Word of God," the special revelation that perfectly shows us God and reveals His will for us. In the Son, Jesus Christ, we see who and what the Father is; in the Son, we see what the Father wants us to be and to become, the "true humanity."

4. How would you describe the "inheritance" God has in store for those who believe in His Son?

Paul affirms in Romans 8:17 that Christians are children of God, thus heirs of God, and joint-heirs with Christ. Sharing Christ's sufferings we shall share in His glory. Paul reminds us that the suffering cannot compare with the glory that we shall know. In eternity, we, as adopted children, will share in all that Christ, the natural Son, shares with the Father. That inheritance can only be described as "glorious." Everything will be new (Revelation 21:5)—all of the imperfect, the flawed, the limited, the mortal will have passed away. Human perception and words, in the final analysis, cannot adequately describe our inheritance.

5. Paul says that we have been "sealed" with the Holy Spirit, who is the "earnest" of our inheritance. What do these two terms mean?

In the ancient world, a seal showed ownership, guaranteed authenticity, or protected something, such as a document or a tomb (see Matthew 27:66). When a person becomes a Christian, that person receives salvation with the accompanying gift of the Holy Spirit (Acts 2:38). In at least the three ways mentioned above, the Holy Spirit acts in believers. The term *earnest* means a down payment, a pledge that more is to come. The gift of the Spirit is God's pledge of the inheritance that is to come. That gift is the down payment in anticipation of the full and final inheritance with the Son.

6. How can a person discover God's purpose in life's choices?

(1) Apply, thoroughly, the principles of the Bible. (2) Pray fervently for God's direction. (3) Seek the insight and counsel of mature Christian friends. (4) Wait on the Lord. (5) Maintain openness and flexibility.

God's Promise to Zechariah

December 13
Lesson 2

LESSON SCRIPTURE: Luke 1:1-25.

PRINTED TEXT: Luke 1:5-17.

DEVOTIONAL READING: Luke 1:67-79.

Luke 1:5-17

5 There was in the days of Herod, the king of Judea, a certain priest named Zechariah, of the course of Abijah: and his wife was of the daughters of Aaron, and her name was Elisabeth.

6 And they were both righteous before God, walking in all the commandments and ordinances of the Lord blameless.

7 And they had no child, because that Elisabeth was barren; and they both were now well stricken in years.

8 And it came to pass, that, while he executed the priest's office before God in the order of his course,

9 According to the custom of the priest's office, his lot was to burn incense when he went into the temple of the Lord.

10 And the whole multitude of the people were praying without at the time of incense.

11 And there appeared unto him an angel of the Lord standing on the right side of the altar of incense.

12 And when Zechariah saw him, he was troubled, and fear fell upon him.

13 But the angel said unto him, Fear not, Zechariah: for thy prayer is heard; and thy wife Elisabeth shall bear thee a son, and thou shalt call his name John.

14 And thou shalt have joy and gladness; and many shall rejoice at his birth.

15 For he shall be great in the sight of the Lord, and shall drink neither wine nor strong drink; and he shall be filled with the Holy Ghost, even from his mother's womb.

16 And many of the children of Israel shall he turn to the Lord their God.

17 And he shall go before him in the spirit and power of Elijah, to turn the hearts of the fathers to the children, and the disobedient to the wisdom of the just; to make ready a people prepared for the Lord.

GOLDEN TEXT: Fear not, Zechariah: for thy prayer is heard; and thy wife Elisabeth shall bear thee a son, and thou shalt call his name John.—Luke 1:13.

Good News for All

Unit 1: Coming of the Good News

(Lessons 1-4)

Lesson Aims

As a result of this lesson, each student should:

1. Have a better understanding of the events surrounding the birth of John the Baptist.
2. Have a growing appreciation for persons like Zechariah and Elisabeth who led righteous lives.
3. Understand that living a righteous life does not insure that one will get everything he or she wants.

Lesson Outline

INTRODUCTION
- A. Always There
- B. Lesson Background

I. ZECHARIAH AND ELISABETH (Luke 1:5-7)
- A. A Compatible Couple (v. 5)
- B. A Righteous Couple (v. 6)
  - *A Blameless Walk*
- C. A Childless Couple (v. 7)

II. TEMPLE SERVICE (Luke 1:8-10)
- A. Zechariah Burns the Incense (vv. 8, 9)
- B. The People Join in Prayers (v. 10)

III. HEAVENLY VISITATION (Luke 1:11-17)
- A. The Angel's Appearance (v. 11)
- B. Zechariah's Response (v. 12)
- C. The Angel's Announcement (vv. 13, 14)
  - *"They Lived Happily Ever After"*
- D. The Son's Character (v. 15)
- E. The Son's Ministry (vv. 16, 17)

CONCLUSION
- A. "They Also Serve"
- B. A Teetotaler
- C. Let Us Pray
- D. Thought to Remember

Visual 2 of the visuals packet says something about Zechariah and Elisabeth, and it speaks to us today. The visual is shown on page 133.

Introduction

A. Always There

When the American Revolution broke out, a young man, like many of his friends, volunteered for service in the Colonial military forces. He fought in several of the early skirmishes of that war, but nothing distinguished his service except that he was there and he survived. Eventually he became a part of the army directly under the command of General Washington and served under him in the nearly disastrous campaign around New York City. About all that could be said about his service was that he survived. He was with Washington at Valley Forge during the terrible winter of 1777-78. Again his service was not outstanding, but he was there doing what was required of him, while many others deserted or shirked their painful duties.

Finally after the Continentals' victory at Yorktown, General Washington singled out the young man, now a corporal, and gave him a special commendation for heroism. "But, sir, protested the corporal, "I never was a hero. About all I did was stay and do my duty."

"Corporal," came the General's reply, "as far as I am concerned, staying and doing your duty is the highest form of heroism."

We know very little about Zechariah and Elisabeth. We are told that they led righteous lives and that Zechariah fulfilled his duty as a priest when he was called upon. This resulted in no newspaper headlines, for sure. Yet in God's eyes they were heroes because they faithfully stayed and carried out their duties.

B. Lesson Background

Last week we began a survey of the New Testament that will take us through the Winter Quarter. The texts we studied from Hebrews and Ephesians gave us a glimpse of God's eternal plan and purpose, and we saw that the central figure in that plan is His Son Jesus Christ.

This week's lesson takes us back to the time when the earthly ministry of God's Son was drawing near. In our text from Luke's Gospel we see a step that God took to prepare His people to receive His Son.

Today's lesson is based on thirteen verses from the first chapter of the Gospel according to Luke. The author of the book of Acts as well as the Gospel account that bears his name, Luke was the companion of the apostle Paul on some of his missionary travels. Luke was a physician (see Colossians 4:14), and most believe that he was a Gentile. The fluent style of his writing indicates that he was readily at home in the Greek language.

One purpose Luke seems to have had for writing his Gospel was to spread the good news of Jesus Christ to Gentiles. He suggests the universality of the good news by tracing Jesus' ancestry back to Adam. He shows Jesus' concern for the poor and for those beyond the Jewish nation.

At the time the events portrayed in today's lesson took place, Rome was the master of the lands surrounding the Mediterranean Sea. Rome granted a good deal of freedom to the people she governed, and so Herod the Great, who was part Jewish, was allowed to rule over Judea. Herod was a clever politician and in many ways a most able ruler. But he became paranoid in his obsession that almost everyone was seeking to take his crown from him, and this led him to commit despicable acts of cruelty. He rebuilt the temple in Jerusalem and built a number of other large and impressive cities and fortifications. But his improvements came at a terrible price in fear and heavy taxes. It was just at this time in history that God, in His infinite wisdom, chose to send His Son into the world.

I. Zechariah and Elisabeth (Luke 1:5-7)

A. A Compatible Couple (v. 5)

5. There was in the days of Herod, the king of Judea, a certain priest named Zechariah, of the course of Abijah: and his wife was of the daughters of Aaron, and her name was Elisabeth.

In order to anchor the birth of John and of Jesus firmly in history, Luke dates these events during the reign of Herod, who became the king of the Jews in 37 B. C. He died in 4 B. C.. Known as Herod the Great, he is the first of several Herods who are mentioned in the New Testament. Herod's reign was significant enough that Gentile readers of Luke's Gospel likely would have known about him. Luke does not give us a precise date for the events mentioned in today's lesson, but from other sources we conclude that they occurred about 6 B. C.

Luke's concern, however, is with Zechariah and Elisabeth. (We may be more familiar with the Greek form of his name, which is "Zacharias.") His name means "Jehovah has remembered," and Elisabeth's name means "God is an oath" or "God is my oath," that is, He is "the absolutely faithful One." Zechariah was a priest of the *course of Abijah.* There were so many priests that they took turns serving in the temple. There were twenty-four courses, or divisions, of priests, and that of Abijah was the eighth (1 Chronicles 24:1-10). Each course served for two weeks each year. Zechariah was a common priest, living in a remote part of Judea, unlike the chief priests who live in and around Jerusalem.

Elisabeth was of the *daughters of Aaron.* As a direct descendant of Israel's first high priest, she, like her husband, was of priestly stock. This would have enhanced their compatibility, which is clearly indicated in Luke 1:60, 63 as well as in the verse that follows here.

B. A Righteous Couple (v. 6)

6. And they were both righteous before God, walking in all the commandments and ordinances of the Lord blameless.

This couple's piety was genuine. They lived upright lives, but not just to be seen of men. They were *righteous before God,* living in the manner that He had commanded in the Old Testament. *Walking in all the commandments and ordinances of the Lord blameless.* This is not to say that their lives were sinless, but their intentions were in line with God's revealed will, and He acknowledged their faithfulness.

A BLAMELESS WALK

Years ago Oliver Lodge said, "Men of culture no longer bother about their sins." There's more than a grain of truth in what he said; many men and women believe that sin is outmoded, that it passed on with the Victorian Age. But I don't believe this idea has anything to do with culture. Some of the most uncouth, uncultured persons that I know deny the reality of sin, while some of the most refined, accomplished, erudite people in my acquaintance readily recognize the existence and threat of sin. Culture has nothing to do with the issue.

One's view of Scripture, however, has everything to do with it. One who believes that the Bible is the Word of God, as it claims to be, recognizes the deadliness of sin and the wisdom of seeking God's remedy for it.

Luke says of Zechariah and Elisabeth, "They were both righteous before God, walking in all the commandments and ordinances of the Lord blameless" (1:6). Unlike Oliver Lodge, they believed what the Scriptures said about sin and righteousness and how God would have one live. They ordered their lives accordingly and received His approval. Oh, for a world filled with such godly couples! —T. T.

C. A Childless Couple (v. 7)

7. And they had no child, because that Elisabeth was barren; and they both were now well stricken in years.

The piety of this couple did not insure that they would be blessed in every way. In ancient Israel, children were considered a great blessing,

How to Say It

ABIJAH. Uh-*bye*-juh.
ELIJAH. Ee-*lye*-juh.
ZECHARIAH. Zek-uh-*rye*-uh.

and a childless wife was looked down upon. Not only was Elisabeth childless, she was past the bearing age and by natural means could never hope to have children.

II. Temple Service (Luke 1:8-10)

A. Zechariah Burns the Incense (vv. 8, 9)

8, 9. And it came to pass, that, while he executed the priest's office before God in the order of his course, according to the custom of the priest's office, his lot was to burn incense when he went into the temple of the Lord.

Because of the great number of priests, lots were cast to determine who would serve on a given day and in what capacity. The burning of incense in the temple was a rare privilege. It has been conjectured that a priest ordinarily received this honor only once in a lifetime. This must certainly have been a highlight in Zechariah's life.

In an attempt to gain the respect of the Jews, Herod had begun to rebuild the temple in 19 B. C. The resulting structure with its courts was much larger and more elaborate than the second temple, which had been built when the Jews returned from the Babylonian captivity. However, the temple proper still followed the same pattern seen in the temple Solomon built, and in the tabernacle before it. In front of the temple was the altar where the sacrificial animals were burned. The altar of incense was located in the Holy Place, right in front of the veil that separated the Holy Place from the Holy of Holies. The incense was burned at the morning and mid-afternoon times of prayer. On those occasions, the officiating priest entered the Holy Place with the incense and burning coals from the altar of burnt-offering. The coals were arranged on the altar of incense. Then, at a signal, the incense was placed on the coals, causing a cloud of smoke to rise. This was accompanied by the officiating priest's prayer of thanksgiving and supplication for peace upon Israel.

B. The People Join in Prayers (v. 10)

10. And the whole multitude of the people were praying without at the time of incense.

Immediately in front of the Holy Place was the court of the priests. The other priests participating in the worship remained here when Zechariah entered the Holy Place. Beyond the court of the priests was the court of the Israelites, and still further removed was the court of women. In these areas the worshipers awaited the signal of the rising smoke. At the sign, they fell upon their faces and prayed.

III. Heavenly Visitation (Luke 1:11-17)

A. The Angel's Appearance (v. 11)

11. And there appeared unto him an angel of the Lord standing on the right side of the altar of incense.

As people on the outside prayed, Zechariah also prayed. Suddenly his prayers were interrupted by the appearance of an angel. The word *angel* means "messenger," and their usual function was to deliver God's messages to humans. Luke does not give us a description of the angel, but usually they looked no different from men. He was standing on the *right side of the altar of incense.* The right side was considered the place of honor (compare Hebrews 1:3). We are not told whether or not the angel was shrouded in dazzling light (see Luke 24:4). If so, we can all the more readily understand Zechariah's response, which is described in the next verse.

B. Zechariah's Response (v. 12)

12. And when Zechariah saw him, he was troubled, and fear fell upon him.

Under these particular circumstances, Zechariah's response was perfectly understandable. We, no doubt, would act in a similar manner. His reaction indicates that he knew immediately that the visitor was no ordinary mortal. He might have become angry or indignant had he thought that the visitor was another man who had improperly intruded into the sanctuary at that very holy moment. His emotion of fear was not that of a coward, but that of a pious man in the presence of the divine. It was the response of Moses when God confronted him through the burning bush (Exodus 3:6), and of Isaiah when he was overwhelmed by a vision of the Lord (Isaiah 6:1-5).

C. The Angel's Announcement (vv. 13, 14)

13. But the angel said unto him, Fear not, Zechariah: for thy prayer is heard; and thy wife Elisabeth shall bear thee a son, and thou shalt call his name John.

The angel's first words were to reassure Zechariah that he had nothing to fear. Angels at other times prefaced their messages with a similar exhortation (see Luke 1:30; 2:10; Matthew 28:5).

Thy *prayer is heard.* Which prayer? Before the altar of incense, Zechariah had just been praying for peace upon Israel. Peace, in its richest sense, would come to Israel through the Messiah and the salvation He would make possible. And so some think the angel referred to this petition.

Others think that the angel meant the personal prayer that Zechariah and Elisabeth had so often made for a child. They point out that the angel's very next words were, *thy wife Elisabeth shall bear thee a son.* Even if they had ceased to offer such a prayer when its fulfillment seemed impossible, they had made such prayers earlier. God does not forget! He may answer prayers with a no, but for reasons of His own, He may delay His answer.

The latter view seems preferable, but perhaps it is not necessary to make a choice. Clearly there is a connection between the two, for the son who was to be born to Zechariah and Elisabeth would go before and announce the coming of the Messiah, through whom salvation would come for Israel.

The son was to be named John, which means "Jehovah is (has been) gracious." The fact that no other family member had borne this name didn't matter (Luke 1:61). This name was significant because it was a mark of God's involvement in the life of the child that was to be born and in the life of the nation.

14. And thou shalt have joy and gladness; and many shall rejoice at his birth.

Needless to say *joy and gladness* would accompany the birth of this son. The joy would be all the greater because it had so long been delayed. Others besides this blessed couple would share in the joy (Luke 1:58). But the angel's promise of joy would not be limited to the family and neighbors. The whole nation, indeed the whole world, would have reason to rejoice at the hopes that the birth of John would bring.

"THEY LIVED HAPPILY EVER AFTER"

Zechariah and Elisabeth were good folks, who believed in God and served Him well. But these good folks had a problem: they had no child, and wanted very much to have one. Through all the years of their married life, they had asked God to help them. And finally He did! In their advanced years He gave them a son; and that boy grew into a hearty man whose life was totally dedicated to the God they served. "And so they lived happily ever after."

Wouldn't it be great if all the good people of the world who wanted children could have them? Don't we all know of similarly devout couples who long for children, and pray to God for them, but who never have them? Why is this?

I don't know the answer. I believe, however, that distinct blessings can come to the childless if they will let them. Otherwise, Romans 8:28 has no meaning. For example, I have observed that childless couples are often the closest couples. Their love, unshared with offspring, grows deeper for each other. No doubt Elkanah was telling the truth when he said to Hannah, "Am not I better to thee than ten sons?" (1 Samuel 1:8).

—T. T.

visual 2

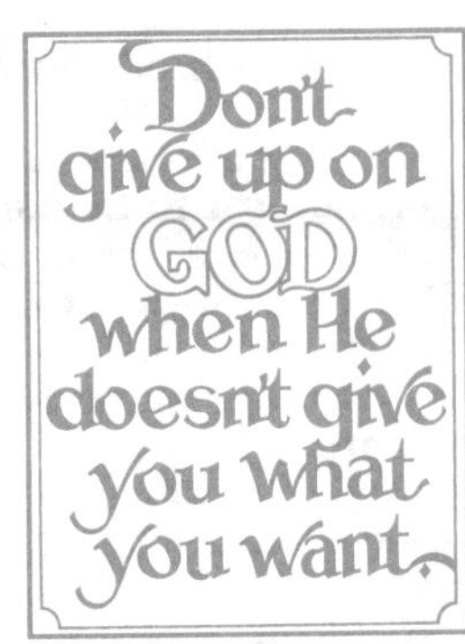

D. The Son's Character (v. 15)

15. For he shall be great in the sight of the Lord, and shall drink neither wine nor strong drink; and he shall be filled with the Holy Ghost, even from his mother's womb.

The world devises many measures to evaluate the worth of a person, but the only standard that really matters is God's standard, and by this scale John would be declared *great.* Later, Jesus would reaffirm this evaluation: "Among them that are born of women there hath not risen a greater than John the Baptist" (Matthew 11:11).

The angel stated that John would abstain from *wine* and *strong drink.* Some feel that this indicates that John was a Nazarite. A Nazarite was a person who was specially consecrated to God. This consecration may have been for a limited period of time or for life. The Nazarite vowed not to drink wine or strong drink, nor eat any product of the vine, nor shave his head during the period of his vow. As in the case of Samson, a person might be dedicated as a Nazarite at or even before birth (see Judges 13:4, 5). In John's case, no mention is made of allowing the hair to go uncut. If John was not a Nazarite as described in the law, the description of him in this verse certainly suggests that he was to be totally consecrated to the Lord in a special way all of his life.

The Old Testament mentions the Holy Spirit in connection with some of the prophets. They were usually directed by the Spirit for only a short period of time. John, by contrast, would *be filled with the Holy Ghost, even from his mother's womb.* This was not to be a temporary indwelling, but would cover his entire ministry. The Old Testament also associates the outpouring of the Holy Spirit with the coming of the Messianic age (Isaiah 61:1; Joel 2:28, 29; compare Matthew 11:5 and Acts 2:17, 18).

E. The Son's Ministry (vv. 16, 17)

16, 17. And many of the children of Israel shall he turn to the Lord their God. And he shall go before him in the spirit and power of Elijah, to turn the hearts of the fathers to the children, and the disobedient to the wisdom of the just; to make ready a people prepared for the Lord.

One of the functions of the prophets was to turn people back to God, to bring them to repentance. This proved to be one very important aspect of John's ministry. In this and in other ways John resembled the prophet Elijah.

John, however, was to have an even greater ministry. He was to *make ready a people prepared for the Lord.* His message of repentance would prepare people to receive the Messiah when He came. The Old Testament closes with the prediction that before the "coming of the great and dreadful day of the Lord," Elijah would return (Malachi 4:5). Jesus pointed out that John the Baptist, who came *in the spirit and power of Elijah,* was the fulfillment of this prophecy (Matthew 11:13, 14).

Conclusion

A. "They Also Serve"

John Milton in his poem *Sonnet On His Blindness* writes of thousands who speed hither and yon to do God's bidding. Then he adds this thought-provoking line: "They also serve who only stand and wait." This line may very well describe the lives of Zechariah and Elisabeth. They were not called to serve in a prominent place where their words would sway thousands. They served instead in a remote rural village far from the splendor of the temple courts. All of his life Zechariah served quietly as a priest, waiting his one opportunity to minister in the temple. But those years were not wasted. He and Elisabeth lived lives of simple piety, lives that served as examples for those who knew them. Who can say how many lives were made better in that village because they lived there?

In the same way, there are untold thousands in the service of the Lord "who only stand and wait." There is a difference between those who are standing and waiting and those who are just standing around. Faithfully they serve in the nursery year after year without anyone much noticing. Or perhaps they are shut-ins who have a telephone ministry or a card writing ministry. And what about those who day after day offer up prayers for the well-being of the saints and the ongoing of God's kingdom? Yet without these quiet and almost unseen saints, the work of the church would be seriously crippled.

B. A Teetotaler

Certain standards were set for John even before he was conceived. He would "drink neither wine nor strong drink." Like the Nazarite of the Old Testament, he was to serve as an example for those about him. The excessive use of alcohol was a problem in that day, although the situation did not begin to compare in seriousness with the situation we face today. If his job was to call men and women to repentance, it was important that his life not contradict his message.

Alcohol is the most serious problem drug in our society today. It causes more problems than all the illegal drugs combined. Nearly half of the fatalities in automobile accidents are attributed to drinking. And how can we count the millions of man hours lost in business and industry, the broken homes, the health problems, the shattered lives?

It is not likely that in the foreseeable future we will have laws seriously restricting the production and sale of alcoholic beverages. Yet we need not give up in despair. By the example of holy lives, we can set standards that can change the lives of others.

C. Let Us Pray

Thank You, dear Heavenly Father, for giving us the example of the faithful lives of Zechariah and Elisabeth. May it be said of us also that we live righteously before You, following the commands of Your Word. In our Master's name we pray. Amen.

D. Thought to Remember

When we pray, God sometimes says, "Be patient. Wait awhile."

Home Daily Bible Readings

Monday, Dec. 7—Obedience to God (Psalm 128)

Tuesday, Dec. 8—God's Grace (Psalm 65:1-8)

Wednesday, Dec. 9—Giving Praise (Psalm 66:1-9)

Thursday, Dec. 10—Giving Thanks (Psalm 67)

Friday, Dec. 11—Zechariah and the Angel (Luke 1:5-17)

Saturday, Dec. 12—Zechariah Is Speechless (Luke 1:18-25)

Sunday, Dec. 13—A Song for a Festival (Psalm 81:1-10)

Learning by Doing

This page contains an alternate lesson plan emphasizing learning activities. Classes desiring such student involvement will find these suggestions helpful.

Learning Goals

After studying this lesson, the pupil will be able to:

1. Identify the miraculous events surrounding the birth of John the Baptist.
2. Explain the nature of John's ministry.
3. Acknowledge willingness to trust God to do what is best for his or her life.

Into the Lesson

Before the class session begins, write on a sheet of newsprint or on the chalkboard these words of John Milton—"They also serve who only stand and wait." Have the words displayed prominently as pupils enter the room.

As the class members arrive, have them form groups of three to five. Ask them to decide if they as a group agree or disagree with Milton's statement. Have them develop a group statement to defend their position. Allow the group five minutes to prepare this.

Then let the groups make their presentations. None should be longer than a minute. Make the transition into the Bible study by stating that today's Bible study presents an excellent example of two people who did wait. Perhaps their example will shed light on the answer to the question.

Into the Word

Make a two- or three-minute presentation of the material included in "Lesson Background." Then have a class member (who has been assigned ahead of time) read Luke 1:5-17 aloud with expression.

Then have the students divide into the same small groups as they did earlier. Have half of the groups develop a character sketch about Zechariah and the other half about Elisabeth based on this lesson's Scripture text. The character sketches should include the following:

1. What character qualities did this person possess?
2. How do you think this person felt as he (she) prayed for a child, but the request was not granted?
3. How did he (she) respond to God during this wait?

Allot five to seven minutes for the groups to do their work. Then let each group report to the entire class.

Continue to examine the text by using the following questions:

1. According to the text, what was to be the nature of John's ministry? (He was to abstain from wine and all other alcoholic beverages, as was required of those who had taken the Nazarite vow. The Holy Spirit would be with him all of his life. Preaching in the spirit and power of the prophet Elijah, John would turn many Israelites to the Lord. He was to make his people ready to receive the Lord.)
2. How do you suppose Zechariah and Elisabeth responded to this?
3. We learn later that John was the forerunner of Jesus. If Zechariah and Elisabeth had known or understood this at the time of this proclamation from the angel, how do you think they would have responded?

Into Life

Send the pupils back to their groups and give each group one of the situations below. Allot five minutes for them to discuss the situation.

Case 1. Jane has been a devoted Christian since she was a young married woman. Though she has prayed persistently for her husband to become a Christian, Tom seemingly has no more interest in the church now than he did twenty years ago. Jane has begun to wonder if God hears her prayers. What would you tell her?

Case 2. Bill's job has become increasingly difficult. His boss has become more and more demanding, in spite of Bill's willingness to do more than he is asked in his job. Bill has prayed for his boss, but there is no change. He wonders if his prayer does any good. What would you tell him?

Case 3. Eva's daughter has been rebellious and uninterested in her parents' faith in Christ. She seems to delight in doing things that shock them. Eva has prayed for many years for her, to no avail. Eva has become discouraged. What would you tell her?

Let each group report to the whole class. Pursue unresolved discussion points about the necessity of trusting in God, of waiting upon God to answer in His timing.

Distribute small index cards to the pupils. Ask them to write a prayer of commitment to God in which they indicate their willingness to wait for His timing in some matter about which they are concerned. Conclude the session with prayer.

Let's Talk It Over

The questions on this page are designed to encourage review of the lesson Scriptures and to promote discussion of the lesson by the class. The answers provided are only discussion starters. Let your class talk it over from there.

1. What are some feelings a married couple might experience resulting from their inability to have a child?

Here are several feelings such couples experience: (1) Frustration. And the harder they try to conceive, the more frustrated they become. (2) Resentment. "It isn't fair that we are not able to have a child." (3) Guilt. They ask, "Are we being punished by God for something we have done?" (4) Tension. Both inner tension and tension in relationships with other persons occurs. (5) Jealousy. Couples with children are the target of this jealousy. (6) Determination. "Whatever it takes to have a baby, we will do. No matter how long it takes or how demanding it is." (7) Trust. There are Christian couples who do what they can, but they leave the outcome to God. If a child is not conceived, many opt for adoption.

2. List some of the emotions parents may experience at the time of the birth of their child.

(1) Happiness. Probably this is the most common feeling. (2) Gratitude. Some are grateful to God for the miracle of birth and the arrival of a healthy child. (3) Relief. "After all these months of waiting and preparation, the baby is here!" (4) Concern. Many parents experience some fear and even anxiety with a birth—is the child healthy, "normal"? (5) Anticipation. Beyond the anticipation of the child's arrival, there is the anticipation of relationship, of growth, of what the baby will become. (6) Wonder. Reflective parents will have a deep sense of wonder—of the miracle of birth, of their participation with God in the creating of new life, the wonder of life itself.

3. What answers may God give to a person's prayers?

Yes. Prayers that are offered in faith, that are aligned with the Lord's will, and that serve the ultimate good of the one praying and others—to these the Father says, "Yes." Answers of this nature tend to be memorable and fulfilling.

No. When God says, "No," the experience becomes difficult. Often the one praying feels angry, frustrated, confused, rejected, or deserted (or all of the above!). Yet the Father does reply in the negative when the prayer runs counter to His will or the best interests of the one praying.

Wait. Sometimes the Father responds neither "Yes" nor "No"; His response is, "Not now." In our impatience, we want an answer *now;* but God's "wait" can foster our growth and maturation. "In His Time" (as with the title of the familiar song) He serves our highest good. A wise and loving Father *would* do just that!

4. John, the son who would be born to Zechariah and Elizabeth, was given a divinely appointed task. What was his life work to be?

Through his preaching of repentance, John would turn many in Israel back to the Lord their God. In so doing, he would "make ready a people prepared for the Lord" (Luke 1:16, 17). John's role was to be that of a herald. In the first-century Mediterranean world, the approach of a notable or significant person was often preceded by a herald who shouted the news. John was to come in the spirit and power of Elijah, as a prophet. He would "foretell," announce the coming of the Messiah, and "forthtell," warn of God's judgment on His people and call them to repentance. John's role was to prepare the way of Jesus the Messiah.

5. What message may John's divinely-mandated abstinence from alcoholic beverages (Luke 1:15) offer us?

It is clear from this text that John was to be a person wholly committed to God, and the accounts of his life and ministry, which are included in the Gospels, show that he was. John's abstinence from alcoholic beverages gives us a healthy and appropriate model for our stewardship of life to God. With the broad range of healthy beverages available to us today, none of us needs to consume alcoholic drinks to meet the needs of our bodies. Abstinence is the best policy!

6. Why does patience seem to be in short supply today?

Our culture spawns and fosters impatience with its focus on instant gratification. Yet the desire for instant gratification typifies immaturity and an infantile mentality. God's call is for patience. How often we read the exhortation in Scripture, "Wait on the Lord"! The experience of Zechariah and Elisabeth reminds us that patience serves God's will and purpose.

God's Promise to the Gentiles

December 20
Lesson 3

LESSON SCRIPTURE: Luke 2:1-40.

PRINTED TEXT: Luke 2:1-7, 22-32.

DEVOTIONAL READING: Luke 2:8-20.

Luke 2:1-7, 22-32

1 And it came to pass in those days, that there went out a decree from Caesar Augustus, that all the world should be taxed.

2 (And this taxing was first made when Cyrenius was governor of Syria.)

3 And all went to be taxed, every one into his own city.

4 And Joseph also went up from Galilee, out of the city of Nazareth, into Judea, unto the city of David, which is called Bethlehem, (because he was of the house and lineage of David,)

5 To be taxed with Mary his espoused wife, being great with child.

6 And so it was, that, while they were there, the days were accomplished that she should be delivered.

7 And she brought forth her firstborn son, and wrapped him in swaddling clothes, and laid him in a manger; because there was no room for them in the inn.

. . . .

22 And when the days of her purification according to the law of Moses were accomplished, they brought him to Jerusalem, to present him to the Lord;

23 (as it is written in the law of the Lord, Every male that openeth the womb shall be called holy to the Lord;)

24 And to offer a sacrifice according to that which is said in the law of the Lord, A pair of turtledoves, or two young pigeons.

25 And, behold, there was a man in Jerusalem, whose name was Simeon; and the same man was just and devout, waiting for the consolation of Israel: and the Holy Ghost was upon him.

26 And it was revealed unto him by the Holy Ghost, that he should not see death, before he had seen the Lord's Christ.

27 And he came by the Spirit into the temple: and when the parents brought in the child Jesus, to do for him after the custom of the law,

28 Then took he him up in his arms, and blessed God, and said,

29 Lord, now lettest thou thy servant depart in peace, according to thy word:

30 For mine eyes have seen thy salvation,

31 Which thou hast prepared before the face of all people;

32 A light to lighten the Gentiles, and the glory of thy people Israel.

GOLDEN TEXT: Fear not: for, behold, I bring you good tidings of great joy, which shall be to all people. For unto you is born this day in the city of David a Saviour, which is Christ the Lord.—Luke 2:10, 11.

Good News for All

Unit 1: Coming of the Good News

(Lessons 1-4)

Lesson Aims

As a result of studying this lesson, each student should:

1. Be filled with wonder at the coming of God's Son into the world.
2. Understand that Jesus is the light of salvation for every person in the world.
3. Be challenged to share with others the good news of the birth of Jesus.

Lesson Outline

INTRODUCTION
- A. Nothing Happened in the Manger
- B. Lesson Background

I. THE BIRTH OF JESUS (Luke 2:1-7)
- A. Historical Setting (vv. 1, 2)
- B. The Trip to Bethlehem (vv. 3-5)
- C. Jesus' Birth (vv. 6, 7)
  Prince of Peace

II. THE PRESENTATION OF JESUS (Luke 2:22-32)
- A. Fulfilling the Law (vv. 22-24)
- B. Simeon's Presence in the Temple (vv. 25-27)
- C. Simeon's Blessing (vv. 28-32)
  The True Light of Christmas

CONCLUSION
- A. Hope Realized
- B. A Baby for the Whole World
- C. Let Us Pray
- D. Thought to Remember

Display visual 3 of the visuals packet throughout this lesson. The visual is shown on page 141.

Introduction

A. Nothing Happened in the Manger

A man once had a dream in which he found himself in a cattle stall. Looking around, he found to his amazement a tiny baby lying in a manger. Thinking aloud, he addressed the baby, "What are you doing here?"

To his surprise, the baby answered him, "I'm not doing anything *here!* In a few days I will leave this manger, and then thirty years after that I will start My church. After that I will do many things through the people who make up that church."

On Christmas Eve every year, hundreds and hundreds of people will throng the square in front of the door of the Church of the Nativity in Bethlehem. If we were to ask them the question, "What are you doing here?" many might have difficulty giving a good answer.

Some might respond, "We aren't doing anything *here,* but when we return to our homes, we will do many things in the name of the One who was born in Bethlehem." While it may be true that the little baby didn't do anything while He was in a manger, He left that manger. Through His church, people have been doing good things in His name ever since. Clearly what happened in Bethlehem nearly two thousand years ago still has the power to capture our imagination and inspire us to serve Him unselfishly.

B. Lesson Background

In 27 B.C., Octavian, more commonly known as Caesar Augustus, became emperor of the Roman Empire, bringing to it stability after years of civil war and internal strife. His long reign, which lasted until A.D. 14, brought peace and prosperity to the Mediterranean. Because his reign saw the flowering of culture, this period often is referred to as Rome's "Golden Age." In many ways it was an opportune time for God to send His Son into the world.

In that day everyone looked to Rome as the center of the empire, the place where the important events happened. God had different plans, however. These plans (as we saw in last week's lesson) involved an aging couple living in a remote Judean village. The events in today's lesson begin in the equally remote Galilean village of Nazareth. There a young maiden, the betrothed of Joseph, was visited by an angel, who informed her that she was to become the mother of the Son of the Highest (Luke 1:26-38).

Shortly after receiving this word, she went to visit her kinswoman, Elisabeth, who was then six months pregnant with John. Their meeting was a time of rejoicing for both women. When Mary returned to Nazareth, however, she had a problem. Before long it became obvious that she was pregnant (Luke 1:39-56). Joseph, not wanting to make a public example of her, decided quietly to break their engagement. But his plan was interrupted by a visit from an angel, who

How to Say It

CYRENIUS. Sye-*ree*-nee-us.
EPHRATH. *Ef*-rath.
QUIRINIUS. Kwih-*rin*-e-us.

convinced him to take Mary as his wife. Without hesitation he followed the orders of the angel (Matthew 1:18-25). This brings us to the beginning of today's printed text.

I. The Birth of Jesus (Luke 2:1-7)

A. Historical Setting (vv. 1, 2)

1. And it came to pass in those days, that there went out a decree from Caesar Augustus, that all the world should be taxed.

The "fulness of the time" had now come. The coming of God's Son into the world was now at hand. The centuries of preparation during the Old Testament period, the annunciation to Mary and Joseph, and the birth of John had all been accomplished. The most important event, the pivotal point in history, was at hand. Yet, without using extravagant language Luke sets forth the birth of Jesus in a calm, straightforward manner.

Luke states that Jesus was born during the reign of *Caesar Augustus* (27 B.C.—A.D.14). By marking this event at a point in history, Luke shows that it is neither myth nor legend but is in the mainstream of human events. Caesar's *decree* went out to *all the world,* that is, the Roman Empire, the world as far as it was ruled by Rome. The decree ordered that an enrollment, or census, be taken. Roman records do not mention this census, but we do know that these were held every fourteen years and that such a census was held in A.D. 6. Projecting backward fourteen years from this date gives us a date within the framework that Luke gives us.

2. (And this taxing was first made when Cyrenius was governor of Syria.)

Luke gives us another reference for anchoring the birth of Jesus firmly in history. He says that the system of taking enrollments on a periodic basis was begun while *Cyrenius,* or Quirinius as most modern translations call him, was governor over the Roman province of Syria. Judea was considered a part of this larger area, although Herod the Great was allowed to rule over the Jews with considerable autonomy. Historical records and archaeological discoveries have shown that Quirinius was governor in some sense of the term both before and after the birth of Jesus, which occurred in about 5 B.C.

B. The Trip to Bethlehem (vv. 3-5)

3. And all went to be taxed, every one into his own city.

The method of the census in Palestine was to have everyone register in his ancestral city or town, perhaps because the family records were kept there. Historical evidence indicates that this method of census taking was used also in Egypt during this period.

4, 5. And Joseph also went up from Galilee, out of the city of Nazareth, into Judea, unto the city of David, which is called Bethlehem, (because he was of the house and lineage of David,) to be taxed with Mary his espoused wife, being great with child.

Joseph lived in *Nazareth,* a small town located in the Galilean hills about fifteen miles west of the southern end of the Sea of Galilee. For Joseph to go to "his own city" meant that he had to travel all the way to *Bethlehem* in Judea. Nor is it likely that he would have taken the shortest route to Bethlehem, for this would have required him to pass through Samaria, and in those days Jews and Samaritans avoided one another whenever possible. As a result, Joseph and Mary would have had to travel nearly one hundred miles. We have become so accustomed to the convenience of modern travel that we can scarcely appreciate how difficult and tiring such a trip would have been. We usually depict Mary riding on the back of a donkey led by Joseph. Such a trip would have taken eight or ten days. We can only guess at the discomfort and fatigue Mary must have experienced on such a trip.

Bethlehem, which means "house of bread," was originally called Ephrath (Genesis 35:19; Micah 5:2). A thousand years earlier, David was born and grew to manhood there. Since Joseph's lineage could be traced back to David (Matthew 1:6-16), it was to Bethlehem that he must go.

Mary his espoused wife. After the angel had made Mary's situation known to him, Joseph had taken Mary for his wife (Matthew 1:18-25). In his account, Luke sets forth the facts of the virgin birth from Mary's viewpoint. Here he states that Mary was the wife of Joseph but indicates her continued virginity by using the term *espoused wife.*

C. Jesus' Birth (vv. 6, 7)

These two verses, sublime in their simplicity, mark the culmination of God's age-old plan to save the world.

6. And so it was, that, while they were there, the days were accomplished that she should be delivered.

While they were there. This expression may mean that Joseph and Mary were in Bethlehem a few days before the child was born. Or it may simply stress the fact that the birth occurred while the couple were *there,* in Bethlehem.

The days were accomplished that she should be delivered. While the conception itself was miraculous, the development in the womb took place in the normal amount of time, and the birth occurred when that time had expired. There is no indication that God intervened to eliminate Mary's inconvenience and suffering.

7. And she brought forth her firstborn son, and wrapped him in swaddling clothes, and laid him in a manger; because there was no room for them in the inn.

Her firstborn son. This clearly implies that after she had given birth to Jesus, Mary bore other children. These were the children of Joseph and Mary. Mark 6:3 names four of the brothers of Jesus and mentions also sisters. (See also Matthew 13:55, 56.)

Wrapped him in swaddling clothes. This statement does not necessarily indicate that Mary, with her own hands, wrapped her babe. It may mean that she gave the directions and Joseph (or anyone else) carried them out.

Laid him in a manger. A manger is a feed trough for animals. Here, perhaps on a bed of straw, the Baby Jesus was placed. Apparently Joseph and Mary had found shelter in a place where animals were lodged. It is possible that they shared that place with other travelers in the crowded town.

There was no room for them in the inn. The little hotel in Bethlehem was crowded, probably because many others came to enroll just as Joseph did. Customarily, the inns were two-story structures built around the four sides of an inner court. The travelers stayed in rooms on the second story, and the animals were stabled on the ground floor. Or perhaps the stables were along one of the outside walls. How often the innkeeper has been berated for being hard-hearted and cruel! Probably he regretted having to turn the inquiring couple away from his inn. Room was simply lacking. It is likely that he showed kindly consideration in allowing them to share the stable with the animals. And so, in such a humble place, the Savior of humankind made His entrance into the world.

PRINCE OF PEACE

One word that could be used to describe world conditions at the time of Christ's birth is *peace.* The "Pax Romana" (Roman Peace) had been in effect, more or less, since 27 B.C. when Caesar Augustus became emperor. From the beginning of his reign, the Mediterranean world had been free from major war. Still, the absence of war could not guarantee the presence of peace.

The Stoic philosopher Epictetus lived later in the first century A.D., when the "Pax Romana" concluded its first century and entered its second. He observed, "While the emperor may give peace from war on land and sea, he is unable to give peace from passion, grief, and envy. He cannot give peace of heart, for which man yearns more than even for outward peace."

How wonderful and satisfying is the peace that the babe of Bethlehem offers! It is an inner tranquillity that surpasses all human understanding. Well did the angels declare "Glory to God in the highest, and on earth peace, good will toward men" (Luke 2:14).

The "Pax Romana" affected only the Roman Empire and the countries that bordered it, and that "peace" eventually came to an end. The stunning truth of the angelic statement lies in the fact that all mankind is eligible for the peace that the Prince of Peace gives, and it lasts a lifetime, and beyond. —T. T.

II. The Presentation of Jesus (Luke 2:22-32)

Forty days passed from Jesus' birth to the time of the event recorded in the last section of our text. Joseph and Mary, with the baby Jesus, had been living in or near Bethlehem. Now they came to the temple in Jerusalem to fulfill the requirements of the law regarding Mary's purification and the child's presentation to the Lord.

A. Fulfilling the Law (vv. 22-24)

22-24. And when the days of her purification according to the law of Moses were accomplished, they brought him to Jerusalem, to present him to the Lord; (as it is written in the law of the Lord, Every male that openeth the womb shall be called holy to the Lord;) and to offer a sacrifice according to that which is said in the law of the Lord, A pair of turtledoves, or two young pigeons.

The law of purification following the birth of a child is recorded in Leviticus 12. After a male child was born, the mother was considered ceremonially unclean for seven days. On the eighth day the son was presented for circumcision, and then for thirty-three more days the mother was not allowed to enter the sanctuary. When the forty days were concluded, she was to make offerings to the Lord. By means of these offerings, she was restored to full communion with all who worshiped Him.

The offerings on this occasion were to be a yearling lamb and a pigeon or turtledove. People too poor to afford the lamb could offer *two pigeons* or two doves. The fact that this was the offering brought by Mary and Joseph is an indication that they were poor.

At this time also, the baby Jesus was presented to God. The firstborn of every species was sanctified to the Lord, in commemoration of the deliverance of Israel's firstborn when they escaped from bondage in Egypt. But the firstborn of a woman, having been publicly consecrated to God, was then redeemed for money (Exodus 12:29, 30; 13:2, 11-15; Numbers 18:15, 16).

B. Simeon's Presence in the Temple (vv. 25-27)

25. And, behold, there was a man in Jerusalem, whose name was Simeon; and the same man was just and devout, waiting for the consolation of Israel: and the Holy Ghost was upon him.

We know nothing about *Simeon* except what we are told here. He was a *just* man in that he was upright before God and man. He was *devout* because he gave himself seriously to serving God and worshiping Him. In his day the priests were corrupt, and the Pharisees, in their efforts to bring religious reform, had become legalistic and arrogant. Yet Simeon, although not in any sense a religious professional, was a truly pious man. We may take heart to know that even when religious corruption seems rampant on every hand, God still has people, often only a small minority, who still love Him and serve Him faithfully.

The *consolation of Israel* was the hope that all pious Jews had for the coming of the Messiah, which would be a time of comfort for the faithful. *The Holy Ghost was upon him.* Simeon believed the promise of Scripture that the Messiah would come; he was *waiting* expectantly. As he did so, he had the rare blessing of being under the constant influence of the Holy Spirit.

26, 27. And it was revealed unto him by the Holy Ghost, that he should not see death, before he had seen the Lord's Christ. And he came by the Spirit into the temple: and when the parents brought in the child Jesus, to do for him after the custom of the law.

We are not told how or when the Holy Spirit communicated to Simeon the fact that he would not die until he had seen the *Lord's Christ,* or "anointed," which is what the word *Christ* means. Sustained by this assurance, Simeon continued in his pious living and patient waiting. Then, just as Joseph and Mary brought the baby Jesus to present Him to the Lord, the Holy Spirit directed Simeon to the temple.

C. Simeon's Blessing (vv. 28-32)

28-32. Then took he him up in his arms, and blessed God, and said, Lord, now lettest thou thy servant depart in peace, according to thy word: for mine eyes have seen thy salvation,

visual 3

The
Light
of Christ
dispels sin's darkness
and draws us
to God.

which thou hast prepared before the face of all people; a light to lighten the Gentiles, and the glory of thy people Israel.

Mary and Joseph must have been surprised when Simeon, a total stranger to them, approached them and asked to hold their baby. If under similar conditions we were approached by a stranger, we would probably be inclined to run or call the police. Fortunately, they lived in "kinder, gentler" days when such behavior would not have been so frightening. On taking the child, Simeon blessed God and then offered up a beautiful hymn or poem.

Simeon was prepared to die in peace now that he had seen God's *salvation,* that is the One through whom that salvation would come. This salvation had been *prepared before the face of all people.* Even though the Messiah would come through the people of Israel and would come as the fulfillment of the numerous prophecies found in the Old Testament, this great blessing would be for the whole world. The Gentiles, all the peoples of the world except the Jews, lived in darkness. For them the coming of the Messiah meant *light* by which they could find their way to God. At the same time the Messiah was the *glory* of the people of Israel. Israel was God's chosen people, and for centuries He had blessed them greatly. But chief among all the honors bestowed by God upon them was the fact that the Christ, who would bring salvation for the whole world, was born of the seed of David.

THE TRUE LIGHT OF CHRISTMAS

Hans Lilje tells the story of a Christmas he spent in a Nazi prison. The commandant took him from his place of solitary confinement to another cell, where he joined two other prisoners. One had a violin, and he played "Silent Night." One had a Bible, and he read the Christmas story. Lilje spoke to them, recalling the sermon he had preached the previous year at Christmas. His text was, "The people that walked in darkness have seen a great light: they that dwell in the land of the shadow of death, upon them hath the light shined" (Isaiah 9:2).

He pointed out to his two fellow prisoners that since they had none of the decorations, none of the festivities, none of the feasts associated with Christmas, all they had left was Christmas itself.

In the darkness of that cell, the abiding presence of Jesus Christ came shining through with brilliance and warmth.

As Simeon's weary eyes gazed upon the babe he held in his arms, he praised God for allowing him this glimpse of His promised salvation. God had fulfilled His promise to all mankind by sending a beacon of hope into a world made dim through sin. Simeon then boldly proclaimed that this babe would light the way of salvation for all humankind. Praise God, that light shines upon us yet today! —T. T.

Home Daily Bible Readings

Monday, Dec. 14—Words of Hope (Isaiah 49:1-6)
Tuesday, Dec. 15—One Is Chosen (Psalm 45:1-7)
Wednesday, Dec. 16—Successor to David's Throne (Isaiah 9:2-7)
Thursday, Dec. 17—The Birth of Jesus (Luke 2:1-7)
Friday, Dec. 18—The Shepherds and the Angels (Luke 2:8-21)
Saturday, Dec. 19—Jesus at the Temple (Luke 2:22-36)
Sunday, Dec. 20—Anna and Baby Jesus (Luke 2:36-40)

Conclusion

A. Hope Realized

God had revealed to Simeon that he would not see death until he had first seen the Messiah. We don't know how many years Simeon had lived with this hope, but the passage of time had not dimmed it for him. Finally it was realized as he held the baby Jesus in his arms. Now he was prepared to leave this life and go on to what God had prepared for him.

We may never be given a special promise, such as the one that God gave to Simeon, but that does not mean that we are without hope. Quite the contrary. Of all religions, Christianity holds out the greatest and most satisfying hope for life beyond this life. We know that the way to that eternal life is through Christ. Realizing this can give us the strength to meet the disappointments of this life with the same calm assurance that Simeon experienced.

B. A Baby for the Whole World

It is interesting to observe the ways that artists around the world have portrayed the Christ child as He lay in His manger bed. To Westerners He is made to look like a Westerner, often with blue eyes and blonde hair. Africans show Him with dark skin and Negroid features. Orientals depict Him as an Oriental. Obviously, such interpretations distort history, for He must have looked like a Jewish baby of the first century.

Yet, if we get beyond our concern for historical accuracy, these varied portrayals of Jesus touch on a very profound truth—Jesus was for all races, all nations. This point was made a number of times in the Old Testament (see Isaiah 42:6; 49:6; 60:1-3; Malachi 1:11). Yet the people of Israel failed to understand. Their pride in being God's chosen people blinded them to the mission God had intended for them and led them to feel that they had an exclusive claim on the blessings the Messiah would bestow. As a result, most of them rejected the Messiah when He finally came.

The question we must ask ourselves is, Do we understand the universal nature of Christ's mission any better than they? We state that we believe God sent His Son to save all the nations, but do we live up to our belief? We rejoice over the coming of God's Son into the world to be *our* Savior, and most appropriately so. May each of us realize that Jesus came to be the Savior for *all*—Jew and Gentile alike. And may we do everything we can to see that those who live in spiritual darkness, whether near or far away, receive the light of God's salvation.

C. Let Us Pray

Dear God and Father, we thank You for sending us Your Son. We marvel at the circumstances of His birth. We thank You for the writers, inspired by the Holy Spirit, who have given us the accounts of Jesus' birth. Even as we become involved in the mystery and marvel of His birth, let us never forget the reason for His coming. May this lesson motivate us to share this wonderful story with others who have never heard it or fully understood its meaning. In the name of the Babe of Bethlehem, we pray. Amen.

D. Thought to Remember

O Holy Child of Bethlehem,
Descend to us we pray;
Cast out our sin and enter in;
Be born in us today.
—Phillips Brooks

Learning by Doing

This page contains an alternate lesson plan emphasizing learning activities. Classes desiring such student involvement will find these suggestions helpful.

Learning Goals

After examining the birth of Jesus and His presentation in the temple, as recorded in Luke 2:1-7, 22-32, the pupil will be able to:

1. Reiterate the events of the birth of Jesus and His presentation in the temple.
2. Explain why Jesus would go through usual Jewish rites and ceremonies.
3. Express gratitude for the birth of Jesus.

Into the Lesson

Have Christmas music playing to set the atmosphere for today's session.

As the class members arrive, have them work in groups of three to five. Ask them to share with each other what their best Christmas was and why it was such a good Christmas. Allot five to seven minutes for this. Then let two or three people share their best Christmas with the entire class (perhaps these can be chosen by the groups).

Make the transition into the Bible study section by reminding the pupils that this lesson will review the events of that first Christmas in Bethlehem. It will remind us of the meaning of Christmas.

Into the Word

Take two to three minutes to present the material in the "Lesson Background" section. Point out that the apostle Paul said that Jesus came in "the fulness of the time" (Galatians 4:4). The *New International Version* translation has, "When the time had fully come." Emphasize that God had prepared the world for this monumental event that would change the course of history.

Refer the pupils back to Luke 2:1-7, 22-32. Develop a discussion using the following questions. (Direct the pupils to appropriate Old Testament Scriptures when discussing questions 5 and 6.

1. Since Joseph and Mary actually lived in Nazareth, why was Jesus born in Bethlehem?
2. What details does Luke give of the birth?
3. What is so striking about the details of this birth?
4. Why would God choose to send His Son in such humble circumstances?
5. According to Luke 2:22-24, what Jewish laws did Joseph and Mary observe on this occasion?
6. What was the historical background and the significance of the presentation of a firstborn child to God?
7. Why would Jesus' parents observe these laws? After all, Jesus came to give something better than the Law.
8. Describe Simeon.
9. What does it mean when it says that Simeon waited for "the consolation of Israel"?
10. How did Simeon respond when he saw the baby Jesus?
11. In a general way, Simeon saw in advance the mission of Christ. Who did he say Jesus came to bless?
12. How do you suppose Simeon felt when he held the baby Jesus?

Into Life

Continue the discussion you have begun by asking the following questions.

1. What do you think is the most appropriate response we can make when we think of Christ's coming into the world?
2. How can we cultivate that kind of response in ourselves and our family members?

Ask the class to work in pairs to continue thinking about our response to Christ's birth. Give each group one of the following questions.

1. Think of your children or grandchildren—or perhaps children with whom you have contact. What are some practical ways to teach them an appropriate response to the wonder of Christmas?
2. What are some things that each of us personally can do to be sure that we capture the wonder of Christmas?
3. What are some practical ways in which our congregation can develop an appropriate response to the wonder of Christmas?

Allot four to six minutes for the groups to do their work. Then list their suggestions on sheets of newsprint, the chalkboard, or an overhead transparency. Encourage each person to select one item from the list to do this year to capture the wonder of Christmas. Let several people share what they have chosen to do.

Conclude the session by singing two or three Christmas carols. Two good choices would be "O Little Town of Bethlehem" and "Silent Night." Close with a prayer of thanksgiving for the gift of the Savior.

Let's Talk It Over

The questions on this page are designed to encourage review of the lesson Scriptures and to promote discussion of the lesson by the class. The answers provided are only discussion starters. Let your class talk it over from there.

1. What does today's lesson teach us about God's control of governmental affairs and "closed doors"?

Human governments and human authorities, at whatever level, ultimately are not in control of life and destiny. In a sentence, the sovereign God is in control of human history. Caesar Augustus exercised his authority by ordering that a census be taken throughout the Roman Empire. And his plans and purposes were carried out. The innkeeper exercised his authority and fulfilled his responsibility in a manner that he thought best. But over and beyond them and what they did stood the God who is in control of all events, the Lord of history. The Christmas story reveals that God's eternal purposes were actually carried forward through the occurrence of these events.

2. What Mosaic laws were Joseph and Mary fulfilling in the event recorded in the second section of today's lesson Scripture?

One Mosaic law had to do with Mary and the other with the baby Jesus, who was her firstborn son. The law excluded a woman from entering the sanctuary until forty days after the birth of a son. At that time she made offerings, and by this means she was declared ceremonially clean and the privilege of worshiping with the community of Israel was again restored to her. (See Leviticus 12:1-8.)

There was also a special law that applied to a woman's firstborn child. When Israel escaped from Egyptian bondage, the firstborn in all the land of Egypt, both human and animal, were slain by the Lord. The firstborn of the Israelites, however, were spared by the application of the blood of the Passover lamb to the doorposts and lintels of the homes of Israel. Thereafter, every firstborn in Israel, whether man or beast, was sacred to the Lord and presented to Him. In the case of animals, the firstborn was sacrificed, or in some instances, redeemed by offering another animal in its place. In every instance, the firstborn of a woman was redeemed by the payment of a ransom fee. It was in connection with the payment of this fee that Joseph and Mary presented the baby Jesus to God. (See Exodus 13:2, 11-15; Numbers 18:15, 16.)

3. List some significant conclusions implied in Simeon's praise and prophecy recorded in Luke 2:29-32.

(1) God is sovereign. (He is Lord of life and history, and He oversees the working out of His eternal plan.)

(2) God keeps His word. (Through the Holy Spirit, the promise was given to Simeon that he would live to see the promised Messiah; and that promise was kept.)

(3) Simeon's life was fulfilled; now he was ready to die. (He could say with contentment, "Now lettest thou thy servant depart in peace.")

(4) God works in the world. (He "prepared" for the coming of Christ through many centuries of Israel's history.)

(5) God's salvation is for *all* people. (The salvation provided by God in the person of Jesus, who was of the lineage of David, was also a light for the Gentiles.) (6) Israel's glory comes to full flowering in Jesus Christ, the Redeemer of the world, who came from their midst. (He is "the glory of thy people Israel.")

4. Many congregations effectively limit their efforts of sharing the good news of Christ to people of a certain race and/or economic level. What do you think of this?

The salvation prepared by God is intended to exclude no one. Therefore, we should strive to open our hearts and our doors to all. It is one thing to say that Jesus is the Savior; it is another thing to say that He is the Savior for all people; it is yet another thing to back up these statements by sharing the gospel with all persons and maintaining an attitude of openness toward them.

5. How can we give peace as a gift to others?

The obvious answer is that we can point them to Jesus Christ, the Prince of Peace. Along with that, however, we can bring some of our neighbors and friends peace merely by listening to their problems and expressing our genuine concern. We can bestow peace on others by asking forgiveness or assuring them of our forgiveness. The gift of peace also may come through our efforts to resolve circumstances that create conflict and frustration in the lives of others.

Jesus Filled With the Spirit

December 27
Lesson 4

LESSON SCRIPTURE: Matthew 3:1—4:11.

PRINTED TEXT: Matthew 3:16—4:11.

DEVOTIONAL READING: John 1:19-34.

Matthew 3:16, 17

16 And Jesus, when he was baptized, went up straightway out of the water: and, lo, the heavens were opened unto him, and he saw the Spirit of God descending like a dove, and lighting upon him:
17 And lo a voice from heaven, saying, This is my beloved Son, in whom I am well pleased.

Matthew 4:1-11

1 Then was Jesus led up of the Spirit into the wilderness to be tempted of the devil.
2 And when he had fasted forty days and forty nights, he was afterward ahungered.
3 And when the tempter came to him, he said, If thou be the Son of God, command that these stones be made bread.
4 But he answered and said, It is written, Man shall not live by bread alone, but by every word that proceedeth out of the mouth of God.
5 Then the devil taketh him up into the holy city, and setteth him on a pinnacle of the temple,
6 And saith unto him, If thou be the Son of God, cast thyself down: for it is written, He shall give his angels charge concerning thee: and in their hands they shall bear thee up, lest at any time thou dash thy foot against a stone.
7 Jesus said unto him, It is written again, Thou shalt not tempt the Lord thy God.
8 Again, the devil taketh him up into an exceeding high mountain, and showeth him all the kingdoms of the world, and the glory of them;
9 And saith unto him, All these things will I give thee, if thou wilt fall down and worship me.
10 Then saith Jesus unto him, Get thee hence, Satan: for it is written, Thou shalt worship the Lord thy God, and him only shalt thou serve.
11 Then the devil leaveth him, and, behold, angels came and ministered unto him.

GOLDEN TEXT: And, lo, the heavens were opened unto him, and he saw the Spirit of God descending like a dove, and lighting upon him: and lo a voice from heaven, saying, This is my beloved Son, in whom I am well pleased.—Matthew 3:16, 17.

Good News for All

Unit 1: Coming of the Good News

(Lessons 1-4)

Lesson Aims

As a result of studying this lesson, the students should:

1. Be able to recount the three temptations mentioned in the text and how Jesus responded to them.
2. Realize that God has provided help for us in meeting temptation.
3. Be more determined to resist the devil's temptations.

Lesson Outline

INTRODUCTION
- A. Learning to Run
- B. Lesson Background

I. JESUS' BAPTISM (Matthew 3:16, 17)
- A. The Presence of the Spirit (v. 16)
- B. The Approval of God (v. 17)

II. THE FIRST TEMPTATION (Matthew 4:1-4)
- A. Food (vv. 1-3)
  When Satan Strikes
- B. Jesus' Response (v. 4)

III. THE SECOND TEMPTATION (Matthew 4:5-7)
- A. To Gain a Following (vv. 5, 6)
- B. Jesus' Response (v. 7)

IV. THE THIRD TEMPTATION (Matthew 4:8-11)
- A. Power (vv. 8, 9)
- B. Jesus' Response (v. 10)
  Method Is Important
- C. Retreat and Respite (v. 11)

CONCLUSION
- A. "The Devil Made Me Do It"
- B. Let Us Pray
- C. Thought to Remember

Display visual 4 of the visuals packet and let it remain before the class throughout this session. The visual is shown on page 149.

Introduction

A. Learning to Run

An alcoholic who had not taken a drink in years was asked if he were ever tempted to drink. "Oh, yes," he replied. "I am frequently tempted. I try to avoid places where I might be tempted—saloons and parties and even friends who drink. But I can't always avoid them."

"How do you handle such temptations?" came the next question.

"My mouth starts to water and my hand begins to shake. I can't keep my mouth from watering or my hand from shaking, but I can run, and that's exactly what I do!"

Jesus was tempted, and if the incarnation means anything, it means that the temptations were real. The desire to accept Satan's offers must have pressed upon Him. When Jesus was faced by these temptations, He met them with His own form of running—He quoted Scripture, and in the end, Satan was forced to run.

B. Lesson Background

Last week's lesson dealt with Jesus' birth and His presentation in the temple. It culminated with the promise that this little Baby would grow up to become a light to the Gentiles, a Savior to the entire world. Following this, Mary and Joseph had to flee to Egypt with the Baby to avoid the wrath of Herod. Eventually they were able to return to Nazareth in Galilee. The only incident that Scripture records of Jesus' youth was His visit to the temple when He was twelve years old. Following that He returned to Nazareth and lived there until He was about thirty.

At this time John the Baptist began his ministry, calling people to repentance and preparing the way for the coming of the Messiah. John soon had a large following, and at the height of his ministry, Jesus came to him to be baptized. At first John refused, insisting that it was more appropriate for himself to be baptized by Jesus. But Jesus insisted that it was fitting for Him to be baptized "to fulfill all righteousness" (Matthew 3:13-15).

I. Jesus' Baptism (Matthew 3:16, 17)

A. The Presence of the Spirit (v. 16)

16. And Jesus, when he was baptized, went up straightway out of the water: and, lo, the heavens were opened unto him, and he saw the Spirit of God descending like a dove, and lighting upon him.

We have no way of knowing the exact location of Jesus' baptism. All we know for certain is that it occurred in the Jordan River (Matthew 3:6). It may very well have been near Jericho at a ford where one of the main travel routes crossed the river. Matthew's description of this scene strongly suggests that Jesus' baptism was by immersion.

As soon as Jesus came out of the water, *the heavens were opened.* This evidently marked some kind of special communion with God or a revelation from Him (see Ezekiel 1:1; Acts 7:56). Then the Holy Spirit descended upon Him *like a dove.* Luke says, "in a bodily form, as a dove" (3:22, *American Standard Version*). It seems probable that others present also saw the dove but did not comprehend the meaning of its lighting upon Jesus. We know that John saw it and understood its significance. This sign had been promised to John to give him absolute assurance of the identity of the Messiah whose arrival he had been proclaiming (John 1:32-34).

B. The Approval of God (v. 17)

17. And lo a voice from heaven, saying, This is my beloved Son, in whom I am well pleased.

On two other occasions later in His ministry, Jesus heard the voice of God. One occurred at the transfiguration on the mountaintop (Matthew 17:5), the other during the last week of His ministry (John 12:23-29). All three came at crucial times. The first came just as He was about to enter His ministry. The second came when His popularity was at its peak, and the third came in the final week as He prepared to die on the cross. In each case these affirmations strengthened Jesus for the task that lay before Him.

II. The First Temptation (Matthew 4:1-4)

A. Food (vv. 1-3)

1. Then was Jesus led up of the Spirit into the wilderness to be tempted of the devil.

Then. Jesus had just been baptized. The time of His great ministry was at hand. The Spirit of God had come to Him, and God's voice from Heaven had proclaimed Him to be God's Son. One might think Jesus would be immune to temptation at such a time of exaltation, but it was not so. The time of exaltation became a special time of temptation. The first decisive leading of the Holy Spirit after His descent upon Jesus was to lead Him forth to bitter combat with the devil. But Jesus was ready for the battle; He was fully prepared. The struggle that was soon to take place would give Him further vital preparation for His ministry to fallen mankind.

It bothers some people that Jesus was *led up of the Spirit.* The Spirit is always supposed to lead us away from temptation not into it, so this line of thinking goes. But that is a shallow misunderstanding of the work of the Spirit. Actually, the Spirit always leads us in the direction we are supposed to go. As a part of *His* ministry, Jesus had to pass through the fires of temptation, and this is where the Spirit led Him.

The *wilderness* into which Jesus was led was probably the wilderness that is located west of the Dead Sea in the southern part of Judea. We are told that John carried on his ministry in the "wilderness of Judea" (Matthew 3:1), and presumably Jesus was baptized in the Jordan where it flows through wilderness for a few miles before it reaches the Dead Sea. It is reasonable, therefore, that the temptation of Jesus took place in the same general area. Today this area is a rugged, barren wasteland with little in it to sustain life. It may have supported more vegetation in Jesus' day, but even then one would have had difficulty finding food or water.

2. And when he had fasted forty days and forty nights, he was afterward ahungered.

When he had fasted forty days and forty nights. We who live in a diet-conscious nation know something of the discomfort that comes from reducing the amount of food we eat. But can we begin to imagine Jesus' physical condition in the desert after eating nothing for this length of time? While one may survive forty days without food, the physical body (apart from a miracle) cannot go forty days without water, and so we assume that Jesus had water during this ordeal. During the rainy season, trickling streams may be found in the desert. We are not to suppose that Jesus suffered this privation because of some masochistic impulse, nor to prove in some macho fashion that He could stand punishment. Probably He was so deep in concentration on God and the ministry into which God was calling Him that for a long time He had no thought of eating. Could one weakness of the church today be that the Lord's people are seldom so wrapped up in prayer and Christian work that they forget to eat?

3. And when the tempter came to him, he said, If thou be the Son of God, command that these stones be made bread.

From verses 2 and 3 of Matthew's account, we might conclude that the devil waited until the forty days had passed, and Jesus was near the point of total exhaustion from His fasting, before he made his advance. Mark's account, however, indicates that the devil tempted Jesus all during the forty days (see Mark 1:13). We conclude, therefore, that the devil tempted Jesus throughout the entire period of forty days and then mounted his supreme assault at the close of the period.

We are well aware that Satan works this way. He is always jabbing and probing, hoping to find a weak place in our defenses. Then when he finds what he thinks is our weakest area, he attacks with full ferocity hoping to cause us to cave in.

If thou be the Son of God. It does not seem likely that Satan was merely daring Jesus to prove that He was the Son of God by performing a miracle. It seems rather that he was trying to get Jesus to doubt God and to use His power for His own benefit. By suggesting that Jesus *command that these stones be made bread,* Satan seemed to be saying, "Look at you; you're near death, and God has deserted you. If you don't take things into your own hands instantly, you will die of starvation. Then how will you do your life's work?"

How many people have been led into sin by a similar lure? "It's too much for you to suffer hardship of any kind," Satan says to us. "You've got to look out for 'number one.' After all, if you don't, who will?" And so, operating under the principle, "A man has to live," many persons excuse any dishonesty or cruelty that seems necessary to promote their physical or material well-being.

WHEN SATAN STRIKES

Albert Barnes, the nineteenth-century Biblical expositor, said, "Satan's temptations are often the strongest immediately after we have been remarkably favoured. Jesus had just been called the Son of God, and Satan took this opportunity to try him. He often attempts to fill us with pride and vain self-conceit when we have been favoured with any peace of mind, or any new view of God, and endeavors to urge us to do something which may bring us low and lead us to sin."

Christmas has just passed, and no doubt each of us has been "remarkably favoured" with gifts and visits of loved ones and the thrill of exciting praise services. For days we have been on a high, filled with exhilaration and joy. But on the journey of life, as on the face of the earth, mountain peaks are always followed by valleys. Therefore, be on guard.

May we learn from Jesus' temptations how cunning Satan is, how he adapts his temptations to times and circumstances, how he makes them artful and plausible. Barnes adds, "How should every one be on his guard at the very *first appearance* of evil, at the first suggestion that may possibly lead to sin!" —T. T.

B. Jesus' Response (v. 4)

4. But he answered and said, It is written, Man shall not live by bread alone, but by every word that proceedeth out of the mouth of God.

Jesus responded by quoting from Deuteronomy 8:3. It seems in this instance that God's word to Jesus was that He should not use His power to provide for His physical needs. Jesus' answer showed that He would neither doubt nor disobey God. He would trust His Heavenly Father to care for Him. Here is help for us all; here is the true way of life; God will care for any person who trusts and obeys Him (see Matthew 6:25, 33).

By turning to Scripture, Jesus gave us an excellent example for dealing with temptation. Of course, in order to quote the appropriate Scripture when it is needed, we must study to know the Word of God. In an age when Biblical illiteracy is a mark of sophistication, we need more than ever to hide the Word of God in our hearts that we might avoid sin.

In our materialistic age, however, the suggestion that the spiritual is more important than the physical does not sell well. A bumper sticker captures the modern mood: "The one who has the most toys at the end of the game wins." Wins what? Not real happiness, not security, not even friends, and certainly not eternal life.

III. The Second Temptation (Matthew 4:5-7)

A. To Gain a Following (vv. 5, 6)

5, 6. Then the devil taketh him up into the holy city, and setteth him on a pinnacle of the temple, and saith unto him, If thou be the Son of God, cast thyself down: for it is written, He shall give his angels charge concerning thee: and in their hands they shall bear thee up, lest at any time thou dash thy foot against a stone.

The holy city is Jerusalem. The *pinnacle of the temple* was a high point of the temple itself, or of one of the other buildings that Herod had built in the temple area. No doubt it was a part of the structure that was in plain view of the worshipers who crowded the courts below.

In His response to Satan's first temptation, Jesus said that a person is to live "by every word that proceedeth out of the mouth of God." Here, in his second temptation, Satan shrewdly turned Jesus' attention to one of God's promises in Scripture concerning Him (Psalm 91:11, 12). If Jesus would cast himself down from this temple pinnacle, Satan implied that Jesus would show that He trusted God's promise to keep Him from harm. Wouldn't this be an example of living by the word God had spoken?

As Jesus looked ahead to His ministry, He knew what it held for Him—three years of slow, patient, and often disappointing teaching and preaching to reach a handful of followers. And then at the end stood the cross. By suggesting that Jesus perform such a spectacular stunt, Satan offered an easy way out. In one bold stroke Jesus could amaze the people and gain a quick following. Jesus intended to win a following, and in His ministry, He did. He won it by doing spectacular things such as healing a paralyzed man, feeding the five thousand, and raising Lazarus from the dead. And then miracles showed that He was the Son of God (John 20:30, 31). But Jesus didn't perform miracles to attract attention to himself or to make His way easier. To the contrary, His miracles at times aroused antagonisms that were life threatening. And each of them had the purpose of meeting need and relieving suffering.

B. Jesus' Response (v. 7)

7. Jesus said unto him, It is written again, Thou shalt not tempt the Lord thy God.

Once more Jesus responded to the devil's offer by quoting Scripture, in this case Deuteronomy 6:16.

By answering as He did, Jesus revealed that Satan had misused God's Word. To do as Satan suggested would not have demonstrated trust in God, nor would it have been living by the word that God had spoken. In reality it would have shown doubt and distrust. Jesus did not need proof that God would keep His word and send angels to save Him from harm. His trust in His Father's care was so complete that no test was needed. Besides, the Scripture clearly forbids such a test, and Jesus was obedient to His Father.

On occasion our service for the Lord may involve us in difficult or dangerous situations. In such situations, we have God's assurance that His protective love overshadows us. Yet this should never be understood in such a way as to encourage our taking unnecessary risks. There is a message here for the brethren who handle poisonous serpents as a part of their worship service just to prove that God will not let them be hurt. Their actions seem to exemplify exactly the kind of thing the devil was tempting Jesus to do. Very different, however, are the actions of a missionary who must invade a serpent-infested jungle to carry the gospel to a remote tribe. The missionary does not enter the jungle in order to seek a confrontation with venomous serpents but to carry out the great commission. And when he goes, he is likely to have some medications available in case he is bitten.

WHEN TEMPTATION COMES . . .

RECOGNIZE *the danger*

RESPOND *with divine truth*

RESIST *with determination.*

THE DEVIL WILL FLEE!

visual 4

IV. The Third Temptation (Matthew 4:8-11)

A. Power (vv. 8, 9)

8, 9. Again, the devil taketh him up into an exceeding high mountain, and showeth him all the kingdoms of the world, and the glory of them; and saith unto him, All these things will I give thee, if thou wilt fall down and worship me.

We have no way of identifying the *exceeding high mountain,* from which this temptation took place. Of course, it is not physically possible to see *all the kingdoms of the world* from a single mountain no matter how high it might be. As a result, some feel that the devil showed Jesus these kingdoms in some kind of a vision. If this was not a vision, Satan may have pointed to the horizon in all directions and described the glory of the lands beyond it.

We see that the temptations Satan put before Jesus had ever-widening appeals: first the satisfaction of His own hunger; then the adulation of Jerusalem; and finally power over the whole world. Again we note that Jesus had come to win the world to himself. In following the path that lay before Him, He would meet resistance, rejection, and finally death. And He knew that even though He would sacrifice His life, a large part of the world would not be won. Satan proposed an easier way. He would withdraw his opposition; he would let Jesus have the world, and He wouldn't have to die to gain it.

If thou wilt fall down and worship me. This was the price tag Satan put on his offer. He would give Jesus the whole world if Jesus would bow to him. With but a little thought, we see the abhorrence of Satan's suggestion. His approach to us may not be as bold and direct. He may simply ask us to compromise a bit: to blur the line that divides right from wrong, to remain silent in the presence of evil. How many persons have sold their integrity and honor for a bit of gold or glory or pleasure? Can we not see that in so doing we are giving ourselves to the devil?

B. Jesus' Response (v. 10)

10. Then saith Jesus unto him, Get thee hence, Satan: for it is written, Thou shalt worship the Lord thy God, and him only shalt thou serve.

God alone is to be worshiped, not idols, nor animals, nor human beings, nor Satan, regardless of how much power he may possess. In its arrogance, this third temptation far surpassed the first two. Satan was suggesting that the whole order of the moral universe be reversed, that the Creator stoop to pay homage to the created. This thought was intolerable, so Jesus would hear no more. "Get out!" He ordered. Once again His response was based on Scripture (see Deuteronomy 6:13).

METHOD IS IMPORTANT

Not long after I became a Christian, one of my old buddies, a World War II veteran who had taken up the beer-drinking habit, said to me, "If you'll drink a bottle of beer with me, I'll give up my drinking." He knew of my conversion to Christ and of my view that such drinking was out of the question in my Christian life.

I thought about his offer for a couple of minutes, rationalizing that my drinking one bottle of beer wouldn't hurt me, and that it might do him a lot of good. But after giving it some thought, I refused. I wanted to have a good influence on him, but I wanted to do it in the right way.

When Satan offered Jesus all the kingdoms of the world and the glory of them, Jesus could have reasoned, "That's what I'm after. I want all the kingdoms to become mine, to honor me." And He does! (Revelation 11:15). But there was a right way and a wrong way to attain this, and the devil's way was as wrong as sin can be. It was not by yielding to the devil, but by fulfilling the Father's plan and purpose that Jesus would lead the peoples of this world to honor Him and His Father. Accomplishments are important, but so is method. —T. T.

C. Retreat and Respite (v. 11)

11. Then the devil leaveth him, and, behold, angels came and ministered unto him.

Home Daily Bible Readings

Monday, Dec. 21—The Birth of Jesus Christ (Matthew 1:18-24)

Tuesday, Dec. 22—Visitors From the East (Matthew 2:1-12)

Wednesday, Dec. 23—The Escape to Egypt (Matthew 2:13-18)

Thursday, Dec. 24—The Return From Egypt (Matthew 2:19-23)

Friday, Dec. 25—The Preaching of John the Baptist (Matthew 3:1-12)

Saturday, Dec. 26—The Baptism of Jesus (Matthew 3:13-17)

Sunday, Dec. 27—The Temptation of Jesus (Matthew 4:1-11)

Satan was forced to leave Jesus in defeat, but Luke 4:13 adds that he left only "for a season." We know that he returned again with the temptations for Jesus to become an earthly king (John 6:15), to put His own will above the Father's will (Matthew 26:39), and to save himself instead of the world (Matthew 27:39-44). Even some of the apostles were instruments in some of his temptations (see Matthew 16:21-23; Luke 9:51-56). This should serve as a warning to us. By the grace of God we may on occasion turn Satan and his temptations away, but we can rest assured that he will return with new temptations.

Following this ordeal, Jesus was ministered to by angels, who brought encouragement for His mind and spirit and perhaps food for His body.

Conclusion

A. "The Devil Made Me Do It"

A comic character of a few years ago had a standard line when caught in some inappropriate activity: "The devil made me do it." If we are honest, we have to admit that on occasion we have used the same or a similar line. There is enough truth in it to make this response plausible. Of course, Satan doesn't make us sin, for we still have the freedom to resist his temptations. But there is no question that Satan is involved any time we sin. Our lesson has some valuable suggestions about how to meet temptations:

1. No one is so righteous that the devil won't tempt him. Even our Lord faced temptation.
2. Satan is clever. His temptations are innocent-appearing and very appealing.
3. The devil tries to get to us at our weakest moments. This may be when we are depressed; but sometimes we are weakest just as we reach a spiritual mountaintop.
4. One of the best ways to overcome temptation is with Scriptural truth. But we have to know Scripture to use it effectively.
5. Even in the most severe temptations, God will provide a way of escape, if we are willing to accept it (1 Corinthians 10:13).
6. Satan is persistent. Be ready always.

B. Let Us Pray

Dear Heavenly Father, help us to recognize temptations when they come, and lead us to accept the way of escape that You provide for each of them. In Jesus' name we pray. Amen.

C. Thought to Remember

"God is faithful, who will not suffer you to be tempted above that ye are able; but will with the temptation also make a way to escape" (1 Corinthians 10:13).

Learning by Doing

This page contains an alternate lesson plan emphasizing learning activities. Classes desiring such student involvement will find these suggestions helpful.

Learning Goals

After examining the temptation of Jesus, described in Matthew 3:16—4:11, the pupil will be able to:

1. Identify the three temptations of Jesus while he was in the wilderness.
2. Explain the significance of each of these temptations.
3. Explain how Jesus overcame temptation.
4. Develop a personal plan for resisting temptation.

Into the Lesson

Before the class session begins, write the word *temptation* prominently on the chalkboard. As the class members arrive, give them paper and pencil and ask them to jot down words that they associate with the word *temptation.* Ask them to share their responses with a neighbor. Allot three or four minutes for this. Then take three or four minutes to let the entire group share with each other their responses. Record these.

Make the transition into the Bible study by stating that temptation is the central theme in today's Bible lesson. Jesus was tempted—and He overcame the temptation.

Into the Word

Begin the Bible study by presenting the material included in the "Lesson Background" section. Then have someone read Matthew 3:16, 17. Lead a brief discussion using these questions:

1. What unusual events surrounded the baptism of Jesus?
2. What was the significance of the voice of God proclaiming His pleasure with Jesus?
3. What was the significance to John of the Spirit's descending like a dove and lighting on Jesus? (See John 1:32-34.)

Have another person read Matthew 4:1-11. Then divide the class into groups of four or five people. Give each group a copy of the questions below and have them discuss them.

1. What were the physical circumstances that preceded Jesus' temptations?
2. Why is it significant that Jesus was severely tempted so soon after His baptism?
3. What was the nature of the first temptation? How did Jesus overcome it?
4. What was the nature of the second temptation? How did Jesus overcome it?
5. What was the nature of the third temptation? How did Jesus overcome it?
6. What did the devil do after the third temptation?

Allot ten to twelve minutes for the groups to work. After the groups have completed their work, use their answers to the questions as the basis for a whole class discussion.

Into Life

Hebrews 4:15 says that Jesus was tempted in every way, just as we are. Continue the discussion by using the following questions:

1. How do you respond to this verse of Scripture?
2. How were Jesus' temptations like the temptations you face?
3. Does it appear that Jesus' temptations differ in any way from those you experience?
4. We have seen how Jesus overcame temptation. How can His example help us?

Divide the class into the same small groups as in the previous section of the lesson. Give each group one of the situations below.

Case 1. Tom travels a great deal on his job. On average he is away from home three nights a week. His work puts him into contact with some attractive women. This is sometimes tempting to Tom, especially when he is particularly lonely. What advice would you give to Tom?

Case 2. Anna has always wanted to be a leader in whatever situation she found herself. She is usually chosen for that role. Sometimes she is tempted to be condescending to those she leads and to manipulate them to get her own way. What advice would you give to Anna?

Case 3. Alan grew up with very few material possessions. Now that he is an adult, he finds it almost second nature to seek more and more money and to buy even more possessions. It gives him a feeling of security to have a growing bank account and all the material possessions that he wants. What advice would you give to Alan?

Give the groups three to five minutes to discuss the situation. Then use their work as the basis for a further discussion about the situations and about how to overcome temptation.

Give each person a small index card. Ask each person to write out a plan for overcoming the strongest temptations he confronts.

Let's Talk It Over

The questions on this page are designed to encourage review of the lesson Scriptures and to promote discussion of the lesson by the class. The answers provided are only discussion starters. Let your class talk it over from there.

1. In the text for this lesson is the statement of God's approval of His Son. What evokes God's approval?

The Father declared that Jesus was well-pleasing to Him because of His spirit of obedience. John the Baptist felt inadequate to baptize Jesus and would have refused, but Jesus insisted that it be done to "fulfill all righteousness." He was doing His Father's will. This perspective and behavior characterized Jesus' life and ministry (John 4:34). What a lesson for all of us!

Children naturally want (and need!) their father's approval. A sense of "the blessing" is bestowed when a father affirms, "You are my child; I love you very much, and I am pleased with you!" We are children of our Heavenly Father. We are assured of His undiminished love for us because of all that He has done on our behalf. We may be just as certain of His approval of us when we are obedient to His revealed will.

2. Was it possible for Jesus to sin? Explain the reasons for your answer.

Theological debate has raged for centuries over this question. In the Latin, the two possibilities were phrased in this way: (1) *non posse pecare* (it was not possible for Jesus to sin); and (2) *posse non pecare* (it was possible for Him not to sin). The second option carries the more weight. If it was not possible for Jesus to sin (option 1), no real temptation could have occurred when Satan made his suggestions to Jesus. That encounter would have been just empty drama, meaningless jousting. But Jesus was truly man (as well as truly God), tempted in all things as we are (Hebrews 4:15). It was possible for Jesus to sin, *but* it was also possible for him *not* to sin (option 2). It was possible that He could live a sinless life and thus be the perfect sacrifice for our sins on Calvary. And that is what He did. He was tempted just as we are, yet He was "without sin" (Hebrews 4:15). God "Made Him [Christ] who knew no sin to be sin on our behalf, that we might become the righteousness of God in Him" (2 Corinthians 5:21, *New American Standard Bible*).

3. At the root of each of the temptations Satan presented to Jesus was a basic question of life each of us must face. What were they?

(1) At what level will you live? Jesus was tempted to use His divine power to satisfy His physical appetite. If He had succumbed to the temptation and changed stones into bread to ease His hunger, He would have chosen the lowest level of existence. He would have made the satisfaction of physical appetites one's most important concern. In refusing this appeal, Jesus chose to live at the highest level: "Man shall not live by bread alone, but by every word that proceedeth out of the mouth of God."

(2) Will you do things God's way? The second temptation was to a short-cut. Instead of taking the long, arduous road to Calvary for the redemption of mankind, Jesus could take a short-cut to glory and win instant followers. If He jumped from the temple pinnacle and suffered no injury or death, the crowds would flock after Him. But Jesus chose to follow the course that God had planned for Him and to trust His Father to fulfill the promises He had made. Therefore He rebutted Satan, "Thou shalt not tempt the Lord thy God."

(3) Who will be supreme? The devil promised Jesus all the world's kingdoms if He would worship him. The temptation of worldly power and glory was rejected in Jesus' choice to give supremacy to God alone: "Thou shalt worship the Lord thy God, and him only shalt thou serve."

4. What is the purpose of fasting and what principles should be followed when a person fasts?

Abstinence from food has gained some recent popularity, both as a physical and spiritual discipline. In Biblical times, fasting usually was intended to help one give complete and serious focus to his or her relationship with God and/or to a significant crisis or concern. Fasting was usually accompanied by fervent prayer. Jesus warned His disciples against fasting as the hypocrites of His day practiced it. They made known the fact that they were fasting so their fellowmen would be impressed by their piety. Such self-advertised piety received no reward from God. Jesus said that fasting is a matter between a person and God only. If one fasts, it is to be a voluntary decision on the part of that individual, and it should be done privately without anyone's knowledge of it.

The Coming of the Holy Spirit

January 3
Lesson 5

LESSON SCRIPTURE: Acts 2.

PRINTED TEXT: Acts 2:1-7, 12-17a.

DEVOTIONAL READING: Acts 2:14-21.

Acts 2:1-7, 12-17a

1 And when the day of Pentecost was fully come, they were all with one accord in one place.

2 And suddenly there came a sound from heaven as of a rushing mighty wind, and it filled all the house where they were sitting.

3 And there appeared unto them cloven tongues like as of fire, and it sat upon each of them.

4 And they were all filled with the Holy Ghost, and began to speak with other tongues, as the Spirit gave them utterance.

5 And there were dwelling at Jerusalem Jews, devout men, out of every nation under heaven.

6 Now when this was noised abroad, the multitude came together, and were confounded, because that every man heard them speak in his own language.

7 And they were all amazed and marveled, saying one to another, Behold, are not all these which speak Galileans?

. . . .

12 And they were all amazed, and were in doubt, saying one to another, What meaneth this?

13 Others mocking said, These men are full of new wine.

14 But Peter, standing up with the eleven, lifted up his voice, and said unto them, Ye men of Judea, and all ye that dwell at Jerusalem, be this known unto you, and hearken to my words:

15 For these are not drunken, as ye suppose, seeing it is but the third hour of the day.

16 But this is that which was spoken by the prophet Joel;

17a And it shall come to pass in the last days, saith God, I will pour out of my Spirit upon all flesh.

GOLDEN TEXT: They were all filled with the Holy Ghost, and began to speak with other tongues, as the Spirit gave them utterance.—Acts 2:4.

Good News for All

Unit 2: Living the Good News

(Lessons 5-9)

Lesson Aims

After this lesson, students should:

1. Have a better understanding of the events that occurred on Pentecost.
2. Understand that the coming of the Holy Spirit on Pentecost was the fulfillment of prophecy.
3. Seek ways to be channels through whom the Spirit-revealed message in the New Testament can be given to a lost world.

Lesson Outline

INTRODUCTION
- A. A New Era Begins
- B. Lesson Background

I. THE COMING OF THE SPIRIT (Acts 2:1-4)
- A. Time and Place (v. 1)
- B. Accompanying Phenomena (vv. 2-4)

II. RESPONSES OF THE ONLOOKERS (Acts 2:5-7, 12, 13)
- A. The Gathering Multitude (vv. 5, 6)
- B. Amazement (v. 7)
- C. Meaning Sought (v. 12)
  The Strange and Unusual
- D. Mocking by Some (v. 13)

III. PETER'S EXPLANATION (Acts 2:14-17a)
- A. Critics Answered (vv. 14, 15)
- B. Prophecy Fulfilled (vv. 16, 17a)
  Filled With the Spirit

CONCLUSION
- A. A Unique Event
- B. Let Us Pray
- C. Thought to Remember

Display visual 5 of the visuals packet and refer to it as you proceed through this lesson. The visual is shown on page 157.

Introduction

A. A New Era Begins

A town had been built along the banks of a large river. There was no bridge across the river, and so the people had to go many miles upstream or downstream to cross to the other side. The town had grown into a small city, but still there was no bridge. For many years the citizens had urged the state to build a bridge across the river, but there never seemed to be enough money in the budget for the project. Finally, however, their petitions were heard and the bridge was built.

Then the day came for the governor to visit their city and dedicate the new bridge. Citizens lined the streets for the parade that was a part of the ceremonies. First came a military color guard, holding high the flags. Then came baton twirlers, and the drum major, strutting before the band that loudly played a majestic marching number. Finally came the open auto carrying the governor and his entourage. Cheers went up as the people voiced their joy at the long-awaited event that would dramatically change their lives, the beginning of a new era.

This in a way resembles what happened on Pentecost. A great crowd had assembled for the feast. This crowd represented the people who for centuries had longed for the coming of the Messiah. Then suddenly came the phenomena that heralded the arrival of the Holy Spirit, whose purpose was to announce the beginning of the Messianic kingdom, an event that would dramatically change their lives.

B. Lesson Background

The general theme for the lessons of this quarter is "Good News for All." Unit 1, the first four lessons, dealt with the coming of Jesus Christ, who is the good news. Today's study is the first lesson in Unit 2, "Living the Good News." The five lessons in this unit deal with God's new community, the church.

Quite appropriately, this first lesson describes some of the events that occurred on Pentecost, when the church had its beginning. In the forty-day period following His resurrection, Jesus made several appearances to His disciples. At the conclusion of this period, He led the eleven out to the brow of the Mount of Olives where He was taken up from them and disappeared in a cloud (Luke 24:50, 51; Acts 1:6-12).

Before Jesus left them, He repeated the commission He had previously given them. The disciples were to be His witnesses, beginning at Jerusalem and then carrying that message to the remotest parts of the world. Before they began this mission, however, they were to return to Jerusalem and wait there until they were empowered from on high. During the ten-day period between the ascension and Pentecost, the disciples and other followers of Jesus, numbering about one hundred twenty, continued to meet and lift up their prayers and supplications. Also during this period, Matthias was chosen to take the place of Judas, who had hanged himself.

I. The Coming of the Spirit (Acts 2:1-4)

A. Time and Place (v. 1)

1. And when the day of Pentecost was fully come, they were all with one accord in one place.

Pentecost was the second of the three great annual religious festivals among the Jews. It fell fifty days after the Sabbath of the Passover (Leviticus 23:15, 16). The name *Pentecost* came from the Greek word for "fifty." This feast was variously called the "feast of weeks," the "feast of first fruits," and the "feast of harvest." It was observed as a kind of thanksgiving day on which the firstfruits of the wheat harvest were offered to God (Exodus 23:16). Pentecost was observed also as an anniversary of the giving of the law on Mount Sinai.

They were all with one accord. Who are *they?* Some hold that it was the twelve apostles only, while others insist that it was the one hundred twenty mentioned in Acts 1:15. English grammar would indicate that the antecedent of *they* is found in the previous verse—the last verse of chapter 1—and is the eleven, now twelve, with Matthias. But Greek does not follow the same grammatical rules, so we can't say for certain.

In one place. Where was the *place* that they met? Some have suggested that it was the upper room where Jesus and His twelve apostles had met for the Last Supper. Others feel it was in the home of a believer or in a room of the temple. Again we have to acknowledge that we don't know. One thing is certain, however: they met *with one accord,* they were united.

B. Accompanying Phenomena (vv. 2-4)

2. And suddenly there came a sound from heaven as of a rushing mighty wind, and it filled all the house where they were sitting.

Suddenly the hour for which they had been waiting came, the moment when they would witness the outpouring of the Holy Spirit. At Jesus' baptism, the Spirit was represented by a dove, but here the symbol is more powerful. We are not told that a strong wind accompanied the Spirit's coming; rather, there was the *sound* as of a mighty wind. This sound filled the room where they were sitting. If this was a room of the temple, then undoubtedly the sound was heard beyond the confines of the room, drawing the attention of the many worshipers in the temple courts.

3. And there appeared unto them cloven tongues like as of fire, and it sat upon each of them.

The sound of the wind was immediately followed by that which looked like tongues of fire coming and resting on them. *Cloven tongues* does not mean forked tongues. The word means "being distributed." Perhaps one flame-like tongue appeared and then separated and a portion came to rest on each of them. Some hold that the fiery-looking tongues rested upon all of the one hundred twenty who were present. While this question cannot be answered with absolute certainty, the context seems to suggest that only the apostles experienced this. This visual image of flame-like tongues resting on each of these men would have strongly reinforced the audible symbol of the Spirit's presence afforded by the sound of the rushing wind.

4. And they were all filled with the Holy Ghost, and began to speak with other tongues, as the Spirit gave them utterance.

Just before Jesus ascended into Heaven, He promised the apostles that they would soon be baptized with the Holy Spirit (Acts 1:5). This event on Pentecost was the fulfillment of that promise. The expressions to "be baptized" and to be *filled* with the Holy Spirit suggest that the apostles were engulfed by the Spirit so completely that in this moment He, rather than their own minds, controlled their words. The result was that they began to *speak with other tongues,* that is, in languages not their own. That these were human languages normally spoken by other national groups is made evident by verses 8-11. The purpose of this gift was twofold: first, it allowed the apostles to communicate more effectively with those Jews who had come from foreign countries and who either did not understand or were not fluent in the language that was spoken by the Jews of Palestine. Since a most vital message was soon to be delivered to them, it was important that they be able to understand it. So, by the Spirit's power, every person present heard and understood the one gospel in their native language. A second purpose was to validate the messengers. The miracle of tongues would help convince the hearers that day that the messengers were indeed sent from God.

As the Spirit gave them utterance. This expression suggests that *what* the apostles said as well as the ability to express the message in a foreign human language came from the Holy Spirit.

How to Say It

MATTHIAS. Muh-*thigh*-us (*th* as in *thin*).
SINAI. *Sye*-nay-eye or *Sye*-nye.

II. Responses of the Onlookers (Acts 2:5-7, 12, 13)

A. The Gathering Multitude (vv. 5, 6)

5. And there were dwelling at Jerusalem Jews, devout men, out of every nation under heaven.

On the occasion of a major religious feast such as Pentecost, Jerusalem was crowded with people. There were, of course, those native born Jews who made their homes there. Also dwelling there were *devout men, out of every nation under heaven.* This phrase describes two groups of Jews. The first were descendants of those people who had been scattered throughout the world as a result of the captivities of Old Testament times. These Jews had spent most of their lives in other lands, but had returned to the holy city to live out the rest of their lives near the temple. The second group were those Jews who had come from various nations, where they were making their homes, to worship at the feast of Pentecost and who thus were only temporarily staying in the city. Verses 9-11 indicate how diverse were the areas from which they had come.

6. Now when this was noised abroad, the multitude came together, and were confounded, because that every man heard them speak in his own language.

The people in the city no doubt heard the sound of wind and rushed out into the streets and into the temple area to find out what was causing all the commotion. By this time, the apostles had left the house or the room of the temple, where they had been meeting when the Holy Spirit came upon them, and they had gone out into the street or the temple court. The flame-like tongues presumably were still hovering above their heads, which certainly would have attracted the gathering crowd's attention. As the people thronged around the apostles, each national group heard these men speak to them in their native language. When one considers all of the extraordinary phenomena that the multitude experienced—the sound of a mighty wind, with no wind; fire-like tongues hovering over a group of men; each person hearing these men speak in his own language—there is little wonder that they were confounded, or bewildered.

B. Amazement (v. 7)

7. And they were all amazed and marveled, saying one to another, Behold, are not all these which speak Galileans?

In the previous verse we were told that the people were bewildered because they heard the message of the twelve in their own language. In this verse we see that their amazement was compounded by the fact that the apostles were Galileans. Galilee was a rather remote province, where there were no great centers of intellectual or religious culture. The standards of education were subnormal. Therefore people from Galilee had a reputation for being ignorant and unsophisticated, a people not likely to have natural linguistic skills. This amazement would cause the people to rivet their attention on the apostles. It might also cause them to attribute their language skills to God rather than to the men themselves.

C. Meaning Sought (v. 12)

12. And they were all amazed, and were in doubt, saying one to another, What meaneth this?

Once more Luke informs us that all the people were *amazed.* He adds, *and were in doubt,* that is, perplexed. Apparently they were so moved by what they had seen and heard that their bewilderment lasted for some time. Without any prior experience similar to this to guide them, they had no way of explaining what it could mean. They were amazed as they realized they were hearing unlearned men speak in the language that was native in the land from which they had come. That amazement grew as they realized that people from other lands were also hearing the message in their native tongues.

These people were aware that this experience was more than just a stunt, some sideshow trick. That is the reason they searched for its meaning. Little did they realize that they were standing at one of the great pivotal points in human history. They were soon to hear the first gospel sermon that would launch the church.

THE STRANGE AND UNUSUAL

It was more than a quarter of a century ago, but I remember the night vividly, as though it were a night last week.

Another missionary and I, serving in old Southern Rhodesia (now Zimbabwe), were novices. Neither of us had lived in Africa's bush country for more than a few months. Hearing drums and strange sounds coming from a distant spot, and seeing the lighted sky from a large campfire, we decided to investigate, to determine what was happening in this part of our newly adopted world. To be honest, we were both a little frightened. The blackness of the African night, coupled with the unusual sounds we kept hearing put a fear in us that contributed to our conclusion that some drunken orgy, or worse, was in progress.

We rode part of the distance, then walked, and wound up half crawling to get as near the activity as we dared (which I must confess wasn't very close!). Using recorders we taped the noises, lingered a while, and then returned to the safety of the mission station, convinced that we had played the roles of heroes.

That illusion was soon dispelled, for on the following night another new missionary went to the gathering, which, it turned out, was a church meeting of local Christians!

The coming of the Holy Spirit on Pentecost was an unusual incident, at first bringing fear and confusion to the people of Jerusalem and causing some to make a false assumption (see Acts 2:13). Soon, however, Peter's explanation of the event brought great rejoicing, which continues to this day (Acts 2:16, 39). —T. T.

D. Mocking by Some (v. 13)

13. Others mocking said, These men are full of new wine.

In every large crowd there are likely to be skeptics who question almost everything, especially those things that may have any religious meaning. Instead of trying to find out the significance of the speaking in tongues, these mockers sought to pass it off with a sneer. For them it was easier to brush away this extraordinary occurrence with a snide remark than it was to examine it. Perhaps they feared that discovering the meaning of this obviously miraculous event might have required them to alter their value systems or change their life-styles. Unfortunately, their number is legion today.

The apostles were speaking to the crowd about "the wonderful words of God" (v. 11). These irreverent mockers could offer no better explanation than that the speakers were drunk. The charge was obviously ridiculous, and Peter dismissed it in the opening remarks of his address that begins in the next verse.

III. Peter's Explanation (Acts 2:14-17a)

A. Critics Answered (vv. 14, 15)

14, 15. But Peter, standing up with the eleven, lifted up his voice, and said unto them, Ye men of Judea, and all ye that dwell at Jerusalem, be this known unto you, and hearken to my words: for these are not drunken, as ye suppose, seeing it is but the third hour of the day.

Peter, standing up with the eleven. Matthias had been added to the group of apostles, taking Judas's place. So once more the apostles numbered twelve. *Men of Judea.* This is translated by the *New International Version* as "Fellow Jews." Perhaps Peter had in mind those who were native to Palestine. *Ye that dwell at Jerusalem* may refer to those who had moved to Jerusalem from other lands or who had come to Jerusalem to observe the feast of Pentecost (see verse 5). He answered the charge that the apostles were drunk by reminding his audience that it was but the *third hour of the day,* nine A. M. according to the way we count time. This was the morning hour of prayer, and devout Jews normally would not eat, much less drink, before this time. So it was highly unlikely that their speaking in tongues was some kind of alcoholic revelry. The keenness of Peter's answer showed that he was not drunk, and his discourse demonstrated it.

B. Prophecy Fulfilled (vv. 16, 17a)

16, 17a. But this is that which was spoken by the prophet Joel; And it shall come to pass in the last days, saith God, I will pour out my Spirit upon all flesh.

Peter completed his rebuttal of the charge of drunkenness by pointing out the real meaning of the speaking in tongues. It was the fulfillment of the prophecy in Joel 2:28-32. In this prophecy Joel looked forward to the coming of the Holy Spirit, which would usher in the Messianic kingdom.

The last days. From Joel's viewpoint, the last days would be the whole period from Christ until the end of the present world order. Not all of what Joel prophesied took place on Pentecost, but Peter indicated that what did happen then was included in Joel's prophecy.

Upon all flesh. Although Peter at the time may not have understood the full implications of this promise, it clearly pointed to the fact that the blessing of the Spirit would not be limited to the Jews but would spread to the whole world. While all did not receive the gift of speaking in tongues, all could receive the gift of the Holy Spirit, which Peter mentioned at the conclusion of his sermon (Acts 2:38).

THE COMING OF THE
HOLY SPIRIT
ANTICIPATED IN PROPHECY
ANNOUNCED BY JESUS
AWAITED BY DISCIPLES
ATTESTED BY POWER
PENTECOST

visual 5

FILLED WITH THE SPIRIT

The story is told that in a certain church school the daily custom in one of the classes was for each of the students to recite a portion of the Apostles' Creed. The first student would begin, "I believe in God the Father Almighty," followed by the second student's, "Creator of heaven and earth," and so on until the entire Creed was spoken. One morning the recitation was proceeding as usual until there was a silence. "What's wrong?" the instructor asked. One of the students replied, "The boy who believes in the Holy Spirit isn't here today."

We in the church claim belief in the Holy Spirit, but sometimes our actions betray our words. Confused because of false claims by some regarding the Spirit, many of God's people act as if the Spirit were an "it" rather than a "He"—living, active, and powerful being. Yet all who have accepted Christ as Savior have received the gift of the Holy Spirit (Acts 2:38).

In his Pentecost sermon, Peter quoted Joel: "In the last days, God says, I will pour out my Spirit on all people" (*New International Version*). Indeed, that very Spirit of God has been poured out and made available. He is given to Christians as a comforter, teacher, guide, intercessor in prayer, and an indwelling gift. Let us not fear His presence, but rejoice because He has come into our lives.

—T. T.

Conclusion

A. A Unique Event

To most the term *Pentecost* signifies only one thing—the coming of the Holy Spirit. This day is of such eternal importance that all the other Jewish Pentecosts are forgotten.

Home Daily Bible Readings

Monday, Dec. 28—The Pentecost Festival (Leviticus 23:15-22)

Tuesday, Dec. 29—The Coming of the Holy Spirit (Acts 2:1-13)

Wednesday, Dec. 30—Peter's Message (Acts 2:14-21)

Thursday, Dec. 31—Peter's Plea (Acts 2:22-28)

Friday, Jan. 1—Peter's Response (Acts 2:29-37)

Saturday, Jan. 2—Peter's Appeal (Acts 2:38-41)

Sunday, Jan. 3—Life Among the Apostles (Acts 2:42-47)

This was indeed a once-for-all occasion. Every phase of it is unique. Repetition of it is impossible and unnecessary.

Coming, as it did, close after the world-shaking events of Christ's crucifixion, resurrection, and ascension, it had upon it the focused rays of prophecy and promise: "I will build my church"; "I will give unto thee the keys of the kingdom of heaven"; "I will send him [the comforter]"; "Repentance and remission of sins should be preached in his name . . . beginning at Jerusalem"; and "Ye shall be baptized with the Holy Ghost not many days hence."

Central figures in this Pentecost were the apostles, once for all chosen by Christ himself. One by one they were removed from earth's scenes when their work was done. Another such Pentecost could not be without other apostles of another Lord and Christ.

There is neither a need nor an occasion for a repetition of the event that occurred on the day of Pentecost. It accomplished its purpose. It brought into the world God's Holy Spirit to empower the apostles for convincing testimony to Christ; to bring the gift of prophecy, by which the New Testament message was revealed; to inspire the teaching which established and built the church; to comfort the faithful; and to transform the world by the entrance of a new power and motivating force. The Spirit having come and His work established, He would have to withdraw and His work be destroyed before another such occasion would be necessary.

In our own time we have an important function as channels of the message the Holy Spirit inspired the apostles to deliver on the day of Pentecost.

We need not claim special inspiration, for we do not have it. We do have, on the other hand, the Spirit-revealed message in the New Testament. The world needs that message as much today as when it first came. And we are the ones who can give it to them.

B. Let Us Pray

Dear Father in Heaven, we thank You that You have sent us the Holy Spirit to be our Comforter in times of stress, our Intercessor when we come to you in prayer. May the Spirit reveal Your will to us through the Scriptures, and may He guide our lives into that unity for which our Master prayed. We ask all of this in Jesus' precious name. Amen.

C. Thought to Remember

The church was begun with the coming of the Holy Spirit on Pentecost. Without the Spirit today, the church would be a lifeless body.

Learning by Doing

This page contains an alternate lesson plan emphasizing learning activities. Classes desiring such student involvement will find these suggestions helpful.

Learning Goals

After studying the coming of the Holy Spirit, which is recorded in Acts 2:1-17a, the pupils will:

1. Be able to recount the events that occurred on the Day of Pentecost.
2. Understand the significance of the Spirit's coming on Christ's messengers.
3. Select one way to share God's message of salvation with someone who is lost in sin.

Into the Lesson

Before the class session begins, prepare an acrostic sheet for each member of your class. Each sheet should have the instructions given below and the words *Holy Spirit* printed on it vertically. As the class members arrive, give each one a copy of the acrostic and ask them to complete it. (The other words shown in the sample are for the teacher's convenience and should be omitted from the sheets given to the pupils.)

Acrostic

What words or phrases come to mind when you think of the Holy Spirit? Complete this acrostic by writing words or phrases that start with each letter of the words *Holy Spirit* and that relate to His coming as recorded in the second chapter of Acts.

H—elper
O—ld Testament prophecy fulfilled
L—anguages
Y—our gift

S—ound
P—entecost
I—ndwells Christians
R—Real
I—n own language
T—ongues of fire

Allot five or six minutes for the students to do their work. When most of them have completed the acrostic, take three or four minutes to complete a master acrostic on the chalkboard, using the contributions of the class members.

Make the transition into the Bible study by stating that the work of the Holy Spirit on the Day of Pentecost is the subject for today's Bible lesson.

Into the Word

Begin the Bible study portion of this session with a brief presentation of the material included in the "Lesson Background" section. Point out that the event presented for study occurred on the Day of Pentecost. Have a class member, assigned ahead of time, give a two- to three-minute report on Israel's feast of Pentecost. Then discuss the following questions.

1. What was the first sign of the coming of the Spirit?
2. What two other phenomena occurred when the Spirit came on Pentecost?
3. What was the purpose of the gift of other languages given by the Spirit?
4. What was the response of the people when they heard these Galileans speaking in their own native languages?
5. How did Peter explain the phenomena that these people were observing?
6. What can we conclude about the function and purpose of the Spirit based upon this passage? (The Spirit's function is to lead people to acknowledge the word of God.)

Into Life

Continue by using the following questions.

1. How did the coming of the Holy Spirit on the Day of Pentecost differ from the modern gift of the the Spirit as it is defined in most churches? (The Spirit enabled the apostles to speak in understandable languages rather than what is often called a prayer language.)
2. On Pentecost the Spirit came forcefully and with visible signs. These manifestations of the Spirit were necessary in the first presentation of the gospel in Jerusalem. But in many other examples of conversions recorded in the New Testament there is no such outpouring of the Spirit. What conclusion may we draw from this regarding evangelism today? (We may well conclude that we need not expect the Spirit to operate in these extraordinary ways.)
3. What one advantage do we today have that those on Pentecost did not have for leading others into the way of Christ? (We have the New Testament inspired by the Spirit to guide us into the way of life eternal.)

Conclude by challenging each pupil to share the message of salvation with one person this week who is outside of Christ.

Let's Talk It Over

The questions on this page are designed to encourage review of the lesson Scriptures and to promote discussion of the lesson by the class. The answers provided are only discussion starters. Let your class talk it over from there.

1. What differences may be noted regarding the way the Holy Spirit is presented in the Old Testament and the way He is presented in the New Testament?

In the Old Testament, God's Holy Spirit is depicted in terms of *power*—as with wind or breath (which energizes). In Ezekiel 37, the vision of the valley of dry bones coming to life again was a picture of captive Israel empowered by God's Spirit to new life in their own land. The prophet Micah noted that he was filled with power by the Spirit of the Lord (Micah 3:8). In the New Testament, the Holy Spirit is viewed essentially as a *person*, rather than power. Thus Jesus refers to the Holy Spirit as "He," not as "it." In John 16:6-15, for example, the Holy Spirit is referred to exclusively as a person. In the Trinity, three *persons* are identified: the Father, the Son, and the Holy Spirit.

In the old dispensation, the Holy Spirit came to relatively few persons, and abode with them temporarily. The newness of the Pentecostal gift was that the Spirit was given to all followers of the Lord and was to remain with them as a permanent gift. When Peter announced the terms on which the multitudes would be received in the new dispensation, he promised not only the forgiveness of sins, but the gift of the Holy Spirit, adding that "the promise is unto you, and to your children, and to all that are afar off, even as many as the Lord our God shall call" (Acts 2:39). The divine gift was to continue in the church of the future as the blessing for every consistent Christian.

2. On the Day of Pentecost, did the apostles speak in tongues unknown to men?

Definitely not! These men spoke in "other tongues" (v. 4) but not "unknown tongues," which needed interpretation. All of the tongues used were familiar to some portion of the audience. What they did facilitated, rather than impeded, communication.

3. What was the purpose of the "gift of tongues" given on Pentecost?

Several purposes may be seen. (1) As the crowds gathered, their attention would have been drawn to these men who were speaking in tongues. (2) The apostles were thus enabled to communicate in the native tongue of every person in the audience. This ensured an accurate presentation and understanding of their message. (3) It was a validation of the messengers. It was obvious that a miracle had occurred. The supernatural nature of this occurrence was confirming evidence that the message that was preached was of God. The speaking in tongues recorded in our lesson is different from that recorded in 1 Corinthians 12, where an interpreter is needed.

4. What symbolic and practical significance may be seen in the fact that the church was established on Pentecost, which was one of Israel's major feasts?

Pentecost came at the end of the grain harvest, and it was celebrated with joyous observance as a kind of thanksgiving day. It was observed also as an anniversary of the giving of the law on Mount Sinai. Both this and the harvest element made it an appropriate symbolic background for the establishment of the church. Joy at the end of wheat harvest was superseded by greater joy at the beginning of Christ's harvest of souls. The anniversary of the giving of the Old Covenant through Moses became the occasion for the establishment of the New Covenant through Christ.

Throngs of people flooded Jerusalem for this feast, coming not only from all of Palestine but from many other lands. When they returned home, they took the gospel of redemption with them. Hence that message was given rapid and wide distribution from its very beginning.

5. What is the role of the Holy Spirit in the lives of Christians today?

He indwells, guides, and empowers. He is God's presence in the lives of His people.

6. How may we summarize the thrust of the Joel passage?

It would be easy to get so involved in an effort to identify the specific literal meaning of each phrase that the overall thrust of the passage would be missed. The prophet was indicating that a great spiritual dynamic would usher in a new era in human affairs. This is precisely what the gospel did.

A Call to Holy Living

January 10
Lesson 6

LESSON SCRIPTURE: 1 Peter 1:3-25.

PRINTED TEXT: 1 Peter 1:13-25.

DEVOTIONAL READING: 1 Peter 2:1-10.

1 Peter 1:13-25

13 Wherefore gird up the loins of your mind, be sober, and hope to the end for the grace that is to be brought unto you at the revelation of Jesus Christ;

14 As obedient children, not fashioning yourselves according to the former lusts in your ignorance:

15 But as he which hath called you is holy, so be ye holy in all manner of conversation;

16 Because it is written, Be ye holy; for I am holy.

17 And if ye call on the Father, who without respect of persons judgeth according to every man's work, pass the time of your sojourning here in fear:

18 Forasmuch as ye know that ye were not redeemed with corruptible things, as silver and gold, from your vain conversation received by tradition from your fathers;

19 But with the precious blood of Christ, as of a lamb without blemish and without spot:

20 Who verily was foreordained before the foundation of the world, but was manifest in these last times for you,

21 Who by him do believe in God, that raised him up from the dead, and gave him glory; that your faith and hope might be in God.

22 Seeing ye have purified your souls in obeying the truth through the Spirit unto unfeigned love of the brethren, see that ye love one another with a pure heart fervently:

23 Being born again, not of corruptible seed, but of incorruptible, by the word of God, which liveth and abideth for ever.

24 For all flesh is as grass, and all the glory of man as the flower of grass. The grass withereth, and the flower thereof falleth away:

25 But the word of the Lord endureth for ever. And this is the word which by the gospel is preached unto you.

GOLDEN TEXT: As he which hath called you is holy, so be ye holy in all manner of conversation.—1 Peter 1:15.

Good News for All

Unit 2: Living the Good News

(Lessons 5-9)

Lesson Aims

As a result of studying this lesson, each student should:

1. Understand that God's standards for human conduct are not arbitrary but are based on His holiness.
2. Understand that human life is brief and quickly passing.
3. Have a growing appreciation for the Scriptures as the revelation of God's standards for human conduct.
4. Be better able to translate Biblical teaching into practical daily conduct.

Lesson Outline

INTRODUCTION
- A. "You Can't Define Holiness"
- B. Lesson Background

I. OBEDIENT CHILDREN (1 Peter 1:13-16)
- A. Mental Activity Required (v. 13)
- B. Modeled After the Father (vv. 14, 15)
- C. Motivated by the Word (v. 16)
  People Become Like Their Gods

II. REASONS FOR REVERENCE (1 Peter 1:17-21)
- A. The Coming Judgment (v. 17)
- B. The Cost of Redemption (vv. 18, 19)
- C. The Consecrated Offering (vv. 20, 21)

III. THE NEW LIFE (1 Peter 1:22-25)
- A. Exceptional Love (v. 22)
  True Love
- B. Everlasting Life (v. 23)
- C. Enduring Word (vv. 24, 25)

CONCLUSION
- A. Holy Is as Holy Does
- B. Let Us Pray
- C. Thought to Remember

Display visual 6 of the visuals packet and let it remain before the class throughout this session. The visual is shown on page 164.

Introduction

A. "You Can't Define Holiness"

Years ago a friend and I, both students in a Bible college, were driving out of the city, heading for our weekend preaching points. As we neared the city limits, we saw a hitchhiker, obviously also a student, and so we stopped and picked him up. It soon developed that he also was a student preacher on the way to his church. He was attending another school in our city, one that had a reputation for putting a strong emphasis on holiness.

It was not long before we were in a rather intense theological discussion, especially about holiness. He insisted that one must have holiness to be saved, a position that both my friend and I readily accepted. Our differences became apparent when we asked him to define what he meant by holiness. "You can't define it, but you'll know when you get it," he insisted. His understanding of holiness was that it was essentially an emotion, and his implication quite obviously was that neither of us had it.

By then we had turned onto the main highway, which gave him an opportunity to change the subject. "Last week I was driving down this highway and I hit ninety going down this stretch," he said.

Just ahead I saw a large speed limit sign: "SPEED LIMIT—50 MPH." Calling his attention to the sign, I asked, "How does your driving ninety in a fifty-mile-an-hour zone square with your doctrine of holiness?"

He paused a moment and then replied, "Brother, you can't define holiness. You just have to get it and then you'll know it."

I will readily agree that holiness involves emotions—awe, humility, love—but it also involves actions. At least that's what Peter tells us in this lesson. While he does not give us a long list of things we must do or things we must avoid, he makes it clear that to be holy we must engage in those activities that bring honor to God and we must avoid those that bring Him dishonor.

B. Lesson Background

The Scripture text for today's lesson is taken from 1 Peter. The introduction to this letter identifies the apostle Peter as its author (1 Peter 1:1). Since Peter according to tradition was martyred about A.D. 67, we are inclined to date this letter somewhat near that time. A major focus of 1 Peter is the future glory that awaits the Lord's people. A fitting and necessary subject in conjunction with this emphasis is holiness. The first chapter of this epistle deals largely with the personal aspects of holiness.

The Greek word here translated "holy" has the root meaning of "separated" or "set aside." The same word is regularly used in the New Testament to designate Christians and is translated "saints." Christians are people who are separated from the world and are consecrated to God. Inherently, the term *holy* has ethical content. Persons who are thus separated and consecrated are not to participate in the world's immorality and impurity. Though Christians are called saints, holy ones, the Scriptures do not imply that moral purity has been realized in their lives. It always assures, however, that such purity is the ideal and that they are obliged to strive toward it.

In our lesson text, God is declared to be holy (1 Peter 1:16). He is completely separated from human beings by His character. He alone is the totally, perfectly pure one. Thus His holiness stands as the model for every human being.

Varied theological winds blow across our land these days. Some make emotions and visible signs their ultimate standard of holiness. Others, neglecting their personal lives, find holiness in social action. Still others seek it in lives of piety, lived in almost complete isolation from the rest of the world. None of these measures up to holiness as presented by Peter in the text for today's lesson. Peter makes rigorous demands for a life-style that is significantly different from worldly life-styles. By living in this manner, Christians will glorify God, for we will thereby "show forth the praises of him who hath called [us] out of darkness into his marvelous light" (1 Peter 2:9; see also Matthew 5:16).

I. Obedient Children (1 Peter 1:13-16)

A. Mental Activity Required (v. 13)

13. Wherefore gird up the loins of your mind, be sober, and hope to the end for the grace that is to be brought unto you at the revelation of Jesus Christ.

In the previous verses Peter has held up the glories of salvation. Now he turns to the kind of life that is compatible with such a hope. *Gird up the loins.* The long robes worn in those days made rapid or vigorous activity difficult if not impossible. And so for one to engage in such activity, he would have to tuck the robe up under his belt or girdle, freeing his legs. Peter applies this figuratively to the mind. There is a notion abroad in some circles that one must park his intellect at the door before he enters church. Nothing could be further from the truth. God requires our physical bodies, our talents, our time, and our minds.

Be sober, and hope to the end. The word *sober* is to be understood in the general sense of self-control, evenness of mind especially under stress. Regardless of life's circumstances, we are to live in the hope (the firm assurance) of *the grace* that we will be given, that is, our final salvation, when the Lord Jesus returns.

B. Modeled After the Father (vv. 14, 15)

14, 15. As obedient children, not fashioning yourselves according to the former lusts in your ignorance: but as he which hath called you is holy, so be ye holy in all manner of conversation.

Peter indicates that Christians are a part of a family, *obedient children.* The family relationship is often used in Scripture to demonstrate our relationship to God. We are not strangers or hired servants, but children.

The first requirement for holiness is a negative one. We are not to conform our lives to worldly standards, but instead are to reject worldly lusts. These must have no place in the lives of those who are children of the Heavenly Father (see 1 John 2:16). In Peter's day many of these *lusts,* especially the sexual lusts, were associated with the worship of pagan deities. Even though his readers had abandoned their pagan religions, that did not mean that automatically they no longer had to wrestle with lusts, which are a part of the human physiological and psychological makeup. We who live in a sex-saturated society know very well how difficult it is to control these desires, but holiness demands it.

He which hath called you is holy. One feature that distinguished Jehovah God from the pagan deities that surrounded Israel was His holiness. Moses' experience at the time of his call (Exodus 3:1-6) and Isaiah's vision in the temple (Isaiah 6:1-5) are but two examples that illustrate this. It follows logically that if one is to worship a holy God, that person must strive to be holy like Him. *Conversation* means much more than one's speech. It refers to one's whole manner of life.

C. Motivated by the Word (v. 16)

16. Because it is written, Be ye holy; for I am holy.

Peter may have been quoting from Leviticus, where this or a similar expression is found in several places (see Leviticus 11:44, 45; 19:2; 20:7, 26). Here is the absolute standard for holiness. The statement is unambiguous and so it cannot be misunderstood; its demands are absolute, and thus it cannot be compromised.

In the Bureau of Standards in Washington, D. C. is a carefully preserved metal bar. Two lines etched in the metal indicate the exact legal length for the yard in the United States. All other linear tools of measurement are based upon it. It is an absolute standard that cannot be changed by political chicanery or popular demand.

So it is with God's demand for our holiness. Oh, we have tried to avoid its requirements.

Sometimes we just ignore them entirely, doing our own thing. At other times we insist that because we live in different times, things have changed. A couple of decades ago leaders of the so-called "new morality" insisted that matters of right and wrong were not determined by any absolute standards, but by the "situation." Or we subtly shift the meanings of words. An unborn baby has now become a fetus. And since a fetus is thus no longer considered a human being, the mother has the freedom to dispose of it any way she chooses. Theoretically, it would be legal to abort a baby an hour before normal birth, while killing it an hour after it was born would be murder. Strange logic indeed! Such logic quickly evaporates in the presence of a holy God.

People Become Like Their Gods

Albert Barnes, Bible expositor of the nineteenth century, said, "It is a great truth, that men everywhere will imitate the god whom they worship. They will form their character in accordance with his. They will regard what he does as right. . . . Hence, by knowing what are the characteristics of the gods which are worshipped by any people, we may form a correct estimate of the character of the people themselves."

As strange as it may seem, one of the gods in Hinduism is Siva, the destroyer, the god of destruction, disease and death. It is claimed for him that in his rage he has "danced" (he is the god of dance) in some terrible fashion over humans who have unwittingly offended him. Except for the intervention of other gods, it is thought that he would have destroyed the whole world on one such escapade.

Siva's consort, Kali, is, if anything, more terrible than he. She is often shown wearing a necklace of human skulls and drinking blood. One of the sects of Kali are the Thugs, who formerly strangled victims as offerings to her.

Praise the Lord, we do not worship such a god. Jehovah, the God of the Bible, is holy, pure and perfect in every way, and He demands that we strive to be holy too. —T. T.

II. Reasons for Reverence (1 Peter 1:17-21)

A. The Coming Judgment (v. 17)

17. And if ye call on the Father, who without respect of persons judgeth according to every man's work, pass the time of your sojourning here in fear.

If, rather, "since" or "as" you pray. Because we are God's children, we may approach Him as *Father,* not as some arbitrary tyrant. We have the assurance that as judge He is impartial, that He

visual 6

does not play favorites, and that He cannot be bribed, as may sometimes occur among human judges.

God's judgment will be based on each person's works. Not that anyone will be saved by good works, for we are saved by grace. Yet the works of one's life are a valid measurement of one's complete commitment and trust in God's grace.

Because we are but sojourners (the *New International Version* has "strangers") in this world, we should live every moment in preparation for the next world. The old spiritual reminds us, "This world is not my home, I'm just passin' through." Surrounded as we are by all the attractive temptations of the world, we forget that all of us are afflicted with a terminal disease. That disease may take any of several forms, but no flesh is immortal. That being the case, we ought to live in fear, not abject, trembling fear, but in reverent fear and awe of Him who holds our destiny in His hands.

B. The Cost of Redemption (vv. 18, 19)

18, 19. Forasmuch as ye know that ye were not redeemed with corruptible things, as silver and gold, from your vain conversation received by tradition from your fathers; but with the precious blood of Christ, as of a lamb without blemish and without spot.

Forasmuch as ye know. Literally, "knowing" or "considering." Peter has already given one reason why we ought to live in reverent fear, and that is we know that we must face God's judgment. Here he gives another reason: we know the high price God paid for our redemption. Peter begins this thought by mentioning what could *not* redeem us. As precious as *silver and gold* are in the estimation of the world, these are simply powerless to save. Peter's original readers seem to have been Christians who had come from a Gentile background, for the word *vain* is used of idolatry (Acts 14:15). The life-style handed down to them from their fathers had been one filled with the debasing sins associated with pagan religions, but from that life-style, and the condemnation to which it led, they had been redeemed.

After stating that the corruptible riches of earth cannot save us, Peter then reminds us that God's plan for human redemption required the shedding of blood. Yet the blood of bulls and goats, sacrifices offered under the Old Testament law, could not take away sin (Hebrews 10:4). Even though most of Peter's readers were from Gentile backgrounds, they knew enough about Old Testament sacrifices to understand what he was saying. The only acceptable sacrifice was the blood of God's own Son, the perfect passover Lamb. John, at the very beginning of Jesus' ministry recognized the role that Jesus would play. He was "the Lamb of God, which taketh away the sin of the world!" (John 1:29).

The mystery of the atonement is beyond our ability to comprehend. Knowing, however, that our redemption from sin required the death of the sinless Son of God should cause each of us to fall before God in humility and holy fear.

C. The Consecrated Offering (vv. 20, 21)

20. Who verily was foreordained before the foundation of the world, but was manifest in these last times for you.

Even before He laid the foundations of the universe, God made plans for human redemption. *Foreordained* here literally means "foreknown." God knew ahead of time that man would fall and would need salvation. God designed the plan of salvation and brought it into operation in *these last times.* Through the centuries God had slowly brought His plan into operation. It finally culminated in sending the Lamb into the world.

21. Who by him do believe in God, that raised him up from the dead, and gave him glory; that your faith and hope might be in God.

The love and power of God that were manifested through Christ bring people to faith in God. Specifically, the power of God to raise Jesus from the grave and glorify Him gives assurance that God will also raise us to new life. This was especially reassuring to those in the first century who were going through the fires of persecution and even facing martyrdom. They could face the executioner's sword with the calm assurance that there was spiritual life beyond this life.

The resurrection of our Lord is at the very heart of the good news. It gives the gospel an evangelistic appeal that no other religion can offer. It provides the one answer for the question that gnaws at the heart of every human being—is there something beyond this life? Jesus' resurrection from the dead and His ascension to glory at the Father's right hand give the believer's faith the character of hope. This hope is the anchor of the soul. We are assured that we will one day be with Him and be made like unto Him.

III. The New Life (1 Peter 1:22-25)

A. Exceptional Love (v. 22)

22. Seeing ye have purified your souls in obeying the truth through the Spirit unto unfeigned love of the brethren, see that ye love one another with a pure heart fervently.

Peter's readers were Christians. By their obedience they had *purified* their *souls.* This was the process that had moved them out of the world into the body of Christ. This, in turn, had led them unto an *unfeigned love of the brethren,* a love that was not false or just for show. The expression *love of the brethren* is frequently used in the New Testament to refer to a love of fellow Christians. The love we have for our brothers and sisters in Christ is to be from the heart, true and pure, and we are to love one another fervently, intensely, with all of our energies strained to the utmost. Truly, our call to holy living demands that we give the best of us all!

TRUE LOVE

Robert Ripley of "Believe It or Not" fame describes what he calls "the longest—and simplest—love letter." It was written by a Frenchman, Marcel de Leclure, in 1875 and addressed to Magdalene de Villallore. The letter contained only one sentence—"I love you"—which was repeated 1,875,000 times, a thousand times for each year in the Christian calendar!

Ripley tells that Leclure did not write the letter personally, but hired a scribe to do the work. Instead of telling the writer to write the sentence 1,875,000 times, Leclure dictated the phrase and required the scribe to repeat it each time before he wrote it. So the phrase, "I love you," was said and written a total of 5,625,000 times! Such love.

We Christians know that speaking about love isn't adequate. Our God, who set the example by sacrificing His Son, wants us to show our love by our actions. Peter tells us, "Seeing ye have purified your souls in obeying the truth through the Spirit unto unfeigned love of the brethren, see that ye love one another with a pure heart fervently" (1 Peter 1:22). That kind of love demands more than talk.

If it is true that a picture is worth a thousand words in helping people grasp reality, how much is a kind and gracious deed worth in helping people to understand love? —T. T.

B. Everlasting Life (v. 23)

23. Being born again, not of corruptible seed, but of incorruptible, by the word of God, which liveth and abideth for ever.

Peter uses the figure of birth to describe the change that occurs when one moves from the world into the kingdom of God. That relationship is not the result of physical conception or physical birth. One is not physically born into the kingdom of God because of the faith of one's parents; the Bible recognizes no such thing as "birthright membership" in the church. Spiritual life, everlasting life, come through *the word of God.* As the potential Christian comes in contact with the word and begins to wrestle with it, intellectual involvement is required.

C. Enduring Word (vv. 24, 25)

24, 25. For all flesh is as grass, and all the glory of man as the flower of grass. The grass withereth, and the flower thereof falleth away: but the word of the Lord endureth for ever. And this is the word which by the gospel is preached unto you.

Peter is quoting from Isaiah 40:6-8. For people who lived in the Near East, expressed how temporary human life and achievements are. The winter rains cause the hillsides to turn green, and wildflowers add their color to the scene. Then the rains cease, and the hot summer sun begins its work. Soon all is brown and dead. How like this are our hopes and ambitions, if they are grounded only in this life!

Vastly different is the prospect for those persons who put their trust in God. We often equate the Word of God with the printed Bible. Obviously, Peter's reference here is broader than that, for much of the New Testament had not yet been written or was not available to his readers. Peter recognizes the gospel of Jesus Christ as the *word of the Lord.* It was preached to them, their salvation was based on it, and it will endure forever. All believers can enjoy complete assurance of their salvation and eternal life with God so long as they continue in that word.

Conclusion

A. Holy Is as Holy Does

"Pretty is as pretty does," my grandmother used to say, indicating that physical beauty is not nearly as important as right behavior. Exactly the same thing is true of holiness.

Holiness begins with an attitude toward God. He is high, and holy, and lifted up. As we study His Word and learn of His majesty and His perfection, we are filled with awe and reverence at His being. Such an attitude immediately brings us humbly to our knees. We recognize that before Him we are miserable sinners, deserving only His wrath. But by His grace He reaches us through His Son, lifts us up, and challenges us to seek His holiness.

We are not left to wonder about the nature of holy living. The attitudes and conduct that God requires of His people are everywhere evident in His Word. A good place to start in a search for these standards for holiness is the Ten Commandments (Exodus 20). Here we find fundamental principles pertaining to our relations with both God and our fellowmen. Jesus' Sermon on the Mount (Matthew 5-7) gives additional guidance. In mentioning the fruit of the Spirit, Paul lists several traits of character that are evidences of holiness (Galatians 5:22, 23). In the same context he also points out behavior that indicates unholiness. In our lesson text for today, Peter sums up the call to holy living by challenging us to become "obedient children." If we are obedient children, we will mold our character after that of our Heavenly Father and will conduct our lives each day as He desires.

B. Let Us Pray

Father, we thank You that You have called us into a saving relationship with You through Your Son, Jesus Christ. Help us to understand that that relationship is only possible if we are willing to live holy lives. We know that we cannot achieve that holiness through our good works but must depend upon Your grace and the guidance of the Holy Spirit. In our Master's name we pray. Amen.

C. Thought to Remember

God has said, "Be ye holy; for I am holy."

Home Daily Bible Readings

Monday, Jan. 4—Glory to God (Psalm 8)
Tuesday, Jan. 5—Full Assurance of Faith (Hebrews 10:19-25)
Wednesday, Jan. 6—Living a Life of Love (1 Corinthians 13:1-7)
Thursday, Jan. 7—The Greatest Gift (1 Corinthians 13:8-13)
Friday, Jan. 8—Living in Christ (1 Corinthians 15:20-28)
Saturday, Jan. 9—A Living Hope (1 Peter 1:3-12)
Sunday, Jan. 10—A Call to Holy Living (1 Peter 1:13-25)

Learning by Doing

This page contains an alternate lesson plan emphasizing learning activities. Classes desiring such student involvement will find these suggestions helpful.

Learning Goals

After examining the directive to holiness in 1 Peter 1:13-25, the pupil will be able to:

1. Identify the characteristics of holiness outlined in this passage of Scripture.
2. Explain why holiness should be the lifestyle of the believer.
3. Evaluate his or her personal holiness.
4. Choose a way to live a more holy life.

Into the Lesson

Display these words prominently for your class members to see as they enter the classroom: *Be ye holy, for I am holy.* Provide paper and pencil and ask each person to complete the following sentence: "When I think of the call to holiness, I—." When they have finished, let each share his or her response with a neighbor. Allot five or six minutes for this activity.

When all have finished, ask for a few volunteers to share their sentence completions with the class. Then make the transition into the text for today by stating that the Bible's call to holy living is the thrust for today's study.

Into the Word

Begin the Bible study by making a brief presentation of the material included in the "Lesson Background" section. Then divide the class into groups of four to six and appoint a leader for each group. Ask each group to complete the following task.

1. Read 1 Peter 1:13-25 aloud in the group.
2. What seems to be the central directive of Peter to believers? (Believers are to be holy, that is, separated from the world, as God is.)
3. What qualities or characteristics should mark the holy person? (Minds prepared for action, self-control [or sober], hope founded in Christ, refusal to conform to the evil desires that marked life before conversion, deep love for other Christians.)
4. What should be the motivation for living a life of holiness? (The desire to obey God who commands us to emulate His character.)
5. What is the part that Jesus Christ plays in this purification that allows us now to live holy lives? (He shed His blood to redeem us.)
6. What does it mean to live in fear (v. 17)? (The idea is not to be terrified of God, but to hold Him in reverence.)
7. Suggest some practical ways that we can demonstrate holiness in our daily lives. Allot ten to twelve minutes for the groups to complete their work.

Develop a discussion centered around the questions used in the groups. Be sure that all of the important points of the text are covered by the answers from the groups.

Into Life

The last question above began the students' thinking about how this applies to their lives. Continue the application by asking class members to respond to the following common statements.

Have the class work in the same groups that they did in the earlier section of the lesson. Give each group one of the statements below. The group should tell what is true about each statement, what is false, and what insights from today's lesson would help a person who makes this kind of statement.

1. "You can't expect me to be perfect. I'm no saint." How could we respond?
2. "I'm only human. You can't expect any more from me." How could we respond?
3. "Holiness is a quality of saints. I'm not one of those yet." How could we respond?
4. "Everybody has to sow a few wild oats." How could we respond?

Allot four to six minutes for the groups to do this. Then use the work of the groups as a basis for discussion.

Point out that we are all called to be holy. Give each student a copy of the "Holiness Checklist" below. Ask them to evaluate themselves.

Holiness Checklist

1. On a scale of 1-5 (5 being best), I would rate my holiness as a
2. I would say that my mind is prepared for action. Yes No
3. I am self-controlled. Yes No
4. My hope for salvation is in Jesus Christ. Yes No
5. I refuse to conform to the evil desires of the world. Yes No
6. I love others and show it. Yes No
7. I would say that I need to do the following to be holy:

Close the session with prayer.

Let's Talk It Over

The questions on this page are designed to encourage review of the lesson Scriptures and to promote discussion of the lesson by the class. The answers provided are only discussion starters. Let your class talk it over from there.

1. Peter states that we are to be holy. What does the word *holy* mean?

In the Bible, *holy* means "separated," or "set aside." To refer to God as "holy" is to recognize that He is separated from us, that He is other than we are. He is other than we are, separated from us, by His character. When we are called to be holy as He is holy, we are challenged to live a life separated from the moral standards of the world, striving to emulate the character of the Father. We are called to be "other than the world is," to be pure as God is, the God who is other than we are.

2. In 1 Peter 1:13, Peter calls for Christians to be "sober," that is, self-controlled. What does this imply?

Self-control implies nothing less than maturity. Self-control is internal control. Each of us chooses between being externally controlled or internally controlled. Things (food, alcohol, drugs, money, job, etc.), events (divorce, the death of a loved one, getting fired, the onset of a serious illness, etc.), and people (spouse, parent, boss, child, ex-spouse, etc.) can control us externally. Toddlers and small children are externally controlled. This is to be expected, because they are *immature*.

The move from external to internal control is the move to maturity. Internal control is self-control; and for the Christian, it is more than this, it is Spirit-control. In Galatians 5:22, 23 the apostle Paul reveals the characteristics of the person who is controlled internally by the Holy Spirit. To be controlled in this way does not imply that things, events, and people cannot hurt you. But it does declare that you can choose whether or not to let them control you. You determine how you will respond to these external control elements in your life. In all relationships and circumstances of life, the Lord calls for His people to be self-controlled, Spirit-controlled.

3. What does the word *purity* mean?

The word *purity* is commonly used with sexual connotations, that is, the avoidance of immoral sexual thoughts and actions. If one is pure in heart, one does not think lustful thoughts. In the Bible, purity is both broader and deeper in its meaning and implications. That which is pure is unmixed, unadulterated, involving only one thing. Soren Kierkegaard wrote a most enlightening work entitled, *Purity of Heart Is to Will One Thing*. Purity of heart is to will one thing—what God wills. It is to be "single-minded." Impurity is to be double-minded. Viewing purity in this light brings an exciting clearness to Jesus' statement in the Beatitudes: "Blessed are the pure in heart: for they shall see God" (Matthew 5:28). Who sees God? Those who will only *one thing*, who will what the Father wills. The call to purity in the Christian life evokes thoughts and behavior that are uncontaminated, unmixed, only what the Father wills. Of course, none of us achieves perfect purity in this life, but purity is to be our longing and our goal.

4. In Scripture, Jesus Christ is referred to as a "lamb." What is the significance of this term as it is used of Him?

John the Baptist referred to Jesus in this manner following His baptism: "Behold the Lamb of God, which taketh away the sin of the world!" (John 1:29). Lambs formed an important part of most sacrifices of Israel's sacrificial system. They were offered in atonement for sin and, in the Passover, to commemorate God's deliverance of Israel from bondage in Egypt. The term *lamb* was used in the description of the redemption the Messiah would bring (Isaiah 53:7). Thus the designation of Jesus as the Lamb of God shows Him to be the Sin Bearer of the world, the one who would bring deliverance from sin's bondage. He is the perfect and final sacrifice for sin.

5. Peter refers to our time on earth as "sojourning" (v. 17). What are the implications of this?

It reminds us that we are not permanent residents in this world. We are "as grass," our time on earth is brief and temporary. Our true home is in Heaven—we were created (and re-created!) to dwell with God forever. As sojourners, we do not give highest value and priority to the temporal, but only to the eternal. Our perspective, our values, our goals—all are transformed by the reality that we are but sojourners.

The Church Is for All People

January 17
Lesson 7

LESSON SCRIPTURE: Acts 11.

PRINTED TEXT: Acts 11:1-18.

DEVOTIONAL READING: Ephesians 2:11-22.

Acts 11:1-18

1 And the apostles and brethren that were in Judea heard that the Gentiles had also received the word of God.

2 And when Peter was come up to Jerusalem, they that were of the circumcision contended with him,

3 Saying, Thou wentest in to men uncircumcised, and didst eat with them.

4 But Peter rehearsed the matter from the beginning, and expounded it by order unto them, saying,

5 I was in the city of Joppa praying: and in a trance I saw a vision, a certain vessel descend, as it had been a great sheet, let down from heaven by four corners; and it came even to me:

6 Upon the which when I had fastened mine eyes, I considered, and saw fourfooted beasts of the earth, and wild beasts, and creeping things, and fowls of the air.

7 And I heard a voice saying unto me, Arise, Peter; slay and eat.

8 But I said, Not so, Lord: for nothing common or unclean hath at any time entered into my mouth.

9 But the voice answered me again from heaven, What God hath cleansed, that call not thou common.

10 And this was done three times: and all were drawn up again into heaven.

11 And, behold, immediately there were three men already come unto the house where I was, sent from Caesarea unto me.

12 And the Spirit bade me go with them, nothing doubting. Moreover these six brethren accompanied me, and we entered into the man's house:

13 And he showed us how he had seen an angel in his house, which stood and said unto him, Send men to Joppa, and call for Simon, whose surname is Peter;

14 Who shall tell thee words, whereby thou and all thy house shall be saved.

15 And as I began to speak, the Holy Ghost fell on them, as on us at the beginning.

16 Then remembered I the word of the Lord, how that he said, John indeed baptized with water; but ye shall be baptized with the Holy Ghost.

17 Forasmuch then as God gave them the like gift as he did unto us, who believed on the Lord Jesus Christ, what was I, that I could withstand God?

18 When they heard these things, they held their peace, and glorified God, saying, Then hath God also to the Gentiles granted repentance unto life.

GOLDEN TEXT: They held their peace, and glorified God, saying, Then hath God also to the Gentiles granted repentance unto life.—Acts 11:18.

Good News for All

Unit 2: Living the Good News

(Lessons 5-9)

Lesson Aims

This lesson should enable students to:

1. Understand that God intended the church to be open to everyone.
2. Appreciate the fact that God's love shed among us can help us learn to accept people who are different from us.
3. Reach out with the gospel to people of various races and cultures.

Lesson Outline

INTRODUCTION
- A. Heavenly Robes
- B. Lesson Background

I. PETER CHALLENGED BY THE CHURCH (Acts 11:1-3)
- A. He Had Preached the Word to Gentiles (v. 1)
- B. He Had Eaten With Gentiles (vv. 2, 3)
  Trespasses or Debts

II. PETER'S RESPONSE TO THE CHARGES (Acts 11:4-16)
- A. Unusual Vision (vv. 4-10)
- B. Urgent Visitors (vv. 11, 12)
- C. Unexpected Validation (vv. 13-16)

III. CASE DISMISSED (Acts 11:17, 18)
- A. Peter's Closing Argument (v. 17)
  Unlikely Companions
- B. The Response of the Church (v. 18)

CONCLUSION
- A. "Red and Yellow, Black and White"
- B. "The Middle Wall of Partition"
- C. Let Us Pray
- D. Thought to Remember

Display visual 7 of the visuals packet and let it remain throughout the session. The visual is shown on page 172.

Introduction

A. Heavenly Robes

According to an old legend, Peter stood at the gates of Heaven welcoming the new arrivals. Coming from all over the world, their skins were of many hues and they wore a variety of costumes. As they approached the gates, Peter ushered each to a dressing room and handed him or her a special robe. "You must wear this robe to be able to enter the gates."

As each emerged from his or her dressing room wearing the Heavenly robe, it was evident that a remarkable change had taken place. The skin of everyone was the same color, and everyone spoke the same language. "I don't understand this," exclaimed one man. "I thought that we would retain our identities in Heaven."

"Oh, you won't lose your identity," replied Peter. "But your identity will no longer be based on such things as the color of your skin or the language you speak. You are not here because of these things. You are here because you are saints, members of the body of Christ."

B. Lesson Background

Were it not for the book of Acts, the history of the early years of the church would be an almost total mystery. We are grateful for Luke, who, guided by the Holy Spirit, gave us this work. It was written about A.D. 63, near the end of Paul's first Roman imprisonment. Today's lesson is based on a portion of Acts 11.

At first thought, we might suppose that the early church, under the leadership of the apostles, would have had no problems. But the church then, as now, was made up of imperfect members, and so problems were certain to arise. Luke was an honest historian and he did not try to ignore or paper over these problems; instead, he presented the facts candidly.

The problem of prejudice toward those who differ from us is not new. It has plagued humankind for thousands of years, and it was at the heart of the problem in the incident in today's lesson. Because prejudice touches just about every culture, it should not surprise us that it appeared in the church. In fact, the Biblical record suggests that prejudice may have been involved in an earlier problem that had surfaced among the first Christians (see Acts 6:1). On that occasion, the Greek-speaking Jewish widows felt that they were being overlooked in favor of the Aramaic-speaking Jewish widows of Palestine. The problem was handled wisely and generously and apparently was solved.

The situation in today's lesson was a more serious one, however, with far-reaching implications. It was more than a dispute between Jewish Christians who came from different cultural backgrounds, as in the case cited above involving the care of the widows in the church. The incident for our study in this lesson involved the ingrained prejudice that Jews had toward all other peoples in the world.

The actions of the apostle Peter prompted the meeting and the discussions that are recorded in our lesson text. By way of background, Peter had been on an evangelistic trip that had taken him to Lydda, a town situated about eleven miles southeast of the coastal town of Joppa. While he was in Lydda, messengers sent by the disciples in Joppa came to him and urged him to return to Joppa with them. Tabitha (or Dorcas), a beloved Christian woman there, had died, and they believed Peter could help her. They were right, for as soon as Peter arrived, he went into the room where she lay, knelt down and prayed, and her life was restored to her. (See Acts 9:32-43.)

Peter remained many days in Joppa, staying in the home of Simon the tanner. While he was there the events occurred that led to his going to Caesarea, the Roman capital of Palestine located farther up the Mediterranean seacoast. His association with Gentiles there precipitated the confrontation recorded in our lesson text.

I. Peter Challenged by the Church (Acts 11:1-3)

A. He Had Preached the Word to Gentiles (v. 1)

1. And the apostles and brethren that were in Judea heard that the Gentiles had also received the word of God.

Peter remained with the disciples in Caesarea "certain days" (Acts 10:48), but just exactly how long that was we have no way of knowing. But one thing we know for certain—news travels fast. Long before Peter returned to Jerusalem, word had already arrived about what he had done in Caesarea. Until this time, the gospel had not been shared with Gentiles. Undoubtedly, the leaders of the church wanted to know by whose authority Peter had undertaken to do it now. Even Peter's position as leader among the apostles did not grant him immunity from this kind of criticism.

B. He Had Eaten With Gentiles (vv. 2, 3)

2, 3. And when Peter was come up to Jerusalem, they that were of the circumcision contended with him, saying, Thou wentest in to men uncircumcised, and didst eat with them.

They that were of the circumcision. These were Jewish Christians who were most zealous of keeping the Mosaic law and the traditions and who held circumcision to be absolutely indispensable.

Neither the law nor the traditions forbade preaching to Gentiles, because, of course, neither dealt with gospel preaching. But the traditions—not the law—were explicit in forbidding familiar association with uncircumcised persons, and this was the principal charge brought against the apostle. He had accepted the hospitality of a Gentile home and had eaten with uncircumcised persons. These actions were incredible violations of Jewish custom. So strong was the traditional prejudice against eating with Gentiles that Peter, at least on one later occasion, reverted to it (see Galatians 2:12).

How to Say It

CAESAREA. Sess-uh-*ree*-uh.
JOPPA. *Jop*-uh.
LYDDA. *Lid*-uh.
TABITHA. *Tab*-ih-thuh.

TRESPASSES OR DEBTS

The story is told of two congregations of similar belief that were located a few blocks from each other in a small community. The leaders of the churches thought the two should merge and become one larger, more effective congregation. It was a good idea, but they couldn't pull it off. It seems they couldn't agree on how to recite the Lord's Prayer. One group wanted, "forgive us our trespasses," while the other insisted on, "forgive us our debts." A local newspaper, reporting on the failed merger attempt, said that one church went back to its trespasses while the other one returned to its debts!

This humorous, and highly unlikely, story points up how easy it is to divide, and how difficult to have unity.

When the Jewish Christians at Jerusalem heard of Peter's work with Cornelius and the other Gentiles of his household, they were disturbed and might well have divided the body of Christ had not good judgment been shown by Peter. His calm and reasoned account of God's leadership in the entire matter eased the tension and kept the church united.

Many matters over which Christians divide are as trivial as the issue of "trespasses" and "debts." That old axiom is worth remembering and practicing: "In essentials, unity; in opinions, liberty; in all things, charity." —T. T.

II. Peter's Response to the Charges (Acts 11:4-16)

A. Unusual Vision (vv. 4-10)

4-6. But Peter rehearsed the matter from the beginning, and expounded it by order unto them, saying, I was in the city of Joppa praying: and in a trance I saw a vision, a certain vessel descend, as it had been a great sheet, let down from heaven by four corners; and it came even

to me: upon the which when I had fastened mine eyes, I considered, and saw fourfooted beasts of the earth, and wild beasts, and creeping things, and fowls of the air.

We don't know who first brought word to the church in Jerusalem of Peter's activities in Caesarea. But to the credit of his critics, they were not willing to base their case entirely on those reports. They directly confronted Peter with their charges and offered him the opportunity to give his side of the story. Such is the manner in which all disputes between members of the Lord's church should be handled.

Instead of trying to argue the rightness or wrongness of what he had done or its theological implications, Peter wisely chose to recount for their information the same events that had convinced him of God's will for the Gentiles. What he told was a summary of the events recorded in Acts 10:9-48.

Peter's account began with his being in the city of Joppa (see "Lesson Background"). One day about noon, when he was on the housetop praying, he fell into a trance and had a vision. He saw *a great sheet* being lowered from Heaven. It was held by the *four corners*, allowing it to sag in the middle and form a *vessel* or basin. Whatever this was, Peter recognized that it came from God. As Peter watched, this great vessel came directly to him. Its approach was personal, and Peter could not avoid it. As he looked attentively on it, he saw that the sheet contained all kinds of four-footed animals, wild beasts, reptiles, and birds. Perhaps not one of those creatures would be acceptable for food according to the law, yet this strange collection had come from Heaven!

7-10. And I heard a voice saying unto me, Arise, Peter; slay and eat. But I said, Not so, Lord: for nothing common or unclean hath at any time entered into my mouth. But the voice answered me again from heaven, What God hath cleansed, that call not thou common. And this was done three times: and all were drawn up again into heaven.

visual 7

Slay and eat. This command was in direct contradiction of the law (see Leviticus 11). By his response, Peter indicated that he knew this command was of God; yet he refused to obey because he had never eaten anything that was considered unclean by the law of Moses. The voice responded by stating that these animals had been cleansed by God. The scene was repeated three times for emphasis, thus preparing Peter to understand that God's cleansing could reach even to people Peter considered most unclean.

B. Urgent Visitors (vv. 11, 12)

11, 12. And, behold, immediately there were three men already come unto the house where I was, sent from Caesarea unto me. And the Spirit bade me go with them, nothing doubting. Moreover these six brethren accompanied me, and we entered into the man's house.

After the vessel was taken back up to Heaven, Peter was left to wonder about the meaning of the vision (see Acts 10:17, 19). Did it have to do only with unclean meats, or did it have some broader meaning? But Peter did not have to ponder the matter long, for at that very moment the answer was at the door.

Standing there were three men who had been sent from Caesarea by Cornelius, a Roman centurion. God had sent an angel to this generous and pious man. The angel had told him to send to Joppa for Peter, giving explicit instructions on how to find him (Acts 10:1-6). We don't know why God chose Cornelius as the one through whom He would open the doors of the church to Gentiles. We just know that God in His infinite wisdom knows best.

Just how fully Peter understood the vision at this point we cannot tell, but all of the circumstances surrounding it surely must have led him to understand that it involved him and this Gentile Cornelius. The nature of the vision itself, the timing of the arrival of the messengers sent by Cornelius, the Holy Spirit's direction that Peter should go with them, and their announcement that God's angel had told Cornelius to send for Peter all pointed to this conclusion. All of these factors convinced Peter that God was behind this entire occurrence and helped Peter to overcome his prejudice toward non-Jews (Acts 10:17-29).

Even though Peter undertook his trip to Caesarea without any hesitation, neither was he totally naive. He knew very well that his actions were likely to face criticism by some of his brethren back in Jerusalem. So wisely he took along six companions as witnesses. Freely he admitted that he had entered the Gentile's home, but he showed that it was of God.

C. Unexpected Validation (vv. 13-16)

13, 14. And he showed us how he had seen an angel in his house, which stood and said unto him, Send men to Joppa, and call for Simon, whose surname is Peter; who shall tell thee words, whereby thou and all thy house shall be saved.

Peter was now repeating to the leaders of the Jerusalem church the information that Cornelius had provided him when he had arrived at the centurion's residence in Caesarea. While most moderns would be skeptical about anyone who reported being visited by an angel, Christians in the first century would not have reacted that way. Many of them would have known about the appearance of angels surrounding the time of Jesus' birth and at His resurrection.

Two things need to be noted here. First, the angel did not bring the message of salvation to Cornelius. God has chosen human beings for this mission, and His purpose has not changed. We need not expect God to send angels as evangelists. That is our job. The second thing is that Cornelius's good deeds did not save him. Although he was a pious and generous man, he still needed the *words* of the gospel to *be saved*.

15, 16. And as I began to speak, the Holy Ghost fell on them, as on us at the beginning. Then remembered I the word of the Lord, how that he said, John indeed baptized with water; but ye shall be baptized with the Holy Ghost.

As I began to speak. Acts 10:34-43 records Peter's words before he was interrupted. He was now convinced that God did not recognize distinctions among peoples, such as those made by Jews toward Gentiles. Therefore he began to share the gospel with those assembled in Cornelius's house. As he did so, the Holy Spirit fell on them, and they began to speak in tongues, just as Peter and the others did on Pentecost when they received the miraculous outpouring of the Holy Spirit. At that moment, he remembered Jesus' promise, which is found in Acts 1:5.

III. Case Dismissed (Acts 11:17, 18)

A. Peter's Closing Argument (v. 17)

17. Forasmuch then as God gave them the like gift as he did unto us, who believed on the Lord Jesus Christ, what was I, that I could withstand God?

At Pentecost, the outpouring of the Holy Spirit upon Peter and the others was convincing proof to those assembled that what occurred was of God and that the message proclaimed had the divine seal of approval. No doubt, some who were now questioning Peter had witnessed this great miracle and had been led to faith in Christ because of it. So when the Gentiles in the home of Cornelius received the same miraculous *gift*, Peter and the Jewish brethren with him knew at once that God was showing His approval of admitting Gentiles into the fellowship of the church. Knowing that the miracle came from God, Peter would not resist God.

UNLIKELY COMPANIONS

Peter Miller and Michael Wittman lived in the same Pennsylvania town in the late eighteenth century. Other than that bond, they had little in common. Peter was a preacher, and Michael an evil-minded man who delighted in opposing and humiliating the preacher. Wittman's choices led him on a path that resulted in his being arrested for treason. He was tried, found guilty, and sentenced to death. Upon learning of this, Peter Miller walked seventy miles to Philadelphia to seek a pardon for his enemy. When George Washington became aware of the circumstances—that Miller was pleading for the life of an enemy—he granted the pardon. As a consequence, these former adversaries became friends.

Peter the apostle and Cornelius the centurion both lived in Palestine in the first century. Other than that, they had little in common. Peter was a Jew, and Cornelius a Roman. But these two became friends through some unusual circumstances. Luke tells how God appeared to both men in order to bring them together. As a result of the vision he had, Peter walked a number of miles to offer the terms of pardon to Cornelius. As a consequence, these unlikely companions became friends. More than that—they became brothers in the Lord. —T. T.

B. The Response of the Church (v. 18)

18. When they heard these things, they held their peace, and glorified God, saying, Then hath God also to the Gentiles granted repentance unto life.

After hearing Peter's report, which was supported by the six witnesses, the leaders of the church accepted it as true. Not only did they hold *their peace,* they also *glorified God* for removing the barriers that previously had kept the Gentiles from repenting and finding new life in Christ.

Conclusion

A. "Red and Yellow, Black and White"

Anthropologists may want to take issue with the racial designations in the familiar children's song, "Jesus Loves the Little Children," but theologians will have to agree that the sentiment of the song expresses the inclusiveness that God intended for His church. Jesus loves not only "all the children of the world," He also loves all the old people and everyone in between. By means of Peter's vision and the subsequent events in the house of the Gentile Cornelius, God made it clear that He intended his message of salvation to reach every person in the world.

Unfortunately, this has to be relearned by every generation. As children grow, too easily adopted are the negative attitudes of exclusiveness and prejudice toward those who differ from them. Once learned these attitudes must be unlearned if the church is to go to the whole world.

Unlearning prejudice has never been easy, either in the ancient world or the modern. But that is one of the principal blessings of the gospel. Human beings whose hearts are touched by the message of salvation and warmed by the power of the Holy Spirit respond in a positive way to people who are different from them. They come to recognize every other human being as a child of God, needing the same hope of salvation. It is often a slow process and one that may have reverses and setbacks (Peter's later example at Antioch, for example), yet it is the only approach that guarantees success in bringing God's human family together.

B. "The Middle Wall of Partition"

In Ephesians 2:14, Paul, addressing the issue of separation between Jews and Gentiles, wrote, Christ "is our peace, who hath made both one, and hath broken down the middle wall of partition between us." Jesus' death on the cross made the gospel available to all persons everywhere. Every Christian must recognize this basic truth and do all in his or her power to work to bring people together in the Lord's church.

Home Daily Bible Readings

Monday, Jan. 11—Saul Persecuted the Church (Acts 8:1-8)
Tuesday, Jan. 12—The Gospel Is Preached (Acts 8:9-13)
Wednesday, Jan. 13—Peter's Sermon (Acts 8:14-25)
Thursday, Jan. 14—The Ethiopian Official (Acts 8:26-40)
Friday, Jan. 15—Peter's Report (Acts 11:1-8)
Saturday, Jan. 16—Peter's Message (Acts 11:9-18)
Sunday, Jan. 17—The Church in Antioch (Acts 11:19-30)

Barriers do exist that naturally tend to keep people apart. One of these is language. This barrier can make Christian fellowship difficult or almost impossible. Yet we cannot label as unworthy of fellowshipping with us everyone who doesn't speak the language we speak. We must learn to find ways to push aside such barriers; but these efforts take time and patience.

We must be careful that we do not unintentionally set up barriers that may divide the Lord's people. One such barrier may be the form of worship a congregation follows. Some may be accustomed to a very formal, liturgical style of worship. Others may prefer a worship style that has some pattern but follows it with less rigidity and encourages more worshiper participation. Still others may prefer a worship style that is almost completely spontaneous with a large amount of participation by the worshipers. There is no Biblical basis for a person's insisting that one style of worship is right and all the others are wrong. In fact, any style of worship that does not violate some clear teaching of Scripture is acceptable to God so long as it is offered sincerely.

We can readily observe differences in the types of music that are preferred in worship. In some worship services, one is likely to hear mainly religious classics. In others, the traditional hymns and gospel songs written in the past two hundred years may be preferred. In still others, the preference may be popular choruses, contemporary music, or even impromptu songs that arise almost spontaneously. Again, so long as God has not indicated precisely the kind of music He wants in a service, we ought not to pass judgment on others whose taste in music differs from our own.

There are other issues that may raise the "middle wall of partition among believers." Groups may differ in their evangelistic methods, or, groups may separate themselves from others on the basis of education and socio-economic status. Methods, education, income, or social status should never be an occasion for raising barriers between groups that otherwise should recognize one another as brothers and sisters in Christ.

C. Let Us Pray

Dear Father, we thank You that You have offered the gospel to all people everywhere regardless of their race, nation, or culture. Please help us to recognize that fact, and shape our lives accordingly. Keep us from the sinful attitude of exclusiveness, which can only divide and weaken the church. In Jesus' name, we pray. Amen.

D. Thought to Remember

"What was I, that I could withstand God?"

Learning by Doing

This page contains an alternate lesson plan emphasizing learning activities. Classes desiring such student involvement will find these suggestions helpful.

Learning Goals

As a result of studying Peter's explanation of his dealings with the Roman centurion, Cornelius, the learner will be able to:

1. Identify the specific criticism leveled at Peter by the church in Jerusalem.
2. Identify the gist of Peter's response to the criticism.
3. Acknowledge that God intended the church to be open to persons of every race and nation.
4. Express an interest in reaching out to various cultures and races with the gospel.

Into the Lesson

Before the class begins, develop a sketch of a person who is most unlike those in your congregation—a person with a different skin color, from a different culture, and with different customs. When the class members arrive, present the sketch of the person. Ask, What response would our congregation make if this person came to worship with us today? Discuss this for three to five minutes.

Make the transition into the Bible study portion of the lesson by stating that a similar occurrence in the early days of the church is the basis of today's lesson.

Into the Word

Review the events recorded in Acts 10:9-48. Point out that Peter's action was unheard of among the Jews, who had a great prejudice against Gentiles, not unlike the prejudice we sometimes have against those who differ from us in any way.

Then have a class member read Acts 11:1-18 aloud. Develop a discussion based on the text. Use the following questions as a guide.

1. What criticism was leveled against Peter? Who led in the criticism? (See verses 1-3.)
2. What did Peter report that he saw in a vision? (This is recorded in verses 4-10.)
3. Why was Peter's vision significant? (Long ago God had given the Jews laws that identified the animals whose flesh they were permitted to eat and those whose flesh they were not to eat. But in this vision God removed those distinctions in order to teach Peter an important truth.)
4. Why did Peter go with the Gentiles from Caesarea? (This is answered in verses 11 and 12.)
5. What did Peter find out when he arrived? (Verses 13 and 14 provide the answer.)
6. What verified the man's story that God had told him to send for Peter? (See verses 15, 16.)
7. What was Peter's conclusion about what he had experienced? (See verse 17.)
8. How did the church respond to what Peter told them? (See verse 18.)

Into Life

Remind the learners that Peter's experience convinced him that God intended the gospel for all people. Ask, What does a lesson such as this have to do with us today? Let the learners share their responses.

Then divide the class into groups of four to six individuals. Give each group one of the situations below.

Situation One. Tom and Karen are planning to go to a remote village in Africa as missionaries. They know that the people there are quite different from those they have known all their lives, and that they worship differently. Some of their friends suppose that Tom and Karen will teach these people to follow our forms of worship. Look at Acts 11:1-18 and also at Acts 15:22-29. How should Tom and Karen respond?

Situation Two. First Church has decided to establish an inner city work. Plans are being made for worship and Christian education. Some on the committee assume that these activities of the new church will be much like theirs. Others say that different customs will require different forms. Look again at Acts 11:1-18 and also at Acts 15:22-29. What would you advise the committee?

Situation Three. Some of the young people in your congregation come to church dressed very casually. They like music that is more informal than is usually used in your church. They even raise their hands when they sing. Some of the congregation is very unhappy with this. Look again at Acts 11:1-18 and also at Acts 15:22-29. What help does this provide for this situation?

Allow each group five to seven minutes to complete their work. Then use their responses as the basis for a class discussion.

Conclude with a prayer for open hearts that we may receive as brothers and sisters in Christ all persons who name Him as their Lord and Savior.

Let's Talk It Over

The questions on this page are designed to encourage review of the lesson Scriptures and to promote discussion of the lesson by the class. The answers provided are only discussion starters. Let your class talk it over from there.

1. What is the root cause of prejudice, and how does one become prejudiced?

Prejudice is rooted in fear. One who is prejudiced feels threatened by groups or persons who are different from him or her. Such a person thinks, "They may usurp my place," or, "They may take what I have," or, "I don't feel secure with people and groups who are not like I am." For the prejudiced person there is always the fear that "I may not be as good or superior as I've wanted to believe I am."

No one is born prejudiced. Prejudice is learned, whether its focus is race, sex, age, or socio-economic status. Parents, extended family, friends, significant others, the culture—all can teach prejudice to children. Prejudice is conveyed by verbal messages (jokes, ridicule, insults, observations, judgments, etc.) and non-verbal messages (tone of voice, facial expressions, gestures, behavior, etc.). And prejudice does not die easily. Peter's prejudice had to be overcome before the Gentiles could be saved, and Jewish prejudice had to be vanquished before the Gentiles were accepted fully into the fellowship of the church.

2. What can be done to prevent prejudiced attitudes from developing in society in general? In the church in particular?

To the extent that prejudice is based on ignorance, information and education can help. Creating situations where people from the differing groups can get together and get acquainted is a healthy preventive. This is true in the church that seeks to represent the universal nature of the gospel.

3. How do you explain the different responses of the Jewish Christians toward Gentiles as recorded in Acts 11:2 and 18?

At first, the Jewish Christians' response to the news of the conversion of Gentiles was based on their ancient and deeply-ingrained prejudice (v. 2). They attacked Peter because he had fellowshipped and eaten with people whom the Jews avoided. This response was simply a conditioned response rooted in long-standing prejudice.

Verse 18 records a quite different response of these Jewish Christians. Peter explained to them the events that had occurred, including his vision from God with the mandate, "What God has cleansed, no longer consider unholy" (v. 9, *New American Standard Bible*). He informed them that the Spirit had directed him to share the gospel with Cornelius. Peter's most persuasive testimony was his report that "the Holy Spirit fell upon them, just as He did upon us at the beginning" (v. 15). When the leaders heard that these Gentiles had also received the miraculous gift of the Holy Spirit, they ceased their objection and glorified God. Let it be said to their credit, when verified testimony was presented to them, they overcame their prejudice and acquiesced to God's will.

4. Peter had a problem with prejudice against the Gentiles prior to God's leading him to Cornelius. Are modern Christians troubled by prejudice toward others? If so, cite some examples.

In many areas, racial differences still give rise to many prejudicial attitudes. Perhaps even more often, differences in culture, education, or wealth create attitudes that limit the church's outreach and ministry. As we see in this lesson, the church is for all people. May each of us eliminate from his or her own heart any attitude that creates a barrier between us and others and prevents the accomplishing of God's will for the church.

5. Did Peter's dramatic experience recorded in today's lesson "cure" him forever of discriminating against Gentiles?

No! Galatians 2:11-14 records a later incident when Peter slipped back into his old pattern of prejudice and discrimination regarding Gentiles. He had visited the church at Antioch, which was composed mostly of Gentile Christians. While there, he shared with them and ate with them. When an influential group of Jewish Christians from the church in Jerusalem came to Antioch, Peter withdrew from fellowshipping and eating with the Gentile Christians, for he was afraid of what the Jews might say. Paul called Peter to task in front of the entire congregation at Antioch. He reminded Peter that by separating himself from the Gentile Christians he was saying, in effect, that observing the old traditions was more important than faith in Jesus Christ.

Learning God's Wisdom

January 24
Lesson 8

LESSON SCRIPTURE: 1 Corinthians 1:1—2:13.

PRINTED TEXT: 1 Corinthians 1:18-31.

DEVOTIONAL READING: 1 Corinthians 2:1-13.

1 Corinthians 1:18-31

18 For the preaching of the cross is to them that perish, foolishness; but unto us which are saved, it is the power of God.

19 For it is written, I will destroy the wisdom of the wise, and will bring to nothing the understanding of the prudent.

20 Where is the wise? where is the scribe? where is the disputer of this world? hath not God made foolish the wisdom of this world?

21 For after that in the wisdom of God the world by wisdom knew not God, it pleased God by the foolishness of preaching to save them that believe.

22 For the Jews require a sign, and the Greeks seek after wisdom:

23 But we preach Christ crucified, unto the Jews a stumblingblock, and unto the Greeks foolishness;

24 But unto them which are called, both Jews and Greeks, Christ the power of God, and the wisdom of God.

25 Because the foolishness of God is wiser than men; and the weakness of God is stronger than men.

26 For ye see your calling, brethren, how that not many wise men after the flesh, not many mighty, not many noble, are called:

27 But God hath chosen the foolish things of the world to confound the wise; and God hath chosen the weak things of the world to confound the things which are mighty;

28 And base things of the world, and things which are despised, hath God chosen, yea, and things which are not, to bring to nought things that are:

29 That no flesh should glory in his presence.

30 But of him are ye in Christ Jesus, who of God is made unto us wisdom, and righteousness, and sanctification, and redemption:

31 That, according as it is written, He that glorieth, let him glory in the Lord.

GOLDEN TEXT: For after that in the wisdom of God the world by wisdom knew not God, it pleased God by the foolishness of preaching to save them that believe.
—1 Corinthians 1:21.

Good News for All

Unit 2: Living the Good News

(Lessons 5-9)

Lesson Aims

After studying this lesson, each student should:

1. Understand that the wisdom of God is greater than the wisdom of man.
2. Understand that God uses what the world regards as foolish and weak to accomplish His purposes.
3. Have a growing appreciation for the preaching of the cross as the power of God.
4. Be bold, in spite of his or her weaknesses, to witness for Christ.

Lesson Outline

INTRODUCTION
- A. The Wise Shall Be Humbled
- B. Lesson Background

I. THE PREACHING OF THE CROSS (1 Corinthians 1:18-25)
- A. Foolishness (v. 18a)
- B. The Power of God (v. 18b)
- C. Foolish Wisdom (vv. 19-21)
- D. Different Responses (vv. 22-25)
  Look Back to Christ

II. THE MAKEUP OF THE CHURCH (1 Corinthians 1:26-29)
- A. The Uncalled (v. 26)
- B. The Chosen (vv. 27, 28)
  But Who Will Stay?
- C. None Should Boast (v. 29)

III. CHRIST AND THE BELIEVER (1 Corinthians 1:30, 31)
- A. The Believer Is in Christ (v. 30)
- B. Glory to God! (v. 31)

CONCLUSION
- A. The Cross
- B. Let Us Pray
- C. Thought to Remember

Display visual 8 of the visuals packet throughout this session. The visual is shown on page 180.

Introduction

A. The Wise Shall Be Humbled

When I was in the seventh grade, I was the checkers champion of my class and more than a little proud of my accomplishment. In fact, I was confident that before the year was over I would be champion of the whole school. One Saturday morning I stopped by the local hardware store, which was a gathering place for farmers and older men from town, who spent their time whittling and exchanging small talk.

"Say, son," one of the men spoke up. "I hear that you are checkers champion of the seventh grade."

"Yes, sir," I proudly replied.

"Why don't you give us a demonstration of just how good you are," said one of the men. That further inflated my ego and I leaped at the opportunity. "You could start out by taking on old 'Uncle' Bill." Uncle Bill was a kind old man but he was slightly retarded. About the only jobs he could get was digging ditches, mowing yards, and trimming trees.

This is going to be a snap, I thought to myself as we set up for the game. I was correct about that, all right. Uncle Bill seemed to be able to anticipate every move that I made, and he "skunked" me the first two games. Only in the third game did I finally manage to get a checker into the king's row. Needless to say, I was properly humbled, a lesson that most young teenagers need.

In a humble way this illustrates man's relationship with God. We come to exalt our wisdom and as a result develop all kinds of social and religious structures that show how much wiser than God we are. But God in His "foolishness," like Uncle Bill, can anticipate every move before we make it, and in His own time and way counter every move that we make. No passage of Scripture better illustrates this than the first two chapters of Paul's first letter to the church at Corinth.

B. Lesson Background

Today's lesson, the fourth in the unit entitled "Living the Good News," deals with the subject of God's wisdom. Understanding how God's wisdom prevails over human wisdom is absolutely essential if we as Christians are to live lives that are pleasing to Him. The church at Corinth was a problem church. First of all, it was a church divided apparently into four different factions, each claiming superiority. But it had other problems—incest, worldliness, remnants of paganism, drunkenness at the Lord's Supper, and disruptions in public worship by some who claimed to be acting under the power of the Holy Spirit. The amazing thing is that Paul could still address these people as "saints" (1 Corinthians 1:2). We sometimes despair of problems in our churches, but if these folk in Corinth were sanctified, then there is hope for our much troubled congregations.

In this letter to them, Paul addressed these problems and offered solutions. He set forth what they must do if they were to live up to the sanctification into which they had been called. Today we might be inclined to discuss why the congregation had so many problems. The city of Corinth was noted for its debauchery. It was a busy seaport and commercial center with all the greed that that brings. The culture of Corinth was saturated with paganism of the most corrupting kind. Further, its problems were compounded by the fact that the population was multinational and multiracial. It is interesting to note, however, that Paul did not use any of these to excuse the Corinthians. He clearly taught that in becoming a Christian, one was obligated to rise above his or her environment.

This letter was written from Ephesus in about A.D. 56, while Paul was on his third missionary journey.

I. The Preaching of the Cross (1 Corinthians 1:18-25)

A. Foolishness (v. 18a)

18a. For the preaching of the cross is to them that perish, foolishness.

In verse 18, Paul divides the human race into two classes—the lost and the saved. For his purposes in this section of his letter, there is no other category. To a generation such as ours that is committed to compromise at every opportunity, this kind of division sounds harsh. But the truth is the truth, and Paul had an obligation to present the truth as God revealed it to him.

To those who perish, the message of the cross is *foolishness.* This may have been aimed especially at the Greeks, who were looked upon as the intellectuals of the ancient world. They sought to find a logical reason for every phenomenon they observed. They could see no logical connection between the death of Christ on the cross and human salvation, and so they regarded that message as foolishness. That God in His wisdom had ordained the connection of the two was a teaching that many Greek intellectuals simply would not believe. Many of our intellectual elite today would have found themselves in harmony with the ancient Greek scholars. How tragic that the wisdom of the world has blinded men and women to the only truths that can bring salvation!

B. The Power of God (v. 18b)

18b. But unto us which are saved, it is the power of God.

Now we see the other side of the coin. If those who are perishing consider the preaching of the cross foolishness, those who are being saved by that same preaching hold it in infinitely higher regard. To them it is nothing less than *the power of God.* Those who are being saved have the vision to see beyond the mere historical facts—that Jesus of Nazareth died on the cross as a purported insurrectionist. Instead, they see in the death of this One the turning point of God's whole plan for human redemption.

C. Foolish Wisdom (vv. 19-21)

19. For it is written, I will destroy the wisdom of the wise, and will bring to nothing the understanding of the prudent.

The apostle Paul continued by quoting from Isaiah 29:14 according to the Septuagint, or Greek version of the Old Testament, and he presented it as the basis for his statements in verses 17 and 18. The inspired apostle saw in Isaiah's statement a prophecy of the power inherent to the preaching of the cross and the utter futility of human philosophy of argument. Thus, Paul had not come to the Corinthians with "wisdom of words" (v. 17), but only with the "preaching of the cross" (v. 18).

20. Where is the wise? where is the scribe? where is the disputer of this world? hath not God made foolish the wisdom of this world?

From prophecy Paul turns to its fulfillment. The *wise* encompasses both classes of persons Paul mentions next. The *scribe* refers to the Jewish scholars who were versed in Rabbinical lore and who split hairs over rituals they thought essential to right living. The *disputer* seems to refer to the Greek "sophists" who argued over minor points of philosophy. The arguments and speculative discussions of these wise men were inconclusive and insufficient to enable human beings to know God or to save them from their sin. In the following verse Paul indicates how *God made foolish the wisdom of this world.*

21. For after that in the wisdom of God the world by wisdom knew not God, it pleased God by the foolishness of preaching to save them that believe.

In the wisdom of God the world by wisdom knew not God. In God's providence humankind was given full rein to speculate concerning the ultimate realities of the world and its Creator. The Greeks had pursued such speculations, but they had all ended in frustration.

The foolishness of preaching. The *New International Version* translates this more accurately "through the foolishness of what was preached." This correctly puts the emphasis on the content of the message rather than on the method used in delivering it. By the proclamation of the message of the cross, which is reputed to be folly by

The Word of the Cross
THE POWER OF GOD
THE WISDOM OF GOD
. . . unto the saved.

visual 8

the wisdom of the world, God saves those who believe that message and thereby shows futility and emptiness of the world's wisdom.

D. Different Responses (vv. 22-25)

22. For the Jews require a sign, and the Greeks seek after wisdom.

Different cultures produce different approaches to meeting life's problems. For the Jews the Book, that is the collection of writings that we call the Old Testament, was their basic guide. These Scriptures had been revealed to them by God, who had authenticated them by various miracles or "signs." From time to time through their long history, God had provided them guidance through His mighty acts—the crossing of the Red Sea, the manna in the wilderness, Elijah on Mount Carmel. Rather than relying upon their reason, the Jews had come to depend upon these signs. And so when Jesus came among them claiming to be the fulfillment of the law and the prophets, they would not believe without an extraordinary *sign* from Heaven (see Mark 8:11).

The Greeks, on the other hand, had for many centuries increasingly emphasized man's intellect as their ultimate guide. They were recognized as the scholarly elite of the ancient world. Yet for all of their emphasis upon *wisdom* or logic, they still had not been able to meet life's ultimate problems.

Most of us today operate from a modern mindset that is essentially scientific. We have come to believe only that which can be measured by scientific standards. So we ask, Can we see it, weigh it, measure it, reduce it to a mathematical formula? If not, we are not likely to be convinced. As a result of this mind-set, many today are likely to reject the claims of the gospel without even examining them. Their situation is like that of the Jews and the Greeks, who locked themselves out of the salvation offered through the cross because it did not fit the mold of their thought patterns.

23. But we preach Christ crucified, unto the Jews a stumblingblock, and unto the Greeks foolishness.

The Jews understood very well the significance of blood sacrifice for the purification from sins. The whole Old Testament system was built on this concept. However, it was impossible for them to understand how the sacrificial death of a human being could accomplish this. Further, the idea of *Christ crucified* was *a stumbling block*, because they envisioned the promised Christ or Messiah as a conquering hero, who would reestablish the Jews as a powerful, independent nation. They could not see the Messiah as Isaiah 53 depicts Him—a suffering and dying servant.

The religions of the Greeks sometimes involved animal sacrifices, but they were efforts to appease the wrath of a god or gods who might be angry with the worshiper for some whimsical reason that had nothing to do with sin. The Greeks felt that philosophy held the answers to humankind's moral and intellectual needs. To them it was an absurdity to announce a person as Savior, especially one who had died a shameful death.

24. But unto them which are called, both Jews and Greeks, Christ the power of God, and the wisdom of God.

There is great irony here. The unbelieving Jews, who sought signs of God's power, rejected Him through whom God's power could be known. And the scoffing Greeks, who valued knowledge and wisdom, turned from the One who was the channel of ultimate wisdom. However, for those of both races who heard and answered God's call, the preaching of the cross was viewed differently. They saw in Christ's death God's means of overcoming the guilt of the sins of all humankind. To them, Christ's death demonstrated *the power of God, and the wisdom of God.*

25. Because the foolishness of God is wiser than men; and the weakness of God is stronger than men.

The foolishness of God and *the weakness of God* both refer to the death of Christ on the cross. To the Greek it seemed *foolishness,* and to the Jew it appeared as *weakness;* but in truth, it was just the opposite.

LOOK BACK TO CHRIST

Duncan Spaeth, Shakespearean scholar and one of Princeton University's beloved professors of the past, also coached the rowing crew. For taking on this extra responsibility he received no remuneration beyond the affection of the oarsmen. When asked why he gave himself to this extra work, he replied, "I would rather teach young men to look backward and go forward than to look forward and go backward.

There is a lesson here worthy of our consideration. We live in a day of great scientific achievement. The technological advances of recent years have been so many as to be overwhelming, and we continually anticipate the unlocking of other secrets of the physical world through ongoing research. But do we look to these advancements with such eager anticipation that we do not bother to look back and learn the lessons of history, experience, and Scripture?

For all of the scientific advancements of our generation, it is painfully evident that humankind's sin problem remains. The remedy was offered at Calvary. The truly wise will look back to Christ and find in Him God's wisdom and power that will insure an eternal future of blessedness.

II. The Makeup of the Church (1 Corinthians 1:26-29)

A. The Uncalled (v. 26)

26. For ye see your calling, brethren, how that not many wise men after the flesh, not many mighty, not many noble, are called.

Ye see your calling, brethren. Paul's thought here is classified by the reading of the *New International Version:* "Brothers, think of what you were when you were called." Of those in Corinth who responded to the gospel, few were wise according to human standards. Not many were leading citizens, nor were they of noble birth. This follows naturally upon what Paul has been saying in the preceding verses.

There were several reasons why not many of the elite were called. Paul has already indicated that the *wise men* regarded the preaching of the cross as foolishness. The *mighty* were not inclined to become Christians because Christianity requires humility, a virtue difficult enough to achieve even by the poor, let alone those who had power. The *noble* were those of established families or those who exercised rule. For a nobleman to become a Christian meant the loss of prestige and perhaps even position, sacrifices that few were willing to make.

B. The Chosen (vv. 27, 28)

27, 28. But God hath chosen the foolish things of the world to confound the wise; and God hath chosen the weak things of the world to confound the things which are mighty; and base things of the world, and things which are despised, hath God chosen, yea, and things which are not, to bring to nought things that are.

Paul continues his explanation of God's design and the utter barrenness of the philosophy and value system of humankind. The word *things* that occurs here is neuter in gender and suggests the contempt that the world had for those persons Paul mentions. Those whom the world regarded as *foolish* (unphilosophical), *weak, base* (of low birth), and who were *despised* as being of no value at all were the very persons whom God chose to humble the wise and the mighty. Paul was not trying to insult the Corinthian church members. His real purpose was to show that God is not limited in what He can do.

We need to keep these things in mind as we evaluate our own situations. God can achieve His purposes without impressive buildings and elaborate programs, as useful as these may be at times. God's Word is at work in miserable slums and primitive tropical villages, and the Word is bearing rich fruit

BUT WHO WILL STAY?

"Hi, Bill. How are you getting on? I guess you've heard that our church recently relocated. Well, you know we were in a poor neighborhood that was deteriorating. We tried to reach the new people, but couldn't seem to attract any of them. Now we've moved to an affluent neighborhood, and our new neighbors seem to be interested; we have visitors every week. I'm calling to see if we can get you and your family back again. Your new home isn't far from our new location, and we do have a lot to offer."

The above situation is an imaginary phone conversation, but its contents are real. All across our land churches are fleeing urban areas where the gospel is sorely needed. This is not said in condemnation, but we Christians must come to grips with this problem and find some means to reach out with the gospel to the poor people of our cities. If we do not, these folk, as well as Christianity, will have a bleak future.

Christianity's strength has always been, even as Paul expresses it in this text, that "not many wise men after the flesh, not many mighty, not many noble, are called." Let's never forget that one of the distinguishing characteristics of Christ's personal ministry was that the poor had the gospel preached to them (see Matthew 11:5). A strategy must be developed that will win the young upper classes while not neglecting the poor downtrodden masses. —T. T.

C. None Should Boast (v. 29)

29. That no flesh should glory in his presence.

Paul now climaxes his argument by showing the reason behind God's design. It was so that no flesh at all may boast itself in God's presence. Human wisdom and philosophy have been shown to be incapable of explaining the ultimate realities of life. The ineffectiveness of worldly power to resolve life's problems is everywhere apparent. So the wise and the strong have nothing whereof to boast. And those persons who are regarded as foolish and weak by the world are in truth wise and strong only by the grace of God through Jesus Christ. Thus, *no flesh* may glory before God.

III. Christ and the Believer (1 Corinthians 1:30, 31)

A. The Believer Is in Christ (v. 30)

30. But of him are ye in Christ Jesus, who of God is made unto us wisdom, and righteousness, and sanctification, and redemption.

Because God sent His only begotten Son to die on the cross, the Corinthian Christians could be *in Christ,* that is, they could be in a special relationship with Christ that would lead to their redemption. *Wisdom and righteousness, and sanctification.* Some scholars believe that these identify steps in the process that leads to *redemption.* Others hold that these are but facets that give different aspects of redemption. In either circumstance, the ultimate goal is redemption, one's eternal salvation. This has been made possible only because Christ died on the cross, a stumbling block to the Jews and foolishness to the Greeks.

B. Glory to God! (v. 31)

31. That, according as it is written, He that glorieth, let him glory in the Lord.

Here the apostle Paul is apparently quoting from Jeremiah 9:24, but it is a paraphrase rather than a direct quotation. This sums up the point Paul has been making in the preceding verses of this text. Salvation came to the human race through the cross, and so for that reason there is no basis for anyone to boast as if he or she had accomplished it through personal efforts. All the glory belongs to Christ and God.

Home Daily Bible Readings

Monday, Jan. 18—Prayer of Thanksgiving (Romans 1:8-15)
Tuesday, Jan. 19—Blessings in Christ (1 Corinthians 1:4-9)
Wednesday, Jan. 20—Divisions in the Church (1 Corinthians 1:10-17)
Thursday, Jan. 21—Power in Christ's Message (1 Corinthians 1:18-25)
Friday, Jan. 22— Union in Christ (1 Corinthians 1:26-31)
Saturday, Jan. 23—The Message About Christ (1 Corinthians 2:1-5)
Sunday, Jan. 24—God's Wisdom (1 Corinthians 2:6-16)

Conclusion

A. The Cross

It is interesting how symbols sometimes change their meaning over a period of time. Take, for example, the cross. In the first century, the cross represented a cruel form of punishment reserved for the worst criminals. Crucifixion was public, and this, combined with the slow, agonizing death it produced, made crucifixion a deterrent to crime. As we have seen in this lesson, Paul showed that by such a horrible means of death God bridged the gap that sin had created between himself and humankind. The cross symbolizes God's concern for justice, mercy, and holiness.

How times have changed. Few people today ever think of the cross as a cruel instrument of torture, and probably few ever give more than passing consideration to the theological implications of the cross. But we see the cross everywhere. It adorns our church steeples and serves as a part of the decor in our sanctuaries. It embellishes our jewelry—necklaces, rings, bracelets, tie clasps, and lapel pins.

These various uses of the cross are not necessarily wrong, but they are often shallow and thoughtless. When we see the cross in our sanctuaries or on our jewelry, may we take time to give serious thought to its true meaning. May we understand that in the crucifixion of Christ God gave evidence of His indescribable love for humankind, and at the same time showed His judgment upon all the wisdom and the power and the glory of this world.

B. Let Us Pray

Dear God, help us to understand better the message of the cross and may we come to understand that our only hope of salvation lies in the preaching of the cross, no matter how foolish that may seem to the world. In our Master's name we pray. Amen.

C. Thought to Remember

When I survey the wondrous cross,
On which the Prince of glory died,
My richest gain I count but loss,
And pour contempt on all my pride
—Isaac Watts

Learning by Doing

This page contains an alternate lesson plan emphasizing learning activities. Classes desiring such student involvement will find these suggestions helpful.

Learning Goals

After examining Paul's teaching in 1 Corinthians 1:18-31, concerning the preaching of the cross, the learner will be able to:

1. Define the "wisdom of God."
2. Explain how the wisdom of God differs from the wisdom of this world.
3. Explain how God uses the weak things of the world to accomplish His purposes.

Into the Lesson

Before the class session begins, prepare for each participant a half-sheet of paper on which you have typed or written this incomplete statement: "When I think of the cross, I think of—" As class members enter the classroom, give one of the sheets of paper to each. Ask them to complete the sentence, then share their responses with two or three other people.

After most people have arrived and have completed this introductory activity, ask several of them to share their responses. Point out how the thinking of most persons today regarding the cross differs from that of the people of the first century. (See the section entitled "The Cross" on page 182.)

This section of your lesson should take no more than eight to twelve minutes.

Into the Word

Explain that the message of the crucified Christ is the focus of today's lesson. Have someone read aloud 1 Corinthians 1:18-31 as the remainder of the class follows along.

Develop a general discussion of the text by using the following questions:

1. How does Paul characterize the message of the cross? (See verse 18.)
2. Why would the message of the cross be foolishness to those who think themselves wise? (See comments under verse 23.)
3. How does Paul characterize the wisdom of the world? (It is in reality foolish, for by it humankind does not know God. See verses 20, 21.)
4. How is the foolishness of God, of which Paul is speaking in this text, greater than the wisdom of the world? (It results in salvation for those who accept it.)
5. How would you define the wisdom of God, on the basis of this Bible text?
6. Paul states that God has chosen those who are regarded as foolish and weak to confound (shame) the wise and the strong (vv. 26, 27). Explain this. (If the gospel is accepted by those whom the wise of the world regard as foolish, will not the world's wise persons be without excuse for rejecting it?)
7. What is the central message of this section of Scripture? (See verses 18, 30, 31.)
8. When you think of the cross and what Christ's sacrifice has accomplished, how do you respond?

Into Life

Divide the class into groups of three to five students each. Give each group newsprint and markers and ask them to make a drawing to symbolize the message of the cross and our response to it. Give each group six to eight minutes to do this. Then have each group show and explain its work and display it on the wall.

Then pursue the following discussion questions.

1. If the message of the cross is, in fact, so important, what kind of response should believers make to it?
2. If the message of the cross is, in fact, so important, what should be the response of the whole church?
3. Display these words of Isaac Watts's hymn, "When I Survey the Wondrous Cross":

> When I survey the wondrous cross,
> On which the Prince of glory died,
> My richest gain I count but loss,
> And pour contempt on all my pride.

Read the words aloud. Then ask, Are those the responses you would like to make? Are there other responses that come to your mind?

4. If we are to count our richest gain as loss and pour contempt on our pride in light of the message of the cross, what kind of action does that call for in our lives?
5. Why is such action of the greatest importance?

Give each person a small index card. Ask each person to write a prayer indicating what his or her response to the message of the cross will be.

Have the groups assemble in the small groups in which they worked earlier. Have the class sing the hymn, "When I Survey the Wondrous Cross." Then have the students pray in their small groups to conclude the session.

Let's Talk It Over

The questions on this page are designed to encourage review of the lesson Scriptures and to promote discussion of the lesson by the class. The answers provided are only discussion starters. Let your class talk it over from there.

1. Why should the church educate its ministers when God's wisdom (not man's) is to be preached?

God did, and does, use many "professionally" untrained workers in calling lost humanity back to Him. Many of Jesus' apostles were in this category. Of course, He trained them and prepared them thoroughly before He left them. Some of God's most notable leaders, for example, Moses and Paul, were well-educated, brilliant men. In the final analysis, whatever is achieved is by God's power, not by man's power. It may be that Will Sweeney, a noted preacher of the first half of the twentieth century, said it best: "God can cut a lot of wood with a dull axe, but He can cut a lot *more* wood with a sharp one!" What God and His church need today is more *sharp* axes! We must offer God the best prepared ministers that is possible, those who handle correctly the word of truth (2 Timothy 2:15). Yet even the best prepared ministers cannot win the world for Christ by themselves; millions of "dedicated amateurs" provide the only hope in accomplishing that divine purpose.

2. Why did God choose to use the so-called foolish, weak, lowly, and despised of earth to accomplish His purpose?

In the Old Testament we first encounter the method God uses to accomplish His purposes in the world. We see it in His choice of Israel through whom His will could be made known. In choosing to work through Israel, God obviously opted for a people without any advantage, from the human point of view. He began with one person, Abraham. After several hundred years had passed, the Israelites were a nation of slaves, uneducated and poor. Possessing no military might or temporal power, what did they have to offer? But God could, and did, show His mighty power through them. *He* established them and blessed them. *He* achieved His purposes through the least likely, least promising people possible.

That pattern continued with the new Israel, the church. Not many wise according to the world, not many mighty, not many noble (Paul reminds the Corinthians) constituted the early church, yet the gospel shook the world of that day. This occurred not from reliance upon human resources, but by the working of God's power. God acted through "the things which are not, to bring to nought things that are" (1 Corinthians 1:28). His method established irrefutably the conclusion that "no flesh should glory in his presence" (v. 29). "Let him who boasts, boast in the Lord" (v. 31, *New American Standard Bible*). *All* is of God!

3. Paul says that the message of the cross is seen as "foolishness" by those who are perishing. How was that true in his day?

The Jews of the first century were looking for the coming of the Messiah, God's anointed one, but they had fashioned in their minds the kind of Messiah He would be. He would come in power and glory to rescue Israel from their oppressors, in the manner of God's mighty and miraculous deliverances in Old Testament times. Their Messiah would *never* suffer the humiliation of death on a cross! The Greeks prized beauty and logical philosophic speculation. The preaching of a crucified Savior was utterly unlovely and unreasonable to them. In both groups, these whose minds were closed to God's revelation of *His* power and *His* wisdom regarded that revelation as foolishness, and they shut themselves out of the salvation He offered.

4. What are the most prevalent reasons why people reject the gospel today?

Several of the main reasons are these: (1)They don't want to change. They want to remain in their "comfort zone." (2) They would have to give up attitudes and actions that they enjoy. Sin, for a time, *is* pleasurable. (3) Long-term habits are hard to break. Accepting the message of the gospel is seen as requiring too much effort. (4) Accepting Christ as Savior might cost them dearly, perhaps alienating them from some of their friends and family members. Some persons lack the courage and strength to stand alone, if need be. (5) Most importantly, Satan does not want them to respond positively to God's message. All his powers and forces are devoted to thwarting the divine message. Satan hasn't given up.

One Body in Christ

January 31
Lesson 9

LESSON SCRIPTURE: Ephesians 4.

PRINTED TEXT: Ephesians 4:1-16.

DEVOTIONAL READING: 1 Corinthians 12:12-27.

Ephesians 4:1-16

1 I therefore, the prisoner of the Lord, beseech you that ye walk worthy of the vocation wherewith ye are called,

2 With all lowliness and meekness, with long-suffering, forbearing one another in love;

3 Endeavoring to keep the unity of the Spirit in the bond of peace.

4 There is one body, and one Spirit, even as ye are called in one hope of your calling;

5 One Lord, one faith, one baptism,

6 One God and Father of all, who is above all, and through all, and in you all.

7 But unto every one of us is given grace according to the measure of the gift of Christ.

8 Wherefore he saith, When he ascended up on high, he led captivity captive, and gave gifts unto men.

9 (Now that he ascended, what is it but that he also descended first into the lower parts of the earth?

10 He that descended is the same also that ascended up far above all heavens, that he might fill all things.)

11 And he gave some, apostles; and some, prophets; and some, evangelists; and some, pastors and teachers;

12 For the perfecting of the saints, for the work of the ministry, for the edifying of the body of Christ:

13 Till we all come in the unity of the faith, and of the knowledge of the Son of God, unto a perfect man, unto the measure of the stature of the fulness of Christ:

14 That we henceforth be no more children, tossed to and fro, and carried about with every wind of doctrine, by the sleight of men, and cunning craftiness, whereby they lie in wait to deceive;

15 But speaking the truth in love, may grow up into him in all things, which is the head, even Christ:

16 From whom the whole body fitly joined together and compacted by that which every joint supplieth, according to the effectual working in the measure of every part, maketh increase of the body unto the edifying of itself in love.

GOLDEN TEXT: There is one body, and one Spirit, even as ye are called in one hope of your calling.—Ephesians 4:4.

Good News for All

Unit 2: Living the Good News

(Lessons 5-9)

Lesson Aims

As a result of studying this lesson, each student should:

1. Understand that Christ intended His church to be one.
2. Realize that Christian leaders are to equip all Christians to serve Christ and to help them become like Him.
3. Work to maintain the unity of the church.
4. Continue becoming more like Christ.

Lesson Outline

INTRODUCTION
- A. Planned Construction
- B. Lesson Background

I. THE CHRISTIAN WALK (Ephesians 4:1-6)
- A. Walk Worthily (v. 1)
- B. Exhortation to Unity (vv. 2, 3)
- C. Examples of Unity (vv. 4-6)

II. GIFTS AND GIVER (Ephesians 4:7-10)
- A. Variety of Gifts (v. 7)
- B. Victorious Christ (vv. 8-10)

III. GIFTS FOR A PURPOSE (Ephesians 4:11-13)
- A. Servant Leaders (v. 11)
- B. Preparation for Service (v. 12)
  Get Them Into Circulation
- C. Unity and Maturity (v. 13)

IV. EXPECTED RESULTS (Ephesians 4:14-16)
- A. Stability (v. 14)
- B. Growth (vv. 15, 16)
  Unknown Heroes

CONCLUSION
- A. "That They All May Be One"
- B. Let Us Pray
- C. Thought to Remember

Display visual 9 from the visuals packet and let it remain before the class throughout the session. The visual is shown on page 188.

Introduction

A. Planned Construction

Several years ago I watched with interest the construction of a large office building. After the steel framework was in place, work was begun on the stone facade. Several truckloads of stone had been hauled in and placed near the area where they would be used. I noticed that the stones, which had already been precut, were many different sizes and shapes.

I noticed the masons never had to stop and cut or shape any of the stones, but whenever they picked up a stone and put it in place, it seemed to fit perfectly. Finally, I asked one of the workers why every stone seemed to fit perfectly without any cutting.

"Oh, that's simple enough, Mister," he responded. "It's all been planned ahead of time." Then he showed me how each stone was numbered and its place plotted on the master plan.

In a way, this suggests how God planned the church. Every member has a place in the master plan, and if the plan had been followed there would have been unity and growth for the church. But something went wrong. Satan managed to slip in and change the numbers on the stones or even bring in stones that did not belong in the plan. The result has been a church that is divided and unable to carry out completely its mission to the world. As tragic as this is, we need not despair. After all, we still have the master plan, the New Testament, which shows us what God expects the church to be.

B. Lesson Background

Any survey of the teachings of the New Testament would, of necessity, include some references to the church. Jesus came to found the church (Matthew 16:18). On Pentecost about A. D. 30, the church actually came into existence (Acts 2). The rest of the New Testament sets forth the growth of the church, while the book of Revelation predicts its ultimate triumph.

This lesson is taken from the epistle to the Ephesians, written by the apostle Paul. (For background information on this letter, see the lesson background section of lesson 1 in this series.)

One of the central themes of the book is the church—how it was a part of God's eternal plan, the provisions God made for its growth, and His concern for its unity.

I. The Christian Walk (Ephesians 4:1-6)

A. Walk Worthily (v. 1)

1. I therefore, the prisoner of the Lord, beseech you that ye walk worthy of the vocation wherewith ye are called.

In the earlier chapters of this letter, Paul had set forth God's purpose for the human race through the church. But Paul was not willing to leave this in the realm of theology that is isolated from real life. As in his epistle to the Romans (chapter 12), he points out that theological statements lead to practical applications for day-to-day living. If men and women have been called into a new relationship with God through the church, then their life-styles should reflect that change. Paul does not give a detailed catalog of all the things Christians should do and not do. Rather, he challenges them to *walk worthy* of their calling. This is a figurative way of saying, "Behave or live in a way that is proper for one who is called to be God's child."

B. Exhortation to Unity (vv. 2, 3)

2. With all lowliness and meekness, with long-suffering, forbearing one another in love.

It may be seen that the thought of unity in the Lord's church underlies much of what the apostle Paul says in the text for this lesson. He begins here by suggesting some practical ways Christians can gain and demonstrate that unity with one another. *Lowliness and meekness.* The qualities of humility and gentleness seldom come naturally. By nature we are more apt to be proud and to demand our own way. But Christians live by a different set of standards, and they have the Lord Jesus as their example. Lowliness and meekness naturally lead to *long-suffering* or patience, the willingness to put up with much that is less than ideal for the sake of unity. These qualities, when adapted by everyone in the church, lead to the development of a warm, loving fellowship. The love and concern that the early Christians showed one another did not escape the notice of their pagan neighbors who grudgingly acknowledged, "How these Christians love one another!"

3. Endeavoring to keep the unity of the Spirit in the bond of peace.

Christian unity is not something that human beings create; rather, it is given through the Holy Spirit. By submitting to the will of God, as mediated through the Spirit, we can experience this unity. *Endeavoring.* The Greek word here means to strive earnestly or, as the *New International Version* has it, "make every effort."

Unity is given by God, but man must make every effort to maintain it. *In the bond of peace.* This suggests the way that unity can be maintained. We must be committed to living in peace with our brothers and sisters in Christ. Each one must put aside selfish ambition and the desire for personal recognition and praise and desire only what is good for the whole church. It goes without saying that bickering and backbiting, on the other hand, are certain to destroy unity. How often over the centuries has the unity of the church been shattered, not by disputes over vital doctrine, but by the pettiness and quarrelsomeness of selfish individuals.

C. Examples of Unity (vv. 4-6)

4. There is one body, and one Spirit, even as ye are called in one hope of your calling.

From the first century, Christians have come from diverse ethnic and religious backgrounds. Thus there have been natural barriers to be overcome in order to achieve oneness in the church. In these verses Paul gives seven examples of unity, which should motivate every Christian to strive to maintain unity among God's people.

One body. When one becomes a Christian, he or she becomes a member of Christ's body, the church. Christ has but *one body,* which is open to all who come to Him as penitent believers. In a sense, it is a contradiction of terms to speak of a divided church, for Christ's body cannot be divided.

One Spirit. There is but *one* Holy *Spirit.* The Spirit is involved in the Christian's entrance into the body: "For by one Spirit are we all baptized into one body" (1 Corinthians 12:13). And the Holy Spirit lives in all Christians everywhere. How then can Christians harbor a spirit of divisiveness?

One hope. Today people come into the church from all kinds of backgrounds. Some of them come with strange and fearful ideas about the future. In Christianity, we do not strive to secure our personal futures at the expense of others. We all have the same hope, a hope for life eternal grounded in the promises of Jesus Christ.

5. One Lord, one faith, one baptism.

One Lord. The statement that Jesus Christ is Lord was used in the early church at the time of baptism. It expressed the truth that Christ is the owner, the ruler, the boss. All of us who belong to Him, therefore, ought to do His will in perfect harmony.

One faith. This is our common belief that Jesus is the Christ. All who share this belief ought not to do anything that would weaken the faith of another. A divisive, antagonistic attitude would do just that.

One baptism. To become one with Christ does not require submission to a series of complicated initiatory rites. In *one baptism* we give public expression of our faith and repentance and we become clothed with Him (Acts 2:38; Galatians 3:27).

6. One God and Father of all, who is above all, and through all, and in you all.

How to Say It

AGABUS. *Ag*-uh-bus.
EPHESUS. *Ef*-eh-sus.

One God. At the heart of the Hebrew covenant relationship with God was the assertion of God's unity; "Hear, O Israel: The Lord our God is one Lord" (Deuteronomy 6:4). Such a concept was practically unheard of in the pagan world. He is *Father of all.* He is not limited to one tribe or one nation, but as the Creator is the Father of every human being. He is *above all.* The false gods, products of human imagination, cannot challenge His power. He is *through all,* that is, He permeates His whole creation, sustaining it by His power. Finally, He is *in you all* in the sense that the church is His temple (1 Corinthians 3:16).

The unity of Father, Son, and Holy Spirit is held up as a model for the unity of the church. It is unthinkable, therefore, that the church, in whom the Father, Son, and Holy Spirit dwell, should be anything but one.

II. Gifts and Giver (Ephesians 4:7-10)

After exhorting Christians to strive for unity and giving examples of unity, Paul now speaks of some differences that exist among us. We have different gifts, different abilities, but these come from the same giver and thus should promote the unity that Christ desires His body to possess.

A. Variety of Gifts (v. 7)

7. But unto every one of us is given grace according to the measure of the gift of Christ.

Two points need to be made about this verse. First, every Christian has received a gift or gifts from Christ. One's gift may not be recognized or it may go unused. But no one may claim that he or she has received no spiritual gifts. The second point is that Christ gives a variety of gifts. The New Testament mentions several of them, but certainly the list is not exhaustive. A vast array of gifts is essential to the growth and development of the church, and Christ has provided these generously. Our responsibility is to discover our gifts and then dedicate them completely to the glory of Christ and His church.

B. Victorious Christ (vv. 8-10)

8. Wherefore he saith, When he ascended up on high, he led captivity captive, and gave gifts unto men.

To further emphasize Christ's giving of gifts, Paul quotes from Psalm 68:18. The picture is that of a conquering hero returning with the prizes of war, which he distributes to his subjects. By His resurrection, Jesus freed us from our captivity to sin and death. Paul pictures Him as ascending to Heaven, leading in chains that

visual 9

which had previously held us captive. Having been freed, we receive gifts from the conqueror.

9. Now that he ascended, what is it but that he also descended first into the lower parts of the earth?

Jesus' ascension had been witnessed by His disciples (Mark 16:19; Acts 1:9). He could not have ascended to Heaven if He had not first descended to earth. *The lower parts of the earth.* It seems best to understand this to mean simply "the earth," which is lower than Heaven.

10. He that descended is the same also that ascended up far above all heavens, that he might fill all things.)

Far above all heavens is a way of referring to the authority that Jesus possesses. His authority is over *all things* in Heaven and earth.

III. Gifts for a Purpose (Ephesians 4:11-13)

A. Servant Leaders (v. 11)

11. And he gave some, apostles; and some, prophets; and some, evangelists; and some, pastors and teachers.

Paul now lists some of the specific spiritual gifts Christ gave to lead His people in the building up of His church. The *apostles* were Christ's authorized representatives specially trained and inspired to teach His word without error and to organize, govern, and guide the churches. *Prophets* were specially inspired to proclaim the message God wanted them to give. One such prophet was Agabus (see Acts 11:28; 21:10, 11). *Evangelists* were those who carried the good news to the unbeliever. These persons were not necessarily inspired as were the apostles and prophets. They had learned the message of salvation from Christ's inspired spokesmen and then repeated it to the unsaved. Persons in every generation have fulfilled this task. *Pastors and teachers.* These two may reflect different functions of the same office. Pastors are shepherds who care for the needs of the flock, while teachers strengthen the faith of the flock by teaching the Scriptures and showing the people how to apply Bible truths to their lives. The pastors in the New Testament were identical to the elders or bishops (see Acts 20:17, 28).

The apostle Paul certainly did not intend this brief list of ministries to be exhaustive. The fact that every Christian has received one or more gifts means that he or she has a ministry. It would be amazing what would happen in our congregations if every member fulfilled his or her given ministry.

B. Preparation for Service (v. 12)

12. For the perfecting of the saints, for the work of the ministry, for the edifying of the body of Christ.

The offices or ministries that Paul mentions were not given for the purpose of providing positions for a select few. Nor were these leaders to be the only ones fulfilling ministry. Today many have the notion that the only people who ought to be engaged in ministry are those professionals whom we designate as ministers, pastors, or preachers. After all, we pay them to do the work. Other versions make the Greek of this text clearer. The *New International Version,* for example, states that the leaders whom Christ gave to the church are "to prepare God's people for works of service, so that the body of Christ may be built up." According to Paul these special ministers are not to do the work all alone. Rather, their main task is to prepare or equip *the saints* so that *the saints* may carry these ministries.

GET THEM INTO CIRCULATION

During the reign of Oliver Cromwell, the British government ran out of silver with which to make the coinage of the land. Cromwell sent men throughout the country in the hope of locating some of the precious metal. His men returned to report that the only silver they could find was in the statues of the saints in various Christian centers. "Good!" he replied, "We will melt down the saints and put them into circulation."

Paul never spoke of melting down the saints; his figure in our text was of building them up (see 4:12). The end that he had in mind however, was akin to that of Cromwell's: he wanted to get them into effective circulation.

God provides leaders to the church for this very purpose. Leaders are not to lord it over God's heritage; rather, they are to "melt down" the saints and build them up into the body of Christ so they can confidently circulate in this world and win others to Him.

God knows that the body of Christ grows and becomes mature when every man and woman in the pew is involved in ministry. The church doesn't need "statues" standing around doing nothing; it needs saints who have been "melted down" and are constantly being circulated doing the work of ministry. —T. T.

C. Unity and Maturity (v. 13)

13. Till we all come in the unity of the faith, and of the knowledge of the Son of God, unto a perfect man, unto the measure of the stature of the fulness of Christ.

The final objective of the ministries that flow from the gifts Christ has given the saints is the building up of the church. This process follows certain logical steps. First, sound teaching leads to the *unity of the faith.* We have sometimes minimized the importance of sound doctrine, supposing that the saints can come to maturity with little understanding of what Christianity is all about. The result has been Biblical illiteracy and a tragic falling away from the faith by some. Second, sound teaching leads to a *knowledge of the Son of God.* Unless we know who Jesus is, we can scarcely know how to obey Him. Finally, sound teaching will lead to a *perfect man* whose life is modeled after the life of Christ. *Perfect* here does not mean moral perfection or sinlessness. It means, instead, mature. This maturity is most readily achieved within the fellowship of the saints.

IV. Expected Results (Ephesians 4:14-16)

A. Stability (v. 14)

14. That we henceforth be no more children, tossed to and fro, and carried about with every wind of doctrine, by the sleight of men, and cunning craftiness, whereby they lie in wait to deceive.

Mature Christians are anchored to the rock, secure in their faith and knowledge of the Son of God. Immature Christians, on the other hand, are like boats driven by every changing wind or wave. The doctrines, or teachings, of men and women carry them first this way and then that. Such teachings are managed by the *sleight* or trickery *of men,* who by their *cunning craftiness* wait to *deceive* the unwary and lead them away from the faith.

B. Growth (vv. 15, 16)

15. But speaking the truth in love, may grow up into him in all things, which is the head, even Christ.

If we follow the sound teaching of the pastors and teachers God gives us, we will grow and approach maturity as Christians. We will resist the deceivers by *speaking the truth,* and we will speak it *in love.* Even sound teaching may fail to reach people if it is not presented lovingly and humbly. Finally, in all that we do, we will try to become more and more like Christ.

16. From whom the whole body fitly joined together and compacted by that which every joint supplieth, according to the effectual working in the measure of every part, maketh increase of the body unto the edifying of itself in love.

Paul compares the church to the human body. When every part is functioning properly, there is unity and harmony of purpose; the body is healthy and growing. So too in the church, the body of Christ. When each member does his or her part in the work of service, the church will grow into what it ought to be. There will be unity and harmony too. since Christ is the head to whom all the members submit, all will be done *in love.*

UNKNOWN HEROES

Passing through Washington D. C., one cannot help noticing the many monuments that have been erected in honor of America's early leaders. The city bears the stamp of such great men as Thomas Jefferson, Patrick Henry, Benjamin Franklin, Andrew Jackson, and Ulysses S. Grant. We have certainly done an admirable job of remembering our national heroes.

As one drives through the capital, the eye is drawn not only to the stately Lincoln Memorial and the towering Washington Monument. Passersby are compelled to observe Arlington National Cemetery also. In these beautiful grounds lie the bodies of many of America's lesser known heroes, memorialized by rows of simple, white crosses. In a sense, these graves represent all who sacrificed their lives to preserve America's independence and uphold the ideals of freedom and democracy. And these too deserve great honor.

In the church the ministries of some cause them to be in the public eye, while others work quietly behind the scenes. The tasks performed by the latter may not always seem great, but they are essential to a healthy church. In fact, Paul says the body of Christ builds itself up "as each part does its work" (v. 16, *New International Version*). Realizing this, may we all willingly use our gifts for the Lord, and may we open our eyes to see and appreciate the work that others render for the kingdom. —T. T.

Home Daily Bible Readings

Monday, Jan. 25—One in Christ (Ephesians 2:11-22)

Tuesday, Jan. 26—A Prayer for Wisdom (Ephesians 3:1-13)

Wednesday, Jan. 27—The Love of Christ (Ephesians 3:14-21)

Thursday, Jan. 28—Show Your Love (Ephesians 4:1-6)

Friday, Jan. 29—Special Gifts (Ephesians (4:7-16)

Saturday, Jan. 30—New Life in Christ (Ephesians 4:17-24)

Sunday, Jan. 31—Members of Christ's Body (Ephesians 4:25-32)

Conclusion

A. "That They All May Be One"

God never intended the church to be divided, but across the centuries the church has been sundered over theological differences, cultural differences, and divisive leadership. Every thoughtful Christian is concerned over these divisions. Divisions have caused fellow Christians to verbally and sometimes physically abuse one another. But worse, divisiveness has hampered the church's evangelistic efforts. An unbelieving world is often turned off by a divided church.

At this late date with so many divisions in the church, we are tempted to feel frustrated and helpless in achieving the unity of which Paul speaks in Ephesians 4. But some things we can do. We can respect the integrity of those with whom we differ. We can enter into dialogue with those whose views differ from ours. When we do, we may find that some of our differences are more verbal than real. We can join together in Bible study and allow the Scriptures to speak to our differences. We can work with other groups on many projects without compromising our convictions. For example, we can work together to feed the hungry or provide shelter for the homeless or oppose pornography in our communities. Above all, we can pray the prayer for unity among believers that Jesus prayed on the night that He was betrayed (John 17:10-23).

B. Let Us Pray

We thank You, Father, that You have given us the church as the ark of our salvation. May each of us strive to be one with our fellow believers and use the gifts that you have given to us to edify the church. In our Master's name, we pray. Amen.

C. Thought to Remember

"The church . . . is essentially, intentionally, and constitutionally one." —Thomas Campbell

Learning by Doing

This page contains an alternate lesson plan emphasizing learning activities. Classes desiring such student involvement will find these suggestions helpful.

Learning Goals

After examining the call in Ephesians 4:1-16 for the unity of the church, the learner will be able to:

1. Identify the basis for church unity as outlined in the text.
2. Explain how the gifts to the church help the church to achieve unity.
3. Identify the results of unity in the church.
4. Select a way to contribute to the unity of the church.

Into the Lesson

As the class members arrive, have them form groups of three or four. Give each group a puzzle that, when completed, will form a picture of a human body. Intentionally omit one piece from the puzzle. Don't mention what you have done as the groups express frustration at having a piece missing. Allot up to ten minutes for this activity.

When the time allotted for this activity has elapsed, make the transition into the lesson by stating that this lesson examines the nature of the body of Christ and its function.

Into the Word

Briefly present the information in the "Lesson Background" section. Then have someone read Ephesians 1:1-16 aloud.

Have the class members continue to work in the groups they were in for the introductory activity. Assign each group one of the following three tasks:

1. Read Ephesians 1:1-16. Focus on verses 1-6. What personal characteristics does Paul urge all in the church to have? What seven examples of oneness in the church does Paul mention? How do these personal characteristics contribute to the church's unity? How do the examples of oneness contribute to unity in the church?
2. Read Ephesians 1:1-16. Focus on verses 7-13. Identify the gifts that Christ has given the church. What is the nature of each gift mentioned? Explain the purpose of each gift. What is each gift's contribution to the unity of the church?
3. Read Ephesians 1:1-16. Focus on verses 14-16. What results are to be expected from the gifts Christ gives the church? How are these results demonstrated in practicality?

Allot up to ten minutes for the groups to do their work. Then call the groups together. Use the answers from each group to serve as the basis for covering the text. After each group has reported, ask these questions:

1. What will be the result if Christians fail to demonstrate in their lives the qualities mentioned in verse 2, or if they refuse to use their gifts for the benefit of the church? (Point out their frustration in the opening activity when one piece was missing from the puzzle.)
2. What attitude should permeate every Christian's service to the church?

Into Life

Use the following questions to continue the discussion you have begun:

1. What is the nature of the unity of the church that is described in Ephesians?
2. Does the unity described in Ephesians require that Christians agree on every matter within the church? Why? What matters must we agree on?
3. Thomas Campbell said, "The church . . . is essentially, intentionally, and constitutionally one." What did he mean as it is considered in the light of this passage?
4. In verse 11 Paul names some spiritual gifts that Christ has given to the church. Name some other gifts He has given.
5. How can we tell if gifts are being used properly in our congregation?
6. How can we contribute to the unity of Christ's body when the church today seems so hopelessly and helplessly divided?
7. How can we contribute to the unity of our own local congregation?

Now give the original groups the missing piece from each puzzle. Have them work on the puzzle again. Of course, this time it can be completed. Ask the class what this teaches us about the church. Reemphasize the need for unity in the church and the results when unity is demonstrated in the church.

Have the class members sing "We Are One in the Bond of Love." If you have time, you may want to sing another song or two about unity.

Conclude the session with a prayer circle. As the class members hold hands, ask three or four persons to offer prayers aloud for the unity of Christ's body on earth.

Let's Talk It Over

The questions on this page are designed to encourage review of the lesson Scriptures and to promote discussion of the lesson by the class. The answers provided are only discussion starters. Let your class talk it over from there.

1. Paul urges all Christians to live in a manner that is worthy of the calling they have received, and he mentions four distinguishing traits of such a life. Identify them and tell how they promote unity in the church.

(1) *Lowliness.* We would speak of this quality as humility. Humility is self-effacement, the willingness to keep oneself in the background. Egotism, by contrast, is an exaggerated sense of one's self-importance. Of the two attitudes, it can easily be seen which promotes harmony within a group. But humility goes further; it acknowledges *the source* of all abilities and achievements. It is opposed to pride or haughtiness of spirit, acknowledging that all is of God.

(2) *Meekness.* This is gentleness, which is opposed to self-assertion. Some may misunderstand meekness, gentleness, as weakness. Far from it! Meekness is power or strength under control. It is one thing to submit to another if one is weak and has no other choice. It is quite something else for a strong person to be submissive and choose the role of a servant. The strength is there; it is under control to be used in the highest good of others

(3) *Long-suffering.* This term implies not merely patient endurance in the face of provocation, but a refusal to give up hope for improvement in a disturbed relationship with another. Long-suffering is expressed in showing forbearance to another, in refraining from demanding what is due.

(4) *Love.* The highest quality or virtue is love, that unconditional self-giving that seeks the highest good of the other. To be like the Father is to love in this way. All qualities and virtues are summed up in this one!

2. What does it mean to "speak the truth in love"?

Speaking the truth in love focuses on the content of what is spoken (truth) and the attitude of the one doing the speaking (love). Truth spoken without love can degenerate into dogmatic arrogance and insensitive legalism. When love pervades the truth, judgmentalism, attacks, and divisiveness will vanish. Christians may rationalize their abusive treatment of brethren with a statement such as this: "I said it because it was the truth." Speaking the truth *in love* with our brethren not only deals the deathblow to harsh, barren attacks upon those with whom we disagree; it also promotes the harmonious functioning of the church, which results in the spiritual health and growth of the Lord's body.

3. If Christ intended His church to be unified ("one"), why is it so divided today?

Due to Satan's craftiness and influence, human beings are led to thwart divine intentions. Even in its infancy, the church became divided when false teaching was disseminated among the believers. That false teaching was confronted and challenged. The result? The unity of the fellowship suffered. Down through the centuries, theological differences have become the ground for division. Cultural, racial, ethnic, and social differences have provided fertile soil for division. One of the greatest causes of disunity in the church is the desire for power. Many human beings are not content unless they are able to control the thinking and the actions of other persons. When two or more persons of this type are in the same sphere of activity, whether in a local congregation or in a wider fellowship, conflict and dissension arise as the parties attempt to establish control. Jesus indicated that this attitude and behavior are pagan in nature (see Luke 22:24-26). How sad that anyone who claims to follow Jesus, the servant Lord, should adopt the motives and methods of the world!

4. In our lesson text, Paul mentions that Christ has given gifts to the church. What four principles may be stated concerning "giftedness" in the church?

(1) *Everyone is gifted.* Christ has given each member of the body a gift or gifts. If someone feels no giftedness, it is because the gift has not been discovered or utilized.

(2) *A variety of gifts have been given.* Not everyone has the same gift. If the body is to be properly equipped, many different gifts are needed.

(3) *Gifts are for ministry.* Christ's gifts are not given to establish positions of prestige or power. They are given so that all may render service for the good of the church.

(4) *Gifts are to edify the church.* The ultimate purpose of all gifts is for the building up of the body of Christ.

Commissioned to Witness

February 7
Lesson 10

LESSON SCRIPTURE: Luke 24:13-53.

PRINTED TEXT: Luke 24:36-53.

DEVOTIONAL READING: Acts 1:1-8.

Luke 24:36-53

36 And as they thus spake, Jesus himself stood in the midst of them, and saith unto them, Peace be unto you.

37 But they were terrified and affrighted, and supposed that they had seen a spirit.

38 And he said unto them, Why are ye troubled? and why do thoughts arise in your hearts?

39 Behold my hands and my feet, that it is I myself: handle me, and see; for a spirit hath not flesh and bones, as ye see me have.

40 And when he had thus spoken, he showed them his hands and his feet.

41 And while they yet believed not for joy, and wondered, he said unto them, Have ye here any meat?

42 And they gave him a piece of a broiled fish, and of a honeycomb.

43 And he took it, and did eat before them.

44 And he said unto them, These are the words which I spake unto you, while I was yet with you, that all things must be fulfilled, which were written in the law of Moses, and in the prophets, and in the psalms, concerning me.

45 Then opened he their understanding, that they might understand the Scriptures,

46 And said unto them, Thus it is written, and thus it behooved Christ to suffer, and to rise from the dead the third day:

47 And that repentance and remission of sins should be preached in his name among all nations, beginning at Jerusalem.

48 And ye are witnesses of these things.

49 And, behold, I send the promise of my Father upon you: but tarry ye in the city of Jerusalem, until ye be endued with power from on high.

50 And he led them out as far as to Bethany, and he lifted up his hands, and blessed them.

51 And it came to pass, while he blessed them, he was parted from them, and carried up into heaven.

52 And they worshipped him, and returned to Jerusalem with great joy:

53 And were continually in the temple, praising and blessing God. Amen.

GOLDEN TEXT: Repentance and remission of sins should be preached in his name among all nations, beginning at Jerusalem.—Luke 24:47.

Good News for All

Unit 3: Sharing the Good News

(Lessons 10-13)

Lesson Aims

This study will help students:

1. Have increased appreciation for the evidence supporting belief in Jesus' resurrection.
2. Be motivated to share the gospel of salvation this week with one person who does not know Jesus as Savior.

Lesson Outline

INTRODUCTION
- A. "Look to Your Marching Orders"
- B. Lesson Background

I. JESUS APPEARS TO HIS DISCIPLES (Luke 24:36-43)
- A. Jesus in Their Midst (v. 36)
- B. The Disciples' Response (v. 37)
- C. Jesus' Reassurance (vv. 38-40)
- D. Further Proof (vv. 41-43)
  Not a Ghost Story

II. JESUS TEACHES HIS DISCIPLES (Luke 24:44-48)
- A. Fulfillment of Scripture (v. 44)
- B. The Disciples' Understanding Opened (vv. 45, 46)
- C. The Disciples Given a Mission (vv. 47, 48)
  Witnesses

III. JESUS LEAVES HIS DISCIPLES (Luke 24:49-53)
- A. Promise of Power (v. 49)
- B. Jesus' Ascension (vv. 50, 51)
- C. The Disciples' Response (vv. 52, 53)

CONCLUSION
- A. "Beginning at Jerusalem"
- B. Let Us Pray
- C. Thought to Remember

Visual 10 of the visuals packet illustrates an important truth. If you use the activity suggested in the "Into the Lesson" section on page 199, wait until the activity is completed before displaying the visual. It is shown on page 197.

Introduction

A. "Look to Your Marching Orders"

On one occasion the Duke of Wellington was attending a meeting at which a young theologian was decrying missions. He insisted that missions were no longer needed and were a waste of money and effort. In addition, missionaries upset and even destroyed native cultures.

Finally the old duke interrupted: "Young man, what were the final orders our Lord gave to His disciples?"

"Well," stammered the surprised speaker, "He told the disciples to go into all the world and preach to all nations."

"Has that order ever been rescinded?" asked the duke.

"Not that I know of," came the reply.

The duke's response was to the point: "I'm not a theologian; I'm an old soldier. One thing I learned as a soldier was that when the commanding officer gave an order, I obeyed it. All I can say to you is, 'Look to your marching orders, young man! Look to your marching orders!'"

B. Lesson Background

Our lessons for this quarter are a survey of the New Testament and have the theme, "Good News for All." In Unit 1 (lessons 1-4), we considered the coming of Jesus Christ. Unit 2 (lessons 5-9) dealt with the church as God's new community, receiving and sharing His grace in its life. Today's lesson begins the third and final unit, entitled, "Sharing the Good News." These last four lessons emphasize the church's outreach to the lost.

The lesson text for today is taken from the final chapter of the Gospel of Luke, and gives us details of two different scenes that occurred following Jesus' resurrection. The first scene took place in a room somewhere in Jerusalem where the apostles (minus Thomas) and other disciples had gathered on the evening of resurrection day.

It had been a hectic day. Hearing the reports of Jesus' resurrection, the apostles' reactions had swung from disbelief, to uncertainty, to growing excitement over the news (see Luke 24:10, 11, 24, 34). Compounding their emotional state was their fear of the Jewish authorities (John 20:19).

As the assembled group discussed the events of the day, two disciples, to whom Jesus had appeared on the way to Emmaus, entered the room. As the two spilled out their story, the excitement of the group must have grown all the more (Luke 24:33-35). Then, even as they were discussing this new information, Jesus suddenly appeared in their midst and showed himself alive to them all.

The second scene occurred forty days later when Jesus led the disciples out to the Mount of Olives. This was their last meeting with Him, for from that place He ascended into Heaven.

I. Jesus Appears to His Disciples (Luke 24:36-43)

A. Jesus in Their Midst (v. 36)

36. And as they thus spake, Jesus himself stood in the midst of them, and saith unto them, Peace be unto you.

This is probably the same appearance of Jesus that is recorded in John 20:19-24. Some of the details are different, however, showing the independence of the Gospel writers. *As they thus spake.* This refers to verse 35. The two disciples who had met Jesus on the road to Emmaus had just come into the room to report of their experience. As they discussed this latest event along with the other momentous events of the day, Jesus appeared in their midst. John tells us that the doors were locked for fear of the Jews (20:19), but locked doors were no barrier to Him who could not be held by the bonds of death.

Jesus' first act was to minister to their needs. They were fearful of the authorities, so His first words, *Peace be unto you,* may have been spoken to calm these fears. But perhaps there was a deeper meaning to His greeting. It may be that He was referring to the ultimate peace that now was theirs because of His death on the cross (see Ephesians 2:14-18).

B. The Disciples' Response (v. 37)

37. But they were terrified and affrighted, and supposed that they had seen a spirit.

Terrified. This may be better translated "startled." These disciples had just been discussing His resurrection, and so one would think that their emotion should have been joy rather than fear at His appearance. We need to understand that they had been on an emotional roller coaster all day long. Further, while they may have believed in the resurrection intellectually, they were not expecting a face-to-face meeting with the risen Lord. It may be that the suddenness of His appearance, as if He materialized out of thin air, caused them to react the way they did. Their immediate response was that they were seeing a ghost, a response that many people today might make under similar circumstances.

C. Jesus' Reassurance (vv. 38-40)

38-40. And he said unto them, Why are ye troubled? and why do thoughts arise in your hearts? Behold my hands and my feet, that it is I myself: handle me, and see; for a spirit hath not flesh and bones, as ye see me have. And when he had thus spoken, he showed them his hands and his feet.

Jesus knew what was troubling them and He immediately took steps to reassure them. He first asked them the cause of their doubts. We ourselves have learned that when we have a problem, the first step toward the solution is to ask why we have the problem or what the problem really is. Once Jesus had started them to think about their doubts, He then offered positive proof that He was not a ghost. After all, ghosts do not have *flesh and bones.* Then He *showed them his hands and his feet,* anticipating that the wounds made while He hung on the cross would be convincing.

D. Further Proof (vv. 41-43)

41-43. And while they yet believed not for joy, and wondered, he said unto them, Have ye here any meat? And they gave him a piece of a broiled fish, and of a honeycomb. And he took it, and did eat before them.

The disciples *believed not for joy,* even after Jesus had shown them His hands and feet. Just two days previously, they had seen Him die on the cross and His body laid in the tomb. His death had brought an end to everything and had plunged them into the darkness of grief and despair. It was, therefore, almost impossible to believe that He now stood in their midst. One moment they must have thought excitedly, "This is Jesus!" and the next, "It's too good to be true; it must be a ghost." Probably most of us at one time or another have experienced such feelings. We reject good news even when it seems obviously true because we fear disappointment should it prove not to be true.

Patiently Jesus took another step to bring them to faith. He had already shown them His hands and feet, demonstrating that He had a physical body. Now he asked for food. By eating food He would clearly show that He was not a ghost. The food available, left over from the evening meal, was *broiled fish.* He was handed a piece, which He then ate, showing beyond a doubt that He was not a ghost. Many manuscripts do not mention the *honeycomb,* and so most recent translations do not mention it.

NOT A GHOST STORY

An episode of Unsolved Mysteries a couple of years ago dealt with the Queen Mary, the great luxury liner that is in permanent dry dock. The point stressed in the episode was that the Queen Mary is thought to be haunted. In the presenta-

How to Say It

EMMAUS. Em-*may*-us.

tion a number of individuals related their stories. One woman told of an incident when she was on an escalator. She turned and saw a man behind her, only to discover upon reaching the top that he had vanished. Another story involved a waitress. One minute she noticed an expressionless woman at one of her tables, and a minute later the woman had disappeared. Other "evidences" were cited also.

This writer remains skeptical, convinced that the evidences cited can all be explained on a rational basis.

The evidences of the resurrection of Jesus, on the other hand, are of a different kind and are far more convincing. The resurrected body of Jesus was seen by numerous witnesses at one and the same time; it could be touched. Jesus could reason with people, and He ate food in their presence. He was no ghost; He was a dead man who had been brought back to life.

Ghost stories are shrouded in mystery and uncertainty and are designed to frighten. The resurrection story is based on fact and brings comfort to those who believe. —T. T.

II. Jesus Teaches His Disciples (Luke 24:44-48)

A. Fulfillment of Scripture (v. 44)

44. And he said unto them, These are the words which I spake unto you, while I was yet with you, that all things must be fulfilled, which were written in the law of Moses, and in the prophets, and in the psalms, concerning me.

When did Jesus give the teachings that are recorded in verses 44-48? Opinions of Bible scholars are divided on this question. Some think that they were given on Easter evening when Jesus appeared to the ten apostles, the two from Emmaus, and perhaps other disciples. Other scholars think that Jesus gave these teachings at indefinite times during the forty days following His resurrection. Although they may have been spoken during later appearances, they certainly seem appropriate in the context of Jesus' appearance to the group assembled on Easter evening.

During the three years Jesus was with His disciples, He had on several occasions pointed out that His life and ministry were a fulfillment of Old Testament prophecies. Some of these are mentioned in the Gospel accounts, but certainly He must have made references to other prophecies that are not mentioned in the Gospels. We may wonder why the disciples were so slow to understand these prophecies. We must realize that they were blinded by traditional Jewish prejudices. As a result, they were looking for an entirely different kind of a Messiah than Jesus proved to be.

The Jews divided the Old Testament into three major divisions—Law, Prophets, and the Writings. Jesus here referred to these three divisions with the *Psalms* representing the third division. He stressed that all three of the divisions contained prophecies concerning Him.

B. The Disciples' Understanding Opened (vv. 45, 46)

45, 46. Then opened he their understanding, that they might understand the Scriptures, and said unto them, Thus it is written, and thus it behooved Christ to suffer, and to rise from the dead the third day.

The enlightenment that the two on the road to Emmaus had experienced earlier (Luke 24:31, 32) was now shared by the other disciples. Scriptures that they had been familiar with all their lives they were now able to understand more fully, especially those Scriptures that spoke of a Messiah who must *suffer,* die, and be raised *from the dead.* He explained that it was necessary for Him to die that man's sins might be forgiven, and that in His resurrection, man's hope of life after death is made impregnable.

C. The Disciples Given a Mission (vv. 47, 48)

47, 48. And that repentance and remission of sins should be preached in his name among all nations, beginning at Jerusalem. And ye are witnesses of these things.

The disciples were led to understand also that the good news of Christ's death, burial, and resurrection was to be preached in order to lead persons to *repentance.* Luke gives abundant evidence in his later work, the Acts of the Apostles, that repentance is used in this verse to cover the whole range of the surrender of one's life to Christ. Only in such complete submission does one find *remission of sins.*

The disciples had been with Jesus from the beginning of His ministry to His resurrection. They had heard His teaching, they had seen His miracles, and they were witnesses of His resurrection. Now they were being sent out to share with others the message of salvation in Christ. They were to begin *at Jerusalem.* That seemed logical enough, for that is where they were and also where Jesus had many followers. But Jerusalem was only the beginning, because they were commissioned to preach this message *among all nations.*

We are not told if the disciples had any questions when so great a challenge was presented to them. Did they wonder how a small handful of men could take this message to the whole world, or where they were going to get the resources to carry out this commission? Perhaps they were shocked into silence by the vast scope of the commission, or perhaps they were quietly confident that He who gave the commission would also provide the means for accomplishing it.

WITNESSES

The Witness is the story of a young boy who quite by chance saw the murder of a man in a men's restroom. I understand that the story, which was made into a TV movie, is based on a real-life situation. Naturally the boy, from whom the story takes its name, became a prime witness against the two men who had committed the murder. The story was complicated by the fact that the murderers were actually law enforcement officers who were engaged in a lucrative drug business. They determined that the boy would never live to witness against them in a courtroom.

Sometimes it's not easy to be a witness. Indeed, it was extremely difficult for this young boy to tell what he had seen and heard.

Not so with our witnessing for the Lord! Not in this time and place. Freely and without fear we can witness concerning the resurrection of Jesus from the dead. No, we weren't there to see Him die on the cross. Nor were we in that locked room on Easter evening when Jesus suddenly appeared to the group of disciples. But we can rely upon the eyewitness testimony of those who were. Taking their story we can tell it to all the peoples of the earth. That story is simple: Jesus Christ has conquered death! —T. T.

III. Jesus Leaves His Disciples (Luke 24:49-53)

A. Promise of Power (v. 49)

49. And, behold, I send the promise of my Father upon you: but tarry ye in the city of Jerusalem, until ye be endued with power from on high.

The closing verses of this chapter parallel what Luke wrote in Acts 1:1-14. The Acts passage has some details that are not mentioned here, and so we need to consider both of these passages for a fuller understanding of Jesus' final meeting with the apostles and His subsequent ascension. On the day of His ascension, Jesus gathered the eleven together for the first time. We don't know where this meeting took place, but it may well have been the familiar upper room. Jesus had already given them their commission to preach His name to all the nations. Now He gave them further preparation to carry out that task.

visual 10

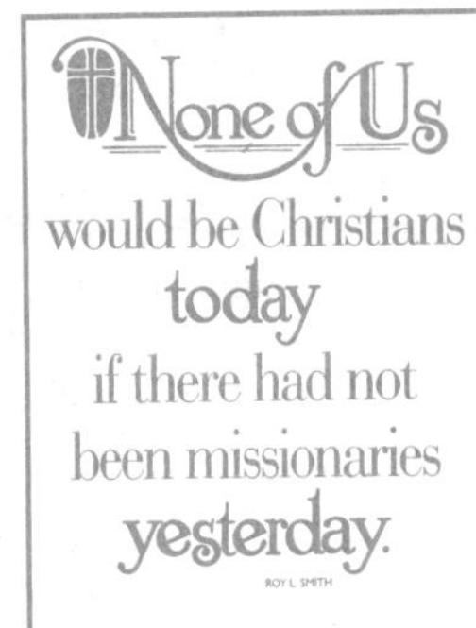

Jesus told them that He would send them *the promise of my Father,* which is the gift of the Holy Spirit (John 14:16, 17). The Holy Spirit would guide them into all truth and also provide them the strength to face the challenge of the commission Jesus had given them. Jesus did not impart the Holy Spirit to them at that time. They were to return to Jerusalem and wait. It turned out that they had to wait ten days until the day of Pentecost (Acts 2).

B. Jesus' Ascension (vv. 50, 51)

50. And he led them out as far as to Bethany, and he lifted up his hands, and blessed them.

If Jesus met with His disciples in the upper room or some other place in Jerusalem, then He probably led them through the city streets, out a gate on the eastern side of the city, and up the slopes of the Mount of Olives. Some may object saying that His enemies would have recognized Him had He walked through the city streets. But this is no problem. We need to remember that even His closest disciples did not recognize Him until they were shown many proofs.

As far as to Bethany. Only the gospel of Luke gives us the location for the ascension. Bethany, located about two miles east of the city of Jerusalem, was the home of Mary, Martha, and Lazarus. Apparently Jesus led the disciples only to the crest of the hill that overlooked Bethany. We have no way of knowing the exact spot where the ascension took place.

The account in Acts indicates that there was additional conversation at this point, following up the discussion that had occurred earlier. Among other things, the disciples asked if Jesus was going to restore the kingdom to Israel at that time, indicating that they still did not fully understand the nature of His kingdom (1:8). At some point in the conversation, Jesus silenced the disciples, *lifted up his hands, and blessed them.* Jesus' final act was to convey to them the divine benediction that would sustain them in the difficult ministry that lay ahead.

51. And it came to pass, while he blessed them, he was parted from them, and carried up into heaven.

Even as Jesus pronounced His blessing upon them, He was taken up into the air. Jesus' body was no longer subject to the ordinary laws of gravity. Acts 1:9 informs us that a cloud received him out of their sight. Jesus had disappeared from their presence before, but this disappearance had an air of finality that indicated His earthly ministry was completed. He had returned to Heaven to assume His place at the right hand of the Father, where He would direct the work of the church through His followers.

C. The Disciples' Response (vv. 52, 53)

52, 53. And they worshipped him, and returned to Jerusalem with great joy: and were continually in the temple, praising and blessing God. Amen.

Acts 1:10, 11 tell us that as they watched Jesus ascend, two men, apparently angels, stood by them. The disciples stood and watched in amazement as Jesus ascended, certainly a normal reaction under the circumstances. But the angels chided them for their curiosity, informing them that Jesus would someday return just as He had left them.

What a transformation the ascension wrought on the disciples! In the forty days following Jesus' resurrection, the disciples had been on an emotional roller coaster, moving from fear to hope to joy. Now all that was behind them. They returned to Jerusalem to the upper room where they must have rehearsed all the things that had happened to them. But they also showed their joy by frequent visits to the temple where they publicly praised God and blessed Him.

Conclusion

A. "Beginning at Jerusalem"

Jesus commissioned His disciples to carry the gospel to the whole world, beginning at Jerusalem. Only a few days later at Pentecost, Peter preached the first gospel sermon, and with amazing results. Three thousand persons accepted the good news and were baptized (Acts 2:41). In spite of persecution and other problems, the church in Jerusalem began to grow. It soon had five thousand members and continued to grow (4:4).

Persecution forced many of the Christians to leave Jerusalem, and wherever they went they carried the gospel with them, making new converts. But as the church reached out, it faced new problems. Gentiles also responded to the gospel. It was not easy for Jewish Christians, with their long history of exclusiveness, to accept Gentiles into the church. After considerable controversy the church was convinced that both Jews and Gentiles should have equal access to the gospel (Acts 15).

In every age, people have felt more comfortable with their own kind, and so they have often limited their evangelistic appeal to people of their own language, culture, or race. As a result, Jesus' name still has not been preached far and wide as He intended it to be.

A valid indicator of a congregation's interest in fulfilling Jesus' commission is its missions budget. How much of the budget is designated for the purpose of sending out the gospel to the peoples of the world who have never once heard it? Bring your own church missions budget to class and examine it in the light of this standard. Such a review might reveal different attitudes toward missions and lead to a profitable discussion. Above all, help students understand that Jesus' commission was for His disciples to begin at Jerusalem and go to all nations, and we today must do our part in fulfilling that commission.

B. Let Us Pray

Dear God, we thank You that You so loved a lost world that You sent Your only begotten Son to die for the redemption of sinful humanity. Help us to understand better the commission our Lord gave to His disciples. Help us to understand that we have the duty of seeing that salvation in His name is preached to all peoples. In our Master's name we pray. Amen.

C. Thought to Remember

"None of us would be Christians today if there had not been missionaries yesterday."

—Roy L. Smith

Home Daily Bible Readings

Monday, Feb. 1—Jesus Is a Witness (Luke 23:26-34)

Tuesday, Feb. 2—Jesus Is Crucified (Luke 23:35-43)

Wednesday, Feb. 3—Jesus' Death (Luke 23:44-56)

Thursday, Feb. 4—The Resurrection (Luke 24:1-12)

Friday, Feb. 5—The Walk to Emmaus (Luke 24:13-27)

Saturday, Feb. 6—Breaking Bread (Luke 24:28-35)

Sunday, Feb. 7—Jesus Appeared to the Disciples (Luke 24:36-49)

Learning by Doing

This page contains an alternate lesson plan emphasizing learning activities. Classes desiring such student involvement will find these suggestions helpful.

Learning Goals

After studying Luke 24:36-53, the pupil will be able to:

1. Identify the final command given by Jesus to His disciples.
2. Explain how this command is to be carried out today.
3. Evaluate the missions emphasis of his or her own congregation in light of the command given by Jesus.
4. Make a plan for personally obeying the command of Jesus.

Into the Lesson

Before the class session, write each word of the following statement on a separate card or piece of paper: "None of us would be Christians today if there had not been missionaries yesterday." Scramble the order of the words. Make one set of words for each four to six people you expect in the class.

As the class members arrive, have them form groups of four to six. Give each group one of the sets of scrambled words and ask them to arrange the words into a sentence. Instruct the group members to react to the message when they have completed it.

Allot six to eight minutes for this. Then let the groups briefly share their responses to the message.

Make the transition into the Bible study by stating that today's lesson provides a background for the statement the groups have found.

Into the Word

Use the "Lesson Background" and your own study to set the scene for the Scripture selected for today's study. Then have a class member, who has been assigned ahead of time, read Luke 24:36-53 aloud.

Develop a discussion centered on the text by using the following questions:

1. How did the disciples respond when Jesus appeared to them? (They were startled and frightened.)
2. What was the purpose of Jesus' first comment to the disciples? (It was to calm their fears.)
3. Noting the disciples' perplexity, what did Jesus have them do first, and why? (He told them to look at His hands and feet to see the crucifixion marks and thus know that it really was He standing before them.)
4. Why did Jesus invite the disciples to handle Him? Look at 1 John 1:1, 2 to help you decide. (Satisfying the physical sense of touch would corroborate what they were seeing with their eyes and hearing with their ears. This sensory verification would remove all doubt that they were simply "seeing things" or "hearing things.")
5. Why did Jesus choose to eat in the presence of His disciples? (This was further verification that He was not a ghost, but that He actually had a body of flesh and bones.)
6. What was the long-range command given by Jesus in this text? (The disciples were to preach among all nations what they had witnessed concerning Him, and to urge people to repent and receive remission of sins.)
7. What does this passage tell us about the ascension of Jesus? (It occurred near Bethany. As Jesus blessed the apostles, He was taken up from them into Heaven.)
8. Read Acts 1:3-9. How is Jesus' command stated there? (The apostles were to be witnesses in Jerusalem, Judea, Samaria, and all the world.)
9. This command was spoken to the Twelve. What application do the words have for believers nearly twenty centuries later?

Into Life

Continue the discussion you have begun by asking, "How should this command of Jesus be carried out today?"

Distribute copies of your congregation's missions budget and describe the nature of the various ministries that are supported. Then divide the class into groups of four to six. Have the groups analyze the missions budget, using the following questions:

1. What does our congregation's distribution of missions' funds reveal about our response to Jesus' command in today's text?
2. Could the missions' giving of our congregation show greater balance in carrying out Jesus' command? How?
3. How can members of our congregation be encouraged to become more personally involved in carrying out Jesus' command?

Allot six to eight minutes for the groups to work. Then discuss their conclusions.

To conclude, distribute small index cards. Have each student write out how he or she personally will obey Jesus command this week.

Let's Talk It Over

The questions on this page are designed to encourage review of the lesson Scriptures and to promote discussion of the lesson by the class. The answers provided are only discussion starters. Let your class talk it over from there.

1. If the resurrection is true (and it is), why are so many Christians apathetic about telling it to others?

It seems that many Christians are afraid to get excited about the good news of Christ's victory over death. Possibly it is a reaction to the emotionalism that is characteristic of some religious groups. Another reason why some are "super cool" about the resurrection is that the reality and importance of it has not really touched their lives. This is sad because it may even indicate a lack of a saved relationship with the Lord. Properly viewed, the resurrection of Christ is the heart of the Christian's faith and he or she can't wait to share it with others.

2. What implications does the resurrection have for Christian living?

The resurrection has significant implications for life. Christians live in faith, hope, and love. We live our lives believing in the One who triumphed over death and the grave. Living in hope means we have the confident expectation that we shall be resurrected even as He was. Love is the hallmark of the One who gave His life for man, and that love is reflected in the lives of His followers.

3. Jesus reminded His apostles that they were witnesses of His death and resurrection. What meanings of the term *witness* did Jesus have in mind regarding them? How may we witness for Him?

A witness is one who has personal knowledge of something, whether through seeing, hearing, or some other means. A witness also is one who testifies to what he or she knows. Jesus was telling His disciples that both meanings of the term applied to them. They knew He had been crucified. They were assured that He had died and had been buried. And He himself had provided the first-hand experience by which they knew He had come back from the dead. But they were not to keep this information to themselves. They were to tell everyone everywhere so that all might find remission of sins in Him.

We, of course, did not witness the life, death, and resurrection of Jesus as the apostles did. Only one generation of persons could do that. But we have their testimony preserved for us in the New Testament. Our role is to share their testimony so that people in our generation can examine it and come to belief in Jesus. As we share that message, we *can* give first-hand testimony about what Christ has done for us. That word, with the example of our changed lives, can have a powerful effect on others.

4. What responses do Christians today make to Jesus' commission that they preach the gospel to the whole world?

There are a variety of responses. Following are some of them:

(1) He didn't mean me. That commission was for His apostles. I'm just an ordinary member of the church. Jesus intended for professionals to fulfill His commission.

(2) I couldn't possibly do that! I don't have the gift or the experience. I'm tongue-tied in situations when the opportunity to witness arises. I'm not articulate or well enough informed to witness.

(3) I'm scared, but I'll trust Him. The thought that I am dealing with the issue of one's ultimate and eternal destination frightens me, but I'll trust the Lord to make me adequate. When I am weak, *His* strength can be manifest.

(4) Let's go! What are we waiting for? Souls are dying every second, babies are being born every second—if we don't get busy, millions of people will die without Jesus, and the population explosion will get so far ahead of us we'll never catch up.

5. What are some common objections to missionary work, and how do we answer them?

It is frequently suggested that heathen people would be better off if missionaries left them alone. These people assume that non-Christians who never hear the gospel will somehow be saved, but that view is not upheld by the Scriptures. Another thoughtless objection is the familiar sentiment that "we have enough of a mission field right here in our own back yard." But that is a selfish limitation of the Great Commission.

Proclaim the Gospel

February 14
Lesson 11

LESSON SCRIPTURE: Romans 10.

PRINTED TEXT: Romans 10:5-17.

DEVOTIONAL READING: 1 Corinthians 9:19-27.

Romans 10:5-17

5 For Moses describeth the righteousness which is of the law, That the man which doeth those things shall live by them.

6 But the righteousness which is of faith speaketh on this wise, Say not in thine heart, Who shall ascend into heaven? (that is, to bring Christ down from above:)

7 Or, Who shall descend into the deep? (that is, to bring up Christ again from the dead.)

8 But what saith it? The word is nigh thee, even in thy mouth, and in thy heart: that is, the word of faith, which we preach;

9 That if thou shalt confess with thy mouth the Lord Jesus, and shalt believe in thine heart that God hath raised him from the dead, thou shalt be saved.

10 For with the heart man believeth unto righteousness; and with the mouth confession is made unto salvation.

11 For the Scripture saith, Whosoever believeth on him shall not be ashamed.

12 For there is no difference between the Jew and the Greek: for the same Lord over all is rich unto all that call upon him.

13 For whosoever shall call upon the name of the Lord shall be saved.

14 How then shall they call on him in whom they have not believed? and how shall they believe in him of whom they have not heard? and how shall they hear without a preacher?

15 And how shall they preach, except they be sent? as it is written, How beautiful are the feet of them that preach the gospel of peace, and bring glad tidings of good things!

16 But they have not all obeyed the gospel. For Isaiah saith, Lord, who hath believed our report?

17 So then faith cometh by hearing, and hearing by the word of God.

GOLDEN TEXT: So then faith cometh by hearing, and hearing by the word of God. —Romans 10:17.

Good News for All

Unit 3: Sharing the Good News

(Lessons 10-13)

Lesson Aims

As a result of studying this lesson, each student should:

1. Understand that righteousness comes through faith, not through observing the law.
2. Have an increased appreciation for the power of the preached word to bring people to Christ.
3. Be better prepared to take the saving word to those who need it.

Lesson Outline

INTRODUCTION
- A. Faith Comes by Hearing
- B. Lesson Background

I. RIGHTEOUSNESS BY LAW (Romans 10:5)

II. RIGHTEOUSNESS BY FAITH (Romans 10:6-13)
- A. Nearness of the Message (vv. 6-8)
- B. Blessings of the Message (vv. 9-11)
- C. Universality of the Message (vv. 12, 13)

III. REACHING OUT WITH THE WORD (Romans 10:14-17)
- A. People Must Hear the Message (v. 14)
- B. Preachers Must Be Sent (v. 15)
  Beautiful Feet
- C. Personal Responses Are Made (vv. 16, 17)
  A Pesky Fly

CONCLUSION
- A. Faith Comes by Hearing and Hearing Again
- B. "Except They Be Sent"
- C. Let Us Pray
- D. Thought to Remember

Display visual 11 of the visuals packet and let it remain before the class throughout the session. The visual is shown on page 204.

Introduction

A. Faith Comes by Hearing

A young minister, noted for his preaching skills, was called to the pulpit of a church in a college town. After he was there for a few months, there was a marked decline in the quality of his sermons. He was quite aware of the situation and went to discuss it with one of his elders, a saintly old man who had served the congregation for many years.

"If I mention anything scientific in my sermon, I know that Professor A, who is head of the science department at the college, will catch any mistake I make," said the preacher. "I'm afraid to make any references to history, because Professor B is a historian and would be critical. And I get tongue-tied trying to keep my grammar straight, because Professor C is in the English Department."

"Well, son," said the old elder, "I wouldn't worry too much about pleasing my critics. Just preach the gospel. They know little enough about that."

In a culture that places a high premium on information, we expect our ministers to be reasonably knowledgeable about all kinds of things. In an effort to satisfy this desire for knowledge, however, there is a temptation to neglect the gospel. Let us never forget that it is through the hearing of the gospel that people are brought to faith in Jesus Christ and find eternal life.

B. Lesson Background

Today's lesson on proclaiming the gospel logically follows last week's lesson on the commission Jesus gave His disciples to carry the gospel to the whole world. In his letter to the Christians in Rome, Paul shows how that commission was being carried out on the practical level.

The epistle to the Romans was probably written from Corinth about A.D. 58 while Paul was on his third missionary journey. Romans is, on the one hand, a profound theological treatise. But Paul never allowed his scholarship to keep him from applying God's truths to everyday Christian living. Romans 10, set in the midst of a theological discussion, reminds us that the ultimate purpose of all theology is to bring people into a saving relationship with Jesus Christ.

In the verses immediately preceding our text (Romans 9:30—10:4), Paul draws a sharp contrast between Christians and unbelieving Jews. Christians are made righteous because of their faith, even though what they do is not altogether righteous. Unbelieving Jews reject the righteousness that God is willing to give to believers. They try instead to make themselves righteous by keeping the law, and they fail. Our lesson continues the contrast.

I. Righteousness by Law (Romans 10:5)

5. For Moses describeth the righteousness which is of the law, That the man which doeth those things shall live by them.

On Mount Sinai God gave His law to Moses, who then gave it to the people of Israel. That law is recorded in the books of Exodus, Leviticus, Numbers, and Deuteronomy. The law itself showed how a person could attain *righteousness;* and that way is seen in the statement at the end of verse 5, which is taken from Leviticus 18:5. The person who obeyed the law in all points would be righteous, and therefore would have the right to live. The life spoken of is more than the continuation of existence; it includes the promise of divine favor and acceptance.

There is a problem, however, and Paul mentioned it earlier in this letter. That problem is this: "All have sinned and come short of the glory of God" (Romans 3:23). No Israelite, indeed no mortal man, has perfectly obeyed the law. By the provisions of the law, therefore, no one had the right to live.

II. Righteousness by Faith (Romans 10:6-13)

A. Nearness of the Message (vv. 6-8)

6, 7. But the righteousness which is of faith speaketh on this wise, Say not in thine heart, Who shall ascend into heaven? (that is, to bring Christ down from above:) or, Who shall descend into the deep? (that is, to bring up Christ again from the dead.)

In this and the following verses, Paul discusses the *righteousness which is of faith.* We will see that this righteousness is ours not because of what we do, but because of what God has done for us. When we believe in Jesus, God takes away our sin and gives us His righteousness instead.

Speaketh on this wise. This "righteousness of faith" is presented as if it were a person speaking, appealing to us. Of course, literally the appeal of this righteousness is contained in the message that Paul and other preachers and teachers of the Word presented.

Say not in thine heart. Beginning here and going through most of verse 8, the apostle Paul makes use of Deuteronomy 30:11-14. That passage was originally written about the law, but Paul adapts it and applies it to the gospel of Christ. The "righteousness of faith" (who is speaking) states that it is not necessary for anyone to *ascend into heaven* to bring Christ down to earth; nor does Christ need to be resurrected *again from the dead* in order for us to be assured that He is divine and that He has power over death. Jesus long ago came to earth, offered himself for our sins, and rose victorious over the grave. That is the gospel message, the good news which has been preached for centuries beginning with Jesus' apostles. And that is the only message we need.

How to Say It

ELISHA. Ee-*lye*-shuh.
ISAIAH. Eye-*zay*-uh.
SINAI *Sye*-nay-eye or *Sye*-nye.

8. But what saith it? The word is nigh thee, even in thy mouth, and in thy heart: that is, the word of faith, which we preach.

What saith it? If we are not to "ascend into heaven" or "descend into the deep" to find the message of the righteousness of faith, where do we find it?

The word is nigh thee. The message is very near each person who is a follower of the Lord Jesus. We already know the message of the righteousness of faith. It is the message that is in our hearts. It is the word that is in our mouths as we share with others the gospel of Jesus.

The word of faith, which we preach. When Paul says *we* here, he means not only himself; he includes us all. Paul has based his remarks in these verses on the passage in Deuteronomy 30, which had reference to the law. The people of Israel were to keep that law in their hearts and speak of it to others so it would be passed on from generation to generation (Deuteronomy 6:6, 7). The word of faith is a better message. May it never slip from our hearts nor be stifled on our tongues.

B. Blessings of the Message (vv. 9-11)

9. That if thou shalt confess with thy mouth the Lord Jesus, and shalt believe in thine heart that God hath raised him from the dead, thou shalt be saved.

The Greek word translated *confess* means to say the same thing, to agree with what another has said. The content of our confession is that Jesus is Lord. We are reminded of the confessions made by Peter (Matthew 16:16) and Thomas (John 20:28), confessions that were approved by Jesus himself. To acknowledge Jesus as Lord is to affirm that He is the Son of God, the Creator of the universe, and most significantly, the Master of one's own life. Jesus accepts no halfway commitments. If He is not Lord of all, He is not Lord at all.

This *confession,* therefore, is an outward, public affirmation of what we believe in our hearts. We believe that God raised Jesus from the dead. That is not all that we believe about Jesus, but it is a central fact. In an age that rejects miracles, some have rejected belief in the resurrection. All kinds of clever efforts have been made to explain it away. But in spite of all of these efforts, the Scriptures clearly teach that the resurrection is at the very heart of the gospel. Indeed, without the resurrection, there is no gospel!

Thou shalt be saved. The way of salvation is summarized in different words in other passages of Scripture (see Mark 16:16; Acts 2:38; 16:31; Romans 8:24; 10:13; Ephesians 2:8). To learn the whole truth about how to be saved, one should read the whole New Testament.

10. For with the heart man believeth unto righteousness; and with the mouth confession is made unto salvation.

Paul has already spoken of the law's demands if one would be righteous (v. 5), and he preceded that by stating that no mortal had ever met those demands (Romans 9:31). Here he states that belief in Jesus is the way unto righteousness. In Philippians 3:8, 9 Paul speaks of this wonderful gift, "the righteousness which is of God by faith."

Confession is made unto salvation. Our belief in Jesus is not to be kept locked in our hearts. It is to be given expression in the words we speak. Both belief and confession have a part in bringing us to salvation.

11. For the Scripture saith, Whosoever believeth on him shall not be ashamed.

Paul here quotes from Isaiah 28:16. Some modern versions translate the latter part of the verse "shall not be put to shame." This seems to reiterate what he has written in the two previous verses: those who believe and confess will be saved; they will not be embarrassed in the final judgment.

C. Universality of the Message (vv. 12, 13)

12. For there is no difference between the Jew and the Greek: for the same Lord over all is rich unto all that call upon him.

There is no difference between the Jew and the Greek. Of course, there were obvious differences between Jews and Gentiles. (Paul uses *Greek* to represent all who were not Jews—Gentiles, in other words.) They spoke different languages, they had different moral standards, they worshiped different gods. But the point Paul is making is that *all* people intrinsically are the same before God. He made all people from one (Acts 17:26). All have sinned and come short of His glory (Romans 3:23). And He desires that all should repent and be saved (2 Peter 3:9). Because He is *Lord over all,* all who call upon God will be granted the riches of His mercy.

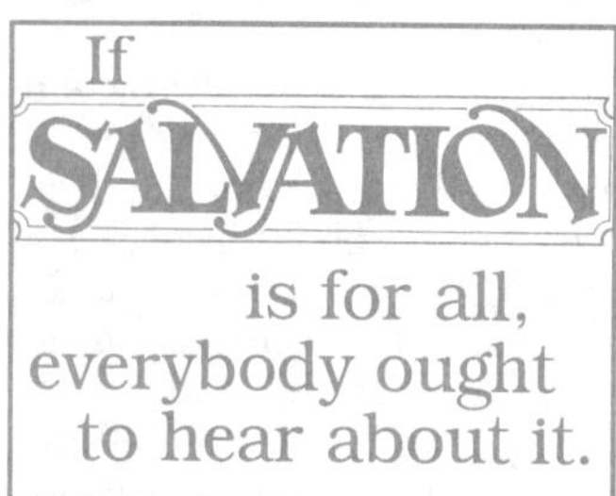
If
SALVATION
is for all,
everybody ought
to hear about it.

visual 11

13. For whosoever shall call upon the name of the Lord shall be saved.

In this passage, Paul has been defining what it means to call upon the Lord. It involves belief in Jesus as the resurrected Son of God; it involves the confession that Jesus is the Lord, the Master of one's life. Implied in all of this is the living of a life consistent with that belief and confession. One who thus calls upon the Lord *shall be saved.*

III. Reaching Out With the Word (Romans 10:14-17)

A. People Must Hear the Message (v. 14)

14. How then shall they call on him in whom they have not believed? and how shall they believe in him of whom they have not heard? and how shall they hear without a preacher?

In the previous verse Paul has affirmed that those who call upon the name of the Lord will be saved. He knows, however, that his statement will raise questions, and so he attempts to answer them in a series of questions of his own. He may have had his fellow Jews specifically in mind, but his questions would apply to Gentiles as well. A non-believer would logically object that he could not *call on him* in whom he did not believe. A remote tribesman in New Guinea would never call upon Jesus for salvation if he did not believe in Him. Nor, for that matter, would a sophisticated pagan living in our contemporary society.

Paul's second question raises the objection that one cannot believe in the Lord if he has never heard about Him. This, too, is logical, for knowledge must always precede faith. The third question deals with the practical problem of getting the message to those who have never heard it. God could have miraculously placed knowledge in the minds of human beings without it ever passing through their five senses. Or He might have sent angels to present the message simultaneously to the whole world. Instead, He chose to convey the message of salvation through preachers. In the first century, oral proclamation was about the only method of carrying a message from one person to another. Today, of course, we have many methods.

B. Preachers Must Be Sent (v. 15)

15. And how shall they preach, except they be sent? as it is written, How beautiful are the feet of them that preach the gospel of peace, and bring glad tidings of good things!

If the people are to hear and believe, the message must come from a preacher. Paul insists that these preachers must *be sent*, sent from God. In ancient Israel many messengers arose, some true, some false. It was not always easy to distinguish between them. Some were authenticated by the miracles they worked—Elijah and Elisha, for example. The messages of some, such as Amos or Isaiah, were authenticated by their moral impact. Other true messengers, because their messages were unpopular, were rejected by the people. Only in his old age was Jeremiah finally recognized as a true prophet.

Today there are many different ideas about how one is called to be a preacher of the gospel. Some feel that such a call must be accompanied by unusual phenomena, even miraculous signs. Others feel that the call comes through the words of Scripture that grip one's heart and move him to act. We have been disappointed in recent years by the moral failure of many prominent preachers. We have been forced again to raise the question about how we can be sure that a preacher is a true messenger of God. We have only one yardstick by which we can make this evaluation—the Bible. If one's message or his life do not measure up to the divine standard, then we are morally obligated to reject him, as painful as that may be.

Paul then adds a tribute to those who are the good news of Jesus by quoting from Isaiah 52:7. The *feet* of the messenger are held up for special praise, not because they are particularly beautiful members of the physical body, but because they symbolize the activity of the messenger in bringing the message to the people.

BEAUTIFUL FEET

Gene Dulin of TCM International tells about a missionary in Southeast Asia who worked to win a remote village to Christ. One day he told the villagers about the love of God that allowed His Son to be nailed to a cross. The members of the tribe had never seen a nail, and when the missionary showed them one and explained how nails had been used to crucify Christ, the entire village accepted Him.

The chief was especially moved and insisted on accompanying the missionary to neighboring villages. Day after day the barefooted chief led the way over rough trails where his feet were cut and bruised by thorns and rocks. The missionary had only to follow the chief's bloody footprints in order to be led to villages where he could preach about Jesus.

Paul, quoting Isaiah, observed "How beautiful are the feet of those who bring good news!" (Romans 10:15, *New International Version*). To those of us in the civilized areas of the world, these words lose a great deal of their meaning; for those in the undeveloped areas, however, as well as for those who lived in the past, they are most appropriate. For such people the feet of good-news-bearing messengers—even dirty, bleeding feet—may be described as beautiful.

—T. T.

C. Personal Responses Are Made (vv. 16, 17)

16, 17. But they have not all obeyed the gospel. For Isaiah saith, Lord, who hath believed our report? So then faith cometh by hearing, and hearing by the word of God.

When Paul wrote, relatively few had yet had an opportunity to hear the gospel. But of those who had heard, not all had accepted the good news. As disappointing as this may have been to Paul, he quoted Isaiah 53:1 to show that God had already anticipated this negative response. In the verses that follow in Isaiah 53, the prophet described the Messiah who would come to save His people. He would be a suffering servant, not a conquering king. Many Jews were not able to accept this view of a humble Messiah, and so they rejected the message. All who do hear the Word of God, however, may come to faith, a faith that saves.

A PESKY FLY

George Whitefield, the famous eighteenth-century English evangelist, preached his first sermon in Gloucester when he was only twenty-one years old. As a result of that first, powerful sermon, a complaint was registered against him that he had driven several people mad! Whitefield's superior was unperturbed by the complaint and stated that it was his hope that the madness would not be forgotten before the next Sunday!

Whether the following ever happened is uncertain, but the story is told of one man who wanted to see the great preacher, but not hear him. (Perhaps he feared the madness mentioned above!) He climbed a tree near where Whitefield was speaking, perched himself on a branch, and stuck a finger in each of his ears. A pesky fly landed on his nose and wouldn't be shook off. At the exact moment that the man removed a hand from his ear to deal with the fly, the preacher quoted Matthew 11:15: "He that hath ears to hear, let him hear."

The man did just that and listened intently to the rest of the sermon. The result of opening his ears was that he also opened his heart. It was true in this case, as it is in all others, that "faith cometh by hearing."

—T. T.

Conclusion

A. Faith Comes by Hearing and Hearing Again

A missionary of a previous generation, who was a pioneer in his field, once affirmed that no one has a right to hear the gospel twice until everyone has had a chance to hear it once. We may respect the desire of this missionary to carry the gospel to the remotest parts of the world in his own generation. But there are some practical problems involved in trying to reach such an idealistic goal.

First of all, there are cultural barriers that must be overcome. For example, the world view of a Hindu is so different from the Christian world view that the gospel makes no sense at all to him the first time he hears it. It might take months or even years of teaching before he could begin to understand what Christianity is all about.

Then there are language barriers. One can hardly respond to the gospel unless one can hear it in his or her own language. Some missionaries work through interpreters, but at best this method of presenting the gospel has its limitations. There are still hundreds of people groups that do not have the Bible available in their own language. Translators are working in many of these languages, but this process takes time. Until these translations are complete, the opportunities for these people to really hear the gospel will be limited.

Political barriers are another problem. Some areas of the world are closed to missionaries. While the gospel may penetrate these barriers through means other than missionaries, these other methods are limited in their effectiveness. We must pray that these political walls will crumble, and in some places they are crumbling. In the meantime, we need to give increased diligence to proclaiming the gospel in those areas that are receptive.

B. "Except They Be Sent"

Every Christian is a preacher. Of course, not every Christian will stand behind a pulpit each Lord's day and publicly proclaim the gospel. Yet every Christian has the responsibility to share the good news with others whether in public assemblies, classrooms, or in private with individuals. Every Christian is sent, commissioned by Christ to carry the gospel to whomever he or she can. A Christian does not have to be formally sent by a synod, a presbytery, or a congregation. The great commission provides all the authority one needs to carry the gospel to those who need it.

Yet we recognize that there is a need for special messengers, persons with special talents and training, to serve as ministers, missionaries, and in other capacities. How are they called? The call begins in the home. As children grow up in a Christian home, they become aware of the gospel and the Great Commission. They are encouraged to direct the talents God has given them towards special ministries. The local congregation shares in the nurturing of the faith of children, always holding high the call for them to carry the gospel to others. Every proclaimer of the gospel is sent of God, but each one is also sent by parents, teachers, preachers, and churches.

As we approach the twenty-first century, there is a growing need for preachers and missionaries. This is especially true in the foreign mission fields. The generation that responded to the call after World War II has reached the age where they are retiring or dying. Replacements must be recruited and prepared to continue these vital ministries. Further, the twenty-first century promises to see the opening of new fields and new opportunities that do not now exist. We must challenge people, young and old, to rise to these opportunities.

C. Let Us Pray

We thank You, Father, that You have sent preachers with the gospel. Unless those messengers had been sent, we would never have known the word of salvation. May we out of gratitude share the word with others. In Jesus' name we pray. Amen.

D. Thought to Remember

"Faith cometh by hearing, and hearing by the word of God."

Home Daily Bible Readings

Monday, Feb. 8—The Law Proclaims (Galatians 3:21-29)

Tuesday, Feb. 9—God's People (Romans 9:1-5)

Wednesday, Feb. 10—God's Promise (Romans 9:6-18)

Thursday, Feb. 11—God's Mercy (Romans 9:19-26)

Friday, Feb. 12—Gospel for Israel (Romans 9:27-33)

Saturday, Feb. 13—Salvation for All (Romans 10:1-13)

Sunday, Feb. 14—Message of Salvation (Romans 10:14-21)

Learning by Doing

This page contains an alternate lesson plan emphasizing learning activities. Classes desiring such student involvement will find these suggestions helpful.

Learning Goals

This study will enable the pupil to:

1. State the basis of the righteousness that God bestows on us in Christ.
2. Affirm the principle that faith occurs when the Word of God is communicated from believers to unbelievers.
3. Identify a way to become involved in the work of preaching the Word of God to others.

Into the Lesson

As class members arrive, have them form groups of three. Give each group the following directions, in written form:

> Imagine that you are now living among a group of people who are not believers in Christ. They know nothing about what it means to be a Christian, but they have expressed to you an interest in how people achieve a perfect life. How would you communicate to them the meaning of righteousness and how one may become righteous?

Allot five or six minutes for the groups to discuss this. Let the groups make brief reports. Make no comments at this time about the strategies chosen.

State that this section of Scripture will provide help in answering these questions.

Into the Word

Briefly present the material included in the "Lesson Background" section. Then read Romans 10:5-17 aloud.

Divide the class members into groups of six and ask them to examine the Scripture text in their groups. Give each group a copy of the following questions as a guide for their study:

1. What did Moses say about a person's attaining righteousness by the law? (One who obeyed the law in all points would be righteous.)
2. According to the gospel, what is the basis of righteousness? (Faith in Jesus Christ as Lord.)
3. What two elements that lead to salvation does Paul mention in this text? (Belief that God raised Jesus from the dead, and confession that Jesus is Lord.)
4. Who can be saved? (All who call on the name of the Lord.)
5. Verses 14 and 15 provide additional details about what must take place if the lost will be saved. What are they? (One must hear the gospel before belief is possible. Someone must communicate the gospel if people are to hear and believe it.)
6. Who is to share the gospel with the unsaved? (Certainly, every Christian is to share the good news of Christ with those who are near. People who live at a distance will hear only if someone is sent to them with the good news.)
7. What is unusual about the description Paul gives of the messenger who brings the gospel of peace? What is the significance of this description? (He sees beauty in the messenger's feet, a body part that we normally do not regard as comely. This signifies the outstanding value of the message.)
8. What is the place of the Word of God in this proclamation process? (Faith comes from hearing the word of God as it is recorded in the Bible.)

In ten minutes call the groups together and use their work as the basis for a discussion to clarify the message of the passage.

Into Life

Develop a general discussion using the following questions:

1. What is the place of the communicator in the process of salvation? Is this the same today as it was in Bible times?
2. Who is responsible to communicate the Word of God?
3. Think back to the plan you made at the beginning of the session. How well does it reflect what today's lesson text says about righteousness and how one may become righteous?
4. Few of us in this congregation have the opportunity to share the gospel beyond a rather narrow circle of friends and associates. What responsibility then does the church have for those in faraway places who have never heard the good news of salvation?
5. What specifically can this congregation do to make the gospel known in this country and throughout the world?
6. What specifically can we in this class do to make the gospel known in this country and throughout the world?

Conclude the session by reading aloud Romans 5:17 from a modern translation of the Bible, and then pray together, thanking God for the salvation He offers us through His Son.

Let's Talk It Over

The questions on this page are designed to encourage review of the lesson Scriptures and to promote discussion of the lesson by the class. The answers provided are only discussion starters. Let your class talk it over from there.

1. What does it mean to confess that "Jesus is Lord"? (Romans 10:9).

The central affirmation of Christians in the early days of the church was that Jesus is Lord. Everyone in the Roman Empire was expected to confess, "Caesar is Lord." During times of persecution, Christians were commanded to confess Caesar as Lord; instead, they would reply, "Jesus is Lord," and go to their deaths. In confessing Jesus as Lord, they were declaring, "Jesus is the Master of my life. He is the Son of God."

People today seem far more ready to confess Jesus as Savior than to confess Him as Lord. They want Him to save them, but they seem reluctant to allow Him to take control of their lives. To confess Jesus as Lord is to affirm His mastery over every area of our lives. It means that we seek and submit to His will in such matters as the use we make of our money, the kinds of entertainment we pursue, our speech, etc. No confession is more all-encompassing and more demanding than this one!

2. It is not enough simply to believe in our hearts that Jesus is Lord; one must also confess "with the mouth." Why is this so?

Thoughts are confined to our minds until we express them. Before such time, they lack objective reality. I can think many thoughts and possess many convictions, but they take on a new quality when I express them in words. Then they are not only inside my head, affecting my life; they are now outside of my body, revealing my convictions, and perhaps affecting the lives of others. Peter may have thought many times about Jesus in terms of His divine nature and mission, but those convictions became "the good confession" only when he spoke them (Matthew 16:16). *Then* Jesus made his astounding response regarding His church and the part that Peter would have in the establishment of it (vv. 17-19). It is God's intention that the whole world should know about Jesus and the salvation He has made possible. How shall the unsaved ever know of Him unless those who believe in Him express orally the conviction they hold in their hearts?

3. What does Paul reveal about one's attaining righteousness by his or her own efforts and thus "earning" salvation?

Paul makes it plain that it cannot be done. This is precisely what the people of Israel were attempting to do. In Romans 10:2, Paul says that they were "ignorant of God's righteousness," and so they were "going about to establish their own righteousness." They sought to achieve righteousness "as if it were by works" (Romans 9:32, *New International Version*). But to do that, one must keep God's law perfectly (Romans 10:5), and no mortal could do that (9:31). Once a person commits a sin, he or she is a sinner and is deserving of punishment (James 2:10).

Paul reveals that God's way of righteousness is far better. It is based on faith, not works. In God's gracious plan, Jesus Christ does for us what we cannot do for ourselves. He fulfilled the law's demands. He is perfect righteousness. Therefore, when we submit to Him, His righteousness becomes ours. We are declared righteous in Him. So Paul concludes in Romans 10:4, "Christ is the end of the law so that there may be righteousness for everyone who believes" (*New International Version*). What good news! All of us are sinners, and we all deserve punishment; but in Christ, God gives us salvation instead. Praise His name!

4. What is the primary mission of the church today?

Paul's series of questions and his conclusion in Romans 10:14-17 underscore the fundamental importance of evangelism. This is the primary mission of the church. When the church couples that mission with ministry, in which those born into God's kingdom are nurtured and brought to maturity, God's intention for the church is realized. When a church forgets its primary mission, however, it may well be that it ceases to be His church, just as a hospital that no longer cares for the sick ceases to be a hospital.

5. In what sense is there no difference between the Jew and the Greek (Gentile)?

There are many obvious differences, of course, such as physical appearance, language, and culture. But the context of Paul's statement in Romans 10:12 is plainly a spiritual one. He means that in the eyes of God, all are sinners, all are equally in need of forgiveness, and the way of salvation through Jesus is open to all.

Serve and Honor

February 21
Lesson 12

Lesson Scripture: Romans 15:1-13.

Printed Text: Romans 15:1-13.

Devotional Reading: Colossians 3:9-17.

Romans 15:1-13

1 We then that are strong ought to bear the infirmities of the weak, and not to please ourselves.

2 Let every one of us please his neighbor for his good to edification.

3 For even Christ pleased not himself; but, as it is written, The reproaches of them that reproached thee fell on me.

4 For whatsoever things were written aforetime were written for our learning, that we through patience and comfort of the Scriptures might have hope.

5 Now the God of patience and consolation grant you to be likeminded one toward another according to Christ Jesus:

6 That ye may with one mind and one mouth glorify God, even the Father of our Lord Jesus Christ.

7 Wherefore receive ye one another, as Christ also received us, to the glory of God.

8 Now I say that Jesus Christ was a minister of the circumcision for the truth of God, to confirm the promises made unto the fathers:

9 And that the Gentiles might glorify God for his mercy; as it is written, For this cause I will confess to thee among the Gentiles, and sing unto thy name.

10 And again he saith, Rejoice, ye Gentiles, with his people.

11 And again, Praise the Lord, all ye Gentiles; and laud him, all ye people.

12 And again, Isaiah saith, There shall be a root of Jesse, and he that shall rise to reign over the Gentiles; in him shall the Gentiles trust.

13 Now the God of hope fill you with all joy and peace in believing, that ye may abound in hope, through the power of the Holy Ghost.

Golden Text: We then that are strong ought to bear the infirmities of the weak, and not to please ourselves. Let every one of us please his neighbor for his good to edification.—Romans 15:1, 2.

Good News for All

Unit 3: Sharing the Good News

(Lessons 10-13)

Lesson Aims

As a result of studying this lesson, each student should:

1. Understand that all Scripture was given for our instruction and encouragement, so that our hope in Christ might be firm.
2. Appreciate the fact that Christ bore the reproaches of others rather than please himself.
3. Name one way in which he or she can serve those who are weak in the faith.

Lesson Outline

INTRODUCTION
- A. "He's My Brother"
- B. Lesson Background

I. THE FELLOWSHIP OF CHRISTIANS (Romans 15:1-6)
- A. Help the Weak (v. 1)
  - *Real Strength*
- B. Please One Another (v. 2)
- C. Heed Christ's Example (v. 3)
  - *What If?*
- D. Study the Scriptures (v. 4)
- E. Glorify God (vv. 5, 6)

II. THE MINISTRY OF CHRIST (Romans 15:7-13)
- A. Christ Receives Sinners (v. 7)
- B. Jesus Ministered to the Jews (vv. 8, 9)
- C. Gentiles Should Rejoice (vv. 10-12)
- D. God Gives Joy and Peace (v. 13)

CONCLUSION
- A. Christ and Culture
- B. Let Us Pray
- C. Thought to Remember

Display visual 12 of the visuals packet and let it remain before the class throughout the session. Refer to it especially as you discuss verses 1 and 2. The visual is shown on page 212.

Introduction

A. "He's My Brother"

Probably most of us have seen the poster or seal advertising Boys town. The poster shows a young boy carrying a smaller boy on his back. The caption reads, "He ain't heavy. He's my brother." No doubt when one is helping a person with whom he feels a close kinship, the burden feels lighter. And that is the way Christians ought to feel when they are helping their weaker brothers.

In real life it doesn't always work out that way. Sometimes the stronger party is not as strong as the person thinks he or she is, and when that person tries to help another, both persons are soon in trouble. And sometimes the weaker party doesn't think he or she needs help, and so that person resists all efforts of assistance.

Yet, Paul's admonition that the "strong ought to bear the infirmities of the weak" still stands. The real key is that the strong learn to please their neighbors rather than themselves.

B. Lesson Background

The underlying theme of the text chosen for today's lesson relates to what the fellowship of the church should be. In the previous chapters of this great letter to the Romans, Paul outlined the failure of both Gentile and Jew to attain righteousness. The Gentile had worshiped nature, and the Jew had followed the law of Moses. Both had failed to reach their goal. Then Christ came, and by His gospel imputed to both a righteousness that would save. They appropriated it by faith in Him. As a result, all were saved by grace. Therefore, all should receive each other in the spirit of Christian fellowship, as brothers and sisters in Christ Jesus.

The immediate background of today's text is found in Romans 14. Disputes had arisen between weak Christians and strong Christians concerning eating meat and observing special days. Brother had been belittling and judging brother in regard to these matters. Chapter 14 records Paul's counsel to the church at Rome, and the first six verses of our text summarize his discussion. The principles he enunciated governing the fellowship of the Roman Christians are just as applicable to the church today. The remaining verses of the printed text show that when all the diverse members of Christ's body are bound together in harmony and peace, God is glorified.

I. The Fellowship of Christians (Romans 15:1-6)

A. Help the Weak (v. 1)

1. We then that are strong ought to bear the infirmities of the weak, and not to please ourselves.

Paul's comments in the verses immediately preceding this verse suggest that *the weak* were those whose consciences would not allow them to eat meat. Paul made it clear that the *strong* should take every precaution to avoid causing the *weak* to stumble or take offense in this matter.

Dealing with a similar problem in the Corinthian church, Paul wrote, "Wherefore, if meat make my brother to offend, I will eat no flesh while the world standeth" (1 Corinthians 8:13).

This principle has much broader application than just to the eating of meat and the observing of special days, subjects that Paul deals with in Romans 14. It covers a whole range of practices and beliefs that sometime arise to cause divisions within congregations. The weak in faith often are swayed by senseless scruples about right and wrong. Those who are strong in faith should be understanding and exercise loving patience toward the weak in order to help them also to become strong. This sometimes requires the strong to overlook many peculiar habits and unusual personality traits on the part of the weak.

Not to please ourselves. Here is another principle that is to guide strong Christians regarding their conduct in the fellowship of the church. They are not to indulge their own will and pleasure. Too often the strong are not willing to reach out to the weak because the strong are thinking first of themselves. They are motivated by pride and self-interest rather than love for the weak. God's plan is that the strong should help the weak, and that the wise should help the ignorant.

Obviously there are limits to the concessions that can be made to the weak. Tolerance cannot go so far as to allow the teaching of false doctrine, nor can it permit practices that divide the church. Mature love requires that false teaching and divisiveness be handled gently and kindly, to be sure, but also firmly.

REAL STRENGTH

Early in 1991 most of us followed the progression of the war in the Persian Gulf with intensity. When it was obvious that the coalition forces would be victorious, General Norman Schwarzkopf gave a briefing to explain the strategy that he and the other military leaders had devised. He stood in front of a large map of that part of the world and pointed to an area in southern Iraq to which our troops had penetrated. He then pointed to the location of Baghdad and explained that it was but a short distance to Iraq's capital from where our troops were positioned. Furthermore, he explained that there was virtually no opposition that could have prevented the conquest of that city had we chosen to advance upon it. He made it clear, however, that the coalition forces would not do that.

It was shortly after this that the United States government, along with others, launched a massive program to provide food and supplies for the fleeing Kurds who opposed Saddam Hussein. It is proper that strong nations express concern for the weak and oppressed.

Those who are truly strong are able to keep their strength in check. This is what Paul is telling us when he writes, "We then that are strong ought to bear the infirmities of the weak, and not to please ourselves." Instead of pushing for our rights, we ought to be willing to relinquish them for the spiritual benefit of our weaker brothers and sisters in Christ. In the church, one's spiritual strength often is best demonstrated in the voluntary restriction of it.

—T. T.

> **How to Say It**
>
> Mesopotamia. Mes-uh-puh-*tay*-me-uh.

B. Please One Another (v. 2)

2. Let every one of us please his neighbor for his good to edification.

This is the attitude that is prompted by the spirit of concern for others. To please our neighbor requires that we restrain our own pet wishes and personal ambitions, and show leniency and sympathy toward him or her. Of course, we must not overlook Paul's qualification here. It is not enough just to please one's neighbor. One might, for instance please an alcoholic neighbor by providing liquor for that person. But this would certainly not be acting in the neighbor's best interest. Paul qualifies how we are to please our neighbor by indicating that it must be *for his good to edification.* Our first concern for our neighbors should be to bring them into a saving relationship with Jesus Christ. Then we must build them up in their faith and help them grow to maturity in their relationship with Him.

C. Heed Christ's Example (v. 3)

3. For even Christ pleased not himself; but, as it is written, The reproaches of them that reproached thee fell on me.

Paul quotes from Psalm 69:9, where the sufferer addresses God. The suffering that he endures is because of his zealous efforts to do God's will. Paul shows that this Scripture is Messianic, having its highest fulfillment in Christ. Thus Christ is speaking these words to God, and they indicate that Christ did not seek to please himself but endured reproach and suffering to do the Father's will.

In fulfilling the Father's will, Christ provided the supreme example of behavior for us. He gave up His Heavenly glory and sacrificed himself for us, a perfect example of unselfish love. Writing in 2 Corinthians 8:9, Paul states it this way: "Though he was rich, yet for your sakes he became poor, that ye through his poverty might be rich." Of course, we cannot begin to measure up to His example of sacrificial love, but we can hold it up as a standard to aim for. Not only in His example but also in His teaching Christ emphasized the principle of self-sacrifice. "Whosoever will come after me, let him deny himself, and take up his cross, and follow me" (Mark 8:34).

WHAT IF?

Have you ever played the game, "What If?" It's a speculative game in which one tries to determine what might have happened if other circumstances had developed or prevailed. In reality it's an act of futility, since what has already happened has indeed transpired. But just for the sake of the illustration, "What if" Christ had chosen to please himself, in contrast to what Romans 15:3 says of Him? What would have been the outcome?

For one thing, He would not have given himself to die an agonizing death on the cross. Indeed, He would not have died at all. He wouldn't have performed miracles of compassion upon others, but would have used His powers for His own gratification. His teaching would have been for the exaltation of himself, rather than for the dissemination of truth that leads others to walk in God's ways. In His time of temptation He might have complied with the devil's requests and thus gained a manipulative control over all the nations.

What if Jesus had pleased himself? Had He done so, would He have been born at all? Why leave the glories of the Heavenly realm to come into this world and be rejected and abused? No, if Christ had pleased himself, there would have been no earthly Christ.

What an example for us, His followers! As our Master was never guided by a principle of self-gratification, neither should we be. —T. T.

D. Study the Scriptures (v. 4)

4. For whatsoever things were written aforetime were written for our learning, that we through patience and comfort of the Scriptures might have hope.

This statement would have been unnecessary had Paul been writing to a totally Jewish audience, but many, perhaps the majority in the Roman church, may have come from Gentile backgrounds. They would have neither an understanding of nor an appreciation for the Jewish Scriptures. Paul has quoted from the Old Testament several times already in this letter, and he wants to make sure that the Gentiles do to cut themselves off from this heritage just because it is Jewish. God had a purpose in giving the Old Testament that extended far beyond the Jewish people.

An understanding of the Old Testament is essential if one is to understand God's purpose toward the human race. That purpose culminates in the coming of Jesus Christ, but it has its roots deep in the Hebrew writings. Here Paul is not primarily concerned with these theological implications of the Old Testament. Rather, he wants to show that the Old Testament provides practical help as Christians live the Christian life. By precept and example, the Old Testament helps develop patience and comfort in Christians and promotes the present possession of their hope in God. This help that the Old Testament gives is as real as it was when Paul wrote these words in the first century. Christians today are sometimes tempted to neglect the Old Testament, feeling that it is often obscure and out of date. We neglect the Old Testament to our impoverishment.

E. Glorify God (vv. 5, 6)

5, 6. Now the God of patience and consolation grant you to be likeminded one toward another according to Christ Jesus: that ye may with one mind and one mouth glorify God, even the Father of our Lord Jesus Christ.

Paul pauses to offer a brief prayer that the Roman Christians settle their differences and be *likeminded* toward one another. This does not mean that they all should have the same opinion about every matter, but that a harmony of feeling should exist among them. All should desire the unity of the church and should live humbly and unselfishly to bring it about. Such conduct would be *according to Jesus* (see Philippians 2:2-5). They did not have to rely solely on their own resources to achieve this spirit of harmony, for God, who is the *God of patience and consolation,* would help them. Paul then states why the church is to be characterized by a spirit of harmony among its members. It is so that all may *glorify God.* Being of one accord all then may unite in uttering praise

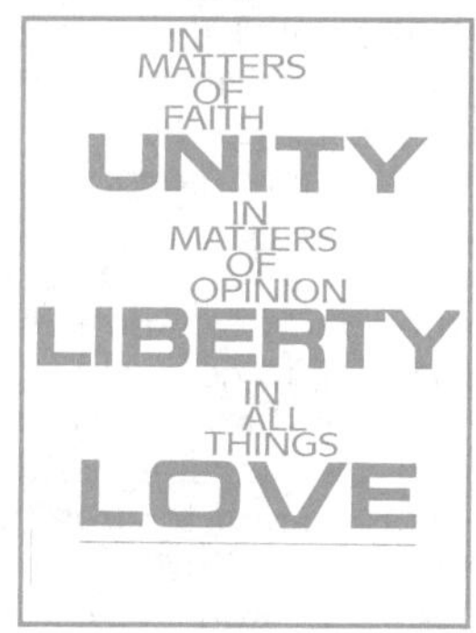

visual 12

to Him. Self-centered, quarreling Christians are likely to be more concerned about gaining advantages over one another than they are about glorifying their Heavenly Father.

God is *the Father,* a term that Jesus frequently used in referring to God. This suggests a warm, personal relationship, not devotion to some distant and unfeeling deity.

II. The Ministry of Christ (Romans 15:7-13)

A. Christ Receives Sinners (v. 7)

7. Wherefore receive ye one another, as Christ also received us, to the glory of God.

Paul now summarizes the argument he has been making. Christians are to *receive . . . one another* in spite of their differences over issues that do not touch on vital faith. Paul clinches his argument by pointing to the example of Christ, who receives all who come to Him, even though they are all sinners. If Christ, who is sinless, can accept sinners, then surely sinners ought to be willing to practice this grace toward other sinners.

But this is not easy to do. Strong Christians feel a responsibility to defend the faith against the activities of weaker Christians that seem to undermine or threaten it. Certainly the essential teachings of the faith must be protected, but many of the things we divide about have nothing to do with these essentials. We must learn the grace of acceptance, which means that we can love a person as a Christian brother or sister without approving of his or her shortcomings or erroneous judgments. After all, that is the only way Christ could accept any of us.

B. Jesus Ministered to the Jews (vv. 8, 9)

8. Now I say that Jesus Christ was a minister of the circumcision for the truth of God, to confirm the promises made unto the fathers.

Jesus was born a Jew, lived according to the Jewish law, and ministered to the Jewish people. In chapters 9-11 Paul has already affirmed the special place the children of Israel enjoyed in God's plan. Unfortunately, through their disobedience they as a nation forfeited this privileged position. But this in no way set aside *the promises made unto the fathers.*

While Abraham was living in Mesopotamia, God formed a covenant with him, and this covenant contained certain promises. God reaffirmed that covenant after Abraham entered the land of Canaan (Acts 7:2; Genesis 12:1-3; 22:17, 18). That covenant was again renewed with Abraham's son Isaac and then with Jacob. In this verse Paul assures readers that God has not set that covenant aside but has fulfilled it through Christ. Paul states that Jesus Christ was a minister *for the truth of God,* that is, to confirm the truth of the promises God made to Abraham, Isaac, and Jacob. In His covenant with them, God promised to bless Abraham and his descendants; but more than that, God promised to bless all the families of the earth. It was this part of the promise that Jesus fulfilled.

9. And that the Gentiles might glorify God for his mercy; as it is written, For this cause I will confess to thee among the Gentiles, and sing unto thy name.

Having shown that God was faithful in His promises to the Jews, Paul now specifies that those promises ultimately included *the Gentiles.* The quotation in this verse is from Psalm 18:49. David, who had been delivered from all of his enemies and raised to dominion over the neighboring nations, gave thanks to God among the heathen. Paul shows that this statement applies also to the Messiah and that it foretells the conquests of His kingdom. Here Christ is seen in the midst of the Gentiles, singing praise to God for their conversion.

C. Gentiles Should Rejoice (vv. 10-12)

10, 11. And again he saith, Rejoice, ye Gentiles, with his people. And again, Praise the Lord, all ye Gentiles; and laud him, all ye people.

In these two verses, Paul adds two more quotations (Deuteronomy 32:43; Psalm 117:1) to show that the Old Testament looked forward to the time when the Gentiles would share God's blessings. Paul thus could show that his own ministry to the Gentiles was not a break with the covenant God had made with the fathers, but was a fulfillment of God's ultimate purpose for the whole human race. The Gentiles, realizing that they were also included in God's covenant, should raise their voices to rejoice.

12. And again, Isaiah saith, There shall be a root of Jesse, and he that shall rise to reign over the Gentiles; in him shall the Gentiles trust.

Paul continues his argument by combining two quotations from Isaiah (11:1 and 10). Jesse was the father of David. The image is of a tree that has died and been cut off, but from the *root* there springs a new shoot. Jesse died, but from him sprang David and his descendants. From this lineage came Jesus the Messiah, whose reign would extend over both Jews and Gentiles. Many Jews were unwilling to accept the fact that the promised Messiah's reign would be universal. The tenor of Paul's comments in the second half of our printed text suggests that the church in Rome may have been troubled over this same issue. From the Old Testament Scriptures Paul quotes that God's mercy, though at first experienced principally by the Jews, was intended for the Gentiles as well. It was Paul's hope that all would understand and accept God's plan, and praise Him with one heart and mind.

D. God Gives Joy and Peace (v. 13)

13. Now the God of hope fill you with all joy and peace in believing, that ye may abound in hope, through the power of the Holy Ghost.

Paul offers another prayer for his readers, reflecting the prayer he had offered in verses 5 and 6. Here the focus is on hope. Jehovah God is *the God of hope,* the one in whom we have the sure hope of eternal life. This hope brings with it both *joy and peace.* Joy comes when one realizes that there is something beyond this life. This is not just the happiness of the moment that may quickly pass, but a deep emotion that pervades every aspect of life. Our hope in God issues also in peace. We can face life with the calm assurance that no matter what happens, God is still in control. Hope, joy, and peace are all grounded in faith. Unless one believes the promises of God, he cannot enjoy any of these blessings. All of these will see fruition through *the power of the Holy Spirit,* who works in our lives in ways that often we do not understand.

Conclusion

A. Christ and Culture

One of the most influential religious books of the twentieth century is H. Richard Niebuhr's *Christ and Culture.* In this book the author shows how across the centuries Christianity has been shaped by the culture in which it has survived. Different cultures have produced different styles of worship, different church organizational structures, and different approaches to the practical applications of Christianity in life situations. All of this may sound rather scholarly and remote from our efforts to make Christianity a vital force in our daily lives. But scholarly or not, none of us can escape our culture. In many different and subtle ways it will shape how we express our Christian faith.

During the Depression of the 1930s the game of Monopoly was introduced and quickly became a popular fad. My cousin owned a copy of the game and it soon became our favorite rainy day activity. However, my grandmother discovered that the game was played with dice. Dice were for gambling, she informed us, and so no dice were allowed in our house. Instead, we had to use a spinner to record our moves.

In two generations our culture has so changed that probably few people would give a second thought to the use of dice in a harmless game. Of course, some may question whether a game such as Monopoly is completely harmless. The idea of gaining a monopoly and bankrupting one's opponents does not impress upon a young person the Christian way to use wealth. Fortunately, we cousins received Christian teachings that offset any negative values that may have been projected by the game. At least none of us became Wall street manipulators or junk bond dealers.

The point of all this is that our Christian faith has become intertwined in and overlaid with values from the world about us. These values become so much a part of our thought patterns that we are scarcely aware of the influence they have on us. To see how we are affected, we need only look at what has happened to two of the great events in the Christian faith—the incarnation and the resurrection, now observed as Christmas and Easter.

Understanding these things and appreciating what Paul has to say about bearing the infirmities of the weak, let us exercise caution in insisting that everyone conform to our standards for the Christian faith. May the spirit of criticism and judging one another depart from us and be replaced by the desire to please others and edify them until they attain maturity in Christ.

B. Let Us Pray

Dear Father, give us the humility to subject our lives to the penetrating light of the Scriptures, and the wisdom to apply the results to our relations with others as we labor for the Lord. In Jesus' name we pray. Amen.

C. Thought to Remember

In matters of faith, unity; in matters of opinion, liberty; in all things, love.

Home Daily Bible Readings

Monday, Feb. 15—Paul's Prayer (Philippians 2:1-11)
Tuesday, Feb. 16—How to Treat Others (Romans 13:8-14)
Wednesday, Feb. 17—Do Not Judge Others (Romans 14:1-12)
Thursday, Feb. 18—Do Not Let Others Fail (Romans 14:13-23)
Friday, Feb. 19—Serve Others, Not Self (Romans 15:1-6)
Saturday, Feb. 20—The Gospel for the Gentiles (Romans 15:7-13)
Sunday, Feb. 21—Paul's Reason for Writing (Romans 15:14-21)

Learning by Doing

This page contains an alternate lesson plan emphasizing learning activities. Classes desiring such student involvement will find these suggestions helpful.

Learning Goals

After studying Romans 15:1-15, the pupils will be able to:

1. Affirm the principle that stronger Christians are to help those who are weaker in faith.
2. Identify ways they can serve those who are weak in faith.

Into the Lesson

Before the lesson begins, place the following statement on the chalkboard or overhead in your classroom for all to see:

Agree or Disagree:

A Christian should never worry about pleasing another person.

As the class members arrive, draw their attention to the statement. Ask them to find two other persons who answer the question as they do. The groups thus formed should then make a case to convince the remainder of the class of the position it has taken. Allow several minutes for the groups to present their cases.

Make the transition into the Bible lesson by stating that today's lesson deals with the principle stated in the agree/disagree statement.

Into the Word

Briefly present the information included in the "Lesson Background" section of the lesson. Then have someone (who has been assigned ahead of time) read Romans 15:1-3 to the class.

Develop a discussion from the Bible passage by using the following questions.

1. Verses 1 and 2 state the central thesis of this section of Scripture. Express that in one sentence. (The strong bear a responsibility for the spiritual well-being of weaker Christians and should be willing to endure personal inconvenience in fulfilling that responsibility.)

2. According to verse 3, what should motivate us to carry out this principle? (The example of Christ.)

3. How do the Old Testament Scriptures assist us in carrying out the principle stated in verses 1 and 2? (They contain examples of godly persons who willingly suffered personal loss for God's cause. See verse 3.)

4. Why is a harmonious spirit among Christians so important? See verses 5 and 6. (The church can thereby be united in glorifying God.)

5. Why is it important for Christians to have an attitude of acceptance of one another? (Acceptance is the key to helping individuals to change and to become better persons. It is especially important for weaker Christians to know that they are accepted by those who are strong. Otherwise, discouragement might overtake them.)

6. On what basis could Paul urge all Christians to maintain an attitude of acceptance toward other Christians? (He mentions two reasons in verse 7. The first is the fact that the sinless Son of God accepts each of us, even though we are sinners. Second, this attitude will result in glory to God.)

7. What great truth regarding God's promises made to the Jewish patriarchs does Paul emphasize in verses 8-12? (By quoting several Old Testament passages, Paul makes it clear that the Gentiles were included in those promises. God's mercy in Christ was for them as well. Therefore Christians should be open to receive all who trust in Him.)

Into Life

Help the pupils understand the importance of the principle that strong Christians should be willing to put up with the imperfections of those who are weak in faith, in the hope that the weak thereby may be brought along to spiritual maturity. Divide the class into groups of four or five. Give each group a copy of the following situation.

Your congregation is in a rapidly changing community. Recently a large number of young adults have become members of your congregation. Most of these young adults have no previous church experience, but they are now earnestly seeking God's way for their lives. Their presence has become challenging to the congregation, however, for they are different from the rest of you. They dress quite casually. They prefer new songs rather than the grand hymns of the faith. They attend services somewhat irregularly. This has begun to cause some tension in the congregation. If we are to observe the principles identified in today's Scripture text, how can this situation be resolved? Who needs to take the initiative?

Allow the groups five to seven minutes to discuss the issue and suggest some specific recommendations. Then let them report their decisions to the whole class. Discuss the situation further if needed. Then close with prayer.

Let's Talk It Over

The questions on this page are designed to encourage review of the lesson Scriptures and to promote discussion of the lesson by the class. The answers provided are only discussion starters. Let your class talk it over from there.

1. What motivates people to serve?

(1) Love and concern. Let's start with the highest motivation. First Corinthians 13 affirms that whatever we do doesn't matter if it isn't motivated by love. When we love the Lord and love people, we will serve. When we are concerned about following the servant Lord, we will serve. Love and concern will flow toward need. Love and concern motivated our Lord.

(2) Fulfillment and meaning. Many people are searching for that which will bring these elements to their lives. They have tried so much and still feel empty. But when they *give* themselves in service to others (ministry), many find the meaning and fulfillment for which they have sought.

(3) A sense of obligation. It is difficult for one to be motivated by love and concern all the time. There are occasions when one serves because a task needs to be done. That motivation has its place, legitimately. However, if one serves most, or all of the time, out of a sense of obligation, that person will miss the joy of the Lord.

(4) The desire for recognition and praise. Some serve for "strokes." They want to be recognized and praised. Those who serve with this motivation are people whose identity and self-worth are drawn from unhealthy and inappropriate sources. Most of us appreciate recognition and praise, but to serve in order to get it is defective.

(5) To obligate and bind others to oneself. Sadly, it must be admitted that there are those who serve for this reason. Power is at the bottom of it. They want to control others, to obligate others to them so they can "call in their debts" when they want to. Although what is done may appear to be "service," it really is manipulation of other people.

2. What is the definition of the word *hope*, as the Bible uses it?

In the popular use of the word, to hope means to desire. To say, "I hope it rains," implies I want it to rain, I desire that it rain. That usually doesn't mean I confidently expect it to rain. But the Biblical term means precisely that—confident expectation. Our hope of eternal life implies our confident expectation that God will raise us from the dead just as He did Jesus Christ. The writer of Hebrews speaks of the certainty of our hope when he describes it as "an anchor of the soul, both sure and steadfast" (6:19). Biblical hope is based on God's character—His reliability, the fact that He does as He promises. The Biblical record, and the experience of Christians, confirms that God always keeps His word!

3. Why are stronger Christians to bear with the failing of weaker Christians?

Paul provides the answer in Romans 15:2. We put up with the failing of the weak for their good, specifically for their edification (that they might be built up). Edification of one another is the highest goal of our fellowship in Jesus Christ. In the matchless fourth chapter of Ephesians, Paul calls for the equipping of the saints (Christians) for the work of ministry—for building up the body of Christ (v. 12). This motive is to control even our speech. In that same chapter Paul challenges us to say "only what is helpful for building others up" (v. 29, *New International Version*).

4. Cite some ways we can care for and edify one another.

Basically, we edify each other by sharing resources. We do this in the following ways. (1) Intellectually—sharing truths and insights, formally and informally. We teach and admonish one another. (2) Relationally—being true and loyal friends, ministering to each other appropriately. The fellowship of the body of Christ functions in this way. (3) Emotionally—being supportive and encouraging. Encouragement may well be the most vital expression of edification. *Everyone* needs encouragement, especially in time of weakness or critical need. The ministry of encouragement builds up brethren! And everyone can be an encourager! (4) "Spiritually." All of the preceding are "spiritual," of course. Here, however, we have in mind praying for others in private and worshiping with them in public. We are fed by intercessory prayer and corporate worship. (5) Materially—through services, money, and gifts to meet concrete needs. People are built up in the realization that others care and will share—tangibly, personally, lovingly.

Teach the Truth

February 28
Lesson 13

LESSON SCRIPTURE: 2 Timothy 2:14—3:9; Titus 2.

PRINTED TEXT: 2 Timothy 2:14-26.

DEVOTIONAL READING: Titus 2.

2 Timothy 2:14-26

14 Of these things put them in remembrance, charging them before the Lord that they strive not about words to no profit, but to the subverting of the hearers.

15 Study to show thyself approved unto God, a workman that needeth not to be ashamed, rightly dividing the word of truth.

16 But shun profane and vain babblings: for they will increase unto more ungodliness.

17 And their word will eat as doth a canker: of whom is Hymeneus and Philetus;

18 Who concerning the truth have erred, saying that the resurrection is past already; and overthrow the faith of some.

19 Nevertheless the foundation of God standeth sure, having this seal, The Lord knoweth them that are his. And, Let every one that nameth the name of Christ depart from iniquity.

20 But in a great house there are not only vessels of gold and of silver, but also of wood and of earth; and some to honor, and some to dishonor.

21 If a man therefore purge himself from these, he shall be a vessel unto honor, sanctified, and meet for the master's use, and prepared unto every good work.

22 Flee also youthful lusts: but follow righteousness, faith, charity, peace, with them that call on the Lord out of a pure heart.

23 But foolish and unlearned questions avoid, knowing that they do gender strifes.

24 And the servant of the Lord must not strive; but be gentle unto all men, apt to teach, patient;

25 In meekness instructing those that oppose themselves; if God peradventure will give them repentance to the acknowledging of the truth;

26 And that they may recover themselves out of the snare of the devil, who are taken captive by him at his will.

GOLDEN TEXT: Study to show thyself approved unto God, a workman that needeth not to be ashamed, rightly dividing the word of truth.—2 Timothy 2:15.

Good News for All

Unit 3: Sharing the Good News

(Lessons 10-13)

Lesson Aims

As a result of studying this lesson, each student should:

1. Have a better understanding of the importance of sound doctrine in the church.
2. Understand that false doctrine and bickering are detrimental to the growth of the church.
3. Have a growing appreciation for the importance of careful study of the Bible.
4. Be able to use the Bible to lead a person to become a Christian.

Lesson Outline

INTRODUCTION
- A. Count the Teeth
- B. Lesson Background

I. WORDS FOR GOD'S WORKMAN (2 Timothy 2:14-19)
- A. Don't Strive Over Words (v. 14)
- B. Handle God's Word Properly (v. 15)
- C. Shun Erroneous Teachings (vv. 16-18)
  Instruments at Our Disposal
- D. Trust and Obey (v. 19)

II. WAYS OF GOD'S WORKMAN (2 Timothy 2:20-26)
- A. Purges Himself (vv. 20, 21)
- B. Flees Youthful Lusts (v. 22)
- C. Avoids Foolish Questions (v. 23)
  The Screams of Those Hurting
- D. Is Gentle and Meek (vv. 24, 25)
- E. Seeks to Free Captives of the Devil (v. 26)

CONCLUSION
- A. Go, Teach
- B. Let Us Pray
- C. Thought to Remember

Visual 13 of the visuals packet highlights actions of the Lord's servant. Refer to it as you proceed through the lesson text. The visual is shown on page 221.

Introduction

A. Count the Teeth

A controversy over how many teeth a horse had once broke out among the monks in a medieval monastery. The argument raged for days and often became bitter. Proponents of each side quoted Aristotle, Plato, and the church fathers to support their positions, but still the question remained unresolved. Finally, a young monk offered what seemed to him to be a very practical suggestion. Why not go find a horse and actually count its teeth?

The older monks were aghast at both the impertinence and ignorance of the young monk. The very idea—trying to solve a scholastic issue by resorting to observation! They turned on the young friar, berating him and otherwise making his life so miserable that he finally was forced to leave the monastery.

We smile at such actions and shrug them off as being medieval. Certainly we would not be guilty of such foolish behavior. Yet to an outsider, our doctrinal disputes must at times seem quite as foolish. When such situations arise, we need to take the advice of the young monk and go to the final source of authority. In the case of religious disputes, that final authority is the Bible. Of course, not everyone understands the Bible in the same way. That's why Paul wrote Timothy to study to show himself approved before God, "rightly dividing the word of truth."

B. Lesson Background

The book of 2 Timothy might very well be called Paul's farewell address. Paul's first imprisonment in Rome is often dated A.D. 61 to 63. It seems a fair conjecture that he was tried and acquitted at Rome and then set free. Various statements in his epistles lead us to believe that he spent the next several years traveling about the lands surrounding the Aegean Sea, evangelizing and visiting the churches he had established earlier. It appears also that he wrote the epistles of 1 Timothy and Titus during these years. Then in A.D. 67, Paul was back in prison in Rome, a victim of Nero's persecution.

Even as Paul pens the words of 2 Timothy, one can almost hear the footsteps of the guards coming down the hall to take him to his execution. "For I am now ready to be offered," he wrote, "and the time of my departure is at hand. I have fought a good fight, I have finished my course, I have kept the faith" (2 Timothy 4:6, 7). Facing imminent death, one is not likely to spend much time on trivial matters. We are justified in believing, therefore, that what Paul wrote in this letter was very close to his heart.

Timothy was urged not to be ashamed to testify of Christ, nor to be ashamed of Paul who was a prisoner for the Lord. Paul called on Timothy to be willing also to suffer for the gospel (1:8, 9). It was imperative that Timothy "hold fast the form of sound words" that he had heard from Paul (1:13), and that he commit these teachings to faithful men who would "be able to teach others also" (2:2). Timothy was a soldier in the Lord's army. Paul, therefore, instructed him to endure hardship and to keep himself focused on the mighty spiritual conflict in which he was engaged (2:3, 4), remembering always that "salvation . . . with eternal glory" awaits those who suffer for the Lord Jesus (2:8-12). In the text for this lesson Paul gives Timothy some specific instructions to help him be a workman who meets with God's approval.

I. Words for God's Workman (2 Timothy 2:14-19)

A. Don't Strive Over Words (v. 14)

14. Of these things put them in remembrance, charging them before the Lord that they strive not about words to no profit, but to the subverting of the hearers.

Verse 14 continues the instructions that Paul has given Timothy in the preceding thirteen verses. The teaching that Timothy has received from Paul, he is to pass on to "faithful men" (v. 2). These were the leaders of the churches that Timothy would be serving. He was to solemnly charge them before God to avoid strife *about words.* We don't know the nature of these word battles. They may have been Jewish in origin, for the Jewish scholars loved to engage in all kinds of disputes over the law. Jesus experienced many such disputes during His ministry. On the other hand, these disputes may have involved some early forms of gnosticism, a pagan philosophy that invaded the church and gave it serious problems in a later period. In 1 Timothy, Paul had given similar warnings (1:3, 4; 4:7; 6:4). Apparently, the problem persisted and further warnings were needed.

Even today scholars sometimes engage in disputes over words and ideas that have little to do with living the Christian life. These battles seem more like games they play rather than teachings that will edify Christians and help the church grow. Not only is such bickering a waste of time (*no profit*), but it may lead men and women away from the faith (*the subverting of the hearers*).

B. Handle God's Word Properly (v. 15)

15. Study to show thyself approved unto God, a workman that needeth not to be ashamed, rightly dividing the word of truth.

This verse makes the study of the Scriptures a divine mandate. One ought to give diligence to handle *truth* in such a way so as not to be an embarrassment to oneself, the church, or before God. The word here translated *rightly dividing* literally means "to cut straight." Figuratively, it could mean to work honestly. The point of the verse is obvious. A good workman will not knowingly or unwittingly handle the word of truth in such a way as to distort it or pervert it, and thus lead people astray.

C. Shun Erroneous Teachings (vv. 16-18)

16. But shun profane and vain babblings: for they will increase unto more ungodliness.

Paul once more returns to the subject of verbal contentions that are disruptive of the peace and harmony of the church. He may have had in mind the same type of disputes mentioned in verse 14. However, the following verses may indicate that something else—the propagation of a serious heresy—was involved. Paul urges Timothy to avoid those who engage in *profane* (godless) talk. To listen to them will only give them encouragement and cause them to *increase unto more ungodliness,* with the potential of doing great harm to the church.

17, 18. And their word will eat as doth a canker: of whom is Hymeneus and Philetus; who concerning the truth have erred, saying that the resurrection is past already; and overthrow the faith of some.

The activities of the babblers are insidious, working swiftly and certainly, gnawing away at the faith of Christians like a *canker,* that is, gangrene. Gangrene is a loathsome affliction that can lead to the loss of limbs, and, left untreated, is fatal. This gives us a graphic picture of just how dreadful heresy may be.

By naming two culprits who were promoting heresy, Paul indicates that this was no theoretical evil. Hymeneus is mentioned along with Alexander in 1 Timothy 1:20. Paul accuses them of having "made shipwreck" of the faith and states that he has delivered them unto Satan so that "they may learn not to blaspheme." This certainly indicates how serious their offense was. Nothing more is known of Philetus.

In this verse Paul is specific regarding the heresy of these two men. They asserted that the resurrection had already occurred. This may mean that they taught that the only resurrection one would experience was at baptism and that Christians should not look forward to a future resurrection at the judgment. Paul's mentioning of this error emphasizes the importance of the proper teaching about the resurrection. There are some today who claim to be Christians, even

How to Say It

HYMENEUS. Hi-me-*nee*-us.
PHILETUS. Fi-*lee*-tus.

some leaders within the church, who deny that Jesus was raised from the dead and that Christians will experience a resurrection at the final judgment. It is not difficult to imagine how Paul would respond to such teaching!

INSTRUMENTS AT OUR DISPOSAL

There is a fable about a servant named Aesop, who was told by his master to prepare a banquet for guests. The servant was to serve the best meat possible. According to the tale, Aesop prepared the banquet and served his choice of meat under covers. When the guests removed the lids, they found cooked tongues. The master was unhappy and he berated Aesop for his choice of meats.

Later, the master instructed Aesop to prepare another banquet. Apparently the master disliked the guests who would be coming to this banquet, so he ordered his servant to buy the worst meat he could find. When these guests uncovered their plates, they too found tongues!

The master was furious, but Aesop explained: "You first wanted the best, so I bought tongues, because tongues have uttered some of the world's greatest truths. Then you ordered me to find the worst. I bought tongues, because tongues have uttered some of the greatest lies."

In these verses Paul issues a strong warning concerning the use of words. As an evangelist, Timothy understood that by the employment of words men and women could be saved. Paul took this opportunity to remind him also of the dangers of the misuse of the spoken word. For this reason Paul challenged him to avoid godless chatter and to have no fellowship with those who spread false teaching.

The tongue can be used to bicker and spread falsehood, or it can be used to teach the truth of God's Word. The choice belongs to each person, for the tongue is but an instrument waiting to be used. —T. T.

D. Trust and Obey (v. 19)

19. Nevertheless the foundation of God standeth sure, having this seal, The Lord knoweth them that are his. And, Let every one that nameth the name of Christ depart from iniquity.

Even though heretics might destroy the faith of some and thereby gain a following, yet *the foundation of God standeth sure.* What is this foundation of which Paul speaks? Various explanations have been given, but in the context it seems best to understand that he means the church. Nothing shall destroy the Lord's church—not heresy, not even the powers of death (Matthew 16:18). The church consists of those who are the Lord's, and it has a *seal.* The seal indicates God's ownership, approval, and protection and gives the assurance that God knows those who are truly His. The seal also indicates that these are the ones who are obedient to God and separate themselves from unrighteousness.

II. Ways of God's Workman (2 Timothy 2:20-26)

A. Purges Himself (vv. 20, 21)

20. But in a great house there are not only vessels of gold and of silver, but also of wood and of earth; and some to honor, and some to dishonor.

It is often a surprise and always a disappointment when some within the church become heretics and apostates. Paul knew that Timothy may have been shocked by this information, and so he draws an illustration from a household. *In a great house,* and it must be a great house because a humble house would not have vessels of gold and silver, one will find all kinds of vessels. Some of these are most valuable and will be carefully protected and used only on special occasions. Other vessels, those of wood and clay, will be used in every day service. Eventually they will become chipped and cracked and will be discarded.

The church on earth is like this, says Paul. It contains true believers, the precious saints who are compared to the gold and silver vessels of the great house. These serve faithfully and remain steadfast and are destined for *honor.* But the visible church contains also those who profess to be believers, but whose practices are inconsistent with their profession. These will know only dishonor in the final judgment.

21. If a man therefore purge himself from these, he shall be a vessel unto honor, sanctified, and meet for the master's use, and prepared unto every good work.

Unlike vessels that cannot change their nature, human beings do not have to remain as they are. Paul is stating that even those who may have become involved in false teaching are not hopelessly captive to it. They may escape from it by purging themselves, that is, separating themselves, from the false teachers and their evil doctrines. If one purges oneself from these "vessels to dishonor," he or she will be *sanctified,* set apart, and prepared to be useful to the Master, our Lord Jesus Christ, in the doing of *every good work.* False teachers and false doctrines insinuate themselves into the church today. Church leaders must be vigilant to protect the flock from these dangers and to rescue any who have fallen for them.

B. Flees Youthful Lusts (v. 22)

22. Flee also youthful lusts: but follow righteousness, faith, charity, peace, with them that call on the Lord out of a pure heart.

One way to avoid moral contamination is to avoid those things that cause it. Paul urges Timothy to actively avoid *youthful lusts,* to flee from them as one would from a hungry lion. These involve a range of sinful activities—pleasure (sex and gluttony), power, and possessions. At the time Paul wrote this letter, Timothy must have been in his mid-thirties or older, and so Paul is not admonishing him as a parent might a teenager. These temptations are certainly not confined to teenagers, and so Paul's warning is appropriate to persons of all ages.

Paul then goes beyond negative admonitions, and urges Timothy to seek *righteousness, faith, charity,* and *peace* with just as much vigor as he uses in fleeing youthful lusts. He is to do this in company with fellow Christians. An individual Christian is stronger in doing what is right when he or she pursues godliness in the company of other Christians.

C. Avoids Foolish Questions (v. 23)

23. But foolish and unlearned questions avoid, knowing that they do gender strifes.

Paul indicates just how serious theological word battles are by adding another warning against them. He described them in 1 Timothy 1:3, 4, and then cautioned Timothy about them in the first verse of today's lesson text. Just as Timothy is to flee youthful lusts, so he is to avoid these worthless questions. Certainly Paul is not attempting to limit free and open discussion, which is an important part of teaching and edification. And he is not saying that Timothy should turn away anyone who is honestly seeking information. He has in mind senseless questions that no one can answer. These are to be avoided because they only produce strife. In verse 15 of our text Paul has given us a better way. We must try hard to be good workers, using God's Word correctly. When it answers our questions, we can repeat its answers with assurance; but we only upset people when we become dogmatic and quarrelsome about unanswerable questions.

THE SCREAMS OF THOSE HURTING

In his classic novel, *Kidnapped,* Robert Louis Stevenson offers an interesting sentence concerning his swashbuckling hero, Alan Breck. Describing Breck's fight with the crew of the Covenant, he writes, "The sword in his hand flashed like quicksilver into the middle of our

visual 13

flying enemies, and at every flash came the scream of a man hurt."

Unfortunately, that statement serves as an appropriate description of what frequently occurs in the church. Too often we Christians view as our opponents those in the congregation who hold opinions that differ from ours. And in our zeal to change them, many a brother or sister is wounded. Though our intentions may be noble, our approach to our fellow Christians often lacks the spirit of gentleness and patience that Paul urges the Lord's servants to manifest.

Paul warned Timothy to have nothing to do with foolish and stupid arguments, which produce ugly quarrels. Furthermore, in his list of qualifications for the office of elder, which he gave to both Timothy and Titus, he emphasized that the spiritual leader must be self-controlled and not quick-tempered. These and other texts make it clear that the Lord's servant must not quarrel. A quarreler may succeed in winning an argument, but in many instances throughout the church will be heard the cries of men and women who are hurt. —T. T.

D. Is Gentle and Meek (vv. 24, 25)

24, 25. And the servant of the Lord must not strive; but be gentle unto all men, apt to teach, patient; in meekness instructing those that oppose themselves; if God peradventure will give them repentance to the acknowledging of the truth.

While Paul's remarks seem directed to Timothy as a leader, they are certainly applicable to all Christians. The Lord's servants are not to *strive,* are not to be quarrelers (v. 23), but are to be *gentle* in their dealings with others. They must be pleasant and gracious, approachable, willing even to suffer ridicule and abuse. Centuries earlier Solomon wrote, "A soft answer turneth away wrath" (Proverbs 15:1). That ancient maxim has never grown out-of-date. An age that values the clever put down or the sharp retort should remember this. The Lord's servants should be *apt to teach,* a requirement given for elders (1 Timothy 3:2). This does not necessarily mean that we must be able to stand before a class in a formal situation and eloquently deliver a lesson. Sometimes the most effective teaching is done in private in one-to-one situations. Assuredly, a Christian needs to be able to tell a person how to become a Christian and how to grow in the faith. But one doesn't have to be a brilliant theologian to do this. A key element in any teaching is patience, the willingness to keep trying to get truths across when the student is either slow to understand or stubbornly rebellious.

We do not work alone as we try to impart the Word of God to others. The Holy Spirit is involved also. God works in ways we don't always understand to bring people to a knowledge of truth. If we are gentle in our manner and meek in spirit, it may be that He will use our instruction to bring to *repentance* those who have taken a stand against the truth.

E. Seeks to Free Captives of the Devil (v. 26)

26. And that they may recover themselves out of the snare of the devil, who are taken captive by him at his will.

The purpose of our teaching is to get people to *recover themselves,* that is, to recover their senses or sober up. Only then can they escape the devil's snare. Some today may deny the reality of the devil, but not Paul. Several figures are used to describe Satan, but he is always depicted as relentless in his efforts to trap human beings. Sometimes he is a roaring lion, at other times a messenger of light, but always he is a menace. When we come to realize this, we will give greater diligence to our teaching.

Conclusion

A. Go, Teach

Someone has observed that the church is always just one generation away from extinction. If the present generation of Christians does not pass its faith along to the next generation, the church will cease to exist. While this view fails to take into consideration God's power to keep His church alive, it points up the vital necessity of teaching. No one is born into the faith. Every person must acquire his or her faith from others or directly from the Scriptures.

The church must do at least two things if it is to survive and grow. First, it must *teach;* second, it must teach the *truth.* In this lesson, Paul emphasizes both of these points. The early church took this commitment seriously. The apostles went everywhere teaching. In the process, they trained others to follow in their steps as teachers. Little wonder the early church grew as it did! The early church did not assume that the burden of teaching fell exclusively upon the apostles and specially trained teachers. Every Christian had an obligation to share the faith with others. The modern church has, in a large measure, lost this concept. Most of us are quite content to allow professionals to do the teaching while we sit comfortably in the pews.

It isn't enough, however, for teachers to teach. If the church is to grow, they must teach the truth. In a land that allows freedom of religion, speech, and press, one is free to teach about anything that one chooses. Some have taken full advantages of these freedoms to propagate the wildest of heresies. We do not want to curtail these freedoms, but we do want to protect people from those who would exploit them for their own purposes. We must have a standard for truth, and that standard is God's holy Word.

Those who know God's Word are less likely to be led astray by every wind of doctrine. Every leader, every teacher, every Christian needs to take seriously the responsibility to teach God's standards both in word and in life.

B. Let Us Pray

Dear Father, give us renewed commitment to study the Scriptures to find Your truths and then to teach them to others. In the name of the Master Teacher, we pray. Amen.

C. Thought to Remember

"And the things that thou hast heard of me among many witnesses, the same commit thou to faithful men, who shall be able to teach others also." 2 Timothy 2:2

Home Daily Bible Readings

Monday, Feb. 22—Be Encouraged (2 Timothy 1:3-14)
Tuesday, Feb. 23—A Worker of Christ (2 Timothy 2:1-13)
Wednesday, Feb. 24—An Approved Worker (2 Timothy 2:14-19)
Thursday, Feb. 25—Work Toward Love (2 Timothy 2:20-26)
Friday, Feb. 26—How Some People Act (2 Timothy 3:1-9)
Saturday, Feb. 27—Sound Doctrine (Titus 2:1-8)
Sunday, Feb. 28—God's Grace (Titus 2:9-15)

Learning by Doing

This page contains an alternate lesson plan emphasizing learning activities. Classes desiring such student involvement will find these suggestions helpful.

Learning Goals

After studying 1 Timothy 2:14-26, the pupil will be able to:

1. List the characteristics of a good workman for God.
2. Identify an area of life in which he or she intends to become a more effective workman for God.

Into the Lesson

As class members arrive, have them form groups of three or four. Each person in the group is to share with the others, telling them about the person who has had the most impact on the development of his or her faith and why that person has had such an impact. Allot five minutes for this activity.

Make the transition into the Bible lesson by stating that today's study will describe an effective workman who can have a similar impact on the lives of others.

Into the Word

Present the material in the "Lesson Background" section. Then read aloud 1 Timothy 2:14-26.

Have the students search the Scripture text for the answers to the following questions as you ask them.

1. What is the effective workman for God to avoid? (Quarreling, profane (godless) chatter, false teaching, evil desires.)
2. What is the effective workman to pursue? (The word of truth, holiness, righteousness, faith, love, peace.)
3. What examples of false teachers did Paul give, and what were they teaching? (Hymeneus and Philetus who were teaching heresy concerning the resurrection.)
4. How does the effective workman deal with the person who opposes the truth of God? (The workman gently and patiently instructs such a one in the hope that he or she will repent and escape the devil's snare.)

Assign the class members to groups of four (perhaps the same groups used earlier in the session). Give each group one of the tasks below.

1. Read 1 Timothy 2:14-26. Write a recipe for producing an effective workman for God.
2. Read 1 Timothy 2:14-26. Draw a sketch that shows a pattern for becoming an effective workman for God.
3. Read 1 Timothy 2:14-26. Develop a three-point sermon outlining how to become an effective workman for God.

Give the groups six to eight minutes to complete their work. Then let them share their results with the rest of the class.

Into Life

Present the following situations to the class members. Ask them how to be effective workmen in each case.

1. You are on a committee to choose teaching materials for your church. Many on the committee want to select materials that, though Bible-based, are clearly in error about how to become a Christian. How can you apply the principle of being a good workman in this situation?
2. A good friend of yours has begun to show an interest in a religious group that denies the sinfulness of humankind, the need for salvation from sin, and the nature of Christ as both God and man. Your friend has been a member of the church for many years. How can you apply the principle of being a good workman in this situation?
3. A person in your Sunday-school class likes to argue, and sometimes raises questions about matters for which there is no definitive answer. It has become discouraging to many in your class. How can you apply the principle of being a good workman in this situation?

(Be sure that students consider all of the characteristics of a good workman as they develop their answers.)

Give each student a copy of the "Good Workman" rating scale below and ask them to fill it out for their private reference.

Good Workman

On a scale of 1-10 (10 being best), how would you rate yourself on the following characteristics of a good workman?

1. Firmly grounded in the Word of God. ____
2. Avoidance of godless chatter. ____
3. Pursuit of holy living. ____
4. Pursuit of righteousness. ____
5. Pursuit of peace. ____
6. Avoidance of foolish arguments. ____
7. Gentleness toward others. ____
8. Ability to teach others. ____

I want to be a better workman by . . .

Let's Talk It Over

The questions on this page are designed to encourage review of the lesson Scriptures and to promote discussion of the lesson by the class. The answers provided are only discussion starters. Let your class talk it over from there.

1. What effect do disputes and arguments have on the church?

(1) They disrupt or destroy peace and harmony in the church. This internal harm is more damaging to the work of the church than any external attack the church's enemies can make. Peace and harmony are not to be preserved at any cost, of course. But these conditions will prevail in the fellowship of the church if each member manifests the spirit of the Lord of the church. They *do* foster maximum utilization of resources in mission and ministry. Disputes destroy, not edify!

(2) They create lasting adversarial relationships. Many people lace the ability (or willingness) to reconcile and foster healing after a dispute or argument. During a dispute, too many tend to view the other party as an enemy. With adversarial relationships come animosity, bitterness, vengefulness, and often the absence of a forgiving spirit. How tragic that those who are brothers and sisters in the Lord become adversaries!

2. What are some ways in which people respond to conflict?

The natural responses are seen in the "fight or flight syndrome." These responses major in self-preservation. Although there are the dominant responses, there is a higher one. Let's consider the primitive way first. (1) *Fight.* When we are attacked or a challenge arises, our adrenalin pumps and we are prepared for battle. The fact is, some people like to fight. They don't run from it; they even seek out a fight. Others fight when they have to. (2) Then there is *flight.* Some, when they are attacked or challenged, run. They will do everything they can to avoid conflict. They are so threatened by conflict that no other alternative is considered. Some, in their effort to avoid conflict, may even deny that any serious problem exists. They will try to pour oil on troubled waters and assume that everything is fine. (3) The highest response to conflict is to *use it for growth.* Neither "fight" nor "flight" serves the highest purpose, to foster growth. Conflict can be a friend in disguise! Few people see it that way, but it's true. Conflict reveals needs (that's a plus), and it can be a source of growth when we resolve conflict creatively (that's a *big* plus). This can be done when the persons involved are guided to view the conflict with the appropriate perspective and when relevant principles are implemented. Men and women who enjoy healthy marriages have long known that creative resolution of conflict is a significant road to growth.

3. As a leader in the Lord's church, Timothy was urged by Paul to correctly handle the word of truth. It is equally imperative for Christians today to do this. What are some basic principles that we should apply in order to properly understand the Bible's message?

A familiar bumper sticker asserts, "God said it, I believe it, and that settles it!" It is a sentiment held sincerely, no doubt, but it is inadequate as a guide for our understanding of the Scriptures' relevance to our lives. As with any category of literature, sacred or secular, rules of interpretation must be applied if we are to correctly understand the intent of the author. The following oft-repeated guidelines for studying the Bible are fundamental. Ask, Who is speaking, to whom is the statement addressed, in what dispensation or time period is it made, and for what purpose? Perhaps, as the bumper sticker states, "God said it." But was the statement made to Moses as a command to the nation of Israel, or is it a statement directed to those who are followers of Jesus Christ? Is the speaker the Lord or one of His authorized messengers, or is the speaker an uninspired human being? Only as we apply principles such as these can we come to an accurate understanding of God's Word and know that we are handling it properly.

4. Paul said to "flee . . . youthful lusts" (2 Timothy 2:22). How does this relate to self-discipline?

Sometimes a temptation is of such a nature that we flirt around with it. We enjoy the temptation so much that we soon cross the point of no return and commit the sin. Then we claim, "I couldn't help myself." We are to flee, run away from, such temptations. If a certain person tempts us to lust and fornication, stay away from that person. If it is a temptation to gossip about an enemy, then do not speak of him or her at all. Satan finds us often enough to test us; we need not go looking for him.

Spring Quarter, 1993

Theme: Believing in Christ

Special Features

Lessons

Unit 1. John: The Word Became Flesh

Unit 2. John: The Great Love

Unit 3. John: Believe in Jesus

Related Resources

The following publications are suggested as additional helps for those who teach the lessons of the Spring Quarter. They may be purchased from your supplier. The prices shown here are subject to change.

John (Standard Bible Studies), by Lewis Foster. This study guide blends different approaches, allowing the reader's interests to flow with John's direction. Order #11-40104, $12.99.

New Testament Maps and Charts. This packet contains eight maps, including those of Palestine and Jerusalem in Jesus' day. Four charts are included also. Order #14-02608, $9.99.

The Only Way, by Lewis Foster. A study of John, chapters 12-21. This book emphasizes the clear teaching of Scripture that there is only one way to real life, the true life, and this is Jesus. Order #11-40048, $2.25.

Why Believe? by Richard Koffarnus. This book is a defense of the Christian faith, presenting a critical review of some popular philosophies of unbelievers. Order #11-40090, $2.25.

Quarterly Quiz

The questions on this page may be used in several ways: as a pretest at the beginning of the quarter; as a review at the end of the quarter; or as a review after each lesson. The questions are based on the Scripture text of each lesson (King James Version). ***The answers are on page 232.***

Lesson 1

1. The Word, who was with God in the beginning, was active in creation. T/F *John 1:3*
2. The Word became a human being, Jesus Christ, and lived among us. T/F *John 1:14*
3. Moses gave the law. What two things did Jesus Christ bring? *John 1:17*

Lesson 2

1. What was the name of the Pharisee who came at night to speak with Jesus? *John 3:1*
2. Jesus told him that no one would see God's kingdom unless he were what? *John 3:3*
3. God sent His Son into the world to ______ the world, not ______ it. *John 3:17*

Lesson 3

1. What did Jesus say He was, as long as He was in the world? *John 3:17*
2. After putting clay on a blind man's eyes, what did Jesus tell him to do? *John 9:7*
3. The blind man saw no purpose in Jesus' command and refused to do it. T/F *John 9:7*

Lesson 4

1. What city did Lazarus live in? *John 11:1*
2. Martha did not believe in the resurrection at the last day. T/F *John 11:24*
3. How many days had Lazarus been dead before Jesus brought him back to life? *John 11:39*

Lesson 5

1. Jesus knew when He would die. T/F *John 13:1*
2. Who put it in Judas Iscariot's heart to betray Jesus? *John 13:2*
3. Which disciple at first refused to let Jesus wash his feet? *John 13:8*

Lesson 6

1. Who ran to tell Peter and another disciple that Jesus' tomb was empty? *John 20:1, 2*
2. Of those two disciples, who was the first to enter the empty tomb of Jesus? *John 20:6*
3. Who did Mary think Jesus was? *John 20:15*

Lesson 7

1. Jesus' appearance to the disciples at the Sea of Galilee was His third appearance to them after His resurrection. T/F *John 21:14*
2. On this same occasion, Jesus spoke about the death of (Thomas, Peter, Nathanael), by which he would glorify God. *John 21:17-19*

Lesson 8

1. What did Jesus promise not to do to the one who comes to Him? *John 6:37*
2. Jesus said, "He that believeth on me hath _______ _______. *John 6:47*
3. Whoever eats the bread that came down from heaven will not do what? *John 6:50*

Lesson 9

1. John the Baptist identified himself as the voice of one crying in the wilderness, uttering the words prophesied by whom? *John 1:23*
2. John the Baptist saw the Spirit descend from Heaven like a ______, and it abode on Jesus. *John 1:32*

Lesson 10

1. What did Andrew tell Peter after spending a day with Jesus? *John 1:41*
2. Who found Nathanael and told him that Jesus was He of whom Moses wrote? *John 1:45*
3. Who asked, "Can there any good thing come out of Nazareth?" *John 1:46*

Lesson 11

1. The woman at the well recognized that the Jews had no dealings with whom? *John 4:9*
2. The person who drinks of the water that Jesus gives will never do what? *John 4:14*
3. Jesus said that those who worship God must worship Him in what manner? *John 4:24*

Lesson 12

1. When Jesus said, "He that believeth on me, . . . out of his belly shall flow rivers of living water," of what was He speaking? *John 7:38, 39*
2. When the chief priests and Pharisees criticized their officers for not apprehending Jesus, who spoke up in Jesus' defense? *John 7:50*

Lesson 13

1. What did Jesus say we are to do, if we love Him? *John 14:15*
2. What did Jesus say He would give to His disciples as His earthly ministry closed and He returned to the Father? *John 14:27*

The Testimony of John

by S. Edward Tesh

RELIGION HAS BEEN DESCRIBED as humankind's upreach and outreach toward God. This search, it is said, began with primitive man. A spring of water, bubbling from the ground, fascinated him. Storms with their thunder and lightning terrified him, as did times of drought or plague. What kept the spring flowing? How could he express his thanks for it? If the water ceased, was it because of something he had done? What should he do? What sacrifice should he make?

In the search for answers to these questions there arose a class of medicine men, shamans, witch doctors, seers, and priests. And so religion grew and developed. But who, of all those doing the searching, ever found God? Their upreach and outreach go on and on. But we ask, as did men of old, "Canst thou by searching find out God?" (Job 11:7).

For the next thirteen weeks our lessons will be based on the Gospel of John. We shall see that the apostle John is not concerned about religion; he doesn't even use the word. Nor does he refer to man's upreach and outreach to God. Instead, he would say, "Let me tell you about God's *down*-reach to man." For the Gospel, from beginning to end, is about God's coming to earth in the person of Jesus Christ to seek and to save the lost.

Believing in Christ

John's purpose in giving his testimony is not clearly stated. It is not written as a treatise on religion, nor merely as an interesting story. In his own words the writer states his purpose clearly and precisely: "In his disciples' presence Jesus performed many other miracles which are not written down in this book. But these have been written in order that you may believe that Jesus is the Messiah, the Son of God, and that through your faith in him you may have life" (John 20:30, 31, *Today's English Version*).

John is deeply in earnest in his writing. For him, the evidence, much of which he received firsthand as an eyewitness, is conclusive. The Jesus whom he saw die on a cross became the living Savior, risen from the grave that could not hold Him. Now John wishes to share that evidence with those he comes in contact with, that they too may believe and have life eternal. Therefore, the title for the thirteen lessons we study this quarter is appropriate: "Believing in Christ" (The Gospel of John).

Basic Considerations

Some may question why our lessons will be "skipping all around" in the book, instead of going straight through from chapter one through twenty-one. The answer involves what we hope to accomplish, with and for our students. To give them a general, overall understanding of the message of John, we might go through the book chapter by chapter. The aim of these lessons for this quarter of study, however, is not an overview of the Gospel. Instead, they seek to focus attention on certain *basic truths* about Jesus, concentrating the study upon these basics to such a degree that the student may never forget them. The lessons also, quite naturally, are concerned to set forth the evidence that sustains and validates the conclusions regarding Jesus.

John: The Word Became Flesh

With the above aim in view, Unit One of our study focuses our attention upon the basic consideration of *who Jesus is.* In the opening verses of his Gospel, John introduces Jesus as the *Word* that was with God—and was God—at creation. John goes on to say, "And the Word was made flesh, and dwelt among us, and we beheld his glory" (John 1:14). He is referring to Jesus Christ as the *incarnation* of God. This is the foundational truth upon which the book stands or falls, and all else that John says is predicated upon it. Jesus was human but also divine, God in the flesh, that He might dwell among us. In Him was *life* and *light,* John tells us, and both of these He would share with the world.

In Him Was Life. Lesson One describes Jesus as the giver of life to those who will receive Him, to whom He gives "power to become the sons of God" (1:12). Lesson Two, *Rebirth Into Eternal Life,* considers the words of Jesus in His conversation with Nicodemus, a ruler of the Jews who recognizes Jesus as "a teacher come from God." Jesus tells him of the necessity, and of the possibility, of being *born again,* "of water and of the Spirit." Only thus may one enter into the kingdom of God and receive eternal life.

In Lesson Three, *Light of the World,* we have demonstrated for us that Jesus *is* the light, as He gives sight to a man blind from birth. Likewise, in Lesson Four, *Coming to Life,* we see Christ's power to give everlasting life, when He raises from the grave His friend Lazarus, who has been dead for four days. Only Jesus, the incarnate Son of God, could provide such light and such life to mankind.

John: The Great Love

As noted above, the religions of the world reflect the efforts of many souls—often devout souls—in their search for God. Some have directed their search outward and upward. Others have said, "Look within, if you would find God." But John says, "Look to Jesus, and behold God in the person of His Son, who came to earth for the express purpose of revealing God to us."

If it be thought incredible that God would thus send His Son to earth, the question might be asked, "Why would He? Why would the Creator and Sovereign of the universe be concerned with the inhabitants of planet earth?"

The answer to this question is just as stupendous as the incarnation itself. It is because "God so loved the world," John says (3:16). The all-righteous God could have looked upon the sinful race with wrath and left humankind to perish in their sins. But no, the God whom Jesus reveals, although His wrath is like a consuming fire against all wickedness, desires that "all should come to repentance" (2 Peter 3:9), that through Christ they may receive forgiveness and life.

The four lessons of Unit Two deal with this theme—*The Great Love.* John reveals God's love as it is demonstrated in the life of Jesus, in His words and in His deeds.

The first lesson of this unit, *Do As I Have Done,* teaches the remarkable truth that the love of God is a love that *serves.* The occasion is the washing of the disciples' feet by Jesus. Jesus their Lord takes a towel and performs this humble task for them. The love that moves Him to do this is a reflection of the love that moved God to send His Son to bless mankind with salvation and life.

Lesson Six, *I Have Seen the Lord,* is the Easter lesson. It makes clear that God's love is available to all. His love for those who mourn is demonstrated by the tender concern of Jesus for Mary, as she weeps by the empty tomb.

In Lesson Seven, *To Love Is to Serve,* Jesus' preparation of a meal for His disciples on the shore of Galilee is a demonstration of love. It is also an example for them to follow. Peter acknowledges his love for Jesus. "Feed my sheep," is the Master's response.

Lesson Eight, *The Bread of Life,* reflects God's compassion. Jesus feeds the hungry. He also provides the *bread of life*—He is the *Bread of life*—and "he that eateth of this bread shall live for ever."

John: Believe in Jesus

John has testified of great things regarding Jesus. He is the Son of God, God in the flesh, who has come to reveal God the Father. Second, the God whom He reveals is a God of *great love.* (See John 3:16.) This is all very wonderful, if it be so. And John is most confident that it is so. Throughout the book he shares reasons why one should *Believe in Jesus* (Unit Three) and receive the life that He alone can give.

In Lesson Nine, *The Witness of John the Baptist,* we have the testimony of this famous man in regard to Jesus. Recognized himself as a man of God and a prophet, the word of John would have carried great weight in his day. He declares that Jesus is the Lamb of God, who takes away the sin of the world, and that He is the Son of God.

The testimony of Jesus' first disciples is presented in Lesson Ten—*We Have Found Him.* These men who left all to follow Jesus were convinced that they had found the Messiah, long ago spoken of by the prophets. They were very ordinary men, but they did marvelous things, and their lives had a most extraordinary effect upon the world for all time to come!

Even the common people, those who were less acquainted with Jesus, recognized Him as one standing in a special relationship with God. Lesson Eleven, *Can This Be the Christ?* relates the verdict of a people who were not even Jews—the Samaritans. Their testimony is like that of other witnesses: "We have heard him ourselves, and know that this is indeed the Christ, the Saviour of the world" (John 4:42).

It is significant that all who confronted Jesus in any capacity were deeply impressed, friend and foe alike. Lesson Twelve, *Confronting the Galilean,* treats this testimony. Some said Jesus was a prophet, others, the Messiah. And others debated the issue. Like a good reporter, the apostle John makes note of all of this.

Unit Three, *Believe in Jesus,* concludes with Lesson Thirteen, *The Promise of the Spirit.* Jesus tells His apostles that after He is gone from them the Holy Spirit from God will come to them. The Spirit will guide them and enable them to do the work Jesus commissioned them to do, that is, to go into all the world and make disciples. But is this promise properly included in a study of the evidence on which we believe? It is when the promise is kept! Just see what happened to these men and what they accomplished in launching the kingdom of God! The handful of disciples has become millions—not through their own power, but through the power of the Spirit that was promised them. Jesus kept His promise.

That You May Believe

by R. David Roberts

WHENEVER ONE TEACHES about the life of Jesus, one confronts unanswered questions: Whatever happened to some of the people only briefly met in the Gospel account (for example, the woman at the well, the official or nobleman and his son, or the young boy with the multiplied lunch of bread and fishes)? Where did Jesus go and what did He do in the "non-described" times? Whom else did He encounter, and what other healings or signs accompanied His ministry? What other statements did Jesus make, even in private conversation, that might be helpful to us today?

Many teachers spend much time conjecturing and wondering, or reconstructing and supposing, but we have no way of knowing those things or answering those questions. Sooner or later, one must leave those unknown aspects and focus on what *is* given to us.

Written for a Purpose

Here is where the simple words in John 20:30, 31 become most helpful: "Jesus did many other miraculous signs in the presence of his disciples, which are not recorded in this book. But these are written that you may believe that Jesus is the Christ, the Son of God, and that by believing you may have life in his name."*

There *were* many other things Jesus said and did. In fact, the last verse of the last chapter in John's Gospel declares that if all that Jesus did had been written, "the world would not have room" for the volumes it would take to record it. But "*these* are written," we are told, "that you may believe."

The Gospel of John—indeed, each of the four Gospels—testifies to the faith of the early Christians. It is an accurate account of events, yes, but it is presented for a singular purpose: that those who read it (or teach it) may *believe* that "Jesus is the Christ." Just to dissect the parts of this book and learn its facts would be to miss the whole intention of the writing. Mere fact-recording did not interest those disciples who were risking their lives to be Christians in the first-century Roman world. They remembered and wrote the facts in order to help others know what they believed and why they were so convinced that Jesus was worth their full commitment.

They did not believe without adequate reason, and they wanted others to know the reason, but most of all they wanted others to believe in Jesus as Lord. Their concern for such faith, of course, was because of their conviction that in Jesus alone could people find real "life."

Teaching With the Right Purpose

When you assume the role of a Bible teacher and take these materials prepared for teaching lessons from the Gospel of John, you need to do so for the right reasons and with the right purpose in mind. No less a conviction than that which is expressed in John 20:31 should be the primary motivation for anyone who is teaching God's Word: we must come to this task with a full conviction that Jesus is the Christ and that people need to believe in Him to have life. Even if we "can fathom all mysteries and all knowledge," and even if we have great gifts for speaking in either the "tongues of men (or) of angels," yet if we do not *love* Jesus Christ as Lord and Savior and the people we teach as those who need to know Him, we are just "a resounding gong or a clanging cymbal" (1 Corinthians 13:1, 2).

In numerous universities across this country there are very highly educated professors of religion who know their material very well. The sad fact, however, is that some of them do not really believe in what they teach. Is it any wonder that many students who take classes in religion in those universities conclude the courses without any personal faith? Such a situation brings to mind Jesus' warning in Matthew 18:6: "If anyone causes one of these little ones who believe in me to sin, it would be better for him to have a large millstone hung around his neck and to be drowned in the depths of the sea." God's primary requirement of those of us who would teach is the conviction that Jesus is, indeed, "the Christ, the Son of God."

Such a convinced faith is what produced the writing of this Gospel, and such a convinced faith is what will compel you to do the very best you can do in teaching each lesson to every student. Nothing less will serve as foundation for such a responsibility.

Eyewitness Testimony

The writers of the Gospels wanted others to believe in Jesus as the Son of God and giver of life, but they did not presume to persuade others merely on the basis of an emotional or spiritual enthusiasm. No matter how convinced they were of Jesus' identity, they had to present facts to those who came along later in order for real faith to be produced in them. Feelings are essential to a person's response to God, but they are not enough for the kind of faith God has in mind.

Obviously, we did not see the events of Jesus' life or hear the actual words of His teachings. We can, nonetheless, believe firmly in Him because of the reliable testimony of those who did witness His life and hear Him speak. That is the gift beyond value of those who lived and died for their faith in the first century: some of them were guided by the Spirit of God to record what they had seen and heard, and we are the beneficiaries of that service today. They told us, in writing, not only what they believed, but why.

For some of them, like Thomas, that faith was not easily formed, because things did not follow normal patterns and the call to believe was above and beyond the usual expectations of life. They did believe, however, through physical evidence and through undeniable experience, and the Gospel accounts record some of that evidence and experience.

Jesus understood the difficulty of believing when things were not normal and usual: He offered His hands and side to Thomas for physical examination. But He also understood that there would be many, like us today, who would believe through the testimony of those eyewitnesses, and He pronounced a blessing for us in our venture of faith (John 20:29).

Faith Comes From Reality Testimony

Faith, though, still demands solid evidence or strong testimony, and we must be careful not to expect people to believe in Jesus just because "everybody else does." That was Paul's testimony in Romans 10:17—"Faith comes from hearing the message, and the message is heard through the word of Christ." If we hope people will believe in Jesus as God's Son and commit their lives to Him, we must make sure they have heard the actual story. Your students deserve the opportunity to hear what has been recorded and to know why Jesus is worth believing.

A college student not long ago indicated that he had ceased to attend Sunday school. His reason was not that he had nothing more to learn, but that he had become aware that the teachers whose classes he had been attending recently had not done their homework and were not really teaching God's Word as written.

That remains one of the biggest challenges of teaching the Bible: to present what is written, fairly and accurately, and to allow God's Word to sink into people's lives today so they may believe. Studying what is written and preparing to teach it honestly and effectively, therefore, are worth the effort, because we are dealing with that which is critical to eternal life. In Romans 10 Paul addressed the questions of how people can believe at all unless they have heard, and of how they can hear unless someone tells them. Recalling the expression of the prophet Isaiah (52:7), Paul concluded his line of questioning with a "beautiful" blessing on those who actually bring the good news (Romans 10:15). Our teaching God's Word is of the utmost importance for people to "have life in his name."

Facing the Ultimate Question

We have indicated that the Gospel writers recorded their testimony because of their faith in Jesus and their conviction that He is the only way to life eternal in God. And we have seen that people today will form their faith in Jesus on the basis of hearing and considering the evidence for His being who He said He was. Yet there is one major question that remains. Do you care what happens as a result of your teaching these lessons? Good teaching is very important, and one must know *about* Jesus to teach about Him. But how vital it is that the teacher *know* Jesus! It is not so important that you be the *best* teacher as that you be *faithful.* Your faith and conviction are essential for teaching this material.

Each of us has different abilities and different strengths, and that is true in teaching. Not everyone can or will be a master teacher. The critical issue for a faithful Christian teacher, though, is, do you care about your students? Do you want *them* to believe? Are you convinced that real life can be found only in Jesus? Do you do what you do as a teacher because you want your students to know Him as Lord and Savior?

All the finest techniques and materials in the world cannot substitute for a genuine concern for the salvation and spiritual maturity of your students. No matter what else you do or how well you do it, you cannot be completely effective as a Christian teacher until that becomes your guiding star to point them, and you, toward Jesus himself.

There are, and always will be, unanswered questions in studying and teaching the Gospels. But the biggest question of all can be answered in the affirmative: Do you believe that Jesus is the Christ, the Son of God? If your answer is yes, and if you seek to lead your students to the same belief, you will be in good company: so believed the apostle John, and for that reason he wrote the Gospel that bears His name.

So we believe, and so we teach!

---

*Scripture quotations in this article are taken from the *New International Version.*

The Light of the World

by Marion W. Henderson

ONE OF THE IMPORTANT CONCEPTS in the Gospel of John is recorded in John 1:4, 5, 9; 8:12; and 9:5. These passages present Jesus as the light of the world. John 1:4, 5 declares that the life that was in Jesus was the light of men, that it shines in the darkness, and the darkness has not understood it. John 8:12 records Jesus' affirmation that He is the light of the world and that the person who follows Him will not walk in darkness, but will have the light of life. Upon the occasion of the healing of the blind man (recorded in chapter 9), Jesus told His disciples that as long as He is in the world, He is the light of the world (v. 5).

John wrote his Gospel account some years after the close of Jesus' earthly ministry, at a time when the church was troubled by heresy. False teachers were claiming to have special insight into spiritual matters and to be "enlightened" in their spiritual perception. There were those who claimed to be Christians and to be walking in the light of spiritual reality, even though they did not accept Jesus as the unique, divine Son of God. John identified Jesus as being the true light because he wanted to present Him as the one through whom true spiritual enlightenment comes.

John's emphasis also highlights the revealing nature of light, which is to penetrate and dispel darkness. Since Jesus is the light of the world, it is His nature to penetrate and dispel the spiritual darkness in which human beings live. "In him was life; and the life was the light of men" (1:4). One purpose for Jesus' coming into the world, therefore, was to explain God to humankind upon the plane of human experience, so that we may know what God is really like (1:18).

To Walk in the Light

Affirming himself to be the light of the world, Jesus said that whoever follows Him will not walk in darkness (John 8:12). That is, a person who is an obedient believer in Jesus will no longer be living in the spiritual darkness of this world. Furthermore, that person will have "the light of life." To learn more of this light and what it means to walk in the light, we turn to John's first epistle.

In 1 John 1:5—2:28 John gives some practical teachings concerning the Christian life. He describes it as a fellowship with God conditioned and tested by one's walking in the light that comes from Him. John begins here by saying that "God is light." Is John contradicting himself? No. The nature of God is light, and the nature of light is to shine and reveal itself. Since "God is light," it is His nature to reveal himself. This He did in Jesus Christ. Thus Jesus could say, "I am the light of the world."

If we are to have fellowship with God, therefore, we must accept His revelation of himself in Jesus Christ and order our lives by it. That is precisely John's intent in his epistle. In the opening verses, he gives his personal eyewitness testimony to the deity of Jesus. He wanted his readers to be just as certain of this fact as he was so that they could have fellowship with one another, and with the Father, and with His Son Jesus Christ (see verses 1-3). This fellowship with God results in one's being cleansed from sin by the blood of Jesus Christ His Son (v. 7).

Test of Righteousness

Having introduced the subject of sin, John goes on to say that if we say we have no sin, we deceive ourselves and the truth is not in us (1 John 1:8). To walk in the light means, therefore, that we not only acknowledge the fact of sin in our lives, but also that we accept the responsibility for it. And certainly, to persist in pursuing evil is proof that one is walking in darkness, regardless of how much he or she may profess to be walking in the light.

When we arrive at the position where we view our sins as God views them and we confess them, He will keep His promise to forgive us our sins (v. 9). The existence of sin in those who are Christians is a fact, but it does not forbid the possibility of fellowship with God for those who penitently acknowledge its presence in their lives. God has provided for its forgiveness and removal for those who are walking in the light of Jesus Christ.

To confess our sins is not only to acknowledge the presence of wrong actions in our lives, but it is to confess them as needing forgiveness, to lay at our own door the full responsibility for them. To deny that we have committed sin is to walk in darkness.

To walk in the light means that we acknowledge our guilt for our sins and that we constantly commit ourselves to keeping God's commandments. The word translated "keep" was used of seamen who carefully observed the direction of the winds and ocean currents and set their course accordingly. We are to observe carefully our conduct and daily bring it into harmony with the will of God as revealed in the Scriptures. John says that the one who habitually fails to keep God's commandments is a liar if he says he knows God. Zeal that is not zeal for keeping God's commandments is merely egotism subtly disguised (1 John 2:3-6).

Test of Love

A second indication that we are walking in the light is to be seen in our attitude toward our fellow Christians. Fellowship with God means that we will love our brothers and sisters in Christ as God loves them. God loves with *agape* love, which means among other things that He loves "in spite of" and not "because of." It carries with it the idea of a willingness to lay down one's life for the object of one's love. One of the necessary ways of showing our love for God is to love our fellow Christians. Not to love them is an indication that we are walking in darkness (1 John 2:9, 10).

We further demonstrate our love for God, and show that we are walking in the light, by not loving the standards of the world or the things of the world (1 John 2:15-17). John describes the love of the world in three ways, and yielding to these lusts crushes the image of God that is in us. The first of these is "the lust of the flesh," which has reference to the baser appetites within us that have their seat in the flesh. The second is the "lust of the eyes." This is desire that has its origin in sight, and includes such things as envy and covetousness. The third is "the pride of life." This pride is based upon what one possesses in material things rather than upon spiritual attainment. It is seen in vain glorious display and arrogant and boastful living. All of these desires are of the world, and not of God. One who loves God and walks in the light of His ways will have no part of them.

Test of Belief

The third test indicating that we are walking in the light is our attitude toward the person of Jesus. Whose Son is He? The false teachers were depreciating the person of Jesus. Some said that He was only a figment of the imagination of the Christians and that He only "seemed" to be. Others said that He was a man who became divine at His baptism when the divine "aeon" (element or Spirit) came upon Him, but that this divine element left Him at the cross, as seen in the cry of Jesus, "My God, my God, why hast thou forsaken me?" (Matthew 27:46).

First John 2:22 states that the one who denies that Jesus is the Christ is a liar. The antichrist, according to John, is the person who refuses to accept Jesus as the Christ. That person denies both the Father and the Son. To John, "antichrist" is a principle of unbelief as well as a person. It is the principle of the rejection of the divinity of Jesus Christ.

If we do not accept Jesus as the Christ, we are not walking in the light of God's revelation given in and through His Son, who came to make God more fully known to us (John 1:18).

To walk in the light means that we look at Jesus in the same way that the Father does. We have no reservations about His identity, nor His person; He is the Christ, the Son of the living God, the Redeemer of mankind.

Walking in the Light Today

To walk in the light of Jesus Christ means we have fellowship with God and with those who are in fellowship with Him. It means that we accept the responsibility for the sin in our lives.

To walk in the light of Jesus Christ means that we are loving our Christian brothers and sisters with the same kind of love that the Father has for them. We are willing to give ourselves in service for them.

To walk in the light of Jesus Christ means that we have the same perspective about the person of Jesus that the Father has. We accept Jesus as God's only begotten Son, whose death on the cross makes possible the restoration of humankind's fellowship with the Father in Heaven (John 20:30, 31).

If we do these things, we will be walking in the light of Jesus Christ and thereby experiencing the manifold blessings of God.

Answers to Quarterly Quiz on page 226

Lesson 1—1. true. 2. true. 3. grace and truth. **Lesson 2**—1. Nicodemus, 2. born again. 3. save, condemn. **Lesson 3**—1. the light of the world. 2. "Go, wash in the pool of Siloam." 3. false. **Lesson 4**—1. Bethany. 2. false. 3. four. **Lesson 5**—1. true. 2. the devil. 3. Peter. **Lesson 6**—1. Mary Magdalene. 2. Simon Peter. 3. the gardener. **Lesson 7**—1. true. 2. Peter. **Lesson 8**—1. cast out. 2. everlasting life. 3. die. **Lesson 9**—1. Isaiah. 2. dove. **Lesson 10**—1. "We have found the Messiah." 2. Philip. 3. Nathanael. **Lesson 11**—1. the Samaritans. 2. thirst. 3. in spirit and in truth. **Lesson 12**—1. the Spirit. 2. Nicodemus. **Lesson 13**—1. keep His commandments. 2. peace.

In Him Was Life

March 7
Lesson 1

LESSON SCRIPTURE: **John 1:1-18.**

PRINTED TEXT: **John 1:1-18.**

DEVOTIONAL READING: **John 1:19-23, 29-34.**

John 1:1-18

1 In the beginning was the Word, and the Word was with God, and the Word was God.

2 The same was in the beginning with God.

3 All things were made by him; and without him was not any thing made that was made.

4 In him was life; and the life was the light of men.

5 And the light shineth in darkness; and the darkness comprehended it not.

6 There was a man sent from God, whose name was John.

7 The same came for a witness, to bear witness of the Light, that all men through him might believe.

8 He was not that Light, but was sent to bear witness of that Light.

9 That was the true Light, which lighteth every man that cometh into the world.

10 He was in the world, and the world was made by him, and the world knew him not.

11 He came unto his own, and his own received him not.

12 But as many as received him, to them gave he power to become the sons of God, even to them that believe on his name:

13 Which were born, not of blood, nor of the will of the flesh, nor of the will of man, but of God.

14 And the Word was made flesh, and dwelt among us, (and we beheld his glory, the glory as of the only begotten of the Father,) full of grace and truth.

15 John bare witness of him, and cried, saying, This was he of whom I spake, He that cometh after me is preferred before me; for he was before me.

16 And of his fulness have all we received, and grace for grace.

17 For the law was given by Moses, but grace and truth came by Jesus Christ.

18 No man hath seen God at any time; the only begotten Son, which is in the bosom of the Father, he hath declared him.

GOLDEN TEXT: The Word was made flesh, and dwelt among us, (and we beheld his glory, the glory as of the only begotten of the Father,) full of grace and truth.
—John 1:14.

Believing in Christ

Unit 1. John: The Word Became Flesh

(Lessons 1-4)

Lesson Aims

When this lesson has been completed, the students should:

1. Have an understanding of the meaning and of the significance of the incarnation.
2. Be able to state the purpose of Christ's coming into the world (v. 12).
3. Be stirred to exercise anew their potential as children of God.

Lesson Outline

INTRODUCTION
- A. The Power to Become
- B. Lesson Background

I. CHRIST AND HIS CREATIVE WORK (John 1:1-5)
- A. The Eternal Word (vv. 1, 2)
- B. His Creative Work (vv. 3-5)
  Light and Life

II. THE HERALD AND THE LIGHT (John 1:6-9)
- A. God's Herald (vv. 6-8)
- B. The Light of the World (v. 9)

III. THE LIGHT REJECTED AND RECEIVED (John 1:10-13)
- A. A World Rejects Its Creator (vv. 10, 11)
- B. The Potential of the Believer (vv. 12, 13)

IV. CHRIST'S DEITY ATTESTED (John 1:14-18)
- A. The Glory of Christ (v. 14)
- B. John the Baptist's Testimony (v. 15)
- C. Jesus' Revelation (vv. 16-18)
  Guilt and Grace

CONCLUSION
- A. The Life-giving Christ
- B. Prayer
- C. Thought to Remember

The statement shown on visual 1 of the visuals packet indicates why the Son of God came to earth. Display the visual throughout this session. It is shown on page 236.

Introduction

A. The Power to Become

When you see an acorn, what do you think of? A squirrel searching for food? Litter on the sidewalk, crushed beneath the feet of passersby? Hold it in your hand and think. You see an acorn, yes? But with the eye of faith you see more, much more. You hold in your hand the potential of a mighty oak, or of a grove of oaks, providing beauty and shade and shelter, or timber for some worthy construction project. The acorn has the power to become all of this.

When you see a child, what mental image is formed? Do you see a nuisance, noisy, with sticky hands? An unwanted baby? Or do you see a future benefactor, a servant of God and man?

Every little child was precious to Jesus because He saw each as in the likeness of God, but precious also because of what the child could become. Even in the sinner Jesus saw great possibility. He condemned sin and also the unrepentant sinner (Matthew 25:41). But to those who would turn from sin He would say, "Neither do I condemn thee: go, and sin no more" (John 8:11). And to those who believe, He promises the "power to become the sons [children] of God" (John 1:12).

What a promise! What potential! No wonder this is called the *gospel,* the "good news." This is what the Gospel of John is all about.

B. Lesson Background

The apostle John was closely associated with Jesus throughout His ministry. As an eyewitness, he was fully qualified to give his testimony. That he himself firmly believed Jesus to be the Son of God and the giver of eternal life is beyond all doubt. For him, such news was too good to keep. He must share it with all the world.

John's interest in writing was not just that of a storyteller. His purpose was evangelistic. He would persuade his readers of the truth of that which he wrote about Jesus, in order that they might believe and "have life through his name" (20:31). He appealed to the intellect, not just to the emotions. From his own knowledge of Jesus, he chose a few of the many *signs* that were available to him in order to accomplish his purpose. These indicate who Jesus is, why He came to earth, and the result of His coming. John states his conclusion at the very beginning, in our text for today. In these eighteen verses he makes some tremendous claims. Anyone who reads them will surely be stirred to read farther, to see how John justifies his claims.

VISUALS FOR THESE LESSONS

The *Adult Visuals/Learning Resources* packet contains classroom-size visuals designed for use with the lessons in the Spring Quarter. The packet is available from your supplier. Order no. 392.

(Teacher, read the verses to the class, but first feel the awesome thrill of the significance of these words, for they are words of life. Truly here we are on holy ground!)

I. Christ and His Creative Work (John 1:1-5)

Although John begins with a rather puzzling reference to an Eternal Word existing with God, it is soon clear that he is referring to Jesus. And right out of the blue he makes this most remarkable claim: Jesus of Nazareth, who was born to a woman named Mary (as the other Gospel writers tell us), actually coexisted with God and was active in the creation of the universe. Before the baby was born in the town of Bethlehem as the Son of man, He was the Son of God with the Father in Heavenly realms.

A. The Eternal Word (vv. 1, 2)

1. In the beginning was the Word, and the Word was with God, and the Word was God.

In the beginning. It is not without reason that John uses these words from the account of creation (Genesis 1:1). Soon he will tell of a new creation to be accomplished by Jesus (John 3:3), and these words indicate Christ's presence at the first creation. *Was the Word.* What word? Is John dealing in riddles? No, not really, for soon he reveals that he is telling of a flesh and blood individual. Why, then, does he identify Jesus as the Word?

First, this term (*davar* in Hebrew) had great significance to the Jewish mind as indicative of the creative power of God. "By the word of the Lord were the heavens made" (Psalm 33:6). God needed only to say, "Let there be light," and there was light (Genesis 1:3). Second, God's word was also recognized as a means of His revelation. He was made known through His word—the spoken word, the written word (the Bible), and the Living Word, Christ Jesus (see Hebrews 1:1-3).

Again, this term was significant because of its connotation in John's day. In the Greek it is *logos,* with a diversity of meaning and wide usage. In Jewish circles the *logos* was related to the personified wisdom of the Old Testament, recognized as being coeternal with God and assisting Him in creation. (See the remarkable passage in Proverbs 8:1, 22-30, and note that Paul identifies Jesus as *the wisdom of God*—1 Corinthians 1:23). The Jewish philosopher Philo, steeped in Greek thought, considered the *logos* to be an intermediary between God and man, bridging the gulf of separation between God and the material universe.

John would say to all of this, "The *logos* about whom men have speculated is now fully known. He was the creative *Word* with God in the beginning. He is the *Wisdom* of God. It is this *logos* who maintains order and sustains the universe. He bridges the gap between Heaven and earth. But more than being *with God,* the Word *was God,* in living relationship with the Father."

2. The same was in the beginning with God.

John emphasizes the eternal nature of the One of whom he speaks. From all eternity He was one with God—in His nature, in purpose, in action.

B. His Creative Work (vv. 3-5)

3. All things were made by him; and without him was not any thing made that was made.

A group known as Gnostics, among the intellectuals of their day, attributed the formation of the universe to an *emanation* from God that was so far removed from Him as to have become a hostile, evil force. So, it was held, all material things were corrupt and evil, and God in his purity would have no contact with such.

"Not so," John would say. Matter is not evil, but is the creation of God and is very good (Genesis 1:31). *All things were made by him,* and not by an evil *emanation.* The verb *were made* is, literally, "were caused to be." God (the *Logos*) brought into being that which did not exist before.

It is God who is self-existent and eternal, not matter. He is the great *I AM* (Exodus 3:14). Is it not more within reason to believe that an all-powerful, all-wise deity has existed from eternity than to suppose that matter was self-creating? And when men of science discover in a distant cluster of galaxies one containing over one hundred trillion stars and extending over an area of six million light years (!), it but overwhelms us anew with God's greatness. It is not surprising, however, for He who has the power of creation can call into being a whole universe as easily as a lump of clay.

4. In him was life; and the life was the light of men.

John has introduced the *Word* as person. Now he speaks of His nature, using two other significant terms—*life* and *light.* The Old Testament distinguishes God from all would-be gods in that He alone is the *living* God. So, also, the *Word* lives. *In him was life,* and the power to bestow life. In creation, life issued from the living One, not from

How to Say It

DAVAR (Hebrew). dah-var.
LOGOS (Greek). *lah*-goss.

dead matter. In introducing Jesus as the giver of life, John is preparing the reader for the prospect of receiving new life at His hand (20:31), abundant life (10:10), everlasting life (3:16).

The life was the light of men. What is light? "The essential condition for vision"? This tells its function, not what it *is.* "The opposite of darkness"? This tells us what it is *not.* We can only know what light is when we experience it. John is concerned that we do not miss the experience of walking in the light that is *life,* which is the *Word,* which is *with God,* which *is God*—Christ the light of the world!

LIGHT AND LIFE

Green plants live and grow by the power of light. Light acts upon cells containing chlorophyll to produce carbon dioxide and water, nourishment to sustain plant life. The process is called *photosynthesis.* Since animals and humans eat plants and/or animals that eat plants, nearly all life depends upon light. Solar energy possesses amazing life-giving properties.

The sun gives physical life, and the Son gives spiritual life. His light energizes nourishment for the soul, just as solar rays energize photosynthesis in plants.

Photosynthesis is a combined form of two Greek words that means "putting together with light." When water and carbon dioxide combine with sunlight, glucose is produced, a substance vital to all living things. When human thought, emotion, and will are combined with "Sonlight," faith is produced—an element that is vital to all human spirits. So, divine light is linked with spiritual life.

The light of Christ feeds and leads us. His truth dispels the darkness of ignorance and fear. Philip P. Bliss was right when he wrote, "No darkness have we who in Jesus abide, the Light of the world is Jesus." —R. W. B.

5. And the light shineth in darkness; and the darkness comprehended it not.

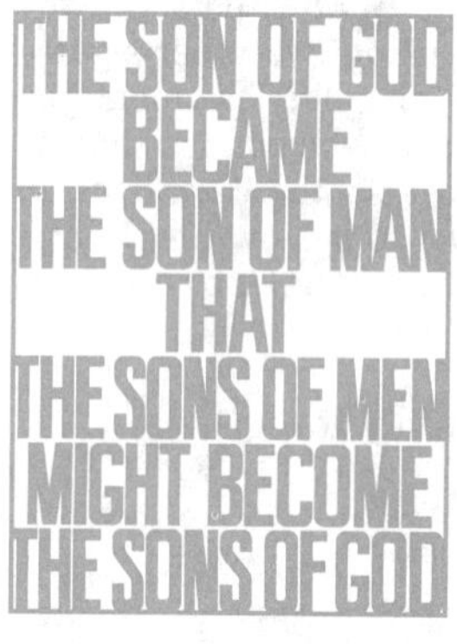

visual 1

Or "the darkness did not overcome it." Either translation is possible. Why can one not comprehend Christ, the true light (v. 9)? Or, why would one want to overcome Him? John gives an answer: "Men loved darkness rather than light, because their deeds were evil" (3:19). Sin in a person's life distorts that person's attitude toward Jesus. But this does not extinguish the light.

II. The Herald and the Light (John 1:6-9)

John gives his testimony about Jesus, believing that the facts he presents will validate the belief that Jesus is the incarnate Son of God. He begins by citing the fact that the One of whom he writes was introduced to the world by a highly regarded person, John the Baptist.

A. God's Herald (vv. 6-8)

6, 7. There was a man sent from God, whose name was John. The same came for a witness, to bear witness of the Light, that all men through him might believe.

John the Baptist was recognized as a prophet and was held in high esteem by the people as a man of integrity, a man of God. That Jesus was endorsed at the outset by such a notable person would be significant, for the word of John the Baptist was recognized as from God.

8. He was not that Light, but was sent to bear witness of that Light.

John the Baptist strongly denied any claim to messiahship. He was sent as God's messenger to announce the Christ (vv. 19-23).

B. The Light of the World (v. 9)

What the sun is to the physical world, Christ is to the spiritual, revealing God to man.

9. That was the true Light, which lighteth every man that cometh into the world.

In verse 11 we note that Jesus' own people, Israel, rejected Him. But He is the light that will illuminate the way for *every person,* making known the pathway to God and with God.

Neither John the Baptist nor the apostle John introduced some new doctrine about which people might argue. They presented a person whose coming was historical fact, one who changed the course of history for all time to come.

III. The Light Rejected and Received (John 1:10-13)

Verses 10 and 11 make a frank and startling admission. There John states that the One of whom he speaks in such glowing terms was rejected by His contemporaries.

A. A World Rejects Its Creator (vv. 10, 11)

10. He was in the world, and the world was made by him, and the world knew him not.

How ironic that the world would not recognize the source of its beginning! So marvellous is the world, and so complex the creatures that inhabit it, that they speak volumes of the power and wisdom of the Creator! But with this testimony of God ever before them, men refused to acknowledge the Creator (Roman 1:25).

11. He came unto his own, and his own received him not.

God had prepared Israel, through Moses and the prophets, for the coming of the one who would reveal the way of God perfectly. Yet, when the *Word* took a body of flesh and came to the house of Israel, they *received him not.* How sad.

B. The Potential of the Believer (vv. 12, 13)

12. But as many as received him, to them gave he power to become the sons of God, even to them that believe on his name.

This is what John's Gospel is all about—the *power to become the sons of God.* (*Sons* is used in the general sense to mean "children.") *As many as received him.* That is "all" who received Him. How broad is God's mercy to those who believe on the name of Jesus: that is, who put their trust in Him! To them is given the power to become the children of God!

13. Which were born, not of blood, nor of the will of the flesh, nor of the will of man, but of God.

The language is figurative, whereby a spiritual reality is understood in the terms of its physical counterpart. This new birth is *not of blood,* not of human parentage. It is not determined by the *will of man.* It is *of God.*

IV. Christ's Deity Attested (John 1:14-18)

The apostle has stated that the creative Word came into the world, bringing to humankind the power to become the children of God. In the remainder of the book he will cite the evidences that validate this claim.

A. The Glory of Christ (v. 14)

14. And the Word was made flesh, and dwelt among us, (and we beheld his glory, the glory as of the only begotten of the Father,) full of grace and truth.

This is the foundational truth of Christianity. By clothing the divine nature in a human body, God broke through the curtain of flesh and shared in human existence. In the person of Jesus of Nazareth, God entered the world of our experience as we all do, through birth. He grew up through childhood and youth to adulthood, subject to the joys and sorrows, the trials and temptations common to us all.

There is an innate longing for God within the human soul. This has stirred many to a lifelong search for God, resulting in the development of various religions. But in Jesus the process is reversed. Here we have God in search of man! Here we have the incarnation—God coming to earth to seek those lost in the darkness of sin to bring them to the light of His love, whereby they may be brought to new life as children of God.

And we beheld his glory. John speaks as an eyewitness (see 1 John 1:1). He and others *beheld* Jesus. This verb refers to a careful and deliberate viewing, a calm scrutiny, not a quick look. As John and the other eyewitnesses thus viewed Jesus, they saw His glory—His grace and truth that shone through all His words, His miracles, and His spotless character.

B. John the Baptist's Testimony (v. 15)

15. John bare witness of him, and cried, saying, This was he of whom I spake, He that cometh after me is preferred before me; for he was before me.

Prophet of God that he was, John the Baptist recognized, without bitterness, the preeminence of Jesus. He *is preferred before me,* or "ranks before me," *for he was before me;* that is, existed before I was born. (More testimony from John the Baptist is given later—John 1:19-34; 3:23-30.) Now, with verse 16, the apostle John resumes his own testimony to Jesus.

C. Jesus' Revelation (vv. 16-18)

16. And of his fulness have all we received, and grace for grace.

This is a continuation of the thought at the end of verse 14. The One who had come from God was "full of grace and truth." Grace is undeserved kindness. It was this that prompted God to send Jesus into the world. And God's grace overflowed through Jesus again and again upon His disciples —*grace for grace,* meaning, perhaps, in one blessing after another.

17. For the law was given by Moses, but grace and truth came by Jesus Christ.

The law was given by God through Moses and it fulfilled its purpose by preparing for Jesus' coming. In Jesus Christ came *grace,* which the law could not supply, that brought pardon for sin, and *truth,* the *reality* toward which all of the types of the law (for example, the sacrifices) pointed.

GUILT AND GRACE

Conservative church leaders are concerned when they hear results of surveys reporting that "Baby-boomers" attend worship primarily to "feel good." Though this good feeling is not always easily defined, the "felt needs" identified by many of this generation seem to be superficial and shallow. Some modern churches have aimed to accommodate and satisfy those needs. Others still wrestle with the dilemma posed by trying to meet human needs without compromising doctrinal convictions.

Whatever our stand on that issue, we can all understand that churchgoers would rather leave worship with assurances of grace than with goadings of guilt. The law, under which the ancient Jews lived, identified and condemned sin, but it could not provide grace to permanently appease the pangs of their guilt. Under the New Covenant, however, no worshipper need leave a Christian church burdened with guilt. "The wages of sin is death, *but* the gift of God is eternal life in Christ Jesus our Lord" (Romans 6:23, *New International Version*).

Jesus brought to humankind the grace of God, whereby the guilt and punishment for sin is completely removed. —R. W. B.

18. No man hath seen God at any time; the only begotten Son, which is in the bosom of the Father, he hath declared him.

Moses had the special privilege, while hidden in a cleft of a rock, to see God after He had passed by. We might say he saw God's passing glory (Exodus 33:18-23). The One of whom John is speaking about, however, came directly from the Father! Only one in such a close relationship could make God fully known. This Jesus did—*he hath declared him.* This means more than what Jesus told us *about* God. It means that Jesus revealed God's nature, His character, His will, and particularly His purpose in sending His Son to earth, which was to bring light and life to humankind.

Conclusion

A. The Life-giving Christ

In the prologue to his Gospel, the apostle John first introduces the Hero of his book as one coming from God, and then he makes clear the purpose of His coming. That one is identified as the eternal *Word,* the very Son of God, who came directly from the bosom of the Father. His mission was to dispel the darkness that engulfs humankind by revealing God's grace, which offers the believer the right to become His child. This is the purpose of His coming, the reason why "the Word became flesh and dwelt among us."

Could John have been mistaken in identifying Jesus as the Son of God and giver of life? He did not think so! Some question the record, saying that between the lines we must seek the "historical Jesus." Well, John *knew* the historical Jesus! The events he records, including the resurrection, occurred in history, and he was an eyewitness of them. He firmly believed that they had universal significance. Since John proclaimed Him, the Jesus he knew has become the redeemer and giver of life to many thousands in every generation. So the "historical Jesus" is very much a part of history, including our own. To as many as receive Him, He still gives the power to become the children of God.

There are two possible responses to the message John brings—belief or unbelief. John depicts the choice as between light and darkness, or as between life and death. He warns us of the condemnation that awaits those who love darkness because their deeds are evil (3:19). Always God's cry is, "Turn ye, turn ye, . . . for why will ye die?" (Ezekiel 33:11).

B. Prayer

Gracious Lord, You have been so good to us! We thank You for the gift of life that is ours, but especially for the privilege of living as Your children, cleansed of our sins and forgiven. Enable us, we pray, to so live as to bring honor to Your holy name. Through Jesus Christ our Lord we pray. Amen.

C. Thought to Remember

There is no greater blessing than the power to become a child of God. This is God's gift to all who believe in Christ Jesus, His Son.

Home Daily Bible Readings

Monday, Mar. 1—The Word Was God (John 1:1-5)

Tuesday, Mar. 2—A Witness to Jesus (John 1:6-13)

Wednesday, Mar. 3—God With Us (John 1:14-18)

Thursday, Mar. 4—John Identifies Himself (John 1:19-28)

Friday, Mar. 5—John Identifies Jesus (John 1:29-34)

Saturday, Mar. 6—We Have Found the Messiah (John 1:35-42)

Sunday, Mar. 7—The Call to Follow (John 1:43-51)

Learning by Doing

This page contains an alternate lesson plan emphasizing learning activities. Classes desiring such student involvement will find these suggestions helpful.

Learning Goals

As a result of completing this lesson students will be able to:

1. Explain the terms that John uses to describe Jesus: *Word, life, and light.*
2. Tell why they are grateful for Christ's visit to earth and what they are doing to receive Him into their lives.

Into the Lesson

Because this is the first lesson of the quarter, you may wish to begin with a brief preview of all thirteen lessons. This will help the lessons have more continuity. Here are three ways you could do this short preview:

1. Prepare thirteen flashcards with an interesting quotation from each lesson on each card. Use these to give a five-minute introduction of the quarter's lessons.
2. Prepare a handout, showing titles, themes, and texts of each lesson. Pass these out to students and briefly go through them.
3. Prepare a bulletin board display that lists themes of all thirteen lessons. Add magazine pictures that illustrate each theme.

Begin today's class with the following discussion exercise. You can go through this activity step by step with the entire class, or you may wish to divide the class into three groups, one question per group.

Say, "Suppose you were God and you wanted to visit earth to tell people of your nature and love. 1. *How would you prepare people on earth for your visit?*" (Try to keep the class from getting ahead of you and into the subject of Christ's visit. Keep the discussion objective at this point.) Some possible answers: Announce your arrival in advance. (God did this with prophecies about Jesus.) Have someone popular and respected ready to introduce you to the public. (John the Baptist filled this role for Christ.) Come at a good time, when the world would be ready and eager for a savior. (Jesus came when the world was prepared—see Galatians 4:4.)

2. *Upon arrival on earth, what credentials would you use to prove that you were in fact God?* Some possible answers: Perform miracles, express love to all, teach the truth.

3. *What would you do to show people that you were a messenger of good will and not harm?* Some possible answers could be: Teach them patiently, do kind deeds for them, comfort them, make sacrifices for them.

Tell the class that today's lesson is about God's actual visit to earth in the form of Jesus Christ. Then give a brief introduction to the book of John. Follow this by having a couple of students (who have been given this assignment in the week before class) read brief biographies of John the apostle and John the Baptist, so your students will know the difference between the two. You can find such information in a Bible dictionary.

Into the Word

Read aloud today's text from John 1:1-18 and ask how Christ answers the questions you just discussed.

Give each student a sheet of paper on which you have written these three words as column headings: WORDS, LIFE, AND LIGHT. Ask them to take two minutes to write down all the positive associations they can think of for each of the three words. For example, under "WORDS" they might list comfort, knowledge, power, beauty, ideas, communication, self-expression. For "LIFE" they might list pleasure, hope, challenge, health, animation. For "LIGHT" they might list guidance, pleasure, security, knowledge, beauty, cheerfulness.

Let several students read their lists, then point out that John uses these three words to describe the nature of Jesus.

Explain each of the three words more fully, looking to the commentary section of this lesson book. Then discuss your students' lists as they relate to Jesus.

Other Scriptures introduce various concepts by using these words. If you have time, you may want to read them. Here are a few: "WORDS"—Psalm 119:103; Proverbs 16:24; 18:21; Isaiah 55:11. "LIFE"—Genesis 2:7; Deuteronomy 30:15; Ecclesiastes 9:4. "LIGHT"—Psalm 119:105; Proverbs 4:18; Ecclesiastes 11:7; John 3:20, 21; 11:9; 1 Corinthians 4:5.

Into Life

After seeing how Jesus was all these wonderful things, ask the class, "Which of these qualities of Christ means the most to you, and why?" Ask for volunteers to tell about specific times when Christ was "light," or "life," or "the Word" in their own lives.

Let's Talk It Over

The questions on this page are designed to encourage review of the lesson Scriptures and to promote discussion of the lesson by the class. The answers provided are only discussion starters. Let your class talk it over from there.

1. John 1:10, 11 shows how remarkable it was that the world rejected Jesus. How may we apply these words to the rejection of Jesus today?

It is still largely the case that although "the world was made by him, . . . the world [knows] him not." Today, of course, scientific theories are given to explain the existence and design of the world, so that many people leave no room in their minds for the concept of a Creator. The grand design of the universe and the manner in which the earth is engineered to meet human needs are facts that proclaim the great Creator and make unbelief a matter of profound foolishness. "He came unto his own, and his own received him not." We inhabit bodies of flesh, which are vulnerable to weariness, pain, and death. Jesus came to be like us and to share our experiences. To know that God's Son lived and died as a human being and rose again here on earth should stir us all to faithful obedience, but many refuse to be stirred.

2. The Gospel of John does not specifically mention the virgin birth of Christ. But how does John 1:14 harmonize with the birth accounts given in Matthew and Luke?

It is striking to see how each of the accounts points to the same great truth, but does it in a different way. Only Matthew (1:23) quotes Isaiah's prophecy regarding the virgin birth. He alone relates how Joseph was able to deal with Mary's unusual pregnancy. Luke is unique in relating Gabriel's appearance to Mary and his explanation (1:35) of how she, although a virgin, could bear the special child. John makes no specific reference to any of these details, but when he tells us that "the Word was God" and that "the Word was made flesh," he suggests the virgin birth. And it is affirmed when he states that the Word who was made flesh was "the only begotten of the Father." This remarkable harmony is one of the lines of evidence that demonstrate the divine origin of the Gospels.

3. Why is it vital that we give extensive attention to the privileges and responsibilities involved in our being the children of God?

We have many reminders of our earthly origin and our proneness to worldly allurements. People say to us, "You're only human!" and they urge us to join them in the pursuit of carnal pleasures. Remembering that we are the children of God makes us aware that we have a higher purpose on earth than seeking pleasure. Or perhaps we can say that as God's children we find our greatest pleasure in trusting, obeying, and serving our Father. He has given us some lofty standards to fulfill, some lofty goals to attain. When the world's standards and goals tempt us, it is good for us to declare, "I'm a child of the Almighty, and He has called me to center my life on things that are purer and nobler!"

4. Jesus has revealed God to us. Why is it important that we view God through Jesus Christ?

Some people regard God as a kindly and indulgent grandfather. With such a viewpoint, they tend to overlook God's righteousness and holiness and excuse their sins as harmless shortcomings. But Jesus has revealed God as One who hates sin, One who demands righteousness from His people. Jesus' own sinless life and His call to holy living give us a more accurate view of the Father. Others view God as unsympathetic to our human plight, harsh and cruel. These persons may regard God as deserving of neglect and scorn. But Jesus again provides a more complete picture. He blended hatred of sin with love for sinners; He combined the call to holiness with compassion for those who fall short of it.

5. Some scholars suggest that we must search for "the historical Jesus," by which they mean that much of what the four Gospels relate is not history, but myth and misrepresentation. How do we respond to this?

While scholarship as such is not to be scorned, it is clear that scholars are sometimes prejudiced and make mistakes. Here is one instance in which some scholars have made a grave mistake, perhaps through prejudice or faulty methods of research or a tendency to conform to the conclusions of others they respect. The Gospel of John has been especially ill-treated by such scholars, partly because it differs so much from the first three Gospels. But John (20:30, 31), like Luke (1:1-4), affirms that what he has written is a narration of historical events, and we have no legitimate reason to question that affirmation.

Rebirth Into Eternal Life

March 14
Lesson 2

Lesson Scripture: John 3:1-21.

Printed Text: John 3:1-17.

Devotional Reading: John 3:22-36.

John 3:1-17

**1 There was a man of the Pharisees, named
Nicodemus, a ruler of the Jews:
2 The same came to Jesus by night, and
said unto him, Rabbi, we know that thou art a
teacher come from God: for no man can do
these miracles that thou doest, except God be
with him.
3 Jesus answered and said unto him, Verily, verily, I say unto thee, Except a man be
born again, he cannot see the kingdom of
God.
4 Nicodemus saith unto him, How can a
man be born when he is old? can he enter the
second time into his mother's womb, and be
born?
5 Jesus answered, Verily, verily, I say unto
thee, Except a man be born of water and of
the Spirit, he cannot enter into the kingdom
of God.
6 That which is born of the flesh is flesh;
and that which is born of the Spirit is spirit.
7 Marvel not that I said unto thee, Ye must
be born again.
8 The wind bloweth where it listeth, and
thou hearest the sound thereof, but canst not
tell whence it cometh, and whither it goeth:
so is every one that is born of the Spirit.
9 Nicodemus answered and said unto him,
How can these things be?
10 Jesus answered and said unto him, Art
thou a master of Israel, and knowest not
these things?
11 Verily, verily, I say unto thee, We speak
that we do know, and testify that we have
seen; and ye receive not our witness.
12 If I have told you earthly things, and ye
believe not, how shall ye believe, if I tell you
of heavenly things?
13 And no man hath ascended up to
heaven, but he that came down from heaven,
even the Son of man which is in heaven.
14 And as Moses lifted up the serpent in
the wilderness, even so must the Son of man
be lifted up:
15 That whosoever believeth in him
should not perish, but have eternal life.
16 For God so loved the world, that he
gave his only begotten Son, that whosoever
believeth in him should not perish, but have
everlasting life.
17 For God sent not his Son into the world
to condemn the world; but that the world
through him might be saved.**

Golden Text: Verily, verily, I say unto thee, Except a man be born again, he cannot see the kingdom of God.—John 3:3.

Believing in Christ

Unit 1. John: The Word Became Flesh

(Lessons 1-4)

Lesson Aims

When this lesson has been completed, the students should:

1. Understand the nature of, and the necessity for, the new birth.
2. Be able to tell what kind of evidence would indicate that one has been born again.
3. Determine to bear evidence in their own daily living that they are children of God.

Lesson Outline

INTRODUCTION
- A. Attitudes
- B. Lesson Background

I. A PHARISEE'S TESTIMONY (John 3:1, 2)
- A. A Man of Distinction (v. 1)
- B. His Appraisal of Jesus (v. 2)
  Closet Christians

II. JESUS' RESPONSE (John 3:3-8)
- A. Startling Announcement (vv. 3-5)
- B. Spiritual Birth (vv. 6-8)

III. QUESTION AND ANSWER (John 3:9-17)
- A. How Can This Be? (v. 9)
- B. Through Faith in Christ (vv. 10-15)
- C. The Gift of God's Love (vv. 16, 17)
  Our Personal Savior

CONCLUSION
- A. Living the Life
- B. Rescue the Perishing
- C. Prayer
- D. Thought to Remember

Display visual 2 of the visuals packet and refer to it in connection with section II of this lesson. The visual is shown on page 244.

Introduction

A. Attitudes

Is the tank half empty or half full of gasoline? Your answer, it is said, will reveal whether you are a pessimist, viewing it as half empty, or an optimist who accentuates the positive—half full. In this particular case, it would seem not to matter very much. But often one's attitude matters a great deal, sometimes causing one to say or do ridiculous things. For example, consider a person who has a biased attitude toward the church in general and Christians in particular. Such a one cannot possibly form a true concept of either the church or Christians. He or she will misconstrue their words, assign base motives for their actions, or even utter falsehoods regarding them.

Many of the Pharisees had a similar attitude toward Jesus. There was one among them, however, who would not prejudge the carpenter from Nazareth. This was Nicodemus, a member of the Jewish ruling council. He was also a scholar and a teacher. More important, he seemed to be free from the bias that infected his associates regarding Jesus. Some of them admitted that Jesus performed miracles, but they said that it was through the power of Satan—even when the miracle was destroying the work of Satan! (See Luke 11:14-18.)

Nicodemus, on the other hand, had witnessed some of the miracles of Jesus and had seen nothing satanic about them. Others might ignorantly denounce Jesus, but Nicodemus wanted to know Him better. So he sought a personal interview with Him. Especially significant is the discussion between Jesus and Nicodemus that developed in this interview.

B. Lesson Background

Believing in Christ is the theme of our lessons from the Gospel of John—a good title, since the apostle declares that his reason for writing is that the readers "might believe that Jesus is the Christ, the Son of God; and that believing [they] might have life through his name" (20:31).

We should note that John does not say, "I *pray* that you might believe," as if one attains faith by praying for it. Nor, with John, is faith a mere existential act, as though one by a simple act of the will could *will* a thing to be so. With the apostle, faith is the acceptance of testimony, the belief of evidence, and it is to that end that he writes.

The evidence that John presents includes (1) deeds of Jesus (among them, miracles that John himself witnessed); (2) teachings of Jesus that amazed His hearers ("Never man spake like this man"—John 7:46); and (3) the testimony of others, such as that of the man born blind whose sight Jesus restored (John 9). The Pharisees said to that man, "Give God the praise: we know that this man [Jesus] is a sinner." The healed man responded, "Whether he be a sinner or no, I know not: one thing I know, that, whereas I was blind, now I see" (John 9:25). It is difficult to argue against evidence like that.

John, however, not only tells us why we ought to believe. He also tells us what we are to believe, as coming from Christ. A very significant part of that teaching is the theme of our lesson today, that which concerns the *new birth.*

I. A Pharisee's Testimony (John 3:1, 2)

Although the minority group, the Pharisees were the most influential sect of the Jews. In the second century B.C. the Syrian Greek rulers of Palestine had attempted to force the Jews to abandon the religion of their fathers and to adopt the ways of the Greek nation. However, the Pharisees resisted vigorously, calling on the people to be faithful to the law of God as given to Moses. It was, one might say, a "back-to-the-Bible" movement or revival, and devout Jewish souls rallied to the challenge.

In time, however, the ideal of the religion of Israel—"to do justly, and to love mercy, and to walk humbly with thy God" (Micah 6:8)—was forgotten because of preoccupation with rigid observance of the ceremonial laws. And by the time of Jesus, the interpretations placed upon the law—the traditions of the elders—had been given as much weight by the Pharisees as the law itself. The Pharisees prided themselves upon their careful observance of all these, and in their zeal considered themselves to be God's favorites.

A. A Man of Distinction (v. 1)

1. There was a man of the Pharisees, named Nicodemus, a ruler of the Jews.

Nicodemus appears in the Scriptures only in John's Gospel; here, again in 7:50, 51, where he rebuked his fellow Pharisees for condemning Jesus unheard; and in 19:39, where it is said that he brought myrrh and aloes to assist in the burial of Jesus. That he was a man of some distinction is indicated by the fact that he was *a ruler of the Jews;* that is, a member of the ruling council of seventy—the Sanhedrin. At times Jesus rebuked the Pharisees face to face for their lack of compassion and justice and for their neglect of faithfulness to the spirit of the law. He did not, however, lay any such charges against Nicodemus; rather, He treated him with respect.

B. His Appraisal of Jesus (v. 2)

2. The same came to Jesus by night, and said unto him, Rabbi, we know that thou art a teacher come from God: for no man can do these miracles that thou doest, except God be with him.

Came to Jesus by night. It is commonly said that Nicodemus was secretive about the interview with Jesus for fear of the ridicule or reprisal of his associates. It may be, however, that he desired only the opportunity to speak with Jesus without interruption.

Thou art a teacher come from God. This is the honest, straightforward appraisal of a leader in Israel, an educated person, a teacher, respected in the community. The certainty of his conclusion was established, he believed, by the miracles that Jesus did, acts that would have been impossible without help from God. The image that Nicodemus had of Jesus was certainly a positive one.

We may wonder what brought him to Jesus. Was it simply a desire to know more about Him? Why would he want to know more? Let it be remembered that God's promise in the Old Testament to send the Messiah was very dear to the hearts of the devout in Israel (see Luke 2:25-32). Nicodemus would share that hope. Now, here is Jesus, *a teacher come from God.* Could this be the Messiah? Is that what was in the mind of Nicodemus? We are speculating, of course, and whatever brought him to Jesus and whatever question he may have had, we cannot know. Before he could say more, Jesus responded with words that must have shaken him sharply.

CLOSET CHRISTIANS

During the days of Roman persecution, Christians gathered for worship in the catacombs. Those secret assemblies kept alive the faith and allowed the church to continue growing. In more recent times, Christians in countries controlled by atheistic Communists have worshiped in secret to avoid harassment, imprisonment, and possible execution.

In recent years, a new era of political and religious freedom has dawned upon the world, and millions of formerly-oppressed Christians can now openly express their faith, own Bibles, and worship in public. Ironically, many disciples in America, where religious freedom has been a privilege for centuries, seem to have gone "undercover," suppressing their faith.

Because he was a rabbi, Nicodemus risked his exalted position in his society by associating with Jesus. Few persons in our society encounter such a risk. Let those Christians who are hiding in a closet of fear come out and boldly declare and demonstrate their faith in Christ. *Professing* Christians must become *practicing* Christians.

—R. W. B.

How to Say It

NICODEMUS. *Nick*-uh-*dee*-mus (strong accent on *dee*).

SANHEDRIN. *San*-huh-drun or San-*heed*-run.

II. Jesus' Response (John 3:3-8)

Remember who Nicodemus was. A Pharisee devoted to God, a teacher of the law (undoubtedly he had expounded the Scriptures to the public many times in the synagogue). He was, of course, an Israelite, one of God's chosen people, a descendant of Abraham. He was zealous to keep God's law in every particular. It is certain that he would have considered himself to be most fortunate, one standing in God's favor.

Jesus, of course, knew all of this and responded as the situation demanded. His words must have startled this devout teacher of the law, but they were exactly the words that he needed to hear—the necessity of the new birth.

A. Startling Announcement (vv. 3-5)

3. Jesus answered and said unto him, Verily, verily, I say unto thee, Except a man be born again, he cannot see the kingdom of God.

Verily, verily, (Greek, *Amen, Amen*). The repetition of the adverb gives emphasis to the solemn truth that is being expressed, meaning: "Note well what I say." *Except a man be born again.* The Greek word translated *again* can also mean "anew" or "from above."

Jesus did not say that Nicodemus needed to make some New Year resolutions. He did not instruct him to keep the law more precisely. He stated that Nicodemus must become a *new* person. He must have new life originating in Heaven. Paul understood this when he wrote, "If any man be in Christ, he is a new creature: old things are passed away; behold, all things are become new" (2 Corinthians 5:17).

He cannot see the kingdom of God. These words must have come as a great shock to Nicodemus. As with all devout Jews, he cherished the day when God would set up a kingdom that would never be destroyed, a kingdom for the people of God (Daniel 2:44; 7:27). As a Jew loyal to God, he anticipated a place in that kingdom. And Jesus was saying that he would not see that kingdom, that is, would not see his hope realized, unless he was born anew. What do you suppose were the feelings of Nicodemus when he heard this?

4. Nicodemus saith unto him, How can a man be born when he is old? can he enter the second time into his mother's womb, and be born?

Nicodemus was puzzled. He was thinking in terms of a literal birth. The absurdity was so obvious, however, that he stated it only to show his bewilderment.

5. Jesus answered, Verily, verily, I say unto thee, Except a man be born of water and of the Spirit, he cannot enter into the kingdom of God.

This answer emphasizes that Jesus meant what He said: *Verily, verily*—truly no one enters the kingdom of God other than by a process called a new birth. It is not a physical birth, but it does include material as well as spiritual elements. This is a birth *of water and of the Spirit,* and it is an absolute necessity for any who would enter the kingdom of God.

The verb *be born* can mean either to be begotten or to be born. In this verse it seems to have both meanings. James says, "Of his [God's] own will begat he us with the word of truth." Paul says, "So then faith cometh by hearing, and hearing by the word of God" (Romans 10:17). We are begotten by the Holy Spirit working through the preaching of the Word. We are born of water as we come forth from the watery womb in Christian baptism to walk in newness of life (Romans 6:4-6).

The new birth is another term for what is commonly called conversion. Or, expressed the other way around, a true conversion to Christ brings such a change in one's life that it may be said that one has actually been born again. From this it is seen that every Christian, if a Christian at all, is a born-again Christian. There is no other kind.

B. Spiritual Birth (vv. 6-8)

6. That which is born of the flesh is flesh; and that which is born of the Spirit is spirit.

Jesus assured Nicodemus that He was not talking about a physical birth at all. He was talking of a spiritual birth. It was this second birth that each person must have.

7, 8. Marvel not that I said unto thee, Ye must be born again. The wind bloweth where it listeth, and thou hearest the sound thereof, but canst not tell whence it cometh, and whither it goeth: so is every one that is born of the Spirit.

Marvel not. Since we are flesh and our relationship to God is spiritual in nature, we should not be amazed that Christ says, *Ye must be born again.* Even such a common phenomenon as

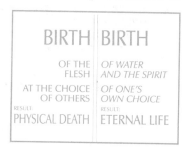

BIRTH	BIRTH
OF THE FLESH	*OF WATER AND THE SPIRIT*
AT THE CHOICE OF OTHERS	*OF ONE'S OWN CHOICE*
RESULT: PHYSICAL DEATH	RESULT: ETERNAL LIFE

visual 2

the wind is not without its mystery. We do not see it, but its presence is observable in its effects. When we hear the rustling of the leaves and see the bowing of the limbs of a tree, we know that a powerful force is present. *So is every one that is born of the Spirit.* When we see a life made knew and transformed, we are aware of the presence and work of the Spirit of God in that person, even though we do not see the Spirit nor understand His working.

III. Question and Answer (John 3:9-17)

A. How Can This Be? (v. 9)

9. Nicodemus answered and said unto him, How can these things be?

Nicodemus was steeped in Pharisaic training, which said that one must save oneself by obedience to the law and a host of man-made regulations based on the law. Therefore, he was unable to grasp what Jesus was saying about entering God's kingdom through a spiritual birth.

B. Through Faith in Christ (vv. 10-15)

10. Jesus answered and said unto him, Art thou a master of Israel, and knowest not these things?

Jesus was not inferring that Nicodemus, an acknowledged scholar, should have known about the new birth. As a doctor of the law, however, this Pharisee would have known of God's promise to give a new heart to His people and to put His spirit in them (Ezekiel 36:26, 27), along with other Old Testament Scriptures about a new covenant that God would make with them (Jeremiah 31:31-33). Nicodemus's study and teaching of the Old Testament should have prepared him for the concepts that Jesus was now discussing. The verb *know* has the meaning of comprehend. "As a master teacher," he is saying, "Do you not understand what I am talking about?"

11. Verily, verily, I say unto thee, We speak that we do know, and testify that we have seen; and ye receive not our witness.

We speak. Apparently Jesus included His disciples. *That we know,* or, what we know and have seen. The disciples, in their preaching tour, had seen the power of God at work (see John 2:1-11, 23), yet their testimony was rejected by the Pharisees—*ye* (plural).

12. If I have told you earthly things, and ye believe not, how shall ye believe, if I tell you of heavenly things?

Recognizing Jesus as "a teacher come from God," Nicodemus would anticipate a "Heavenly" message from Him. But if Nicodemus did not believe what Jesus taught about a person's need for spiritual rebirth, how would he believe when Jesus told him about Heavenly matters—about God's plan to redeem the lost world by sending His own Son to die for it?

13. And no man hath ascended up to heaven, but he that came down from heaven, even the Son of man which is in heaven.

Try as he may, no man in his seeking for God has ever *ascended up to heaven,* to search out these "heavenly things" of which Jesus speaks. The great truth of salvation through Christ is ours, not because human beings sought for and found it, but because God sent His Son *from heaven,* as the Son of man, to reveal it. Jesus is this *Son of man,* the same as the *Word* that was with God from the beginning (John 1:1). He would identify himself with us through this name, *Son of man.*

14, 15. And as Moses lifted up the serpent in the wilderness, even so must the Son of man be lifted up: that whosoever believeth in him should not perish, but have eternal life.

On one occasion when the children of Israel sinned through unbelief, they were bitten by poisonous serpents and many died. God told Moses to raise up a bronze serpent on a pole, and those who would look on it would live (Numbers 21:5-9).

Even so must the Son of man be lifted up. Sin has infected all the world, and without a cure all will perish. The only remedy is that Christ be lifted up for all to see. Then those who look to Him in faith—*whosoever believeth in him*—will not perish, *but have eternal life.*

C. The Gift of God's Love (vv. 16, 17)

The new birth of which Jesus spoke is birth to eternal life, to citizenship in the everlasting kingdom of God. No one deserves it, no amount of money can buy it, no one can earn it. It is the gift of God's love.

16. For God so loved the world, that he gave his only begotten Son, that whosoever believeth in him should not perish, but have everlasting life.

Jesus' words to Nicodemus end with verse 15; here we return to John's testimony. These words are called the Golden Text of the Bible, justifiably so. Here we see the unfathomable *love* of God; the object of His love, *the world* (sinful humanity); the expression of that love, *he gave* (here we have the incarnation); the nature of His gift, *his only begotten Son* (the *Word* that was with God from the beginning); the recipient of the gift, *whosoever*; the basis on which the gift is received, *believeth in him;* the result of belief, *everlasting life.* All of the above is an elaboration of

John 1:12—"As many as received him, to them gave he power to become the sons of God."

17. For God sent not his Son into the world to condemn the world; but that the world through him might be saved.

God's purpose in sending Jesus was our salvation. Jesus said, "The Son of man is come to seek and to save that which was lost" (Luke 19:10). We are lost without Christ, or He would not have come! He was sent, not *to condemn the world*—it was already condemned by its wickedness (vv. 18, 19). He offers salvation to "whosoever" (v. 16). Those who persistently reject His offer of love will perish, foregoing the hope of eternal life. The message is, Receive the Lord and be saved.

OUR PERSONAL SAVIOR

Each generation seems to produce its own saviors of the world. Whether it's flower children or ecologists, their goals are similar: to conserve/create a world culture free from war, waste, and want. These are commendable causes.

All saviors condemn "sins," but most are selective in the sins they preach against. If they promote love, they preach against hate. If their agenda favors socialism, they castigate capitalism. If their primary goals are clean air and conservation of resources, they are against pollution and wastefulness.

Jesus came to condemn sin—*all* sin. He said: "The reason the Son of God appeared was to destroy the devil's work" (1 John 3:8, *New International Version*).

Christ condemned sin, and in so doing saves us *from* sin. His primary mission was to "seek and to save the lost." To make our salvation possible, He paid the penalty for our sins, and was victorious over the last enemy, Death. Thus, we can live and be forgiven, because Christ came not to punish and destroy us, but to save and renew us. —R. W. B.

Conclusion

A. Living the Life

If one is born anew, it follows that the old life has died. Paul writes that in baptism this dead one is "buried with Christ" and rises to walk "in newness of life" (Romans 6:2-4). But how can we know that a new birth has really occurred? Is it not apparent as we see signs of the new life? And what are they? The Scriptures tell us.

For example, Peter urges those whose faith has brought them to Christ, to add to their faith virtue, knowledge, temperance, patience, godliness, brotherly kindness, and love (2 Peter 1:5-7). Certainly these things should be evident in the life of one who is born again.

We can witness one's being "born of water" in baptism, but how can we know that that person is born of the Spirit? Paul tells us that the "fruit of the Spirit" is love, joy, peace, long suffering, gentleness, goodness, faithfulness, and self control (Galatians 5:22, 23). The greatest visible evidence that one has been born of the Spirit is a life that bears these fruits. May we all examine our *own* lives as we consider these words of Jesus: "By their fruits ye shall know them" (Matthew 7:20).

B. Rescue the Perishing

When Fanny Crosby wrote the words of the hymn "Rescue the Perishing," it was commonly understood that one who rejected Jesus as Savior *would perish*. To say that God is too good to permit this is to misunderstand the case. It is precisely because God *is* good, and because of His love, that He sent Jesus to offer to us life in the place of death. But what claim has anyone on the love of God who rejects His gift of love, Jesus His Son?

Consider this. The steps of every human being lead into the grave, with none coming out. Except Jesus. Victorious over sin and death, He desires to free us from them both. If we reject Him, what other hope remains?

C. Prayer

For the love that sent Christ to be our Savior we thank You, Lord. We do believe in Him and desire the life that He gives. Help us to live daily in a manner to honor You. In Jesus' name, amen.

D. Thought to Remember

High position in life, excellency of achievement, noble ancestry—none of these entitles one to spiritual privilege. If one would enter the kingdom of God, he or she must be born again.

Home Daily Bible Readings

Monday, Mar. 8—Born of the Spirit (John 3:1-8)

Tuesday, Mar. 9—Christ Lifted Up (John 3:9-15)

Wednesday, Mar. 10—Christ, the Way (John 3:16-21)

Thursday, Mar. 11—He Must Increase (John 3:22-30)

Friday, Mar. 12—He Is Above All (John 3:31-36)

Saturday, Mar. 13—Eternal Life in Christ (John 17:1-11)

Sunday, Mar. 14—Born of God (1 John 4:7-12)

Learning by Doing

This page contains an alternate lesson plan emphasizing learning activities. Classes desiring such student involvement will find these suggestions helpful.

Learning Goals

As a result of this lesson, the students will:

1. Be able to describe the process of new birth and tell why it is essential.

2. Examine their lives to see if they exhibit the characteristics of one who has been spiritually reborn.

Into the Lesson

Before class, find some old magazines and tear out pictures of babies, expectant mothers, and children of different ages. Distribute these pictures to the students to serve as a visual trigger for the discussion to follow.

Write these questions on the chalkboard.

1. What is a child's life like before it is born? (Confined, dark, etc.)

2. What are the *pluses* of childbirth? (Draws husband and wife together, over in a relatively short time.)

3. What are the characteristics of a newborn child? (Dependent, vulnerable, growing, cute.)

4. What is there about children that makes the birth process worth the trouble? (Pleasure, fellowship, potential achievement, etc.)

After you have written these questions on the board, tell the class, "Today's lesson is about the new birth, recorded in John 3. Before we look at the text, let's consider these questions on the board." Keep this discussion less than fifteen minutes in length.

Into the Word

Ask for two male volunteers to come to the front of the class and sit in chairs facing each other. Give each of the men a Bible opened to John 3 and say, "(First man's name) will play the part of Jesus, and (second man's name) the role of Nicodemus. I'll be the narrator, and will you two read your parts from the text when it's your turn?"

Begin reading, "There was a man of the Pharisees, named Nicodemus, a ruler of the Jews: the same came to Jesus by night, and said to him,

First man reads his part,

etc.

When you have finished this group reading of the text, thank the volunteers and let them return to their seats. Refer to the commentary in today's lesson quarterly and briefly explain to the class who the Pharisees were and who Nicodemus was. Then ask the class the following questions, encouraging them to look to the Bible texts shown in parenthesis for help in answering.

1. Do "religious" people ever need to be born again? (See vv. 1, 10.)

2. What is the difference between making a New Year's resolution and being born again? (vv. 3, 5.)

3. How is being born again like the physical birth of a child? How is it different?

4. Why is the wind (v. 8) such a good illustration of one's birth of the Spirit?

5. What all is included in the new birth? (vv. 5, 6. See other passages such as Romans 10:10; Acts 2:38; Romans 6:4.)

6. Why doesn't being born again make one instantly into a mature Christian, and what problems occur because of that?

If answers to these questions are not easy to come by, ask the class to look up some of the cross references to John 3 in their Bibles and read them aloud for more help.

Into Life

Ask three or four of your oldest class members to come and sit facing the class to act as an opinion panel. Direct the following questions to them individually, or ask them to confer on their answers and answer as a team, whichever they prefer.

1. Why does it often get harder to make radical change as one gets older? (People get set in their ways, too tired to change, etc.)

2. Some people seem to have incentive to change as they get older. What can happen as one ages that might make that person even more ripe for a radical change? (Death of a loved one, dissillusioned with the world, skills acquired, etc.)

3. What keeps people from *believing* they can change their lives with God's help?

4. What caused you personally to decide to be born again? What was the experience like for each of you?

5. What made your conversion a rewarding experience? What special joys make Christianity worthwhile for you?

If you have time: There is always the possibility that certain of your class have not been born again. This would be a good time to explain in detail the conversion experience.

Let's Talk It Over

The questions on this page are designed to encourage review of the lesson Scriptures and to promote discussion of the lesson by the class. The answers provided are only discussion starters. Let your class talk it over from there.

1. Bible students have long speculated as to why Nicodemus came to Jesus by night. How may this apply to those who come to Jesus today?

Some have concluded that fear of his fellow Jewish leaders led Nicodemus to seek out Jesus at night. This may be an erroneous conclusion, but even if it is not, we should not think less of Nicodemus. The point is that he did come to Jesus, and it is desirable that human beings come to Jesus today, whether publicly or privately. Certainly we know of Christians who chose to be baptized into Jesus Christ in a private setting, and their faith in Him is just as strong as that of people whose decision was very much a public matter. If Nicodemus came by night so that he might investigate the character and claims of Jesus in an unhurried manner, that is commendable. Many today also make their decision for Jesus on the basis of a carefully-reasoned investigation.

2. Why do we need to emphasize the difference between being born again and self-improvement?

Books and public speakers on the topic of self-help abound. Many of the writers and speakers claim to represent a Christian viewpoint. There is no doubt that some of the principles and problem-solving techniques they present can be helpful to Christians. It is a matter of concern, however, that non-Christians reading or hearing these presentations may derive a false idea of what is involved in becoming a Christian. Jesus' teaching about the new birth leaves no room for the idea that we can make ourselves Christians by purifying our thoughts, elevating our goals, and improving our habits. We should add that merely attending church, giving to charitable causes, and devoting ourselves to aiding our neighbors do not in themselves make us Christian. "Ye must be born again" is a vital emphasis.

3. How can the blowing of the wind be a reminder to us of spiritual truth?

It often blows unexpectedly, and with great force. This can serve as a reminder of how awesome is the reality of the new birth in a sinner's life. In Acts 2:2 "a sound from heaven as of a rushing mighty wind" was one aspect of God's display of power on Pentecost. The wind can serve as a reminder of the power of God's Holy Spirit indwelling Christians. That power may not work in us in the miraculous way it worked on Pentecost, but it can strengthen us to combat temptation and to perform our labor in the Lord. We should thank God for the way in which He has given us the wind, the rain, and snow from heaven (Isaiah 55:10, 11), and the sun, moon, and other heavenly bodies (Psalm 19:1) as object lessons of spiritual truth.

4. It seems a bit strange to read in John 3:14, 15 that Jesus is compared with the bronze serpent lifted up in the wilderness. How shall we explain such an unusual comparison?

The serpent appears in the Bible as a symbol of evil. Indeed, Revelation 12:9 speaks of "That old serpent, called the Devil, and Satan." Why should the holy Son of God be described in connection with such a symbol? Perhaps here in the Gospels we have an indication of the same truth Paul spoke of when he said that Jesus was "made . . . to be sin for us" (2 Corinthians 5:21) and that He was "made a curse for us" (Galatians 3:13). These Scriptures emphasize Jesus' willingness to identify himself with our sin, to bear our guilt on the cross. Of course, we could say that the emphasis in John 3:14, 15 is not on a comparison between Jesus and the bronze serpent, but on the comparative benefits the Israelites received by looking on the bronze serpent and those we gain by responding in faith to Jesus' death on the cross.

5. We may have become so familiar with John 3:16 that it has lost some of its power for us. How can we gain renewed appreciation for this verse?

One of the best ways is to use it in our efforts to evangelize friends and neighbors. We can point out that they are part of "the world" that God loves and that they are among the "whosoever" who are called to believe in God's Son and gain eternal life. Another way is to use this verse as the focus for praise to God. We can thank Him for the wideness of His love, for the giving of His Son to live and die and rise again, for making it possible for us to believe, and for extending to us the hope of eternal life.

Light of the World

March 21
Lesson 3

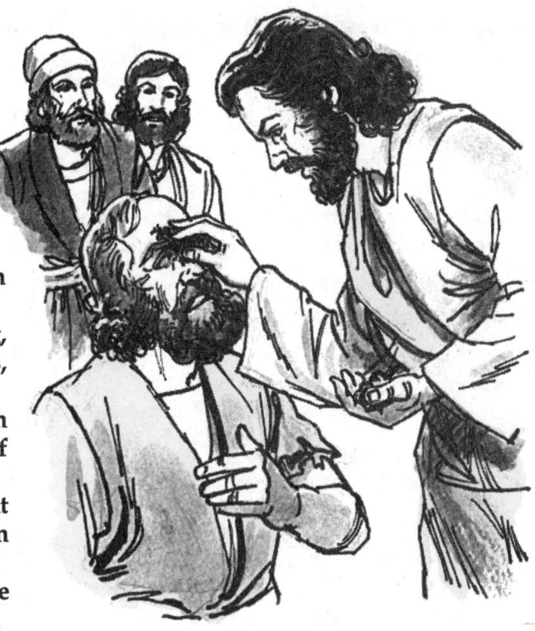

Lesson Scripture: John 9.

Printed Text: John 9:1-12, 35-41.

Devotional Reading: John 8:48-59.

John 9:1-12, 35-41

1 And as Jesus passed by, he saw a man
which was blind from his birth.
2 And his disciples asked him, saying,
Master, who did sin, this man, or his parents,
that he was born blind?
3 Jesus answered, Neither hath this man
sinned, nor his parents: but that the works of
God should be made manifest in him.
4 I must work the works of him that sent
me, while it is day: the night cometh, when
no man can work.
5 As long as I am in the world, I am the
light of the world.
6 When he had thus spoken, he spat on the
ground, and made clay of the spittle, and he
anointed the eyes of the blind man with the
clay,
7 And said unto him, Go, wash in the pool
of Siloam, (which is by interpretation, Sent.)
He went his way therefore, and washed, and
came seeing.
8 The neighbors therefore, and they which
before had seen him that he was blind, said,
Is not this he that sat and begged?
9 Some said, This is he: others said, He is
like him: but he said, I am he.
10 Therefore said they unto him, How
were thine eyes opened?
11 He answered and said, A man that is
called Jesus made clay, and anointed mine
eyes, and said unto me, Go to the pool of
Siloam, and wash: and I went and washed,
and I received sight.
12 Then said they unto him, Where is he?
He said, I know not.

. . . .

35 Jesus heard that they had cast him out;
and when he had found him, he said unto
him, Dost thou believe on the Son of God?
36 He answered and said, Who is he, Lord,
that I might believe on him?
37 And Jesus said unto him, Thou hast
both seen him, and it is he that talketh with
thee.
38 And he said, Lord, I believe. And he
worshipped him.
39 And Jesus said, For judgment I am
come into this world, that they which see not
might see; and that they which see might be
made blind.
40 And some of the Pharisees which were
with him heard these words, and said unto
him, Are we blind also?
41 Jesus said unto them, If ye were blind,
ye should have no sin: but now ye say, We
see; therefore your sin remaineth.

Golden Text: I am the light of the world.—John 9:5.

Believing in Christ

Unit 1. John: The Word Became Flesh

(Lessons 1-4)

Lesson Aims

Upon the completion of this lesson, the students should be able to:

1. Explain why it is significant that Jesus should be called the light of the world and why He merits that title.

2. Resolve to walk in the light that has been revealed to us through Christ.

Lesson Outline

INTRODUCTION
- A. An Experience of Darkness
- B. Lesson Background

I. A BLIND MAN RECEIVES SIGHT (John 9:1-7)
- A. Blindness and Sin (vv. 1, 2)
- B. An Opportunity to Show God's Works (vv. 3, 4)
- C. Command and Response (vv. 5-7)

II. THE BLIND MAN'S TESTIMONY (John 9:8-12)
- A. The Perplexed Neighbors (vv. 8-10)
  Identity Crisis
- B. The Facts, Only the Facts (vv. 11, 12)

III. JESUS REVEALS HIMSELF (John 9:35-41)
- A. The Healed Man Believes (vv. 35-38)
- B. The Willfully Blind (vv. 39-41)
  None So Blind . . .

CONCLUSION
- A. From Darkness to Light
- B. Prayer
- C. Thought to Remember

Display visual 3 of the visuals packet before the class and let it remain throughout the session. Refer to it in connection with verses 39-41. The visual is shown on page 253.

Introduction

A. An Experience of Darkness

Have you ever been in a cave deep in the earth when the guide extinguished all the lights? If you have, you remember how really dark darkness is in the absence of even a trace of lumination. It is an eerie feeling, and for some, quite frightening. In a cave you may stand with eyes wide open and still be just as blind as if you had no eyes at all. Without light, we would all be totally blind.

But the guide has promised that the lights will be off for just a minute. Even so, that minute is so long that before it is up, some in the group are saying, "Turn the lights back on." And when they are turned on, many in the group are likely to cheer. In an experience of this kind, in just sixty seconds one may come to a much greater appreciation for light than he or she has ever known before.

What is light? Men of science have labored the question for years. And whether they speak of it in terms of waves of luminous energy or as quantums of energy, or both, it is difficult to improve on the dictionary definition of light as "that which makes vision possible." Without light, our eyes would be totally useless.

Transfer these thoughts from the natural to the spiritual realm and you will get an understanding of what our lesson is all about. Christ is the light of the world. Without Him our souls grope in complete darkness. Illumined by His light, we see opening before us the way to God. Our lesson presents evidence to validate this.

B. Lesson Background

The event we are studying in this lesson occurred in the third year of Christ's ministry. By now His acquaintance among the people had broadened widely. Some among them would have made Him king because of His miraculous powers (John 6:15). Others considered Him to be a threat to the welfare of the nation, and soon they would be plotting how best to get rid of Him (John 11:47-53).

It is ironic that these enemies did not question the validity of His miracles (11:47). They admitted their fear that because of the greatness of His wondrous deeds everyone would believe on Him (v. 48). Remember? Faith, or belief, is the acceptance of evidence. Specifically John writes, "Then many of the Jews which . . . had seen the things which Jesus did, believed on him" (v. 45).

Our lesson centers around a blind man whom Jesus healed. More remarkable, the man had been born blind; his eyes had never functioned. The healing bears witness that Jesus was, as Nicodemus said, "A teacher come from God." But it testifies to more than this. The preceding chapter records Jesus' declaration, "I am the light of the world: he that followeth me shall not walk in darkness, but shall have the light of life" (8:12). This was a tremendous claim. But John believed it! And he wanted others to believe it also. So he included the account of how the light of the world brought light, literally, to one who had never known it before. In doing this, Jesus gave validation for His claim to be the light from Heaven.

I. A Blind Man Receives Sight (John 9:1-7)

After Jesus had declared himself to be the light of the world, the Pharisees said that He was bearing witness to himself and that it was a false witness (John 8:12, 13). As Jesus left the temple precincts, He soon came upon a blind man and was thus presented the opportunity to demonstrate the truth of His claim. By bringing this man out of his physical darkness into the light of this world, would He not demonstrate that He had the power also to bring the souls of men from the darkness of sin into the light of God's forgiveness and acceptance?

A. Blindness and Sin (vv. 1, 2)

1. And as Jesus passed by, he saw a man which was blind from his birth.

Jesus had an awareness that led Him to take note of those in need. Verse 8 tells us that the man was a beggar. He was near the temple, where he could appeal to the worshipers of God for help. In every age it has been the people of God, more than others, who have responded to human need.

2. And his disciples asked him, saying, Master, who did sin, this man, or his parents, that he was born blind?

Who did sin? This question of Jesus' disciples reflected a common misconception held in that day, that the suffering of great misfortune was a sign of sin in the life of the sufferer or of a close relative. "He is probably getting what he deserves," many would have reasoned.

Many an infant has come from the womb with defects, because of parental sin. But it simply is not true to say that every birth defect is the fault of the parents. The disciples asked the wrong question, did they not? Should they not have said, "Lord, here is a poor soul in desperate need. What can we do to help him?" In any case, Jesus made it clear that suffering, of itself, does not mark the one suffering as a great sinner.

B. An Opportunity to Show God's Works (vv. 3, 4)

3. Jesus answered, Neither hath this man sinned, nor his parents: but that the works of God should be made manifest in him.

Jesus did not say that the man or his parents had lived sinless lives. The question was, "Who sinned to bring about this affliction?" And Christ's answer was, *neither.* This man's suffering was in no way a judgment from God.

But *that the works of God should be made manifest in him.* That is, that God may work in him, and for him, and through him, making him a testimony to others, to the glory of God. This does not mean that God decreed that the man be born blind *in order that* God's work could be displayed in healing him. Jesus was not revealing the cause of the man's blindness; rather, He was announcing what would be its result. He was saying that, by the grace of God, even unmerited suffering may serve a glorious purpose. It is this latter that is the work of God. He works in us and through us to bring victory out of defeat. In being the one through whom the reality of God's mercy was shown, this blind man served in a way that others could not.

4. I must work the works of him that sent me, while it is day: the night cometh, when no man can work.

I must work. Some of the earliest manuscripts have, "We must work," which suggests that Christ included His disciples in the statement. The works of God were such things as Jesus had been doing: healing the sick, feeding the hungry, calling men to repentance, announcing the coming of the kingdom of God. We must do the works God asks of us *while it is day;* that is, so long as life shall last. *The night cometh.* This signifies death, which brings an end to one's earthly labors.

C. Command and Response (vv. 5-7)

The disciples saw the blind man and thought, "Who sinned, to cause this?" Jesus saw him and thought, "This man is in need; I will help him."

5. As long as I am in the world, I am the light of the world.

As long as. Jesus knew that His time on earth was short. In about six months would come the Passover, the last supper, and the crucifixion.

I am the light of the world. Jesus had said this before, adding, "He that followeth me shall not walk in darkness, but shall have the light of life" (8:12). Why did He repeat that claim now? Because the miracle of healing He was going to do would give light to a man who had lived in darkness until now, and would be evidence to the truth of His claim.

6. When he had thus spoken, he spat on the ground, and made clay of the spittle, and he anointed the eyes of the blind man with the clay.

When he had thus spoken, and not before. He had said that He must do the works of God, that He was the light (from God). He now proceeds to do a work such as only God could do.

He . . . made clay of the spittle, and anointed the eyes. There were times when Jesus healed a person with a word or a touch, and the healing was instantaneous. We are not told why He used clay made with spittle on this occasion or why He sent the man away to receive healing a little later. Various answers have been given, but most are unsatisfying. If we must speculate, perhaps it is best to say that Jesus used this method to arouse the blind man's faith and to demonstrate it in his obedience. We will see in a latter portion of today's text (vv. 35-38) that Jesus desired to give light not only to the blind man's eyes, but also to his soul.

7. And said unto him, Go, wash in the pool of Siloam, (which is by interpretation, Sent). He went his way therefore, and washed, and came seeing.

What a clear, straightforward example of what, under other circumstances, would be called "saving faith." The blind man did not say, "What use is this clay in my eyes?" "Why the pool of Siloam? Do you mean to say there is something in that water that will restore my sight?" Not at all. However strong or weak, his faith, leading him to do what Jesus commanded, saved him, that is, brought him his sight. His faith caused him not to *question* Jesus, but to *obey* Him. *He went . . . and washed, and came seeing.*

II. The Blind Man's Testimony (John 9:8-12)

A. The Perplexed Neighbors (vv. 8-10)

8. The neighbors therefore, and they which before had seen him that he was blind, said, Is not this he that sat and begged?

Mention of the man's *neighbors* suggests that, in all likelihood, he went home soon after he had received his sight. It is not surprising that he would want his parents and close acquaintances to be among the first to know of his good fortune.

Day after day the blind beggar had sat at the entrance of the temple, asking alms of those who passed by. He was, then, a familiar sight, though some might only have given him a passing glance. But now, here he was, walking, and with 20/20 vision. The change in the man's appearance and bearing would have been striking and would have caused even those who knew him best to wonder if they were "seeing things." Could this possibly be the man they had known to be totally blind? Some thought so, and in what was tantamount to an affirmation, asked, *Is not this he that sat and begged?*

9. Some said, This is he: others said, He is like him: but he said, I am he.

Various ones expressed their opinions. "Yes, it is." "Well, it looks like him." The man formerly blind must have been somewhat amused at all of the speculation going on, but he settled the discussion with the straightforward announcement, *I am he.*

The internal, or inherent, evidence in this account is overwhelming in establishing its authenticity. This is no "made up" story, but the account of what happened, the way it happened. Notice the varied and precise detail of the interchange between the neighbors and this man (vv. 8-12), and so on through the story (vv. 13-34). It seems quite likely that John secured the record from the man himself, the firsthand record of how a man blind from birth was made to see through faith in and obedience to Christ Jesus. And John recorded this "that ye might believe that Jesus is the Christ" (John 20:31).

10. Therefore said they unto him, How were thine eyes opened?

The fact of the miracle was not questioned. These neighbors wanted to know only *how* the healing was accomplished.

IDENTITY CRISIS

Celebrities sometimes report that a fan who sees them on the street will say, "I know you! You're . . . uh . . ." When the famous person helps the fan by identifying himself or herself, the fan says, "No, no! You're . . . uh . . ." What an identity crisis—not for the celebrity, but for the fan!

Some of the neighbors of the man born blind were not sure of his identity when they saw him seeing. They actually argued about who he was, apparently in his presence. Finally, he convinced them by insisting upon his own identity. Then he told them of his personal experience with "a man that is called Jesus."

No one is ever quite the same after being with Jesus. The courage and bold witness of Peter and John impressed the Sanhedrin, and the Jews "took note that these men had been with Jesus" (Acts 4:13, *New International Version*). The pages of the New Testament, and of secular history as well, are filled with examples of lives transformed by an encounter with Christ. It is in Him that we first learn who we really are and what kind of person God wants us to be. —R. W. B.

B. The Facts, Only the Facts (vv. 11, 12)

The man was so straightforward in his report of the events as to be completely disarming. He made no claims about the one who had brought the healing. He evidently did not know that

How to Say It

NICODEMUS. *Nick*-uh-*dee*-mus (strong accent on *dee*).
SILOAM. Sigh-*lo*-um.

visual 3

some regarded his benefactor to be the Messiah, for not once did he speak in those terms.

11. He answered and said, A man that is called Jesus made clay, and anointed mine eyes, and said unto me, Go to the pool of Siloam, and wash: and I went and washed, and I received sight.

He answered and said, A man that is called Jesus. Isn't that precious? It seems that, until now, he had never met the one who helped him, though he may have heard of Him. "This man came along—Jesus, they called Him—He made clay and anointed my eyes. He told me what to do. I did as He said, and I received my sight."

12. Then said they unto him, Where is he? He said, I know not.

Having learned *how* the blind man had been healed his neighbors and acquaintances quite naturally desired to see the one who had effected the healing. The man, however, did not know where Jesus was.

Verses 13-34, omitted from our printed text, tell of the Pharisees' interrogation of this man concerning his healing. This group had already condemned Jesus in their hearts, and they were greatly disturbed because of the miracle and the fact that Jesus healed the man on the Sabbath. How were they to explain it, if it were not from God? They asked the man how it happened, and in simple terms he told them. But they replied, "This man [Jesus] is not of God, because he keepeth not the sabbath day" (v. 16). Yet even some among the Pharisees raised the question, "How can a man that is a sinner do such miracles?" Then they asked the man, "What do you have to say about Him, since He opened your eyes?" And the man replied, "He is a prophet." (Notice that the Pharisees acknowledged the miracle.)

Some were not convinced that the man really had been born blind, so they summoned his parents and questioned them. "Is this your son, who ye say was born blind? how then doth he now see?" (v. 19). Note the insinuation: "Who ye *say* was born blind." "We know that this is our son," they replied, "and that he was born blind" (v. 24). But they denied any knowledge of who it was that opened his eyes, or how it was accomplished.

Still unsatisfied, they questioned the blind man once again. When he persisted in declaring Jesus to be a man of God, they became angry and cast him out of the synagogue.

III. Jesus Reveals Himself (John 9:35-41)

To be cast out was to be ostracized by the community, to be classed as a non-person, perhaps to suffer abuse, a most unpleasant fate. And this was the sad state of one who just a day or so before had been so elated. He was still in deep need, and Jesus again responded.

A. The Healed Man Believes (vv. 35-38)

35. Jesus heard that they had cast him out; and when he had found him, he said unto him, Dost thou believe on the Son of God?

Jesus . . . when he had found him. The man likely was in some out-of-the-way place, but Jesus, the Good Shepherd, sought and found him. In his depressed state, the man may have felt that he had lost the world, but, as B. W. Johnson stated, Jesus was "ready to give him heaven!"

Dost thou believe on the Son of God? He had believed Jesus as *a man of God* and, in obeying Him, received his sight. But he was now asked the question of ultimate faith, belief in Christ as the Son of God. (Some early manuscripts read *Son of man*, a title of Jesus associated with the one coming "with the clouds of heaven"—Daniel 7:13. It is the same Jesus, the divine Son of God.)

Many believe that Jesus was kind and good, a great teacher who revealed what God is like. But that is not enough.

36, 37. He answered and said, Who is he, Lord, that I might believe on him? And Jesus said unto him, Thou hast both seen him, and it is he that talketh with thee.

Who is he, Lord. This man had not seen Jesus until this moment, so perhaps he was not aware that the One before him was responsible for his healing. To the extent of his knowledge, he had believed in the One who had healed him. His reply here revealed his willingness to believe as further light was given him.

Thou hast seen him. Jesus said, "I am He who sent you to the pool of Siloam.

38. And he said, Lord, I believe. And he worshipped him.

With all his heart and soul the man believed what he had just heard, and did not hesitate to confess his faith. *Lord, I believe,* and he worshiped Jesus as Lord.

B. The Willfully Blind (vv. 39-41)

39. And Jesus said, For judgment I am come into this world, that they which see not might see; and that they which see might be made blind.

In the presence of Jesus, the light from God, every soul passes judgment upon himself or herself. *They which see not.* These are the ones who lack the true knowledge of God, who are lost in sin, but who acknowledge their need and receive the light when it shines in their hearts. They are made to see. But those *which see,* that is claim to be enlightened and admit to no need of Christ, ultimately cut themselves off from God's saving light.

40, 41. And some of the Pharisees which were with him heard these words, and said unto him, Are we blind also? Jesus said unto them, If ye were blind, ye should have no sin: but now ye say, We see; therefore your sin remaineth.

Are we blind? Scornfully, the Pharisees who were near Jesus (to find fault?) said to Him, "Surely You don't mean to say that You must enlighten us, do You?" These proud teachers of the law claimed to be spiritually enlightened, and so they willfully closed their eyes to the light Jesus offered. If they had admitted blindness (as explained under verse 39), their sins would have been forgiven. But they would not, so they remained in their sins.

NONE SO BLIND . . .

The only sightless person I knew as a child was a man named Al. One time when Al was sick, I went with my father to take him a hot meal that my mother had prepared. I marvelled at the way Al recognized Dad's voice. I also knew that Al could identify friends by the sound of their footsteps, even before they spoke to him. I have always been impressed by the way blind folk "see" with their other senses.

The key to such adaptations is *desire.* We all know that sighted persons usually see only what they want to see. We see only when we open our eyes. Jesus frankly told the legalistic Pharisees that they were spiritually blind. They refused to see reality, to acknowledge the truth, when it was presented to them. "None are so blind as those who will not see." The man born blind, however, received not only the physical sense of sight; through faith, he received forgiveness of sin, and thus spiritual vision.

The gift of sight is precious; the gift of vision is priceless. Without sight people are handicapped; without vision, people perish (Proverbs 29:18).

—R. W. B.

Home Daily Bible Readings

Monday, Mar. 15—Before Abraham, I Am (John 8:48-59)

Tuesday, Mar. 16—Delivered From Blindness (John 9:1-7)

Wednesday, Mar. 17—The Man Called Jesus (John 9:8-12)

Thursday, Mar. 18—He Is a Prophet (John 9:13-23)

Friday, Mar. 19—I Was Blind, Now I See (John 9:24-34)

Saturday, Mar. 20—Lord, I Believe (John 9:35-41)

Sunday, Mar. 21—Jesus the Shepherd (John 10:1-9)

Conclusion

A. From Darkness to Light

Can you imagine the amazement with which the blind man in our text viewed the world about him when he first received his sight? He may have heard it described by others as he groped through sightless years. But now he could see for himself, and he was in an entirely new and glorious world. So it is with the soul that is illumined by Christ, the light that is from above.

One who is without God lives in spiritual darkness. That person may be a slave to carnal passion and pleasure, and driven by envy and malice. If not deliberately defiant of God, such a person is certainly deceived by the prince of this world, Satan. That person is alienated from God, having no hope in the world (Ephesians 2:12).

Jesus came to bring the light of God into our lives, thus dispelling the darkness that engulfed our souls. He shows us God's mercy and love, opening our eyes to the beauty of life in Him and to the glories of Heaven awaiting us. Let us, therefore, praise God for Him who brought us light. Further, let us walk in that light and share it with those who are still stumbling in sin's darkness.

B. Prayer

Father, we pray that the light, Christ Jesus, may illuminate the path that we walk daily. As we journey in that light, may it drive sin's darkness from us, and shine through us that others too may see Jesus. In His name, amen.

C. Thought to Remember

"One thing I know, that, whereas I was blind, now I see!" What greater evidence is there than this that Christ is the light of the world?

Learning by Doing

This page contains an alternate lesson plan emphasizing learning activities. Classes desiring such student involvement will find these suggestions helpful.

Learning Goals

As a result of this lesson, the students will:

1. Be able to tell the difference between physical blindness and spiritual blindness.
2. Ask God to heal them of any blindness that may exist in their hearts.

Into the Lesson

Wear some dark sunglasses to class, just to arouse curiosity in the lesson topic.

Divide the class into two informal groups and give each of them a topic for a rapid brainstorm. Ask one group to list answers to the question, "What's so great about being able to see well?" Ask the other group to brainstorm the question, "What's so bad about being blind?"

Write their answers on the board when they are finished, and discuss them briefly. All will certainly agree that the ability to see well is a blessing for which one should be most grateful.

Point out that today's lesson is about blindness and sight, both physical and spiritual. The central thought of the lesson may be summed up in Jesus' words, "For judgment I am come into this world, that they which see not might see; and that they which see might be made blind" (John 9:39).

Into the Word

Because of the good action scenes in this lesson Scripture text, this is an ideal text to involve some students in a pantomime of the event for our study. During the week before class, contact class members to take the part of the following characters: Jesus, the blind man, the disciples (2), the neighbors (2), the parents (2), and the Pharisees (2). If you can't get that many volunteers, just get someone for Jesus, the blind man and the Pharisees. Ask them to read over the ninth chapter of John to get familiar with the story.

At this time, call your actors to the front of the classroom. Slowly read the entire ninth chapter, as the class acts out the parts.

Alternative: If your class is too shy to act, let them stay in their seats, but assign different class members to read the "lines" that fit their appointed characters. You be the narrator.

Now tell the class you would like to quiz them over the text they have just dramatized, to see how much they really understood. (This quiz is in the student book also.) The questions are true/false.

1. Jesus said that the blind man and his parents were perfect, sinless people. (False. He meant that they had not done any specific sin to cause this man's blindness.)
2. Jesus said, "The night cometh, when no man can work." (True. He may have been referring to the fact that we all die or that the world will get so wicked that no one can help much.)
3. Jesus spit on the blind man's eyes. (False. He spit on the ground, v. 6.)
4. When Jesus put the clay on the blind man's eyes, the man opened his eyes and was able to see. (False. He had to go wash in the pool before he could see.)
5. Jesus healed the blind man on a Sunday. (False. It was the Sabbath, a Saturday, v. 14.)
6. The blind man did not really know who Jesus was until some time after he was healed. (True. "A man that is called Jesus," he said, v. 11; see also verse 36.)
7. The blind man's parents testified that their son was indeed born blind. (True, v. 20.)
8. The Pharisees treated the blind man as a hero and honored him in the synagogue. (False. They cast the blind man out of the synagogue, v. 34.)
9. Jesus compared sin to blindness. (True. He suggested that humility leads to spiritual sight, and that pride keeps one blind to one's spiritual need and thus chained to his or her sin, vv. 39-41.)

Into Life

Point out that there are different kinds of and degrees of eye problems. Write the following vision defects in a vertical list on the chalkboard: Total lack of vision, nearsighted, farsighted, cataracts, tunnel vision, blind spots, color blind, optical illusions.

Ask the class to discuss some of the spiritual counterparts of each of these kinds of blindness. For example, some church members are nearsighted, meaning that they see only their own little needs and no one else's. After they have identified and briefly discussed these spiritual vision problems, ask the class to suggest some ways we can overcome these forms of spiritual blindness. Then close the session with prayer for better spiritual vision.

Let's Talk It Over

The questions on this page are designed to encourage review of the lesson Scriptures and to promote discussion of the lesson by the class. The answers provided are only discussion starters. Let your class talk it over from there.

1. Few today would regard blindness as a result of someone's sin, but some may tend to look down on people who are blind. If so, how can such a tendency be corrected?

While Jesus healed the blind as a way of demonstrating His divine power, He also certainly did it out of compassion for such persons. We are expressly told in Matthew 20:34 that Jesus' compassion was a factor in His restoring sight to two blind men. His example should inspire us to a similar regard for all who struggle with physical handicaps. However, if we have the opportunity to become well-acquainted with persons who are blind, we may find our compassion being equaled by admiration for them. Persons without sight have proved that they can study, work, and serve the Lord effectively right alongside of those who are able to see.

2. The healing of the blind man in today's text brought glory to God. How have disabled modern-day believers brought glory to God through their handicaps?

Certain prominent persons come to mind, such as Fanny Crosby, who wrote over five thousand hymns in spite of blindness; and Joni Earickson Tada, who, although a quadriplegic, has served the Lord well as a writer, artist, and musician. Countless others less well known, who are blind, deaf, lame, or disabled by illness or accident have performed the tasks of minister, musician, teacher, youth worker, writer, and the like. These persons have inspired their fellow Christians by laboring in spite of their handicaps, by refusing to allow their physical handicaps to cripple their spirits, and by daring to take on fresh challenges in the cause of Christ. Their example should lead us all to examine the areas of weakness in our own lives and to develop the determination to surmount them for the glory of God.

3. Why is Jesus' title "the light of the world" one that we should emphasize today?

Although we possess artificial lighting, we are just as much in need of spiritual light as were the people of Jesus' day. Indeed, the threat of moral and spiritual darkness seems to be engulfing our society. We live in a confusing era with issues of importance being debated on every side. Abortion, euthanasia, homosexuality, the ever-growing menace of the occult and Satanism—these are just a few of those issues that vex us. Jesus Christ offers light through His Word to guide us in making the right decisions regarding such matters.

4. Jesus' dealings with the man born blind involved ministering both to his physical and spiritual needs. Why is it vital that we carefully consider Jesus' example here?

It is easy to stress one aspect of ministry to the virtual exclusion of the other. We're aware of religious organizations that pour their energies into combating political oppression, malnutrition, disease, poverty, and illiteracy, but appear to give scant attention to preparing people for eternity. However, many churches and individual Christian leaders have been criticized for focusing on saving men's souls without regard for saving their bodies and minds from earthly woes. If we keep Jesus' example in view, we will provide food for the malnourished, and make sure they receive the bread of life (John 6:35); we will teach the masses to read and write, and see that they have the Bible; we will demonstrate our concern for the healing of their bodies and the saving of their souls.

5. What are some examples of how the blindness of unbelief afflicts our society?

Humanism asserts that it holds the keys to human progress apart from belief in God and the Bible and dependence on prayer. The humanist is confident that he sees what is best for humankind, but he is blind to what is real. The worldly person dreams of material acquisition and sensuous pleasure and thereby blinds himself or herself to the glories of Jesus Christ (see 2 Corinthians 4:4). Those people who dabble in the occult or devote themselves to New Age philosophies or practices are confident that they have gained a special insight into the nature of things and a special power to succeed, but they have blindly allied themselves with Satan's cause. And even within the church there are many who regard themselves as enlightened because they have discarded those parts of the Bible they claim are outdated or irrelevant. But this also is a form of blindness.

Coming to Life

March 28
Lesson 4

Lesson Scripture: John 11:1-44.

Printed Text: John 11:1-4, 21-27, 38-44.

Devotional Reading: John 11:45-54.

John 11:1-4, 21-27, 38-44

1 Now a certain man was sick, named Lazarus, of Bethany, the town of Mary and her sister Martha.

2 (It was that Mary which anointed the Lord with ointment, and wiped his feet with her hair, whose brother Lazarus was sick.)

3 Therefore his sisters sent unto him, saying, Lord, behold, he whom thou lovest is sick.

4 When Jesus heard that, he said, This sickness is not unto death, but for the glory of God, that the Son of God might be glorified thereby.

. . . .

21 Then said Martha unto Jesus, Lord, if thou hadst been here, my brother had not died.

22 But I know, that even now, whatsoever thou wilt ask of God, God will give it thee.

23 Jesus saith unto her, Thy brother shall rise again.

24 Martha saith unto him, I know that he shall rise again in the resurrection at the last day.

25 Jesus said unto her, I am the resurrection, and the life: he that believeth in me, though he were dead, yet shall he live:

26 And whosoever liveth and believeth in me shall never die. Believest thou this?

27 She saith unto him, Yea, Lord: I believe that thou art the Christ, the Son of God, which should come into the world.

. . . .

38 Jesus therefore again groaning in himself cometh to the grave. It was a cave, and a stone lay upon it.

39 Jesus said, Take ye away the stone. Martha, the sister of him that was dead, saith unto him, Lord, by this time he stinketh: for he hath been dead four days.

40 Jesus saith unto her, Said I not unto thee, that, if thou wouldest believe, thou shouldest see the glory of God?

41 Then they took away the stone from the place where the dead was laid. And Jesus lifted up his eyes, and said, Father, I thank thee that thou hast heard me.

42 And I knew that thou hearest me always: but because of the people which stand by I said it, that they may believe that thou hast sent me.

43 And when he thus had spoken, he cried with a loud voice, Lazarus, come forth.

44 And he that was dead came forth, bound hand and foot with graveclothes; and his face was bound about with a napkin. Jesus saith unto them, Loose him, and let him go.

Golden Text: I am the resurrection, and the life: he that believeth in me, though he were dead, yet shall he live.—John 11:25.

Believing in Christ

Unit 1. John: The Word Became Flesh

(Lessons 1-4)

Lesson Aims

After this lesson the students should:

1. Be able to quote John 11:25 and to explain how the events of today's lesson show Christ to be the resurrection and the life.
2. Be challenged to deeper faith in Jesus as God's Son our Savior and the giver of life.
3. Cultivate awareness of those around them who are burdened and need a word of encouragement and loving concern.

Lesson Outline

INTRODUCTION
- A. When a Loved One Is Stricken
- B. Lesson Background

I. ILLNESS STRIKES A FRIEND (John 11:1-4)
- A. The Family in Bethany (v. 1)
- B. The Sister Who Anointed Jesus (v. 2)
- C. Jesus Notified (vv. 3, 4)
  Sick to God's Glory

II. MARTHA TALKS WITH JESUS (John 11:21-27)
- A. Faith and Disappointment (vv. 21, 22)
- B. Reassurance From Jesus (vv. 23-26)
- C. A Confession of Faith (v. 27)
  Can You Believe It?

III. FAITH SUSTAINED—THE BROTHER LIVES (John 11:38-44)
- A. Jesus' Purpose—Martha's Protest (vv. 38-40)
- B. Jesus' Prayer (vv. 41, 42)
- C. God's Answer (vv. 43, 44)

CONCLUSION
- A. What If Jesus Had Failed?
- B. Prayer
- C. Thought to Remember

Refer to visual 4 of the visuals packet as you consider Jesus' words recorded in verse 4 of the text. The visual is shown on page 261.

Introduction

A. When a Loved One Is Stricken

Into every life some shadows must fall, with their accompanying sorrow. It may be a crippling accident, a lingering illness, the death of a loved one. And the child of God does not escape. Even Paul, man of God that he was, had an illness that persisted in spite of his prayers that it be taken away (2 Corinthians 12:7-10).

When the child of God experiences such sorrow, are we to conclude that he or she has been abandoned by the Lord? When the one dearest to us on earth dies, must we grope through the dark valley alone? Oh, no. The darkness may engulf us, but Jesus is the light of the world; and He will shine the light of His life and of His love upon us, if we trust Him. (See John 8:12.) Furthermore, since He was victorious over death and the grave, we can rest on His promise when He says, "I am the resurrection, and the life: he that believeth in me, though he were dead, yet shall he live" (John 11:25). The events recorded in the text for this lesson will demonstrate the truth that Jesus is the resurrection and the life.

B. Lesson Background

As we continue our lessons in the book of John, let us recall the apostle's basic theme and purpose in writing. Christ, the living Word that was with God and that was God from the beginning, became flesh to bring the light of God to a dark world, to bring life to a dying world. To those who believe on His name He gives the power to become the children of God (1:12). Light and life—eternal life—are inherent in Christ, and these He would share with every human being. John writes to present the evidence that this is so (20:31). A significant bit of that evidence is the subject for our study today, the raising of Lazarus from the dead.

Jesus opened the eyes of the man born blind (last week's lesson) around the time of the feast of Tabernacles (October). Afterward He remained a while in the area of Jerusalem to teach. Many of the Jews, hearing Him and seeing His miracles, believed in Him. Opponents said, "He hath a devil, and is mad; why hear ye him?" Others said, "These are not the words of him that hath a devil. Can a devil open the eyes of the blind?" (10:20, 21).

John then reports that Jesus was in Jerusalem at the feast of Dedication, which was observed in December, but gives no indication of where He was in the meantime (John 10:22). During this period, the animosity directed toward Jesus increased. His enemies were especially incensed by His frequent reference to God as *my Father* and charged Him with blasphemy, threatening again to stone Him. When they sought to apprehend Him, He escaped and went to the region of Perea, east of the Jordan River (John 10:23-42). We find Him there as our lesson begins. Spring and the final Passover would soon come.

Of all the miracles that Jesus did, the raising of Lazarus certainly was the most significant.

Jesus had restored others to life—the daughter of Jairus (Mark 5:21-43), and the widow of Nain's son (Luke 7:11-16.) In each of these cases, however, the individual had just died, and skeptics say that they were just in a state of suspended animation. Such an argument is foolish, to say the least. But this could not have been the case with Lazarus, for he had been dead four days, and bodily decay had begun.

Unbelievers deny outright the possibility of such a miracle. They suggest, instead, that we really have here a parable or an allegory, which is not intended to be taken literally. On the face of it, however, it is certain that John intended for it to be taken literally, and there is nothing to indicate otherwise. Notice how straightforward the account, including numerous little details, such as one would find in an actual event recorded as evidence.

I. Illness Strikes a Friend (John 11:1-4)

Those who are familiar with the life of Jesus know that He had no home of His own. "The foxes have holes," He said, "and the birds of the air have nests; but the Son of man hath not where to lay his head" (Matthew 8:20). Frequently, however, there were offers of hospitality along the way, and these Jesus accepted.

A. The Family in Bethany (v. 1)

One of the homes where Jesus was a welcome guest was in Bethany, a small town located just two miles southeast of Jerusalem. Here in the home of Mary, Martha, and Lazarus Jesus could find both shelter and a warm welcome. Quite naturally they were dear to Him. John tells us that "Jesus loved Martha, and her sister, and Lazarus" (11:5). This, however, did not prevent illness from striking this home.

1. Now a certain man was sick, named Lazarus, of Bethany, the town of Mary and her sister Martha.

Presumably the parents were not living, but the children had each other. The home belonged to Martha (Luke 10:38). Was she, then, the oldest? Perhaps, and Lazarus may have been the youngest of the three. In any case, the brother seems to have been very dear to his sisters. And now he was sick with a serious illness.

B. The Sister Who Anointed Jesus (v. 2)

2. (It was that Mary which anointed the Lord with ointment, and wiped his feet with her hair, whose brother Lazarus was sick.)

It may seem strange that this verse is inserted here. The anointing to which John refers took place after the resurrection of Lazarus. (See John 12:1-3.) But we must remember that John wrote his Gospel long after these events had occurred. Matthew and Mark had recorded this anointing many years earlier, and so probably most Christians knew about it. But Mary's name was not given in those accounts. John here identifies her and distinguishes her from the other Marys associated with Jesus.

> **How to Say It**
>
> JAIRUS. Jay-*eye*-rus or *Jay*-ih-rus.
> PEREA. Peh-*ree*-uh.
> SADDUCEES. *Sad*-you-seez.

C. Jesus Notified (vv. 3, 4)

3. Therefore his sisters sent unto him, saying, Lord, behold, he whom thou lovest is sick.

Therefore, meaning "as a consequence." Their brother was sick; they needed help. So the sisters naturally thought of Jesus and hastened to get word to Him.

4. When Jesus heard that, he said, This sickness is not unto death, but for the glory of God, that the Son of God might be glorified thereby.

This was an enigmatic statement calculated to make the hearers think deeply. Not long afterward, Jesus said bluntly that Lazarus was dead. Putting the fact that he was dead with the declaration that *this sickness is not unto death, but for the glory of God,* the disciples would be able to understand that Jesus was about to raise Lazarus from the dead as He had raised Jairus' daughter and the son of a widow at Nain. So Jesus meant that the final outcome would not be death for Lazarus. He would live, and Mary and Martha would be reassured of Jesus' love for them and their brother. But more than this, they would know that the One who was their friend is the Savior, even from death!

There is another consequence of the illness of Lazarus. God would be glorified when Jesus called for Lazarus's deliverance from death in the name of the Father. In addition, the miracle of raising Lazarus from the dead would so galvanize the enemies of Jesus that they would not rest until they saw Him killed (11:45-53). The final result, then, of the death of Lazarus would be *that the Son of God might be glorified.* And how was this to be? He was to be crucified, but the cross would become His greatest glory when followed by His resurrection. (See John 7:39; 12:23.)

Having received word of the illness of Lazarus, Jesus stayed where He was for two more days (John 11:6), and Lazarus died (v. 14).

So the scene was set. Jesus was ready to visit His friends—and to face His enemies. The danger was recognized by Thomas, who said, "Let us also go, that we may die with him" (v. 16). How great was Jesus' love for Lazarus, love that would bring Him back to Bethany! How great His love for the world that would soon bring Him to the cross!

SICK TO GOD'S GLORY

"I'm sick to death of this!"

"I'm sick to death of that!"

"I'm sick to death of you!"

Frustrated persons often resort to such exaggerated outbursts to vent their anger. It simply means, "I am tired of this treatment or of these circumstances; I'm weary of this situation." Both *sick* and *to death* are hyperboles in most cases, though sometimes tensions, conflicts, and abuse do indeed make victims sick enough to actually die. In any case, the phrase itself, *sick to death,* is significant in light of today's text.

Jesus said that Lazarus was not "sick unto death." This good friend of Jesus was sick "for God's glory." In the natural circumstances of Lazarus's affliction, God (and Christ) used the occasion as an opportunity to dramatize the miraculous, life-giving power of the Lord.

Still today, Christians can use the circumstances of sickness and impending death to glorify God. The late Luke Perrine, former president of St. Louis Christian College, witnessed to hospital patients and personnel continually during his hospital confinements. And literally thousands of lesser-known believers all over the world are testifying to God's grace and glory as they lie on their death beds at this moment. They are sick "to God's glory." —R. W. B.

II. Martha Talks With Jesus (John 11:21-27)

Of the two sisters, Mary seems to have been the more contemplative, whereas Martha was more active. When word was received of Jesus' coming, it was Martha who hurried to meet Him. In spite of the fact that He had delayed His coming, she had never doubted His love for them, and her faith in Him never wavered.

A. Faith and Disappointment (vv. 21, 22)

Some detect a note of rebuke in Martha's remark. It may have been only disappointment, although rebuke comes readily to mind.

21. Then said Martha unto Jesus, Lord, if thou hadst been here, my brother had not died.

If thou hadst been here—but you were not! Why? You healed so many others, yet our brother had to die. Why didn't you come when we needed you so much? (How often have *we* delayed making a visit, or calling a friend, or writing a letter, until it was too late? We need to cultivate awareness of those around us who are burdened and need a word of encouragement. Can you think of such a person just now?—*Lesson aim three.*)

Jesus, however, had not forgotten His friends. His delay in responding immediately to the news of the illness of Lazarus was not due to neglect; it was by design. His purpose was to do something far greater than to heal a sick body. (So it is, oftentimes, when God does not respond immediately to our calls upon Him.)

If there was a note of remonstrance in Martha's voice, it immediately gave way to a confidence so daring as yet to keep hope alive in her heart, even though her brother was dead.

22. But I know, that even now, whatsoever thou wilt ask of God, God will give it thee.

Martha put no limits on Jesus' power. Nor should we. Some do, however, asking questions such as, "Did Jesus really walk on water, or what?" The apostle John would have thought it ludicrous to question the miracles of Jesus. The question is not, "How can one dead four days be restored to life?" but, "What think ye of Christ? whose son is he?" (Matthew 22:42).

John had heard the words and witnessed the miracles of Jesus and was fully persuaded that He was the Son of God. Granted this, miracles are to be expected, not questioned! Whatever Christ asks of God—*God will do it.*

Martha expressed confidence, but what did she expect Jesus to do? She herself was puzzled about the matter, as we shall see.

B. Reassurance From Jesus (vv. 23-26)

23, 24. Jesus saith unto her, Thy brother shall rise again. Martha saith unto him, I know that he shall rise again in the resurrection at the last day.

Martha believed in the resurrection, as did the Jewish people in general (except the Sadducees). When Jesus said, *Thy brother shall rise again,* He meant, "He shall rise here and now," but Martha's thoughts were of the final resurrection. This she believed. This was her faith. Soon that faith would be greatly expanded.

25, 26. Jesus said unto her, I am the resurrection, and the life: he that believeth in me, though he were dead, yet shall he live: and whosoever liveth and believeth in me shall never die. Believeth thou this?

How bold a statement! How audacious! Martha believed in the resurrection to come. Jesus said, *I am the resurrection, and the life: he that believeth in me, though he were dead, yet shall he live.* These are the claims of Jesus that inflamed His enemies. Are these the words of a deranged fanatic? Or, are they the pronouncement of the most wonderful truth man has ever heard? A truth that only the One who has come from God could utter? Every soul who hears these words must answer that question, and how great that question is! Presently, for Martha and for all the world, Jesus would demonstrate that His words were true. And, in a short while He would remove all doubt when He himself would come forth from death and the grave.

Teacher: Have the class read together several times the words of the Golden Text—see page 257—for the purpose of memorizing them.

I am the resurrection. Does a person, knowing that death is inevitable, desire to be raised from the dead? Desire it not! Instead, let your desire be for Jesus, for He *is* the resurrection. His is the power that opens every grave and gives life to the lifeless, because in Him is life, and from Him life proceeds.

He that believeth in me, though he were dead, or, "even though one dies," *yet shall he live.* Believe in Jesus—not in the resurrection, not in the immortality of the soul, not in the good things you have done in this world: *Believe in Jesus.* Only if we trust Him who is *life,* do we receive life, abundant and eternal. We go to Him who conquered death, to Him who is the resurrection, if we would be raised again. If we do not put our trust in this One who has proven altogether trustworthy, to whom will we go?

C. A Confession of Faith (v. 27)

27. She saith unto him, Yea, Lord: I believe that thou art the Christ, the Son of God, which should come into the world.

Martha was convinced and did not hesitate to make the confession that must come from the lips—and the heart—of every one who would follow Jesus. She believed that Jesus was *the Christ.* Centuries before, the Hebrew prophets had spoken of one who was anointed of God, who would come and lead His people to salvation. The Hebrew *Messiah* and Greek *Christ* mean "anointed." Martha believed that Jesus was He. Further, she believed that He was *the Son of God,* that He had a unique relationship with the Father. Peter acknowledged the Lord in like fashion (Matthew 16:16). Paul calls this "the good confession" (1 Timothy 6:12, *The New King James Version*). And in Romans he writes, "If thou shalt confess with thy mouth the Lord Jesus, and shalt believe in thine heart that God hath raised him from the dead, thou shalt be saved" (Romans 10:9; see also Matthew 10:32).

visual 4

CAN YOU BELIEVE IT?

Ripley's Believe It Or Not was a popular feature of many newspapers for several years. He reported stranger-than-fiction facts that intrigued his readers. People, though perhaps less gullible and more skeptical, are still fascinated by facts that "blow their minds," as it were. The human intellect is titillated by information and/or happenings that seem to be supernatural or supernormal. Witness the popularity of television shows such as *That's Incredible!* and *Incredible Breakthroughs.*

Our future-shock era has been marked by so many wondrous and awesome discoveries and achievements that *incredible* and *unbelievable* seem to be the only adjectives to describe them.

Jesus was asking Mary and Martha to believe an absolutely incredible truth—that He had power over death. It was hard to believe then, and it is hard to believe now. Our medical miracles and technological advances cannot overcome death. We must still accept by *faith* that Jesus is "the resurrection and the life."

Jesus proved His outrageous claim by raising Lazarus—and Jairus's daughter, and the son of the widow from Nain. His own resurrection is the ultimate evidence. "Christ has indeed been raised from the dead . . . Thanks be to God! He gives us the victory through our Lord Jesus Christ" (1 Corinthians 15:20, 57, *New International Version*).

Do you believe this? —R. W. B.

III. Faith Sustained—the Brother Lives (John 11:38-44)

Having made her glorious confession, Martha went back to get Mary, apparently at Jesus' request (v. 28). Mary hurried out to Jesus, and when she met Him she greeted Him the same way Martha had (vv. 29-32). Kneeling before Jesus, Mary could not hold back her tears. Jesus was so moved by her sorrow that He also wept (vv. 33-36).

A. Jesus' Purpose—Martha's Protest (vv. 38-40)

38, 39. Jesus therefore again groaning in himself cometh to the grave. It was a cave, and a stone lay upon it. Jesus said, Take ye away the stone. Martha, the sister of him that was dead, saith unto him, Lord, by this time he stinketh: for he hath been dead four days.

Jesus . . . groaning in himself. The verb involves stress, often the result of anger, but here, perhaps, the result of deep emotion. *Take ye away the stone.* Jesus came to the tomb for one purpose, to restore the life of Lazarus. But Martha, until now, had not dared hope for such a miracle, and so she voiced a polite protest. To open the tomb would be both an embarrassment and a desecration.

40. Jesus saith unto her, Said I not unto thee, that, if thou wouldest believe, thou shouldest see the glory of God?

Jesus did not criticize Martha for her wavering faith. Instead, He summarized with a question what He had previously told her. Then He reassured her that she would indeed witness God's glorious power.

B. Jesus' Prayer (vv. 41, 42)

41, 42. Then they took away the stone from the place where the dead was laid. And Jesus lifted up his eyes, and said, Father, I thank thee that thou hast heard me. And I knew that thou hearest me always: but because of the people which stand by I said it, that they may believe that thou hast sent me.

Father, I thank thee that thou hast heard me. Jesus prayed these words for the benefit of those standing by. He wanted them to know that God honored His prayers. He said it so that, when God answered, these people might *believe that* God had sent Him—the incarnation. Here is the word *believe* again. Not belief as in a creed, not faith as the acceptance of the unknown, but faith as the result of evidence. Christ had prayed. Would God answer?

C. God's Answer (vv. 43, 44)

43, 44. And when he thus had spoken, he cried with a loud voice, Lazarus, come forth. And he that was dead came forth, bound hand and foot with graveclothes; and his face was bound about with a napkin. Jesus saith unto them, Loose him, and let him go.

He that was dead came forth. Jesus had spoken truth. The Father heard the Son, just as Jesus was sure He would. Death, the "final enemy," the scourge of humankind, is powerless before Him who is "the resurrection, and the life." As Jesus had shown himself to be the light of the world in giving sight to the blind, he now gave evidence that He is the conqueror over death.

Bound hand and foot with graveclothes. Even the appearance of Lazarus is given. The suggestion that being bound would prevent movement is overstated. Obviously, the binding would not be that severe. In any case, no graveclothes can hold the person of one in the grave when Jesus calls, "Come forth."

Conclusion

A. What If Jesus Had Failed?

Suppose Lazarus had not come forth when Jesus called? Suppose Jesus had failed? Surely His claims would have been questioned and He himself rejected. But Jesus did not fail. His offer of life and immortality is genuine, without fraud or deceit. From the heart of every soul in the face of death there may come the cry of Paul: "O wretched man that I am! who shall deliver me from the body of this death?" From Paul also comes the answer: "I thank God through Jesus Christ our Lord" (Romans 7:24, 25). Christ *is* the resurrection and the life.

B. Prayer

We thank You, Heavenly Father, for sending Your Son, who abolished death and brought life and immortality to light. Help us to live daily a life illuminated by His presence. Then, when death claims these mortal bodies, let us be clothed with the immortality that is in Christ. In His name we pray. Amen.

C. Thought to Remember

"I am the resurrection, and the life: he that believeth in me, though he were dead yet shall he live." Believe in Him—and live!

Home Daily Bible Readings

Monday, Mar. 22—For the Glory of God (John 11:1-11)

Tuesday, Mar. 23—He Will Rise Again (John 11:12-23)

Wednesday, Mar. 24—I Am the Resurrection (John 11:24-29)

Thursday, Mar. 25—Jesus Wept (John 11:30-37)

Friday, Mar. 26—Unbind Him and Let Him Go (John 11:38-44)

Saturday, Mar. 27—Jesus Must Die (John 11:45-53)

Sunday, Mar. 28—Looking for Jesus (John 11:54-57)

Learning by Doing

This page contains an alternate lesson plan emphasizing learning activities. Classes desiring such student involvement will find these suggestions helpful.

Learning Goals

As a result of this lesson, the students will:

1. Express some of their questions and emotions about grief, death, and hope of resurrection.
2. Be able verbally to defend their faith in Jesus' power over death, based on the historical facts of Lazarus's resurrection.

Into the Lesson

Lessons on death can be upsetting to anyone who has had a recent death of a close relative or friend. But they can also serve to reinforce the Christians' hope of ultimate victory over death. Keep this victory in focus as you proceed through this lesson.

Give each student paper and pencil as they arrive. To begin today's session, say, "All of us have attended gatherings where we have experienced mixed emotions, such as a wedding or graduation, where people are happy and sad at the same time. The death of a faithful Christian is another one of these times. On your paper, list some of the negative and positive feelings and thoughts you might experience at a funeral for a Christian friend."

Give the class three or four minutes for this, then collect the papers and read them aloud. Make the transition into the lesson by stating that today's lesson is about just such an occasion, the death of a good friend of Jesus.

Into the Word

Divide the class into two groups and give each student an index card. Tell the class that they are to pretend that they are journalists in the time of Christ. Group one are journalists for the *Jerusalem Journal* (a sympathetic, religious paper) and group two for the *Bethany Blab* (a critical, expose tabloid). Assign the characters in today's text (Mary, Martha, Lazarus, Jesus, or a disciple) to the students in both groups as the subject for an interview. Have the students write down three or four questions they might ask their interviewer to help them flesh out their story.

Read the text aloud and give them about five minutes to write their questions. Some questions they may write are, "Martha, how did you feel toward Jesus when He didn't arrive in time to save your brother?" Or, "How did you know your brother was really dead? Maybe he was in a coma."

Let the class members share their questions, after first telling the class whether they are from the journal or the tabloid and which character they are interviewing.

As you go along, urge students to use their collective imagination and the text to answer as many questions as they can. Point out that this is a speculative exercise, but that it will help them to "get inside" the characters of today's lesson.

If you have time, discuss some of the following questions as well:

1. How does the raising of Lazarus compare with the raising of the widow's son (Luke 7) and Jairus's daughter (Mark 5). (Lazarus was dead for a longer period of time, he had already been buried, and bodily decay would have already begun.)
2. Why didn't Jesus miraculously remove the grave stone and graveclothes while He was at it?
3. Why did Jesus weep, when He knew He was about to raise their loved one back to life?

Into Life

Point out that a number of important truths may be drawn from today's lesson text. Ask the class to name as many as they can think of. Write their suggestions on the chalkboard and add additional ones from the list below. Comment on each briefly.

1. Even close friends of Jesus sometimes suffer.
2. Jesus has genuine sympathy for human grief.
3. Death for the Christian is a prelude to joy.
4. Jesus *is* life.
5. Christians can be of great comfort to each other in times of grief.
6. The death of a good person can cause many others to think about life and eternity and their own mortality.
7. Public prayers, such as the one Jesus prayed at Lazarus's raising, can be of real comfort to those listening.
8. Because of the resurrection, we will be reunited with those who have died in faith; they are not forever gone.

Ask the class to tell which of these truths means the most to them and why.

To close the session, have each student write a brief prayer to express his or her thanks for the hope of resurrection that is ours in Jesus. Ask several volunteers to share their prayers with the entire class.

Let's Talk It Over

The questions on this page are designed to encourage review of the lesson Scriptures and to promote discussion of the lesson by the class. The answers provided are only discussion starters. Let your class talk it over from there.

1. The raising of Lazarus was one of the most significant of Jesus' miracles. Why is this so?

Jesus' delaying of His arrival in Bethany, His conversations with Martha and Mary, the command to remove the stone from the tomb's entrance, the powerful call to Lazarus to come forth—all these factors added to the drama. And we are given more of the details of this miracle than of most of the others. But the most striking of all the features of this miracle, and one that has significance for every person who has ever lived, is the fact that Jesus raised from the dead a person whose body had lain in the grave for four days. Decomposition of the body had already begun. Yet even this could not prevent the raising of him who was dead. There is no way for an unbeliever to explain away the reality of such a mighty work.

2. Many have experienced disappointment because God has delayed in granting a request. How can we deal with such disappointment?

Martha and Mary were disappointed at Jesus' failure to respond promptly when they informed Him of their brother's illness. But the way in which Jesus responded after delaying was much more wonderful than an earlier healing would have been. Perhaps we too have known situations in which the delayed answer to our prayer was clearly superior to what we initially hoped for. There is no doubt that God sometimes delays answering prayers because we are not yet ready for the answers. An unrepented sin, an attitude of resistance to God's will, a need for some further growth in our understanding or commitment—these are factors that can delay the answers. We must continue to pray persistently (Luke 18:1-8), and we must work at removing the delay-causing factors.

3. Are we guilty of putting limits on Jesus' power? If so, in what ways do we do it?

Some Bible teachers limit Jesus by proposing naturalistic explanations for the miracles described in the Gospels. They deny that He was born of a virgin and that He actually arose from the dead. We dare not join in with their faithless tampering with Biblical facts. But even those who accept the Bible without reservation may limit Jesus. We may do this by assuming that certain persons are beyond Jesus' power to attract and save, or by lamenting that our congregation, which is part of the body of Christ, is unable to grow or to make an impact on the community. Still another way is by resigning ourselves to the impossibility of overcoming some besetting personal attitude or habit. "I can do all things through Christ" (Philippians 4:13) is the answer to this tendency to limit our Lord.

4. This lesson reminds us that our faith must reside in Jesus himself as "the resurrection, and the life." Why is this reminder needed?

Our faith can be misdirected to other human beings, to an institution, or to certain doctrines or traditions. It hardly needs to be said that faith in any of these can be severely damaged, as for example when a respected Christian leader is found to have "feet of clay." To cultivate faith in Jesus himself we need to spend much time poring over His words and deeds recorded in the Gospels. Our faith will be deepened if we talk about Him with our Christian friends, and make use of the vast store of hymns, poems and other literature that friends of Jesus in past eras have written to reflect their perceptions of Him and fellowship with Him.

5. While Martha's faith was remarkably strong, it nevertheless seems to have wavered a bit. How may this observation help our faith?

Martha's reaction when Jesus commanded that the stone be removed from the tomb's entrance may have resulted from a momentary sense of embarrassment or from a temporary wavering of her faith. Jesus' response to her in John 11:40 seems to indicate this. It may trouble us somewhat to think of someone so close to Jesus struggling to maintain faith, but it was no different than the struggles Peter and the rest of the apostles experienced. Here again is a mark of the authenticity of the Gospel accounts, and here is a fresh reminder that the people closest to Jesus were subject to the same weaknesses as we. They grappled at times with doubt, but because they knew Jesus, faith won out. When we encounter moments of wavering faith, we can identify with Martha, Peter, and the rest, and let faith win out in us also.

Do As I Have Done

April 4
Lesson 5

LESSON SCRIPTURE: John 13:1-20.

PRINTED TEXT: John 13:1-16.

DEVOTIONAL READING: John 13:31-36.

John 13:1-16

1 Now before the feast of the passover, when Jesus knew that his hour was come that he should depart out of this world unto the Father, having loved his own which were in the world, he loved them unto the end.

2 And supper being ended, the devil having now put into the heart of Judas Iscariot, Simon's son, to betray him;

3 Jesus knowing that the Father had given all things into his hands, and that he was come from God, and went to God;

4 He riseth from supper, and laid aside his garments; and took a towel, and girded himself.

5 After that he poureth water into a basin, and began to wash the disciples' feet, and to wipe them with the towel wherewith he was girded.

6 Then cometh he to Simon Peter: and Peter saith unto him, Lord, dost thou wash my feet?

7 Jesus answered and said unto him, What I do thou knowest not now; but thou shalt know hereafter.

8 Peter saith unto him, Thou shalt never wash my feet. Jesus answered him, If I wash thee not, thou hast no part with me.

9 Simon Peter saith unto him, Lord, not my feet only, but also my hands and my head.

10 Jesus saith to him, He that is washed needeth not save to wash his feet, but is clean every whit: and ye are clean, but not all.

11 For he knew who should betray him; therefore said he, Ye are not all clean.

12 So after he had washed their feet, and had taken his garments, and was set down again, he said unto them, Know ye what I have done to you?

13 Ye call me Master and Lord: and ye say well; for so I am.

14 If I then, your Lord and Master, have washed your feet; ye also ought to wash one another's feet.

15 For I have given you an example, that ye should do as I have done to you.

16 Verily, verily, I say unto you, The servant is not greater than his lord; neither he that is sent greater than he that sent him.

GOLDEN TEXT: I have given you an example, that ye should do as I have done to you.—John 13:15.

Believing in Christ

Unit 2. John: The Great Love

(Lessons 5-8)

Lesson Aims

At the close of this lesson the students should:

1. Be able to name the occasion and to tell the circumstances of the washing of the disciples' feet by Jesus.
2. Be committed to the principle that the ultimate joy in life consists in serving, not in being served.

Lesson Outline

INTRODUCTION
- A. Others
- B. Lesson Background

I. JESUS' HUMBLE SERVICE (John 13:1-5)
- A. The Motivation—Love (v. 1)
  - *You Ask How Much I Love You . . .*
- B. The Circumstances (vv. 2, 3)
- C. The Washing of Feet (vv. 4, 5)

II. PETER'S INDIGNATION (John 13:6-11)
- A. Christ's Service Refused (vv. 6-8)
  - *By and By*
- B. An Embarrassed Acceptance (vv. 9-11)

III. JESUS' ACTION EXPLAINED (John 13:12-16)
- A. The Master's Position (vv. 12, 13)
- B. The Master's Example (vv. 14-16)
  - *Tell and Show*

CONCLUSION
- A. The Deadly Effect of Pride
- B. Christ Our Example
- C. Prayer
- D. Thought to Remember

Display visual 5 of the visuals packet and let it remain before the class. The visual is shown on page 269.

Introduction

A. Others

The teacher of the Intermediate Boys' Class at Sunday School was G. H. Crumpler. He is remembered for a number of things, one of which was his interest in the boys at all times. If one of them was ill, as soon as he learned of it he called by telephone and followed this with a visit, if circumstances warranted.

He is remembered also for his love for the church as the family of God. He delighted in the Scripture that tells us that "Christ also loved the church, and gave himself for it" (Ephesians 5:25). It was his desire that we all work together that we might have a church as Christ wanted it to be, "a glorious church, not having spot, or wrinkle, or any such thing" (Ephesians 5:27). And so he stressed brotherhood and the family spirit, with all sharing love for one another and helping one another.

This sense of togetherness was enhanced by two framed mottoes on the walls of the classroom. One of these said, *Shake hands with the other fellow.* The second, in spite of its brevity, was most impressive, bearing one simple word: *Others.* These mottoes reflected the spirit of the teacher, and somehow the boys in that class seemed to know that, and in their hearts they wanted to be like Mr. Crumpler.

It has been said that "we are all just as selfish as we dare to be." We think selfish thoughts and our first priority seems to be to "take care of number one"—ourselves. We want our share of things, our share of honors, our rightful place in society, or in the church, or in the home. If this is an accurate appraisal of our mood and spirit, then the Scripture that is ours for study today has a message for us!

B. Lesson Background

As a result of the raising of Lazarus, the nation's leaders met and formally decided to put Jesus to death. Not only so, but they began plotting how to do it (John 11:45-53). Jesus then left the immediate area of Jerusalem and went to a remote village named Ephraim, which many think was located about fourteen miles northeast of Jerusalem. There He remained in seclusion with His disciples (v. 54). A number of weeks passed, during which Jesus concluded His ministry in Perea, east of the Jordan, before once again making His way back to Bethany in preparation for the final Passover.

Jerusalem thronged with people, many of them pilgrims who had come to keep the Passover. When they learned that Jesus was in Bethany and that He was coming to the feast in Jerusalem, the crowds came out to meet Him. Jesus rode on a donkey, and the crowds of people that were with Him soon were joined by those coming out of the city. The people cut palm branches and laid them and their garments before Him. Singing and shouting, they welcomed Him as their king and ushered Him into the city. He entered the temple, surveyed the situation there, and then returned to Bethany to spend the night.

On Monday, He returned to the city and cleansed the temple for the second time, driving out those who were buying and selling there. On this day He also caused a fig tree to wither (Mark 11:12-19). On Tuesday He made His last visit to the temple, teaching many things in parables. This was also a day of discourse with and denunciation of the nation's leaders. When it had ended, these men met and plotted how they might kill him without arousing the public (Matthew 26:1-5).

Apparently, Jesus spent Wednesday in retirement at Bethany, while the rulers pursued their conspiracy against Him. On Thursday He sent two disciples into the city to make preparation for the Passover meal. Then in the evening he entered Jerusalem and went to the "large upper room" that had been prepared. At some point, perhaps before they began to eat the Passover meal, there was a dispute among the disciples as to who should be considered the greatest (Luke 22:24). That may have been the circumstance that led to the action of Jesus in today's lesson.

I. Jesus' Humble Service (John 13:1-5)

How important is one's position in life? For many, prestige, wealth, and acclaim seem to be the chief aim of existence, and the major portion of their energy is spent in their quest for these. They would say, "Assert yourself, dominate, let people know who is boss." Even the disciples of Jesus seemed not to have been free from such a spirit. Jesus, however, taught them an entirely different outlook regarding the seeking of honors. Instead of "assert yourself" as proof of your position, He would say "exert yourself" to improve the position of those around you.

A. The Motivation—Love (v. 1)

The opening verse is introductory to all that Jesus said and did during this last evening with His disciples. His every action and word were motivated by love.

1. Now before the feast of the passover, when Jesus knew that his hour was come that he should depart out of this world unto the Father, having loved his own which were in the world, he loved them unto the end.

In view of the emphasis upon the love of Jesus in this verse, we would explain it as follows. As Jesus came to this farewell meeting with His disciples, even before the meal had begun, He was conscious of the fact that He himself, the Passover Lamb of God, was facing a sacrificial death. Even in an hour so filled with distress for himself, His thoughts and concerns were for others, for His little band of followers who would be left without Him. He had loved them from the first —even Judas!—with an abiding love. Now, John records, *he loved them unto the end.* This could mean that He loved them until He was taken away and crucified. Or it could mean "to the utmost." He had always loved them, but now He would demonstrate that love to the utmost.

YOU ASK HOW MUCH I LOVE YOU . . .

For centuries, poets and lyricists have been measuring the dimensions of love. Browning said, ". . .let me count the ways." Songs say, "Love is a many-splendored thing," and, "Love makes the world go 'round."

Romantic love has been celebrated in thousands of poems, songs, novels, films, and paintings. It possesses the power to inspire not only art and rhymes, but adoration and surrender.

As powerful as romantic love is, *agape* love is superior. This divine love seeks the highest good for its object. It is totally unselfish. As Jesus demonstrated in today's text, His kind of love is humble and serving. After He washed His friends' feet, He went to Calvary to show them "the full extent of His love" (v. 1, *New International Version*). *Agape* is self-effacing and sacrificial.

We don't need to wonder if, or how much, God loves us. He revealed "his love for us in this: While we were still sinners, Christ died for us" (Romans 5:8, *New International Version*).

—R. W. B.

B. The Circumstances (vv. 2, 3)

2. And supper being ended, the devil having now put into the heart of Judas Iscariot, Simon's son, to betray him.

Supper being ended. Literally, "supper taking place," or "during supper."

Judas Iscariot was present with Jesus, even though he had already agreed upon the sum of thirty pieces of silver as payment for delivering Jesus into the hands of His enemies (Matthew 26:14-16). And Jesus knew this!

The devil . . . put into the heart of Judas . . . to betray him. "The devil made me do it." Do we ever say that? The truth is, he may tempt us, as he tempted Jesus (Matthew 4:1-11), but the devil has no power to *make* us do anything. James advises us to "resist the devil, and he will flee from you" (James 4:7). The covetous heart of Judas and his peevish nature were an invitation to the devil to enter and take over. Though Judas

How to Say It

ISCARIOT. Iss-*care*-e-ut.

would betray Jesus, still Jesus would wash his feet along with the others. But this service that Jesus was about to perform is remarkable for a greater reason.

3. Jesus knowing that the Father had given all things into his hands, and that he was come from God, and went to God.

In New Testament times, sandals were the common footwear. Because the roads were dusty, one could not walk far without having dirty feet. Consequently, when guests arrived at a home, it was a common courtesy of the host to arrange for the washing of their feet. Although the host himself would not do it, he would generally see to it that was performed. It was a menial task, one performed by a servant. In the upper room, however, there was no servant. One of the disciples, therefore, should have performed the task. Some—perhaps all—may have thought about it. But for any to volunteer might be considered an admission of inferiority. So no one did. The leader of the group, therefore, prepared to render the neglected service.

Who was this who was about to perform the menial service of washing feet? It was He into whose hands God had given all things, He who had come from God and who would return to take His place by the right hand of God! And Jesus, all the time, was conscious of this.

C. The Washing of Feet (vv. 4, 5)

The failure of the twelve to attend to the matter at hand may have been an oversight. More likely, it was pride that kept them from responding to the need. No one of them would demean himself or compromise his dignity by performing such lowly service. Jesus would teach them that *service to others is never demeaning*, even to the Son of God!

4, 5. He riseth from supper, and laid aside his garments; and took a towel, and girded himself. After that he poureth water into a basin, and began to wash the disciples' feet, and to wipe them with the towel wherewith he was girded.

He riseth from supper. The meal was served on a low, u-shaped table, and those who ate reclined on cushions or couches, with their feet away from the table. The disciples had already taken their places. As Jesus arose, we may be sure that they had not the faintest idea of what He was about to do. They had been concerned about *greatness* (Luke 22:24), perhaps in connection with the order in which they would recline around the table. Jesus—without saying a word—would give them a lesson on *true greatness!*

Laying aside the outer, flowing robe, which was the usual attire, Jesus became a servant to all. The sandals of all would have been removed, exposing their dusty feet, when they entered the room. *He poureth water into a basin.* Water from the basin was then applied by hand to the feet of each, which were then wiped by the towel.

II. Peter's Indignation (John 13:6-11)

We can only wonder what may have been the thoughts of eleven of the disciples as they watched Jesus. Perhaps they were ashamed. We are not left to wonder about what Peter thought, however. Here was Jesus, their Lord, performing the task of a menial servant. To Peter, it was intolerable.

A. Christ's Service Refused (vv. 6-8)

6. Then cometh he to Simon Peter: and Peter saith unto him, Lord, dost thou wash my feet?

By the time Jesus got to Peter, the latter had made up his mind. He would not let the Master suffer this indignity any longer. His question, *Lord, dost thou wash my feet?* was more shocked protest than question. The pronouns are emphatic, both of them. "*You*, Lord, are going to wash *my* feet? Never! That is preposterous!" Peter didn't say this, but the nature of his remark implied it.

7. Jesus answered and said unto him, What I do thou knowest not now; but thou shalt know hereafter.

"You, Peter, and the rest, have been arguing about who will be the greatest, and by greatest you mean, according to this world's measure of greatness. In that frame of mind you cannot begin to comprehend what I am doing." *But thou shalt know hereafter.* Jesus would soon explain His actions (vv. 12-16). They, and we, must understand that greatness in the eyes of God is not to be conceived in terms of how much control we may gain over others, but by how one may meet the needs of others. The disciples would not fully understand this truth until after Jesus gave himself on the cross for the sins of the world and was raised again by the power of God.

By and By

"Why you doin' that?" says a three-year-old.

"If I told you, you wouldn't understand."

"Why?"

"Because you haven't gone to school yet. You haven't had enough experience yet."

"Why?"

"You don't know the words I would have to use to explain it to you."

"Why?"

"Look, by and by you'll be old enough to understand what I'm doing. Right now you can help me by moving your foot off that drop cord!"

Youngsters can be exasperating with all their questions. They can't begin to understand everything adults say and do. So, we sometimes have to tell them to wait patiently until they have learned how to learn.

When Peter balked at His Master's washing his feet, Jesus patiently promised, as to a child, "Later you will understand."

Our carnal minds often have difficulty grasping spiritual truths. We must be content to wait for greater insights, "for we'll understand it better by and by." —R. W. B.

8. Peter saith unto him, Thou shalt never wash my feet. Jesus answered him, If I wash thee not, thou hast no part with me.

Ah, Peter! So devoted to the Master. The rest might suffer Jesus the indignity of washing their feet, but not Peter. Never! He was indeed devoted to the Lord, but his was an uninformed devotion. He really would fight to the death on behalf of the Christ—but for the Christ of his own imagination. Like so many whose image of God is one of their own making, Peter's image of Christ was what Peter thought the Christ ought to be, and the Christ he would follow did not go around washing feet!

Peter was thinking only of what was happening at the moment, but Jesus had the entire scope of His humiliation and sacrificial death for the sins of mankind in mind. He was saying, "Peter, unless you accept me as I am and receive the cleansing that I alone can give, you will have no share in the fruits of my redemptive work."

B. An Embarrassed Acceptance (vv. 9-11)

9. Simon Peter saith unto him, Lord, not my feet only, but also my hands and my head.

Impetuously, in keeping with his nature, Peter overreacted. He desired to meet any requirement for continued fellowship with the Lord. If Jesus insisted on washing his feet, so be it. He was more than willing—*not my feet only, but also my hands and my head.* He had not yet caught the significance of what Jesus was doing.

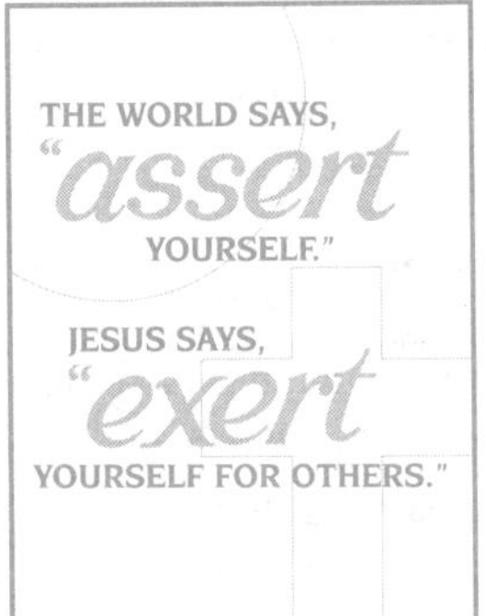

visual 5

10, 11. Jesus saith to him, He that is washed needeth not save to wash his feet, but is clean every whit: and ye are clean, but not all. For he knew who should betray him; therefore said he, Ye are not all clean.

On the surface this has reference to the practice of bathing entirely before coming to a banquet. When one had taken a bath, only his feet needed cleansing when he arrived at the place where the meal would be eaten in order to be wholly acceptable. Deeper than this surface meaning, of course, is the thought of spiritual cleansing. Sins are washed away when one turns to God in sincere faith, repentance, and baptism (Acts 2:38; 22:16), so that repetition of this act is unnecessary. For the removal of the stain of sins committed afterward, the apostolic injunction found in Acts 8:22 would apply.

Ye are clean, but not all. By these words, Jesus revealed that He knew one was present in the room who was not cleansed as the other eleven were.

III. Jesus' Action Explained (John 13:12-16)

Jesus taught that "there is more happiness in giving than in receiving" (Acts 20:35, *Today's English Version*). But do we believe it? He teaches that the way to true greatness is the way of service (Matthew 23:11). This is not the way of the world. There, people like to lord themselves over others (Matthew 20:25). Their pride causes them to seek positions of preeminence. But the way of Jesus is just the opposite; it is the way of humble service, and anyone who would follow Him in truth must learn this lesson.

Jesus was just one day away from crucifixion. Soon He would depart this earth, leaving His disciples to proclaim the good news of the kingdom of God. He knew that it was essential that they understand and commit themselves to the way of glory through service.

A. The Master's Position (vv. 12, 13)

12, 13. So after he had washed their feet, and had taken his garments, and was set down again, he said unto them, Know ye what I have done to you? Ye call me Master and Lord: and ye say well; for so I am.

Ye call me Master and Lord . . . so I am. This was no boast, but a simple statement of fact. He was the Son of God. The Father had put all things into His hand. But instead of coming among us to be served, He came to serve the whole world.

B. The Master's Example (vv. 14-16)

14, 15. If I then, your Lord and Master, have washed your feet; ye also ought to wash one another's feet. For I have given you an example, that ye should do as I have done to you.

No one anymore can say it is beneath his dignity to wash the feet of others! To do so would be to put one's self above the Master, for He did not hesitate to do this.

I have given you an example—an example of humble service. As long as there were dusty feet in Palestine, there was a need for this washing. But as long as the world shall stand, there is the need for the followers of Jesus to follow His example of humble service.

16. Verily, verily, I say unto you, The servant is not greater than his lord; neither he that is sent greater than he that sent him.

With this solemn pronouncement, Jesus concluded the discussion. He, the Master, had given His disciples the example of humble service. It would be totally inappropriate and unacceptable, therefore, for any disciple to claim that performing lowly service for others is beneath his or her dignity. Such pride has no place in the life of one who would follow Jesus.

Tell and Show

The statistics vary from one educator to the next, but to underscore the value of audio/visual/activity aids in teaching, they quote percentages like these: Students remember 13% of what they *hear;* 50% of what they *see:*; 78% of what they *see* and *hear;* and 90% of what they *see, hear* and *do.*

More than once Jesus had told His disciples that humility was an essential of discipleship (see Matthew 18:4; 20:26, 27). Repetition likely raised their comprehension and retention of the idea. But could anything have impressed the concept of humility upon their hearts more than Jesus' demonstration of it in the upper room? Who among His closest followers would ever forget the experience of having his feet washed by the Son of God?

Here is the best example of the Lord's tell-and-show method of teaching. Though we weren't there, we too learn the lesson of humility more forcefully by our vicarious identification with the scene. And all of us will learn the value of humility best of all when we serve each other and our hurting world. —R. W. B.

Home Daily Bible Readings

Monday, Mar. 29—Jesus Is Anointed (John 12:1-6)

Tuesday, Mar. 30—The King Is Coming (John 12:12-19)

Wednesday, Mar. 31—Jesus Predicts His Death (John 12:23-36)

Thursday, Apr. 1—Jesus Washes the Disciples' Feet (John 13:1-11)

Friday, Apr. 2—The Servant Role (John 13:12-17)

Saturday, Apr. 3—Jesus Predicts His Betrayal (John 13:18-30)

Sunday, Apr. 4—Bear Witness to Christ (John 15:18-27)

Conclusion

A. The Deadly Effect of Pride

Pride is an expression of selfishness. It is a "me first" attitude that prompts all kinds of spiteful and vicious behavior. And it is self-defeating. Pride causes one to speak and act in ways such as these: "I don't get the recognition that is due me, so I refuse to participate." "The solo part that I should have had was given to another, so I won't sing anymore." "I was given an insignificant place on the program, so they can have it. I'm through!" Poor souls, how we are abused! But wait! Let us turn again to that upper room and see Jesus, girt with a towel, kneeling and washing the feet of His disciples. Then hear Him say, "the servant is not greater than his Lord!"

B. Christ Our Example

In forbidding Jesus to wash his feet, Peter thought he was honoring his Lord, sparing Him this indignity. In fact, he was denying the very principle that brought Jesus to earth, for He "came not to be ministered unto, but to minister, and to give his life a ransom for many" (Mark 10:45). His death for our sins was the supreme example; the washing of feet was an application of the principle to everyday living.

To help us follow His example, let the word *Others* be stamped on our right hand with invisible ink. We may be sure our Lord will take note. And maybe it will remind us that the way of Jesus is through service to others.

C. Prayer

Impress upon our hearts, O God, the truth that the more we serve others, the more like our Master we become. In His blessed name, amen.

D. Thought to Remember

If you know these things, Oh the joy that comes when you do them. (See John 13:17.)

Learning by Doing

This page contains an alternate lesson plan emphasizing learning activities. Classes desiring such student involvement will find these suggestions helpful.

Learning Goals

After this session has been completed, the students will:

1. Be able to give in a few words a Biblical definition of the servant attitude.
2. Render more unselfish service with their family and friends.

Into the Lesson

Before class, locate some "glitzy" magazines. You may want to go through them and remove anything that might be inappropriate for use in a Sunday-school class.

Begin by giving each student a magazine. Ask them to tear out one or two pictures that they think portray selfishness, worldly position, or worldly power. Allow no more than three or four minutes for this. Collect the pictures and hold them for use later in the lesson.

Into the Word

Establish the background for today's study by putting the following calendar on the chalkboard or on poster paper on the wall.

SUNDAY: Triumphal entry into Jerusalem
MONDAY: Cleansing of temple
TUESDAY: Teaching in the temple
WEDNESDAY: Return to Bethany
THURSDAY: Passover meal
FRIDAY: Crucifixion
SATURDAY: Jesus in the tomb
SUNDAY: The resurrection

Comment briefly on the events of the days leading up to Thursday of this week (see "Lesson Background").

Now have a student, whom you have asked ahead of time, read aloud the Bible text for this lesson. After the reading, point out that the event we are studying in this lesson occurred at a time of intense emotion and confused feelings and attitudes. The Passover was in progress, Jesus' popularity was at an all-time high, but hatred of Jesus by His enemies was also high. Ask the class to speculate as to the thoughts and attitudes of the following people in the upper room that night:

1. Jesus (tired, afraid, wanting to teach disciples more),
2. Judas (Impatient, cautious),
3. Peter (proud, self-centered, desirous of Jesus' blessings),
4. Other disciples (proud, self-centered, embarrassed about Peter).

After the class speculates, lecture briefly on the Scripture text. Refer to comments under verse 3 to explain the practice of foot-washing. Emphasize Jesus' willingness to perform this menial task, and His command that His disciples do likewise. Then ask the class to suggest activities in our culture that might compare with it. For example: polishing someone's shoes, carrying luggage for someone.

Now refer to the pictures that the students tore out of the magazines earlier. As you hold each one up, ask, "How does this relate to the attitude Jesus demonstrated in today's text?"

Read aloud the following agree/disagree statements, and discuss each one briefly.

1. It's possible to be rich and famous and still be a humble servant.
2. The president of an institution should sweep his own office floors and wash his own windows in order to show his servant's attitude.
3. All janitors are humble people.
4. It's always wrong to seek honor and glory. (Read Romans 2:6, 7.)
5. Someone who truly serves others will likely become rich and famous.
6. The way we go about achieving success is more important than success itself.
7. Small, private acts of service can be more significant than great public acts of service.
8. People often serve others for selfish reasons.

Try to get class members to validate their opinions by the Scriptures whenever possible.

Into Life

Reproduce the following evaluation chart on a handout to give to class members at this time. Ask them to rate themselves in each area or activity of life. Close the session by challenging each to greater service for others.

My Level of Servanthood

AREA	LOW	MEDIUM	HIGH
Family			
Job			
Church			
Driving			
Shopping			

Let's Talk It Over

The questions on this page are designed to encourage review of the lesson Scriptures and to promote discussion of the lesson by the class. The answers provided are only discussion starters. Let your class talk it over from there.

1. Apparently Judas Iscariot was among those whose feet Jesus washed. What does this suggest regarding the extent of our service?

It brings to mind the counsel Paul gave in Romans 12:20: "Therefore if thine enemy hunger, feed him; if he thirst, give him drink: for in so doing thou shalt heap coals of fire on his head." We are to render Christian service to our enemies, to the undeserving, and to the unlovely. Such people may be in the church or outside of it. They may be neighbors, people we work with, or even our relatives. Our service to them may not be appreciated, but we must still attempt to minister the love of Christ to them. Judas seems to have been unmoved by Jesus' humble service, but we can hope that the ones we serve will become ashamed of their harshness toward our service and will be led to return our love. And we can further hope that our service will draw them to the Lord who has inspired us to serve them.

2. In Palestine during Bible times, foot-washing was one aspect of extending hospitality to houseguests. What may be some present-day counterparts in the church? How important is it that all members participate in these?

Parallels may be seen in the practice of welcoming visitors into the church building. We may merely give them a smile, a friendly handshake, and, if they are newcomers, direct them to their proper classroom or to a pew. Or we may welcome them by assisting them in hanging up overcoats, introducing them to members of their age group, showing them where restrooms are, etc. In some cases it may be necessary to assist elderly persons in climbing steps or to provide an umbrella escort service from the parking lot when it is raining. Every member should be ready to go out of his or her way to extend such humble hospitality to make visitors feel welcome in God's house.

3. Sometimes humility dictates that we must accept someone else's efforts to minister to us. Why is this an important consideration?

Peter's resistance to Jesus' washing of his feet has many parallels in today's church. To refer back to one item in the previous answer, there may be some elderly persons who refuse assistance in climbing steps because they insist on "doing it by myself." As a result they may endanger themselves and deprive another of the opportunity to serve them. Another example of such reluctance to accept service is the family that experiences a financial reversal and is too embarrassed to accept help with food, clothing, utility payments, etc. from the church. We need to remember that while Jesus came to minister, He also graciously accepted the ministry of others to Him. Two women who anointed Jesus' feet on two different occasions are examples. (See Luke 7:36-50; John 12:1-8.)

4. How is there "joy in serving Jesus"?

To receive a word of sincere gratitude from someone we have served is a heartwarming experience. A person to whom we have ministered may become a Christian partly through our efforts, or a fellow believer may draw closer to the Lord, and that can fill us with an indescribable satisfaction. One of the richest rewards, however, is the fellowship we have with Jesus Christ through serving in His name. He healed the sick, and while we may not have healing power, we can still feel that we are working with Him when we visit hospitals and nursing homes. He comforted the bereaved and while we may not be able to raise the dead, we can serve in harmony with Him by offering our compassion and concern to saddened families in funeral homes.

5. What are some examples of how pride can hinder members from serving in the church?

Pride can lead some to refuse any kind of service that does not involve a goodly measure of authority and prominence. Consequently, some of the "little" tasks in the church may go undone. Pride can make a person hypersensitive to criticism so that one is inclined to give up his or her job at the first hint of dissatisfaction on the part of another member. On the other hand, a person because of pride may require a great deal of praise for his or her work. If praise is not received, such a person may decide to quit working. Pride may produce an unhealthy attitude of competitiveness. Not all competitiveness need be unhealthy, but when it leads to jealousy, bickering, and a determination to "show up" someone else, it can wreak havoc in the church.

I Have Seen the Lord

April 11
Lesson 6

LESSON SCRIPTURE: John 20:1-18.

PRINTED TEXT: John 20:1-16.

DEVOTIONAL READING: John 20:19-23.

John 20:1-16

1 The first day of the week cometh Mary Magdalene early, when it was yet dark, unto the sepulchre, and seeth the stone taken away from the sepulchre.

2 Then she runneth, and cometh to Simon Peter, and to the other disciple, whom Jesus loved, and saith unto them, They have taken away the Lord out of the sepulchre, and we know not where they have laid him.

3 Peter therefore went forth, and that other disciple, and came to the sepulchre.

4 So they ran both together: and the other disciple did outrun Peter, and came first to the sepulchre.

5 And he stooping down, and looking in, saw the linen clothes lying; yet went he not in.

6 Then cometh Simon Peter following him, and went into the sepulchre, and seeth the linen clothes lie,

7 And the napkin, that was about his head, not lying with the linen clothes, but wrapped together in a place by itself.

8 Then went in also that other disciple, which came first to the sepulchre, and he saw, and believed.

9 For as yet they knew not the Scripture, that he must rise again from the dead.

10 Then the disciples went away again unto their own home.

11 But Mary stood without at the sepulchre weeping: and as she wept, she stooped down, and looked into the sepulchre,

12 And seeth two angels in white sitting, the one at the head, and the other at the feet, where the body of Jesus had lain.

13 And they say unto her, Woman, why weepest thou? She saith unto them, Because they have taken away my Lord, and I know not where they have laid him.

14 And when she had thus said, she turned herself back, and saw Jesus standing, and knew not that it was Jesus.

15 Jesus saith unto her, Woman, why weepest thou? whom seekest thou? She, supposing him to be the gardener, saith unto him, Sir, if thou have borne him hence, tell me where thou hast laid him, and I will take him away.

16 Jesus saith unto her, Mary. She turned herself, and saith unto him, Rabboni; which is to say, Master.

GOLDEN TEXT: Mary Magdalene came and told the disciples that she had seen the Lord.—John 20:18.

Believing in Christ

Unit 2. John: The Great Love

(Lessons 5-8)

Lesson Aims

This study should enable the students to:

1. Relate the experience of Peter and John and Mary Magdalene at the open tomb.
2. Explain what caused both John and Mary to believe that Jesus was risen.
3. Live with a deeper consciousness of the presence of the living Christ in their lives.

Lesson Outline

INTRODUCTION
- A. Love's Triumph
- B. Lesson Background

I. MARY'S ALARMING DISCOVERY (John 20:1, 2)

II. PETER AND JOHN AT THE TOMB (John 20:3-10)
- A. John, First to Arrive, Hesitant (vv. 3-5)
- B. Peter, Impetuous, Unhesitating (vv. 6, 7)
- C. John, the First Believer (vv. 8-10)
  Magic and Miracles

III. CHRIST APPEARS TO MARY (John 20:11-16)
- A. Angels at the Tomb (vv. 11-13)
  The Confiscated Christ
- B. Jesus the Lord Unrecognized (vv. 14, 15)
- C. Recognition and Confession (v. 16)

CONCLUSION
- A. The Result
- B. Prayer
- C. Thought to Remember

Display visual 6 of the visuals packet throughout this session. The visual is shown on page 276.

Introduction

A. Love's Triumph

"The Great Love" is the title of the second unit of lessons in this quarter of study. It is the purpose of these lessons to give insight into the nature of the One who came to earth as God's envoy. In view of the sinfulness of man, God might have sent an avenging angel to execute judgment on the earth. Instead, because "God is love" (1 John 4:8), and because He so loved the world, "he gave his only begotten Son, that whosoever believeth in him should not perish, but have everlasting life" (John 3:16).

In last week's lesson, the love of Christ was demonstrated in His washing of the disciples' feet. Jesus did not hesitate to give himself to this humble task. Presently, however, He would demonstrate the magnitude of His love by giving himself on the cross, a sacrifice on behalf of sinful man. Our lesson today deals with the resurrection of Jesus. This may be said to be love's triumph, for in this our Lord gained the victory, victory over sin and over death, victory for every one who has fallen under the curse of sin—every one, that is, who will receive Him as Lord and Savior (John 1:12).

B. Lesson Background

To gain the widest possible knowledge of the events related to the crucifixion of Jesus, one must study the record of each of the four Gospel writers. We will mention only a few of the circumstances as a background for our study today.

The crucifixion took place on Friday. Since the Sabbath would begin at sundown, the Jews desired a hasty removal of the three bodies from the crosses in order that the Sabbath not be desecrated. John tells of the breaking of the legs of the robbers, and the piercing of the side of Jesus (19:31-37).

Joseph of Arimathea asked Pilate for the body of Jesus and, with the help of Nicodemus, hastily prepared it for burial. It was then placed in Joseph's own tomb, which was near the place of the crucifixion (Matthew 27:57-60; John 19:38-42). Mary Magdalene and Mary the mother of James (sometimes called "the other Mary") stayed for a while at the tomb that evening (Matthew 27:61).

Saturday was the Sabbath, a day of rest. For those who were waiting to complete the preparation of the body of Jesus for final burial, it must have been a long day. But finally, as Sunday morning began to dawn, a number of women hastened toward the tomb with spices to perform this last act of devotion. Mark 16:1 mentions Mary Magdalene, Mary the mother of James, and Salome. John did not mention these other women. By the time he wrote, the synoptic accounts had already been written and were widely known. John, therefore, felt no need to mention all the details included in the other Gospels. He was concerned only with the role played by Mary Magdalene.

I. Mary's Alarming Discovery (John 20:1, 2)

The sight of the empty tomb filled Mary with distress. She came with the other women to render one last act of devotion to the Lord. But now it seemed that even that last bit of comfort would be denied to them.

1. The first day of the week cometh Mary Magdalene early, when it was yet dark, unto the sepulchre, and seeth the stone taken away from the sepulchre.

The women started out for the tomb while it was still dark, and they arrived there just as the sun was rising on the first day of the week (Mark 16:2). As they made their way, their chief concern was how they were going to remove the stone that had been rolled across the mouth of the sepulchre. When they arrived, however, they were amazed to see that the stone already had been taken away. Matthew tells us that the angel of the Lord had descended from Heaven and had rolled back the stone from the door (Matthew 28:2). Since John is concentrating on Mary Magdalene, he does not include these details in his account. He simply reports that Mary found the tomb open.

2. Then she runneth, and cometh to Simon Peter, and to the other disciple, whom Jesus loved, and saith unto them, They have taken away the Lord out of the sepulchre, and we know not where they have laid him.

Then she runneth. It appears that just as soon as Mary saw that the stone had been moved from the entrance, she ran to tell Peter and *the other disciple, whom Jesus loved* (that is, John). The other women, however, stayed at the tomb and entered it. Mary was not present, then, when the angel declared to the women that Christ was risen (Mark 16:5-7). And the women would have been gone before Peter and John arrived at the tomb (Mark 16:8).

They have taken away the Lord. Why would Mary say this? What would you have said? Suppose you should visit a cemetery to be at the graveside of one whom you hold dear, only to find an open grave and an empty casket? Would you not conclude that someone had taken the body? So did Mary. Until that time, the footprints of all humankind had led into the grave. There were none coming out.

Some suggest that the idea of the resurrection began in the mind of this highly emotional woman and was then taken up by others after her. Upon seeing the empty tomb, however, Mary came to no such conclusion. She could only suppose that the body had been taken, and this is what she said to the disciples. She had seen Jesus die and had seen that body sealed in a tomb (Matthew 27:55-61). The idea of resurrection would never have occurred to her—until she had seen the risen Lord and heard Him call her name (John 20:16). Not until then would she even consider a resurrection possible. After that, for her it would be undeniable. But when first reporting to the disciples, she knew only deep distress.

How to Say It

ARIMATHEA. Air-uh-muh-*thee*-uh (*th* as in *thin*).
MAGDALENE. *Mag*-duh-leen or Mag-duh-*lee*-nee.
RABBONI. Rab-*bo*-nye.
SALOME. Suh-*lo*-me.

We know not. Here is evidence that other women had been with Mary that morning in the garden, even though John makes no reference to them by name.

II. Peter and John at the Tomb (John 20:3-10)

In the account of what follows, note the circumstantial details: The persons involved—Peter and that "other disciple." They did not walk, they "ran both together." But the other outran Peter. He looked in the tomb but did not enter. Peter barged right in. He saw the graveclothes just so. Then the other entered, saw, and believed. This sounds like the account of an eyewitness, doesn't it? Of course it does, for it is. This is evidence in the record itself, "internal evidence," as to its authenticity.

A. John, First to Arrive, Hesitant (vv. 3-5)

3, 4. Peter therefore went forth, and that other disciple, and came to the sepulchre. So they ran both together: and the other disciple did outrun Peter, and came first to the sepulchre.

That other disciple. This undoubtedly was John, who identified himself only as the disciple "whom Jesus loved" (v. 2). John was one of the younger apostles, perhaps the youngest. This could account for his outrunning Peter and getting to the tomb first.

5. And he stooping down, and looking in, saw the linen clothes lying; yet went he not in.

Why didn't John enter the tomb? Was it out of respect for the dead? Did he consider this to be holy ground? Or did he first wish to collect his thoughts? Whatever the cause, he looked inside the tomb but did not enter.

B. Peter, Impetuous, Unhesitating (vv. 6, 7)

6, 7. Then cometh Simon Peter following him, and went into the sepulchre, and seeth the linen clothes lie, and the napkin, that was about his head, not lying with the linen clothes, but wrapped together in a place by itself.

There was no hesitancy with Peter. Arriving at the tomb, he *went into the sepulchre.* There, lying orderly before him, were the linen bandages that had been wrapped around Jesus' body. And nearby, the napkin that had been about His head lay neatly folded. Peter must have thought it strange that these were lying neatly and not tossed in a pile, as they surely would have been had a grave robber unwound them from the body. Or, if a body snatcher were involved, why would he have discarded the graveclothes at all? Peter may have wondered at this, but for the moment it did not occur to him that the empty tomb could not be due to grave robbers.

C. John, the First Believer (vv. 8-10)

8. Then went in also that other disciple, which came first to the sepulchre, and he saw, and believed.

Of all persons of all ages who have believed that Jesus is the Christ, our risen Lord and Savior, apparently John was the first. In reporting this event, however, he was in no way boasting; he didn't even give his name. Simply, and as a matter of fact, he stated that the *other disciple* entered the tomb, *and he saw, and believed,* as if to say, "Could it have possibly been otherwise?"

Note the basis of his faith. He saw and believed. His faith was based on evidence. He had known Jesus firsthand, had heard His words, experienced His love, witnessed His miracles. Now he stood at the spot where, the night before, the body of Jesus, taken from the cross, had lain.

The graveclothes were there, but they enveloped no body. The tomb was empty. Empty, in spite of the imperial seal that had sealed it, in spite of the Roman soldiers that had guarded it! (See Matthew 27:62-66.)

But now it was empty. Suddenly the truth broke upon John's consciousness like a flash. "Of course the tomb is empty; no tomb could hold the body of the Son of God!" All of the facts that John knew about Jesus pointed in this direction, and now he understood why.

Thank God, and thank John, that evidence has been preserved for us, committed to writing by the apostle, written, as he himself says, that we may believe "that Jesus is the Christ, the Son of God; and that believing [we] might have life through his name" (John 20:31). John would not live forever on earth, but the written word would live; and that word is adequate to produce faith in the heart of the one who will receive it. Jesus himself inferred as much. In His prayer for His disciples, He included a prayer for us also! Hear His words: "Neither pray I for these alone, but for them also which shall believe on me through their word" (John 17:20).

We need no special revelation from God in order to believe in His Son. A special revelation was what the rich man in Hades desired for his brothers back on earth, so they might be spared his torment. He wanted Lazarus to be sent back from death to warn them. But Father Abraham said to him, "If they hear not Moses and the prophets [God's Old Testament Scriptures], neither will they be persuaded, though one rose from the dead" (Luke 16:31). If one will not hear John and the other New Testament writers, what kind of miracle or what Heavenly vision is going to be convincing?

This is not to slight the work of the Holy Spirit. John himself wrote that the Spirit "will convict the world of sin, and of righteousness, and of judgment" (John 16:8, *New King James Version*). But such conviction comes when the Spirit-inspired word is preached. Jesus tells us, "It is the Spirit who gives life," and then adds: "the words that I speak to you are spirit, and they are life" (John 6:63, *New King James Version*). And so they are, John would say, to all who believe and obey.

MAGIC AND MIRACLES

I have seen David Copperfield make a huge jetliner disappear. I have seen him also vaporize the Statue of Liberty. When I saw his magic, I believed. That is, I believed that Copperfield is a master illusionist. I *do not* believe that the airplane and the statue actually vanished. I am a believer in his skills as a magician, not that what seemed to happen actually took place. He fooled me, and I am fascinated by his ability to play tricks on my eyes. I have been amused and entertained by his magical illusions.

No one was playing tricks on John's eyes. "He saw" the empty tomb and the graveclothes, "and believed." Knowing the rest of the story, we can legitimately conclude that John believed in the resurrection of Christ. Later, he was arrested (with Peter) for "proclaiming in Jesus the resurrection of the dead" (Acts 4:2, *New International Version*).

Just as I can recognize a skillful work of magic, John knew a miracle when he saw one. He had seen five thousand men fed with a boy's

visual 6

lunch. He had seen a blind man given his sight. He had seen Lazarus raised from the dead. He had seen and believed. The empty tomb was no illusion. John knew that, once again, he was witnessing a miracle. His faith in Jesus as "the resurrection and the life" was confirmed. —R. W. B.

9. For as yet they knew not the Scripture, that he must rise again from the dead.

Some think that the disciples of Jesus were easily misled into thinking that He arose from the dead because they were eagerly awaiting it, expecting it to occur. Nothing could have been further from the truth. The disciples thought that He was the Messiah, that He would lead them in throwing off the yoke of Roman subjugation, and when He was crucified, their hopes were dashed (see Luke 24:17-21). These disciples were familiar with the Old Testament Scriptures, but even so, *as yet they knew not the Scripture, that he must rise again from the dead.* Scriptures such as Psalms 16:10, 11; 110:1, 4; and Isaiah 53:11, 12 referred to Christ's resurrection, but as yet these disciples had not understood that. Thus they did not immediately interpret the event that they were witnessing as fulfilling Old Testament prophecies. It was only as Jesus spoke with them later that they began to understand what the Scriptures had predicted concerning Jesus' suffering, death, and resurrection (Luke 24:25-27, 45-47).

10. Then the disciples went away again unto their own home.

That is, each went to his place of abode. Disciples from Galilee and elsewhere would likely have stayed in the homes of friends in the city.

III. Christ Appears to Mary (John 20:11-16)

We do not know if Mary, for some reason, delayed her return to the tomb. But after Peter and John left, Mary returned to the tomb. She found herself alone there, or so she thought.

A. Angels at the Tomb (vv. 11-13)

11, 12. But Mary stood without at the sepulchre weeping: and as she wept, she stooped down, and looked into the sepulchre, and seeth two angels in white sitting, the one at the head, and the other at the feet, where the body of Jesus had lain.

In Mark 16:9 we read, "Now when Jesus was risen early the first day of the week, he appeared first to Mary Magdalene." The women who had come to the tomb with Mary early that morning had tarried while she ran to find Peter and John. They were told by an angel to go and tell the disciples that Jesus was risen. Then they departed. In the meantime, Peter and John had come to the tomb, and now they were gone. Mary, now alone with her grief, looked inside the tomb and saw two angels.

13. And they say unto her, Woman, why weepest thou? She saith unto them, Because they have taken away my Lord, and I know not where they have laid him.

Woman, why weepest thou? Why didn't the angels tell Mary that Jesus was risen as they had told the other women? Why ask her this question? Because she had no cause for weeping, for even now her Lord was there—not in the tomb where she had hoped to find His pierced body, but outside the tomb, standing behind her as she looked within.

THE CONFISCATED CHRIST

Almost daily reports tell of new violations of Christians' rights to express their faith. No-prayers-in-school is just the tip of the iceberg, it seems. Students are not allowed to participate in free-time Bible studies on school property; teachers must not even carry a Bible or keep one on their desks. *Creation* cannot be taught in public schoolrooms, not even as an alternate theory with *evolution.* Baccalaureate services for graduates are being dropped, or replaced with "award ceremonies" or something else equally innocuous. Nativity scenes on public property are outlawed in many communities, and carols and crosses, as well. Like Mary in the garden, we cry, "They have taken away my Lord."

The forces of evil may "have taken away [our] Lord," but we know where He is. He is risen! And we can still testify to His resurrection by our pursuit of holiness and by defending our faith with bold witness. —R. W. B.

B. Jesus the Lord Unrecognized (vv. 14, 15)

14. And when she had thus said, she turned herself back, and saw Jesus standing, and knew not that it was Jesus.

Perhaps her tear-dimmed eyes kept Mary from recognizing Jesus, but in reality no explanation is necessary. Until now, in her mind, Jesus was dead. She had seen Him die! This person behind her had to be somebody else!

15. Jesus saith unto her, Woman, why weepest thou? whom seekest thou? She, supposing him to be the gardener, saith unto him, Sir, if thou have borne him hence, tell me where thou hast laid him, and I will take him away.

Since, in her mind, Jesus was dead, she supposed that the one speaking to her must be the *gardener,* or caretaker. There are others who suppose many things about Christ, even that He is so loving that He will overlook our sins. Christ will forgive us our sins if we repent and follow Him. But He says quite clearly, "Except ye repent, ye shall all likewise perish" (Luke 13:3). Whatever curious or odd things people may suppose about Jesus, this does not alter who He really is, the risen Savior, the Son of God. How many will never know the salvation He brings and the life He gives because they fail to recognize Him!

C. Recognition and Confession (v. 16)

16. Jesus saith unto her, Mary. She turned herself, and saith unto him, Rabboni; which is to say, Master.

Once Jesus had spoken her name, the special sound of that familiar voice was unmistakable and brought instant recognition. *Mary!* What joy must have filled her soul! *She turned herself.* Like Mary, many whose hearts are burdened with grief keep their eyes on the tomb and give way to despair. But she turned herself, and there beside her stood the Lord. And the despair gave way to unspeakable joy.

Then Mary responded, *Rabboni.* This Aramaic term is equal to the Hebrew *Rabbi,* meaning *Teacher,* and embodies both devotion and respect, such as "honored and beloved Teacher." With this one word Mary confessed that she recognized the Lord. Henceforth, to share the joy of the resurrection faith with all who would come after her, she could say, "I have seen the Lord." And this made all the difference in the world in her life.

Conclusion

A. The Result

For Mary, the effect of her experience was immediate. Tears for the dead gave way to rejoicing; the Savior lived. Sorrow gave way to joy. Is this not precisely the kind of change that knowledge of the resurrection would bring?

For those who heard Mary's claim, the result was *disbelief* until they too had seen the Lord. Then the change that came in their lives was almost unbelievable. The fear that had caused them to hide after the death of Christ gave way to a boldness that took them to the temple itself to proclaim salvation through the risen Christ. They would be beaten, imprisoned, forbidden to preach in His name. But that would not silence them. Galilaean bumpkins would become eloquent as they spoke of a living Jesus.

The results in the world were just as amazing. Christ's resurrection was first preached just seven weeks after it occurred (Acts 2). And to whom? To those who had cried out, "Crucify him!" "You did this," Peter said, "but God has raised Him up." Why didn't the enemies of Jesus bring forth His dead body and squelch this rumor for all time? They could not. The tomb was still empty! In deep sorrow and fear, the multitudes were cut to the heart, Peter tells us (Acts 2:37). And when they were told what to do to receive forgiveness for their sins, three thousand responded.

With this most unlikely group as charter members, the church began. And *this* is the church? Oh, the mercy of God and the power of God, that Christ should begin with the very ones who had brought about His death!

The results of faith in the risen Lord are just as amazing today. There are still those who are concerned about sin and God's forgiveness, those who mourn whose sorrow is turned to hope and gladness, those who are dead in their inner being who receive new life. Could all of this—the change in Mary's life, in the lives of the apostles, in the three thousand, and in the lives of thousands today—possibly have resulted if that which Mary believed to be true was a lie?

The tomb of Jesus is still empty. How did it happen? One's eternal destiny depends upon how he or she answers that question.

B. Prayer

Lord, we rejoice this day in the glorious reality of the resurrection. May our remembrance that we serve a living Savior make every day a day of victory and a time of celebration and joy. In the Savior's name we pray. Amen.

C. Thought to Remember

We were not there, so we cannot say with Mary, "I have seen the Lord." But we can say, "I believe that Jesus is the Christ, the Son of God." And we can have new life in His name.

Home Daily Bible Readings

Monday, Apr. 5—Jesus Sentenced (John 19:1-16)
Tuesday, Apr. 6—The Via Dolorosa (John 19:17-21)
Wednesday, Apr. 7—The Crucifixion (John 19:22-27)
Thursday, Apr. 8—Jesus' Death (John 19:28-37)
Friday, Apr. 9—The Empty Tomb (John 20:1-9)
Saturday, Apr. 10—Jesus Appears to Mary (John 20:10-18)
Sunday, Apr. 11—Jesus Appears to the Disciples (John 20:19-30)

Learning by Doing

This page contains an alternate lesson plan emphasizing learning activities. Classes desiring such student involvement will find these suggestions helpful.

Learning Goals

As a result of this lesson, students should:

1. Be able to retell the story of the discovery of the empty tomb.
2. Be able to explain what the resurrection means for their lives.

Into the Lesson

Ask your students to bow their heads as you read aloud the following story.

"It's five o'clock Sunday morning. You Ralph Jones, have tossed and turned all night, your mind spinning with memories of a troubled week. Your best friend, Gene Smith, passed away after a heart attack. You were at his side in the hospital when he died. Thoughts of the funeral roll through your mind. Old friends of his were there, and you were a pallbearer. After the service on Friday, you lingered awhile. The maintenance crew lowered the casket and filled the grave.

Unable to lie in bed any longer, you quietly dress and slip out of the house. As you arrive at the cemetery, the first rays of the sun are tinting the sky a bright lavender and pink. Memories of happy times with Gene flood your mind. Almost reluctantly you shuffle over to the place where you said your last goodbye. Then suddenly you stop cold. The gravesite has been disturbed! The marker has been tipped over, and someone has been digging. Then you spot it—the casket, lying open on its side.

"Graverobbers!" you wonder out loud. "Who would do something like this?"

A pickup truck is parked nearby, and a maintenance man is standing beside it. You run to him. "Excuse me, sir, but what's going on here? Have you moved a grave or what?"

The man smiles a familiar smile and says, "Ralph! Relax! It's me, your friend Gene. I'm alive and well!"

At this point ask the class to express how they might feel if this really happened to them. (Shock, bewilderment, etc.) Tell them that the disciples had some of the same kinds of reactions at the resurrection of Jesus.

Into the Word

Begin by having a contest called "a race to the tomb." Put two paper circles on the wall to represent "tombs." Divide the class into two groups and give the leader of each group seven paper "footprints." Name one group, "Simon Peter," and the other group, "John." Give each leader a list of the following questions and see which group can be first to answer all of them, *proving each answer with a verse reference from today's text.* Each answer puts a footprint on the wall in the race to the tomb.

1. Who was the first woman to arrive at the grave of Jesus, according to John? (Mary)
2. Who was the first man to arrive at the tomb of Christ? (John, "the other disciple")
3. Which disciple first entered the tomb? (Peter)
4. Which disciple first believed the resurrection had taken place? (John)
5. Where were the two angels in the tomb sitting? (One at the head, and one at the feet, where Jesus' body had lain)
6. What same three words did the angels and Jesus say to Mary? (Why weepest thou?)
7. When Mary at last recognized Jesus, what did she call Him? (Rabboni)

After the contest, read the text and explain it as necessary.

Next, consider the facts that lead us to believe that Jesus was raised from the dead. Some of them are listed below. Ask the class to prioritize the list and to tell which of these proofs means the most to them.

1. The fulfilled prophecies
2. The empty tomb and missing security guards
3. Appearances of angels
4. The testimony of eyewitnesses
5. The graveclothes
6. Jesus' resurrection appearances
7. The impact of the resurrection on history
8. The changed behavior of the disciples

Into Life

Divide the class into groups of four. Give each group a sheet on which is written the phrase "Because Jesus rose from the dead . . ." followed by these references: Romans 6:5, 11; Ephesians 1:18-23; Ephesians 2:5-7; Colossians 2:13; Colossians 3:1-4; 1 Peter 1:3-5. Each group is to complete the phrase with thoughts found in each of the passages. Allow the groups several minutes to do their work; then let the groups share their answers with the class. Close by having the students pray together in their groups.

Let's Talk It Over

The questions on this page are designed to encourage review of the lesson Scriptures and to promote discussion of the lesson by the class. The answers provided are only discussion starters. Let your class talk it over from there.

1. The Gospel accounts contain a number of variations in their descriptions of Jesus' resurrection appearances. Why should these be seen as a help, and not a hindrance, to our faith?

Among the variations are the listing of the women at the tomb, the number of angels who appeared to them, and the various appearances to some or all of the apostles. These demonstrate the independence of the four accounts. Rather than indicating contradictions, these variations can be arranged so as to show that they are complementary. Each writer emphasized those facts that fit in with his purpose in writing, and each thereby provided a part of the total picture. If the individual accounts seem a bit confusing, it may be that this was the Holy Spirit's way of giving us a feel for the glorious confusion of resurrection Sunday. Reports and rumors must have been circulating throughout that day until the disciples were made certain of the undeniable truth that Jesus had risen.

2. Unbelievers have suggested that the resurrection can be explained away on the basis of His followers' emotional reaction to Jesus' tragic death. How do Mary Magdalene's words and actions fit in with such a suggestion?

John's account certainly shows that Mary's emotions were stirred. But did they cause her to leap hysterically to the conclusion that Jesus had risen? No. To the contrary, she reported to Peter and John that some persons had removed Jesus' body. She returned to the tomb a little later, and her emotional state is indicated by the mention of her weeping (John 20:11). But her exchanges with the two angels and with Jesus himself show that she was not swept away in an emotional ecstasy of belief. She still held to the belief that some person had taken Jesus' body. She became convinced of Jesus' resurrection only when He clearly revealed himself to her.

3. Both Peter and John entered the empty tomb and saw the graveclothes. Whereas John quickly came to belief in Jesus' resurrection, Peter was slower in doing so (compare John 20:8 and Luke 24:12). What was the difference between these two men?

We cannot state with certainty why one of these two men believed immediately and the other did not. However, we do know of Peter's inclination to speak and act impetuously. Perhaps on this occasion his mind raced on in indignation toward those whom he thought had removed Jesus' body. The evidence of Jesus' resurrection was before him, but he did not take time to consider it. In the meantime, John must have pondered the manner in which the tomb had been opened, with the breaking of the Roman seal. He must have observed that the graveclothes appeared almost undisturbed, contrary to what one would have expected had graverobbers been involved. The same two options are open to people today: to fail to consider the evidence for Jesus' resurrection or to carefully weigh it.

4. How can we rate the quality of John's testimony, which he records in his writings?

John testified of "that which was from the beginning, which we have heard, which we have seen with our eyes, which we have looked upon, and our hands have handled, of the Word of life" (1 John 1:1). These words dispel any idea of John as a superstitious speculator or a wild-eyed dreamer. He used his full range of senses to confirm that what he wrote about Jesus was real. Both in regard to Jesus' death (John 19:35) and His resurrection (John 20:8), John put his reputation as an honest man and accurate observer on the line by boldly stating what he saw. Later, as the books of Acts and Revelation show, John put his very life on the line for the truths he and his fellow apostles taught. It is foolish, therefore, for anyone to think John's testimony may be lightly dismissed.

5. After Christ's resurrection, the apostles exhibited a powerful new boldness. Why was this significant, and what does it say to us?

The apostles' boldness was in itself a testimony to the reality of the resurrection. Even the hardened Jewish leaders were impressed with it (Acts 4:13). We also must be impressed as we contrast the fearful and shaken band of apostles after the crucifixion with the confident, courageous spokesmen for the gospel we read of in Acts. This raises the question, "Where is our boldness?" If we believe that Jesus Christ has risen, conquering sin and death, we also should possess confidence and courage in speaking out for Him.

To Love Is to Serve

April 18
Lesson 7

LESSON SCRIPTURE: John 21.

PRINTED TEXT: John 21:12-22.

DEVOTIONAL READING: John 21:1-14.

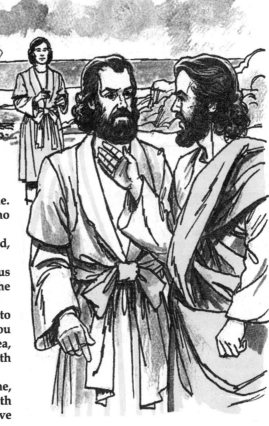

John 21:12-22

12 Jesus saith unto them, Come and dine.
And none of the disciples durst ask him, Who
art thou? knowing that it was the Lord.
13 Jesus then cometh, and taketh bread,
and giveth them, and fish likewise.
14 This is now the third time that Jesus
showed himself to his disciples, after that he
was risen from the dead.
15 So when they had dined, Jesus saith to
Simon Peter, Simon, son of Jona, lovest thou
me more than these? He saith unto him, Yea,
Lord; thou knowest that I love thee. He saith
unto him, Feed my lambs.
16 He saith to him again the second time,
Simon, son of Jona, lovest thou me? He saith
unto him, Yea, Lord; thou knowest that I love
thee. He saith unto him, Feed my sheep.
17 He saith unto him the third time,
Simon, son of Jona, lovest thou me? Peter
was grieved because he said unto him the
third time, Lovest thou me? And he said unto
him, Lord, thou knowest all things; thou
knowest that I love thee. Jesus saith unto
him, Feed my sheep.
18 Verily, verily, I say unto thee, When
thou wast young, thou girdedst thyself, and
walkedst whither thou wouldest: but when
thou shalt be old, thou shalt stretch forth thy
hands, and another shall gird thee, and carry
thee whither thou wouldest not.
19 This spake he, signifying by what death
he should glorify God. And when he had
spoken this, he saith unto him, Follow me.
20 Then Peter, turning about, seeth the disciple whom Jesus loved following; which
also leaned on his breast at supper, and said,
Lord, which is he that betrayeth thee?
21 Peter seeing him saith to Jesus, Lord,
and what shall this man do?
22 Jesus saith unto him, If I will that he
tarry till I come, what is that to thee? follow
thou me.

GOLDEN TEXT: Lovest thou me? . . . Feed my sheep.—John 21:17.

Believing in Christ

Unit 2. John: The Great Love

(Lessons 5-8)

Lesson Aims

The study of this lesson should enable the students to:

1. Relate the incident of Christ's post-resurrection appearance on the shore of the lake.
2. Explain what is meant to say that Christianity is a historical religion.
3. Resolve anew to show their love for Christ by serving the needs of others.

Lesson Outline

INTRODUCTION
- A. A Historical Religion
- B. Lesson Background

I. THE MASTER'S LOVING EXAMPLE (John 21:12-14)
- A. The Invitation (v. 12)
  Christian "M. O."
- B. The Service (v. 13)
- C. The Significance (v. 14)

II. PETER'S TEST AND HIS FUTURE (John 21:15-19a)
- A. A New Test of Peter's Love (vv. 15-17)
- B. Peter's Future (vv. 18, 19a)

III. PETER'S SECOND CHANCE (John 21:19b-22)
- A. Christ's Invitation (v. 19b)
- B. Peter's Decision (vv. 20-22)
  Minding Your Own Business

CONCLUSION
- A. Peter's Faithful Service
- B. Do We Love Jesus?
- C. Prayer
- D. Thought to Remember

Visual 7 of the visuals packet highlights the thought emphasized in verses 15-17 of the text. The visual is shown on page 285.

Introduction

A. A Historical Religion

Of the eleven or so major religions of the world, only Judeo-Christianity may be defined as a *historical* religion. By this is meant that it resulted from a series of definite historical events, occurring over a period of some two thousand years. They began with the experience of Abraham and culminated with Jesus Christ and His disciples. The summation of this development may be found in Hebrews 1:1, 2: "God, who at sundry times and in divers manners spake in time past unto the fathers by the prophets, hath in these last days spoken unto us by his Son."

Although there are some who raise questions about "the historical Jesus," it is a rare individual who would venture to say that Jesus never lived. At a definite place in time and history He appeared on this earth, and the world has never been the same since! He wrote no books, established no university, assembled no armies, explored no continent, conquered no territories. And when He died, at the age of thirty-three, His death was that of a common criminal. Yet today, around the earth, His followers number in the millions. People of all races honor Him as the living Savior. Our every calendar, marking the passing of the years, finds its reference point in the year of Jesus' birth.

How can we account for such an influence, stemming from such an apparently unlikely source? Quite simply. God promised His people Israel that through the family of David He would send One who would establish an everlasting kingdom, a kingdom of truth and righteousness. And God kept His promise. True, some were not pleased with God's choice. They could not visualize as acceptable a kingdom in which love was to be the ruling motive, and greatness was to be attained by serving others.

Yet, from among the common folk, there was a group who recognized Jesus as the promised Messiah. To any observer, they probably would be considered unlikely prospects for launching the kingdom of God on earth. Some might even describe them as "a rag-tag" group. But Jesus taught them, commissioned them, and promised to be with them until the end of the age. Today, all the world bears witness to the result. Our lesson is one small but significant event in the record telling us how it all came about.

B. Lesson Background

After the resurrection, Jesus made a number of appearances to His disciples. The first was to Mary Magdalene. On that same day, He appeared to other women, to Peter, to two in the countryside, and to the eleven in the upper room. All of this was in the vicinity of Jerusalem. In addition, Jesus gave instruction that He would meet the disciples also in Galilee. Anticipating this meeting, some of them went northward to wait.

Peter, always the impetuous one, saw no reason to sit idly by while awaiting Christ's coming, and so he said, "I go a fishing" (John 21:3). And the others joined him.

After a night of toil, however, they had caught nothing. As day was dawning and they were returning to shore, someone called out to them to cast their net one more time, on the right side of the boat. This they did and they had a great catch of fish. Immediately John said, "It is the Lord" (John 21:7). On hearing this, Peter jumped into the water and hastened to shore. There he found Jesus, with a fire of coals and with fish laid thereon, and bread. This would be a very significant meeting of Peter with his risen Lord.

I. The Master's Loving Example (John 21:12-14)

Jesus had taught His disciples to love one another, even to love their enemies. He had also taught them that, "whoever desires to become great among you, let him be your servant" (Matthew 20:26, *New King James Version*). Remember, the night before the crucifixion He had washed the feet of His disciples, demonstrating the love that expresses itself in serving others.

Now the crucifixion was past. Jesus was the risen Lord; He had shown himself to be the Son of God with power. Yet even now as He met with the disciples, He chose for himself the role of servant. Thus would He reinforce His lesson for them about the meaning of true love and of true greatness. The great Son of God served breakfast to the hungry disciples.

A. The Invitation (v. 12)

12. Jesus saith unto them, Come and dine. And none of the disciples durst ask him, Who art thou? knowing that it was the Lord.

Come and dine. The disciples had been toiling strenuously for hours during the night, and all would have been hungry. How like the Master to thoughtfully provide for those in need. Breakfast was ready and waiting, prepared by the Master's hand.

When Jesus had first appeared to the group of disciples in Jerusalem following His resurrection, they "were terrified and affrighted, and supposed that they had seen a spirit" (Luke 24:37). Not until He had shown them His wounded hands and feet and had eaten with them were they convinced that it was He (Luke 24:40-43). Now, after such evidence, none dared question who this was. It was unnecessary; they knew *that it was the Lord.*

CHRISTIAN "M. O."

Most police stories refer at least once to some criminal's "M. O." The *modus operandi* is a thief's or murderer's method of operation. Very often, the M. O. discerned in a crime is a clue that helps investigators identify suspects. Certain thieves always rob convenience stores—even specific chains of them. Serial killers can sometimes be identified by the weapon they use or by clues they leave at the scene of each crime—"trademarks" of a sort.

The disciples recognized Jesus in the semi-darkness of early morning, not so much by His appearance as by His behavior. Christ's M. O. was service. First, He brought their unsuccessful night of fishing to an end by directing them to a tremendous catch of fish. Then He provided and served breakfast to the disciples, who really should have been serving the Master. This seemed to be a postscript to the lesson Jesus taught them when He washed their feet: Greatness in the kingdom belongs to humble servants.

Jesus' life-style was service; that was His method of operation. Obviously, His followers likewise can be identified by the M. O. of servanthood. If you were arrested for being a Christian, would there be enough evidence to convict you? —R. W. B.

How to Say It

AGAPAO (Greek). ah-gah-*pah*-oh.
MAGDALENE. *Mag*-duh-leen or Mag-duh-*lee*-nee.
PHILEO (Greek). fil-*leh*-oh.

B. The Service (v. 13)

13. Jesus then cometh, and taketh bread, and giveth them, and fish likewise.

Jesus then cometh. This seems to suggest that the disciples hung back after Jesus invited them to come and dine. He, therefore, came to them, giving them of the bread and the fish, which He himself had provided. Just as He had washed the feet of each disciple, one after the other, now He served their food.

C. The Significance (v. 14)

14. This is now the third time that Jesus showed himself to his disciples, after that he was risen from the dead.

John is apparently referring to those appearances that Jesus made to the disciples as a group. The first was in the evening of resurrection Sunday, when the disciples were gathered behind closed doors "for fear of the Jews" (John 20:19). Thomas was not present on that occasion. A week later, the next Lord's Day evening, Jesus appeared again to the disciples, and this time Thomas was present (John 20:26). After this experience he too believed. Now this third appearance to the group served as further evidence of the resurrection. For Peter, however, who three times denied his Lord, it also provided an opportunity to learn that his commission to serve in the kingdom was still valid, if he would have it so.

II. Peter's Test and His Future (John 21:15-19a)

Jesus knew in advance the time of His death. He also knew what a traumatic effect His death would have on His disciples. When they left the upper room and came to the Mount of Olives, He said, "All ye shall be offended because of me this night" (Matthew 26:31). Literally, He said, "You will be caused to stumble because of me." The language is figurative, indicating what their reaction would be when they saw Him in chains, taken away by Roman soldiers.

On that occasion Peter vigorously declared that although all others might be "offended," he would never be. He would remain steadfast no matter what happened (v. 33). Yet before the night was over, he denied even that he knew Jesus (vv. 69-75). Now Jesus directed himself to salvaging what was left of Peter's vaunted courage and devotion.

A. A New Test of Peter's Love (vv. 15-17)

15. So when they had dined, Jesus saith to Simon Peter, Simon, son of Jona, lovest thou me more than these? He saith unto him, Yea, Lord; thou knowest that I love thee. He saith unto him, Feed my lambs.

Simon, son of Jona. Note that Jesus addresses Peter by his earlier name *Simon* and not by the name *Peter* that He himself had bestowed on him (Luke 6:14). *Peter* means "rock" or "stone," which Peter eventually would become. But not yet. He failed the test of his loyalty when Jesus was given His mock trial. He was not yet a rock.

Lovest thou me more than these? Did Jesus mean, "Do you love me more than you love these things—boats, nets, and other fishing gear?" Some think so. It seems more likely, however, that Jesus meant, "Do you love me more than these disciples standing here love me?" Peter had boasted that even if all the rest should forsake Jesus, he never would. Yet among the disciples, he is the only one in the record who publicly denied loyalty to the Master. Did Peter still place himself above his fellow-disciples?

Lovest thou me? The Greek word for love that Jesus used was *agapao,* which suggests an attitude of intelligent goodwill toward another, the willingness to do what is best for the one loved. It is interesting that the Lord did not ask, "Do you pledge your faithful loyalty?" Peter had done that before and had failed the test. But, "Do you love me?" There can be no stronger tie than the bond of love to keep one faithful to the Lord.

Thou knowest that I love thee. Peter responded by using the word *phileo,* which referred to a warm, personal attachment, such as one has for a dearest friend. The boastful note was gone from Peter's words. He could not erase the memory of his denial from the record. "But Lord," he would say, "you *know* that I love you, in spite of what I did. You know the affection I have for you." The love to which Peter referred was not of a lesser quality than the love of which Jesus spoke in His question, but it was love of a different kind. Both terms are used of God's love for man. In John 3:16, we read that God so loved (*agapao*) the world, that He gave His Son in response to the deep need of the world for salvation. And in John 16:27 when speaking to His disciples, Jesus said, "The Father himself loveth (*phileo*) you." He has warm affection for those who are dear to Him.

In the mind of Jesus, and in reality, there can be no true love that remains passive and unexpressed. Love is not an emotion; it is a way of life. It delights to serve. But, from a practical viewpoint, how can one who loves Christ serve *Him?* The Lord gave the answer in His words to Peter: *Feed my lambs.* How typical of Jesus that His thoughts were of others. He was concerned about those who would believe on Him through the word of the apostles (John 17:20). Many would be weak and immature, in need of spiritual food. Peter was to give them instruction, guidance, and encouragement. Always one may find ample opportunity to show his or her love for Jesus by ministering to the needs of others.

16. He saith to him again the second time, Simon, son of Jona, lovest thou me? He saith unto him, Yea, Lord; thou knowest that I love thee. He saith unto him, Feed my sheep.

Lovest thou me? Jesus again used the verb *agapao*—the love of intelligence and purpose. And again Peter answered using *phileo*—the love of deep affection. "Tend my sheep," Jesus replied. That is, be a shepherd to the flock of God, whether the old or the young.

17. He saith unto him the third time, Simon, son of Jona, lovest thou Me? Peter was grieved because he said unto him the third time, Lovest thou me? And he said unto him, Lord, thou knowest all things; thou knowest that I love thee. Jesus saith unto him, Feed my sheep.

Lovest thou me? This time Jesus used the term for *love* Peter had used. It was as if Jesus were saying, "All right, Peter, do you really have the warm, personal affection for me that you claim?"

Peter was grieved. Why? Was it because he felt that Jesus might doubt his love? Peter was aware that Jesus knew all things. How could Jesus not know the affection Peter had for Him? Once again, Jesus responded, *Feed my sheep.*

Why did Jesus ask Peter three times if he loved Him? Was it to remind Peter that he had denied his Lord three times. Perhaps so. But there is a less subtle explanation as well. The lesson that Jesus was teaching Peter was of such importance that the apostle must never forget it. And so, the repetition: To love is to serve; to love Christ is to serve Him; and to serve Him is to serve those who are His. Do you love the Lord? Jesus gives us the one, simple test by which we may answer the question truthfully, "Yes." *Feed my sheep.*

B. Peter's Future (vv. 18, 19a)

18, 19a. Verily, verily, I say unto thee, When thou wast young, thou girdest thyself, and walkedst whither thou wouldest: but when thou shalt be old, thou shalt stretch forth thy hands, and another shall gird thee, and carry thee whither thou wouldest not. This spake he, signifying by what death he should glorify God.

The words of verse 18, taken simply, could be said of almost any person experiencing the aging process. Young persons can put on their clothes in a flash and be ready to dash off in whatever direction they choose. The elderly may need some help, both in getting dressed and in having the steady hand of others for support.

In verse 19, however, John makes clear that these words of Jesus indicated in some way how Peter would meet his death. The stretching forth of the hands suggests his being bound—or crucified! *Another shall gird thee,* or, "a stranger will bind you fast" (*New English Bible*), and *carry thee whither thou wouldest not.* Contrary to the desire of his flesh, Peter would be taken to the place of execution.

Whether Peter understood this or not, Jesus made clear to him that the future held something ominous in his life. The way of Christ is not always a bed of roses. Fear for his own safety and welfare had led Peter to deny Jesus at the time of His crucifixion. Before he committed his life anew to the Master, he must understand that to follow Jesus might take him all the way to a cross himself. According to tradition, he *was* crucified. Unwilling to have anyone compare his crucifixion to Christ's, he asked to be crucified upside down.

visual 7

III. Peter's Second Chance (John 21:19b-22)

A. Christ's Invitation (v. 19b)

When Jesus foretold that Peter would deny Him, He also told Peter that He had prayed for him (Luke 22:32). Isn't that great? And he added, "When you come back, strengthen the brethren." The time for Peter to make that decision had come, and Jesus invited him to do so.

19b. And when he had spoken this, he saith unto him, Follow me.

The discussion about Peter's love for Jesus was ended. Three times he said, *I love thee.* It was enough. If Peter's faith in Christ was tempered with love, he was ready to rejoin the ranks of those who would serve Him; and so Christ invited, *Follow me.*

B. Peter's Decision (vv. 20-22)

Like so many of us, Peter had the tendency to consider his call to service in the light of what others might do. We may match the gift of others, but don't press me to give more. I will do my fair share of the calling, but what about Tom, Dick and Harry?

20, 21. Then Peter, turning about, seeth the disciple whom Jesus loved following; which also leaned on his breast at supper, and said, Lord, which is he that betrayeth thee? Peter seeing him saith to Jesus, Lord, and what shall this man do?

Peter was overly concerned about what John was going to do for the Lord. It may have been a legitimate interest, but it had absolutely nothing to do with his own response to the Master's call to service that had come to him. Jesus made this clear.

22. Jesus saith unto him, If I will that he tarry till I come, what is that to thee? follow thou me.

Regardless of what Christ's will for others may be, each person must obey what he or she knows the Lord has asked of him or her.

MINDING YOUR OWN BUSINESS

The late Clovis Chappell once published a sermon for young people entitled, "If I Were You, I'd Mind My Own Business." The thrust of the message, of course, was that Christians

Home Daily Bible Readings

Monday, Apr. 12—Jesus Appears Again (John 21:1-8)
Tuesday, Apr. 13—Jesus Dines With the Disciples (John 21:9-14)
Wednesday, Apr. 14—Jesus Challenges Peter (John 21:15-19)
Thursday, Apr. 15—Who Will Remain (John 21:20-25)
Friday, Apr. 16—Wait for the Spirit (Acts 1:1-5)
Saturday, Apr. 17—Jesus Is Lifted Up (Acts 1:6-11)
Sunday, Apr. 18—Judas Is Replaced (Acts 1:12-16, 21-26)

should concentrate, without distractions or petty preoccupations, upon our God-given purpose, the supreme task of our lives.

Peter had difficulty, it seems, minding his own business. He loved Jesus and had pledged his loyalty no less than three times during one meal, but his concentration was distracted by a preoccupation with comparisons of his own commission with that of others. The Lord rebuked him, "Don't concern yourself with the opportunities, privileges, and successes of others. Focus your thoughts, energies, and talents upon the task that I have given *you*. Concentrate on following me, no matter what others do."

How about you? Do others seem to labor in "greener pastures" ? Are others experiencing greater success and receiving greater rewards? Christ wants you to focus upon your own gifts and ministries. To follow Him faithfully, we must keep our eyes upon Him. We must mind our own business. —R. W. B.

Conclusion

A. Peter's Faithful Service

A familiar Scripture states that "pride goeth before destruction, and a haughty spirit before a fall" (Proverbs 16:18). Another reminds us that "when pride cometh, then cometh shame" (11:2). Both of these Scriptures find verification in the experience of Peter. Professing proudly that he would not be like others, who might abandon Jesus in difficult times, Peter renounced the Lord altogether when physical danger threatened.

So Peter abandoned Jesus in the Lord's hour of greatest need. But the Lord did not abandon Peter. As we have seen, He prayed for Peter and called him once again to be His follower. First, however, He made clear that Peter's relationship to the Lord was firmly founded in love and not on some fancied privilege of rank or position. This was His call to Peter, and the commission was to demonstrate that love in service.

We know from the Biblical record, brief though it may be, that Peter responded to the call and accepted the commission to become a shepherd of the flock of God. Years later, he would write to the elders of the churches of Asia Minor, urging them to be shepherds of God's flock. And for the young men he would advise humility. "God opposes the proud," he would say. "Humble yourselves, therefore, under God's mighty hand, that he may lift you up in due time" (1 Peter 5:2-6, *New International Version*). Peter should know. He had known the pride that can cast down. He learned humility that could serve the Lord with the utmost dignity. And he knew the love in his heart for Jesus that could find fulfillment only in loving service for his Lord.

B. Do We Love Jesus?

We sing, "Oh, how I love Jesus" and "I love Him because He first loved me." But do we? How is Jesus to know that we love Him? Just by hearing us sing the songs? No, He will know it only when He sees us actively engaged in the work of His kingdom. Christ had a mission to perform in this world—to bring life and immortality to light through the gospel. Now His mission of love and mercy has become our mission, if we are truly children of God. Hear His challenge once again directed to us: "Do you love me? Feed my sheep." That is what Jesus would say to all who want to follow Him. He does not ask, "Are you qualified to serve? Do you have the proper educational background?" But, *Do you love me?* He knows that only love will make us willing—yes, and eager—to follow Him, not only in word but in deed. It is a weak faith and a weak commitment that pleads inability to render service in the Lord's kingdom. *Love will find a way.* So Christ's question-"Lovest thou me?"—remains crucial to each of us; so too does His challenge, "Tend my sheep."

C. Prayer

Lord, by Your mercy You have given us new life through Jesus, Your Son. Forgive us our past failures, we pray. This day may our love for Christ our Savior find expression in some definite service that we render to others in His name. We pray in His name. Amen.

D. Thought to Remember

To love the Lord is to serve Him, and to serve Him is to serve others.

Learning by Doing

This page contains an alternate lesson plan emphasizing learning activities. Classes desiring such student involvement will find these suggestions helpful.

Learning Goals

As a result of participating in this class session, the students:

1. Will express their determination to be loyal to Christ.
2. Will select one way in which they will try to reach someone for Christ this week.

Into the Lesson

Describe to the class your favorite breakfast; then ask them the following questions. Keep this discussion light, fun, and brief.

1. What's your favorite breakfast?
2. Does your mate ever serve you breakfast in bed? How does it make you feel?
3. Do any of you ever have fish for breakfast?

Point out that today's lesson is about a fisherman, Simon Peter, who failed his Lord but was given another chance. Have the class turn to John 21.

Into the Word

Using the material included in the lesson background section, give a brief lecture to set the stage for this lesson. Note especially that this was the third time Jesus had appeared to the group of disciples (see under verse 14). Ask the class members to read the text aloud, taking turns.

During the week before class, write the following questions (including the numbers) on paper "fish." Put them in a bucket or pan and let students draw out a fish. Have the student who drew question 1 read it aloud, and ask the class to answer the question. Do the same for all nine questions.

Fish Questions

1. How is serving someone a meal a really good expression of love and service? (It is personal, takes sacrifice, money, etc.)
2. Much of our business today is conducted over meals. Why, and how can we use this principle in church work?
3. Why do you suppose Jesus waited until after breakfast to quiz Simon Peter?
4. Why do you think Jesus grilled Simon in front of all the other disciples? (He had boasted in front of all of them, for one thing.)
5. Why do you suppose Jesus asked Peter three times about his love? (Peter had denied Jesus three times; or maybe Jesus was just forcing Peter to think hard.)
6. Although Simon Peter had publicly denied Jesus three times, he did indeed love Him. How is it that we too may love Christ and yet deny Him?
7. Jesus told Peter, "Feed my sheep." What did He mean? How should we today do it?
8. Peter expressed concern about John's discipleship (v. 21). Jesus told Peter to mind his own business. Why is it that we sometimes are more concerned about others' commitments than about our own? Why is this dangerous?
9. How may we be encouraged by Simon's rehabilitation?

Allow about twenty minutes for this discussion, then put the following points on the board. Ask the class to vote on which they think are the three most important points in today's text.

Lessons From John 21

1. We can recover from bad failures.
2. Love is best shown by service to people.
3. It is folly to be more concerned about others' commitments to Christ than our own.
4. We need to be loyal to Christ under fire.
5. We should not make rash commitments.
6. God's forgiveness is bigger than we can ever imagine.
7. We serve Christ when we tend His sheep.

Ask the class to tell why they made the selections they did.

Into Life

Put the following words and phrases on the board or on poster board: *bait, hooks, boat, net, stringer, lures, sonar, fish line, patience, dock, guide, tacklebox, life vest, fishing license, game warden, lake, river.*

Point out that Christian service is a kind of fishing for men's souls. Ask the class to draw some analogies between fishing for fish and fishing for men, using the items listed on the poster as a trigger for their thoughts.

Here are some ideas to get them started:

1. Use good bait. (Teach the Word of God.)
2. Keep your equipment clean. (Live a godly life.)
3. Go where the fish are. (Get out into the world.)
4. Keep your line in the water. (Patience.)
5. Set the hook. (Ask people for decisions.)

Close with prayer, thanking God that He is patient and forgiving and doesn't lock us out of serving Him because of our past failures.

Let's Talk It Over

The questions on this page are designed to encourage review of the lesson Scriptures and to promote discussion of the lesson by the class. The answers provided are only discussion starters. Let your class talk it over from there.

1. Before the crucifixion Peter had boasted that he was, in effect, a better disciple than the others. Do we ever think that we are better Christians than others? What is the danger of this?

Paul spoke of some believers who "measuring themselves by themselves, and comparing themselves among themselves, are not wise" (2 Corinthians 10:12). It is easy to become complacent when we favorably compare ourselves with weak or worldly believers. But even if we are stronger spiritually than they are, we may still be far short of what God wants us to be. Seeing ourselves as better than others may tempt us to move closer to what we perceive their level of spirituality to be. We may reason that if they can engage in certain worldly habits, we should be able to also; if they can "coast along" as Christians without making any sacrifices, why should we make those sacrifices?

2. Jesus' commands to Peter to "feed my lambs" or "feed my sheep" may seem applicable only to ministers and elders. But how are they applicable to all Christians?

The mention of lambs may remind us of the vast responsibility we have of teaching the Word of God to children. Jesus can be seen here as speaking to Christian parents, teachers in Sunday schools and vacation Bible schools, and Christians who work in children's homes and day-care centers. Of course, "lambs" could refer to newborn Christians, and certainly all veteran members of the church should be concerned that babes in Christ be taught and nurtured. But whether working with children or adults, with experienced believers or with new converts to the faith, every Christian should look for opportunities to strengthen other Christians in their faith.

3. Should we be more careful to warn those who are considering becoming Christians that they may face many struggles and pressures because of their faith? Why or why not?

In trying to win the lost to Christ, we may feel that we should stress only the positive aspects of becoming a Christian. Perhaps we assume that new converts will learn gradually that the Christian life has its difficulties, and that they will learn to adjust to them. Is it possible though, that some of those who have drifted away from Christ and His church have done so because they were not prepared for the peculiar trials Christians face? In Luke 14:25-33 Jesus described how vital it is for those who would follow Him to count the cost. If we urge prospective converts to do this, we may see some of them shy away from becoming Christians. But we may see others becoming stronger, more steadfast Christians because they are forewarned.

4. Peter was concerned about what John was going to do. How are Christians hindered in their work for the Lord by excessive concern for what other Christians are or are not doing?

The example of other Christians should encourage us to do more for Christ. To stir up the Corinthians to generosity on behalf of the Christians in Judea, Paul pointed to the example of the churches of Macedonia (2 Corinthians 8:1-5). As we learn of churches and individuals who are having exceptional success in evangelism or missions support or stewardship, it should stimulate us to do greater work in these areas. Often, however, we look at what others are doing, complain that we do not have the talents or resources they have, and then fail to use what we do have. Or we look at what others are not doing, and we use their inactivity as an excuse for our own lack of effort.

5. A glorious truth that we learn from Peter's experience is that the Lord is willing to restore to His service those who have denied Him.

The sexual misconduct of some church leaders in recent times has damaged the Lord's cause and may properly be called a denial of Him. Some of those leaders have been restored through humble penitence before the Lord and public acknowledgement of their sin, with a request for forgiveness on the part of those they have injured. Christians can also deny Christ by using profane, ungodly language, by becoming enslaved to drugs or alcohol, or by being consumed by greed. But restoration is available through sincere repentance and an honest effort to undo the effects their denial has had on other persons.

The Bread of Life

April 25
Lesson 8

LESSON SCRIPTURE: John 6.

PRINTED TEXT: John 6:35-51.

DEVOTIONAL READING: John 6:22-29.

John 6:35-51

35 And Jesus said unto them, I am the bread of life: he that cometh to me shall never hunger; and he that believeth on me shall never thirst.

36 But I said unto you, That ye also have seen me, and believe not.

37 All that the Father giveth me shall come to me; and him that cometh to me I will in no wise cast out.

38 For I came down from heaven, not to do mine own will, but the will of him that sent me.

39 And this is the Father's will which hath sent me, that of all which he hath given me I should lose nothing, but should raise it up again at the last day.

40 And this is the will of him that sent me, that every one which seeth the Son, and believeth on him, may have everlasting life: and I will raise him up at the last day.

41 The Jews then murmured at him, because he said, I am the bread which came down from heaven.

42 And they said, Is not this Jesus, the son of Joseph, whose father and mother we know? how is it then that he saith, I came down from heaven?

43 Jesus therefore answered and said unto them, Murmur not among yourselves.

44 No man can come to me, except the Father which hath sent me draw him: and I will raise him up at the last day.

45 It is written in the prophets, And they shall be all taught of God. Every man therefore that hath heard, and hath learned of the Father, cometh unto me.

46 Not that any man hath seen the Father, save he which is of God, he hath seen the Father.

47 Verily, verily, I say unto you, He that believeth on me hath everlasting life.

48 I am that bread of life.

49 Your fathers did eat manna in the wilderness, and are dead.

50 This is the bread which cometh down from heaven, that a man may eat thereof, and not die.

51 I am the living bread which came down from heaven: if any man eat of this bread, he shall live for ever: and the bread that I will give is my flesh, which I will give for the life of the world.

GOLDEN TEXT: I am the living bread which came down from heaven: if any man eat of this bread, he shall live for ever: and the bread that I will give is my flesh, which I will give for the life of the world.—John 6:51.

Believing in Christ

Unit 2. John: The Great Love

(Lessons 5-8)

Lesson Aims

When this lesson has been completed, the students should:

1. Have an understanding of the concept of Jesus as the bread of life.
2. Be able to state what God's will is for humankind.
3. Be motivated to seek daily for spiritual strength through Christ Jesus.

Lesson Outline

INTRODUCTION
- A. Friendly Neighbors
- B. Lesson Background

I. JESUS, THE BREAD OF LIFE (John 6:35, 36)
- A. Satisfying Soul Hunger (v. 35)
  - *Bread or Truth?*
- B. Seeing Is Not Believing (v. 36)

II. THE FATHER'S WILL (John 6:37-40)
- A. Sure Reception (vv. 37, 38)
- B. See, Believe, and Live (vv. 39, 40)

III. MURMURINGS OF UNBELIEF (John 6:41-46)
- A. The Incarnation Questioned (vv. 41, 42)
- B. Hear, Learn, Come (vv. 43-46)

IV. A PROMISE OF LIFE ETERNAL (John 6:47-51)
- A. Believe in Christ and Live (v. 47)
- B. Manna and the Bread of Life (vv. 48-50)
  - *Bread in the Desert*
- C. Christ, the Living Bread (v. 51)

CONCLUSION
- A. Eat and Live
- B. Prayer
- C. Thought to Remember

Display visual 8 of the visuals packet and refer to it as you deem appropriate. The visual is shown on page 293.

Introduction

A. Friendly Neighbors

Apparently many people today do not have any neighbors. They may live in a two-block area that houses a thousand or more persons, or in a residential area of nice homes where everyone "minds his own business." But many seem not to have the time nor the inclination to cultivate contacts with those about them.

Many of the older ones among us can remember when it was different. The people who lived up and down our block were neighbors. The celebration of an anniversary often became a community affair. Summer evenings might see many gathered in the park, sharing homemade ice cream and angel food cakes. At other times, aspiring young musicians might gather in one home or another, with proud parents in an adjoining room to visit and to listen.

Of all the circumstances that drew us together, however, it was in times when someone was having difficulty that the genuine concern of the neighbors was revealed. If one had overburdening medical bills, the neighbors responded, some with sacrifice. When a death occurred, the neighbors would show their love by providing food for the stricken family. This, they knew, could not heal the grief. But it said, better than words, "We care." It was the response of loving hearts to the needs of a friend.

I am sure the food was appreciated, but it could not restore the dead. God's power is required for that. How wonderful it is, then, that God himself, our divine Neighbor, showed His concern about our need in the face of death. In love He responded by sending His Son. To be our Savior? Yes. Our shepherd? Yes. The light of the world? Yes. And as we see in today's lesson, Jesus came to us as the bread of life. God's promise is that he who partakes of this bread shall live forever.

B. Lesson Background

The feeding of the five thousand occurred near the northeastern shore of the Sea of Galilee. On that occasion, in view of the great miracle involved, some said, "This is of a truth that Prophet that should come into the world" (John 6:14). They would, if they could, make Him their king. Realizing their intentions, Jesus withdrew into a mountain by himself (John 6:1-15).

That night, as the disciples were returning by boat to the west shore of the lake, Jesus came to them walking on the water. The next day, many of those who had been fed by Jesus the day before came by boat to Capernaum and found Jesus there (vv. 16-24). He rebuked them mildly, saying that they followed Him only because they hoped He would fill their stomachs. He told them not to labor for food that perishes, but to labor for the food that endures unto everlasting life (v. 27). This is food that the Father gives, this is bread from Heaven that gives life to the world. "Then said they unto him, Lord, evermore give us this bread" (John 6:34). At this point Jesus gave His discourse on the bread of life in the synagogue there.

I. Jesus, the Bread of Life (John 6:35, 36)

The followers of Jesus will share of their substance with the needy. But barns full of grain cannot guarantee a life that is worth living nor be of any value when the body has breathed its last. Thus, Jesus addressed the concerns of the soul.

A. Satisfying Soul Hunger (v. 35)

35. And Jesus said unto them, I am the bread of life: he that cometh to me shall never hunger; and he that believeth on me shall never thirst.

The bread of life. What bread is to the body, Jesus is to the soul of man. Without food, these bodies of ours are doomed to weakness, helplessness, and death. Without Christ, there is spiritual weakness, paralysis, and death.

All things that breathe may be said to exist, whether it be a human being or the ox in the field. But God desires for human beings more than mere existence, more than the life of an ox. He wants us to have abundant life here and eternal life hereafter. For this reason God sent Jesus, "the true bread from heaven" (John 6:32). Wholesome food can satisfy the hunger of the body, enabling it to function. The soul's hunger can be satisfied only in Christ.

He that cometh to me . . . he that believeth on me. The parallel construction indicates that the two thoughts are equal. What Jesus means by coming to Him includes believing in Him, and believing in Him includes coming to Him. Belief that brings one to full commitment to Jesus is what satisfies the hunger of the soul.

He . . . shall never hunger . . . never thirst. Jesus was speaking of the needs of the human soul, spiritual needs. Some may deny any such need. "Thank you," they may say, "but we are getting along very well without God. We haven't experienced any spiritual hunger." At the moment they may feel that way, but theirs is a life without hope (Ephesians 2:12) and without the peace that passes understanding (Philippians 4:7), which come through Christ. And when they do finally come to think of the *bottom line* of their existence, theirs will be a spirit bound by the awareness of its own limitations, restless in its own uncertainties, and despairing of any certain knowledge of truth. Jesus alone can supply the soul's every need.

Home Daily Bible Readings

Monday, Apr. 19—Feeding the Five Thousand (John 6:1-14)
Tuesday, Apr. 20—Jesus Calms the Storm (John 6:15-21)
Wednesday, Apr. 21—Doing the Works of God (John 6:22-29)
Thursday, Apr. 22—The Bread From Heaven (John 6:30-40)
Friday, Apr. 23—Jesus, the Source of Life (John 6:41-50)
Saturday, Apr. 24—Spirit and Life (John 6:51-65)
Sunday, Apr. 25—The Holy One of God (John 6:66-71)

BREAD OR TRUTH?

My father-in-law helped prepare Easter breakfast at his church for several consecutive years. I remember hearing him complain about "Easter Christians" and "freeloaders" who would show up only for that annual feed, sometimes without even attending the sunrise worship service. I suspect that most congregations include a few inactive members who consistently appear at the "eatin' meetin's." Such folk are not unlike the crowd who followed Jesus to Capernaum because He had fed them bread and fish the day before. Jesus rebuked them for their superficial discipleship.

Humans who hunger for bread will always outnumber those who hunger for truth. On foreign fields, the former are sometimes called "rice Christians." They "convert" to Christianity because (and only as long as) the missionary feeds them. Fortunately, not all indigenous believers are so shallow. And discerning evangelists on foreign soil are careful to distribute *truth* proportionately with *bread.*

Christ's bread metaphor was difficult for carnal hearers to comprehend. But believers grasped by faith the spiritual truth that Jesus satisfies the deepest hungers of the soul. His spirit fills our own until living is abundant and everlasting. Bread and bodies don't last; truth and life are forever. —R. W. B.

B. Seeing Is Not Believing (v. 36)

36. But I said unto you, That ye also have seen me, and believe not.

In matters of faith, some people are like the man who was so set in his opposition to certain foods that he would say, "Even if it was good, I wouldn't like it." Unreasonable? Yes, but this is the way it is when one's prejudices rule one's thinking. These people had been fed at the hands of Jesus. Yet some of them failed altogether to comprehend the significance of the miracle they had seen. "What great power," they thought.

How to Say It

CAPERNAUM. Kuh-*per*-nay-um.

"This man ought to be our king, for with such power, think what He could do to our enemies!"

In light of Jesus' miracles and what He had already said to them (vv. 27-33), they should have understood that He was the Son of God, come from Heaven. But their eyes were closed to any such thought. Here was the evidence before them, as plain as day. They had seen Jesus do these mighty things, but they believed not.

II. The Father's Will (John 6:37-40)

Jesus made remarkable claims. God was His Father, He said, and He himself was the bread of life. And He would impart everlasting life to all whom the Father gave Him. This was God's will.

A. Sure Reception (vv. 37, 38)

37. All that the Father giveth me shall come to me; and him that cometh to me I will in no wise cast out.

All that the Father giveth me. This is not to say that the Father is selective in regard to who shall be saved and who lost, except that the saved will be those who respond to Christ in faith. Observe that this verse says, *him that cometh to me.* We must decide whether or not to respond to Christ's invitation. Those who come to Jesus are given to Him by the Father, and Jesus will never turn any such away.

38. For I came down from heaven, not to do mine own will, but the will of him that sent me.

I came down from heaven. If Jesus were only a man, this statement is preposterous, as those who would reject Him would note (vv. 41, 42). In this case, Jesus was either suffering great delusions or He was a great deceiver. But the life and teachings of Jesus do not reflect delusion and certainly are not the life and teachings of a deceiver. Acknowledging that He did come from Heaven, one can comprehend His remarkable life and deeds. Otherwise, how does one account for them?

Furthermore, the quality of life that is experienced by those who follow Him is evidence that the source of that life is with God. "Do you expect to go to Heaven when you die?" someone asked a devoted follower of Jesus. "Go to Heaven?" he responded. "Why, man, I live there!" Many without Christ can testify to their experience of Hell on earth. Many who have accepted Christ as Savior and Lord can testify to the joy they have experienced in the fellowship of Christ and of His people, a little bit of Heaven here and now and a foretaste of eternity.

The will of him that sent me. Jesus elaborates on the Father's will in the verses that follow.

B. See, Believe, and Live (vv. 39, 40)

39. And this is the Father's will which hath sent me, that of all which he hath given me I should lose nothing, but should raise it up again at the last day.

This is the Father's will. In Revelation 4:11 it is stated that all things were created and have their being by the will of God (*New International Version*). Otherwise, in the New Testament the term, *the will of God,* is used of His purpose to bless humankind through Christ or of what God wishes to be done by us who are in Christ. Both point to our salvation in Him. How very important, therefore, salvation must be to our God.

Peter states that God is "not willing that any should perish, but that all should come to repentance" (2 Peter 3:9). Elsewhere we read, "As I live, saith the Lord God, I have no pleasure in the death of the wicked; but that the wicked turn from his way and live: turn ye, turn ye from your evil ways; for why will ye die, O house of Israel" (Ezekiel 33:11).

40. And this is the will of him that sent me, that every one which seeth the Son, and believeth on him, may have everlasting life: and I will raise him up at the last day.

John's record of events in the life of Jesus is given in order that we may "see" *the Son,* and thus seeing Him will believe and have life (John 20:31). On God's side the key word of the book is *love,* but for us the key word is *believe.* Verse 36 above refers to those who have seen and believe not. They have no further claim on Christ. In the present verse, the one who sees and believes on the Son has the promise of resurrection to eternal life. Those who are chosen of God to be saved, therefore, are those who believe on the Son (and come to Him, verse 35). It is the will of God that all who do this, thus partaking of the bread of life, live forever.

III. Murmurings of Unbelief (John 6:41-46)

Those who were eyewitnesses were amazed by the life of Jesus. It is true that He made great claims, but they were accompanied by great signs and wonders. Some of the Pharisees said, "This man is not of God." But others asked, "How can a man that is a sinner do such miracles?" (John 9:16).

visual 8

Bread of heav'n, on Thee we feed,

For Thy flesh is meat indeed;

Ever let our souls be fed

With this true and living bread.

—JOSIAH CONDER

A. The Incarnation Questioned (vv. 41, 42)

41, 42. The Jews then murmured at him, because he said, I am the bread which came down from heaven. And they said, Is not this Jesus, the son of Joseph, whose father and mother we know? how is it then that he saith, I came down from heaven?

The Jews. This is John's characteristic way of referring to the Jewish leaders who were hostile to Jesus. Some of them, of course, were in the synagogue, and they objected to Jesus' claim to deity. They knew that He had been brought up in Nazareth as a son of Joseph and Mary, and they naturally supposed that He had been born in a natural way to those who were thought to be His parents. But now He said, *I came down from heaven.* How could He be from Heaven when they knew He was from Nazareth? This question was at the heart of their murmuring.

B. Hear, Learn, Come (vv. 43-46)

Jesus did not attempt to explain the incarnation, how the divine Son could be present in Jesus of Nazareth. Of course, He would not claim that He came physically from Heaven, as if in some super spaceship. He entered the world as any human being comes, by birth; in His case, to the virgin Mary. Physically, He was altogether human, but His spirit was from God.

Such an explanation would have fallen on deaf ears, however. Instead of this, Jesus made the observation that only those who hear and learn from God will come to Him. God's teaching, and God's invitation, will be the drawing power that brings souls to Jesus.

43, 44. Jesus therefore answered and said unto them, Murmur not among yourselves. No man can come to me, except the Father which hath sent me draw him: and I will raise him up at the last day.

Murmur not. It is sometimes said that we talk when we should be listening. As long as we continue our murmuring, we make it impossible to gain any insight relative to solving the dilemma confronting us.

No man can come to me, except the Father which hath sent me draw him. In verse 37 Jesus said, "Him that cometh to me I will in no wise cast out." Clearly, the promise of Jesus is to those who *come to him.* The human will must act to establish one's relationship to God through Christ. No one comes unless he or she wills to come. To some Jesus said, "Ye will not come to me, that ye might have life" (John 5:40). Jesus desires to impart the life; but if one does not come to Him, Jesus will not compel that person to do so. He does not overpower the will of one who refuses to follow Him, but calls for a positive response, saying, "Let him that is athirst come. And whosoever will, let him take the water of life freely" (Revelation 22:17). Whosoever will may come.

Yet Jesus also says, *No man can come to me, except the Father which hath sent me draw him.* We must exercise our will in coming to Jesus, but this coming is in response to the love that God has shown in giving His Son for our salvation. God draws us, not by overpowering the human will, but by calling us to respond to His offer of life. Jesus' comments in the next verses help to clarify this.

45, 46. It is written in the prophets, And they shall be all taught of God. Every man therefore that hath heard, and hath learned of the Father, cometh unto me. Not that any man hath seen the Father, save he which is of God, he hath seen the Father

It is written. Isaiah 54:13 states that "all thy children shall be taught of the Lord" or "by the Lord." God draws by teaching, His ultimate message being the gospel, the good news about Christ. It is this gospel, Paul reminds us, that is "the power of God unto salvation to every one that believeth" (Romans 1:16). All who are thus *taught of God,* who listen to the teaching and learn, come to the Son. Those who turn a deaf ear to the teaching are the ones who do not come.

Not that any man hath seen the Father. It is not through a personal interview with God that one learns of Him. Only the Christ has seen God, and we learn of the Father through Him.

IV. A Promise of Life Eternal (John 6:47-51)

Having dealt with the murmuring that had occurred, Jesus now returned to His discussion on the bread of life.

A. Believe in Christ and Live (v. 47)

47. Verily, verily, I say unto you, He that believeth on me hath everlasting life.

Earlier in His sermon, Jesus stated the will of God that every one who sees the Son and believes in Him may have everlasting life (v. 40). Now he states that whoever believes *hath everlasting life*. By this He implies that some of the blessings of Heaven are experienced by believers here and now.

B. Manna and the Bread of Life (vv. 48-50)

48, 49. I am that bread of life. Your fathers did eat manna in the wilderness, and are dead.

The people had asked Jesus to show them a sign or miracle, such as God's giving Israel manna, or "bread from heaven" in the wilderness (John 6:30, 31). Jesus would give them a greater sign! He is the bread that imparts and sustains spiritual life. By contrast, the manna, although from God, fed only the physical body, not the soul or the spiritual nature. Consequently, the fathers died, even though they had manna to eat.

50. This is the bread which cometh down from heaven, that a man may eat thereof, and not die.

The bread which cometh down from heaven. This entire passage is filled with Jesus' claims to deity. Because He was God and came from the Father in Heaven, Jesus could offer bread that gives eternal life to humankind, thus banishing spiritual death. As the bread of Heaven, He alone has life within himself. Apart from Him we have no promise of that life. Only those who eat this bread shall live.

BREAD IN THE DESERT

During the war in the Persian Gulf, Iraqi troops surrendered by the thousands. The typical POW came to the allies' side of the front lines, white flag waving, with tattered uniform, raw knuckles from digging trenches in sand, fatigued, and malnourished. These soldiers from Iraq were trying to survive on half a cup of water and three tablespoons of rice per day. Ironically, they surrendered with relief, knowing that they would enjoy far better treatment and rations as prisoners of the allied forces. They found "bread" in the desert installations of the enemy.

Though they were desperately hungry for food, the Iraqis valued even more the safety of surrendered status, the promise of peace and the hope of a future. Like the manna that the Hebrew children ate in the wilderness, physical food's life-sustaining properties are only temporary.

Jesus wants His followers, indeed, all nations, to seek and work for "soul food"—spiritual nourishment of eternal sustenance. Work for the faith that is infinite, and share the Living Bread with the empty and desperate seekers in your private world. —R. W. B.

C. Christ, the Living Bread (v. 51)

51. I am the living bread which came down from heaven: if any man eat of this bread, he shall live for ever: and the bread that I will give is my flesh, which I will give for the life of the world.

I am the living bread. The use of the figure of the *living* bread underscores the necessity of our receiving Christ if we would have life. Since there is no *living* bread to be found anywhere else, we must *eat of this bread* if we would have eternal life. *The bread that I will give is my flesh.* In verses 53-56, Jesus said that we are to eat His flesh and drink His blood if we would live. At the outset this is shocking language, but of course Jesus spoke figuratively. He yielded His body of flesh to suffer for us, becoming our sacrifice for sin. Unless we partake of that sacrifice, accepting Him as our Savior and partaking of His nature, we have no part in the life that He offers. Thus do we eat the living bread.

Conclusion

A. Eat and Live

The ultimate hunger that a human being experiences is the hunger for life itself. If we develop our talents and use them for personal gain in this life only, if we have no thought of life beyond in which there is to be judgment with both reward and punishment, what final significance does life itself have? There is no answer to the inner hunger for life if there is no Heaven.

In this sermon on the bread of life, Jesus comes again and again to this ultimate hunger of the soul that finds satisfaction in the world's only Savior. Death and the day of judgment are repeatedly emphasized as this Savior offers himself to the world as the bread of life. He promises to give His life for the divine purpose of giving eternal life to all who will accept Him as Christ and Lord. Let us who are His carry His invitation to everyone: "Eat of this bread and live!"

B. Prayer

Heavenly Father, we thank You for daily bread that sustains our mortal bodies. More than this, we are grateful for Your promise of life more abundant through Jesus, Your Son and our Savior. Help us this day to eat of the living bread by partaking of His nature, to the end that we may be like Him. In His name we pray. Amen.

C. Thought to Remember

The ultimate hunger of the soul is satisfied only when one partakes of Christ, for He is the bread of life.

Learning by Doing

This page contains an alternate lesson plan emphasizing learning activities. Classes desiring such student involvement will find these suggestions helpful.

Learning Goals

As a result of this lesson, the students will:

1. Be able to describe how Jesus can satisfy their deepest hungers.

2. Seek to fulfill their spiritual hunger with spiritual bread and not with earthly pleasures.

Into the Lesson

Divide your class into three work groups and appoint a leader for each group. Give each group leader a sheet of posterboard and a felt marker. If you wish, cut the posterboard in the shape of a large slice of bread for effect.

Instruct the first group to draw a contrast between the state of hunger and the state of nourishment. Have them list their comparisons on the posterboard. Here are some examples.

Hunger	*Nourishment*
craving,	satisfaction
fatigue, sickness	energy, good health
depression	optimism

Ask the group to be prepared to describe both states and how they feel when they are in that condition.

Instruct the second group to define spiritual hunger and spiritual food, using the following Scriptures as a help. Have them summarize their conclusions on the posterboard. *Scriptures:* Matthew 5:6; Luke 6:25; 1 Corinthians 3:2; 10:14-17; Psalm 34:8-10.

Instruct the third group to make a simple chart or design that contrasts and compares Jesus with manna. Have them refer to the following Scriptures: John 6:35, 48-51; Exodus 16:15, 35; Numbers 11:6; Deuteronomy 8:3-5; Revelation 2:17.

Allow about fifteen minutes for the groups to work.

Into the Word

Whether the groups are finished or not, begin with group one, asking them to show their chart on hunger versus nourishment. Then probe them further with questions such as, "When in your life were you the hungriest?" or "What are you like to live with when you are hungry?"

When they have described the state of hunger and fulfillment, read aloud today's text. Briefly explain how Jesus used the phenomenon of hunger to teach about spiritual food.

Now ask the second group to show their poster and define spiritual hunger and spiritual food. Be sure that mention is made of the different kinds of hungers that are involved in spiritual hunger. For example, longing for fellowship, desire for truth, hope of Heaven, craving for holiness.

At this point lead a discussion by using the following questions:

1. Is hunger a good or bad thing? Why, why not?

2. Can physical, material things ever give a measure of spiritual fullness?

3. How does hunger differ from lust?

4. Will we ever be fully fed, spiritually, in this life? If not, why try?

5. Are spiritual things sometimes less than satisfying? If so, why?

Now ask the third group to draw their comparison between Christ and manna. This will illustrate the fact that Jesus is fully-satisfying, spiritual, eternal food.

Into Life

Read the following case study to the class and then discuss the two questions that follow it.

Case Study

Jill works as a writer for a prestigious firm in a large city. She designs newsletters, ghostwrites speeches, and produces scripts for videos. She loves her work and works overtime most evenings and weekends. She makes a lot of money and enjoys many benefits. She dresses like a movie star, drives an expensive car, and lives in a luxury apartment. Although she is single, she dates occasionally and has a network of friends she calls on a regular basis.

Jill attends church on Sunday morning, but she doesn't go to Sunday school or other activities of the church. She often feels that Christians are socially out of touch or hypocrites, neither of which she can tolerate. She does read a devotional book at breakfast every day and she tries to model a Christian life at work.

In spite of all that's good in her life, Jill feels so lonely and empty that she often contemplates doing sinful things to meet her needs.

1. What could Jill be doing or not doing that might cause her to feel so spiritually empty?

2. What should Jill (and we) do to feel more fulfilled by spiritual things?

Let's Talk It Over

The questions on this page are designed to encourage review of the lesson Scriptures and to promote discussion of the lesson by the class. The answers provided are only discussion starters. Let your class talk it over from there.

1. What are some comparisons we can make between physical bread and Jesus, the bread of life?

Bread is produced by what we could call a violent process. The grinding of the grain, the sifting of the flour, and the baking of the loaves are essential if we are to have bread for our tables. Then that bread must be sliced or broken before we can use it. This reminds us of Jesus' bruising, crushing, searing, experience on the cross in order to become available to us as the bread of life. We may admire bread's golden brown surface and savor its fresh-baked aroma, but it does us no good until we eat it. Likewise, people may hold Jesus Christ in high regard as a teacher and humanitarian; they may speak of His remarkable influence on human history; but until He is made part of their lives, they will receive neither the spiritual nourishment nor everlasting life, which He gives.

2. Why is hunger, both physical and spiritual, something for which we should be thankful?

Hunger is beneficial, for it spurs us to give our bodies what they need for health and strength. Even so, spiritual hunger leads us to read the Bible, to pray, to worship, and to fellowship with other Christians. Without the experience of physical hunger, we might neglect eating, and grow weak and sickly. Without spiritual hunger, we might forego worship and Bible study, and our faith would become sluggish and impotent. We remember that Jesus said, "Blessed are they which do hunger and thirst after righteousness: for they shall be filled" (Matthew 5:6). Therefore, we should say, "Thank You, God, for this blessed hunger and thirst."

3. God's will is that those who are lost in their sins should be saved. How should this truth affect us?

God made an ultimate sacrifice by sending His Son to earth to die so that human beings could be saved. How much of a sacrifice are we willing to make in order to bring salvation to the lost? God "wants all men to be saved and to come to a knowledge of the truth" (1 Timothy 2:4, *New International Version*). Are we satisfied with seeing our own family saved or our own neighbors or our countrymen, or do we have a vision of salvation for all races and nations? It is clear that if Jesus made it His mission "to seek and to save that which was lost" (Luke 19:10), we who are His body, His church, must make that our mission. We must throw into it our mental and physical energies, our financial resources, and our very hearts and souls.

4. What is it about Jesus that draws people to Him?

The timelessness of Jesus' teachings draws some to Him. Even non-Christians often express an appreciation for the Sermon on the Mount, the parable of the good Samaritan, and other teachings of Jesus. Jesus' love and compassion possess a drawing power. When we read in the Gospel narratives that He healed lepers, restored sight to the blind, and granted forgiveness of sins, we are touched to realize that such a caring person lived on this earth. Jesus' power, displayed in miracles such as His stilling of the storm and raising of the dead, is impressive and draws others to Him. Most of all, Jesus' sacrificial death on the cross draws people. He said, "And I, if I be lifted up from the earth, will draw all men unto me" (John 12:32). There is something about the depicting of this Savior nailed to the cross that can melt the human heart.

5. Jesus' hearers were shocked and disturbed when He spoke of giving His flesh as bread for people to eat. Why did He use such language, and why do we need to emphasize Jesus' shocking statements today?

Some speakers and writers today thrive on controversy for controversy's sake. Others use sensational statements or claims merely to draw the attention of people to themselves. Jesus was not interested in pointless controversy or sensationalism, but He was concerned about making people think. One result of His discourse on the bread of life is recorded in John 6:66: "From that time many of his disciples went back, and walked no more with him." These no doubt included many who were attracted to Jesus only by His miracles, but were unwilling to think through His amazing claims. Jesus seeks followers who will ponder His words and works and will for their lives.

The Witness of John the Baptist

May 2
Lesson 9

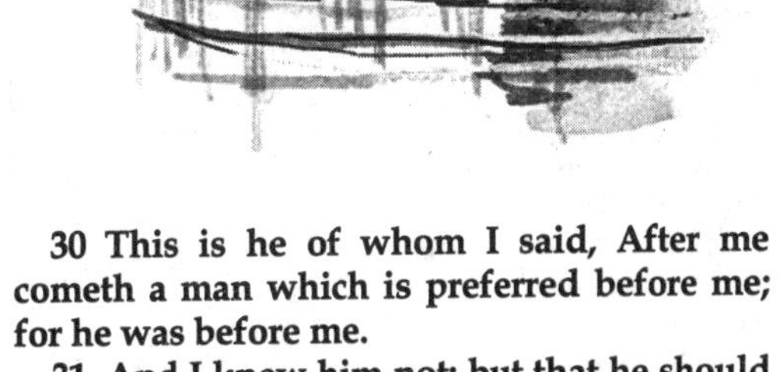

Lesson Scripture: John 1:19-34.

Printed Text: John 1:19-34.

Devotional Reading: John 1:35-42.

John 1:19-34

19 And this is the record of John, when the Jews sent priests and Levites from Jerusalem to ask him, Who art thou?

20 And he confessed, and denied not; but confessed, I am not the Christ.

21 And they asked him, What then? Art thou Elijah? And he saith, I am not. Art thou that Prophet? And he answered, No.

22 Then said they unto him, Who art thou? that we may give an answer to them that sent us. What sayest thou of thyself?

23 He said, I am the voice of one crying in the wilderness, Make straight the way of the Lord, as said the prophet Isaiah.

24 And they which were sent were of the Pharisees.

25 And they asked him, and said unto him, Why baptizest thou then, if thou be not that Christ, nor Elijah, neither that Prophet?

26 John answered them, saying, I baptize with water: but there standeth one among you, whom ye know not;

27 He it is, who coming after me is preferred before me, whose shoelatchet I am not worthy to unloose.

28 These things were done in Bethabara beyond Jordan, where John was baptizing.

29 The next day John seeth Jesus coming unto him, and saith, Behold the Lamb of God, which taketh away the sin of the world!

30 This is he of whom I said, After me cometh a man which is preferred before me; for he was before me.

31 And I knew him not: but that he should be made manifest to Israel, therefore am I come baptizing with water.

32 And John bare record, saying, I saw the Spirit descending from heaven like a dove, and it abode upon him.

33 And I knew him not: but he that sent me to baptize with water, the same said unto me, Upon whom thou shalt see the Spirit descending, and remaining on him, the same is he which baptizeth with the Holy Ghost.

34 And I saw, and bare record that this is the Son of God.

Golden Text: I saw, and bare record that this is the Son of God.—John 1:34.

Believing in Christ

Unit 3. John: Believe in Jesus

(Lessons 9-13)

Lesson Aims

When this lesson is completed, the students should:

1. Be able to identify John the Baptist and explain the importance of his testimony regarding Jesus.
2. Be able to relate John's two-fold identification of Jesus (as the Lamb of God and as the Son of God) and tell the significance of each.
3. Consider again who they are in relationship to God, to Christ, and to His church.

Lesson Outline

INTRODUCTION
- A. The Problem of Identity
- B. Lesson Background

I. JOHN IDENTIFIES HIMSELF (John 1:19-25)
- A. Who Are You? (v. 19)
- B. Neither Messiah nor Prophet (vv. 20, 21)
  The Unmessiah
- C. The Voice of a Herald (vv. 22, 23)
- D. John's Role Questioned (vv. 24, 25)

II. JOHN ANNOUNCES THE MESSIAH (John 1:26-28)
  Advance Men

III. JOHN TESTIFIES OF JESUS (John 1:29-34)
- A. The Lamb of God (vv. 29-31)
- B. The Son of God (vv. 32-34)

CONCLUSION
- A. Who Is Jesus?
- B. Who Am I?
- C. Prayer
- D. Thought to Remember

Display visual 9 of the visuals packet and let it remain before the class throughout the session. The visual is shown on page 301.

Introduction

A. The Problem of Identity

Requests for identification are common in today's world. For that reason we carry with us a driver's license bearing our picture, a Social Security card with its identifying number, and the cards that identify our relationship to various groups and services. If we would travel in a foreign land, we must have a passport to prove our identity; otherwise we might be detained.

Sometimes persons suffering amnesia do not know who they are. As a matter of fact, psychologists tell us that everyone, at some time or other, either consciously or subconsciously, wrestles with the problem of who he or she is. Some young persons face an identity crisis when they reach their teen years. Perhaps the parents have criticized so often and so severely that the child actually comes to believe that "I am a nobody," or "I am a bad person." It is not surprising, therefore, that the one who has identified himself or herself in that way acts accordingly.

The identity of Jesus of Nazareth is the concern of the Gospel of John throughout, and particularly so in the Scripture we study today. John's conclusion was that Jesus is the Son of the living God, through whom we may have eternal life (John 3:16). In order that we might identify Jesus in this way and live, the writer, the apostle John, included as evidence the testimony of various witnesses as well as the record of many events in the life of Jesus. It is only natural that he began with the testimony of John the Baptist, since this was given at the very beginning of Jesus' ministry.

John the Baptist knew precisely who he himself was. Some might wonder if John were the Messiah. "Oh no," he said, and then he identified himself as the forerunner, the one preparing the way for the Messiah, the one announcing His arrival. There was no identity crisis with John the Baptist. He knew he was the forerunner. He also knew and declared the identity of Jesus. A study of this lesson should help us to a clearer insight into our own identity as related to God and to Jesus.

B. Lesson Background

"Why are our lessons skipping all around the Gospel of John?" Have you asked this question? We have had eight lessons in this study already, and here we are back at the first chapter! The arrangement of lessons, however, has not been haphazard.

Our first four lessons dealt with the fundamental truth underlying the Gospel of John; namely, that in Jesus "the Word became flesh and dwelt among us." Jesus is the living Word, bringing light and life to humankind. But what brought Jesus to earth?

Our second group of four lessons answered this question by saying that the love of God prompted the incarnation. The love of Jesus also led Him to serve humankind, even unto death.

Today we begin our final unit of study, in which we have five lessons on the theme, "Believe in Jesus." Basically, this will involve a study of some of the evidence showing that the incarnation was a reality. Reemphasized will be the truth that because of God's love, Jesus came to this earth so that "whosoever believeth in him should not perish, but have everlasting life" (John 3:16). We begin, as we have indicated, with the testimony of John the Baptist.

John the Baptist was a powerful preacher who condemned sin and evil and called for repentance. "Jerusalem, and Judea, and all the region round about Jordan" went out to hear John, Matthew tells us, "and were baptized of him in Jordan, confessing their sins" (Matthew 3:5, 6). Because of the great success that John was having and perhaps because of the tone of authority in his voice, many wondered if this might not be the Messiah for whom Israel had been looking.

From Galilee Jesus came to the Jordan to be baptized by John. He did so, not because He had any sins to confess, but in order "to fulfil all righteousness" (Matthew 3:15). At Jesus' baptism, "the Holy Spirit descended on him in bodily form like a dove" (Luke 3:22, *New International Version*). After being baptized, Jesus withdrew into the wilderness, where He was tempted by the devil for forty days (Luke 4:1). Our lesson begins when the period of temptation had ended, and Jesus was making His way back again to the Jordan.

I. John Identifies Himself (John 1:19-25)

Whenever one gives testimony in an important matter, we naturally want to know if that person is a reliable witness. We want to know something about him or her. We understand, therefore, the question put to John the Baptist by the priests and Levites. They wanted John to identify himself.

A. Who Are You? (v. 19)

19. And this is the record of John, when the Jews sent priests and Levites from Jerusalem to ask him, Who art thou?

This is the record of John, or more precisely, the "witness" or "testimony" of John, meaning, his testimony with reference to Christ. It was only incidental that John the Baptist testified to who he himself was. The writer of this Gospel account, John the apostle, was chiefly concerned with recording testimony that showed Jesus to be the Son of God. It was, therefore, both natural and logical that he begin with the first public pronouncement of that truth—and that was made by John the Baptist.

The occasion was the coming of a delegation of priests and Levites to question John. They were sent from Jerusalem by the religious leaders, the Sanhedrin. These leaders were responsible for overseeing the temple and the worship of the people there. That worship included the sacrificing of sin-offerings on behalf of the people. But here was John, calling on sinners to repent and turn away from sin, preaching a "baptism of repentance for the remission of sins" (Mark 1:4). And large crowds were coming out to hear him. Clearly an investigation of this one who was invading their prerogative was in order.

Who art thou? As we read the complete record we gather that the question really means, "Who are you? What do you think you are doing? And by whose authority?" Before John could clarify his role in God's scheme of things, he must dispel any misconceptions the people might have about him.

B. Neither Messiah nor Prophet (vv. 20, 21)

20. And he confessed, and denied not; but confessed, I am not the Christ.

And he confessed. The Greek verb may mean "to confess" or "to admit." But often it signifies a declaration, such as a declaration of faith, or of a great truth. Plainly John declared, *I am not the Christ.* Undoubtedly among the masses the question had been raised, "Could this be the Messiah from God for whom we have waited so long?" And in Jerusalem the authorities were likely disturbed by the idea that this fellow might have some delusions that he was the Messiah, the Christ. But John flatly denied any such claim.

THE UNMESSIAH

The psychoses of Jim Jones, evangelist turned killer, included a "Messiah complex." He thought he was a latter-day Christ, anointed by God to be prophet, priest, and king. Obsessed with usurped authority, he subjected his followers to increasing demands and oppression, until finally he ordered the mass suicide that shocked the entire world. Jones was consumed with carnal ambition for power; his subservient followers fed that lust. He wasn't the first spiritual leader to think of himself more highly than he ought to think. Pride does, indeed, go before destruction.

How to Say It

BETHABARA. *Beth-ab*-uh-ruh (strong accent on *ab*).
PEREA. Peh-*ree-uh.*
SANHEDRIN. *San*-huh-drun or San-*heed*-run.

John the Baptist, by contrast, gave us a superb example of the humble spirit that is characteristic of true greatness in God's kingdom. Many may have suspected that John was the Messiah. He did not hesitate one moment, however, to tell them, "I am not the Christ." John knew himself and his mission. He was humbly yet boldly preparing his audience for the inauguration of Christ's ministry.

Our task is the same: to point people to Jesus. Selfish pride and power can distract any one of us from our guiding purpose. Remember, Jesus is the way; no one can come to the Father except through Him. —R. W. B.

21. And they asked him, What then? Art thou Elijah? And he saith, I am not. Art thou that Prophet? And he answered, No.

Art thou Elijah? In Malachi 4:5 it is stated that Elijah would come before the "day of the Lord." Before the birth of John the Baptist, an angel told his father that John would go before the Lord "in the spirit and power of Elijah" (Luke 1:17). Also, Jesus himself said that John the Baptist was the Elijah who was to come (Matthew 17:10-13). Undoubtedly the text in Malachi is to be understood figuratively. Those who questioned John apparently expected a literal return of Elijah from the dead. Hence, John answered, *I am not.*

Art thou that Prophet? Literally, *the* prophet. This seems to be a reference to the prophet that God promised to raise up "like unto" Moses (see Deuteronomy 18:15-19). John correctly understood that passage to refer to the Messiah himself (see Acts 3:19-23), so he answered, *No.*

C. The Voice of a Herald (vv. 22, 23)

22. Then said they unto him, Who art thou? that we may give an answer to them that sent us. What sayest thou of thyself?

Who art thou? Identify yourself! The delegation needed something to tell those who had sent them.

23. He said, I am the voice of one crying in the wilderness, Make straight the way of the Lord, as said the prophet Isaiah.

I am the voice of one crying. John's words were from Isaiah 40:3 and would have been familiar to his hearers. The picture is that of a herald for a king. Before modern means of communication, heralds were very important persons, making public pronouncements in the name of or on behalf of the king. And when a herald announced that the king planned to visit a province of his realm, the roads would be made ready so that there would be no obstacles in his way. "This," John said, "is who I am; I am the herald of a king, and my king is the Lord." He was announcing the coming of the Lord and calling everyone to repent of their sin, thus preparing the way for His entrance into their hearts. So it was John the Baptist, himself a prophet of God (see Matthew 11:7-10), who first introduced the Son of God to the world.

D. John's Role Questioned (vv. 24, 25)

24, 25. And they which were sent were of the Pharisees. And they asked him, and said unto him, Why baptizest thou then, if thou be not that Christ, nor Elijah, neither that Prophet?

The members of the investigating committee were of the Pharisees, the strictest sect of the religious leaders. So they pressed on in their inquiry. Judging from what these men said here, the people of that day associated some form of ceremonial cleansing with the appearance of the Messiah (see Ezekiel 36:25; Isaiah 52:15; Zechariah 13:1). John, however, said that he was not the Messiah. Neither was he Elijah, nor the prophet like Moses. They demanded, therefore, that he justify this innovation of baptism. John did not answer their question precisely, but took this as an opportunity to announce the presence of the Messiah.

II. John Announces the Messiah (John 1:26-28)

26, 27. John answered them, saying, I baptize with water: but there standeth one among you, whom ye know not; he it is, who coming after me is preferred before me, whose shoe-latchet I am not worthy to unloose.

What John was doing was in preparation for the appearing of the Messiah. "Repent," he had said, "for the kingdom of heaven is at hand" (Matthew 3:2). This could mean only one thing. The Messiah was about to appear.

I baptize with water. John acknowledged that he had introduced an important change. His authority for such an action was based on his role as the forerunner for the Messiah. A dramatic change in the way God would deal with humankind was in the offing. It was proper that a change of such magnitude should be announced in a striking manner.

The baptism of Jesus and the revelation of His identity to John had already occurred. John knew who the Messiah was, so he could say to his audience that this One was even now standing among them. A glorious One, too, John might add, for he did not consider himself worthy even to be the servant who would loose His sandal straps.

How did these inquirers respond to this great announcement? How great was their desire to meet this One of whom John spoke? Did they clamor to hear more? Apparently not. Their interview with John was finished, so they could now turn and walk away, no more concerned about Jesus than some today who suddenly develop a condition of deafness whenever Jesus is presented to them seriously.

ADVANCE MEN

When the president visits a city, he is preceded by dozens of "advance men" who make detailed preparations for his visit. The time he spends there is tightly scheduled. Travel routes are selected and meticulously checked for optimum safety, speed, and comfort. Federal and local law-enforcement personnel join forces to protect our chief. Advance men provide an important service, to the president and to our nation.

John the Baptist considered his job to be very important, one for which he was not even worthy. He was an advance man for Jesus Christ, the Son of God. John was humbled by the opportunity to herald the coming of Christ. It was his privilege to cry, "Prepare ye the way of the Lord."

All Christian service is similar to that of an advance man. We are commissioned to prepare the way for Christ's coming again. Of first importance is our personal spiritual readiness to meet Him. Helping others to prepare for His return is our next priority. When He comes, every eye will see Him, every knee will bow before Him, and every tongue will confess that He is Lord. What a privilege to help plan for the celebration! —R. W. B.

28. These things were done in Bethabara beyond Jordan, where John was baptizing.

In Bethabara, or, properly, *in Bethany beyond Jordan,* not to be confused with the Bethany on the Mount of Olives. Some think that the Bethany where John was baptizing was east of the Jordan near Jericho. Others think it was farther north, about thirteen miles south of the Sea of Galilee.

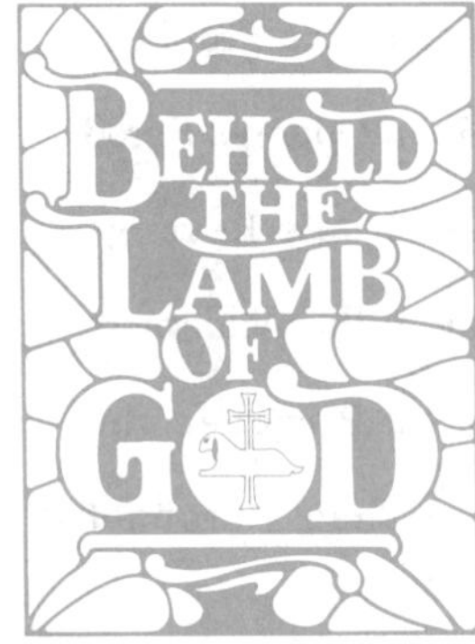

visual 9

III. John Testifies of Jesus (John 1:29-34)

A. The Lamb of God (vv. 29-31)

29. The next day John seeth Jesus coming unto him, and saith, Behold the Lamb of God, which taketh away the sin of the world.

The next day. This was the day after the delegation from Jerusalem had interrogated John. On this day, Jesus came again to the place where John was preaching, and John seized the opportunity to identify Jesus for his audience and to bear witness to who He was.

The Lamb of God. It is significant that John introduced Jesus as *the* Lamb of God. In the mind of Israel, lambs were associated with sacrifice. As for the Messiah, they expected Him to sit on David's throne and reign as a victorious king. Christ Jesus *would* reign over an eternal kingdom. But first, in keeping with prophecy, He would become a sacrificial offering for the sins of the world. (See Isaiah 53:7).

30. This is he of whom I said, After me cometh a man which is preferred before me; for he was before me.

John reminded his audience of his statement of the day before (v. 27). On that occasion he spoke of Christ in veiled terms. Here now he added clarification. Jesus came *after* John in the sense of His physical birth and public ministry. But John knew that Jesus ranked far above him in power and glory because of who He was. *For he was before me.* Clearly this is a reference to Christ's preexistence before His coming to earth.

31. And I knew him not: but that he should be made manifest to Israel, therefore am I come baptizing with water.

John knew enough about Jesus to shrink from baptizing Him at first (Matthew 3:14). But he did not know Him at that time in the sense that he had not yet received the proof God had promised that would remove all question regarding the Messiah's identity. John's statement in the following verses make this clear.

That he should be made manifest to Israel. Once again John declared that his mission was to point people to the Christ.

B. The Son of God (vv. 32-34)

32. And John bare record, saying, I saw the Spirit descending from heaven like a dove, and it abode upon him.

John bare record. That is, he gave his testimony as an eyewitness and as a prophet of God. *I saw the Spirit descending.* John reported what had occurred when Jesus came up out of the water at His baptism (Matthew 3:16).

33, 34. And I knew him not: but he that sent me to baptize with water, the same said unto me: Upon whom thou shalt see the Spirit descending, and remaining on him, the same is he which baptizeth with the Holy Ghost. And I saw, and bare record that this is the Son of God.

He that sent me; that is, God himself. It was God who told John how he would be able to identify the Messiah. He *baptizeth with the Holy Ghost* (or, Holy Spirit). On two occasions after His ascension Jesus sent the baptism of the Holy Spirit. First, upon the apostles on the Day of Pentecost (Acts 1:5; 2:3, 4), and then when the kingdom was opened to Gentiles (Acts 10:45-47). *This is the Son of God.* What a claim for John to make! But, he said, *I saw* and therefore, "I testify (as one under oath) to this truth."

Conclusion

A. Who Is Jesus?

The acceptance or rejection of the testimony of the Gospel accounts regarding the true identity of Jesus is not just an academic exercise. It makes all the difference now and in the world to come whether or not Jesus Christ is the Lamb of God that takes away the sin of the world, as the Scripture says. If He is, then we can be cleansed of our sins, experience life as children of God, and end this earthly existence with the hope and assurance of eternal life in the Father's kingdom. But it all depends upon who Jesus is.

It does not matter who anybody else may have been or is—great teacher, learned philosopher, generous benefactor, or dedicated humanist. The best they can do for us is to escort us to our graves! Not one of them can do more.

On the other hand, Jesus, the bread of life, provides that living bread that assures us eternal life (John 14:19). But He was put to death! He died *for our sins.* But the tomb in which He lay is empty, and has been for two thousand years! No tomb could hold the Lord of life.

As the Lamb of God, Jesus can take away the guilt and punishment of our sins. As the light of the world, He can illumine our darkest night. As the Word of God, He can give direction to our lives, and as the door, He can provide entrance for us to the very presence of God.

John the Baptist was certain that Jesus was the *Lamb of God* and the *Son of God.* John the apostle was sure and has left evidence in this Gospel that has led even skeptics to believe "that Jesus is the Christ, the Son of the living God." To every person who has ever considered this evidence, there comes the question: "What think ye of Christ? whose Son is he?" Our eternal future rests upon our answer to that question.

B. Who Am I?

"Mama, is this me?" a little girl asked when she awoke one morning, after her mother had moved the sleeping child during the night from one bedroom to another. Do we not all, at one time or other, feel that we are in a strange place and wonder who we really are? Am I a vile sinner, condemned forever to live in guilt and shame? Or am I cleansed from sin and forgiven? Am I nothing more than an animal whose rotting flesh will return to earth's soil? Or was I made in the likeness of God, with a spiritual nature that transcends the material?

Am I a lost sheep, unloved and alone in a desolate place? Or am I enfolded in the arms of the Good Shepherd who gave His life for me? Am I an unwanted child or an orphan, without family that I can call my own? Or am I a son, a daughter, in the family of God that circles this earth and that is found even in my own little neighborhood?

Who am I? Am I a nobody? Or am I an heir of God and joint heir with Jesus Christ? Our answer to all such questions will be determined according to our identity of Christ.

C. Prayer

Lord, as we think of Your love shown through Jesus, we are overwhelmed. Such love is beyond wonder. Jesus, the Lamb of God, bore our sins. By this expression of Your grace, we have been made members of Your family. Please help us to live as the children of God ought to live, continuing together in unity and love. Amen.

D. Thought to Remember

One cannot know one's own true identity until he or she knows and acknowledges who Jesus is.

Home Daily Bible Readings

Monday, Apr. 26—The Birth of John (Luke 1:57-66)

Tuesday, Apr. 27—Zechariah's Prophecy (Luke 1:67-80)

Wednesday, Apr. 28—John Opposes Herod (Mark 6:14-20)

Thursday, Apr. 29—Herod's Revenge (Mark 6:21-29)

Friday, Apr. 30—A Way in the Wilderness (Isaiah 40:3-8)

Saturday, May 1—John Preached the Christ (Luke 3:15-20)

Sunday, May 2—More Than a Prophet (Matthew 11:7-15)

We Have Found Him

May 9
Lesson 10

Lesson Scripture: John 1:35-50.

Printed Text: John 1:35-50.

Devotional Reading: Matthew 10:1-10.

John 1:35-50

35 Again the next day after, John stood,
and two of his disciples;
36 And looking upon Jesus as he walked,
he saith, Behold the Lamb of God!
37 And the two disciples heard him speak,
and they followed Jesus.
38 Then Jesus turned, and saw them following, and saith unto them, What seek ye?
They said unto him, Rabbi, (which is to say,
being interpreted, Master,) where dwellest
thou?
39 He saith unto them, Come and see. They
came and saw where he dwelt, and abode
with him that day: for it was about the tenth
hour.
40 One of the two which heard John speak,
and followed him, was Andrew, Simon
Peter's brother.
41 He first findeth his own brother Simon,
and saith unto him, We have found the Messiah, which is, being interpreted, the Christ.
42 And he brought him to Jesus. And when
Jesus beheld him, he said, Thou art Simon the
son of Jona: thou shalt be called Cephas,
which is by interpretation, A stone.
43 The day following Jesus would go forth
into Galilee, and findeth Philip, and saith
unto him, Follow me.
44 Now Philip was of Bethsaida, the city of
Andrew and Peter.
45 Philip findeth Nathanael, and saith unto
him, We have found him, of whom Moses in
the law, and the prophets, did write, Jesus of
Nazareth, the son of Joseph.
46 And Nathanael said unto him, Can there
any good thing come out of Nazareth? Philip
saith unto him, Come and see.
47 Jesus saw Nathanael coming to him, and
saith of him, Behold an Israelite indeed, in
whom is no guile!
48 Nathanael saith unto him, Whence
knowest thou me? Jesus answered and said
unto him, Before that Philip called thee, when
thou wast under the fig tree, I saw thee.
49 Nathanael answered and saith unto
him, Rabbi, thou art the Son of God; thou art
the King of Israel.
50 Jesus answered and said unto him, Because I said unto thee, I saw thee under the
fig tree, believest thou? thou shalt see greater
things than these.

Golden Text: We have found the Messiah.—John 1:41.

Believing in Christ

Unit 3. John: Believe in Jesus

(Lessons 9-13)

Lesson Aims

At the conclusion of this lesson the students should:

1. Be able to name the first disciples of Jesus, tell what kind of men they were, and how they came to be His followers.

2. Explain what evidence is found in this lesson to indicate who Jesus is.

3. Look for opportunities to introduce Jesus to others.

Lesson Outline

Introduction
- A. Come and See
- B. Lesson Background

I. Andrew and John Find Christ (John 1:35-39)
- A. John the Baptist's Testimony (vv. 35, 36) *The Leader's Leader*
- B. Andrew and John's Response (vv. 37-39)

II. Peter, Found for Christ (John 1:40-42)
- A. Andrew's Testimony (vv. 40, 41) *The Order of Andrew*
- B. A New Name for Simon (v. 42)

III. Philip and Nathanael Are Found (John 1:43-49)
- A. Jesus Finds Philip (vv. 43, 44)
- B. Philip Finds Nathanael (v. 45)
- C. Nathanael's Doubt (v. 46)
- D. Nathanael's Amazement (vv. 47-49)

IV. Jesus' Promise of Great Things (John 1:50)

Conclusion
- A. No Disappointment
- B. Prayer
- C. Thought to Remember

Display visual 10 of the visuals packet and discuss its statement in connection with verse 41. The visual is shown on page 309.

Introduction

A. Come and See

A young minister six years out of Bible college was called to serve a church in the Northwest, in the state of Washington. He and his wife and two small children were graciously received and immediately fell in love both with the people and with the surroundings. While calling upon one family of the congregation, the couple expressed how delighted they were to be where they were. At this, the man of the house said, "Well, let me warn you. If you live here as long as three years, you will never be satisfied to live anywhere else. Just try it and you will see."

Well, we lived there more than three years, before returning east. And although we dare not say that we are dissatisfied, we must admit that at times our hearts have a longing for that Northwestern land.

One who has not had an experience of this kind cannot understand the attachment one may develop to a locality. The many remarkable claims published by the Chamber of Commerce sound too good to be true. To the skeptic, one can only say, "Come and see. Live here yourself awhile! Only then can you know the reality of the appeal of this country."

That is the nature of the witness to Jesus in today's lesson Scripture. A number of disciples were attracted to Jesus. One of them was Philip, who told Nathanael that Jesus of Nazareth was the Messiah. When Nathanael voiced his skepticism, Philip could only say, "Come and see." Walk with Jesus awhile. Live in His presence; hear His teachings; observe His life. Then you will learn, firsthand, who He is.

B. Lesson Background

John has discussed the incarnation—the foundational truth upon which his book stands. Jesus, the eternal Word of God, became flesh and dwelt among us, and gives light and eternal life to as many as receive Him. Thus, by the grace of God, life may be ours, and all of this is so because of the infinite love of God. This is John's explanation of why Jesus came.

That love was demonstrated by Jesus in humble service, such as washing feet and in feeding the hungry. Such love would also provide the bread of life for all who would ask.

Having stated these two great themes, John provides his readers the evidence that establishes their truth. The theme of our final lessons in John, then, is why we should believe. Last week the point was made that we believe because Jesus' identity was announced to the world by one who was recognized in his time as a great man of God and a prophet, John the Baptist. This herald of the Lord was certain in his own mind that Jesus was the Christ—even before Jesus had begun His ministry!

Today's evidence focuses upon the witness of the disciples of Jesus, those persons who were His close associates for three years or longer. We will note that their encounter with Jesus was extraordinary, even from the beginning of that relationship. In point of time, our lesson follows immediately upon the events we considered last week. John had introduced Jesus as the Lamb of God and as the Son of God. Reacting to John's testimony, certain persons sought out Jesus and became His disciples for life. The effect that Jesus had upon their lives is a matter of record and bears testimony to who He is, the Son of God, the Messiah.

I. Andrew and John Find Christ (John 1:35-39)

The fame of John the Baptist and his influence in Israel must have been quite extensive. "Jerusalem, and all Judea, and all the region round about Jordan" went out to hear him, "and were baptized of him in Jordan, confessing their sins" (Matthew 3:5, 6). And many authorities believe that Bethabara, the scene of last week's and this week's lesson, was located at a ford just a few miles south of the Sea of Galilee. Thus John would have preached virtually the whole length of the Jordan and would have influenced persons from all regions of the nation.

A. John the Baptist's Testimony (vv. 35, 36)

John had declared from the beginning that he was the forerunner, the herald of the Christ. He had introduced Jesus. Now, with Jesus once again in the vicinity, he pointed Him out to his own group of followers.

35, 36. Again the next day after, John stood, and two of his disciples; and looking upon Jesus as he walked, he saith, Behold the Lamb of God!

The next day after was the day following John's identification of Jesus as the Lamb of God and the Son of God (see last week's lesson). *John stood,* or, "was standing" with *two of his disciples.* From verse 40 we learn that one of these was Andrew, Simon Peter's brother. The other, though his name is not given, was undoubtedly John the apostle, the writer of the book. (Never, in this gospel, does the writer refer to himself by name.) As disciples, these two would have been close followers of John, who remained to assist him while the multitudes came and went. But when John made it clear that Jesus was the long-awaited Messiah, these men were ready to leave John and follow Jesus.

Behold (see!) *the Lamb of God!* On the day before, John had identified Jesus by this title. Now he addressed these two disciples personally. And since he had made it clear that he was only the herald of the Christ, his directing of their attention to Jesus could be understood as an invitation to them to follow Him.

How to Say It

BETHABARA. *Beth-ab*-uh-ruh (strong accent on *ab*).
BETHSAIDA. Beth-*say*-uh-duh.
CAPERNAUM. Kuh-*per*-nay-um.
CEPHAS. *See*-fus.
PETROS (Greek). *peh*-tross.
SHALOM (Hebrew). shah-*lome*.

THE LEADER'S LEADER

After primary elections are over, losers concede to winners, and they usually encourage their own supporters to get behind their party's candidate. Their former opponents become the leaders of choice. Putting party loyalty before personal pride, losing candidates throw their influence and the votes of their supporters behind the campaign of party winners. It is strategic political policy, and it makes good sense.

John the Baptist and Jesus never vied for office; they did not compete for any position of leadership. John said repeatedly, "He [Jesus] must increase; I must decrease." When Christ came on the scene, John pointed his followers to "the Lamb of God." He recognized that Jesus was God's Messiah, and humbly directed disciples to Him. The Lamb of sacrifice would become the Lord of resurrection. John counted it a privilege merely to announce His coming.

We too have the privilege of heralding the coming of Jesus. The attention of the world must be drawn to Him and His promised return.

"He is Lord; He is Lord!
He is risen from the dead, and He is Lord.
Every knee shall bow, every tongue confess
That Jesus Christ is Lord." —R. W. B.

B. Andrew and John's Response (vv. 37-39)

37. And the two disciples heard him speak, and they followed Jesus.

They *heard* and they *followed.* We see from this that the first disciples of Jesus became His followers because they believed the testimony of John the Baptist. In every example of conversion to Christ in the New Testament, someone first tells the individual about Christ, the Lord and Savior. As one person who knows Christ testifies to another, others also become His followers. The effectiveness of personal testimony appears again in verses 41 and 45.

38. Then Jesus turned, and saw them following, and saith unto them, What seek ye? They

said unto him, Rabbi, (which is to say, being interpreted, Master,) where dwellest thou?

Apparently the two disciples followed Jesus at a distance as He left the crowd. Jesus gave them full opportunity to show their determined interest, and then halted until they overtook Him.

What seek ye? Jesus was not asking for information, but was opening a conversation, and it would be a life-changing conversation. As a result of it, Andrew and John—two fishermen—would become followers of Christ. Never would they return to their nets except for a short time. They would be fishers of men.

In reply, the two addressed Jesus as *Rabbi*. The term was a title of highest respect among the Jews. It was used with the meaning of *master*, or *teacher*. Their addressing Jesus as teacher is a clear indication of their interest in receiving instruction from Him. The question, *Where dwellest thou?* may then be understood to mean, "Give us your address. We would like to visit you sometime." They desired an opportunity to have an uninterrupted conversation with Jesus, which would be rather difficult out in the open.

39. He saith unto them, Come and see. They came and saw where he dwelt, and abode with him that day: for it was about the tenth hour.

Come and see. Jesus' answer must have been more than they expected. He invited them to accompany Him at once. We are not told *where he dwelt* at this time. Having so recently come from the temptations in the wilderness, He may have been camping out in the hills nearby.

And abode with him that day. Commentators differ as to whether John used the Jewish or the Roman method of reckoning time. If the Jewish, *the tenth hour* would have been 4:00 P.M., since the day began at daybreak. It seems best, however, to regard this as Roman time, which is the same as ours. Thus the tenth hour would have been 10:00 A.M. The two disciples would have been able to spend several hours in conversation with Jesus and still have had time for Andrew to go find his brother and bring him to Jesus on that same day.

II. Peter, Found for Christ (John 1:40-42)

A. Andrew's Testimony (vv. 40, 41)

40, 41. One of the two which heard John speak, and followed him, was Andrew, Simon Peter's brother. He first findeth his own brother Simon, and saith unto him, We have found the Messiah, which is, being interpreted, the Christ.

Andrew, Simon Peter's brother. It may seem strange to us that Andrew is identified in this manner. When John wrote his Gospel account, however, the name of Peter was widely known, whereas many who would be reading this book would not readily identify Andrew.

He first findeth his own brother Simon. This may mean that the first thing Andrew did was to find Simon. Or, it may be that Andrew was the first to find his brother, but that the other disciple (John) also sought his own brother (James).

We have found the Messiah. We may be certain that when Andrew found his brother, these words were spoken with the utmost fervor and conviction—with such conviction that Peter did not hesitate to return with Andrew to Jesus. Andrew had not received any training in soul-winning. He had not made a study in how best to present the message. But in all earnestness he bore his testimony about Jesus to his brother, and in a single statement of five words (three in Greek or Hebrew) he gained this brother for Christ. Although Andrew may not have been one of the better known apostles, his contribution to the kingdom of God is incalculable as a result of his bringing his brother to the Lord.

THE ORDER OF ANDREW

Pollsters report that the largest percentage of church members visited their church the first time because a relative, friend, neighbor, or coworker invited them. Such statistics are significant because they show how few people choose a church on the basis of professional clergy-type contact and influence. The true evangelists are people of the pew. Friendship evangelism has proven to be far more effective than formal calling programs or any other structured outreach.

Andrew is a classic case-in-point. After being with Jesus for a while one day, he went to his brother, Simon, with the good news. Perhaps no one else could have been as effective as Andrew in bringing Peter to Christ. These brothers knew each other intimately, and trusted each other fully. Peter might have looked askance at a stranger who claimed to have found the Messiah. But he listened to Andrew and went himself to see Jesus.

The surest way to carry out the commission of Christ is for us who are Christians to evangelize our own private worlds—the people with whom we regularly come in contact. The most likely prospects are those who will trust our judgment and respect our convictions. —R. W. B.

B. A New Name for Simon (v. 42)

42. And he brought him to Jesus. And when Jesus beheld him, he said, Thou art Simon the son of Jona: thou shalt be called Cephas, which is by interpretation, A stone.

Notice the situation. Peter was brought to Jesus. And what were the first words the Lord spoke to him? Did He say, "Shalom, welcome, please come in"? No. He said ("out of the blue" we might say), "You are Simon, but you will be called Cephas." Was this not an unusual way to greet a stranger? What was the significance of such a greeting?

By saluting Simon in this manner, Jesus showed that He knew his identity and past, and His bestowal of a new name showed that Jesus knew Simon's future. *Cephas* is Aramaic and means "a stone." The Greek equivalent is *petros* (Peter), and it was by this name that the apostle would become known. Jesus thus designated the stability of Peter's character and personality in the future.

At the time of this meeting, however, Peter was as unstable as Jell-O, impetuous, audacious, sometimes bold, sometimes fearful. But Jesus could look into his heart and see what it was possible for him to become, and what he would become. We know the story of Peter's life. We know the struggles he had. We also know that this fisherman from Galilee became as firm as a piece of stone in his labor for Christ. Jesus knew this as He saw Simon standing by his brother Andrew.

III. Philip and Nathanael Are Found (John 1:43-49)

A. Jesus Finds Philip (vv. 43, 44)

As we have seen, some who became Jesus' disciples, such as Andrew and John, sought Jesus and were welcomed by Him. Peter was brought to Jesus by his brother Andrew. In the case of Philip, Christ himself sought out the disciple. The time had come when Jesus would pursue His public ministry in Galilee. Before departing from the regions of the Jordan, however, He called Philip to become His follower.

43, 44. The day following Jesus would go forth into Galilee, and findeth Philip, and saith unto him, Follow me. Now Philip was of Bethsaida, the city of Andrew and Peter.

Jesus would go forth; that is, He decided to go, *into Galilee,* accompanied, it seems, by His newly-won disciples. But first He found Philip and invited him to become His disciple. When he was called, Philip responded at once. Quite likely he had heard about Jesus from Andrew and Peter. His presence in the area where John was preaching, and his ready acceptance of Jesus' invitation, suggest that Philip too was one of John's disciples. *Bethsaida* was a little fishing village located, it would seem, not far from Capernaum.

visual 10

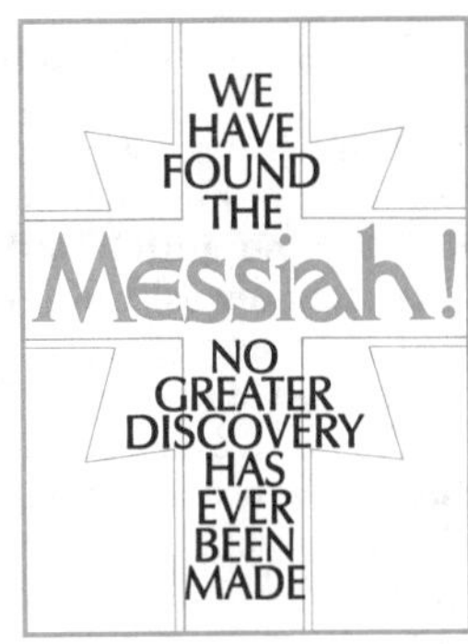

B. Philip Finds Nathanael (v. 45)

45. Philip findeth Nathanael, and saith unto him, We have found him, of whom Moses in the law, and the prophets, did write, Jesus of Nazareth, the son of Joseph.

Philip findeth Nathanael. That is, Philip looked for him until he found him. In announcing the Messiah to his friend, Philip said, *We have found him.* Quite likely the *we* referred to Peter, Andrew, and John. Philip testified person-to-person to Nathanael, but he would have him know that he was not alone in bearing witness.

Of whom Moses . . . and the prophets, did write. Moses said that God would raise up a prophet to whom all should listen (Deuteronomy 18:18). And the prophets told of the coming righteous one who would establish God's everlasting kingdom. Nathanael knew these Scriptures and anticipated the coming of the promised one. *We have found him,* Philip said. Messiah had come. He was *Jesus of Nazareth, the son of Joseph.* This identification of Jesus was such as would appear on an ID card as an official designation, giving the name, the place of residence, and the name of the father (real or supposed). Legally, Joseph was Jesus' father. We do not know when Jesus' followers learned of His virgin birth.

C. Nathanael's Doubt (v. 46)

46. And Nathanael said unto him, Can there any good thing come out of Nazareth? Philip saith unto him, Come and see.

Can there any good thing come out of Nazareth? Some suggest that Nathanael's scoffing remark was typical of the jealousy between small towns. It may be, however, that he was questioning whether the Messiah could come out of Nazareth. Had any of the prophets made any such prediction regarding that town? (In this connection, see John 7:52.)

Rather than argue the worth of Nazareth, Philip wisely suggested instead the pragmatic test of personal investigation and evaluation: *Come and see.*

D. Nathanael's Amazement (vv. 47-49)

47-49. Jesus saw Nathanael coming to him, and saith of him, Behold an Israelite indeed, in whom is no guile! Nathanael saith unto him, Whence knowest thou me? Jesus answered and said unto him, Before that Philip called thee, when thou wast under the fig tree, I saw thee. Nathanael answered and saith unto him, Rabbi, thou art the Son of God; thou art the King of Israel.

An Israelite indeed, in whom is no guile. The name *Israel,* one who prevails with God, was given to *Jacob,* a trickster, late in his life. But there was nothing of the trickster in Nathanael. He was genuine, through and through.

Thou art the Son of God. Amazed that Jesus knew so much about him, Nathanael at once acknowledged Him to be the Son of God. Undoubtedly, Nathanael had heard John the Baptist give his testimony about Jesus. He knew the words of Moses and the prophets. Now, amazed, he saw already in Jesus enough to convince him that He was God's Son, hence, *the King of Israel* (see Psalm 2).

IV. Jesus' Promise of Great Things (John 1:50)

50. Jesus answered and said unto him, Because I said unto thee, I saw thee under the fig tree, believest thou? thou shalt see greater things than these.

Thou shalt see greater things. Verse 51 helps us understand this verse. Once again Jesus referred to the story of Jacob of old, this time to the occasion when Jacob saw a vision of a ladder reaching from earth to Heaven with angels ascending and descending on it (Genesis 28:10-17). Nathanael and the other disciples would come to see that Jesus was the Son of God and the Son of man, the connecting link between God and man, who by the sacrifice of himself would reconcile man to God.

Home Daily Bible Readings

Monday, May 3—Disciples Given Authority (Matthew 10:1-7)
Tuesday, May 4—Disciples Given Instructions (Matthew 10:8-15)
Wednesday, May 5—The Call to Endure (Matthew 10:16-23)
Thursday, May 6—Be Like Your Teachers (Matthew 10:24-28)
Friday, May 7—A God of Detail (Matthew 10:29-33)
Saturday, May 8—A Sword That Separates (Matthew 10:34-42)
Sunday, May 9—Good News to All (Matthew 11:1-6)

Conclusion

A. No Disappointment

In this lesson we have studied about some of Jesus' first disciples and their efforts to bring others to Him. Andrew announced to his brother, Simon, "We have found the Messiah," and he brought him to Jesus. Philip went to Nathanael with this good news, but Nathanael hesitated. Whereupon Philip invited Nathanael, "Come and see."

Some may see in Philip's words justification for a "let's-give-it-a-try" approach to Christian living. But such an approach reflects a wrong mental attitude. To say, "We'll give it a try," is to admit that "it might not work." This attitude invites defeat. Surely this was not Philip's intent.

When Philip invited Nathanael to "come and see" Jesus, there wasn't a shred of doubt in his mind as to what Nathanael would find in Him. Philip was sure that Jesus was the one of whom Moses and the prophets had written, and he was equally certain that Nathanael would recognize that Jesus was the Christ, once he was in His presence and heard Him speak.

With an assurance akin to Philip's, we may invite the lost to "come and see" Jesus. For nearly two thousand years, the honest consideration of the testimony of John and the other Gospel writers has led innumerable persons to proclaim Jesus as the Christ, the Son of God, and to commit their lives to Him. In so doing, they have found the way of life, abundant and eternal. *Come and see!*

B. Prayer

God of all mercy, we have heard Your call to become Your children through Christ Jesus, our Savior. We do not claim that we are worthy of such honor. Indeed, we acknowledge that all have sinned, and we claim only the forgiveness that You have provided through Christ Jesus, the Lamb of God that takes away the sin of the world. Help us, like Andrew and Philip, to bring a loved one or friend to Jesus, whom we have found to be our Lord and our Savior. In His name we pray. Amen.

C. Thought to Remember

It is wonderful to enjoy the love and the fellowship of Christ. That joy is increased when we share it with others.

Learning by Doing

This page contains an alternate lesson plan emphasizing learning activities. Classes desiring such student involvement will find these suggestions helpful.

Learning Goals

As a result of participating in this session, your students will:

1. Identify three methods of evangelism.
2. Choose at least one way to be a witness for Christ this week.

Into the Lesson

The following statements relate to modern methods of evangelism. To begin today's session, read the statements aloud and let the students give the answers orally. The answers are in italics.

1. This method is used to broadcast the gospel over a wide area (*radio evangelism*).
2. Due to the popularity of this medium, many Christian groups use (*TV evangelism*) to reach others.
3. A popular summer program, designed to reach boys and girls for Jesus. (*VBS*)
4. You can teach others in our own home by leading a (*home Bible study*).
5. The Sunday morning teaching sessions of the church are often called (*Bible school*).
6. The church was begun on the Day of Pentecost by means of this form of evangelism. (*Preaching*)
7. The informal sharing of the gospel by one person with another is called (*personal evangelism*).

List the answers on the board and add other methods of evangelism your students can suggest. Let them discuss which they consider to be most effective. Then say, "Today, we are going to look at successful methods of evangelism used by the disciples. Let's compare them with the methods we've discussed."

Into the Word

Provide each student with paper and pencil. Then tell them that we have divided the lesson text into three passages: verses 35-39, 40-42, and 43-50. Ask each student to write a short sentence to explain each verse, and then a brief summary of the method of evangelism used in each passage. Their outlines should resemble the following:

John 1:35-39

v. 35 John the Baptist was standing with two of his disciples.
v. 36 John identified Jesus as the Lamb of God.
v. 37 The two disciples followed Jesus.
v. 38 In response to Jesus' question, the two asked Jesus where He dwelt.
v. 39 Jesus invited them to come and see, and they spent the day with Him.

Summary: John used his influence as a prophet and teacher to point others to Jesus.

John 1:40-42

v. 40 Andrew was one of the two disciples of John who followed Jesus.
v. 41 Andrew immediately shared his discovery with his brother, Peter.
v. 42 Andrew brought Peter to meet Jesus.

Summary: Andrew's enthusiasm for the Lord caused him to bring his brother to Jesus.

John 1:43-50

v. 43 Jesus called Philip to be a disciple.
v. 44 Philip was from Bethsaida.
v. 45 Philip told Nathanael about Jesus.
v. 46 Nathanael doubted Philip and was challenged to see for himself.
v. 47 Jesus gave indication of His divinity.
v. 48 Jesus gave added proof of His divinity.
v. 49 Nathanael acknowledged Jesus' deity.
v. 50 Jesus promised great things to come.

Summary: Philip's persistence caused Nathanael to come and see Jesus for himself.

Ask the students to share their work. Write on the board the best outline point for each verse and make a composite summary for each section. Then ask these questions:

1. What characteristics did these methods of evangelism have in common? (Each sought to introduce a person to Jesus so that that person could personally evaluate Him.)
2. What made these methods effective? (They depended on a person's meeting Jesus, not merely hearing about Him.)

Into Life

Today's lesson may be summed up in two words: "*Who?* and *How?* Who do we know (relatives, friends, neighbors, club members) who need to know Jesus? (Have each student write the names of two persons on their papers.) How can we be helpful in causing these persons' to "meet" Jesus? Read the list of modern methods of evangelism mentioned in the opening activity. Ask the students to select from that list one method they will use this week to be an evangelist for Jesus.

Let's Talk It Over

The questions on this page are designed to encourage review of the lesson Scriptures and to promote discussion of the lesson by the class. The answers provided are only discussion starters. Let your class talk it over from there.

1. How is Jesus' effect upon the lives of His disciples a demonstration of His identity as the Son of God?

Many have noted how outwardly unremarkable were the men Jesus gathered around Him as His closest followers. To begin a great spiritual enterprise such as the church, it might seem that scholars, orators, and people of wealth and influence would be needed at the outset. But Jesus chose fishermen, a tax collector, and other common Galileans to lead in this undertaking. We may note also that Jesus chose a group that featured potential conflicts within it. These included the curious combination of Simon the Zealot, who was a nationalist, with Matthew the tax collector, who had collaborated with the Roman rulers. Jesus molded this band into a force through which He built a church that has endured for almost two thousand years. That certainly testifies to His divine character.

2. Evangelism has a simple pattern: a Christian speaks to another person about Jesus, and that person becomes a follower of Jesus. Is it that simple for us? If not, why not?

Evangelism would seem less fearful if we could learn to speak more naturally about Jesus. It is not too difficult to talk to others about religion in general or the church or the Bible. But people need to hear about Jesus himself. When we who are Christians are together in our classes, our fellowship gatherings, and even our casual meetings, we need to practice speaking about Jesus. That will help us become more comfortable in mentioning Him during our conversations with non-Christians. Of course, not every such conversation will result in the winning of a follower for Jesus, but a simple, sincere testimony may at least plant the gospel seed (note 1 Corinthians 3:6-8).

3. Is enthusiasm the most vital characteristic of the person who seeks to tell others about Jesus Christ? Why or why not?

The answer to this question surely is no, because error can be presented with enthusiasm just as truth can be. Knowledge of the truth and the ability to state it clearly are more important, but these can be more effective when they are enthusiastically presented. We do not want to stifle the zeal of new converts who are eager to share their newly-found faith with their families and friends, but it is important that their zeal be complemented by the understanding of basic doctrines and the Scriptures that describe them. On the other hand, long-time believers who have mastered the fundamental teachings of Scripture may require an occasional "pumping up" of their enthusiasm. In Romans 10:2 Paul spoke of the Jews' having "a zeal of God, but not according to knowledge." We must have the zeal *and* the knowledge.

4. Nathanael was ready to reject Jesus because He was from Nazareth. What are some facts about Jesus that lead people today to reject Him?

Nathanael's question, "Can there any good thing come out of Nazareth?" could be reworded in our time. Some might ask, "Can there any good thing come out of the Bible?" We live in an era when the Bible has been dissected, debated, and discounted. Jesus' association with the Bible may be to His disadvantage in the minds of some people. Others might ask, "Can there any good thing come out of the church?" When Jesus' church becomes known for disharmony, indifference, or lack of love and compassion, observers may be led to reject Him. Another question is, "Can there any good thing come out of 'Christian nations'?" When Christianity becomes identified with a particular race, culture, or nation that has a poor reputation, the cause of Christ suffers.

5. What is wrong with the "let's-give-it-a-try" approach to Christian living?

We may ask the person who wants to give the Christian faith a try, "What results do you expect from your try?" If one hopes to have all of one's problems resolved in a few weeks' time, or to gain prompt financial success or domestic harmony, one's try will likely end in failure. The New Testament leaves no room for an experimental approach to Christianity. Jesus expects full commitment from those who would be His disciples. That's what He meant when He said, "If any man will come after me, let him deny himself, and take up his cross, and follow me" (Matthew 16:24).

Can This Be the Christ?

May 16
Lesson 11

LESSON SCRIPTURE: **John 4:1-42.**

PRINTED TEXT: **John 4:7-15, 20-26.**

DEVOTIONAL READING: **John 4:43-54.**

John 4:7-15, 20-26

7 There cometh a woman of Samaria to draw water: Jesus saith unto her, Give me to drink.

8 (For his disciples were gone away unto the city to buy meat.)

9 Then saith the woman of Samaria unto him, How is it that thou, being a Jew, askest drink of me, which am a woman of Samaria? for the Jews have no dealings with the Samaritans.

10 Jesus answered and said unto her, If thou knewest the gift of God, and who it is that saith to thee, Give me to drink; thou wouldest have asked of him, and he would have given thee living water.

11 The woman saith unto him, Sir, thou hast nothing to draw with, and the well is deep: from whence then hast thou that living water?

12 Art thou greater than our father Jacob, which gave us the well, and drank thereof himself, and his children, and his cattle?

13 Jesus answered and said unto her, Whosoever drinketh of this water shall thirst again:

14 But whosoever drinketh of the water that I shall give him shall never thirst; but the water that I shall give him shall be in him a well of water springing up into everlasting life.

15 The woman saith unto him, Sir, give me this water, that I thirst not, neither come hither to draw.

. . . .

20 Our fathers worshipped in this mountain; and ye say, that in Jerusalem is the place where men ought to worship.

21 Jesus saith unto her, Woman, believe me, the hour cometh, when ye shall neither in this mountain, nor yet at Jerusalem, worship the Father.

22 Ye worship ye know not what: we know what we worship; for salvation is of the Jews.

23 But the hour cometh, and now is, when the true worshippers shall worship the Father in spirit and in truth: for the Father seeketh such to worship him.

24 God is a Spirit: and they that worship him must worship him in spirit and in truth.

25 The woman saith unto him, I know that Messiah cometh, which is called Christ: when he is come, he will tell us all things.

26 Jesus saith unto her, I that speak unto thee am he.

GOLDEN TEXT: We . . . know that this is indeed the Christ, the Saviour of the world.—John 4:42.

Believing in Christ

Unit 3. John: Believe in Jesus

(Lessons 9-13)

Lesson Aims

After this lesson, the students should:

1. Be able to relate the story of Jesus' interview with the woman of Samaria, including the results.
2. Be able to explain the manner in which Jesus obtained the interest of the woman and how He directed the course of the conversation.
3. Be alert to opportunities for opening a conversation on spiritual matters.

Lesson Outline

INTRODUCTION
- A. Erasing Blackboards
- B. Lesson Background

I. UNUSUAL MEETING (John 4:7-9)
- A. Opening the Conversation (v. 7)
- B. Circumstances of the Meeting (v. 8)
- C. Curiosity Indicating Interest (v. 9)

II. PUZZLING OFFER (John 4:10-15)
- A. The Gift of God (v. 10)
- B. Bewilderment (vv. 11, 12)
- C. The Living Water (vv. 13, 14)
  Thirsty Again
- D. The Woman's Request (v. 15)

III. JESUS TEACHES ABOUT WORSHIP (John 4:20-26)
- A. A Change of Subject (v. 20)
- B. Worship in Spirit and in Truth (vv. 21-24)
  True Worship
- C. The Speaker Is Messiah (vv. 25, 26)

CONCLUSION
- A. Life's Turning Points
- B. Prayer
- C. Thought to Remember

Visual 11 of the visuals packet highlights the main thoughts concerning the "living water" Jesus offers. The visual is shown on page 318.

Introduction

A. Erasing Blackboards

In days gone by, one of the joys in elementary school was to be given the *privilege* of erasing the blackboards and dusting the erasers. (The latter was done outside the building by beating two erasers together to get out the chalk dust.) The question of why we considered it to be a privilege to do so unpleasant a task never entered our heads. But obviously, when the teacher said, "Mary, you may erase the blackboards today," she was conferring some kind of honor. And immediately others would volunteer.

It doesn't require a degree in psychology to realize that the teacher, in this case, was imparting to the student a feeling of importance and of worth. Some children have been criticized so often that they have lost all sense of worth and self-respect. It is a wise teacher who can awaken new confidence in such a student.

Jesus was the master teacher. This was clearly shown in His conversation with the woman at the well, which is the text for this lesson. With an attitude of respect, Jesus opened the conversation on a topic of mutual interest—water to drink. Note the following factors as He led this chance listener to a consideration of profound truth.

1. First, He had a message for her of vital importance. 2. He was genuinely concerned for her welfare. 3. In no fashion did He speak to her in a condescending manner. 4. He secured her attention by asking her a favor, and thus also gave her a feeling of importance. 5. He began with reference to what was common and well known (water) and moved on to a discussion of the things of God. 6. He stimulated interest by arousing curiosity. 7. With an innocent request, "Go, call thy husband" (v. 16), He brought her to a consideration of the life-style she had adopted, and to a tacit admission of guilt (v. 19). 8. When she would evade the issue by changing the subject, He used her newly formed perception of Him as a basis for further vital teaching.

Teacher: familiarize yourself with the above, and at this point read the Scripture text to the class. Include verses 16-19.

B. Lesson Background

John the Baptist had baptized Jesus and had announced Him as the Lamb of God and as the Son of God. "He must increase," John said of Jesus, "but I must decrease" (John 3:30). John continued his ministry, but soon Jesus was making more disciples than he (John 4:1). The Pharisees took note of this, and from that time their eye of scrutiny was continuously upon Jesus. He was not frightened, but He desired to continue His ministry and His training of the apostles without interruption. And so for the time being, he left Judea to go into Galilee.

For this journey there was a choice of two routes. He could go straight northward from Jerusalem, through Samaria. Or, He could go east to the Jordan, cross over and head north through Perea, and then cross back over the river west into Galilee. Obviously, the second route was farther, but usually the Jews took the longer way because of the hatred between Jews and Samaritans. On this trip, however, Jesus chose to go through Samaria. He did not share any hatred or prejudice against them, but would gladly take God's offer of life to a people whom others considered as outcasts.

Traveling through Samaria, Jesus and His disciples approached the city of Sychar, nestled in the valley between Mount Gerizim and Mount Ebal. Nearby was Jacob's well. (The well exists today, still yielding water). It was noon when Jesus and His disciples arrived here. The disciples went into town to buy food. Jesus, tired and thirsty, sat on the curb of the well to rest.

I. Unusual Meeting (John 4:7-9)

A. Opening the Conversation (v. 7)

7. There cometh a woman of Samaria to draw water: Jesus saith unto her, Give me to drink.

As Jesus rested, *a woman of Samaria* (that is, the province of Samaria in which the city of Sychar was located) came out from the city to draw water. We wonder what her thoughts were as she arrived at the well and saw a man here, a Jew, no less! Was she upset—even angered to find a stranger here? Was this an awkward situation, an embarrassing moment? If so, Jesus defused the situation with a humble request, *Give me to drink.* He spoke to her as one thirsty soul to another. Thirst is one thing they had in common. And He would put himself in her debt by accepting a favor from her. Thus He began a conversation in a situation that otherwise might have known only a cold silence and would have perpetuated the enmity between Jews and Samaritans.

B. Circumstances of the Meeting (v. 8)

8. (For his disciples were gone away unto the city to buy meat.)

Although there was hostility between the Jews and Samaritans, apparently they had some dealings with each other, for the disciples had gone into Sychar to buy food for the group.

C. Curiosity Indicating Interest (v. 9)

9. Then saith the woman of Samaria unto him, How is it that thou, being a Jew, askest drink of me, which am a woman of Samaria? for the Jews have no dealings with the Samaritans.

The woman was curious and had every right to be. The barrier that existed between them was, in her sight, quite formidable. He was a Jew, one of a people who hated and disdained the Samaritans. To add to her wonder, He was a man speaking to a Samaritan *woman.*

For the Jews have no dealings with the Samaritans. It is not certain whether these words were spoken by the woman or added by John for the benefit of his non-Jewish readers.

When the Assyrians conquered the northern kingdom in 721 B.C., they deported many of the Israelites, allowing the very poor to remain. The Assyrians then brought in foreigners to resettle the land. These intermarried with the Israelites who remained, and the result was a mixed race—the Samaritans—despised by the Jews in the southern kingdom for that reason. The antagonism between the Jews in the southern kingdom and the Samaritans was intensified during the time of the return of the Jews from Babylonian captivity, when the Samaritans were not allowed to share in the rebuilding of the temple (535 B.C.). The animosity continued between the two peoples from that time until the time of Christ.

II. Puzzling Offer (John 4:10-15)

Jesus now, in gentle fashion, moved the conversation from a drink of water and the animosity between races to spiritual matters.

A. The Gift of God (v. 10)

10. Jesus answered and said unto her, If thou knewest the gift of God, and who it is that saith to thee, Give me to drink; thou wouldest have asked of him, and he would have given thee living water.

The gift of God, of which Jesus spoke, was salvation or everlasting life, which would be made available through Him. Of course, the woman had no way of knowing of God's gift; nor did she know who Jesus was. Therefore, she had no reason to ask Him for this gift (the living water) that He was willing to give.

Living water. This designation was commonly used of the water bubbling forth from a spring or at the bottom of a well, in contrast to water gathered in a pool or cistern. In other words, flowing

How to Say It

ASSYRIANS. Uh-*sear*-ee-unz.
BABYLONIANS. Bab-uh-*low*-nee-unz.
EBAL. *Ee*-bal.
GERIZIM. *Gair*-ih-zim or Guh-*rye*-zim.
PEREA. Peh-*ree*-uh.
SHECHEM. *Shee*-kem or *Shek*-em.
SYCHAR. *Sy*-kar.

water. And that is how the woman understood the expression when Jesus used it. As the conversation progresses, it becomes clear that Jesus was speaking of everlasting life, which comes to a person when God dwells within him or her.

B. Bewilderment (vv. 11, 12)

The woman was puzzled, not realizing that Jesus was speaking figuratively of God's offer of the gift of everlasting life. He had asked for water, but now offered her *living water.* The water in Jacob's well was *living water,* in her view; that is, not stagnant. But Jesus could not give her this, for He had just asked for a drink himself. And so, her question.

11, 12. The woman saith unto him, Sir, thou hast nothing to draw with, and the well is deep: from whence then hast thou that living water? Art thou greater than our father Jacob, which gave us the well, and drank thereof himself, and his children, and his cattle?

Because she took His words literally, the woman was confused. Jesus had no vessel by which to draw water from a well. Furthermore, the well was *deep.* If the well was the one that today bears the name of Jacob's well, it was more than one hundred feet deep. How could He get at the spring water that bubbled up at the bottom of it?

Our father Jacob. The Samaritans claimed descent from Jacob through Joseph and his sons, Ephraim and Manasseh. The woman was obviously proud of her descendancy from Jacob, and there was a bit of challenge in her question: "Are you greater than he?" The way her question is stated in the Greek indicates that she expected a negative answer. Yet, the fact that she asked the question suggests that she was beginning to think that Jesus was someone special.

C. The Living Water (vv. 13, 14)

Jesus did not give a yes or no answer to her question, and He would not be drawn into a discussion of the ancestry of the Samaritans. He simply stated the differences between what Jacob had left his descendants and what He himself offers.

13, 14. Jesus answered and said unto her, Whosoever drinketh of this water shall thirst again: but whosoever drinketh of the water that I shall give him shall never thirst; but the water that I shall give him shall be in him a well of water springing up into everlasting life.

Whosoever drinketh of this water shall thirst again. This the woman knew from experience. Nothing of this earth satisfies *permanently*—not even water from Jacob's well. However, man has a thirst greater than that for water, and that is his soul's thirst for God. Augustine spoke of this when he said, "Thou hast created us, O God, for thyself, and our souls find no rest until they rest in Thee."

Jesus has the answer for the soul's thirst. *Whosoever drinketh of the water that I shall give him shall never thirst.* To deny the soul's thirst for God leads to spiritual death. The remedy is not to deny our spiritual need, but to satisfy it. This Jesus can and will do for us. When He says that the one who drinks of the water that He gives shall never thirst, He means that that person's soul will never be *thirsty* again. Such a one will always have within himself or herself the means of satisfying the soul's longing for God. (Jesus' promise of water that shall be *a well of water springing up into everlasting life* is comparable to the promise of the Holy Spirit as God's abiding presence in the lives of His followers. See John 7:39.)

THIRSTY AGAIN

One of the earliest symptoms of diabetes is unquenchable thirst, sometimes accompanied by insatiable appetite. Diabetics are unable to drink enough to satisfy their thirst. Non-Christians are similarly affected in their souls. Thirst for possessions and pleasure is never fully quenched. Humanists and secularists drink and drink at the fountains of fortune and frivolity, but they can never get enough to fill their empty hearts. They are always thirsty again.

"Everyone who drinks this water will be thirsty again," Jesus told the woman at the well. Regular intake of water is essential to physical life and health; the truth of Jesus is vital to spiritual life and growth. Drinking from Christ's cup is the only way to satisfy forever the longings of one's soul.

Emptiness is a common symptom of the spiritual epidemic that is rampant among fast-track, workaholic, social climbers in secular society. The disease even has affected some in the church. As Jesus promised, however, thirsty souls can be satisfied when they draw from the right wells. "Blessed are those who hunger and thirst for righteousness, for they will be filled" (Matthew 5:6, *New International Version*).

—R. W. B.

D. The Woman's Request (v. 15)

15. The woman saith unto him, Sir, give me this water, that I thirst not, neither come hither to draw.

Sir, give me this water. Although still puzzled, the woman asked for the *living water* of which Jesus spoke, not knowing that He was referring to things spiritual. She asked for water; He would show her the way to new life as a child of God. The first step required that she deal with the sin in her life. Notice how, without accusations, He introduced the subject. (Read verses 16-18.)

Jesus did not denounce her as a "vile sinner." Instead of using harsh words of condemnation, He gently led her to see herself as she really was, a sinner in need of God's loving forgiveness. Because He knew so much about her personal life, she naturally concluded that He was a prophet (v. 19).

III. Jesus Teaches About Worship (John 4:20-26)

The woman had been made to face the sin in her life. Perhaps in an effort to draw Jesus' attention away from her own life-style, she raised the issue about the correct place to worship. The Jews and Samaritans had conflicting ideas about this subject.

A. A Change of Subject (v. 20)

20. Our fathers worshipped in this mountain; and ye say, that in Jerusalem is the place where men ought to worship.

This mountain is a reference to Mount Gerizim, at the foot of which the village of Sychar lay. The Samaritans said that this was the place that God had chosen "to put his name there" (Deuteronomy 12:5).

The *fathers* (for example, Abraham and Jacob) had erected altars to God at Shechem, which was near Mount Gerizim (Genesis 12:6, 7; 33:18-20). The Jews, however, insisted that the central place of worship was Jerusalem.

B. Worship in Spirit and in Truth (vv. 21-24)

21. Jesus saith unto her, Woman, believe me, the hour cometh, when ye shall neither in this mountain, nor yet at Jerusalem, worship the Father.

Again, Jesus would not allow himself to be drawn into a discussion of a subject of controversy between the Samaritans and the Jews. Instead, He took the subject of worship, which the woman introduced, and turned the emphasis away from the place where one worships to the Person who is worshiped. He was saying that the worship of the Father could not be restricted *only* to *this mountain* or to *Jerusalem.* God is the Lord of all, and Jesus implied that He could be worshiped anywhere.

22. Ye worship ye know not what: we know what we worship; for salvation is of the Jews.

Here Jesus states that the worship of the Samaritans was done in ignorance. How could it be otherwise, since they accepted only the five books of Moses and rejected all the books of prophecy and poetry of the Old Testament? Jesus went on to say that *we* (the Jews) *know what we worship.* The Jews accepted the entire Old Testament, and thus were exposed to all of what God had revealed of himself. These Scriptures clearly indicate that the salvation God would offer through His Son would proceed from the Jews.

23, 24. But the hour cometh, and now is, when the true worshippers shall worship the Father in spirit and in truth: for the Father seeketh such to worship him. God is a Spirit: and they that worship him must worship him in spirit and in truth.

Jesus now turned to the "how" of worship. For many in that day, worship was considered a matter of observing prescribed ceremonies in the proper place. But true worship is much more. First, it must be done *in spirit.* Worship is homage rendered to God with one's entire heart and mind. If we "worship" without the involvement of our spirits, we do not worship at all—we simply go through the motions. Second, true worship is *in truth.* It is directed to God as He is revealed in Scripture. It is the feeling and the expression of adoration or praise to God as He really is, and not as we may think He ought to be.

TRUE WORSHIP

Expressions change. Persons who used to "carry chips on their shoulders" or had "axes to grind" are now people "with an attitude." So, the word *attitude* has taken on a negative connotation. Having an attitude has come to mean some sort of personality defect.

In reality, of course, attitudes can be either bad or good. Attitude is a state of mind, affected by opinions, philosophy, biases, temperament,

Home Daily Bible Readings

Monday, May 10—The Water of Life (John 4:1-14)

Tuesday, May 11—True Worship (John 4:15-24)

Wednesday, May 12—Can This Be the Christ? (John 4:25-30)

Thursday, May 13—White for Harvest (John 4:31-38)

Friday, May 14—A Personal Experience (John 4:39-42)

Saturday, May 15—Looking for Signs (John 4:43-48)

Sunday, May 16—The Second Sign (John 4:49-54)

and faith. One's attitude can produce either virtues or vices. What you think of yourself, what you believe about God, and how you feel about others—all determine your attitude toward life, morality, and society in general. Behavior is designed by attitude.

Jesus taught that worship is as much an attitude as it is an activity. "In spirit and in truth" means that the place and accoutrements of worship are incidental when compared to one's state of mind and the condition of one's heart. Awe and reverence for God are basic to true worship. Integrity and sincerity are essential. What goes on in the worshiper's heart and mind during a service of worship determines whether or not one has truly worshiped.

What is your attitude as you sing, pray, give offerings, commune, and hear God's Word?

—R. W. B.

C. The Speaker Is Messiah (vv. 25, 26)

25, 26. The woman saith unto him, I know that Messiah cometh, which is called Christ: when he is come, he will tell us all things. Jesus saith unto her, I that speak unto thee am he.

I know that Messiah cometh. As previously mentioned, the Samaritans lacked the prophetic books of the Old Testament, in which are found so many of the references to the Messiah. Yet the Scriptures they accepted contained God's promise that He would raise up a great prophet like Moses. "I will . . . put my words in his mouth," God said, "and he shall speak . . . all that I shall command him" (Deuteronomy 18:18).

Was the Samaritan woman astonished to learn that Jesus was the Messiah? "Overjoyed" would be a better word, for she hastened to report to the men of Sychar, saying, "Is not this the Christ?" (v. 29). After hearing Him, they were equally certain and enthusiastic in their belief that Jesus was "indeed the Christ, the Saviour of the world" (v. 42).

Conclusion

A. Life's Turning Points

If we were to speak of turning points in life, what thoughts would come to your mind? Would you think of some occasion such as graduation from high school or college? Marriage? A move to a new location? The attainment of a coveted position? These are significant events, but they are not necessarily turning points. They are only mileposts along the way. A true turning point in life is a point at which a significant change takes place in the course of that life.

Suppose you were interviewing a prisoner in the state penitentiary. In answer to your question, "Where did you go wrong?" do you think that person would say, "It was when I committed my first murder"? Or, "When I robbed my first bank"? Oh, no. More likely it would be, "When I took my first drink," or, "When I stole my first quarter," or, "When I began lying to my folks," or, "When I began going with the wrong crowd." Some little incident that seemed innocent at the time was, in reality, the turning point, the first step on the downward path.

Many persons who now live in fellowship with Jesus Christ experienced a turning point, an event that started them on the road to faith in Him. One says, "It was when I was invited to a Bible-school class in which I saw Christ demonstrated in the lives of the students." Another says, "It was when I started dating my wife. She insisted that I attend church with her, and I did." Or yet another, "Because of a plane delay I was waiting in an airport, talking with a fellow beside me. In a calm and sincere manner, he spoke to me of Christ and of what it means to be a Christian. That was the turning point of my life."

All of these, like the meeting of the woman of Samaria with the Stranger at the well, were very ordinary occasions. They became turning points, however, when during the occasion the person who was lost met Jesus. But someone had to be present to make the introduction! May God help us to be alert to every such opportunity.

B. Prayer

O Lord, our God, we praise Your name for Your goodness to us, for the love and mercy that You have shown to us. We know that eternal life, the living water that You have offered through Your Son Jesus Christ, is intended for everyone. Help us to be alert to opportunities for making Christ known and for inviting others to join us in following Him. In His precious name we pray. Amen.

C. Thought to Remember

"The Spirit and the bride say, Come. . . . And let him that is athirst come. And whosoever will, let him take the water of life freely" (Revelation 22:17).

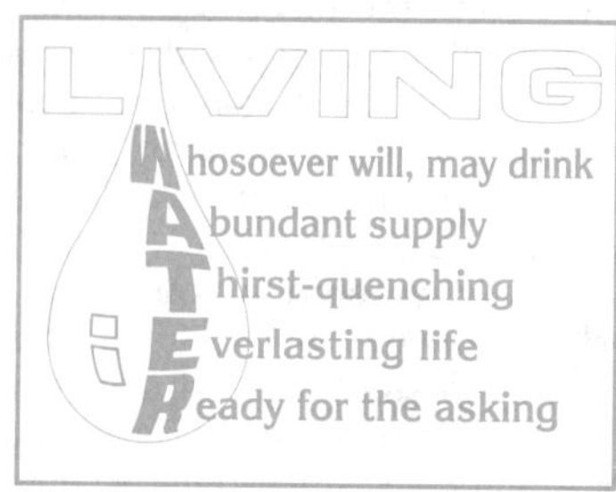

visual 11

Learning by Doing

This page contains an alternate lesson plan emphasizing learning activities. Classes desiring such student involvement will find these suggestions helpful.

Learning Goals

As a result of this lesson, students:

1. Will be able to tell the story of Jesus and the woman at the well.

2. Will look to Christ, not to material things, to satisfy their spiritual thirst.

Into the Lesson

Begin class by telling about a time when you were terribly thirsty. As you relate your story, slowly pour small amounts of soda pop into a clear glass from time to time. For example, "We had been fishing all day in one-hundred-degree heat, but we forgot to take along the cooler of soft drinks. The fish were biting so well that we hated to leave. We finally did, though, and by the time we got to a convenience store our lips were cracked, we were so weak we could hardly stand up, and all we could think about was liquid."

Now ask the class, "What is the purpose of thirst?" After they have answered that question, ask, "What are the signs of spiritual thirst?" Discuss this for about three minutes.

Point out that today's lesson deals with a woman who had a deep spiritual thirst, and presents Jesus' remedy for it.

Into the Word

Divide the class into groups of three or four (or more) students, depending on the size of your class. Put the following italicized statements, and the questions that accompany each, on separate sheets of paper and give each of your groups a sheet.

Read John 4:7-30 aloud, then ask the groups of students to discuss their questions and try to answer them from the text. Give them fifteen minutes for this.

The thirst for God cannot be satisfied with earthly things (vv. 10, 13, 14).

1. What are some human needs that only God can satisfy? (Example: desire for forgiveness.)

2. Seeking some things is like drinking salt water to quench thirst. Name some things like that. (Example: money.)

Marriage and intimacy do not meet all the needs of the human heart (v. 18).

1. What does marriage *not* do for people?

2. Why do we sometimes expect so much from our mates and marriage itself? How can we change that?

Spiritual needs transcend race and gender (vv. 9, 10, 27).

1. What are some of the human needs common to all races of people in all cultures?

2. What are some of the human needs that both men and women have in common, and how does Christ meet those needs?

Sin needs to be confronted, but there is a right and a wrong way to confront sinners (vv. 16, 17).

1. How was Jesus tactful with the woman at the well? Give examples of how we can use tact when speaking about Christ to those outside of Him.

2. How can sin be a force to lead a person to God?

Jesus knows everything about everyone, so He can meet our needs precisely (vv. 18, 29).

1. Why should we be open with God?

2. What are some things you are glad God knows about, and why?

After the time is up, have the groups report their conclusions to the whole class. Let the class discuss and add additional thoughts.

Into Life

Give each student a sheet on which you have listed the human needs shown in italics below. Ask them to circle the three needs that are most important to them at this time in their lives. Have them do this anonymously. Then collect the sheets and read aloud the needs indicated.

Human Needs

hope love security companionship worship
forgiveness change wisdom strength truth
meaning vocation goals rest faith health
beauty patience success stability discipline
holiness money freedom challenge solitude
happiness willpower sympathy attention

Point out that some of our needs, even spiritual ones, will not be fully met in this life. On the other hand, many of these needs can be met by the church—by people helping people.

Discuss ways that the needs indicated by your class members can be met by other members of your class. List these ways on the board.

Put your class back into the groups they were in earlier, and give each group several of the lists of needs that were checked in the last exercise. Ask each group to pray for each other's specific needs.

Let's Talk It Over

The questions on this page are designed to encourage review of the lesson Scriptures and to promote discussion of the lesson by the class. The answers provided are only discussion starters. Let your class talk it over from there.

1. When we are seeking to share our faith in Jesus Christ with another person, why is it helpful to emphasize what we have in common with that person?

Some non-Christians tend to regard Christians as oddities. When they find that believers in the Lord share their interests in automobiles, sewing, fishing, baking, etc., some of that aura of oddness is removed. Sometimes what the non-Christian and the Christian have in common is strong enough to form something of a bond between the two. For example, each may have a child serving in the armed forces in some far-off place, or each may have suffered from a recent serious illness. As 1 Corinthians 9:19-22 shows us, Paul considered it important to find common ground with people whom he wished to win to the Lord. He summed up this approach by declaring, "I am made all things to all men, that I might by all means save some."

2. The lesson writer observes that "nothing of this earth satisfies permanently." In what ways have we found that to be true?

No pleasure can satisfy for long. We have surely anticipated at some time the pleasure of a meal, a ballgame, a vacation, or a meeting with old friends. After the occasion was past, perhaps we felt the frustration brought on because of the fleeting nature of such pleasure. No material object can satisfy for long. For the first few days or weeks after acquiring a new car or a new piece of furniture for our home, we may derive deep satisfaction from it, but the satisfaction soon fades. No achievement can satisfy for long. Graduation from high school, a job promotion, the winning of an award in athletics or music—these are bright moments that are quickly forgotten. There is much wisdom in the observation that "only what's done for Christ will last."

3. Jesus demonstrated wisdom and compassion in the way He led the Samaritan woman to face her sin. How can we follow His example in this?

It is vital that non-Christians be led to face their sins. People can claim to believe in Jesus Christ and accept Him as Savior without taking the critical step of repentance. But this cannot be described as conversion. There were occasions when Jesus bluntly denounced sin (see Matthew 23:13-39), but here He progressed gently in awakening the woman to the need in her life. At no time did He reject or condemn her because of her sin. When we see Jesus working in such a masterful way to win this woman, it should impress us to pray that we might be able to reproduce His approach. Here is one area in which we will want to ask for wisdom (James 1:5) and for a heart of compassion.

4. If you have done evangelistic calling, you have probably encountered persons who raised various religious questions in order to avoid discussing their own spiritual needs. How do we deal with such persons?

This is a difficult situation to handle, but we may answer the question by simply saying that we must be single-minded and persistent in our effort to bring the person to the point of admitting his or her own need for Christ. We note that Jesus took the woman's religious question (John 4:20), discussed it, and led her right back to the matter of faith in Him. We remember that Philip did this with the Ethiopian eunuch (Acts 8:30-35). Jesus is the focus of the entire Bible. Therefore, if we become familiar with God's Word, we should be able to begin with any Scripture under discussion and from it turn the questioner's attention to Jesus.

5. For many persons there are potential turning points in which they are especially susceptible to be influenced for Christ. How can we recognize these occasions so that we can utilize them in our evangelistic efforts?

In Acts 16 we read of two noteworthy conversions. Verse 14 tells of Lydia, "whose heart the Lord opened, that she attended unto the things which were spoken of Paul." She was susceptible to Christian influence, because she was already engaging in worship. So let us be alert for those who are seeking God, and be ready to guide them to the true water of life. Verses 25-34 describe the experience of the Philippian jailer. He was susceptible to Christian influence because of the crisis of an earthquake and the possible escape of his prisoners. Crises related to health, income, family, etc. often cause people today to be receptive to the gospel.

Confronting the Galilean

May 23
Lesson 12

Lesson Scripture: John 7:37-52.

Printed Text: John 7:37-52.

Devotional Reading: John 7:1-13.

John 7:37-52

37 In the last day, that great day of the feast, Jesus stood and cried, saying, If any man thirst, let him come unto me, and drink.
38 He that believeth on me, as the Scripture hath said, out of his belly shall flow rivers of living water.
39 (But this spake he of the Spirit, which they that believe on him should receive: for the Holy Ghost was not yet given; because that Jesus was not yet glorified.)
40 Many of the people therefore, when they heard this saying, said, Of a truth this is the Prophet.
41 Others said, This is the Christ. But some said, Shall Christ come out of Galilee?
42 Hath not the Scripture said, That Christ cometh of the seed of David, and out of the town of Bethlehem, where David was?
43 So there was a division among the people because of him.
44 And some of them would have taken him; but no man laid hands on him.
45 Then came the officers to the chief priests and Pharisees; and they said unto them, Why have ye not brought him?
46 The officers answered, Never man spake like this man.
47 Then answered them the Pharisees, Are ye also deceived?
48 Have any of the rulers or of the Pharisees believed on him?
49 But this people who knoweth not the law are cursed.
50 Nicodemus saith unto them, (he that came to Jesus by night, being one of them,)
51 Doth our law judge any man, before it hear him, and know what he doeth?
52 They answered and said unto him, Art thou also of Galilee? Search, and look: for out of Galilee ariseth no prophet.

Golden Text: This is the Christ.—John 7:41.

Believing in Christ

Unit 3. John: Believe in Jesus

(Lessons 9-13)

Lesson Aims

At the conclusion of this lesson, the students should:

1. Be able to tell something of the observance of the feast of Tabernacles and of how Jesus' message was related to that observance.
2. Understand how the public viewed Jesus at this time and possible reasons why.
3. Reexamine the basis of their concept of Christ, whether based on hearsay or on evidence.

Lesson Outline

INTRODUCTION
- A. Hearsay or Evidence?
- B. Lesson Background

I. JESUS OFFERS LIVING WATER (John 7:37-39)
- A. Believe and Drink of the Water (vv. 37, 38)
- B. Believe and Receive the Holy Spirit (v. 39)
  Thirsty

II. BELIEVERS AND UNBELIEVERS (John 7:40-43)
- A. Acclamation (vv. 40, 41a)
- B. Rejection (vv. 41b-43)
  The Great Divide

III. JESUS' ENEMIES THWARTED (John 7:44-52)
- A. Frustrated Citizens (v. 44)
- B. Empty-handed Guards (vv. 45-49)
- C. A Believing Ruler (vv. 50-52)

CONCLUSION
- A. Examine the Evidence
- B. Prayer
- C. Thought to Remember

Display visual 12 of the visuals packet and let it remain before the class throughout this session. The visual is shown on page 324.

Introduction

A. Hearsay or Evidence?

Anyone who has watched crime movies on TV has seen it. At one point during the testimony the defense attorney will say, "Your Honor, I object. What the witness is saying is only *hearsay,* and is not admissible as evidence." "Objection sustained," says the judge, "strike that from the record."

We all know, or should know, how unreliable hearsay testimony is. But hearsay is very subtle, and if it is repeated often enough, many accept it as fact.

One's conclusion based on hearsay testimony will be just about anything one wants it to be! Robert Browning's *The Ring and the Book* demonstrates this in a most convincing way. One chapter is entitled "Half-Rome," revealing what many in Rome believed in regard to a murder that had been committed. Read this chapter and you are sure their conclusion was right. Then read the next chapter, "The Other Half-Rome," and you will change your mind and say, "*This* must be right." But the following chapter, "Tertium Quid," presents a third view held by others, a view that again seems most plausible. The lesson for us is that conclusions based on hearsay alone must always be suspect.

The events recorded in today's lesson text took place just about six months before Jesus' crucifixion. For about three years He had taught, both in Judea and in Galilee. Now He was in Jerusalem when the city was thronging with people. Rumors were flying. Word was circulating that Jesus was a wanted man, and people were taking sides. For many, their position was based almost altogether on hearsay. But now Jesus was in their midst. They would have opportunity to see and to hear Him firsthand. Now they must judge for themselves who He was.

B. Lesson Background

The setting for the events in today's lesson was the feast of Tabernacles, the third of the three great annual Jewish festivals (the other two being Passover and Pentecost). The festival continued for seven days, climaxing with a special "holy convocation" on the eighth day (Leviticus 23:36). The time was late September or early October.

As the festival season approached, Jesus was in Galilee. At this time "he wished to avoid Judaea because the Jews were looking for a chance to kill him" (John 7:1, *The New English Bible*). But Jesus' own brothers chided Him for not going to the great gathering of people in Jerusalem. They thought that He ought to make himself known. "No one who wants to become a public figure acts in secret . . . show yourself to the world," they said (7:4, *New International Version*). Urging His brothers to go on up to the feast, Jesus added, "For me the right time has not yet come" (7:8).

In the meantime, the authorities in Jerusalem were looking for Jesus, quite confident that He would come for the festival. And there was much discussion among the people about Him. "What do you think?" one would ask. "Oh, He is a good man," some said. "No He isn't," others said. "He is a deceiver." (Can you imagine that

How to Say It

NICODEMUS. *Nick*-uh-*dee*-mus (strong accent on *dee*).
PHARISEES. *Fair*-ih-seez.
SADDUCEES. *Sad*-you-seez.

the influence of Christ upon the world is the work of a deceiver?) But in Jerusalem no one dared to speak His name above a whisper for fear of being jerked off the street and dragged away for questioning (vv. 11-13).

After His brothers had gone to the feast, Jesus also went—"not openly, but as it were in secret" (v. 10). If He had gone with the crowds to Jerusalem, He would have been instantly recognized by some who, in the excitement of the occasion, might have tried by force to make Him their leader. This doubtless would have led to a showdown with those in power. Jesus wanted to avoid such a confrontation, for His mission was not a political one.

So He came to Jerusalem unnoticed about the middle of the week, and went up to the temple and began teaching the people (v. 14). The Jewish authorities marveled that an uneducated man could speak in such a scholarly fashion. How could it be? they wondered among themselves (v. 15). It was simple, really, Jesus would have them know. His teaching was not His own, He told them, but God's who sent Him (v. 16).

Many who heard Jesus speak believed on Him (v. 31). But the Pharisees and chief priests sent some of the temple guards to arrest Him (v. 32). Our lesson text begins in the midst of His discussion with them.

I. Jesus Offers Living Water (John 7:37-39)

The purpose of the feast of Tabernacles was twofold. First, it was a commemoration of Israel's wanderings in the wilderness following the exodus from Egypt. The people lived for seven days in booths made of tree branches and palm fronds. Thus they remembered this time in their history and God's remarkable care of them.

Second, the feast was a kind of fall harvest festival. As such it involved both thanksgiving for God's past bounty and prayers for future blessings. Water was significant in the observance. Each day a priest would take a golden pitcher, draw water from the pool of Siloam, and take it into the temple. There, with the sound of cymbals and trumpets and the shouting of rejoicing multitudes, the water was poured out at the altar. At the climactic moment the people recited Isaiah 12:3: "With joy shall ye draw water out of the wells of salvation."

This particular ceremony is not mentioned in the Old Testament, and was apparently added sometime after the institution of the feast. Because this feast commemorated Israel's wilderness wanderings, it is thought that this ceremony was a reminder of God's miraculous provision of water for the people at that time (see Exodus 17:6).

A. Believe and Drink of the Water (vv. 37, 38)

Naturally, the people were well acquainted with the ceremonies associated with the feast of Tabernacles, so they were well prepared to understand the spiritual content of Jesus' words.

37, 38. In the last day, that great day of the feast, Jesus stood and cried, saying, If any man thirst, let him come unto me, and drink. He that believeth on me, as the Scripture hath said, out of his belly shall flow rivers of living water.

Jesus stood. Customarily Jesus sat as He taught (Matthew 5:1) as did the rabbis, and He had likely been teaching daily in the temple. But now so momentous were His words that He stood up and cried out for all to hear. Just imagine the sound of His voice resounding against the temple walls!

His message was the message of life, as we see over and over again in the book of John. In John 1:4 we read, "In him was life and the life was the light of men"; In John 3:36, "He that believeth not the Son shall not see life"; and in John 5:26, "For as the Father hath life in himself; so hath he given to the Son to have life in himself."

In the text before us the figure is that of *water of life,* or *living water.* The figure was especially significant, since for seven days water had been poured out at the altar as a symbol of God's blessing, and the people had chanted the verse from Isaiah that spoke of drawing water from the wells of salvation. Jesus was saying, in effect, "Are you anxious about water? I will give you the water of life. Do you thirst for a drink from the wells of salvation? This too I will give you."

When Jesus spoke to the woman at the well, He stated that anyone who drank of the water He gives would find lasting satisfaction—everlasting life (see John 4:14). That is His meaning here, as He offered himself as the Redeemer of humankind.

And *out of his belly,* that is, from the life of the one who has Christ within, *shall flow rivers of living water.* Those who receive the life that Christ offers share it, in turn, with others.

Thus it has been, ever since the church began. The apostles, as witnesses of Christ's glory and as recipients of the *living water,* shared with all others who would receive it, and they with others, down to the present time. And so the waters from the river of life from Christ Jesus continue to flow, bringing the life that comes by faith in Christ to thirsty souls around the globe.

B. Believe and Receive the Holy Spirit (v. 39)

39. (But this spake he of the Spirit, which they that believe on him should receive: for the Holy Ghost was not yet given; because that Jesus was not yet glorified.)

This spake he of the Spirit. Jesus had said nothing to the people about the Holy Spirit. In the present verse John explains that the living water about which Jesus had been speaking foreshadowed or symbolized the Holy Spirit, *which they that believe on him should receive.* Later, Jesus promised His disciples that the Holy Spirit would come (John 14-16). But not yet, for *Jesus was not yet glorified.* Glorified? What does John mean? He means that Jesus had not yet suffered the abuse of a criminal, not yet suffered execution, not yet conquered death by His resurrection, nor yet ascended on high to sit at the Father's right hand. That is how He would be glorified. And the Holy Spirit would not come until after all this had taken place.

On the Day of Pentecost the promised Holy Spirit did come upon the apostles gathered in Jerusalem, enabling them to proclaim the gospel message with its promise of the gift of the Holy Spirit to obedient believers (Acts 2:1-4, 38). Only then did the mission of Christians to share the water of life with the world begin.

THIRSTY

I didn't know what *thirsty* was until I toured Egypt. I became only too well acquainted with thirst, however, riding for one very long night on a train from Cairo to Luxor. It was midsummer, too hot to travel with windows closed. Open windows, though, let in not only night air, but desert dust and grit as well. Sometime after midnight, I crawled from my lower berth, removed an emergency water flask from a wall bracket, and gulped the contents. I didn't even try to remove the layer of dust that had accumulated on top of the stale water. I just had to slack my thirst before my dry throat choked me to death.

Spiritual thirst can seem unquenchable, too. Millions strive to satisfy dry souls by desperate drinking at worldly waterholes. Possessions, pleasure, pursuit of power—all are empty wells. Only when we come to Christ, the source of living water, will our spiritual thirst be stopped. Repentant believers receive God's Spirit in Christian baptism (Acts 2:38) and find the "rivers of living water" that Jesus promised. Joyfully we sing John W. Peterson's hymn:

Drinking at the springs of living water,
Happy now am I, my soul they satisfy;
Drinking at the springs of living water,
O wonderful and bountiful supply! —R. W. B.

visual 12

II. Believers and Unbelievers (John 7:40-43)

Remember the meeting of Jesus and the woman of Samaria. When she returned to the city and told the men that she had just met the long-awaited Christ, some believed on Him because of her testimony. When they asked Jesus to remain with them, He stayed two days, "and many more believed because of his own word" (John 4:41). Then the men said to the woman, "Now we believe, not because of thy saying: for we have heard him ourselves, and know that this is indeed the Christ, the Saviour of the world" (John 4:42). Wherever Jesus went, many believed on Him when they witnessed the marvelous things He did and heard His words.

A. Acclamation (vv. 40, 41a)

40, 41a. Many of the people therefore, when they heard this saying, said, Of a truth this is the Prophet. Others said, This is the Christ.

Many . . . when they heard this saying. That is, "these words," meaning the things Jesus had been saying, over and over again, during the festival, concluding with His invitation given here.

Of a truth this is the Prophet. Some thought that Jesus was the prophet "like unto" Moses, whom God promised to send (Deuteronomy 18:15-19). Acts 3:19-23 shows that that prophet was the Christ. Whether or not these persons understood the prophecy to refer to the Christ is not certain. "I . . . will put my words in his mouth," God had said of the prophet to come. At one point during His teaching at this feast Jesus affirmed, "My teaching is not my own. It comes from him who sent me" (John 7:16, *New International Version*).

Others said, This is the Christ (the Messiah). These hearers were more definite; they believed that Jesus was the promised Messiah and boldly affirmed their belief.

B. Rejection (vv. 41b-43)

41b-43. But some said, Shall Christ come out of Galilee? Hath not the Scripture said, That Christ cometh of the seed of David, and out of the town of Bethlehem, where David was? So there was a division among the people because of him.

Every person who had any contact with Jesus was impressed, and amazed, by this man from Galilee. The Jews, including those hostile to Him, marveled at His learning (John 7:15). Those who considered Him to be a prophet believed Him to be an important one—like Moses, and some of these folk were in the crowd at the feast. Those who saw Him as the Messiah regarded Him as the one they had been waiting for who would deliver Israel. They too were in the crowd, as we have seen. But there was a third group in the crowd—those who rejected the idea that He was the Christ, as is seen by the following question?

Shall Christ come out of Galilee? The question indicates that those who raised it were not acquainted with the circumstances surrounding Jesus' birth. These critics were correct in pointing out that *Christ cometh of the seed* (or offspring) *of David.* This is confirmed in Jeremiah 23:5 (and elsewhere). And David's people, of the tribe of Judah, were from the south, not from the regions of Galilee. They were correct also in stating that the Messiah would come *out of the town of Bethlehem.* This is what the prophet Micah said, seven hundred years earlier (Micah 5:2). Their mistake was in assuming that because Jesus spent most of His life in Nazareth, He must have been born there.

Jesus *was* the offspring of David, and the account of His birth in Bethlehem may be read in the opening chapters of Matthew and Luke. Jesus, if asked, would surely have answered any earnest inquiry relative to the place of His birth. As to those whose minds were already set against Him, if Christ's own life and teachings and miracles were not adequate as a basis of faith in Him, it would not have helped if He had shown these critics a birth certificate from Bethlehem.

THE GREAT DIVIDE

Harry Truman was a president whom many Americans either loved or hated. That is often the case with decisive, outspoken leaders. His strong personality and forceful administrative style either turned off constituents or turned them on. Other presidents and leaders have prompted similar reactions.

Response to Jesus has always been mixed, too. "There was a division among the people because of him." Those who opposed Him did so vehemently; they felt strongly that He was an impostor and a blasphemer. Many who embraced Him as Messiah, on the other hand, were so convicted that they literally gave up their lives for their faith in Him.

Jesus predicted that He would divide people, even families (Luke 12:51-53). A real difference in the response of people today is that so many behave as though they can "take Him or leave Him." Such indifference and lukewarmness is unmistakably condemned by Christ (Revelation 3:16). Christians must develop the capacity for one hundred percent commitment. Like Joshua, we must be willing to make a definite choice and say, "As for me and my household, we will serve the Lord" (Joshua 24:15, *New International Version*). —R. W. B.

III. Jesus' Enemies Thwarted (John 7:44-52)

A. Frustrated Citizens (v. 44)

44. And some of them would have taken him; but no man laid hands on him.

Knowing that the Pharisees and priests wanted this man, it is not surprising that some *would have taken him* and delivered Him to these leaders. *But no man laid hands on him.* In verse 30 we are told why this was so: "Because his hour was not yet come." When the time came for Jesus to take those steps that led to Calvary, it would be according to God's clock and not by the design of Christ's enemies.

B. Empty-handed Guards (vv. 45-49)

45, 46. Then came the officers to the chief priests and Pharisees; and they said unto them, Why have ye not brought him? The officers answered, Never man spake like this man.

Earlier, mutual enemies—Pharisees and Sadducees (most of the priests were Sadducees)—joined in sending temple officers to arrest Jesus, so threatened did they feel by Jesus' popularity (John 7:32). It is remarkable that the officers refused to take Jesus. More remarkable was their reason for not doing so—*Never man spake like this man*—which equals, "This is the greatest teacher who ever lived." Among the Pharisees there were proud teachers of the law. Now they were told that this unlearned Galilean excelled them all.

47-49. Then answered them the Pharisees, Are ye also deceived? Have any of the rulers or of the Pharisees believed on him? But this people who knoweth not the law are cursed.

Are ye also deceived? Or, led astray. The Pharisees took the position that only the illiterate masses were taken in by the teachings of Jesus. The Pharisees were experts in the law, and they felt that that knowledge made them pious. In their view, the people, mere rabble who were ignorant of the law, were wicked. So they ridiculed the guards for siding with the common people.

C. A Believing Ruler (vv. 50-52)

50-52. Nicodemus saith unto them, (he that came to Jesus by night, being one of them,) Doth our law judge any man, before it hear him, and know what he doeth? They answered and said unto him, Art thou also of Galilee? Search, and look: for out of Galilee ariseth no prophet.

The answer to the Pharisee's question in verse 48 is *yes.* There was a ruler who believed that Jesus was "a teacher come from God" and that His miracles were genuine miracles (John 3:2). Nicodemus was no uneducated yokel but one of their own respected teachers. "In all fairness, give Jesus a hearing before you judge Him," he said.

The Pharisees answered Nicodemus by speaking evil of the Galileans. In doing this they did not speak with the voice of wisdom, but of prejudice, hatred, and ignorance. The way of justice (and of common sense) is to hear a person before one judges him or her. We wish that all persons would be so wise as to do this with Jesus.

Conclusion

A. Examine the Evidence

Read the book of John. What impression do you get of his concept of Christ? From the very first verse to the last, there is never a doubt about John's belief. Jesus is God's creative Word, the long-awaited Messiah, the Son of God, the Light of the World, the Life, the Truth, and the Way.

There are those today who view Jesus differently—some speaking favorably of Him, others derisively. What is the basis for their views? Unless those who state their views have considered the evidence, then in every case their conclusions are based on hearsay, on what they have heard or what others have written as their opinions.

John's faith was not based on hearsay. He was an eyewitness of that which he reported concerning Jesus' deeds and His teachings, including the report of the resurrection appearances. In legal terms, John's book might be termed a *deposition.* He himself considered it to be a presentation of the facts in the case as he had observed and heard them.

In our lesson today, the options are two. Jesus *was* an uneducated young Galilean overcome with thoughts of self-importance, or else He *is* the Son of God, our living Savior and our Lord.

From the Biblical standpoint, our decision regarding Jesus is literally a matter of life and death, a matter of far too great importance to be decided by hearsay. May God help every person who examines the evidence to do so honestly and make the right decision.

B. Prayer

O Lord, our God, Creator of all life, we thank You for this precious gift You have given us. You have created us a little lower than the angels, and how marvelous is the work of Your hands! But we have marred Your creation. We have defiled these bodies. We have misdirected our intellect. We have corrupted our souls. But thanks be to You for the cleansing You provide in Christ Jesus. Help us to live as the redeemed of the Lord, partakers of that new and eternal life He has given. In His name we ask. Amen.

C. Thought to Remember

Jesus invites any who thirst to come to Him and drink. But how will those who are thirsty of soul know of His offer of living water *unless someone tells them?*

Home Daily Bible Readings

Monday, May 17—Jesus in Galilee (John 7:1-9)
Tuesday, May 18—Jesus Teaches (John 7:10-15)
Wednesday, May 19—The Authority of Jesus (John 7:16-24)
Thursday, May 20—The People Marvel (John 7:25-31)
Friday, May 21—Come and Drink (John 7:32-39)
Saturday, May 22—This Is the Christ (John 7:40-44)
Sunday, May 23—Nicodemus Defends Jesus (John 7:45-52)

Learning by Doing

This page contains an alternate lesson plan emphasizing learning activities. Classes desiring such student involvement will find these suggestions helpful.

Learning Goals

After this lesson, the students will:

1. Be able to identify the two claims Jesus made for himself as recorded in the text.
2. Be able to explain what Jesus meant when He said, "Whoever believes in me, as the Scripture has said, streams of living water will flow from within him" (John 7:38, *New International Version*).
3. Decide on one personality change they will make in their lives with Jesus' help.

Into the Lesson

As the class members arrive, call their attention to the incomplete statements below. Distribute these on sheets of paper. The sheets will be used also at the end of the class session.

FINISH THE SENTENCE

1. The most attractive Christian personality I have ever known personally is—
2. He/she impressed me this way because—
3. If I were to state a reason for his/her winsomeness, it would be—

Ask the students to complete their sentences and to share their responses with two or three other people. Use the results of these small-group discussions for a brief general discussion to launch into the lesson.

Make the transition into the Bible study by pointing out that today's narrative reveals that Jesus' personality and work attracted many people. The passage also presents the principle by which the personalities of His followers can be transformed.

Into the Word

Read John 7:37-52 aloud. Then instruct the class to work within the groups already formed during the introductory section of the lesson.

Give each group a sheet of paper and ask them to write at the top of the sheet the two column headings shown on the chart in the next column. Have the students in each group examine the lesson text and work together to fill in the information included in the chart.

Allot six to eight minutes for this study, then use their work as the basis for a class discussion of the text. Emphasize the uniqueness of Jesus' personality and His appeal to those who knew Him.

Jesus' Claims	Responses
"I can quench a person's thirst."	"He is the Prophet."
	"He is the Christ."
"Whoever believes in me, out of him will flow streams of living water."	"He is an impostor."
	"There has never been a person who has taught like this man."
	"None of the rulers or of the Pharisees believe on Him."
	"He should not be condemned before He receives a fair hearing."

Into Life

Ask the groups to look at their charts and decide the importance of Jesus' claims for us today. They should see that (1) Jesus offers eternal life, and we need to accept His offer; and (2) The closer we live to Jesus the greater is the work of the Holy Spirit in our lives.

Allot three minutes for the activity above. Then use the students' responses as the basis for a discussion. These questions may help.

1. How can Jesus' claim to satisfy thirst affect your life?
2. In what ways are streams of living water demonstrated in the lives of Christians?
3. How has the presence of the Holy Spirit had a transforming influence in your life?
4. How does our living close to Jesus affect the personality we project to others?
5. What areas of your life and personality need yet to be transformed?

Summarize the discussion, emphasizing particularly the changes that have occurred and need yet to occur in the lives of class members. Then say, "Imagine expressing our feelings to Jesus himself about what He taught concerning His claims and His transforming power. What would you write? Let's each use the reverse side of our sheets, and write a letter to Jesus saying how we will let Him change us." Let students write their letters, then close with prayer.

Let's Talk It Over

The questions on this page are designed to encourage review of the lesson Scriptures and to promote discussion of the lesson by the class. The answers provided are only discussion starters. Let your class talk it over from there.

1. There seem to be many persons today who regard Jesus as a good man, but nothing more. What is wrong with such a conclusion?

Such persons focus their attention exclusively on Jesus' words and deeds that reflect kindness, compassion, and love. They ignore the claims He made and the evidence He set forth through His miracles that demonstrated His true identity as the Son of God. As many Christian teachers have pointed out, we must either accept the truthfulness of Jesus' claims, or we must conclude that He was either a deceiver or He was seriously deluded in regard to His identity. If He was a deceiver who encouraged His followers to think of Him as the Son of God when He was not, then we cannot call Him a good man. If deluded into believing He was divine, then He was a dangerously misguided man. And again, as such we cannot call Him a good man.

2. The living water must flow into us and out from us to others. Why does this truth need to be emphasized?

We are familiar with what happens to water that is impeded in its flowing. It becomes stale and stagnant. Something similar can happen to believers in Christ who sit in classes and worship services week after week, receiving a constant flow of spiritual instruction, but who never pass on the life-giving truths to others. These are the persons who frequently lament, "I'm not getting anything out of church anymore!" But because they have not channeled these truths out to their friends and neighbors, these persons have become insensitive to the beauty and the power of divine truth. Jesus' exhortation to His apostles is applicable to such persons: "Freely ye have received, freely give" (Matthew 10:8).

3. The officers' declaration, "Never man spake like this man," is an impressive testimony. In what ways might Jesus' speaking have impressed them?

Perhaps they were impressed as the hearers of the Sermon on the Mount were. Those hearers "were astonished at his doctrine: for he taught them as one having authority, and not as the scribes" (Matthew 7:28, 29). Or perhaps they felt the force of Jesus' wisdom as His enemies would later feel it. These enemies tried to trap Him with "loaded" questions, but He answered them so wisely that "from then on no one dared ask him any more questions" (Mark 12:34, *New International Version*). Or it may be that the power of His personality was so exhibited by His words that these men were drawn to Him in the same way as those fishermen/disciples who responded when He said, "Follow me, and I will make you fishers of men" (Matthew 4:19).

4. The fact that Nicodemus was a ruler who was willing to give Jesus a fair hearing is a reminder that Christ has attracted many highly-intelligent, well-educated persons to be His disciples. Why is this an important observation?

Perhaps we have met persons who rejected the gospel on the basis of their supposedly superior intellect or education. And perhaps our own faith was shaken when we heard them scoff at the truths we hold dear. But however learned these persons may be, no matter how keen their powers of reasoning, their intellectual equals may be found among the men and women who are firm believers in Jesus Christ. The ranks of Jesus' disciples have included scientists and statesmen, professors and philosophers, and people in all areas of human achievement. Paul referred to the gospel as "the foolishness of God" (1 Corinthians 1:25), but both the wise and the simple, the educated and the uneducated, may come to see it as "wiser than men," as the very wisdom of God.

5. What are some common ways in which people reach their conclusions regarding Jesus Christ?

It is frightening to think that many persons have formed their concept of Jesus on the basis of certain popular films such as *Jesus Christ Superstar* or *The Last Temptation of Christ.* Others have read novels or books of theology that present a distorted picture of Jesus. Still others may know only what they hear by word of mouth. All of this reminds us of how vital it is that we encourage people to read the Gospels for themselves. If they can be made to see that the Gospels are interesting, stimulating reading material, they can come to form their opinion of Jesus by viewing Him through the testimony of those who knew Him best.

The Promise of the Spirit

May 30
Lesson 13

LESSON SCRIPTURE: John 14.

PRINTED TEXT: John 14:15-27.

Devotional Reading: John 16:5-15.

John 14:15-27

15 If ye love me, keep my commandments.
16 And I will pray the Father, and he shall
give you another Comforter, that he may
abide with you for ever;
17 Even the Spirit of truth; whom the
world cannot receive, because it seeth him
not, neither knoweth him: but ye know him;
for he dwelleth with you, and shall be in you.
18 I will not leave you comfortless: I will
come to you.
19 Yet a little while, and the world seeth
me no more; but ye see me: because I live, ye
shall live also.
20 At that day ye shall know that I am in
my Father, and ye in me, and I in you.
21 He that hath my commandments, and
keepeth them, he it is that loveth me: and he
that loveth me shall be loved of my Father,
and I will love him, and will manifest myself
to him.
22 Judas saith unto him, not Iscariot, Lord,
how is it that thou wilt manifest thyself unto
us, and not unto the world?
23 Jesus answered and said unto him, If a
man love me, he will keep my words: and my
Father will love him, and we will come unto
him, and make our abode with him.
24 He that loveth me not keepeth not my
sayings: and the word which ye hear is not
mine, but the Father's which sent me.
25 These things have I spoken unto you,
being yet present with you.
26 But the Comforter, which is the Holy
Ghost, whom the Father will send in my
name, he shall teach you all things, and bring
all things to your remembrance, whatsoever I
have said unto you.
27 Peace I leave with you, my peace I give
unto you: not as the world giveth, give I unto
you. Let not your heart be troubled, neither
let it be afraid.

GOLDEN TEXT: The Comforter, which is the Holy Ghost, whom the Father will send in my name, he shall teach you all things, and bring all things to your remembrance, whatsoever I have said unto you.—John 14:26.

Believing in Christ

Unit 3. John: Believe in Jesus

(Lesson 9-13)

Lesson Aims

At the end of the lesson the students should:

1. Be able to tell what the promised Spirit would do for and through the apostles (the mission of the Holy Spirit).

2. Understand that the Holy Spirit guides us to a life of holiness and to salvation through the inspired Word of God—the Bible.

Lesson Outline

INTRODUCTION
- A. An Endangered Species
- B. Lesson Background

I. THE DIVINE COUNSELOR (John 14:15-18)
- A. Need for Loving Obedience (v. 15)
- B. The Spirit of Truth (vv. 16, 17)
- C. Christ's Promise to Return (v. 18)
  Chosen Children

II. THE FELLOWSHIP OF LOVE (John 14:19-21)
- A. The Promise of Life (v. 19)
- B. Oneness in God's Love (vv. 20, 21)

III. THE SECRET OF GOD'S PRESENCE (John 14:22-27)
- A. The Question (v. 22)
- B. The Answer (vv. 23, 24)
- C. The Leading of the Spirit (vv. 25, 26)
- D. The Gift of Peace (v. 27)
  Heavenly Peace

CONCLUSION
- A. A Promise Kept
- B. The Presence of the Spirit
- C. Prayer
- D. Thought to Remember

Display visual 13 of the visuals packet and let it remain before the class. The visual is shown on page 334.

Introduction

A. An Endangered Species

Did you ever hear of the *snail darter?* It is a species of fish, quite small, found only in isolated places in Tennessee. Is it highly significant? In the minds of some, yes, because it classifies as an endangered species. In Tennessee today one may visit the impressive Tellico Dam. But even after construction of the dam had begun, all work toward the completion of the multi-million-dollar project was halted for *more than two years.* Why? Because environmentalists were afraid it would mean the extinction of the *snail darter.* It was only after the tiny fish was found to exist elsewhere that opposition to the dam subsided. More and more people are concerned about the endangered species on this planet.

At the time of the event recorded in our lesson text, the disciples of Jesus were an endangered species. Of the twelve apostles, one had defected. Another, one of the most stalwart, would soon deny that he even knew Jesus. Nearly two months after the crucifixion of Jesus, the total number of disciples was just 120 (Acts 1:15). Today they number in the millions. Something happened that kept Christianity from becoming extinct upon the death of the 120. That is what our lesson is about.

B. Lesson Background

The event we are studying in this lesson took place in the upper room. It was night, and Jesus was with the eleven apostles. Judas had already gone out to tell the chief priests where they might find Him. Soon Jesus would be arrested, bound, and led away to a mock trial and execution. So now He was speaking to the eleven for the last time before His death, and He knew this, even if they did not.

The group had kept the Passover, and Jesus had instituted the Lord's Supper. Henceforth they were to break the loaf and share the cup in memory of Him. In memory? What did He mean? "Yet a little while I am with you," Jesus said (John 13:33). Then He was going away. When they questioned Him about it, He spoke of the Father's house, and said, "I go to prepare a place for you" (14:2).

Jesus knew that He was going to His death, but the disciples were puzzled. Was He not the Messiah, the Son of God? Wasn't He going to establish the kingdom of God among men? But later this evening they would see the beginning of the end, and tomorrow they would see Him die. He really was leaving them! What about the kingdom? What kingdom? It hadn't even started yet, and Jesus was leaving the responsibility of it upon their shoulders! What could these eleven, distraught, very ordinary men do, without Jesus, to launch a movement that would sweep the world, a movement that would engage the support of some of the noblest, the best, the most intellectual men and women of many nations of all times? The responsibility for all this was to be thrust upon them.

What *could* they do? Let the critic of the church and of Christianity answer that question. List the possibilities before the disciples, their qualifications, their inherent power, their influence. Add all of these together, and on a scale from one to ten, what were their chances of success? Don't you think we should add a zero to that scale? Their cause was hopeless, zero, nil, zip—*except for the promise Jesus gave them.* This, too, is what our lesson is all about. The lesson is entitled, "The Promise of the Spirit." We might reword the title, "An Endangered Species and What Jesus Did About It."

I. The Divine Counselor (John 14:15-18)

Several times in His ministry Jesus stated that He had come from the Father. Now He told the disciples plainly that He was going to leave them and return to the Father (John 13:33; 14:2, 12). But His disciples would not be without the divine presence.

A. Need for Loving Obedience (v. 15)

15. If ye love me, keep my commandments.

Verses 15 and 16 go together. The latter gives the promise of the Holy Spirit; verse 15 states the condition that must precede the Spirit's coming. *If ye love me, keep my commandments.* True love must be expressed in word and in deed. A short while earlier this very evening, Jesus gave His disciples a "new commandment" to "love one another" (John 13:34). How can the Holy Spirit of God possibly abide in the midst of a people where love is lacking? Or with those who are willfully disobedient?

B. The Spirit of Truth (vv. 16, 17)

16. And I will pray the Father, and he shall give you another Comforter, that he may abide with you for ever.

In the opening verse of this chapter Jesus encouraged the disciples not to be troubled over His leaving, but urged them to continue to believe in God and in Him. In verses 13 and 14 He stated that they could be assured that their prayers would be answered. Here, now, is a further reason for a calm and untroubled spirit. Jesus would make request of the Father, and He would send them *another Comforter* to help them. This Comforter would be with them forever. Jesus used the term *paraclete,* which can also mean adviser, advocate or defender, and, in general, a helper. The Holy Spirit would be *another* Comforter, doing for the disciples what Jesus had done while He was with them.

17. Even the Spirit of truth; whom the world cannot receive, because it seeth him not, neither knoweth him: but ye know him; for he dwelleth with you, and shall be in you.

> **How to Say It**
>
> ISCARIOT. Iss-*care*-e-ut.
> LEBBEUS. Leh-*bee*-us.
> THADDEUS. Tha-*dee*-us.

The Spirit of truth. The Spirit is designated thus, because He would guide them into all truth (John 16:13), keeping them from error as they communicated the good news of salvation, which God would have all the world to know. There was no New Testament at this time, as the written Word of God. Some of these men would have a part in writing it, led by the Spirit. But for the time being, the message would come from the lips of the disciples, inspired by the Spirit.

Whom the world cannot receive. The term *the world* often refers to those who have given themselves completely to the pursuit of the things of this world—possessions, pleasure, power—and who often are openly hostile to the things of God. Such persons value only that which gratifies their physical senses. Hence, while they are in this state, they cannot receive the Spirit. They neither see nor acknowledge Him because they have determined not to do so.

But ye know him; for he dwelleth with you. In verse 16, Jesus used the future tense when He said the Father "shall give you another Comforter." Here Jesus projects himself into the future and, using the present tense, speaks as though the Spirit were already dwelling with them, so certain was He of the Spirit's coming to them.

On the Day of Pentecost the Holy Spirit would come to abide with them and be in them, helping them as they proclaimed the gospel.

C. Christ's Promise to Return (v. 18)

18. I will not leave you comfortless: I will come to you.

Comfortless. The word is, literally, *orphans.* The meaning is "desolate." The disciples would be crushed by the death of Christ, as children would be by the loss of father and mother. But Jesus would return to them—for forty days after the resurrection, and after that, in the Spirit, forever. In verse 23 it is stated that both the Heavenly Father and the Son would come and make their abode with those who love Him and keep His commandments.

CHOSEN CHILDREN

Motherless children have always been the special concern of civilized societies. Many charities make orphans their projects of priority. Benevolent citizens most generously respond to the appeals of needy children without families. Christians especially champion the cause of orphaned youngsters. "Pure religion" looks after orphans and widows (James 1:27).

Jesus used language that tugged at heartstrings when He promised not to leave His disciples "as orphans." Christ does not forsake us, leaving us without consolation, protection, and affirmation. By the Holy Spirit, He remains with us, comforting and giving us peace "beyond understanding."

Christians have been adopted as God's children through Jesus Christ (Ephesians 1:5). Like all adopted children, we know we are special, for we have been *chosen* to be a part of God's family. —R. W. B.

II. The Fellowship of Love (John 14:19-21)

A. The Promise of Life (v. 19)

19. Yet a little while, and the world seeth me no more; but ye see me: because I live, ye shall live also.

Yet a little while. On the morrow Jesus would be crucified, and with the sealing of His body in the tomb, *the world* would see Him for the last time until the second coming. *But ye see me.* The verb indicates continued action. The disciples would go on seeing Jesus—visibly, for forty days until the ascension, and with the eyes of faith after that.

Because I live, ye shall live. This is man's one certain hope of immortality. Some grasp for hope in the fact that among all cultures there is a concept of life beyond the grave, a concept that must be Heavenly inspired. Perhaps so. Others speak of the inequalities of life. Surely, beyond the grave, all will be made right, they think. Perhaps so. Others advance the argument of the *unfinished life.* Man's days may be cut short. Can he not anticipate a time of fulfillment? Perhaps. And that is all we can say for all of man's arguments for immortality—perhaps.

Among all the philosophers on this earth who have pondered the matter, among all the sacred religious leaders whom men may follow, only one gives a certain hope of eternal life. Jesus alone makes this life possible by His own death on the cross for our sins, and validates His offer by His resurrection from the grave. *Ye shall live also.* What a great promise! Not perhaps. Not I hope so. But *ye shall live.*

B. Oneness in God's Love (vv. 20, 21)

20. At that day ye shall know that I am in my Father, and ye in me, and I in you.

At that day. This, apparently, is a reference to the Day of Pentecost. Jesus was returning to the Father and had promised His disciples that He would send the Holy Spirit. On Pentecost the Spirit would come with power (Acts 2:1-4). The disciples would know by this that Jesus had reached His destination in Heaven, as He said. They would understand in a fuller sense the deity of Christ, and they would begin to experience the reality of daily fellowship with God the Father, and with Christ Jesus the Son.

21. He that hath my commandments, and keepeth them, he it is that loveth me: and he that loveth me shall be loved of my Father, and I will love him, and will manifest myself to him.

Being Christian is not adherence to a creed. It is a way of life, a life of fellowship with God, made possible through Christ. This fellowship, from beginning to end, is founded on love. God so loved the world that He gave His Son. Christ loved us, and gave himself for us. And He said, "By this shall all men know that ye are my disciples, if ye have love one to another" (John 13:35).

Our first love, naturally, is to God, for sending His Son to bring us this life. It is folly, however, to say we love God, unless we keep His commandments. If our love for God is genuine, obedience will follow. Active obedience, in turn, is evidence of our love. And as we keep Christ's commandments, we are loved by Him and the Father in return.

Will manifest myself to him. This manifestation to the believer is in the Spirit through the Word. The one who loves Christ will experience the Spirit's working to convict of sin, to lead to repentance, to give assurance of salvation, and to impart the peace of God that passes understanding.

III. The Secret of God's Presence (John 14:22-27)

A. The Question (v. 22)

22. Judas saith unto him, not Iscariot, Lord, how is it that thou wilt manifest thyself unto us, and not unto the world?

This Judas was not the betrayer of Jesus, but was that apostle also known as Lebbeus, or Thaddeus. He misinterpreted what Jesus had been saying. Jesus had been speaking of a manifestation that was spiritual in character, but Judas seems to have been thinking in physical terms. Was he still thinking of Jesus as a worldly Messiah who would restore the kingdom to Israel? (Compare Acts 1:6.) How, Judas wondered, would Jesus be able to establish His reign over all the nations if He manifested himself only to His little group of disciples, and not to the world?

B. The Answer (vv. 23, 24)

Without directly correcting Judas's misinterpretation of His words, Jesus continued to speak of God's abiding presence in the lives of His followers. In verse 21 we noted that God loves that person who loves and obeys Jesus. This is not a call to observe a set of rules and regulations, but a call to show one's delight in Christ by walking in His way. God will honor such a person with His presence, since that person has honored His Son.

23. Jesus answered and said unto him, If a man love me, he will keep my words: and my Father will love him, and we will come unto him, and make our abode with him.

Both God the Father and Jesus the Son will abide with the person who loves Christ and keeps His words. This coming, begun on Pentecost and continuing throughout the Christian dispensation, will be ultimately fulfilled when Christ returns to claim His own.

24. He that loveth me not keepeth not my sayings: and the word which ye hear is not mine, but the Father's which sent me.

It follows logically that one who does not love Jesus will not follow His *sayings,* that is, His teaching, as the rule and guide for his or her life. But to reject that teaching is a very serious matter, for Jesus' teaching is the very truth of God.

C. The Leading of the Spirit (vv. 25, 26)

25, 26. These things have I spoken unto you, being yet present with you. But the Comforter, which is the Holy Ghost, whom the Father will send in my name, he shall teach you all things, and bring all things to your remembrance, whatsoever I have said unto you.

The abiding presence of God, as above stated, is assured to all who love and obey the Son. Now a special promise was given to the apostles.

These things. The reference is inclusive, embracing all that Jesus had taught, *being yet present,* that is, while on earth with them. Jesus would soon leave them, but the Father would send the Holy Spirit to comfort and to guide. The Spirit would guide them into all truth (John 16:13), thus equipping them fully for their awesome task of telling the world of the ways of God and the way of life.

D. The Gift of Peace (v. 27)

27. Peace I leave with you, my peace I give unto you: not as the world giveth, give I unto you. Let not your heart be troubled, neither let it be afraid.

How remarkable is this pronouncement of peace! It calls to mind a painting titled *Peace,* which shows a tree in a storm, battered by the wind. On a limb is a nest and on the the nest a bird, with her two little ones tucked underneath. That is peace! Jesus would hear the maddening crowd on the morrow crying, "Crucify him!" But in the upper room He spoke of *my peace.* And He wants to share it with us! *Let not your heart be troubled,* He says, *neither let it be afraid.* Truly this is God's Son!

HEAVENLY PEACE

When our son was growing through his "terrible twos," he was quite uninhibited in public places. On one of those rare occasions when we were eating in a restaurant, he was especially vociferous, and I was especially sensitive to all the attention I thought he was drawing to our table. As I was studying the menu, Sam asked loudly, "What you gonna have, Dad? What you gonna have?"

"I think I'd like some peace and quiet," I muttered.

"A PIECE OF CORN?!?" Sam practically shouted.

I was easily embarrassed in those days, and easily angered, too. It seemed as though everyone in the restaurant turned to watch my ears get beet red.

I am happy to report that I am not so easily embarrassed these days, nor am I easily angered by children's antics. Our nest is empty, and though peace is still a valued possession, quiet is no longer the premium it once was.

Spiritual peace, of course, doesn't require constant quiet. It is the deep contentment and confidence of the soul that cannot be disturbed by any temporal turbulence. It is eternal calm. Nothing in the world can bring such peace—only God, through Christ, by His Spirit. —R. W. B.

Home Daily Bible Readings

Monday, May 24—A Place Prepared (John 14:1-7)

Tuesday, May 25—The Authority of God (John 14:8-14)

Wednesday, May 26—A Counselor Is Promised (John 14:15-20)

Thursday, May 27—Keeping His Commandments (John 14:21-25)

Friday, May 28—Jesus Leaves Peace (John 14:26-31)

Saturday, May 29—The Spirit's Witness (Romans 8:12-17)

Sunday, May 30—The Spirit's Intercession (Romans 8:18-27)

Conclusion

A. A Promise Kept

Jesus had been with His disciples for three years. Before leaving them, He promised them "another Comforter" who would abide with them forever (v. 16). He also said that He himself and God the Father would come to and abide with those who exhibit the obedience of love (v. 23). The promised Comforter was the Holy Spirit, who would enable them to recall all Jesus had said. He would also teach them "all things" necessary for the establishing and ongoing of His kingdom.

On the occasion when Peter confessed Jesus as the Christ, the Son of the living God, Jesus had said, "Upon this rock [this truth, this solid ledge of rock] I will build my church" (Matthew 16:16-18). Now as Jesus spoke to the disciples in the upper room, the church was yet in the future. He was entrusting it to these men, with the promise that the Holy Spirit would come to them, empowering them and guiding them "into all truth" (John 16:13). After the resurrection, Jesus would commission the eleven apostles to disciple all nations, and would promise again to be with them always (Matthew 28:19, 20).

The promised Holy Spirit came with enabling power on the Day of Pentecost (Acts 2:1-4). Peter, using "the keys of the kingdom" (Matthew 16:19) for the first time, opened the door to the way back to God for the very persons who had demanded Jesus' death when He stood before Pilate. "What shall we do?" the stricken sinners cried, indicating that they now believed in Jesus. Peter, led by the Spirit, told them what to do, adding that they would then receive the indwelling Spirit as a gift (Acts 2:38). Three thousand responded and were baptized (Acts 2:41).

What a testimony Pentecost was to the power of God working in the lives of a few ordinary persons. And this was only the beginning! The book that is called *The Acts of the Apostles* may rightfully be named *Acts of the Holy Spirit*, for these men could never have done what they did by themselves *alone*. Jesus knew that. So He promised them the Holy Spirit, and He kept His promise. Because He did, the church has stood for nearly two thousand years, calling men and women to faith in Jesus Christ, that they "might have life through his name" (John 20:31).

B. The Presence of the Spirit

Every Christian has a promise of the actual presence and power of the Holy Spirit in the heart and life. "Ye shall receive the gift of the Holy Ghost" (Acts 2:38). Just how does the Holy Spirit accomplish His work in our lives? Who but God himself can fathom such a divine mystery? If we are puzzled by this question, we may note that the work of Jesus is no less puzzling. He too is with us. "Lo, I am with you alway, even unto the end of the world." "Where two or three are gathered together in my name, there am I in the midst of them." Just how does Jesus work in our hearts and lives? What does He do and say in the midst of those assembled in His name? We cannot answer with certainty, but we know that both Jesus and the Spirit work for our good.

We can be sure that Jesus does not today say anything that contradicts what He said through His inspired apostles and messengers who proclaimed the gospel in the beginning. We can be certain that the Holy Spirit does not say anything to anyone today to contradict what He has caused to be written for the ages. We can be assured that the Holy Spirit today expects us to obey what He inspired Paul to write—and Paul's frequent praise of the written Word of God urges us to study the Scriptures with all diligence. We can expect guidance, strength, and help from the Holy Spirit, but nothing contradictory to the New Testament.

C. Prayer

Heavenly Father, we rejoice to know that there is a way of forgiveness, a way of salvation, a way to citizenship in Your everlasting kingdom that is clearly revealed in the teachings of the Spirit-guided apostles. Let us not be troubled by the doctrines of men. May our concerns be all the things of Jesus as taught by His inspired apostles. May they be our all-sufficient guide for salvation and godliness. We pray in the name of Jesus. Amen.

D. Thought to Remember

Distraught by the departure of Jesus, the handful of His disciples who were left could never have launched the church on its course except by the power and leading of the Holy Spirit.

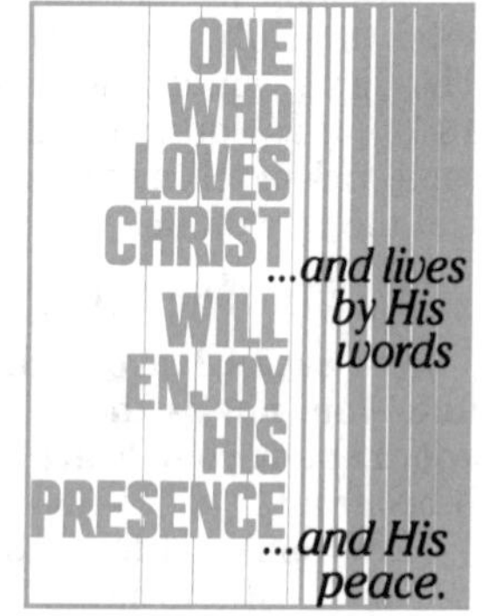
ONE
WHO
LOVES
CHRIST
...and lives by His words
WILL
ENJOY
HIS
PRESENCE
...and His peace.

visual 13

Learning by Doing

This page contains an alternate lesson plan emphasizing learning activities. Classes desiring such student involvement will find these suggestions helpful.

Learning Goals

As a result of this lesson, the students:

1. Will be able to describe Jesus' promise of the Holy Spirit.
2. Will seek reassurance in prayer and in obedience to Christ's commands.

Into the Lesson

Have four volunteers form a panel of parents in front of the class, two fathers and two mothers. Assure them that this is only an opinion panel, and that they need not be experts.

Pose the following situation and ask their opinions:

"Suppose your employer suddenly transfers you to a town five hundred miles away. You must leave immediately. Your family will remain at home to sell the house before coming to join you. You expect this to take at least three months."

1. What kinds of feelings and thoughts would you have about this change?
2. What reassurances would you give your family? Exactly what would you say?
3. What instructions would you give to your children?

Allow no more than ten minutes for this discussion.

Into the Word

Point out that today's lesson deals with Jesus' preparation of His disciples for His coming death and departure to Heaven. Though He was leaving them, He reassured them of His continued presence in their lives. Like a father or mother, He spoke to them tenderly of both promises and commands.

Have the students team up in pairs. Instruct half of the pairs to read the text and find all the commands that Jesus gave His disciples. Here are some they should find:

v. 15 "Keep my commandments"
v. 21 "Keep my commandments"
v. 23 "Keep my words"
v. 27 "Let not your heart be troubled."

Ask the other half of the pairs to locate all the promises and reassurances that Jesus gave. Here are some they should find:

v. 16 "The Father will give you another Comforter"
v. 19 "You will live"
v. 20 "You will know that the Father, Son, and disciples are united
v. 21 "The Father and I will love you"
v. 26 "The Comforter will teach you all things, and remind you of what I taught you"
v. 27 "My peace I give to you."

Give the groups ten minutes to work, then ask the "commands" group to give their answers. Lead a class discussion with these questions:

1. What is the motive for keeping Christ's commands, and why is that alone sufficient?
2. Can we actually control our hearts and let them not "be troubled"? How can we do this?

Ask for a report from the "promises" group, then discuss these questions:

1. Which of these promises means the most to you, and why?
2. How has Jesus kept these promises to you?

Ask the class to respond to the following agree/disagree statements, to help them see these truths in the context of real life.

AGREE/DISAGREE

1. Having the Comforter (Holy Spirit) means that you will never again be anxious or upset.
2. It's possible to keep the commandments of Christ and yet not really love Him.
3. It's possible really to love Christ and yet not keep His commandments.
4. The Holy Spirit was promised to the apostles in a way not promised to us.
5. The Holy Spirit uses the Scriptures to bring us consolation and encouragement.
6. Jesus expects too much of us today when He says, "Let not your heart be troubled."

Into Life

Give each student a copy of the following letter and ask them to fill in the blanks. When they have done this, have them gather in groups of four. Ask as many as will to share their concerns in their groups, and then to pray for one another in closing.

Dear Lord, sometimes when I read your Word I feel ______________________________.

When I look at the condition of the world around me, I wonder ____________________.

Lord, I try to keep Your commands, but it isn't easy, because ______________________.

Your devoted servant

Let's Talk It Over

The questions on this page are designed to encourage review of the lesson Scriptures and to promote discussion of the lesson by the class. The answers provided are only discussion starters. Let your class talk it over from there.

1. If we were to choose a small group of men to launch an enterprise to influence the whole world, how would our choices compare with those of Jesus when He selected His apostles?

Surely we would look for men of stable temperament. Peter, who was prone to emotional ups and downs, and James and John, to whom Jesus gave the nickname, "The sons of thunder" (Mark 3:17), probably would have failed to meet such a standard. We would look for men of courage. The apostles' behavior during the time of Jesus' arrest and trials and following His death makes them suspect on this point. In all likelihood, we would want our group to have an above-average education, the kind the apostles woefully lacked. We would also want our group to work together harmoniously—another area in which the apostles had shortcomings.

2. How is the Holy Spirit a comforter or counselor to us?

The Scriptures were inspired by the Holy Spirit. Thus, as we read them with an open heart and mind, we allow the Holy Spirit to minister to us. The Holy Spirit can use the words and examples of Jesus himself and His apostles to minister comfort to our hearts. Paul indicated that "the God of all comfort . . . comforteth us in all our tribulation, that we may be able to comfort them which are in any trouble, by the comfort wherewith we ourselves are comforted of God" (2 Corinthians 1:3, 4). The Scriptures are also the instrument by which the Holy Spirit can counsel us or guide us. The New Testament sets forth many principles of behavior from which we can derive counsel in times of spiritual and moral decisions. Among these are Romans 14:19; 1 Corinthians 6:19, 20; 10:31; Galatians 5:13. In studying the Bible we fill our minds with these words of comfort and counsel, so that the Holy Spirit can use them in His ministry to us.

3. Jesus' promise, "Because I live, ye shall live also," must have rung in the apostles' minds through all the trials they encountered. Why is this promise especially effective?

This promise sums up in few words a truth that is discussed in greater detail in other places in the New Testament. It is more succinct than Jesus' memorable promise to Martha in John 11:25, 26 or the beautiful promise recorded in Revelation 14:13. First Corinthians 15, the "resurrection chapter of the Bible," contains many striking statements, but nothing there offers a better description of what the resurrection means to us than this one. We too can find encouragement in tough times by thinking of the glorified Christ and this precious promise.

4. A beautiful aspect of Jesus' teaching in John 14-16 is His description of a kind of circle of love that exists among the Father, the Son, and the saved. John 14:23, 24 is one place where this is found. How is this idea of such a circle of love helpful to us?

First, we think about the amazing love that exists between the Father and the Son. (See Matthew 3:16, 17.) It is found in John's Gospel in John 3:35; 5:20; 15:9; 17:26. That love led the Son to perfect adherence to the Father's will. Next, we ponder how we have been privileged to enter such a relationship of love. To view God's love for us in this way should lead us to exclaim with John, "Behold, what manner of love the Father hath bestowed upon us, that we should be called the sons of God" (1 John 3:1). It should also inspire us to the kind of obedience to the Father that Jesus His Son exemplified.

5. Jesus promised the apostles that the Holy Spirit "shall teach you all things, and bring all things to your remembrance" (John 14:26). How does this promise apply to us?

This is not a promise that we can apply directly to ourselves. We should not expect the Holy Spirit to give us visions and unique, special enlightenment pertaining to the truth. Rather, it is a promise we enjoy through the apostles' testimony recorded in the New Testament. Thanks to the literary labors of the apostles, we learn "all things that pertain unto life and godliness, through the knowledge of him that hath called us to glory and virtue" (2 Peter 1:3). As we read the New Testament, we allow the Holy Spirit to teach us and stir our memories concerning what we must know and do as disciples of Jesus. Peter noted this when he told his readers that one purpose in his writing was "to stir you up by putting you in remembrance" (2 Peter 1:13).

Summer Quarter, 1993

Theme: Following God's Purpose

Special Features

Lessons

Unit 1: Joy in Serving Christ

Unit 2: Christ Above All

Unit 3: Newness Through Christ

Related Resources

The following publications are suggested to provide additional help on the subjects of study presented in the Summer Quarter. They may be purchased from your supplier. Prices are subject to change.

Galatians/Ephesians (Standard Bible Studies), by LeRoy Lawson. Storytelling technique makes this study enjoyable while providing solid Biblical analysis. Order #11-40109, $12.99.

Philippians-Thessalonians (Standard Bible Studies), by Gary Weedman. This book illuminates Paul's message of hope, encouragement, and joy found in these letters. Order #11-40110, $9.99.

Teach With Success, Revised, by Guy P. Leavitt; revised by Eleanor Daniel. Offers ideas for successful teaching and includes an update on terms and trends. Order #18-03232, $9.99.

Timothy-Philemon (Standard Bible Studies), by Knofel Staton. This book focuses on Paul's practical help for all who serve Christ. Order #11-40112, $9.99.

Quarterly Quiz

The questions on this page may be used in several ways: as a pretest at the beginning of the quarter; as a review at the end of the quarter; or as a review after each lesson. The questions are based on the Scripture text of each lesson (King James Version). ***The answers are on page 344.***

Lesson 1

1. What did Paul pray that the Philippians' love would do? *Philippians 1:9*
2. Did Paul's imprisonment hinder or help the spread of the gospel? *Philippians 1:12*
3. What privilege do Christians have besides that of believing in Christ? *Philippians 1:29*

Lesson 2

1. How could the Philippian Christians make Paul's joy full? *Philippians 2:2*
2. How is Jesus' name placed in relation to other names? *Philippians 2:9*
3. What are Christ's people to be doing with the word of life? *Philippians 2:16*

Lesson 3

1. How is the rejoicing of Christians different from the rejoicing of others? *Philippians 3:1*
2. What things seem worthless when compared with knowing Christ? *Philippians 3:8*
3. If legal righteousness is not enough, what righteousness is enough? *Philippians 3:9*

Lesson 4

1. When will we rejoice in the Lord if we follow Paul's advice? *Philippians 4:4*
2. What should go to God along with our requests? *Philippians 4:6*
3. In what was Paul content? *Philippians 4:11*

Lesson 5

1. Where is our hope? *Colossians 1:5*
2. Who has made us fit to have a part in the inheritance of saints? *Colossians 1:12*
3. Jesus is head of the church. In what else is He preeminent? *Colossians 1:18*

Lesson 6

1. Name four things that may despoil Christians if they are not on guard. *Colossians 2:8*
2. How much of God's complete fullness dwells in Christ? *Colossians 2:9*
3. Name three things not to be used in judging a Christian's life. *Colossians 2:16*

Lesson 7

1. What do we seek when we have been raised with Christ? *Colossians 3:1*
2. With whom is your life hid? *Colossians 3:3*
3. What is "the bond of perfectness" that is to be put on over all the other good things of the Christian life? *Colossians 3:14*

Lesson 8

1. For what two attributes of Philemon did Paul give thanks? *Philemon 4, 5*
2. What did Paul prefer to do instead of giving an order? *Philemon 8, 9*
3. What did Paul propose to do about Onesimus' debt to Philemon? *Philemon 18, 19*

Lesson 9

1. What part of us conspired with our flesh to make us "children of wrath"? *Ephesians 2:3*
2. What other attribute of God worked with His love to give us life? *Ephesians 2:4, 5*
3. With what did Paul want Christians to be filled? *Ephesians 3:19*

Lesson 10

1. By what were some of those far from God made near? *Ephesians 2:13*
2. By what were both Jews and Gentiles reconciled to God? *Ephesians 2:16*
3. For what are Christians built together into a holy temple? *Ephesians 2:21, 22*

Lesson 11

1. Christians walk in love. Who gives them an example of how to do it? *Ephesians 5:2*
2. Christians do not share in the works of darkness. What do they do instead? *Ephesians 5:11*
3. Christians do not get drunk with wine. What fills them instead? *Ephesians 5:18*

Lesson 12

1. Christians submit to the Father, Son, and Holy Spirit—and to whom else? *Ephesians 5:21*
2. Why should Christian children obey their parents? *Ephesians 6:1*
3. In whose nurture and admonition do Christians bring up children? *Ephesians 6:4*

Lesson 13

1. How much of God's armor do we need in our Christian warfare? *Ephesians 6:11*
2. Whose wiles do we resist? *Ephesians 6:11*
3. What is the sword of the Spirit that we can use in our battle? *Ephesians 6:17*

Following God's Purpose

by Knofel Staton

THE STUDIES FOR THIS QUARTER are drawn from four different New Testament books—Philippians, Colossians, Philemon, and Ephesians. There are at least three things these books have in common.

1. They were all written by the same person, the apostle Paul.

2. Each was written while Paul was a prisoner.

3. Each deals with specific situations that have parallels in today's culture.

Bridging the Centuries

The Bible teacher is a significant person in God's scheme, for he or she bridges the centuries. There is an important gap between a culture of donkeys and one of automobiles, between a culture of sandals and one of shoes, between a culture of hand-delivered letters and one of electronic mail.

That gap is not so wide when we look at it from another angle. There were marriages then, and there are marriages today. We read of divorces then and today, competitive gods then and today, alternative life-styles then and today, sin then and today.

The Bible teacher provides the "golden gate bridge" that allows the teaching of the apostles to leave the first-century shoreline and touch the twentieth-century shoreline. When the Bible teacher plugs today's situations into God's truth written long ago, God works through His Word to do today what He did through His Word long ago.

It is important for teachers to remind their classes that each student becomes God's bridge to those outside of Christ. Christians are models for Christianity. While many of the people on earth are illiterate, everybody reads other people. Most of those who are literate do not read the Bible very much during any one week. Paul reminded the Christians in Corinth that they were a living letter, "known and read of all men" (2 Corinthians 3:2, 3). This is true of us today.

Aiming Toward God's Purpose

Since this quarter's study is entitled, "Following God's Purpose," it is important to consider what God's purpose is for every person. It is not just that we go to a prepared place, Heaven. It is also that we become a prepared people. God's purpose, His aim, and His desire for us is that we grow toward Christlikeness. That is, our attitudes, actions, and reactions are to be like those of Christ.

That purpose is seen in the following verses: Romans 8:29—"To be conformed to the likeness of His son . . ."; 2 Corinthians 3:18—"And we . . . are being transformed into His likeness . . ."; Ephesians 4:13— "Until we all reach unity in the faith and in the knowledge of the Son of God and become mature, attaining to the whole measure of the fullness of Christ"; Ephesians 4:24—"And to put on the new self, created to be like God in true righteousness and holiness." (Those quotes are from the *New International Version.*)

Since that is God's purpose, it is important for the teacher to approach every lesson with the question, "How can this lesson help my students become more like Christ?" Christians should be open to continual change. They should set aside their ego to make way for the Christ. If Christ is kept on the outside, there will always be something wrong on the inside.

An "Upper" in the Midst of a "Downer"

The principles taught in the lessons of this quarter are very positive ("up"), but written by someone who was in a very "down" predicament. Paul was a prisoner, but he looked beyond the valley to see the mountaintops.

More than likely every student in your class will experience at least one disappointment, one downer, one setback, one depressing time. Continually remind the students that we are reading words from someone whose body was in distressing circumstances, but whose spirit rose above the circumstances.

Our attitude determines our altitude, our insight determines our outlook. Often the way we talk determines the way we walk.

Stinking thinking is always sinking thinking. Resurrection thinking is always elevative thinking. Paul exhibited resurrection thinking in these letters—a model for what he wants the readers to do in their lives. It is important for us to remember that our thinking is not beyond our control. Even when we cannot escape from depressing circumstances, we can think about things that are true, honest, just, pure, lovely, and of good report (Philippians 4:8). Furthermore, we can keep our actions in line with our thinking.

The Quarterly Overview

The thirteen lessons of this quarter's study are divided into three units. *Unit One*, entitled "Joy in Serving Christ," covers the first four lessons and is drawn from Philippians.

Lesson 1 outlines a worthy life that is possible even though a person may be in an unfair situation. Instead of focusing on the unfairness of it all, Paul remembered with thanksgiving people who were his friends. His heart was filled with affection for them, and he told them about that affection. Instead of saying, "I want out of here," Paul looked for the good of his readers and expressed his prayer that their lives might abound. He encouraged them to live their lives in a manner worthy of what God has done for us in Christ, regardless of how bad the circumstances might be.

Lesson 2 encourages the students to live a life of unity amid diversity by maintaining an attitude of humility both in their fellowship with God and in their fellowship with the people around them. The lesson then shows how Christ set the example in His unselfish attitudes and in His serving activities. The highest greatness comes through the lowliest services.

Lesson 3 encourages the students to stick with Christ and His way, in spite of competition, opposition, barriers, and failures. There are many priorities pulling us in different directions at the same time, but the principles of this lesson are as up to date now as they were in the first century.

Lesson 4 zeroes in on positive thinking amidst negative surroundings. This lesson challenges the students to give up being negative. It shows what the power of a positive attitude can do in, for, and through a person.

Unit Two is entitled "Christ Above All" and includes the next four lessons. The first three of them come from Colossians, and the last comes from Philemon. This unit spotlights the fact that Christ is above all, which is the theme of Colossians.

In the midst of the rise of humanism, the new age, and many cults, *lesson 5* stresses the reality of Jesus as the exact image of the invisible God, the role of Jesus as head of the church and integrator of all creation, and the supremacy of Christ's power in the individual Christian. Any student who believes that all of life on earth is controlled only by natural laws will need this lesson.

Lesson 6 deals with a situation in which Christians are attracted to new and faddish ideas and trends. What does a Christian do with the law system of the past, when he is to be under love rather than law? Have we really been freed from our sins, or should we continue to live in guilt?

Lesson 7 stresses the kind of change that has happened and continually happens in the life of the Christian. We all wrestle with the problems of controlling sinful desires, filthy language, slanderous talk, and unforgiving spirits.

Lesson 8 provides the students with a model of being a reconciler when wrong actions have separated people into possible opponents.

Unit Three is entitled, "Newness Through Christ." It covers the final five lessons, which are drawn from the book of Ephesians. This unit deals with the unity that Christ brings: what that unity is, how it is achieved, who is to live a life of unity, and the circles of relationship in which Christ's unity is to be most visible.

Lesson 9 teaches the two ways to die and the two ways to live, with a Biblical and functional concept of the meaning of grace.

Lesson 10 teaches clearly how God through Christ bridged our broken relationships, and describes our new relationships to others who are in Christ. As Christians we must not only know that we have been united to others, but we must also actually relate to them as our real brothers and sisters.

Lesson 11 concerns the demonstration of the Christian life-style in the midst of an un-Christian world. Christians are to have a positive moral influence in the communities in which they live, and this lesson gives practical ways to do it.

While lesson 11 talks about relationships in the community, *lesson 12* discusses relationships within the family. Emphasis is put on the roles and responsibilities of the wife, the husband, the children, and the parents.

Lesson 13 concludes the series by emphasizing the practical and functional resources God provides for the Christian in coping with contemporary problems.

The lessons for this quarter have been written with the first century and the twentieth century in mind. The lesson writer has tried to capture what the apostle Paul intended his letters to do in, for, and through the people of the first century. But the writer has tried also to beam these lessons to the situations of the students living in the last decade of the twentieth century. Paul's teachings are linked to up-to-date issues, contemporary problems, and current illustrations and application.

God drew a target for His people in the first century—to grow into Christlikeness in their relationships with Him, with others, and with self. God continues to draw the same target for people in the twentieth century.

A Purpose for Living

by Carl Bridges, Jr.

LET ME INTRODUCE YOU to two friends of mine, Tim and Butch. They are alike in many ways, but in a way that counts, they are quite different.

Tim is a mechanic who works in the auto shop of a large department store. He has a wife and two grown daughters. Not too long ago he finished college by correspondence. Butch works as a crew boss for the road department of the city where he lives. He and his wife are raising a young grandson they have adopted. Butch goes to night school in an adult education program.

Both of my friends are decent, hardworking family men. They are good at their jobs. They don't have obvious bad habits, and everyone who knows them likes them. So what's the difference between them?

The difference lies in their purpose for living. Tim is a vibrant, committed Christian whose life revolves around his faith. He worships regularly and makes decisions based on what he thinks God wants him to do. Even though he goes to work every day and carries on his life much as other people do, he sees everything he does as an expression of his love for God.

Butch, on the other hand, is not an active Christian. Though his name is probably still on a church's roll book somewhere, he has ignored the church so long that his faith is no longer a factor in his life. He doesn't smoke, drink, or swear, and he wants the best for his grandson; but this kind of good behavior seems to come more from his idea of decency than from a direct response to God.

The overall purpose of Tim's life is to please God. Butch's life purpose appears to be just getting by.

Lower and Higher Needs

Butch and Tim, and all of us, are motivated by many of the same things. We all want peace and privacy; we all fear pain and death. The need for love and acceptance drives us; fear of being rejected sometimes paralyzes us. Reward us, and we will usually do what we are asked; threaten us, and we will run away or fight back.

Beyond these factors that motivate all of us to do what we do, some of us have higher purposes. We want to please God, we want to help others. We want to make our world more like Heaven and our lives more like Christ's.

We might, then, describe men like Tim and Butch in this way: Butch has lower-level desires and needs that make him what he is, but he doesn't have any apparent larger purpose for his life. Tim's life, though it is driven by many of the same needs as Butch's or anyone else's, also has the larger purpose of pleasing God.

If it is fair to describe Butch and Tim like this, it is also fair to describe anyone in similar terms. A Christian is driven by many of the same lower-order needs as a non-Christian, but the Christian has—or ought to have—the ultimate purpose of pleasing God as well.

A Purpose for Living: Pleasing God

Why, then, did God put us here? What purpose do we have for living? We find in Paul's prison epistles (Ephesians, Philippians, Colossians, Philemon) several reasons for living. Some of them have to do with God, and others have to do with other people.

Paul opens his letter to the Christians in Ephesus with a statement of who we are in Christ. God, Paul says, has "blessed us in Christ with every spiritual blessing in the heavenly places" (Ephesians 1:3*). He has chosen us "in Christ before the foundation of the world to be holy and blameless before him in love" (1:4). He has "destined us for adoption as his children through Jesus Christ" (1:5). In addition, God has redeemed us (1:7), or bought us back from our state of sin. He has revealed His will to us (1:9) and chosen us as His heirs (1:11). God has given us the Holy Spirit as a "seal," a guarantee that we will inherit what He has promised us (1: 13, 14).

These grand words point to one of our reasons for living: to live out our destiny as God's children. We are not simply physical creatures, as a biologist might look at us, or citizens, as a politician might see us. We are not just husbands or wives, parents or children, bosses or workers. We are special creations of God, created to live with Him forever and enjoy His glory.

All this may sound a little abstract. If I have such a high destiny in God's future, what does that mean for my present life?

In Ephesians 2, Paul tells us. There he draws a contrast between our former lives in sin, when we were "dead through the trespasses and sins in which [we] once lived" (2:1, 2), and our present lives in Christ, in which God has "raised us up with him and seated us with him in the heavenly places in Christ Jesus" (2:6). God has saved us "by grace . . . through faith" (2:8), Paul says, making us new people in Christ. God's purpose for all this is the "good works" that He has "created" us for, works that He has "prepared beforehand to be our way of life" (2:10).

That's what these fine-sounding words mean for our daily lives. We are people who have a high destiny in Christ. We are to live out that destiny in works of service to God and to people. Our purpose for living is to please God and thereby live up to what He has made us.

This, then, is a big difference between Tim and Butch, between any Christian and any non-Christian. Butch's reason for living is vague; his purposes and goals are all short-term concerns. He wants to make a living, take care of his family, and enjoy life. Tim, on the other hand, has these same goals plus one more, the goal of becoming everything God wants him to be, of living up to the "heavenly call of God in Christ Jesus" (Philippians 3:14).

A Purpose for Living: Helping Others

We not only have this first purpose, the purpose of living up to our destiny as God's children. We also have an interpersonal reason for living; we want to live our lives in a right relationship with the people around us.

Paul points out to the Ephesian Christians that God has brought Jews and Gentiles together through the death of Christ (Ephesians 2:11-22). The two groups, once separated and hostile, now belong to the same "household of God" (2:19). They are parts of the same "holy temple in the Lord" (2:21) and members of the "one body" of Christ (2:16).

Paul goes on in Ephesians 4 to elaborate the "one body" image. Several unifying factors lie at the heart of the Christian faith: "one body . . . one Spirit . . . one hope . . . one Lord, one faith, one baptism, one God" (4:4-6). Because of these, we as Christ's people are one on earth, no matter where we came from or what we look like. We work together "building up the body of Christ" (4:12). We tell each other the truth (4:25; compare Colossians 3:9); we control anger (4:26); we "share with the needy" (4:28). We say things that build up our brothers and sisters (4:29); we forgive (4:32; compare Colossians 3:13) and love and protect each other. Our purpose for living is no longer self-centered, focusing on our jobs and our families and our personal needs. We now live for others, meeting the needs of the other members of the body of Christ.

Paul's own life serves as an illustration of this other-centered way of living. Imprisoned in Rome and uncertain of his fate, Paul describes his conflicting thoughts in the first chapter of his letter to the church in Philippi.

Paul is torn between a desire to "depart and be with Christ," which he says will be "far better" (Philippians 1:23), and a wish "to remain in the flesh." This, he says, "is more necessary for you" (1:24). "Living is Christ," he believes, and "dying is gain" (1:21). His reason for staying alive rather than dying, for postponing the joys of being with Christ, is to bring help and support to his Christian brothers and sisters in the Philippian church.

If right now I faced the choice of living or dying, I would choose living. But I'm not so sure I would choose it for Paul's high motives. I would want to stay alive simply because I don't want to die. There are things I want to experience, places I want to go. If I faced such a choice, other people's needs would likely be pretty unimportant to me. How about you?

Paul's little letter to Philemon gives us another illustration of this other-centered reason for living. While few in the Roman world would show concern for a slave, and a runaway at that, Paul has taken Onesimus in hand and dealt with him like a son (Philemon 10). He writes Onesimus' master Philemon and begs him to take Onesimus back as "more than a slave, a beloved brother . . . both in the flesh and in the Lord" (16). Paul lives to serve others.

Different People, Different Purposes

Here then is the difference between Tim and Butch. One lives for himself. It's not that we would call him a selfish person, but that his sights are set too low. All he really wants out of life is living. All he hopes for is in this world. All he wants to do is please himself and his immediate circle of friends and family, with little reference to the God who made him.

The other man has the same needs and goals as the first, but he has a higher purpose as well. He wants to please God, because of what God has done for him, and because he is a member of Christ's body, the church. Both Tim and Butch are ordinary people, with ordinary human needs; but Tim has gone a step farther, has set his sights a notch higher. He knows who he is in relation to God and God's people, and so he has a purpose for living.

How about you? What makes you tick? What motives drive you? May God grant that you don't just want to please yourself. May He help you live up to your destiny as a child of God, doing what you can for God's other children.

---

*Scriptures are quoted from the *New Revised Standard Version.*

The Secret of Contentment

by Charles E. Cook

AMONG THE FREQUENT COMMERCIALS on television is the one in which an attractive woman extols the benefits of a certain haircare product. Her closing words are, "And I'm worth it!" The suggestion is obvious: "You're worth it too, and if you don't have this product you will miss something that can make you happier and more beautiful." The commercial, like many others, is designed to produce a feeling of discontent, out of which a sense of need will become so strong that purchase it I must!

We desperately need to learn what the apostle Paul had learned. In his letter to the Christians at Philippi, he wrote, "I have learned to be content whatever the circumstances. I know what it is to be in need, and I know what it is to have plenty. I have learned the secret of being content in any and every situation" (Philippians 4:11, 12).* Incredible! This man was writing as a Roman prisoner. What an affirmation of sufficiency!

How does a person reach such a state of mind? What makes it possible for one to honestly say, "The circumstances of life couldn't be worse, but I myself couldn't be better"? Is this a form of insanity resulting from prolonged deprivation, a philosophical irrationality that ignores reality, or an immature naivete that just doesn't understand the situation? Certainly not in the case of Paul. Never was there a person who had a firmer grip on reality. He said, "I know what it is to be in need, and I know what it is to have plenty" (Philippians 4:12).

Paul lived in no world of dreams and fantasies. He described the conditions under which he carried out his ministry in realistic and vivid terms: "In great endurance; in troubles, hardships and distresses; in beatings, imprisonments and riots; in hard work, sleepless nights and hunger; in purity, understanding, patience and kindness; in the Holy Spirit and in sincere love; in truthful speech and in the power of God; with weapons of righteousness in the right hand and in the left; through glory and dishonor, bad report and good report; genuine, yet regarded as impostors; known, yet regarded as unknown; dying, and yet we live on; beaten, and yet not killed; sorrowful, yet always rejoicing; poor, yet making many rich; having nothing, and yet possessing everything" (2 Corinthians 6:4-10). There it is: "Having nothing, and yet possessing everything!"

This is precisely what Paul was attempting to explain to his dear friends in Philippi who had sent him some gifts by way of Epaphroditus. He was deeply grateful for their thoughtfulness and kindness, but he wanted them to know that he was not depending on their gifts for his inner joy and contentment. Just how do you say to someone, "Thanks for everything, but I really don't need anything"? You might say it like this: "I rejoice greatly in the Lord that at last you have renewed your concern for me, but . . . I have learned the secret of being content in any and every situation" (Philippians 4:10, 11).

What is this secret that Paul had learned? How can we learn it?

Consider God's Purpose

How easy it is for us to focus on the circumstances of life first and then evaluate our relationship to God by our evaluation of the circumstances! It is natural to look at the divine/human relationship from the human perspective. So often we ask, "Why did God let this happen?" Or, "What have I done to deserve this?" Or again, "If God is a loving God, how can He allow something like this?"

We must remember that the pendulum of life swings back and forth between good news and bad news, joys and sorrows, prosperity and need. Strength of character comes, not from yielding to life's circumstances, but from trusting in the one who said of himself, "I the Lord do not change" (Malachi 3:6). James reminds us that "every good and perfect gift is from above, coming down from the Father of the heavenly lights, who does not change like shifting shadows" (James 1:17).

We should look at the divine/human relationship from the perspective of divine purpose. Instead of interpreting God's character by life's changing circumstances, we should respond to the circumstances confident of God's unchanging integrity and faithfulness. This is a secret of true contentment.

Look Beyond the Temporal

The youth minister at our church has a wooden plaque that reads, THINK ETERNITY. Every time I see it I am reminded of how easy it is for us to become so concerned with the issues of the moment that we lose sight of the issues that are eternal. We must continually ask ourselves, "How important is this, ultimately?" "What difference does it really make in terms of the eternal consequences of life?" A friend of mine often asks, "How important will this be one hundred years from now?"

Of course, we all live in the moments of each day. That cannot be avoided. Those moments combine to make the days, weeks, months, and years that eventually make a lifetime. But we must learn to interpret the meaning of each momentary experience in the light of God's eternal purpose. Paul had learned to do this. He wrote, "And we know that in all things God works for the good of those who love him, who have been called according to his purpose" (Romans 8:28). Paul was committed to the eternal purpose of God, regardless of what the temporary circumstances might be.

In the midst of his description of many life-threatening circumstances, Paul wrote, "For our light and momentary troubles are achieving for us an eternal glory that far outweighs them all. So we fix our eyes not on what is seen, but on what is unseen. For what is seen [life's circumstances] is temporary, but what is unseen [God's purpose] is eternal" (2 Corinthians 4:17, 18).

It is so easy for us to lose our perspective on life. The more demanding and difficult the situations we face, the narrower our perspective seems to become. We are unable to see beyond the moment and ourselves. We begin to function on the basis of our feelings rather than the facts. We misinterpret what, under other circumstances, we might understand quite clearly.

The way to prevent this is to step back, take our eyes off the circumstances, and turn them upon our Creator, whose eternal purposes can and will be realized regardless of any temporary situation. "Trust me," He is saying; "I have everything under control."

Have Confidence in Christ's Sufficiency

To feel contentment we must place our confidence in the sufficiency of Christ. Paul was reminded of this when he struggled with his tormenting "thorn in the flesh" and finally realized that Christ's grace was sufficient. He concluded, "I delight in weaknesses, in insults, in hardships, in persecutions, in difficulties. For when I am weak, then I am strong" (2 Corinthians 12:10).

These are the affirmations of a man who had experienced the worst that life can bring and had recognized that it is no match for the best that Christ promises. Paul understood that contentment comes from accepting our own limits and allowing the unlimited grace and power of Christ to be the source of our strength. He measured his ability to deal with life's circumstances by the sufficiency of the resources of God in Christ. "I can do everything through him who gives me strength" (Philippians 4:13).

It is easy to find people who know how to say, "I can't." "I can't take it anymore." "I can't bear the thought of it." "I can't do without it." "I can't help it." "I can't stand that person." "I can't live a victorious Christian life." "I can't, I can't." The list is endless and the refrain is monotonous. But the answer to all of these self-imposed limitations is not just to tell ourselves we must roll up our sleeves and try harder. Nor is the answer found in convincing ourselves that if we just ignore life's problems long enough they will go away. Rather, the way to cope with life and live with contentment is to find our sufficiency in the One who has already given us everything we need for living.

When you feel discontented and a voice whispers in your ear, "You deserve more and better in life," just whisper back, "Thank you very much, but "His divine power has given [me] everything [I] need for life and godliness" (2 Peter 1:3). Understanding and accepting this truth is the real secret to contentment.

---

*Scripture quotations are from the *New International Version.*

Answers to Quarterly Quiz on page 338

Lesson 1—1. abound more and more. 2. help. 3. suffering for His sake. **Lesson 2**—1. by living in harmony. 2. above them. 3. holding it forth. **Lesson 3**—1. it is in the Lord. 2. all things. 3. righteousness from God by faith. **Lesson 4**—1. always. 2. thanksgiving. 3. in whatever state he was. **Lesson 5**—1. in Heaven. 2. the Father. 3. all things. **Lesson 6**—1. philosophy, vain deceit, tradition, rudiments of the world. 2. all of it. 3. food, drink, special days. **Lesson 7**—1. the things above. 2. with Christ in God. 3. charity. **Lesson 8**—1. love and faith. 2. beseech. 3. pay it himself. **Lesson 9**—1. the mind. 2. mercy. 3. the fulness of God. **Lesson 10**—1. by the blood of Christ. 2. by the cross. 3. for a habitation of God. **Lesson 11**—1. Christ. 2. reprove them. 3. the Spirit. **Lesson 12**—1. one another. 2. this is right. 3. the Lord's. **Lesson 13**—1. all of it. 2. the devil's. 3. the word of God.

A Worthy Life

June 6
Lesson 1

DEVOTIONAL READING: 2 Corinthians 5:1-15.

LESSON SCRIPTURE: Philippians 1.

PRINTED TEXT: Philippians 1:3-14, 27-30.

Philippians 1:3-14, 27-30

3 I thank my God upon every remembrance of you,

4 Always in every prayer of mine for you all making request with joy,

5 For your fellowship in the gospel from the first day until now;

6 Being confident of this very thing, that he which hath begun a good work in you will perform it until the day of Jesus Christ:

7 Even as it is meet for me to think this of you all, because I have you in my heart; inasmuch as both in my bonds, and in the defense and confirmation of the gospel, ye all are partakers of my grace.

8 For God is my record, how greatly I long after you all in the bowels of Jesus Christ.

9 And this I pray, that your love may abound yet more and more in knowledge and in all judgment;

10 That ye may approve things that are excellent; that ye may be sincere and without offense till the day of Christ;

11 Being filled with the fruits of righteousness, which are by Jesus Christ, unto the glory and praise of God.

12 But I would ye should understand, brethren, that the things which happened unto me have fallen out rather unto the furtherance of the gospel;

13 So that my bonds in Christ are manifest in all the palace, and in all other places;

14 And many of the brethren in the Lord, waxing confident by my bonds, are much more bold to speak the word without fear.

. . . .

27 Only let your conversation be as it becometh the gospel of Christ: that whether I come and see you, or else be absent, I may hear of your affairs, that ye stand fast in one spirit, with one mind striving together for the faith of the gospel;

28 And in nothing terrified by your adversaries: which is to them an evident token of perdition, but to you of salvation, and that of God.

29 For unto you it is given in the behalf of Christ, not only to believe on him, but also to suffer for his sake;

30 Having the same conflict which ye saw in me, and now hear to be in me.

GOLDEN TEXT: Let your conversation be as it becometh the gospel of Christ.
—Philippians 1:27

Following God's Purpose

Unit 1: Joy in Serving Christ

(Lessons 1-4)

Lesson Aims

The study of this lesson is designed to help the student:

1. Engage in regular intercessory prayer.
2. Practice encouraging others.
3. Trust in the majesty of God while going through setbacks in life.

Lesson Outline

INTRODUCTION
- A. Remembering What?
- B. Lesson Background

I. A LIFE WORTHY OF REMEMBERING (Philippians 1:3-8)
- A. With Thanksgiving (v. 3)
- B. With Joyful Intercession (v. 4)
- C. For Fellowship (v. 5)
- D. With Confidence (v. 6)
  - *Confident Expectation*
- E. With Affection (vv. 7, 8)

II. A LIFE WORTHY OF EXPANDING (Philippians 1:9-14)
- A. Love (v. 9)
- B. Character and Conduct (vv. 10, 11)
- C. Understanding (vv. 12-14)
  - *Overcoming Circumstances*

III. A LIFE WORTHY OF THE GOSPEL (Philippians 1:27-30)
- A. In Unity (v. 27)
  - *A Worthy Life*
- B. In Courage (v. 28)
- C. In Conflict (vv. 29, 30)

CONCLUSION
- A. A Promotion and an Assignment
- B. Prayer
- C. Thought to Remember

Visual 1 of the visuals packet highlights the points of Paul's prayer that are discussed in verses 3-8. The visual is shown on page 348.

Introduction

A. Remembering What?

Someone has said a well-trained memory is one that lets you forget everything that isn't worth remembering. How can we forget the worthless? Here are some suggestions:

1. Fill your mind with the positive by recalling things that are worth remembering.
2. Mention those things to God in prayer—not once, but over and over.
3. Find at least one positive thing in the negative situation and dwell on that. Think about the good in the bad, the marvelous in the mess, the sweetness in the sourness.
4. Speak about and encourage the positive aspects in another person in spite of the negative aspects.

B. Lesson Background

Paul wrote Philippians during the two years he was a prisoner in Rome (Acts 28:30, 31). While there, Paul could have thought like this: "Had I not become a Christian, I could have been one of the most popular leaders in Judaism—respected, well paid, and in great demand. But here I am a long way from home and chained to a guard. What a mess!"

Instead, Paul thought about the positive aspects of his ministry. He thought back to his work in the city of Philippi. It would have been very easy for him to think about the negative aspects of that. He was arrested, tortured, and then thrown into prison. But Paul dwelt on the positive. He knew that God's grace was greater than man's disgrace, and that the power of the Creator was greater than the oppression of the circumstances. In what we would call a discouraging situation, Paul wrote encouraging words; and we will see some of them included in this lesson.

I. A Life Worthy of Remembering (Philippians 1:3-8)

A. With Thanksgiving (v. 3)

3. I thank my God upon every remembrance of you.

Paul is a prisoner, but instead of thinking of himself he thinks of others. When he thinks of others, he also thinks about God. He says, *I thank my God.* That's because Christianity is *the* relational religion. In Christ we are not just related to God, but also to all others who come to the Father through Jesus. When Paul thinks about the people at Philippi, he immediately shows his attitude of gratitude. Wouldn't it be wonderful to have such relationships with others that every time they think of us, they are filled with gratitude? What do people think when they think of you? Do they think, "Out of sight, out of mind"? Do they think, "He/she isn't worth remembering"? Do they recall, "He/she hurt me deeply"? Do they say, "I am thankful for him/her"?

B. With Joyful Intercession (v. 4)

4. Always in every prayer of mine for you all making request with joy.

We can note here some dimensions of Paul's prayer life. This is a prayer not only of thanksgiving, but also of intercession. It is a prayer that makes requests for the sake of others.

Jesus modeled intercessory prayer. He said to Peter, "But I have prayed for thee, that thy faith fail not" (Luke 22:32). Not only did He pray for others while He was on earth; He is continuing to intercede for us while He is in Heaven. At the right hand of God He is making intercession for us (Romans 8:34; Hebrews 7:25; 9:24).

Paul's intercessory prayer is offered *with joy.* This Greek word for *joy* is based on the same root as the word for *thank* in verse 3. Thanksgiving comes out of something we delight in, and Paul delights in the Philippian people. He makes his requests *with joy* because he knows that God hears his prayers, that God is able to answer his prayers, and that the Philippians will be open to receive God's answers.

C. For Fellowship (v. 5)

5. For your fellowship in the gospel from the first day until now.

The word for *fellowship* (*koinonia*) doesn't just mean a handshake or a hug or pie and coffee in the fellowship hall. It means a partnership, a sharing in the life of others. It is not just attending a meeting, but attending to people.

When Paul speaks about their fellowship *in the gospel,* he is recalling that they participated in spreading the gospel by sharing their finances with Paul (4:15, 16). The same Greek word for *fellowship* is translated *contribution* in Romans 15:26. Real fellowship is to contribute something of yourself to the lives of others.

When Paul says, *From the first day until now,* he makes it clear that the Philippians have remained consistent in their concern and involvement. They have not run hot and cold, up and down, in and out.

D. With Confidence (v. 6)

6. Being confident of this very thing, that he which hath begun a good work in you will perform it until the day of Jesus Christ.

One of the reasons Paul can pray with joy (v. 4) is that he has confidence in God, who has begun His work in the lives of those people. God has not begun something good in our lives to let it die, has not picked us up to drop us, has not adopted us to abandon us.

What is the *good work* that God has begun in us? He has restored us to His image in which man was created (Genesis 1:26, 27). He has made us new creatures (2 Corinthians 5:17). He has shared with us His divine nature (2 Peter 1:4) so we can grow up into the likeness of Christ (Ephesians 4:15).

However, we must allow that good work to continue in us. It is possible for us to suppress what God has started. When that happens, we should not blame God, but ourselves.

VISUALS FOR THESE LESSONS

The *Adult Visuals/Learning Resources* packet contains classroom-size visuals designed for use with the lessons in the Summer Quarter. The packet is available from your supplier. Order no. 492.

CONFIDENT EXPECTATION

Bill was more than discouraged. He was desperate. His new job was a nightmare. He felt out of place in the office. Everyone else seemed so confident, so secure!

Bill was working extra hours to get used to the new equipment, but was making more mistakes than were acceptable. Sleep came hard at home, and Bill found himself cross and critical of his wife and children, which was not like him. Bill was ready to quit! The new position had promised so much, but it was creating frustration, fear, and failure.

Then an older employee said, "Bill, I've noticed you're having a hard time. Would you let me help you a little? I know these machines and can speed up your learning. I'm sure you can handle the job, and I'd like to help you."

The results were phenomenal. Very soon Bill was a confident, competent worker.

All of us need someone who believes in us and feels sure we can achieve success. Haven't you been helped by someone? Can't you help someone else? Come alongside and give that person a needed lift. This is what the Lord does for us. Paul is confident that He will continue to help us till the day when all we have become, through His love and guidance, will be judged.

—W. P.

E. With Affection (vv. 7, 8)

7. Even as it is meet for me to think this of you all, because I have you in my heart; inasmuch as both in my bonds, and in the defense and confirmation of the gospel, ye all are partakers of my grace.

How wonderful to live such a life that others not only have us on their minds but also in their hearts, in their affections! *It is meet* is an archaic way of saying *It is right* or It *is appropriate.*

Some people could say, "You are on my list," or "You are on my nerves," or "You worry me"; but Paul says the Philippians are in his heart. Our minds and hearts are not separate. Our intellect and our emotions are not in conflict. There is not only rationality in Christianity, but also emotion. To eliminate either is to mar God's nature within us. It is sad if we allow emotions to arise over a baseball team, but not over God's team—our brothers and sisters in Christ.

What do we do when we hold people in our hearts? We pray for them, go to bat for them, encourage them, speak good of them, forgive them, long for them, share materially when they are in need, and bring healing to their hurts.

The Philippians were *partakers* with Paul. They were sharers in his imprisonment *(in my bonds)* and in the *defense and confirmation of the gospel.* In both of these they shared his *grace:* that is, the ministry, the privilege of proclaiming the gospel, that God had graciously given to Paul (Ephesians 3:8). His imprisonment was part of that gift, for it brought new opportunities to preach (Acts 28:30, 31). The Philippians shared this grace, not only by supporting Paul, but also by their own preaching and suffering (Philippians 1:29, 30). How do we feel when we are persecuted or ridiculed or mistreated because of our Christian witness? Do we consider it a grace, a gift, a privilege?

8. For God is my record, how greatly I long after you all in the bowels of Jesus Christ.

My record means *my witness*. Paul is saying God knows his longing is sincere and deep. Probably one of the best proofs of a positive relationship is that a person longs to be in another's presence. Isn't that how we felt when we first fell in love?

Loving and longing go together. Love for the Philippians is seen in Paul's longing. It was like Jesus' love for them. (The ancients referred to one's affections when they used the term *bowels.*) Our love for the church is shown by our longing to be there when the church is meeting. If we are finding excuses to be absent when God's people meet for worship and fellowship, perhaps we need to fall in love all over again with Christ and His bride, the church.

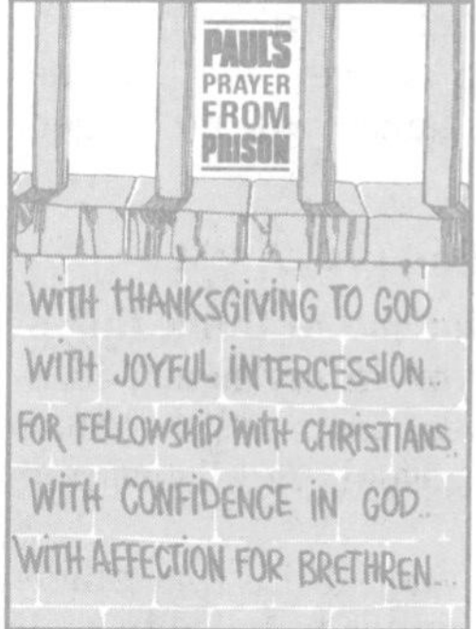
PAUL'S
PRAYER
FROM
PRISON
WITH THANKSGIVING TO GOD..
WITH JOYFUL INTERCESSION..
FOR FELLOWSHIP WITH CHRISTIANS.
WITH CONFIDENCE IN GOD..
WITH AFFECTION FOR BRETHREN...

visual 1

II. A Life Worthy of Expanding (Philippians 1:9-14)

The worthy aspects of a life deserve to be expanded. Paul mentions several such aspects.

A. Love (v. 9)

9. And this I pray, that your love may abound yet more and more in knowledge and in all judgment.

Paul has expressed his love and longing for the Philippians. Now he prays that their love *may abound yet more and more.* How does love abound? It abounds in at least two ways.

1. By including more people. Someone has said, "He drew a circle that shut me out, Rebel, heretic, a thing to flout. But love and I had the wit to win: We drew a circle that took him in."

2. By doing more for others. Love is not just an emotion. Real love acts *in knowledge and in all judgment.* We need to know what it is to love someone else, particularly in our day when the idea of love is so perverted. If we really want to know what love is and make the right decisions (*judgment*) about love, we need to study the life of Jesus. He was God's love in visible form.

Now the big question—Is your love stagnant or growing? Is it dead or alive?

B. Character and Conduct (vv. 10, 11)

10. That ye may approve things that are excellent; that ye may be sincere and without offense till the day of Christ.

There is a significant connection between verses 9 and 10. When our love grows in knowledge and discernment, we become wise enough to recognize and *approve things that are excellent.* In knowing what is excellent and loving it, we develop good character, *sincere and without offense.* If we are sincere, what we appear to be on the outside squares with what we are on the inside. We are not trying to fool people. What you see is what you get.

Without offense is a way of saying that we do not cause others to stumble into sin. We do not lure people into wrongful deeds.

11. Being filled with the fruits of righteousness, which are by Jesus Christ, unto the glory and praise of God.

Good character is shown in good conduct. *Righteousness* is in character; *the fruits of righ-*

teousness are good deeds. We do not produce them by ourselves, but *by Jesus Christ,* by following His teaching and example so that He lives in us and acts through us. Thus led by the Savior, we do not do good to win praise for ourselves, but *unto the glory and praise of God.*

C. Understanding (vv. 12-14)

12. But I would ye should understand, brethren, that the things which happened unto me have fallen out rather unto the furtherance of the gospel.

In difficult circumstances it may be hard to keep growing in love and character and conduct. It is easier to complain than to be grateful. It is easier to ask God why than to follow God's way. It is easier to look down rather than look up. But Paul kept looking up. His imprisonment might be expected to hinder the spread of the gospel, but God's power was able to make it help instead. The messenger was chained, but the message was free. In the next verses we see how that happened.

13. So that my bonds in Christ are manifest in all the palace, and in all other places.

Paul was held in a house instead of a prison cell, but he was constantly guarded (Acts 28:16). Probably he was chained to the guard. What an opportunity! Every time Paul wrote a letter, the guard could read it. Every time Paul spoke and counseled with people, the guard would overhear. When there was no one else to talk to, Paul could preach to the guard. What a captive audience! In off-duty hours the guard would tell his fellow soldiers what he had heard, and another guard would be listening to Paul. Even people from Caesar's household became Christians due to Paul's imprisonment (Philippians 4:22).

OVERCOMING CIRCUMSTANCES

Buchart Gardens in Victoria, British Columbia, Canada, is one of the most visited of all the tourist attractions Vancouver Island has to offer. The floral plantings, amidst towering trees, rocky slopes, and precipice heights make the garden a vision of beauty at any season.

The manicured lawns, ponds, and glistening fountains all remind visitors of the beauty of creation and the ability of man to place, in several hundred acres, the plants, paths, and open spaces to delight the eyes and bring peace to the soul of the beholder. At night, with the illumination of spotlights and floodlights, Buchart Gardens becomes a magic paradise, never to be forgotten.

It is hard to believe that much of the area was once a commercial rock and gravel business that defaced the original natural beauty. With planning, and hard work, what was scarred and marred is an area of delight, and productivity.

Jesus enters into scarred lives to perform an even more wonderful transformation. Paul used the dismal circumstances of his imprisonment to preach the glory and rebirth possible in Christ. The Roman palace guard, hearing the good news, came to know the Savior who could change life's misery into eternal triumph.

When you see others marred by sin, reach into their lives with Jesus, and discover the healing He can bring to them and to you. Replace despair with the beauty of faith, hope, and love. —W. P.

14. And many of the brethren in the Lord, waxing confident by my bonds, are much more bold to speak the word without fear.

Other Christians saw that Paul was continuing to preach the gospel boldly even when he was a prisoner (Acts 28: 30, 31). That encouraged them to be fearless in preaching the same gospel. So Paul's imprisonment not only helped him reach people he could not have reached if he had been free (v. 13); it also helped others reach people Paul could have reached if he had been free.

If we are in difficult circumstances, shouldn't we look beyond them to see how God can use them to bring good into the lives of others?

III. A Life Worthy of the Gospel (Philippians 1:27-30)

A. In Unity (v. 27)

27. Only let your conversation be as it becometh the gospel of Christ: that whether I come and see you, or else be absent, I may hear of your affairs, that ye stand fast in one spirit, with one mind striving together for the faith of the gospel.

The word *conversation* here means conduct, the whole way of life. We are not only to talk the walk, but also walk the talk. Our life-style should be one that *becometh the gospel of Christ:* that is, one suitable to the message we believe and share. People should be able to see that Christians *stand fast in one spirit.* Instead of watching Christians fuss and fight with each other, the community needs to see that we are a family and that we love one another in spite of our differences. We are *striving together,* not against each other, *for the faith of the gospel.* We proclaim the faith not only by what we say, but by the way we live.

A WORTHY LIFE

Jim and Joan Yost are missionaries among primitive tribespeople in Irian Jaya, Indonesia. One of the early converts was a man named Aeko. Aeko stood out in a crowd, as he was over six feet tall, an unusual height among the Comoro people.

Aeko liked Jim Yost and would sit at his feet each time Jim preached. He became one of the first believers among his people. Through his witness his wife and children and their spouses soon became followers of Jesus.

Although Aeko was seldom sick, the years began to diminish his strength and stamina. One day his sister, Ohare, came bursting into the Yosts' home with news that Aeko was dying. Jim was not at home, so Joan made the journey by canoe with Ohare in driving rain. Deep in the jungle, in a pole house, Aeko lay on the floor, his head cradled in his wife's arms. He was composed, talking of the Lord and how all of his family members had become Christians. He died before Jim could arrive.

As Aeko was laid in his grave, his most valued possessions were placed with his body. This was Comoro custom. There were no tools, bows, or instruments of warfare. The things his family placed as his most precious possessions were his New Testament books, a songbook, and his literacy books that he never fully understood. These books were his treasure.

Aeko lived in a way worthy of the gospel he believed. The Word was his treasure. If you should die tonight, what would your family think is most important of all you possess?

—W. P.

B. In Courage (v. 28)

28. And in nothing terrified by your adversaries: which is to them an evident token of perdition, but to you of salvation, and that of God.

When we are firm in our faith in spite of all opposition, this is *an evident token*, a clear indication, that the opponents are lost and we are saved. Our salvation is not due to our courage, however; it is *of God.* From our courage in the face of adversity the non-Christians get a clear message that our God is greater than theirs, that our hope is more firm than theirs, that our future is more secure than theirs, and that our fellowship is more loving than theirs.

C. In Conflict (vv. 29, 30)

29. For unto you it is given in the behalf of Christ, not only to believe on him, but also to suffer for his sake.

What a privilege it is not only to *believe* in Christ, but also to *suffer for his sake.* Our suffering is slight. We are not prisoners as Paul was; we are not persecuted as the Philippians were. But we do give up some comfort and pleasure in order to invest money and time and energy in Christian work, and we do endure some scorn and ridicule. Whatever distress we endure has two good results: It makes us stronger in the faith, and it shows others that we have a faith worth suffering for.

30. Having the same conflict which ye saw in me, and now hear to be in me.

We Christians are actively engaged in a great *conflict* with the devil and evil. The devil would like us to think that we are in it all alone, but Paul reminds the Philippians that the agony they are going through is the same kind he has endured and is enduring.

We do not fight the battles alone, and we do not win them alone. We need each other. In our conflict a worthy life does its part with unity, courage, and victory through suffering.

Conclusion

A. A Promotion and an Assignment

On the day I received the promotion to technical sergeant, the colonel said, "Now let's see if he can live up to that promotion. We are going to give him this assignment . . ." With a promotion comes responsibility.

In Christ, we have been promoted—we have been lifted up to become a new creation. With the promotion comes an assignment: we are to live a life worthy of Him who has promoted us.

B. Prayer

Thank You, Father, for believing that we can be worthy of the sacrifice of Your Son. Help us to be worthy of that sacrifice in the way we think and live. In Jesus' name, amen.

C. Thought to Remember

God's majesty is greater than our mess.

Home Daily Bible Readings

Monday, May 31—Partakers Together of God's Grace (Philippians 1:1-11)
Tuesday, June 1—Rejoice! Christ Is Being Proclaimed (Philippians 1:12-18)
Wednesday, June 2—A Life-style Worthy of the Gospel (Philippians 1:19-30)
Thursday, June 3—We Share Both Suffering and Comfort (2 Corinthians 1:3-11)
Friday, June 4—God Establishes and Commissions Us (2 Corinthians 1:12-22)
Saturday, June 5—Christ Always Leads Us in Triumph (2 Corinthians 2:12-17)
Sunday, June 6—Preach Christ as Lord, and Serve (2 Corinthians 4:1-6)

Learning by Doing

This page contains an alternate lesson plan emphasizing learning activities. Classes desiring such student involvement will find these suggestions helpful.

Learning Goals

Students in today's class should:

1. List what Philippians 1:3-30 says about *prayer, fellowship, or trials.*

2. Choose one way to improve their prayer life, enrich fellowship with a Christian leader, or face a trial.

Into the Lesson

Before class, write the following familiar verse on the chalkboard: "I thank my God every time I remember you" (Philippians 1:3, *New International Version*). Ask class members, in pairs, to discuss with each other, "Whom would you say this about? Why?" After a few minutes, allow two or three volunteers to share what they have discussed, and then ask the whole class, "Can you think of someone who would say this about you?" Ask class members to decide, "What goes into a relationship of this quality?"

Tell the class that today begins a study of Paul's letter to the Philippian Christians. His relationship with them will be one dimension of this study; their relationships with each other will be another.

Into the Word

Be prepared to slowly read today's text (Philippians 1:3-30) to your class, or play a tape recorded rendition of the passage for them. Before students hear the text, number them by threes so that each class member is either a "one," a "two," or a "three."

Those in group number one are to listen for everything this passage says about *prayer.* Those in group two are to listen for everything the passage says about *fellowship.* Those in group three are to listen for everything it says about *trials.*

As class members listen to the text, they should follow along in their Bibles or with some other printed version of the text (student books or a copy of the text that you have duplicated for them). Each student should write his or her assigned number beside the appropriate verses.

Next, have students group in twos or threes with others who have the same number. Give them about five minutes or less to compare notes and discover how their marked Bibles are the same or different. Ask them to write a summary, in one or two sentences, of what the passage says about their assigned topic.

Ask one or two representatives of the "ones" to read their summary sentences. Then hear one or two "twos," followed by one or two "threes." You may wish to copy their sentences on the chalkboard. Or have the class members write them on overhead projector transparencies or pieces of newsprint. (If the latter, mount these on the wall. You may want to refer to them throughout the class session.)

Discuss with the class:

1. What was the nature of Paul's relationship with the Philippians? In what sense do you suppose they were partners with him?

2. What does Paul say he is praying for? How do you suppose his concern for the Philippians was a factor in his leadership of them?

3. What seems to be the relationship between love and knowledge in verses 9-11? How does this contrast with the tendency in today's culture to connect love only with feeling?

4. What are Paul's *physical* trials? What are his *emotional* trials? (List these on the chalkboard or newsprint pad as students identify them.)

5. Which of Paul's trials are easiest for you to relate to? Which would be hardest for you to bear? What surprises you about Paul's reactions to his trials? Comforts you?

Into Life

Distribute pencils and paper. Ask class members to complete at least one of the following sentences for sharing with those they grouped with in the first Bible-study activity:

1. Paul's example has challenged me to change my prayer life in this way:

2. Paul's example has prodded me to deepen my fellowship with some Christian leader in this way:

3. Paul's example has encouraged me to face a significant trial in my life this way:

Allow the small groups to hear each other's sentences. Then, if you have time, you may wish to ask a few class members to share them with the whole group. Thank each one for his or her contribution and example.

End with prayer. Perhaps you will choose to ask class members to pray in their small groups. Ask members to pray for each other and encourage each other to act on the sentences they have completed. When most of the groups are silent, close the session with your own prayer.

Let's Talk It Over

The questions on this page are designed to encourage review of the lesson Scriptures and to promote discussion of the lesson by the class. The answers provided are only discussion starters. Let your class talk it over from there.

1. Paul begins his letter to the Philippians by announcing that he and Timothy are "servants of Jesus Christ." The Greek word means slaves. Are we also slaves of Christ?

Most of us are slaves to something. Drugs, money, work, pleasure, and TV are in control of many. A sinner is a slave of sin (John 8:34). Jesus himself took the form of a slave (Philippians 2:7) in order to redeem us from slavery to sin. Being free from sin we are slaves of righteousness (Romans 6:18). This is a willing slavery, even an eager one. We desire to show our gratitude to our Savior by doing His will in giving, serving, obeying, forgiving, meeting the needs of others.

2. Paul encouraged the Philippians by his prayers and confidence. He knew the value of encouragement, for he had been encouraged by Barnabas (Acts 9:26-28). How does our congregation encourage outsiders and newcomers?

When people visit our congregation, are they welcomed regardless of their wealth or poverty, style of dress, nationality, or religious tradition? What do we do to make sure they are accepted? Do they get a verbal welcome? Are they invited to a small group or class? Are they asked out to dinner? Are they informed of various church functions? Would a Barnabas Club in the church help encourage outsiders and new members?

3. Paul records things that happened *to* him and things that happened *through* him. List some of your experiences in which you become a channel of blessing?

To Paul came imprisonment, and it was not pleasant; but through him God's message continued to go out. His imprisonment provided new opportunities to reach his guards and visitors (Acts 28:16-20, 30, 31). Someone wrote, "Two men look out through prison bars; one sees the mud and one the stars." What do you see? What do others see in you? Has some unhappy experience given you an opportunity to help someone either spiritually or materially? Has a joyous experience provided such an opportunity? Have you been looking for opportunities of that kind?

4. Whether Paul was to live or to die, he meant for Christ to be magnified: that is, to become more influential and more honored (Philippians 1:20). How can Christ be magnified in our bodies when we face danger, doubt, disaster, or despair?

Paul was courageous in danger. What situations of our time call for us to speak or act "with all boldness"? Strong convictions produce boldness. How are convictions developed till they are strong enough to make us bold? Do you recall a time when you by bold words or actions made a difference in what happened? In Acts 16 we read of a dark midnight when Paul was in jail and Christ was magnified through his singing. Has your life ever been a comfort to someone in the midst of despair? What midnight hours have found you singing?

5. Paul pens his philosophy of life in the words, "For to me to live is Christ, and to die is gain" (Philippians 1:21). What does it mean to you that Christ is your life? How is death your gain?

Often we hear of someone who lives for his family, or his fun, or his money. Paul teaches us that Christ is the reason for living. The whole of God's nature is in Christ (Colossians 2:9), and Christ in you is your hope of glory here and hereafter (Colossians 1:27). In all the areas of our need, of our failure, and of our fears, Christ is the answer. We need to trust Him and do His will. Death is gain, not just because it ends earthly troubles, but because it means being with Christ (Philippians 1:23). What a great philosophy! If I go on living, Christ is my life. If I die, I will live with Christ.

6. In the *New International Version*, Philippians 1:27 begins, "Whatever happens, conduct yourselves in a manner worthy of the gospel of Christ." How do we do that?

We simply act like Christians all the time. What does a Christian do when the light turns green and the car in front does not move? When a careless clerk hands him too much change? When a little income can easily be hid from the tax man? When a sick neighbor's grass needs to be cut? We really know, don't we?

Being a Christian is a privilege. Behaving as a Christian is a responsibility. Watch your conduct!

Christ, Our Model

June 13
Lesson 2

DEVOTIONAL READING: **John 14:1-14.**

LESSON SCRIPTURE: **Philippians 2:1-18.**

PRINTED TEXT: **Philippians 2:1-16.**

Philippians 2:1-16

1 If there be therefore any consolation in
Christ, if any comfort of love, if any fellow-
ship of the Spirit, if any bowels and mercies,
2 Fulfil ye my joy, that ye be likeminded,
having the same love, being of one accord, of
one mind.
3 Let nothing be done through strife or
vainglory; but in lowliness of mind let each
esteem other better than themselves.
4 Look not every man on his own things,
but every man also on the things of others.
5 Let this mind be in you, which was also
in Christ Jesus:
6 Who, being in the form of God, thought
it not robbery to be equal with God:
7 But made himself of no reputation, and
took upon him the form of a servant, and
was made in the likeness of men:
8 And being found in fashion as a man, he
humbled himself, and became obedient unto
death, even the death of the cross.
9 Wherefore God also hath highly exalted
him, and given him a name which is above
every name:
10 That at the name of Jesus every knee
should bow, of things in heaven, and things
in earth, and things under the earth;
11 And that every tongue should confess
that Jesus Christ is Lord, to the glory of God
the Father.
12 Wherefore, my beloved, as ye have al-
ways obeyed, not as in my presence only,
but now much more in my absence, work
out your own salvation with fear and trem-
bling:
13 For it is God which worketh in you
both to will and to do of his good pleasure.
14 Do all things without murmurings and
disputings:
15 That ye may be blameless and harm-
less, the sons of God, without rebuke, in the
midst of a crooked and perverse nation,
among whom ye shine as lights in the world;
16 Holding forth the word of life; that I
may rejoice in the day of Christ, that I have
not run in vain, neither labored in vain.

GOLDEN TEXT: Let this mind be in you, which was also in Christ Jesus.
—Philippians 2:5.

Following God's Purpose

Unit 1: Joy in Serving Christ

(Lessons 1-4)

Lesson Aims

This lesson is designed to help students:

1. Determine whether their attitudes nourish unity or feed disunity.

2. Measure their greatness by their level of service.

Lesson Outline

Visual 2 of the visuals packet illustrates the comments of explanation under verse 9. The visual is shown on page 357.

Introduction

A. He Modeled It

Benjamin Franklin wanted to interest the people of Philadelphia in lighting the streets. He knew just talking about it wouldn't work, so he modeled it. He hung a beautiful lantern in front of his own place. He kept the glass brightly polished and lit the wick every evening.

It wasn't long before Franklin's neighbors began placing lights in front of their own homes. Soon the whole city was not only interested in street lighting, but also enthusiastic about it.

Instead of just telling us what godly living is like, Jesus modeled it so we not only would become interested in it, but also would do it with enthusiasm.

B. Lesson Background

Paul has been writing to the Christians in Philippi about standing courageously together in one spirit, so the enemies of Christianity can see the strength of Christian unity in the face of difficulty (Philippians 1:27-30). Now he continues to urge unity within the church.

I. The Life of Unity (Philippians 2:1-4)

A. Some Motivations for Unity (v. 1)

1. If there be therefore any consolation in Christ, if any comfort of love, if any fellowship of the Spirit, if any bowels and mercies.

These motivations come from above and are copied in our own lives. The Greek word for *consolation* is sometimes translated *encouragement.* By its derivation it indicates that someone is called to our side to support and help us. That one is *Christ.* If we are in Him, we hasten to the side of others to support and help them in time of need. The word *comfort* denotes the soothing tenderness we find in God's *love.* This too we copy in our own lives and express to those who are in distress. *Fellowship* means sharing, partnership. If God's *Spirit* has chosen to be a partner with us, we ought to be partners with every brother and sister in Christ. One cannot walk in close harmony with the Father, Son, and Holy Spirit without maintaining harmony also with God's people on earth. The ancients used the word *bowels* as we use *heart.* From the heart of God come the *mercies,* the tender compassion that lifts our burdens and brings us joy; and from our hearts a like compassion flows to our brothers and sisters who are burdened. All these things we learn from God are not just feelings inside of us. They are motivations: they move us to outward acts of helpfulness.

B. Some Elements of Unity (v. 2)

2. Fulfill ye my joy, that ye be likeminded, having the same love, being of one accord, of one mind.

Paul rejoiced in the Philippians' fellowship with him in the gospel (1:3-5). Here he states that his joy in them would be complete if they would be *likeminded,* united in mind and heart. To be likeminded does not mean we all bury our individuality and become just alike. There are no two leaves alike, no two sets of fingerprints alike, no two clouds alike, no two snowflakes alike; and there are no two people alike. Because of our differences we need one another. However, in Christ we find unity amid our diversity.

Paul expressed the thought of unity in different words. *Having the same love* means that we all love one another as God loves us. *Being of one accord* means that we are knit together in our very souls. To be *of one mind* is to share the same attitude—the attitude of unselfish service that is seen in the following verses.

C. Some Attitudes for Unity (vv. 3, 4)

3. Let nothing be done through strife or vainglory; but in lowliness of mind let each esteem other better than themselves.

Vainglory is the attitude that demands respect instead of trying to merit it. Nothing hurts unity more than arrogance, the superior attitude that says to another, "You need me, but I don't need you"; or, "I am right, you are wrong"; or, "I am in charge, so you march to the beat of my drum." Such an attitude produces *strife.*

Lowliness of mind is not an inferiority complex, a feeling of unworthiness that makes us helpless. It means taking a place under others to hold them up, to support and help them. To *esteem other better* than ourselves is not to degrade ourselves; it is to lift up others. It is to limit our own desires so as to give others the benefit of our prayers, our forgiveness, our service, and our sacrifice. Success is not seen in who gets ahead of others, but in who helps others get ahead. Imagine the unity we would have in the church, the family, and the nation if each person would esteem others thus.

4. Look not every man on his own things, but every man also on the things of others.

Considering *the things of others* involves the following: (1) Not to be envious; (2) To protect the things of others; (3) To be grateful for the things of others. The *things of others* include the hopes, the wishes, the dreams, the interests, the goals, the advancement of others. To have these in mind is to affirm, "I am my brother's keeper."

SELF-INTEREST?

The Turner Christian Retirement Homes in Oregon are open to people over fifty-five. Many of the residents have been Christians for over half a century. Some of the joy of being part of this community is found in the care members have for the welfare of all who live there.

If someone is sick, food is lovingly prepared and brought to that household. Lawns are mowed, gardens are watered, and household chores well done. Each nearby neighbor feels a genuine responsibility and desire to meet others' needs. All are self-committed to keep the grounds clear, orderly, and therefore a pleasure to visitors and homeowners alike.

Is Turner a Utopia? No, but it is a community of Christians who have learned to look out for the interests of others. It is a good place to live because love and service have become a part of daily living through the more than fifty years it has existed.

Really now, when you think it through, serving the interests of others is also in your own self-interest. If our world could learn this lesson, the ills of our age could be healed. When we give, we receive more than we offer. In the blessing of serving, we who minister are the most truly blessed.

Begin at home, and then reach out to your community. In serving others we also minister to our Lord Jesus. He said, "Inasmuch as ye have done it unto one of the least of these my brethren, ye have done it unto me." Caring does have its rewards! Jesus said also, "Come, ye blessed of my Father, inherit the kingdom prepared for you" (Matthew 25:31-40). —W. P.

II. Our Model for Unity (Philippians 2:5-11)

A. His Attitude (vv. 5, 6)

5. Let this mind be in you, which was also in Christ Jesus.

Our model, our example, is *Christ Jesus.* We are to think as He thinks. His attitudes, actions, and reactions can be ours because He lives in us through His Spirit.

WHAT'S ON YOUR MIND?

The mind has always been the source from which all actions good or evil flow. The centuries have not changed this truth. In the poem "Paracelsus," Browning wrote, "Measure your mind's heights by the shadow it casts." In the play *Henry VI,* Shakespeare penned these words: "Tis but a base ignoble mind that mounts no higher than a bird can soar."

The condition of our mind determines the position of our soul. What we place in our mind can produce the "shadow," the influence our speech and acts have upon all around us. Paul said, "Let this mind be in you, which was also in Christ Jesus." Letting the mind of Christ be our mind is an act of our will. It should be the basis of our Christian experience.

The computer adage, "garbage in, garbage out," is true of our thinking. Therefore we should allow no garbage in our mind. Elsewhere Paul wrote, "Seek those things which are above, where Christ sitteth on the right hand of God" (Colossians 3:1). If we set our mind on such things, the outpouring of our mind will benefit and bless our life. It will also influence for good the lives of others. The conversion of our mind is the key to our salvation and Christian life.

A little boy said it well: "When test time comes I can't write anything. I just didn't get the right stuff in my head anyplace, so I can't get the right stuff to come out!" His problem is one many adults share.

What's on your mind? If Christ fills it, then its "shadow" will be OK. —W. P.

6. Who, being in the form of God, thought it not robbery to be equal with God.

Jesus shares the very nature of God. "In him dwelleth all the fulness of the Godhead bodily" (Colossians 2:9). He is "the image of the invisible God" (Colossians 1:15). He is "the express image" of God's person (Hebrews 1:3). He is God who put on human flesh (John 1:1, 14). That's why He could say, "He that hath seen me hath seen the Father" (John 14:9).

Thought it not robbery to be equal with God. As we see it in the *King James Version,* this means equality with God properly belongs to Jesus; He did not steal it. As the *American Standard Version* translates, it means Jesus did not think His equality with God was something to be grasped and clung to. Unselfishly He was willing to lay aside His divine glory and take the form of a man in order to die for humankind. Do we have the same mind in us? Can we let go of status in order to be servants? Can we stop trying to be masters of others in order to let God be master of us? Are we willing to accept the fact that we have been created in the image of God and can be re-created in His image without trying to make ourselves little "gods"? Can we be God's companions instead of His competitors?

B. His Humility (vv. 7, 8)

7. But made himself of no reputation, and took upon him the form of a servant, and was made in the likeness of men.

Jesus was willing to give up the privilege of His status for the purpose of His service. Someone has observed that the best way to test a person's character is not to give that person responsibilities, but to give the individual privileges and see what he or she does with them. Does the person cling to them or share them? Does he or she use them to promote self or to propel others?

Jesus is God, but His favorite term for himself is "son of man." *Made himself of no reputation* is literally *emptied himself.* Jesus poured out His Heavenly glory and accepted earthly poverty. He gave up mansions above for a manger below. All the fulness of divine nature still was in Him (Colossians 2:9), but it was not visible to everyone.

8. And being found in fashion as a man, he humbled himself, and became obedient unto death, even the death of the cross.

Certainly it was humbling for God to appear as a man, but Jesus *humbled himself* more than that. In the form of a man He *became obedient unto death.* He put His Father's will above His own will, and man's salvation above His own life. He who was sinless allowed all the sins of humanity to be laid on Him, and for them He was executed as a criminal on *the cross.* He who was life eternal, with the Father from the beginning, submitted himself to death. He who was the Good Shepherd became the sacrificial lamb of God for the sin and guilt of humanity.

The real mark of greatness is not seen in how much we are willing to suffer for what we have done wrong, but in how much we are willing to suffer to help other people who have done wrong.

C. His Exaltation (vv. 9-11)

9. Wherefore God also hath highly exalted him, and given him a name which is above every name.

We all like to be promoted, don't we? We like to move from where we are to a higher place, and we like to move as directly as possible. Some of us are willing to trample on others as we go. It may seem that the shortest way to the top is to be arrogant, to claim authority, to dominate those about us. Jesus said that is the way of the Gentiles, the heathen. "But it shall not be so among you," He added, "but whosoever will be great among you, let him be your minister; and whosoever will be chief among you, let him be your servant." Jesus himself showed what He meant: He came to serve rather than to be served (Matthew 20:25-28).

The way of real greatness does lead from where we are to a higher place, but it leads through humble service. Jesus left Heaven's glory "to minister, and to give his life a ransom for many" (Mark 10:45). He who was always perfect became our perfect Savior through His suffering (Hebrews 2:10). When He had served well, He was lifted to a higher place. That is the route of greatness for us also. Jesus repeatedly said the one who is greatest is the one who is serving others (Luke 22:24-27).

Jesus has a name *above every name.* List all the great historical leaders; none match up to Jesus. Do you know of choirs performing cantatas to celebrate the birth or resurrection of Napoleon or George Washington or even Abraham Lincoln? But they do for Jesus.

10. That at the name of Jesus every knee should bow, of things in heaven, and things in earth, and things under the earth.

Every knee without exception will someday bow before Jesus. If we do it now, with humble submission and willing obedience, we can be saved. If we resist Him until He comes back, we will be condemned. The point is that every person who has ever lived will finally come to acknowledge that Jesus is Lord. We should do it now before it is too late.

11. And that every tongue should confess that Jesus Christ is Lord, to the glory of God the Father.

Not only will every person bow his knee to His lordship, but every person also will speak up and *confess that Jesus Christ is Lord.* If we do it before He returns, "confession is made unto salvation" (Romans 10:10). But if we wait until He returns, that confession will bring judgment, for in it we will be admitting the lordship that we denied. The truth remains—*Jesus Christ is Lord,* whatever our response is now.

When we acknowledge Jesus, we are also affirming God. Confession of Jesus is made *to the glory of God the Father.* The Son is not in competition against the Father; the Father is not jealous when Jesus is proclaimed Lord of lords and King of kings. That is God's goal, and He is honored when it is reached.

III. The Application Today (Philippians 2:12-16)

A. Our "Work-out" (v. 12)

12. Wherefore, my beloved, as ye have always obeyed, not as in my presence only, but now much more in my absence, work out your own salvation with fear and trembling.

Paul had been with the Philippian Christians at an earlier time, and they had obeyed the inspired instructions he had given. He wanted them to continue their obedience now, though he was absent. This suggests that our obedience also should be consistent whether someone is with us or we are alone, whether those who see us are Christian brothers or total strangers, or even enemies of Christ.

Paul does not say we are to work for our salvation. That would indicate trying to earn something we do not have. To *work out* our *salvation* is to develop what is already present. Miners and manufacturers work out the metal and produce many useful and beautiful things. So we work out our salvation and produce thoughts and words and deeds that are both helpful and beautiful. God has put something in us through salvation—His divine nature (2 Peter 1:4). He

visual 2

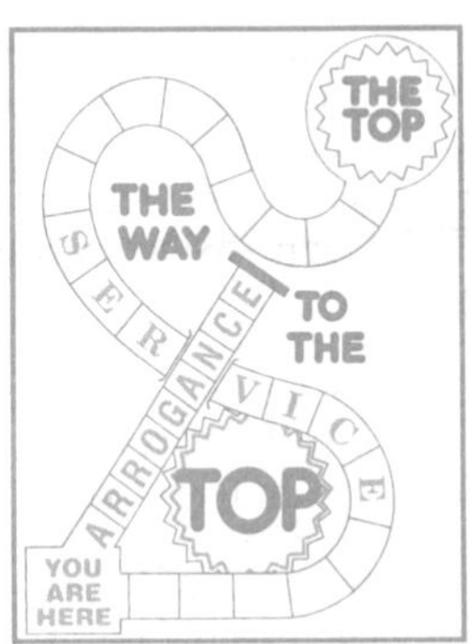

wants us to *work out* that divine nature until we become conformed to the image and rightness of Jesus (Romans 8:29).

Fear and trembling does not mean we are terrified, but we stand in awe and reverence in the presence of almighty God. We are not to become so familiar with Him that we lose our sense of awe before His majesty.

B. God's "Work-in" (v. 13)

13. For it is God which worketh in you both to will and to do of his good pleasure.

We are to work out what God has worked in. God himself is at work in us through the Holy Spirit. When the Spirit lives in us, God is our special guest (1 Corinthians 6:19). We may not think we are willing to do God's work, but He is at work within us. When strong temptation would lead us to do wrong, God helps us *to will,* to desire to do right. Besides that, He gives us power *to do* what pleases Him. He energizes us with His presence to accomplish His purpose. He is not only outside of us giving commands; He is also inside of us with guidance and strength.

C. Results (vv. 14-16)

14. Do all things without murmurings and disputings.

What is your talk like when guests are in your home? You want them to feel good in your presence, don't you? Knowing that God is our guest within, we keep our talk pleasant; we *do all things without murmurings and disputings.* We do not want to make Him uncomfortable. One of the things He hated in Old Testament times was the murmuring and complaining of His people. He still does not like grumbling.

Murmuring is grumbling. *Disputing* is arguing. The church is not to be a gossip club or a debating society. Murmuring and disputing create disunity instead of unity. They indicate pride rather than humility. Can't we take a firm stand for right without descending to unworthy bickering?

15. That ye may be blameless and harmless, the sons of God, without rebuke, in the midst of a crooked and perverse nation, among whom ye shine as lights in the world.

Not only are we to talk the walk, but we are also to walk the talk. People with a positive talk can be people with a positive walk—*blameless and harmless. Sons of God* are to be characterized by godly life-style. *Blameless* does not mean faultless, but we live such a life that people are not constantly pointing their fingers at us or charging us with hypocrisy. The word *harmless* primarily means unmixed, pure. We do not mix goodness with evil. We do not dilute our Christian commitment with worldly culture. Christians are to be where the darkness is, but are to be there *as lights*, showing the right way to all who are willing to follow it.

16. Holding forth the word of life; that I may rejoice in the day of Christ, that I have not run in vain, neither labored in vain.

Holding forth the word of life is displaying the good news of Christ. Holding it means we do not lose our grip on that truth. Holding it *forth* means holding it before others so they can see it and accept it. If the Philippians do that, all Heaven and earth will know it when Christ comes again. Then Paul will rejoice to see that his work with them was well done. Likewise those who taught us will rejoice if we continue to hold forth the word of life. In Heaven there will be a grand reunion of all of God's people as they celebrate together. It will be one grand party!

HOLD FAST AND HOLD FORTH

On March 12, 1991, Eleanor Hammond went home to be with the Lord. For fifteen years she had served as a missionary in Japan with her husband, Al. Their ministry left Christians and churches firmly founded on the Word of God. Now Al serves as a professor in San Jose Christian College.

Eleanor's deep devotion to Christ, the church, and her family left an impression that will be a heritage cherished by many of the faithful in years to come. She loved God and let Him rule in her life. She loved the Scriptures and spent much time reading them. She loved music and played in the orchestra at Crossroads Bible Church. She loved her family and taught them to know and serve her Lord.

On the day of Eleanor's death, Al was teaching at the college. When he returned home at 2:45 that afternoon, he learned that his wife of thirty-nine years had died. The sad news was given by her son-in-law, Curt Lueck, and his wife Sharon, who are missionaries to Japan. Curt had offered prayer and words of assurance, then had read the Scripture to Eleanor. Her last word as he finished reading the Bible was, "Amen."

After many years of "holding forth the word of life," Eleanor was still holding fast to that word. She had finished her course. She was HOME. Her life had steadily followed the Word of God in the Bible because she knew the living Word, Jesus Christ. May her "Amen" be ours as we hold fast and hold forth the word of life, and as we "shine as lights in the world." —W. P.

Conclusion

A. Love of Power or Power of Love

How would you caption a painting to depict the basic attitude of most people of our day? Surely you would not be far amiss if you named it, "The Love of Power." Contrast this with the painting that is displayed in an art museum in Europe. It is a picture of Jesus washing the feet of His disciples. Underneath that picture are the words, "The Power of Love."

Jesus showed us the power of love when He put on our flesh, lived among us, and died for us. Which attitude is more dominant in our lives, the love of power or the power of love?

B. Prayer

Thank You, Father, for allowing Your Son Jesus to put on our flesh so that we may put on His Spirit. We thank You that the Son of God became a son of man so that we can become Your children. In His name, amen.

C. Thought to Remember

The greatest one among you is the one who is doing the most for the most people.

Home Daily Bible Readings

Monday, June 7—Follow Christ's Example (1 Peter 2:18-25)

Tuesday, June 8—Hold Fast the Word of Life (Philippians 2:12-18)

Wednesday, June 9—Honor Faithful Servants of Christ (Philippians 2:19-30)

Thursday, June 10—Christ Our Reconciler (2 Corinthians 5:16-21)

Friday, June 11—Christ Our Standard (2 Corinthians 13:5-14)

Saturday, June 12—Walk in Christ's Spirit (Galatians 5:13-25)

Sunday, June 13—Love as Christ Loved (John 15:12-17)

Learning by Doing

This page contains an alternate lesson plan emphasizing learning activities. Classes desiring such student involvement will find these suggestions helpful.

Learning Goals

Students in today's class should:

1. Discover Christian attitudes that Paul lists in Philippians 2.
2. Choose at least one Christian to whom they can do a better job of demonstrating these attitudes.
3. Choose at least one non-Christian with whom they will seek to share Christ.

Into the Lesson

Duplicate the following sentence so that each class member can have his or her own copy:

It is (easier) (harder) for me to get along with church people today than five years ago.

To begin today's session, distribute the sentence (or write it once on the chalkboard for members to copy) and ask members to circle either *easier* or *harder* to make the sentence true for them. Then ask members to find partners, share their answers, and explain why they chose as they did. You may allow a few to tell the whole class how they reacted to this sentence.

Explain that today's lesson is about the relationships of the Philippian Christians with each other, and about Paul's instructions telling how to make them stronger. The class discussion already in this session may indicate that these are lessons very relevant for today as well!

Into the Word

You may wish to ask a class member to read aloud Philippians 2:1-11 before giving students instructions about the following activities. Then tell them they are to *choose one* of the following to complete in about ten minutes. (Students may do these alone or in groups, as you wish. If the class is small enough to divide into thirds, you may copy the instructions below and assemble materials for each of these activities in a different corner of the room. Students may go to the corner of the activity they choose.)

Activity one: Study verses 1-4 again. Write a newspaper ad or a radio commercial inviting people to come to a local congregation. This church has perfectly obeyed what Paul teaches here. Describe the church in your advertisement.

Activity two: Study verses 5-11 again. Draw a symbol of the ideal Christian attitude as it is described here. Use shapes, colors, textures, or pictures to summarize the teachings in these verses.

Activity three: Write a poem or prayer expressing thanks to Christ for His attitude that allowed Him to come to earth. Mention some or all of the characteristics of verses 5-11 in your prayer. Ask God to help you develop the same characteristics in your own life.

After students have finished, allow time for some to share with the class. Save the sharing of activity three until the end of the class period.

Probe students' understanding of the Scripture with the following discussion questions:

1. Which part of the attitudes described in verses 2-4 strikes you as most challenging? Why?
2. Try to pretend you were Jesus. Which part of what He did (vv. 5-11) would have been hardest for you?
3. (Read verses 12, 13.) What might be the relationship between verse 12 and the first eleven verses of the chapter? What's the difference between working *for* our salvation and working *out* our salvation? (See the explanation of verse 12 in the earlier part of the lesson.) What about the example of Jesus in verses 5-11 causes you the greatest fear and trembling (that is, reverence and awe)?
4. (Read verses 14-16.) List each of the elements in Paul's instruction. What is the relationship between unity and evangelism?

Into Life

Distribute blank paper and pencils and ask students to make two lists: The first should contain "five people in the church you know very well." The second should show "five people outside the church you know very well."

Tell students to look at the first list (the one with church people). Ask, "How have you been demonstrating to these folks the attitudes Paul describes here? Is there one toward whom your attitude most needs to change? Circle that name."

As they look at the second list (people outside the church), ask students to consider whether they have held out the word of life to each of them. Once again, they should circle one name, this time the name of the person they feel would be the most open to receiving the good news of Christ.

Allow time for the students to pray about the names they have circled. End the class session with some or all of the poems and prayers composed in activity three.

Let's Talk It Over

The questions on this page are designed to encourage review of the lesson Scriptures and to promote discussion of the lesson by the class. The answers provided are only discussion starters. Let your class talk it over from there.

1. One of the hallmarks of Christ's church is a kind of love that is able to unite people of every conceivable background. What does love do in your life to maintain unity?

Love influences us by softening our hard hearts so we feel the joys and pains of others. Love forgives and accepts another. Love gives and shares to such a degree that we respect another's point of view. Love expresses itself in unselfishness, and soon we may discover some areas in which we are wrong and others in which we are right.

The church is not a club of people who are all alike, who have similar financial situations or similar educations. Real Christians can be recognized because they are knit together in common service to Christ and others in a spirit of love, whatever their differences (John 13:35).

Has the church failed in this area? Have we decided it isn't necessary to love each other as the Lord asked us to love? Are we saying it can't be done? Is it too costly?

2. Paul indicates in his letter how we are to get along with other Christians. What do you and another Christian have in common, so that you are united to that person?

Every Christian has received Christ. One who has received Christ has received forgiveness and new life. That person is a child of God, and therefore is my brother or sister. No matter what his or her size, shape, or color, that person has received Christ, the same Christ who is in me. The other Christian also has responded to the love of God, and in this way has experienced what I have experienced. God's love for the other person is as great as His love for me. We can get along together because each of us has received Christ and responded to His love.

3. List some differences the example of Jesus makes in our attitudes towards others?

If I humble myself, God will exalt me. If I wish to follow Him, I must be willing to take up my cross. If I die with Christ, I shall be raised with Christ. Is this not the teaching of Paul in the sixth chapter of Romans?

It is hard to accept the mind of Christ and keep our own selfish attitudes. We must learn that the way to a resurrection is through a cross. God is glorified when I humble myself and put myself in the right position. The way to exaltation is through self-abasement. Jesus taught us that when a grain falls into the ground and dies, it will bring forth much fruit. Our farming community depends on that promise yearly. For life to be present and fruit to be enjoyed, death must come. The way to the throne is through the tomb. The way to the crown is through the cross.

4. What does it mean to be "likeminded, having the same love, being of one accord, of one mind"?

When soul is knitted with soul, love with love, and mind with mind, we are united. However, I don't think the apostle Paul is saying all of us must be of the same mold. Wouldn't we get tired if everyone were singing the very same note? If a pianist plays a C and then adds an E with the C, it sounds good. No conflict there. The notes are different, but they unite beautifully. Add a G with the C and E. Still no conflict. It is all C major, but the three notes are different. Add another C. You can vary the chord. How about C minor? All of these notes speak together. They are united but varied. A monotone is boring, but Christian unity is harmony. It is the more beautiful because there are so many variations.

5. Why are we called to work out our own salvation, if it is God in us who does the work? (vv. 12, 13). What difference does God make as He works in us? What difference do we make as we work out our salvation?

If God is to work in us He must enter us. This happens when we become Christians. We receive the gift of the Holy Spirit, God in us (Acts 2:38). We become different. We move from death to life; we change from enemies to friends of God, from aliens to His children. We are new creatures.

But God does not take possession of us by force. He does no work in us unless we cooperate. His Spirit inspires the Holy Bible that tells us what to do; His Spirit in us gives us power to do it; but we must supply the will. We must try to be more like Christ, to shine as lights in the world.

Keep On Keeping On

June 20
Lesson 3

DEVOTIONAL READING: Romans 15:1-13.

LESSON SCRIPTURE: Philippians 3.

PRINTED TEXT: Philippians 3:1-16.

Philippians 3:1-16

1 Finally, my brethren, rejoice in the Lord. To write the same things to you, to me indeed is not grievous, but for you it is safe.

2 Beware of dogs, beware of evil workers, beware of the concision.

3 For we are the circumcision, which worship God in the spirit, and rejoice in Christ Jesus, and have no confidence in the flesh.

4 Though I might also have confidence in the flesh. If any other man thinketh that he hath whereof he might trust in the flesh, I more:

5 Circumcised the eighth day, of the stock of Israel, of the tribe of Benjamin, a Hebrew of the Hebrews; as touching the law, a Pharisee;

6 Concerning zeal, persecuting the church; touching the righteousness which is in the law, blameless.

7 But what things were gain to me, those I counted loss for Christ.

8 Yea doubtless, and I count all things but loss for the excellency of the knowledge of Christ Jesus my Lord: for whom I have suffered the loss of all things, and do count them but dung, that I may win Christ,

9 And be found in him, not having mine own righteousness, which is of the law, but that which is through the faith of Christ, the righteousness which is of God by faith:

10 That I may know him, and the power of his resurrection, and the fellowship of his sufferings, being made conformable unto his death;

11 If by any means I might attain unto the resurrection of the dead.

12 Not as though I had already attained, either were already perfect: but I follow after, if that I may apprehend that for which also I am apprehended of Christ Jesus.

13 Brethren, I count not myself to have apprehended: but this one thing I do, forgetting those things which are behind, and reaching forth unto those things which are before,

14 I press toward the mark for the prize of the high calling of God in Christ Jesus.

15 Let us therefore, as many as be perfect, be thus minded: and if in any thing ye be otherwise minded, God shall reveal even this unto you.

16 Nevertheless, whereto we have already attained, let us walk by the same rule, let us mind the same thing.

GOLDEN TEXT: I press toward the mark for the prize of the high calling of God in Christ Jesus.—Philippians 3:14.

Following God's Purpose

Unit 1: Joy in Serving Christ

(Lessons 1-4)

Lesson Aims

This lesson is designed to help the students:

1. See what aspects in our lives really make an eternal difference.
2. Tell what is God's goal for each of us.
3. Shape their present and future according to God's will, letting the past be past.

Lesson Outline

Display visual 3 of the visuals packet and let it remain before the class throughout the session. The visual is shown on page 365.

Introduction

A. Keep On Going

To produce a pound of honey, the bee must visit fifty-six thousand cloverheads. Each head has sixty flower tubes, so the bee must dip into three and a third million of them to give us one pound of honey. A bee may fly as far as eight miles to gather her little load. How many miles did she fly, and how many hours did she labor, to gather the honey you poured on your pancakes?

The bee can be a model encouraging the Christian to keep on keeping on. Some unknown author wrote the following:

One step won't take you very far;
You've got to keep on walking.
One word won't tell folks who you are;
You've got to keep on talking.
One inch won't make you very tall;
You've got to keep on growing.
One single deed won't do it all;
You've got to keep on going.

B. Lesson Background

San Francisco has a large area known as "Chinatown"—a little bit of China away from China. Orange County in southern California has an area called "Little Saigon." Philippi might be called "Little Rome." It was a "colony" (Acts 16:12). Its people were citizens of Rome. Rome was not known for its belief in one God; neither was Philippi. Probably Philippi did not even have ten Jewish men when Paul visited. It was a city of many different religions.

Paul realized that the Christians in Philippi were in a hostile environment. There were many influences in the city that could lure them away from their Christian commitment. Sounds like our town today, doesn't it?

It is not easy to be a Christian in a society where the educational system, the mass media, the entertainment world, and the politicians are not supportive of Christianity. In such an environment, we need to be encouraged consistently to keep on keeping on. That's what Paul does for the Philippians.

I. Attitudes for Keeping On (Philippians 3:1-6)

A. Be Celebrating (v. 1)

1. Finally, my brethren, rejoice in the Lord. To write the same things to you, to me indeed is not grievous, but for you it is safe.

Finally does not mean Paul is ending the letter. Elsewhere in his writings the same word is translated *besides,* or *moreover.* Here it indicates that Paul is changing the subject.

The word *brethren* is plural, and so is the verb *rejoice.* All the Christians are to rejoice. Christians should show their joy in front of all the people in Philippi, and of our town. Christians should not be "down in the mouth"; they should outlive, outlove, and out-celebrate all those around them. Christian rejoicing is *in the Lord.* Pagans ancient and modern are more likely to rejoice in sensual pleasure.

As Christians we can *rejoice in the Lord* because He is good, He does not treat us as our sins deserve, He cares about us, He knows us by name, He erases our negative past, He enjoys our presence, He has an inheritance reserved for us, and He is preparing a fabulous eternity for us. He is a Lord full of promises, and One who keeps His promises.

On what do we depend for our joy? The weather? Our health? Our wealth? Our jobs? In what do we find a reason to celebrate?

Paul has called for rejoicing before (2:18), but he is not slow or reluctant to *write the same things* again. For the readers *it is safe* because the Lord's promises are sure and Christians can safely rely on them.

B. Be Cautious (v. 2)

2. Beware of dogs, beware of evil workers, beware of the concision.

There are "joy killers" among us. They are referred to here as *dogs*—not the word of house pets, but for dogs who run in packs in the streets and attack to destroy. These can be either nonreligious people or religious fanatics who are trying to get us to change our religion.

Some "joy killers" are *evil workers* who say we can't have fun unless we are immoral. The mass media and the entertainment world persistently picture sin as "fun." Christians need to show how wrong they are by celebrating godly lives with joy.

Concision refers to those who demanded circumcision as the mark of God's people. They were like dogs snapping at Paul's heels constantly, insisting that no one can be saved without being a Jew as well as a Christian. There will always be people telling us that we must have something besides Jesus, that we cannot be complete Christians unless we do as they do. They say we must obey *their* rules: "You cannot be a Christian if you go to a movie, or if you drive an expensive car." The forbidden list goes on and on. We must not allow such people to take away our joy. *Beware*—do not let them delude you or take you in.

C. Be Confident (vv. 3-6)

3. For we are the circumcision, which worship God in the spirit, and rejoice in Christ Jesus, and have no confidence in the flesh.

The Jews used circumcision as the identifying mark of God's people. *We are the circumcision* means *we are God's people.* We are confident in that claim, not because of the external sign of circumcision, but because of an internal reality—His Spirit living in us. We worship Him with and in that Spirit. Worship is not an external show, but an inner attitude. Is that really true in us? Or do we bow our heads without really praying? Are we silent during Communion, with our thoughts on what we will do in the afternoon?

We *rejoice in Christ Jesus.* We are not rejoicing in keeping rules, in external signs, in our spiritual gifts, in our attendance records, but in our relation to Jesus Christ. We rejoice because we love Him and He loves us.

We *have no confidence in the flesh.* We are humble about who we are, what we have, and what we have done. We put our confidence in Jesus.

FALSE CONFIDENCE

One of the sad records in American history is the one that tells of the rise and fall of General Benedict Arnold. Arnold fought courageously in the great victories at Ticonderoga in 1775 and at Saratoga in 1777. This battle, with Burgoyne of the British, is considered by some historians to be the turning point of the war. Such were Arnold's valor and leadership that he was given the command of Philadelphia in 1778. Confidence in him was complete, and his past successes seemed to indicate more in the future. But in Philadelphia he lived luxuriously and was reprimanded for abuse of his authority. He was transferred to West Point in New York, which was an important command for blocking the British soldiers and fleet along the Hudson River.

Smarting under the reprimand in Philadelphia and feeling his excellent record as a military commander was not appreciated, Arnold, along with British Major John Andre, plotted West Point's surrender to the British. Andre was captured in this mission, and Benedict Arnold was forced to flee to the British side. In 1781 he sought exile in England. In the memory of a nation his excellent leadership and many successes are overshadowed by his betrayal of his command and of his country.

Self-esteem and false confidence in his ability and skill led to excesses that brought reprimand. Self-esteem and resentment at the reprimand led to betrayal and the stigma of traitor. Too much self-esteem, too much confidence in our ability, our achievement, or our heritage is what Paul calls "confidence in the flesh." Such false confidence may lead us to betray our Lord and become enemies of all that He alone can do for us. False confidence in ourselves is the enemy of complete confidence in Jesus Christ. —W. P.

4. Though I might also have confidence in the flesh. If any other man thinketh that he hath whereof he might trust in the flesh, I more.

Confidence in the flesh is confidence in one's own ability, accomplishments, position, or wealth. Isn't it easy to think that we don't need

Christ when we have so many other things going for us? We have bank accounts, education, jobs, insurance, doctors, counselors, grocery stores—but a Christian knows we need more.

5. Circumcised the eighth day, of the stock of Israel, of the tribe of Benjamin, a Hebrew of the Hebrews; as touching the law, a Pharisee.

If anyone could have trusted in self, Paul could have. He was from the prestigious family—*Benjamin.* His parents followed the Jewish practices to the letter, having him *circumcised* on *the eighth day.* He advanced in Judaism above his peers and became *a Hebrew of the Hebrews.* He was one of the elite, a Pharisee. Everywhere he went, he was recognized and admired.

Suppose a person is born into the Rockefeller family, drives a Mercedes, and has a law degree from Harvard. Does that kind of person need Christ? Yes, of course. There is only one way to God and Heaven, and that is Christ.

6. Concerning zeal, persecuting the church; touching the righteousness which is in the law, blameless.

As far as his peers were concerned, Paul did everything right. His morality was above reproach. *Concerning zeal,* he was *persecuting the church,* which was thought to be the enemy of his religion. When it came to fulfilling the requirements of the Jewish *law,* he was *blameless.*

It is easy for people who are not bad to think they don't need Christ. Don't you know some people who think they are even better than the people who go to church? It is easy to rest upon our own morality, but it is fatal. The wages of sin is death, and no one is sinless except Jesus.

II. Preparation for Keeping On (Philippians 3:7-11)

A. Calculate Correctly (vv. 7, 8)

7. But what things were gain to me, those I counted loss for Christ.

It's okay to have influence, status, wealth, and good morals, but if we calculate correctly we understand that those things are not significant in comparison with what we have in Christ. All of them are not enough for eternity. That's what Paul means when he says, *Those I counted loss for Christ.* He is not saying they are no good, but that he is not depending on them for eternity.

8. Yea doubtless, and I count all things but loss for the excellency of the knowledge of Christ Jesus my Lord: for whom I have suffered the loss of all things, and do count them but dung, that I may win Christ.

Paul once depended on the things listed in verses 5 and 6 to give him a place of honor, influence, and wealth. But he traded them all for the *excellency,* the superior value, of knowing *Christ.* This does not mean he knows *about* Christ, but he knows Christ *personally.*

He is talking about a relationship with Jesus. Jesus is his Lord, his Master, his King as well as his Savior. For the sake of that relationship Paul has given up the things he valued before. He has discarded them as if they were *dung,* refuse, garbage. In the light of eternity, they have no value whatever.

B. Be in Christ (vv. 9, 10)

9. And be found in him, not having mine own righteousness, which is of the law, but that which is through the faith of Christ, the righteousness which is of God by faith.

Paul wants to *be found in him,* not found in the "Who's Who" of Palestine. He once tried to make himself righteous by keeping the law (v. 6), but now he knows that is not good enough. He no longer counts on himself to live without sin; he counts on God to forgive his sin because he believes in Jesus. Thus his *righteousness* does not come from his own efforts; it comes from *God* by reason of Paul's *faith.* Being forgiven and brought into a right relationship with Christ, Paul can relate to other people as Christ does; with compassion, with mercy, with forgiving, with corrections, with understanding, with love. Such relationships come from being made "right" through the forgiveness Jesus provides.

10. That I may know him, and the power of his resurrection, and the fellowship of his sufferings, being made conformable unto his death.

Without Christ we were dead in sin, but the power that raised Jesus from the dead gave us a new life on earth (Ephesians 2:4-6) and will raise us to new life in Heaven. This is accomplished through God's Spirit living in us.

When we link up with the power of the Holy Spirit and let Him guide our relationships, we may also share in the kind of suffering Christ experienced. Why? Because those who are merciless cannot stand those who are merciful, those who bear grudges cannot stand someone who forgives, those who are rough cannot stand someone who is gentle, those who are prejudiced cannot stand someone whose heart is open to all. So be a gracious person—but get ready to be treated ungraciously. Our goal makes all the suffering seem trivial (Romans 8:18).

RICHES IN CHRIST

Jonathan Swift, the Irish-born English satirist, died in 1745; but he left a statement that ought to haunt us all. Here are his words: "Nothing is so hard for those who abound in riches as to conceive how others can be in want." In Christ we know unlimited wealth, but how dimly we see the plight of those who lack that wealth! How slow we are to share what we possess!

As we look around us we see the hungry and homeless, but do we see them simply as victims of their own decisions? When we see the spiritually deprived and destitute, do we see them as people who have chosen their way and should be allowed to follow it without any interference?

As Christians we have faced Jesus and realized that in Him and in Him alone are unlimited resources for time and eternity. We have cried with Paul, "I count all things to be loss . . . that I may gain Christ, and may be found in Him" (*New American Standard Bible*). Receiving from Him the wealth we need for time and eternity, we must begin to see our world as poor, lost, and hopeless without our Lord Jesus. When we see the world thus truly, we will share what we have received. We will sacrifice whatever it takes of our talents, wealth, and time to offer Christ to those who have no eternal riches.

Don't let people remain in spiritual poverty while we hold Jesus just for ourselves! To do so is to withhold from them what Paul gained by forfeiting all he once had thought was of value.

—W. P.

C. Focus on the Goal (v. 11)

11. If by any means I might attain unto the resurrection of the dead.

Not only do we walk in newness of life here, but we also look forward to being raised from the dead in the future. No matter what opposition we have, we cannot be killed permanently.

III. The Act of Keeping On (Philippians 3:12-16)

A. Keep Maturing (vv. 12-14)

12. Not as though I had already attained, either were already perfect: but I follow after, if that I may apprehend that for which also I am apprehended of Christ Jesus.

Perfect means mature. God wants all of us to mature into Christlikeness (Romans 8:29). Maturity does not come overnight. We are to be daily in the process of being transformed from our likeness into His (2 Corinthians 3:18). Jesus has *apprehended* us—that is, has taken hold of us—to bring about that transformation. Like Paul, we keep trying to take hold of that maturity for which Christ has taken hold of us.

13. Brethren, I count not myself to have apprehended: but this one thing I do, forgetting those things which are behind, and reaching forth unto those things which are before.

visual 3

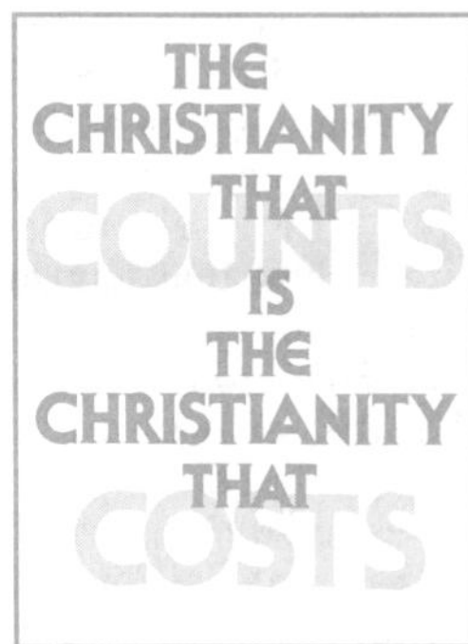

One of the ways to keep maturing is to let the past be the past. The past can interfere with our maturing into Christlikeness in two ways: (1) We can allow past sins, failures, and weaknesses to discourage us and stop us from pressing on. (2) We can allow past accomplishments to satisfy us and stop us from pressing on. But yesterday's life should not determine today's life.

Paul regretted his sin of persecuting the church, but he did not let it keep him from growing into Christlikeness. Neither did he allow his accomplishments as a Jew or as a Christian to keep him from growing.

14. I press toward the mark for the prize of the high calling of God in Christ Jesus.

Press toward is at the heart of this lesson on keeping on. Not letting anything in the past slow us down, we exert all our strength of body and mind to move toward our goal, to become more like Jesus.

What is the *prize of the high calling of God in Christ Jesus?* It is Heaven, but it is far more than just a place. It is also being like Christ. That's God's goal for all of us. When we see Jesus, we will become like Him (1 John 3:1-3). With that in view, we press on to become like Jesus here and now. Christ is living within us. We need to let Him control us so thoroughly that we can say with Paul, "It is no longer I that live, but Christ liveth in me" (Galatians 2:20, *American Standard Version*). We must let His Spirit fill us till He overrides our spirits. Then we will see the fruit of His Spirit in our lives.

PRESS ON!

On August 3, 1492, Columbus sailed from Spain in command of three ships, the *Santa Maria*, the *Nina*, and the *Pinta*. Thus began one of the most important voyages ever made from Europe. Its purpose was to find a new route to the spice-rich East Indies.

Seventy days later the little fleet reached an island Columbus named San Salvador. It is in what is now the Bahamas, just off the Florida coast. On that first of his four sailings to America, Columbus also discovered Cuba and Hispaniola.

Columbus thought the world was round, and therefore he could sail west to reach the East Indies. The world indeed is round, but much larger than that navigator thought. His voyage nearly ended in disaster. Food and water ran low. His sailors almost mutinied, demanding that the ships turn back. Only with confidence in his belief and with iron discipline did Columbus reach the "new world."

"Sail on! Sail on!" This was his daily command. He was on an important mission, and in his mind there was no turning back.

Paul's words are, "I press on!" Having found in Christ the promise of a new and eternal world of forgiveness and freedom from sin's guilt, he would not turn back. The promised prize of eternal life lay before him. No matter what the obstacles, he was reaching forward to that goal.

Our lives need to follow this model of "pressing on," even when doubters attack our faith and circumstances make it easier to give up the Christian journey. Press on! Just ahead is the new world Jesus promised and revealed. —W. P.

B. The Mature Mind (vv. 15, 16)

15. Let us therefore, as many as be perfect, be thus minded: and if in any thing ye be otherwise minded, God shall reveal even this unto you.

As noted under verse 12, *perfect* means mature, grown up. With the help of God, we who are in Christ have matured to some degree already: we have been growing. Now with God's help we must keep on growing, and that takes our best effort as well as His help. Let us *be thus minded:* let us make up our minds to do our best. Our best effort begins with how we think. We must allow Christ to capture our minds. We are to bring every thought into captivity, make every thought obey Christ (2 Corinthians 10:5). Our behavior comes out of our beliefs; our practices come out of our perceptions; our conduct comes out of our thinking. Therefore we set our minds on the Christian way; and if *in any thing* our minds leave that way, *God shall reveal* the right as we give ourselves to the study of His Word.

16. Nevertheless, whereto we have already attained, let us walk by the same rule, let us mind the same thing.

We have learned much about the Christian way, but it is not enough to know the way. We are also to *walk* in the way. We have made some progress toward our goal. We have become somewhat like Christ, and we have done it by the help of God and our own earnest effort. Then let us keep on keeping on in the same way. Let us live up to what we have learned. Let us always keep our goal in mind, and keep moving toward it.

Home Daily Bible Readings

Monday, June 14—Be Faithful Even to Death (Philippians 3:1-11)

Tuesday, June 15—Press on Toward the Goal (Philippians 3:12-21)

Wednesday, June 16—The Savior Will Come (Philippians 3:17-21)

Thursday, June 17—Give Yourselves in Service (Romans 12:1-8)

Friday, June 18—Follow Christ's Example (Romans 12:9-20)

Saturday, June 19—Bear One Another's Burdens (Galatians 6:1-5)

Sunday, June 20—Do Good to All People (Galatians 6:6-10)

Conclusion

A. Perseverance Produces

Plato wrote the first sentence of his famous *Republic* nine different ways before he was satisfied. Noah Webster labored thirty-six years writing his dictionary. Milton rose at four in the morning every day in order to have enough time to write his *Paradise Lost.* Gibbon spent twenty-six years writing *The Decline and Fall of the Roman Empire.* Sir Walter Scott put in fifteen hours a day at his desk. He averaged writing a book every two months. Isaac Newton seldom went to bed before two in the morning. Hemmingway went over the manuscript of *The Old Man and the Sea* eighty times. Edison tried six thousand different experiments before he came up with the light bulb. Goodyear took ten years to develop hard rubber. Lincoln lost nearly a dozen elections before he was elected President of the United States.

Perseverance indeed produces results.

B. Prayer

Thank You, Heavenly Father, for Your persistence. You have kept on keeping on in loving us. We thank You that You have not given up on us, and promise you will not. Help us not to give up on ourselves. Through the indwelling Christ, amen.

C. Thought to Remember

Triumph is just *umph* added to *try.* It was the preacher Spurgeon who said, "By perseverance the snail reached the ark." That's triumph!

Learning by Doing

This page contains an alternate lesson plan emphasizing learning activities. Classes desiring such student involvement will find these suggestions helpful.

Learning Goals

As students participate in today's class session, they should:

1. Paraphrase Paul's challenge to lifelong faithfulness.
2. List factors that will help them to stay faithful to Christ for the rest of their lives.

Into the Lesson

If you teach young adults, ask students to find a partner and tell each other a story. Their stories should begin with one or the other of the following sentences:

1. "Here's someone past age sixty who's been a Christian all of his or her life. . . ."
2. "Here's someone whose faith faltered by the time he was middle-aged. . . ."

Ask volunteers to share a story they *heard.* After several have spoken, discuss with the class: "Why do some Christians remain faithful while others fall away? Have you ever been surprised by the moral and spiritual failure of a Christian you admired? Have you been able to explain why he or she didn't stay faithful?"

If you teach middle adults, ask students in groups of two or three to make two lists:

1. Factors that can encourage Christians to *keep* their faith.
2. Factors that can prod Christians to *give up* their faith.

After five minutes ask students to call out items on the lists, one after the other. Write the items on your chalkboard. When the lists are complete, ask the class to help you choose the five best responses on each list.

Discuss briefly: "Does either list convince you? Are the reasons for being faithful stronger than the reasons for falling away?"

If you teach senior adults, ask each member of your class to complete this sentence: "One reason I'm still a Christian today is . . ." (If your class is too large for every member to speak, ask for volunteers to answer. Or ask everyone in a certain part of the room to answer—for example, all the ladies on the left half, or everyone in the first two rows.)

Whichever opening you choose, bridge into Bible study by telling class members that today's lesson looks at a passage from Philippians that should encourage us to keep on living for Christ our whole life.

Into the Word

Depending on your time and your preferences, choose one or both of these Bible-study activities for today's session:

Complete the outline. Refer to the lesson outline on page 354. Divide the class into three sections. Assign a different Roman numeral heading to each section of the class. In small groups or pairs, class members should write sentences or phrases under their assigned heading to explain what the verses mean and how the heading fits this paragraph.

After several minutes, ask students to read their sentences. If more than one group worked on each heading, be sure to let a representative from each group report.

As class members share, ask questions and share insights or commentary to clarify any misunderstandings they may be displaying. Be sure to answer any questions as they arise.

Make a chart. Ask students to concentrate on verses 4-6 as they make a chart titled, "Paul's Causes for Confidence." The left side of the chart should be a column with this heading: "The source of his confidence." Students should list reasons Paul was confident as they find them in these verses.

The right column in the chart is headed, "Why this gave him confidence." Beside each reason for Paul's former confidence listed on the left, students are to write an explanation for why Paul might have once relied on it.

After enough time for students to do their work, make one chart on the chalkboard as students share what they have written in their study.

Into Life

If you have time, you may challenge students to rewrite verses 4-6 as they might be done by someone living today. How might our contemporaries try to use their religious heritage, their family roots, their social standing, or their economic prominence to justify themselves before God?

Or you may challenge students to write a description of themselves as they anticipate they will be ten or twenty years from now. They should describe their job situation, their family life, and most importantly their involvement in the church and their relationship with Christ.

Ask students, "What factors will help you stay faithful to Christ for the rest of your life?"

Let's Talk It Over

The questions on this page are designed to encourage review of the lesson Scriptures and to promote discussion of the lesson by the class. The answers provided are only discussion starters. Let your class talk it over from there.

1. Paul tells us to "rejoice in the Lord," and in chapter 4:4 he says to do it "always." How do we experience this kind of joy?

Nehemiah 8:10 records that weeping people were told, "The joy of the Lord is your strength." To disciples saddened because He was about to leave them, Jesus spoke of keeping His commandments and abiding in His love. He said this that they might have full joy (John 15:10, 11). Joy "in the Lord" is not sensual pleasure. It is a joy that we can have in our times of deepest grief. We feel this joy as we realize that Christ loves us even though the day may be filled with trouble. Christ is unchanging. As our day passes and we commit sins, we know He forgives us; and this produces joy. There are distasteful experiences often. So what do we do? Do we get upset about circumstances? Or do we rejoice because we are in the Lord and our eternal future is secure?

2. The text calls us to be discerning disciples, to watch out for such troublemakers as Paul called "dogs," and "evil workers." Are we so comfortable that we have become careless, unconcerned about mistaken teaching that may infiltrate the church?

There were people seeking to undo what Paul had done, insisting that all Christians must become Jews. There are people now who are looking for a fight. They always criticize. There are evildoers who major in minors, and they always seek to get their own way. There are people who mix truth with error, even as those who wanted all Christians to be Jews. The result of such efforts is the same today as it was in Paul's day—confusion and division. We must be aware of dangers and keep on keeping on in true Christian teaching and living.

3. What have we lost as a result of our conversion? What have we gained?

Paul had been proud of his heritage and his advancement in the Jewish religion; but all that lost its value when he saw the greater value of being a Christian. Have you given up some of your heritage? Are there some things that once were very important to you, but now take secondary positions? Comparing Acts 26:9 with Acts 9:20, we see that Paul set out to exterminate the church of Jesus Christ, but then turned to building it. Do you see any similar change in your life as a result of your conversion? Can you recall sins that have been forgiven, and ideas, interests, and intentions that have been changed? How does the gain of salvation compare with what you have lost?

4. Do we find the Christian life monotonous and dull? One reason may be that we stop too close to the place where we got into the kingdom. How can we be pushing on toward maturity as Christians?

Verses 10 and 11 suggest some principles of growth that are illustrated in Paul's life: no resurrection without crucifixion; no fruit without dying; no victory without a battle; no life in Christ without death of self. The Christianity that counts is the Christianity that costs. Paul gladly paid the price, and he challenges us to do the same.

Another aspect of growth is our willingness to take risks. A child risks falling as he learns to walk or to ride a bike. What risks should the Christian be taking in order to grow?

Nutrition and exercise are vital to growth. A Christian needs to feed on God's Word and exercise in Christian work, and both food and exercise are more enjoyable when taken with a congenial group.

5. In our minds we usually know what we should do, but how do we move our knowledge into action?

Have you ever been at a meeting where everyone agreed that "something ought to be done," but nothing was? The way to get things done is to go to work and do them. Knowledge affects our hearts, and sometimes makes us weep; but tears are not effective till we add effort and action. Paul's letter was stained with his tears because what he knew stirred his emotions (Philippians 3:18), but progress came by pressing on, not by crying (v. 14). Seeing things happen as a result of our involvement produces more action. Obedience added to faith makes Christianity exciting. Our need leads us to depend on God, and with Him all things are possible. God is at work in your life, both to will and work for His good pleasure (Philippians 2:13).

Rejoice in the Lord

June 27
Lesson 4

DEVOTIONAL READING: **Romans 5:1-11.**

LESSON SCRIPTURE: **Philippians 4.**

PRINTED TEXT: **Philippians 4:4-20.**

Philippians 4:4-20

4 Rejoice in the Lord always: and again I say, Rejoice.

5 Let your moderation be known unto all men. The Lord is at hand.

6 Be careful for nothing; but in every thing by prayer and supplication with thanksgiving let your requests be made known unto God.

7 And the peace of God, which passeth all understanding, shall keep your hearts and minds through Christ Jesus.

8 Finally, brethren, whatsoever things are true, whatsoever things are honest, whatsoever things are just, whatsoever things are pure, whatsoever things are lovely, whatsoever things are of good report; if there be any virtue, and if there be any praise, think on these things.

9 Those things, which ye have both learned, and received, and heard, and seen in me, do: and the God of peace shall be with you.

10 But I rejoiced in the Lord greatly, that now at the last your care of me hath flourished again; wherein ye were also careful, but ye lacked opportunity.

11 Not that I speak in respect of want: for I have learned, in whatsoever state I am, therewith to be content.

12 I know both how to be abased, and I know how to abound: every where and in all things I am instructed both to be full and to be hungry, both to abound and to suffer need.

13 I can do all things through Christ which strengtheneth me.

14 Notwithstanding, ye have well done, that ye did communicate with my affliction.

15 Now ye Philippians know also, that in the beginning of the gospel, when I departed from Macedonia, no church communicated with me as concerning giving and receiving, but ye only.

16 For even in Thessalonica ye sent once and again unto my necessity.

17 Not because I desire a gift: but I desire fruit that may abound to your account.

18 But I have all, and abound: I am full, having received of Epaphroditus the things which were sent from you, an odor of a sweet smell, a sacrifice acceptable, well-pleasing to God.

19 But my God shall supply all your need according to his riches in glory by Christ Jesus.

20 Now unto God and our Father be glory for ever and ever. Amen.

GOLDEN TEXT: Rejoice in the Lord always: and again I say, Rejoice.—Philippians 4:4.

Following God's Purpose

Unit 1: Joy in Serving Christ

(Lessons 1-4)

Lesson Aims

The study of this lesson is designed to help the student:

1. Identify attitudes and actions that result in joy.
2. See and enjoy the benefits of generous giving.
3. Rejoice in the Lord.

Lesson Outline

INTRODUCTION
- A. A Recipe for Joy
- B. Lesson Background

I. BUILDING JOY (Philippians 4:4-9)
- A. By Good Relationships (vv. 4, 5)
  - *Rejoice!*
- B. By Thankful Prayer (vv. 6, 7)
- C. By Right Thinking (v. 8)
  - *The Upward Look*
- D. By Right Living (v. 9)

II. GENEROSITY GIVES JOY (Philippians 4:10-16)
- A. Joyous Thanks (vv. 10-13)
  - *The Right Source*
- B. Joyous Commendation (vv. 14-16)

III. RESULTS OF GENEROSITY (Philippians 4:17-20)
- A. It Puts Credit to Our Account (v. 17)
- B. It Pleases God (v. 18)
- C. It Invites Gifts From God (v. 19)
- D. It Gives Glory to God (v. 20)

CONCLUSION
- A. The Power of a Positive Attitude
- B. Prayer
- C. Thought to Remember

Display visual 4 of the visuals packet. It relates to Paul's teaching in verses 4-10 of the text. The visual is shown on page 373.

Introduction

A. A Recipe for Joy

Some unknown author has written the following as a recipe for joy:

Forget the kindness that you do,
As soon as you have done it;
Forget the praise that falls on you,
The moment you have won it.

Forget the slander that you hear,
Before you can repeat it;
Forget each slight, or spite, or sneer,
Wherever you may meet it.

Remember every kindness done
To you, whate'er its measure;
Remember praise by others won,
And pass it on with pleasure.

Remember every promise made,
And keep it to the letter;
Remember those who lend you aid,
And be a grateful debtor.

Remember all the happiness
That comes your way in living;
Forget each worry and distress,
Be hopeful and forgiving.

Remember good, remember truth,
Remember heavens above you,
And you will find through age and youth
True joy and hearts to love you.

B. Lesson Background

Paul called for an end to hard feeling between two women in the church (Philippians 4:2, 3). Disunity can turn our minds from the positive to the negative, from the helpful to the hurtful, from joy to grieving, from contentment to complaining. So Paul concludes this letter with a recipe for being joyful, positive, contented, and generous. If we use his recipe, we will have not only a more positive relationship with others, but also a more positive relationship with ourselves: we will have less stress, strain, and anxiety. All these affect our physical health. This lesson does not feed our spiritual nature only, but also our emotional, social, mental, and physical makeup.

I. Building Joy (Philippians 4:4-9)

A. By Good Relationships (vv. 4, 5)

4. Rejoice in the Lord always: and again I say, Rejoice.

The note of joy runs throughout this letter (1:4, 18, 25; 2:2, 17, 18, 28, 29; 3:1; 4:1, 4, 10). When Paul tells us to *rejoice,* he is talking about our reaction to whatever we encounter. We cannot control the actions of others, but we can control our reactions. To let others control them is to give up our own control of our lives. Paul does not say to *rejoice* only when things are going well, but to rejoice *always.* The reason for rejoicing is not that everything is going well, but that we are *in the Lord.* That means we have a constant companion who loves us and whom we love, and He is the Master of Heaven and earth. If we let earthly circumstances destroy our joy, it is because we are looking at the circumstances rather than at our relationship with the Lord.

REJOICE!

Charles H. Spurgeon, a great preacher of an earlier generation, told this story about good news a friend of his received.

The first bearer of the news came with a sad and solemn face to say the friend had been left an inheritance of ten thousand pounds sterling. At the current rate of exchange that would be about twenty thousand U.S. dollars. The hearer of this news simply laughed, considering the information to be false.

Later a member of his family burst into the room and cried, "You're a rich man! Mr. Jones left you ten thousand pounds sterling!" Spurgeon's friend then jumped up with a smile and began to rejoice over his good fortune.

Joy is contagious. When we carry or receive the good news of Jesus, we should let our life and attitude express our joy at all the riches we have received. "Rejoice in the Lord."

There is too much anxiety in our world. Sometimes it limits our expression of joy over all that is ours in Jesus Christ. Rejoice in Him always, and you need be anxious for nothing as you make your requests known to God. Rejoice in the Lord today! —W. P.

5. Let your moderation be known unto all men. The Lord is at hand.

We live among people, and we are to live so they will know our *moderation.* The Greek word means basically that we are fair and reasonable; but fair and reasonable people are also gentle and kind, and sometimes that is what the Greek word means. Gentleness and kindness enhance good relationships. Who among us likes to be with an overbearing, quarrelsome person? When we want a companion, do we call up someone who is arrogant and insulting?

Moderation is not only in what we do, but in what we say as well. The fastest horse in the world cannot catch a word spoken in anger. Such words run wild. We can say "I'm sorry," but we cannot call them back. Moderation stops them before they are spoken. Thus it brings joy instead of grief to those about us, and then like a boomerang it circles back to bring joy to our own lives.

When people make it hard to be kind, we need to remember *the Lord is at hand.* Jesus may appear at any time; we want to be pleasing to Him at all times. But He is *at hand* in another sense too. He is a resident guest within us here and now, in the person of the Holy Spirit. His Spirit is the Spirit of kindness. If our kindness is not enough, we can draw on His.

How to Say It

EPAPHRODITUS. E-paf-ro-*dye*-tus.
MACEDONIA. Mass-eh-*doe*-nee-uh.
PHILIPPI. Fih-*lip*-pie or *Fil*-ih-pie.
PHILIPPIANS. Fih-*lip*-pee-unz.
THESSALONICA. *Thess*-uh-lo-*nye*-kuh (strong accent on *nye; th* as in *thin*).

B. By Thankful Prayer (vv. 6, 7)

6. Be careful for nothing; but in every thing by prayer and supplication with thanksgiving let your requests be made known unto God.

Be careful for nothing does not mean we are to be careless. The Greek word for *careful* suggests being divided, pulled apart. We are not to be so overanxious that we are distracted, torn apart, unable to concentrate and do our best. What really matters is what happens in us, not what happens to us.

Prayer is an antibiotic to keep us from going to pieces. Prayer is chatting with God. We can chat in a negative way, filling our talk with complaints, blaming God, making excuses—but that is not the way Paul recommends. Rather, our *supplication* and *requests* are to be wrapped in *thanksgiving.*

In every thing does not mean we are to be thankful *for* everything. We are not thankful because we are sick, or because we lose a job or a home or a loved one. But even in such tragedies there are other things to be thankful for. We are to see them and keep on giving thanks. "In all things God works for the good of those who love him" (Romans 8:28, *New International Version*). Trust Him and thank Him.

Let your requests be made known—and be specific. Some prayers are too general. If you say, "Bless my family," what do you mean by that? What blessing do you need? God knows (Matthew 6:8), but making specific requests helps you to know and to be thankful when your prayer is answered.

7. And the peace of God, which passeth all understanding, shall keep your hearts and minds through Christ Jesus.

God's *peace* is the opposite of being torn apart or going to pieces. Peace comes through joy in the Lord (v. 4), closeness to the Lord (v. 5), and communication with the Lord (v. 6). Such peace *passeth all understanding.* Physicians, psychologists, and philosophers cannot analyze it; but God gives it when our relationship with Him is right.

God's peace *shall keep your hearts.* Quite literally, anxiety troubles the heart. The arteries narrow, the blood pressure goes up, the heart works harder, the possibility of blockage increases. God's peace avoids this stress. God wants us to enjoy living, not just endure it. But this promise is no less precious when we take *hearts* to mean our emotions. Too often we are upset over trivial things, distracted, torn in our feelings and thinking. Such things are better committed to the Lord in thankful prayer. We do what we can about the distressing things, of course; but we do it with trust in the Lord, not with heartbreaking anxiety.

C. By Right Thinking (v. 8)

8. Finally, brethren, whatsoever things are true, whatsoever things are honest, whatsoever things are just, whatsoever things are pure, whatsoever things are lovely, whatsoever things are of good report; if there be any virtue, and if there be any praise, think on these things.

We are to be selective in our thinking. If we want to be joyful, we need to think about good things. Too often we allow hurts, sins, and disappointments to affect the way we think about people and situations. Then our disconsolate thinking interferes with our joy and our relationships with others. Don't gossip; don't slander anyone. One of the marks of maturity is to get more satisfaction in keeping a secret than in telling one. Another mark of maturity is to pass on the good instead of the bad.

We should think positively about ourselves as well as about others. Perhaps nobody knows the trouble we've seen, but why keep trying to tell them? It only makes them and us miserable. Tell the joyful things!

THE UPWARD LOOK

The huge garbage dump for the eleven million people of metropolitan Manila burns continually. It is aptly named "Smokey Mountain." Several shanty villages exist on this ever growing refuse site. Children are born there. People die there. Accidents happen there. In short, life continues in the decaying, burning, dangerous environs of "Smokey Mountain." No one calls that an ideal home. Its inhabitants are the poorest of Manila's thousands of poor. They are scavengers, seeking anything in the refuse that can be cleaned, repaired, traded, or sold to gain food. Missionaries do work there, and they bring hope where otherwise there would be only despair.

One of the women who lives on "Smokey Mountain" said it well: "We live in a taste of Hell, but I know Jesus. I have promise of a house in Heaven, and that gives me hope. When the pain and toil overwhelm me, I look up! No, not at the sky. I look to Him who is coming on those clouds someday. He is coming for me! I take an upward look in my mind and see all that is good in my Lord. He died for me. Looking at Him who is pure and holy, I know I will be like Him one day. This keeps me going."

We are not living on "Smokey Mountain," but there is so much hurt in all of our lives that we find relief by thinking of the blessings of Christ.

—W. P.

D. By Right Living (v. 9)

9. Those things, which ye have both learned, and received, and heard, and seen in me, do: and the God of peace shall be with you.

It is not enough to hear about doing right; we are also to act out what we hear. It is not enough to think good thoughts; we must also do good deeds. Then we will receive God's peace that keeps us from going to pieces. And joy will be ours, too.

II. Generosity Gives Joy (Philippians 4:10-16)

A. Joyous Thanks (vv. 10-13)

10. But I rejoiced in the Lord greatly, that now at the last your care of me hath flourished again; wherein ye were also careful, but ye lacked opportunity.

There was a lot for Paul to be unhappy about: (1) He was a prisoner, chained to a guard. (2) He recalled a time when no one but the Philippians had given support to his evangelistic campaign. (3) More recently he had received no support from the Philippians. Instead of complaining, Paul rejoiced: *Now at the last your care of me hath flourished again.* He did not ask why their care had stopped. He knew it was because they *lacked opportunity.*

They could not send help when he was at sea, or when he was marooned on an island (Acts 27:1—28:10). Even when he received nothing from them, he knew they were *careful.* This *careful* is not the same word that means *anxious* in verse 6. Here it means they were thinking of him. Paul rejoiced in that instead of complaining about his problems.

11. Not that I speak in respect of want: for I have learned, in whatsoever state I am, therewith to be content.

Persons who are content enjoy what they have without envying others who have more; they are grateful for what they have and do not complain about what they do not have. Content persons are not lazy ones who don't care about making any improvements, but do appreciate what good things there are among the bad.

12. I know both how to be abased, and I know how to abound: every where and in all things I am instructed both to be full and to be hungry, both to abound and suffer need.

Being content is not the natural result of tough circumstances. We choose to be content. Paul decided he was not going to let the external situation control his internal disposition. He trained himself to be content in poverty (*abased*) and with riches (*abound*), to be appreciative when he ate luxuriously (*full*) and when he was without food (*hungry*). He knew how to be content when he had more than he could use (*abound*) and when he did not have enough (*suffer need*). Real happiness is in what we are and what we do, not in what we have. Some people who have very little are content, while others who have more than they can spend are miserable. Who do you think had more joy—Howard Hughes or Mother Teresa?

13. I can do all things through Christ which strengtheneth me.

In this context, doing *all things through Christ* does not mean escaping from confinement, walking on water, or flying to the moon. It means all the things Paul was doing: keeping on with his ministry and being content in affluence and in poverty, in excess and in want, when cared for by others and when neglected, in jail or in freedom. However, the principle can be applied more widely. We must not lose sight of the fact that nothing is impossible with the Lord. His arm is never too short. His power is never diluted. His love is never distant. He can do all things! Psalm 115:3 says our Lord is in Heaven and does whatever He pleases. May we never suspect that the God of power went to sleep after the death of the apostles. He is not dead, asleep, or impotent. If we do not believe He can do more than we can, we will not pray meaningfully. If we think life can be no more than we humans can make it, we will not be able to rejoice always. What a weak and pessimistic way to live! Ralph Waldo Emerson once said, "All I have seen teaches me to trust the Creator for all I have not seen."

THE RIGHT SOURCE

As a small boy, Jim knew his dad could do anything. He was a preacher, church planter, rancher, hunter, fisherman, loving father, companion, disciplinarian, and friend. If Dad had faults, Jim couldn't see them. With Dad's help and protection Jim felt that he too could do anything.

visual 4

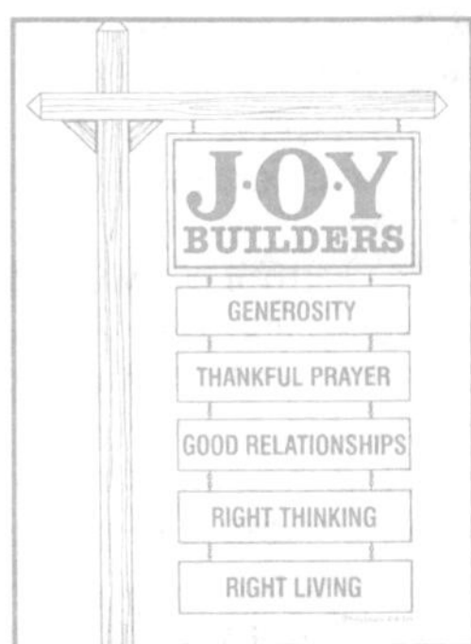

One afternoon at Sunset Beach in Oregon, Jim accidentally stretched that belief to its limit. Playing in the edge of the water, he got in too deep. Dad saw the trouble and raced into the water, though he couldn't swim. With strength not his own, he got to Jim and brought him to shallow water.

"I knew you would get me out," Jim said.

Soberly Dad answered, "Jim, I can't swim. The good Lord had to give me strength to get you. I never could have done it myself."

That is our situation as we see people in need and "going under" for the last time in the clutches of sin, shame, and hurt. Sometimes we ourselves are going under. No, we can't save anyone, but God can! The apostle Paul says, "I can do all things through Christ which strengtheneth me."

Strength means power, ability, and protection. Misused, it means abuse, weakness, and injury. Be sure your strength is from the right source and used in the right way. —W. P.

B. Joyous Commendation (vv. 14-16)

14. Notwithstanding, ye have well done, that ye did communicate with my affliction.

One way to stop being weak and pessimistic is to reach out and help someone else. Good therapy for depression is to find someone in trouble and help that person out of it.

Taking our minds off ourselves keeps us from thinking the world owes us something. Mark Twain said, "Don't go around saying the world owes you a living. The world owes you nothing. It was here first." Instead of thinking about his affliction, Paul saw the positive aspects of it. One of them was the help he had from the Philippians, and he happily commended them for it.

15. Now ye Philippians know also, that in the beginning of the gospel, when I departed from Macedonia, no church communicated

with me as concerning giving and receiving, but ye only.

Sometimes we may be reluctant to share what we have for another's material needs, but it is the unselfish who become joyous and give joy. The Philippians were that kind of people. Paul looked back over the years to a time when they were the only supporters he had. God uses people to help people. God's provisions are always greater than man's poverty. God's supply is always greater than man's need. God's grace is always greater than man's disgrace.

16. For even in Thessalonica ye sent once and again unto my necessity.

A generous person doesn't give just once in order to get some points racked up in Heaven; such a one gives over and over again. That's what Paul was commending the church at Philippi for doing. They lost no time in starting to give. *Thessalonica* was the first place Paul stopped to preach after he left Philippi.

III. Results of Generosity (Philippians 4:17-20)

Paul mentions four results of giving joy by being generous.

A. It Puts Credit to Our Account (v. 17)

17. Not because I desire a gift: but I desire fruit that may abound to your account.

Paul was not praising the Philippians in order to get more from them, but in order to get more for them. God does keep a record of our generosity. When we share with the poor, we are making a loan to God. He will repay us (Proverbs 19:17).

B. It Pleases God (v. 18)

18. But I have all, and abound: I am full, having received of Epaphroditus the things which were sent from you, an odor of a sweet smell, a sacrifice acceptable, well-pleasing to God.

Epaphroditus was the messenger who took the Philippians' offering to Paul. By reason of it Paul now had all he needed. But their offering was not just a gift to Paul. It was a sacrifice that God accepted, one that pleased Him. Whatever we do to God's people, we do to God. Remember how plainly Jesus taught this (Matthew 25:34-40).

C. It Invites Gifts From God (v. 19)

19. But my God shall supply all your need according to his riches in glory by Christ Jesus.

We cannot outgive God. He will supply the needs of those who are generous, those who are using what they have to help others. To give to God's people in need is inviting God to give to us. He meets our needs so that through us He can meet the needs of others.

D. It Gives Glory to God (v. 20)

20. Now unto God and our Father be glory for ever and ever. Amen.

All our Christian rejoicing is in Christ. He provides the good things that bring joy; He gives the insights and the promises that enable us to rejoice in circumstances that are not good. In all our joy and for all our joy we give glory, honor, and praise to *our Father* in Heaven.

Conclusion

A. The Power of a Positive Attitude

A nine-year-old boy was taking his first airline flight. When the airplane flew into a severe thunderstorm, he was terribly frightened. Looking at a man sitting beside him, he said, "Aren't you afraid?"

The man could see how the boy was feeling. "No," he said with a wide grin. "This is really fun."

Immediately the boy's face changed. Fear and tension left him. He, too, began to have fun. It was like a roller coaster ride. Such is the power of a positive attitude.

B. Prayer

Thank You, Father, for being powerful and not weak—for being up and not down—for being great and not small—for being magnificent and not mean. In Jesus' name, amen.

C. Thought to Remember

"I can do all things through Christ which strengtheneth me."

Home Daily Bible Readings

Monday, June 21—Rejoice in the Creator God (Psalm 33:1-12)
Tuesday, June 22—Rejoice in the Reigning God (Psalm 96)
Wednesday, June 23—Rejoice in the Sustaining God (Psalm 104:24-35)
Thursday, June 24—Rejoice in the Saving God (Psalm 118:19-29)
Friday, June 25—Rejoice in the God of Peace (Philippians 4:1-7)
Saturday, June 26—Rejoice in the Strengthening God (Philippians 4:8-13)
Sunday, June 27—Rejoice in the God of Grace (Philippians 4:14-23)

Learning by Doing

This page contains an alternate lesson plan emphasizing learning activities. Classes desiring such student involvement will find these suggestions helpful.

Learning Goals

Students in today's class should:

1. Discover Paul's advice for how we can be joyful, positive, contented, and generous.
2. Decide which of these qualities they most need to develop in their own lives.

Into the Lesson

Write this sentence on the chalkboard before students arrive: "Stress is a problem that threatens to unravel our society."

To begin today's class, ask students to brainstorm ideas and evidences that support that sentence. List their ideas on the chalkboard as they shout them out in a ninety-second time period.

When time is up, count the ideas. Ask students to look at all of them and decide how many could be true for them. Are we Christians as plagued by stress as the rest of our society?

Today's text, although it never mentions the word *stress,* helps us develop attitudes to battle it.

Into the Word

The lesson writer has summarized today's text with four words: Joyful, positive, contented, and generous. How does Paul present a recipe for each of these attributes in this text? That's the question class members should answer as they participate in today's class session.

Divide the class into fourths, and assign each of these attributes to a different quarter of the class. Students should survey the text and then write a "Recipe for Joy" or "Recipe for Positive Thinking" or "Recipe for Contentment" or "Recipe for Generosity." Their "recipes" should give Paul's teaching on the assigned subject from this passage. If students wish, they can actually write their summaries as a recipe. ("Take two cups of gentleness and mix slowly with heaping measures of grateful prayers," etc.)

After eight or ten minutes, allow students to share their recipes with the whole class. Use your study of the first lesson plan to answer questions or correct students' misunderstandings as they arise.

Into Life

Ask class members to write a response to one of the following paragraphs, whichever one they choose. The bad attitudes demonstrated by each of these people could be remedied by a proper understanding of today's text. Students should use teachings from this passage to answer one of these people.

- I just wish you could understand what my problems are really like. If you had to live on my tiny little pension . . . If you had to exist in this bug-infested hole of an apartment . . . If you had to survive on beans and rice and handouts from the government . . . If you were too poor to buy a decent Christmas gift for your grandkids or a church outfit for yourself . . . If you had to live *just one week* the way I have to live, then you'd be weary and maybe a little bitter too. Life for me is trying to survive from one measly Social Security check to the next one. Somehow I thought it would have all ended so much better than this.
- Someday life will settle down for me and for our family. Someday. But now is the time for me to reach my career goals, establish my financial security, and create a nest egg. If I don't work hard now, there will be no money for my kids' college. If I don't get ahead now, I'll never be able to afford to retire. Oh, sure, I know plenty of people get by on less income. But they don't have the goals I have, the potential I have, the dreams I have. They're happy to let everyone else get ahead at their expense. But that's not me. I can see security and the fulfillment of all my dreams ahead of me. Someday we won't live this way. Someday I'll be home in the evenings. Someday we'll take vacations. But not now.

After class members have written their responses, ask several to read what they've written. How do they feel about the case studies? Do they know anybody who has demonstrated the attitudes of these people?

Display the words *joyful, positive, contented,* and *generous* on flashcards that you've prepared before class. Ask students to decide which of these qualities they most need in their lives.

Ask them to write the word in their student book or on a slip of paper you provide. Under the word they should write some of the verse references from Philippians 4 that encourage us to demonstrate the quality they have chosen.

Challenge students this week to read—or memorize—the verses they've written down and to pray about the quality they need.

Close the class session by reading "A Recipe for Joy," which is the introduction to the first lesson plan. Close with sentence prayers.

Let's Talk It Over

The questions on this page are designed to encourage review of the lesson Scriptures and to promote discussion of the lesson by the class. The answers provided are only discussion starters. Let your class talk it over from there.

1. Much of Christian teaching is concerned with living beyond death. Heaven and hell are often mentioned. How does Paul's teaching prepare us for living before we die?

Christianity is an experience of life that enjoys divine love down here on earth. The love of God is shown by His giving. A lovely thing about Christian love is that it originated with God. He took the initiative, but His love is demonstrated by the attitude of His people. The Christian life is a life of joy. There is joy in meeting people, influencing them for Christ, and leading them to greater heights of commitment and service. The Christian life is a life of prayer and thanksgiving (vv. 6, 7), a life of noble thinking and doing (vv. 8, 9), a life of giving and receiving (vv. 10-20).

2. There was a disagreement between two women in the Philippian church (vv. 2, 3). How do you handle disagreements?

Paul could have taken sides with one of the quarreling women if he had thought that was best, but he chose to admonish both of them to work *out* their problem—and he urged another good Christian to help them. The important thing was to *deal* with the problem in the spirit of Christian love. The two ladies should not continue to wrangle, and neither should they turn back to back and never speak to each other again. If they could not agree, they should disagree in friendly fashion.

3. The lesson writer encourages us to overcome anxiety. How do you handle your anxious spirit?

Parents say to their children, "Be careful!" Paul says to Christians, "Don't be careful." These bits of advice are not contradictory. The word *careful* does not have the same meaning in both. We need to use our heads and act sensibly and safely, as parents tell their children. But as Paul tells us, we do not need to be anxious and worried. Whatever problem may make us anxious, we need to be prayerful and worshipful about it. We must relate it to the Lord. With great reverence, with great respect, and with a sense of holy awe, we present it to the Lord; but we refuse to be pressed into the ground by the problem. Notice also that we are to come before God with a thankful attitude. Thank Him that He hears your prayer and that He is adequate to meet the anxious concern.

4. A present-day problem is that of loneliness. Why is loneliness so common? Is it possible that God permits loneliness so we will turn to Him?

Leaders often find themselves lonely. In Numbers 11:14 we find Moses crying out, "I am not able to bear all this people alone." Death of loved ones leads to loneliness. The desertion of friends leaves one lonely, as Paul points out in 2 Timothy 4:10, 11. Sometimes a person is lonely because he or she is faithful to God (Jeremiah 15:15-17). Whatever the cause of loneliness, relief can be found in communion with God (Philippians 4:6, 7).

5. Sometimes God provides for people through other people's generosity. To whom are you generous?

Often we are generous to people who are generous to us. It appears that a higher standard of sharing is seen when we share with someone in need, though we will get nothing in return (Luke 14:12-14). We need to be sensitive to the distress of others. Jesus taught that through the good Samaritan story (Luke 10:30-37). Three men passed along and saw a need, but only one did anything about it.

6. What principles have you discovered that encourage you to keep on sharing?

Here are some principles easily seen in the Scriptures:

1. If you have received, give (Matthew 10:8). People have the opportunity of sharing when they have the blessing of receiving.

2. If you give, you will receive (Luke 6:38). Christians are not depleted when they give. God will not let us outgive Him.

3. The more you give, the more you will receive (Luke 6:38). The more we allow to flow through us to others, the more God pours in. The outflow determines the input. Be generous, and you will have the joy of the generosity of others. Be abandoned in giving to God, and God will be abandoned in giving to you. Be overflowing in superlative measure, and God will overflow in superlative measure to you.

The Preeminent Christ

July 4
Lesson 5

DEVOTIONAL READING: **1 Corinthians 3:10-23.**

LESSON SCRIPTURE: **Colossians 1.**

PRINTED TEXT: **Colossians 1:3-5a, 11-23.**

Colossians 1:3-5a, 11-23

3 We give thanks to God and the Father of our Lord Jesus Christ, praying always for you,

4 Since we heard of your faith in Christ Jesus, and of the love which ye have to all the saints,

5a For the hope which is laid up for you in heaven.

. . . .

11 Strengthened with all might, according to his glorious power, unto all patience and long-suffering with joyfulness;

12 Giving thanks unto the Father, which hath made us meet to be partakers of the inheritance of the saints in light:

13 Who hath delivered us from the power of darkness, and hath translated us into the kingdom of his dear Son.

14 In whom we have redemption through his blood, even the forgiveness of sins:

15 Who is the image of the invisible God, the firstborn of every creature:

16 For by him were all things created, that are in heaven, and that are in earth, visible and invisible, whether they be thrones, or dominions, or principalities, or powers: all things were created by him, and for him:

17 And he is before all things, and by him all things consist:

18 And he is the head of the body, the church: who is the beginning, the firstborn from the dead; that in all things he might have the preeminence.

19 For it pleased the Father that in him should all fulness dwell;

20 And, having made peace through the blood of his cross, by him to reconcile all things unto himself; by him, I say, whether they be things in earth, or things in heaven.

21 And you, that were sometime alienated and enemies in your mind by wicked works, yet now hath he reconciled

22 In the body of his flesh through death, to present you holy and unblamable and unreprovable in his sight:

23 If ye continue in the faith grounded and settled, and be not moved away from the hope of the gospel, which ye have heard, and which was preached to every creature which is under heaven; whereof I Paul am made a minister.

GOLDEN TEXT: He is before all things, and by him all things consist.—Colossians 1:17.

Following God's Purpose

Unit 2: Christ Above All

(Lessons 5-8)

Lessons Aims

The study of this lesson is designed to help the students:

1. Understand Jesus' relationship to God, creation, humankind, and especially the students themselves.
2. Appreciate Christ's sacrifice for him.
3. Be reconciled to God and show their reconciliation in their way of life.

Lesson Outline

Visual 5 of the visuals packet emphasizes the description of Christ given in verses 15-20. The visual is shown on page 381.

Introduction

A. God With Skin On

A little boy woke up in the middle of the night to flashes of lightning and crashing of thunder. In fear he started to cry. From another room his father called, "What's the matter?"

"I'm scared," he called back.

"Don't be scared," the father said calmly, "God will take care of you."

"I know," said the trembling boy, "but I need somebody with skin on."

All of us need someone with skin on. God met our need when Jesus came to earth. He was God with skin on.

B. Lesson Background

Last month we studied the letter to the Philippians, which Paul wrote from his Roman imprisonment. Now we turn to Colossians, another letter written during that same imprisonment. Probably Paul had never visited the Colossians, but the gospel had been carried through all that region while he was teaching in Ephesus (Acts 19:10). Epaphras may have been the one who took the gospel from Ephesus to Colossae, and he brought news from Colossae to Paul in Rome (Colossians 1:7, 8). Apparently he reported that some false teachings were making headway there. We shall learn more about them in the next two lessons. Paul wrote this letter to correct the errors and to encourage the Christians to apply their Christian beliefs to behavior.

I. Christian Effectiveness (Colossians 1:3-5a)

A. Prayers (v. 3)

3. We give thanks to God and the Father of our Lord Jesus Christ, praying always for you.

Probably we have grossly underestimated the power of the prayers of others for our Christian effectiveness. Paul was *praying always* for the Christians in Colossae. Since we Christians are linked to one another in Christ, shouldn't we be praying for one another more?

Have we attributed our effectiveness to things we can see—the budget, the building, the staff—more than to what we can't see—prayers that undergird us? We may someday discover that our Christian lives float on the prayers of others. Jesus evidently knows that, for He is constantly praying for us (Romans 8:34; Hebrews 7:25). Shouldn't we join Him?

Why not prepare a small notebook with pages numbered 1 through 31 and begin to pray for a certain person or situation each day of the month? The list may include family members, leaders in the church, other church members, friends, people with whom you work, missionaries, governmental leaders, and more. Keep it current by adding people mentioned in the Sunday-school class or from the pulpit. Make the prayers specific and practical. Then note God's answers.

Giving Thanks

An old blues song emphasized the phrase, "I ain't got nobody, and nobody cares for me." The kids in one school called it the "ghost song." Their emphasis was on "no body," because their physical education teacher made fun of their physical weakness. As their condition improved, however, they changed the words to the song and sang, "I do have some body, and that body cares for me."

Accidentally they hit on a truth we need to know, share, and live by. When we have "nobody" we are alone, hurting, and needing someone to love us and care about our well-being. How good it is to have someone help our spiritual development as the physical education teacher helped the physical development of his students!

Paul prayed for the believers in Colossae, rejoicing in their faith and confirming their hope. By his concern their spiritual health was revived and their strength in the Lord increased.

Do you know "somebody" who has "nobody"? Is there someone whose spiritual renewal you can help until that person knows that in Christ he or she is "somebody"?

Everybody does need somebody, and you can be God's tool for new life and hope if you reach out to someone as Jesus did to you. —W. P.

B. Faith and Love (v. 4)

4. Since we heard of your faith in Christ Jesus, and of the love which ye have to all the saints.

The Colossian Christians had *faith* and *love*, and they had them in the right objects. Their *faith* was *in Christ Jesus,* and their *love* was *to all the saints.*

Everybody has faith. We have to have faith to eat a meal at a restaurant, to drink water out of a faucet, to breathe air that we cannot see. We cannot live five minutes without faith. But in what do we place our faith for eternal life? To place it in anything on earth is to place it in something that is temporary and will one day burn up (2 Peter 3:10).

Notice that the Colossians had love for more than just some of the saints—the ones they liked. They had love for *all* the saints. They loved the whole family.

How to Say It

Colossae. Ko-*loss*-ee.
Epaphras. *Ep*-uh-fras.

This verse illustrates the twofold relationship that all Christians are to develop—a relationship with God and a relationship with one another. Christianity is never to be just mystical—just between us and God—or just social—just between us and others. Christianity involves a relationship with God and with others—both.

C. Hope (v. 5a)

5a. For the hope which is laid up for you in heaven.

Our lives are based upon looking up (in Christ Jesus), looking around us (to all the saints), and looking ahead of us (in Heaven). What is it that is laid up for us in Heaven? It is what we hope for—our eternal salvation, our eternal home, the transformation of our mortality to immortality, our weakness to strength, and our humanness to Christlikeness.

What makes us effective is not only what has happened in the past, but what we are hoping for in the future. Hope of the future is a major motivation for what we do right now. People who hope to get a college degree will go through many difficulties to realize that hope. Our forefathers hoped to start a new country, and they went through the hardships of pioneering. Future hope is a powerful motivation for present happenings. If someone would write down all that we are doing now, would one be able to identify what we are hoping for?

II. Christian Privileges (Colossians 1:11-14)

A. Our Inner Power (v. 11)

11. Strengthened with all might, according to his glorious power, unto all patience and long-suffering with joyfulness.

This is a power-packed verse. Note three forceful words: *strengthened, might, power. According to his glorious power,* God's power, we are *strengthened with all might.* God's power strengthens us when His Spirit lives in us (Ephesians 3:16). He does not necessarily equip us to do sensational or miraculous things, though He can do such things if He chooses. But He constantly empowers us to live through the daily nitty-gritty of life.

This verse gives three results of this power: *all patience, long-suffering,* and *joyfulness.* The word for *patience* literally means "remaining under." It refers to standing firm under the burden of a difficult situation. God's power gives to us stick-to-it-ive-ness. All Christians go through difficult times, and we have observed their endurance.

Long-suffering means putting up with difficult people and situations. No one meets only people who are "easy to get along with." By putting up with difficult people, we grow into the kind of character Jesus modeled for us. The same Spirit that was in Him is in the Christian.

Joyfulness is that inner quality that keeps us floating through the troubled waters while everyone else is drowning. *Joyfulness* is buoyancy. It is not the result of what happens around us, but of what has happened inside of us.

B. Our Inheritance (v. 12)

12. Giving thanks unto the Father, which hath made us meet to be partakers of the inheritance of the saints in light.

We have an inheritance in Heaven. It is reserved for us (1 Peter 1:4) as a seat is reserved at a baseball game or concert. No one can take it away from us. When God reserves something, you can be sure it will be there for you.

One of the beautiful words in this verse is *partakers.* To partake is to take a part, a share. We will share our inheritance with all *the saints in light.* There will be no jealousies. We will rejoice that God shares His inheritance with us all. There is no greed in Heaven, just enjoyment. Shouldn't we start practicing that now? Why get upset over what we inherit from men, when our inheritance that comes from our Heavenly Father is guaranteed?

C. Our Transfer (v. 13)

13. Who hath delivered us from the power of darkness, and hath translated us into the kingdom of his dear Son.

There are only two kingdoms, the kingdom of God and the kingdom of Satan. We are in one or the other. Whenever we are converted to Christ, God transfers us from the kingdom of Satan (*the power of darkness*) *into the kingdom of his dear Son.* With that transfer, we have a new king—Jesus.

We cannot make the transfer ourselves; God does it. But God transfers no unwilling immigrants. We cannot get into His Son's kingdom unless we believe in His Son, unless we want to make Him our king and obey Him, unless we make our wish known. Then the transfer is completed in baptism: our sins are washed away (Acts 22:16) and we begin a new life in Christ's kingdom (Romans 6:4).

D. Our Forgiveness (v. 14)

14. In whom we have redemption through his blood, even the forgiveness of sins.

Redemption is like a ransom that releases a hostage or a kidnap victim. Without Christ, we are slaves of sin (John 8:34). We are not ransomed with money, but with "the precious blood of Christ" (1 Peter 1:18, 19). Jesus took the penalty of our sins and gave us *forgiveness.* What God forgives, He erases. What God erases, he forgets. He will remember our sins no more (Hebrews 8:12).

III. The Christ (Colossians 1:15-23)

A. His Relationship to God (v. 15)

15. Who is the image of the invisible God, the firstborn of every creature.

The Christ is God's *image,* "the exact representation of His nature" (Hebrews 1:3, *New American Standard Bible*). Do you want to know what God is like? He is like Jesus. How would God act and react in any given situation? Look at Jesus. He demonstrates the character of His Father.

Among the Jews, the *firstborn* was next to the father as head of the family. The Christ is with His Father as head of all creation. The next two verses develop this thought

B. His Relationship to Creation (vv. 16, 17)

16. For by him were all things created, that are in heaven, and that are in earth, visible and invisible, whether they be thrones, or dominions, or principalities, or powers: all things were created by him, and for him.

The Christ was Co-Creator with God the Father. Everything that was made was made through Him (John 1:1-3). All things were created not only *by* Him, but also *for* Him. All of creation was designed to participate in carrying out God's plan and purpose. All of creation is responsive to God. He can intervene in what we call the "laws of nature"; and when He does, all creation obeys Him. Human beings are the only part of creation that has been given the freedom to hear a command of God and choose not to obey it.

17. And he is before all things, and by him all things consist.

In the past Christ created all things, and *by him all things consist* in the present. That means He now is holding everything together. What keeps this earth in one piece? Jesus does. We talk about the law of gravity, but that is only His law. He made it along with everything else, and He rules it along with everything else. An electric watch quickly leaves the control of the watchmaker. It runs by itself till the battery is exhausted. But our world does not work like that. The law of gravity and other "natural laws" continue to function because the Creator continues to wish it. When He says "Stop!" that will be the end of the world.

In the meantime the Creator is in charge. He can speak, and the waters of the Red Sea divide.

He can speak, and lions lose their appetites. He can speak, and fire burns without consuming. All of nature recognizes the voice of the Creator. Wouldn't it be great if all humans would?

THE ETERNAL ORDER

Two doctrines of authority emerged in the Middle Ages. One was "the divine right of kings." Rulers held that God had given kings their right to rule, and therefore any resistance to a king was rebellion against God. The other doctrine was "apostolic succession." The Bishop of Rome claimed the right to rule in the spiritual realm because he was the successor of Peter, who was given "the keys of the kingdom of heaven."

Terrible conflicts finally broke autocratic authority in both the secular and spiritual realms. Such conflicts came as believing men turned again to the Word of God and rediscovered the authority of Christ. He is the Creator. He made all things in the beginning, and He holds all things together now. He is preeminent: Christ alone is head of the church, which is His body! This is the eternal order, determined before the world began.

To worship Christ, exalt Him, and submit to His beneficent rule will give you peace, hope, and a secured future. Any other course is disobedience to God, for God made Christ preeminent and gave all authority into His hands.

—W. P.

C. His Relationship to the Church (vv. 18, 19)

18. And he is the head of the body, the church: who is the beginning, the firstborn from the dead; that in all things he might have the preeminence.

As Christ is over all of creation, He is also over the church. His rule is wrapped in love, but He is the ruler, the keeper, the life giver. The physical body would die if the head were removed, and so it is with the church. If the directions of the head are not received and followed, that is insanity.

The church cannot have two heads. No human being has the right to control it. Dictatorship must go, for we have only one Lord. People in the church who demand their own way are in competition with the church's only head—and that is disastrous.

The body, the church is the ongoing presence of Christ on earth. The twentieth-century body of Christ should do for Him what His first-century body did. It should make Him visible: it should show His nature and character, His kindness and helpfulness, His righteousness and truth.

visual 5

The Creator of all creation is also *the beginning* of the church. He is its foundation (1 Corinthians 3:11) and its builder (Matthew 16:18). as the firstborn of all creation (v. 15) He is over all creation; As *the firstborn from the dead* He is over all those who rise to everlasting life. *In all things* now and forever He has *the preeminence.*

It is tragic when individuals allow their traditions or prejudices or preferences to override the will of the Lord Jesus Christ. When we have no word from Jesus, of course there is room for our preferences; and we must allow others to have room for their preferences without fighting about it and thus hurting the body and grieving the Head.

19. For it pleased the Father that in him should all fulness dwell.

Jesus was not just a partial image of the Father; He was the full image. "All the fulness of the Godhead" (Colossians 2:9), all of God's character and nature, dwelt in Jesus. That's why He could say, "He that hath seen me hath seen the Father" (John 14:9). God showed His character, His nature, His will in Jesus.

The beautiful thing is that God now wants to do that in Christ's body—"the church, which is his body, the fulness of him that filleth all in all" (Ephesians 1:22, 23). What the Father is in His character and nature, we are to be. All of us are to be daily growing into the likeness of Christ, and thus we are to mirror the image of the Father. We are to "put on the new man, which after God is created in righteousness and true holiness" (Ephesians 4:24).

D. His Reconciliation (vv. 20-23)

20. And, having made peace through the blood of his cross, by him to reconcile all things unto himself; by him, I say, whether they be things in earth, or things in heaven.

Christ died to reconcile us to God; and not only us, but *all things* in earth and sky. In ways we do not fully understand, the whole creation is suffering because of the sins of mankind (Romans 8:22). In the redemption of mankind the whole creation "shall be delivered from the bondage of corruption into the glorious liberty of the children of God" (Romans 8:21).

21, 22. And you, that were sometime alienated and enemies in your mind by wicked works, yet now hath he reconciled in the body of his flesh through death, to present you holy and unblamable and unreprovable in his sight.

Our sins, our *wicked works*, made us aliens and enemies of God. But Jesus, His only Son, paid the penalty for our sins. Forgiven, we are as holy and blameless as if we had never sinned. By the same sacrifice that reconciled us to God, He reconciled us to each other (Ephesians 2:11-22). Are we helping to promote unity among all of God's people, or are we helping the devil spread disunity? Christ sacrificed His life to reconcile us. Reconciled, we are to be His ministers, His servants, to reconcile others (2 Corinthians 5:17-20). We also will have to make some sacrifices. We will have to let go of our pet peeves and preferences as well as our sins. God wants very much to reconcile all mankind. We must let His longing be more important to us than our personal preferences.

23. If ye continue in the faith grounded and settled, and be not moved away from the hope of the gospel, which ye have heard, and which was preached to every creature which is under heaven; whereof I Paul am made a minister.

Christ died to take way our sins and make us holy and blameless (v. 22), but His sacrifice will be unavailing unless we live for the cause for which He died. We ourselves must cling to our *faith* in Christ. We must cling to the *hope* held before us in *the gospel.* We must live for Him who died for us. Then we can be sure of living with Him forever.

WRAPPING THE GIFT

In 1776, thirteen colonies in North America signed a Declaration of Independence. With this document they expressed their dream of freedom, equality, and justice for all; but that vision was not easily realized.

Our forefathers fought and died to be free. They thought and prayed to create a Constitution defining the freedom and government they wanted to pass on. Wars, westward expansion, purchases of land, prayer, faith, and dependence on God gave us America. The gift came wrapped in the sacrifice and service of many. If we are to maintain this gift and pass it on to our children, it has to be continually rewrapped in our own sacrifice and service.

Jesus came among us with a new revelation to create a new people, His church. He wrapped His gift of grace in His sacrifice. By His work Christians are a new creation, free in Christ and in Him reconciled to God. We cannot make a sacrifice like His, but we must "continue in the faith" in order to take possession of all our Lord has given to us by going to Calvary. —W. P.

Conclusion

A. The Incomparable Christ

We can never exhaust the subject of who Jesus is and what Jesus does. Nothing can compare to Him. He is the bread of life, the eternal water, the rock, the good shepherd, the sacrifice, the deliverer, the ransom price, the gem of great price, the lily of the valley, our passover, our friend, the living way, the resurrection and the life, the door, the way, the truth, and the life, the Savior, the Messiah, the Redeemer, the cornerstone, the forgiver, the lover, the holy one, the perfect one, the sinless one, the understanding one, the wisdom of God, the presence of God, the great physician, and more. The list of metaphors could go on and on. He is the incomparable, preeminent Christ.

B. Prayer

We thank You, Our loving Father, for being willing to say good-bye to Jesus from Heaven so that through Him You can say hello to us in Heaven. We thank You that He descended so we can ascend, that He died so we can live, that He took our sins so we can be forgiven. You are our magnificent Father. We thank You; we love You, we praise You. Amen.

C. Thought to Remember

The twentieth-century body of Christ is to do for Jesus what His first-century body did.

Home Daily Bible Readings

Monday, June 28—Christ, the Word of Truth (Colossians 1:1-8)
Tuesday, June 29—Christ, Our Example (Colossians 1:9-14)
Wednesday, June 30—Christ, the Fullness of God (Colossians 1:15-20)
Thursday, July 1—Christ, Revelation of God's Glory (Colossians 1:21-29)
Friday, July 2—Christ, Our Reconciler (Romans 5:6-11)
Saturday, July 3—Christ, the One Who Justifies (Romans 5:12-16)
Sunday, July 4—Christ, the Righteous (Romans 5:17-21)

Learning by Doing

This page contains an alternate lesson plan emphasizing learning activities. Classes desiring such student involvement will find these suggestions helpful.

Learning Goals

As students participate in today's class session, they should:

1. See the uniqueness of Jesus, as He is presented in Colossians 1.
2. Praise God for the special place Jesus has in their lives.

Into the Lesson

Write this question on the chalkboard for students to see as they arrive for today's session: "What's so special about Jesus?"

To begin today's discussion, ask class members if they have ever known someone who does not believe in Christ? Do they have a friend or co-worker who is an atheist, or perhaps a Moslem or Hindu? Have they talked with their friend about Jesus? What was the result?

Ask class members to brainstorm a list of attributes that belong to Jesus alone. What are some ways He is unlike anyone else who has ever lived?

After about two minutes of putting their answers on the chalkboard, tell class members that today's passage answers the very question they have been addressing today. Since so many in our world are saying that allegiance to Jesus is not necessary, Christians should know why they are putting their faith in Him.

Into the Word

Class members should look at Colossians 1:3-20 to see how this passage answers four questions: What Has God Done? Who Is Jesus? What Have the Colossians Done? What Should the Colossians Do?

You may decide to divide the class into fourths. Each quarter of the class should take one of the four headings and look at this whole passage to see how it answers the question they have been assigned.

Or, for something different, ask each group to listen for answers to one of the questions as you read the text.

Or ask all class members to listen for answers to only one of the questions as you read the text. Then move to the second question and read the text again, perhaps from a different translation. Read the text aloud four times, perhaps with a different reader each time. With each reading the class jots down verse references under a separate heading. Then discuss with the whole class. Maybe you will put the headings on a wall and jot down verse references under each one.

As a help to you, here is a summary of the passage's teachings under each of the four points:

What Has God Done?

Provided hope in Heaven (v. 5).

Provided the word of truth, the gospel (v. 5).

Provided power for spiritual growth (v. 6).

Demonstrated grace (v. 6).

Filled the Colossians with knowledge of His will and spiritual wisdom (v. 9).

Qualified Christians to share in "the inheritance of the saints in the kingdom of light" (v. 12, *New International Version*).

Rescued us from the power of darkness and brought us into the kingdom of His Son (v. 13).

Provided redemption, the forgiveness of sins (v. 14).

Invested Jesus with all His fullness (v. 19).

Provided Jesus so that we may be reconciled to God (v. 20).

Who Is Jesus?

The image of the invisible God (v. 15).

The firstborn over all creation (v. 15).

The Creator of all things, the source of unity in the universe (vv. 16, 17).

The head of the church (v. 18).

What Have the Colossians Done?

Developed faith in Jesus (v. 4).

Loved the saints (v. 4).

What Should the Colossians Do?

Live a life worthy of the Lord, pleasing Him in every way (v. 10).

Bear fruit in every good work (v. 10).

Grow in the knowledge of God (v. 10).

Receive God's strength that leads to endurance and patience (v. 11).

Joyfully give thanks to God (v. 12).

Into Life

Ask class members to think of hymns that affirm one or some of the truths about Jesus taught in this passage. If there is time, students may do this as an activity; distribute hymnals for their search.

Close by singing one of these hymns.

Or close with sentence praise prayers. Each prayer should focus on an attribute or role of Christ, especially one presented in this text. Ask class members to pray only one sentence.

Let's Talk It Over

The questions on this page are designed to encourage review of the lesson Scriptures and to promote discussion of the lesson by the class. The answers provided are only discussion starters. Let your class talk it over from there.

1. It seems normal for Christians to pray for others when they are ill. What other concerns are properly included in our prayers for family and friends?

Of course our concern is not limited to family and friends. Paul prayed for the Colossians even though he did not know most of them personally. We too may pray for people far away, but we pray more specifically when we know the people and their needs. It is proper to pray for increasing faith, for the growth and peace of congregations, for the well-being of families, for the ability to stand under temptation, and for the peace people need in order to live properly. While we pray for the spiritual welfare of those we love, we do not forget their physical and material welfare. Jesus taught His disciples to ask for daily bread as well as deliverance from evil (Matthew 6:9-13). In our prayers for others as well as ourselves, it is proper to pray about every area of life Jesus mentioned in that famous model prayer, also about the things mentioned in Paul's prayers for the Colossians (Colossians 1:9-12).

2. How does hope become a motivating force for our faith and love?

Human beings live with a future orientation. We look ahead and live for what is to be. We dream and plan where we can be and what we can have if we continue on a certain course of action. Our dreams become a motivating factor in the decisions we make: we take action to make our dreams a reality.

Before us lies the prospect that we shall share an inheritance with the saints, and that we shall live eternally with God. This gives us reason to develop our faith, to study the Scriptures and strengthen our "assurance of things hoped for" (Hebrews 11:1, *American Standard Version*). Hoping to live with God for ever, we make it our aim to live with Him now. That leads us to learn to love all those whom God loves. Thus hope calls us to continue and increase in faith and love.

3. How can a person with God's help build the strength to endure "long-suffering with joyfulness"?

We cannot learn the skills of football or golf just by reading books and watching instructional videos. We have to take the field and learn by experience. So also we learn endurance and patience by experience, by going through difficult situations that try us and cause us pain.

On the other hand, books and videos prepared by experts can help greatly in learning football and golf. They guide us in our experience so it will be most helpful. So also the Word of God can help greatly as we try to develop our endurance in the difficulties of life. It teaches us to be firm and steadfast, to trust God and love our fellowmen, to look forward to the end of earthly troubles and the joys of Heaven.

We need to pray for ourselves as Paul prayed for the Ephesians, that God will strengthen us "according to his glorious power." Then we need to rely on His strength and simply refuse to give up our faith or to do wrong. Thus we bear the load and become stronger because of our trials and temptations.

4. If Christ is head of the church, how can we think of the church as a democracy or a republic with representative government?

We can't. The Bible describes the church as a kingdom (Christ is its head), not a democracy or a group governed by representatives of its members. This means that the members of the church should not choose their elders to represent them, but to represent Christ. Those who oversee the activities of the church should not be chosen because they think as we think, but because they think as Jesus thinks. They should be chosen because they are spiritual men well acquainted with the Scriptures and devoted to them, men who will look to Christ for guidance. He can lead His church through such leaders. They seek direction from above for the church. Important decisions should be prayerfully made on the basis of God's Word, not on the feelings of the congregation.

5. The first chapter of Colossians presents other-world goals (share in the inheritance of saints, verse 12, and goals for this world (live a life worthy of the Lord, verse 10). Which kind of goals should be our primary aim?

There is no need to make a distinction between two kinds of goals, for the same faith and the same kind of life bring us toward both, and we need God's help to reach either.

The Sufficient Christ

July 11
Lesson 6

Devotional Reading: Hebrews 10:11-25.

Lesson Scripture: Colossians 2.

Printed Text: Colossians 2:5-19.

Colossians 2:5-19

5 For though I be absent in the flesh, yet am I with you in the spirit, joying and beholding your order, and the steadfastness of your faith in Christ.

6 As ye have therefore received Christ Jesus the Lord, so walk ye in him:

7 Rooted and built up in him, and stablished in the faith, as ye have been taught, abounding therein with thanksgiving.

8 Beware lest any man spoil you through philosophy and vain deceit, after the tradition of men, after the rudiments of the world, and not after Christ.

9 For in him dwelleth all the fulness of the Godhead bodily.

10 And ye are complete in him, which is the head of all principality and power:

11 In whom also ye are circumcised with the circumcision made without hands, in putting off the body of the sins of the flesh by the circumcision of Christ:

12 Buried with him in baptism, wherein also ye are risen with him through the faith of the operation of God, who hath raised him from the dead.

13 And you, being dead in your sins and the uncircumcision of your flesh, hath he quickened together with him, having forgiven you all trespasses;

14 Blotting out the handwriting of ordinances that was against us, which was contrary to us, and took it out of the way, nailing it to his cross;

15 And having spoiled principalities and powers, he made a show of them openly, triumphing over them in it.

16 Let no man therefore judge you in meat, or in drink, or in respect of a holyday, or of the new moon, or of the sabbath days:

17 Which are a shadow of things to come; but the body is of Christ.

18 Let no man beguile you of your reward in a voluntary humility and worshipping of angels, intruding into those things which he hath not seen, vainly puffed up by his fleshly mind,

19 And not holding the Head, from which all the body by joints and bands having nourishment ministered, and knit together, increaseth with the increase of God.

Golden Text: As ye have therefore received Christ Jesus the Lord, so walk ye in him.—Colossians 2:6.

Following God's Purpose

Unit 2: Christ Above All

(Lessons 5-8)

Lesson Aims

This lesson is designed to help the student:

1. Realize that Christ supplies all the guidance and support we need to live and grow as Christians.
2. Faithfully follow Christ, not being turned aside by any fashionable fad.

Lesson Outline

Visual 6 of the visuals packet illustrates Paul's thoughts in verse 8. The visual is shown on page 387.

Introduction

A. Christ Above All and in All

Here is a prayer that highlights the sufficiency of Christ for times like these:

"Christ, be with me; Christ, be the one in the front and the one in the rear. Christ, be within me, below me, and above me. Be at my right hand and at my left. Be in my home, in my car, in my work, and in my leisure. Christ, be in my heart and control my emotions. Be in my mind and capture my thinking; be in my mouth and guide my speaking; be in my eye and govern my choice of what to look at. Be in my hands and touch what You would touch the way You would touch it. Be in my ears and help me listen to what You would hear and refuse to pay attention to what You wouldn't. Christ, be in my feet; and let's walk together today."

B. Lesson Background

The opening verses of Colossians 2 express Paul's deep concern for the Colossian Christians and others whom he has not met personally. He wants their hearts to be encouraged, joined closely in love, and rich in understanding of God's way. Our text begins with more details of things that concern him.

I. Some Concerns of Paul (Colossians 2:5-8)

A. For Their Faith in Christ (v. 5)

5. For though I be absent in the flesh, yet am I with you in the spirit, joying and beholding your order, and the steadfastness of your faith in Christ.

Paul is a prisoner far from the Colossians, but he rejoices as if he were with them. We all do something like that at times. While the body is in one place, the mind and emotions are somewhere else. Paul finds joy in two things among the Colossians. First is their *order.* They are well organized and disciplined, like soldiers marching together in the ranks. Then Paul rejoices at the *steadfastness* of their *faith.* Their confidence and trust are strong, not shaken by any fad, folly, or false teaching. Their steadfast faith is *in Christ,* of course. Otherwise it would not have brought such joy to Paul.

B. For Their Walk in Christ (v. 6)

6. As ye have therefore received Christ Jesus the Lord, so walk ye in him.

We take our place in Christ when we receive Him, and we show that we are in Him by the way we *walk.* That means the way we live day by day. Our walk is not just what we do on Sunday; it includes what we do every day in every situation. Our weekday activities may be different from what we do on Sunday, but we should not have a change of character. The kind of character we show on the Lord's Day should be carried through every day.

"Can two walk together, except they be agreed?" (Amos 3:3). If we are to walk in Christ, we must agree with Him about the right way to live. Are we agreeing with Him in the way we spend our money? In forgiving those who have hurt us? In caring for the poor in our communities? In letting go of prejudices? In not being nitpicky and complaining? In the way we talk? In giving our employer a full day's labor?

KEEPING AT IT

"Johnny, why haven't you mowed the lawn? It's your job, you know. You chose it yourself." His father's voice had an edge that got Johnny's attention.

"Dad, it was last fall when I chose it. It wasn't so hard then. But now it needs mowing every week. I don't have time for it."

Johnny's Dad didn't seem very much impressed. "Son, it's your job. You chose it, and I expect you to do it. If you don't, we won't have that fishing trip I promised, and you still have to choose another job to do."

Johnny did mow that lawn all summer. He got not only the promised fishing trip, but also an unexpected check as a bonus.

Paul tells the Colossians, "As you have therefore received Christ Jesus the Lord, so walk ye in Him." Remember your vows and keep at the task of living in His love and grace as you mature in your faith. When tempted to give up, keep doing each day what you committed yourself to do when you accepted Him as Lord of your life. The rewards are worth it! —W. P.

C. For Their Maturity in Christ (v. 7)

7. Rooted and built up in him, and stablished in the faith, as ye have been taught, abounding therein with thanksgiving.

Rooted refers to our beginning; *built up* to our maturing. When we plant something we expect it to take root and grow. Its growth will be of the same kind as the root. Rooted in Christ, we are to grow in Christlikeness. We must let go of concepts, priorities, feelings, activities, and practices that do not reflect our root, and we must hold to those that do.

To be *stablished* is to be strong *in the faith* that we *have been taught,* so strong that we will be unshaken in all the storms of life. *Abounding* in a faith so firm, we can find in every situation a reason for *thanksgiving.*

D. For Their Continuation in Christ (v. 8)

8. Beware lest any man spoil you through philosophy and vain deceit, after the tradition of men, after the rudiments of the world, and not after Christ.

To *spoil* is to loot or rob, as conquering troops spoil a city they have captured. There are many things in the world that are trying to rob us of our Christian faith, and so to take away our eternal life as well. Four of these spoilers are mentioned in this verse: *philosophy, vain deceit, tradition of men,* and *rudiments of the world.*

Various kinds of *philosophy* are capturing Christians today. For example, humanism teaches that there is no God above humans, that God is only an idea created by humans. This *philosophy* is running wild in many universities today. It makes fun of Christianity. It denies creation and says evolution is the way we began.

Vain deceit is any kind of teaching that produces nothing eternal. Such teaching is empty and useless. Materialism, for example, teaches that our worth is measured by how much we make, where we live, what we drive, and how much we have accumulated. Bumper stickers put it this way: "The one who dies with the most toys wins." What does he win? He loses his toys along with his life.

Tradition of men. Jesus and His disciples were criticized because they did not keep the tradition of the elders (Mark 7:5). Had Jesus kept all their traditions, perhaps they would not have crucified Him—but they would have kept Him from teaching the truth.

It is okay to have traditions; we all do. But it is not okay to condemn others because they do not value our traditions as we do. Traditions must not destroy the unity of Christ's body, the church. We have traditions about many things: the time of worship, the length of a worship service, the order of worship, the style of music, when to use the Lord's Prayer in worship, whether the choir should wear robes or not. None of these is established by the Bible. Then let none of them disturb the harmony that is taught in the Bible.

Rudiments primarily means things put in a row, and so it came to mean various bits that compose something: letters of the alphabet, basic elements of the earth, stars of the sky. Here Paul speaks of *rudiments of the world.* Perhaps he

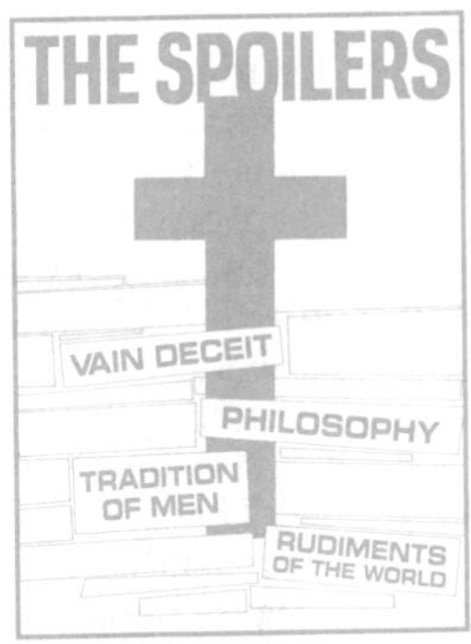

visual 6

is saying that all the worldly things that oppose Christ are rudimentary, incomplete, inadequate, insufficient. On the other hand, Christ is sufficient, as the following verses show. How silly to let any insufficient thing turn us away from Him!

II. The Character of Christ (Colossians 2:9-15)

A. He's the Fullness of God (v. 9)

9. For in him dwelleth all the fulness of the Godhead bodily.

No sentence better describes Christ's place in the world than this one. All that deity is was dwelling in Jesus Christ on earth. List all the characteristics of God—they were in Jesus. The fullness of deity did not dwell in philosophy, vain deceit, traditions of men, or rudiments of the world—but in Jesus. God was in Christ doing the miracles; God was in Christ feeding the poor; God was in Christ accepting the outcast; God was in Christ being a friend to the lonely—God was always in Christ.

B. He's Head of All (v. 10)

10. And ye are complete in him, which is the head of all principality and power.

Ye are complete in him does not mean we now are all we can be as Christians. It means that in Christ we have all we need to become all we can be. We do not need to be Jews as well as Christians; we do not need to accept some human philosophy or tradition. We need to know Christ, to follow His example and teaching, to become more like Him. He is superior to the philosophies, the traditions, and the rudiments of the world. He is *the head of all principality and power:* in Him we have the best wisdom and power there is. We need to utilize these and mature. That happens as we become less self-centered and more Christ-centered.

TO BE COMPLETE

One of the problems many pastors and counselors hear is this: "Something is lacking in my life. I just don't feel fulfilled." In many ways people are trying to be "fulfilled" and feel good about themselves.

A Korean orphan, who had experienced loss and rejection, and was later adopted into a Christian family in Oregon, expressed the feeling very well: "I never knew my parents. The first family that took me decided they didn't want me. That decision left a 'hole' in me nothing could fill for a long time. Then you came to get me, and I was afraid you wouldn't want me either. But you said, "I hope you are as excited about today as we are. We have waited a long time to have a son. You are the answer to our prayers. We love you, Son." The boy and his mother and dad put their arms around each other and cried.

Later the adopted boy said, "I've never felt alone or rejected again, but it took a long time for the 'hole' in me to be filled."

To be complete, all of us need the "holes" in our lives filled. Paul says in Jesus is all of God, and all we need to be whole. We are "complete in Him." It's a wonderful feeling. Share it with others.

—W. P.

C. He Includes the Outsiders (v. 11)

11. In whom also ye are circumcised with the circumcision made without hands, in putting off the body of the sins of the flesh by the circumcision of Christ.

Circumcision is a term the Jews used to mean God's people. If you were circumcised, you were one of God's. If you were not circumcised, you were not one of His (Ephesians 2:11, 12).

Here the apostle Paul indicates that anyone who is in Christ belongs to God, regardless of their race, IQ, nationality, gender, or denominational affiliation. *The circumcision of Christ* is not a surgical operation; it is forgiveness that gets rid of *the sins of the flesh.* That makes us God's people, regardless of how far from God we were before.

D. He Raises the Dead (v. 12)

12. Buried with him in baptism, wherein also ye are risen with him through the faith of the operation of God, who hath raised him from the dead.

Our first "resurrection" came through *baptism.* In it we were *buried* because we were dead to sin, and from it we were raised to a new life (Romans 6:1-4). Our second resurrection will come when Jesus appears again. In our first resurrection, we were raised *with* Him; in the second resurrection, we will be raised *to* Him (1 Thessalonians 4:16, 17).

E. He Forgives (v. 13)

13. And you, being dead in your sins and the uncircumcision of your flesh, hath he quickened together with him, having forgiven you all trespasses.

Quickened means *made alive.* Before we died to sin (Romans 6:2), we were *dead in* our *sins,* as we read in our text. But God made us alive by forgiving our sins upon our faith, repentance, and baptism (Acts 2:38). Thus we are reconciled, justified, forgiven, redeemed, cleansed, saved. As stated here in verses 12 and 13, God, who raised Jesus from the dead, has forgiven us and made us alive *together with him.* But God saves us through Christ, and so we can say also that Christ raises the dead and Christ forgives. He has not forgiven just a few of our sins, but *all trespasses.* Since Christ has forgiven us, we should be quick to forgive others also. Remember, Christ now lives in us.

F. He Liberates From Legalism (v. 14)

14. Blotting out the handwriting of ordinances that was against us, which was contrary to us, and took it out of the way, nailing it to his cross.

The laws of the Old Covenant were nailed to the cross with Christ. We no longer live in legalism, but in love; not in fear but in faith; not in hopelessness but in hopefulness.

Does that mean we can live any way we wish, since the rules and regulations have been nailed to the cross? Of course not. We do not live according to law, but we do live according to Christ. The law is reduced to a four-letter word—l-o-v-e. Since love does no harm to another person, love fulfills the law (Romans 13:8-10).

But be careful, because love requires more than law does. For instance, the law said, "Thou shall not commit murder," but love is not even angry with his brother (Matthew 5:21, 22). The law says, "Do not commit adultery," but Christ teaches us not even to look at another in lust (Matthew 5:27, 28).

We are not free to do anything bad; we are free to live godly lives filled with the fruit of the Spirit (Galatians 5:22, 23) because God's Spirit lives in us, not because of commands outside of us. It is not that we now have the right to do as we please, but because of the indwelling Spirit we now please to do what is right.

G. He Triumphs Over All (v. 15)

15. And having spoiled principalities and powers, he made a show of them openly, triumphing over them in it.

The *principalities and powers* refer to the evil forces—the devil and his demons. When Christ died to take away our sins, He wiped out what the devil worked in. When He arose from the grave, His victory over death was a victory over all the powers of earth and Hell that oppose Him. They are defeated; He is triumphant!

But be careful! The devil still can tempt us, influence us, lure us, entice us. He is like a lion seeking whom he may devour (1 Peter 5:8): But our victorious God holds him in check. God will not let any temptation be more than we can resist (1 Corinthians 10:13). If we give way, it is our own fault. If we trust in Christ and do our best, the devil is helpless against us.

III. Christian Commitment (Colossians 2:16-19)

A. Don't Depend on a Shadow (vv. 16-18)

16. Let no man therefore judge you in meat, or in drink, or in respect of a holyday, or of the new moon, or of the sabbath days.

Some Jewish Christians wanted all Christians to keep the old Jewish laws of diet and of special days. The church had decided that it was not necessary (Acts 15:1-31), but some still insisted. Most of us do not face exactly the same problem now, but still many earnest Christians judge our Christianity by our observance of rules of conduct not stated in the New Testament: Don't shop on Sunday. Don't go to movies. Don't watch television. Probably you know of others.

Paul says, *Let no man therefore judge you* by such standards. Of course we can't keep others from forming judgments in their own minds, but we need not accept their judgment and be bound by their rules. We need to study the life and teaching of Jesus and decide for ourselves what is pleasing to Him. As Paul wrote in another place, "Let every man be fully persuaded in his own mind" (Romans 14:5).

17. Which are a shadow of things to come; but the body is of Christ.

The Old Testament regulations were *a shadow.* A shadow is not permanent, but in its time it more or less imperfectly represents the real thing. The Old Testament rules foreshadowed the rule of Christ, under which we do His will without a host of minute rules. The many rules that Christians make now are a shadow of Christ's government, an attempt to define His will in more detail than it is defined in His Word. We may do well to examine any such rule thoughtfully. Is it a valid expression of Christ's will as we see it in the Scriptures? But *the body* is that of *Christ.* He is the real thing; His Word is always valid.

18. Let no man beguile you of your reward in a voluntary humility and worshipping of angels, intruding into those things which he hath not seen, vainly puffed up by his fleshly mind.

Voluntary humility aptly names the attitude of one who makes his own minute rules and lives by them. He is humble in submitting to them even if it requires some sacrifice; but his humility is *voluntary:* it is according to his own will.

We have no information about the *worshipping of angels* in Colossae. Possibly some Christians thought they were more humble and pious because they offered worship to angels as well as to God. Or possibly they claimed to imitate the worship offered by angels, and therefore thought they were more pious than others.

Intruding into those things which he hath not seen is no less puzzling. As we see it in the *King James Version*, it seems to suggest that a man is claiming to know about things that no one knows, such as the way angels worship. But the word *not* is missing in so many of the ancient manuscripts that some versions read, *Dwelling in those things he has seen.* Some students take this to describe a man who claims to see visions or special revelations; others take it to mean one who claims to be scientific and to believe only what he can see. At least the last phrase of the verse is clear. We are reading about a man who is *vainly puffed up by his fleshly mind.* Whatever piety this fellow pretends, he is really a conceited, egotistical man with his unspiritual mind set on his own power or profit or pleasure. Look out for him! If you fall for his line, he will *beguile you,* lead you away from your allegiance to Christ, make you his follower; and you will lose *your reward* in Heaven. Or perhaps, as some students think, the first part of the verse means, *Let no man deny you your reward.* This is similar to "Let no man judge you" in verse 16. Don't let that puffed-up fellow be the referee and tell you that you can't get your reward in Heaven unless you follow him. Whatever we make of the mysterious phrases in this verse, the warning is plain: Don't be one of the thousands who flock after a puffed-up popular preacher who has some brave new idea not found in God's Word.

BEWARE OF FRAUD

Fraud by mail has become a menace. Smooth-talking salesmen on TV and telephone promise superior goods at bargain basement prices, and our desire for "a good deal" can make us victims.

For only $9.95 one ad offered something guaranteed to kill insect pests in your home. When you received your merchandise you could not deny that it would work, but all you got was a rolled-up newspaper.

Perhaps you preferred the guaranteed ant killer for only two dollars, plus postage. You received two small blocks of wood with the instructions, "Place the ant on block one and strike firmly with block two."

Unfortunately many frauds are not just inexpensive jokes, but rob older persons of their life savings.

Paul writes about similar cheating in the Spiritual realm: "Let no man beguile you of your reward." Schemes of salvation are frauds if they offer anything instead of Christ as a way back to God. Beware lest they rob you of all you are promised in Him. —W. P.

B. Do Depend on Christ (v. 19)

19. And not holding the Head, from which all the body by joints and bands having nourishment ministered, and knit together, increaseth with the increase of God.

Not holding the Head. Here is the basic fault of the fellow described in verse 18. He has let go of Christ in order to glorify himself. How do we answer him and all the people who condemn us, criticize us, put us down because we do not hold their traditions and teachings? We simply hold to the Head, Jesus.

Not only are we joined to the Head; we are also *knit together.* All of us are the *joints and bands,* the parts of Christ's body, the church. We are united to each other; we ought to be nourishing each other.

Be committed to Christ, not customs. Be committed to fellow Christians without being committed to all their traditions. As we do that, we can grow into the likeness of Christ. That is how we increase *with the increase of God.*

Home Daily Bible Readings

Monday, July 5—Christ Reveals God's Treasures (Colossians 2:1-7)

Tuesday, July 6—God's Fulness Dwells in Christ (Colossians 2:8-15)

Wednesday, July 7—Christ Is Head of the Church (Colossians 2:16-23)

Thursday, July 8—Christ Frees Us From Slavery (Galatians 5:1-12)

Friday, July 9—Christ Fulfilled the Scriptures (1 Corinthians 15:3-8)

Saturday, July 10—Christ Is God's Word to Us (Hebrews 1:1-13)

Sunday, July 11—Christ Is Our Perfect High Priest (Hebrews 7:23-28)

Conclusion

A. Unity, Liberty, and Love

Augustine said it, but Alexander Campbell popularized it. It is a slogan that should have a place in all our lives: "In essentials unity, in non-essentials liberty, in all things love."

B. Prayer

Father, help us to grow so that we can see how sufficient and how complete is Your fullness in Jesus, and then open us to the truth of Your fullness in our lives. Amen.

C. Thought to Remember

"In him dwelleth all the fulness of the Godhead."

Learning by Doing

This page contains an alternate lesson plan emphasizing learning activities. Classes desiring such student involvement will find these suggestions helpful.

Learning Goals

Students in today's class should:

1. Discover several characteristics that make Christ and His teachings unique and above all others.
2. Refute several false ideas that diminish the superiority of Christ and His way.
3. Evaluate whether and how they have put Christ above all in their lives.

Into the Lesson

Before class, prepare five flash cards; on each write one of the following words: *He, Is, All, I,* and *Need.* In the week before this class session, collect newspaper or magazine advertisements that show how our society seeks after many solutions and satisfactions other than Christ for life's problems. The ads may portray the pursuit of wealth, of knowledge, or of status. You may find an ad for a cult or humanistic self-help seminar or book.

Bring these ads to class for a display on a bulletin board or one wall of your classroom. Mount them, with the five flash cards scattered among them so that the sentence, "He is all I need," is scrambled.

To begin today's session, ask students to get up from their seats if necessary and examine the ads. What do the ads indicate about the values and priorities of our society? What are people today seeking?

Do not mention the five flash cards at first. See if a class member looks at them and figures out the sentence they make. Discuss with your class, "Does our society believe what the flash cards say? Is Jesus enough for people today? Do we Christians really believe He is enough for us?"

Today's lesson builds on last week's study by listing attributes of Christ and calling us to make Him first and to rely on Him alone.

Into the Word

Recall what things in last week's lesson showed that Jesus is unique. Tell class members to look for more ways He is unique as someone reads today's text aloud.

After the Scripture reading, ask class members to share a few characteristics of Christ they heard. Point out that Paul is encouraging the Colossians to depend on Christ instead of anything else—any other person, idea, or philosophy.

Focus on verse 8: The commentary in this book describes the *philosophy, vain deceit, tradition of men,* and *rudiments of the world* that Paul tells the Colossians to avoid.

Divide the class into thirds. Each third should concentrate on one of the first three items in this list: philosophy, vain deceit, or tradition of men. Ask students to discuss, in twos or threes, how people today follow these instead of Christ. Then you can use comments from this book to explain "rudiments of the world."

Next, look at the following list of ideas. (The list is also printed in the student book for your students' convenience.) Ask class members, probably in twos or threes, to refute each idea on the list with teaching from our text. They should list the verse reference of the teaching beside each idea, and then write a sentence that contradicts the idea and summarizes the truth presented in Colossians. (To help you, the verse references are printed below, as well as a sample correct sentence for number 1.)

1. Jesus was a good man, but nothing more (v. 9). (All the fullness of the divine nature is in Jesus.)
2. If I'm good enough, God will let me go to Heaven without believing in Jesus (vv. 10-13).
3. Baptism has no connection with salvation (vv. 12, 13).
4. There are many paths to Heaven (vv. 8-10).
5. We can find satisfaction enough in the philosophies and traditions of humankind (v. 8).
6. The essence of Christianity is what we do *not* do (vv. 20-23).

Into Life

After refuting each of the above false statements, discuss some or all of these questions:

1. Why is it easier to follow philosophies, traditions, or the ideas of human beings than to trust Christ?
2. Of the four categories listed in our study of verse 8, which do you think is the most influential today? Why?
3. How has one of these ever threatened to take Christ's place in your priority list?
4. How would today's discussion help you encourage or advise someone trapped by one of these false priorities?
5. How has today's study caused you to reevaluate where you are putting your trust?

Let's Talk It Over

The questions on this page are designed to encourage review of the lesson Scriptures and to promote discussion of the lesson by the class. The answers provided are only discussion starters. Let your class talk it over from there.

1. How is order important to the Christian life and to the growth of the church?

Paul was glad to see the order of the Colossians. *Order* was a word used of the disciplined array of soldiers in the ranks. A well-ordered, disciplined life is most effective in self-improvement as in other efforts. Christian growth usually consists of many small changes that come through regular, orderly habits of prayer, Bible reading, and efforts to live by the Bible. Each of the changes is almost imperceptible, but together they add up to a major transformation as we grow to become more Christlike. The analogy applies to congregations as well. Churches that experience disorder very seldom grow.

2. Paul calls us to be rooted in Christ. How does the analogy of a plant's roots apply to the success of our Christian life?

The roots of a plant are unseen, but they keep the plant alive. A shallow root system supports a puny plant. The roots must grow with the plant as it matures. Without such growth a plant can never reach its potential.

As the root system of a plant is unseen, so are the spiritual roots of the Christian life. They connect the unseen inner person with the unseen Savior. Christians must take care that this part of their spiritual being is developing so that they will be able to remain healthy in their quest for maturity.

3. How can Paul say we have put off the sins of the flesh when we know we still struggle with the same sins that plagued us before we were baptized?

We all know that baptism, forgiveness, and the gift of God's Spirit do not mean we will never be tempted again. After we have been forgiven, sooner or later we will face the temptation to return to sin once more. When we turn to Christ, however, we receive an added power to resist the old temptations. This added power gives us the ability to conquer even the strongest temptations, but the victory may come with a great struggle. We need to approach each struggle with faith in the power of God, but also with our own determined effort. Biblical writers admonish us to act like what we really are, children of God. We have been bought with a price, and we must learn to live for the One who now owns us (1 Corinthians 6:20).

4. If we are no longer bound by law, where do we find a standard for our moral life?

The law that was nailed to the cross was the covenant that God gave to Moses. Christ replaced it with a New Covenant by which sins are forgiven (Jeremiah 31:31-34). The moral standards of the New Covenant are as plain as those of the Old Covenant, but the emphasis is moved from outward acts to the thoughts and intents of the heart. The law forbade murder; Jesus said danger lies in anger that can lead to murder. The law forbade adultery; Jesus warned against lust (Matthew 5:21, 22, 27, 28). Right actions flow from a right heart. We are to learn the broad principles by which Jesus lived. These principles are plain in the New Testament. They will produce right actions in accord with the ethical standard of God.

5. Where is the responsibility for personal growth as a Christian?

I have heard Christians say they are not growing because they are not being fed. They place the responsibility for their spiritual growth upon the church, a Bible-school class, or the preacher. Leaders do have a responsibility to "feed the flock of God" (1 Peter 5:2), but our text makes it clear that each person also is responsible for his or her own growth. When our relationship with Christ is right, God causes natural growth to come to members of the body (v. 19). If we are not growing properly, perhaps we should think about our personal walk with God.

6. Why is it important that we understand the basis of our Christian faith?

There has always been a struggle for the minds of men. Verses 8 and 16-18 describe that struggle in Paul's day. In our time we have seen communist leaders trying to control the thinking of their people by force. Many other mistaken philosophies are trying to win control with persuasion. It is important for us to understand that our Christian faith is firmly grounded in facts. Jesus showed himself to be the Son of God by His miraculous power. We can trust His Word and example to lead us in God's way.

Life in Christ

July 18
Lesson 7

DEVOTIONAL READING: 1 Corinthians 12:12-26.

LESSON SCRIPTURE: Colossians 3.

PRINTED TEXT: Colossians 3:1-17.

Colossians 3:1-17

1 If ye then be risen with Christ, seek those things which are above, where Christ sitteth on the right hand of God.

2 Set your affection on things above, not on things on the earth.

3 For ye are dead, and your life is hid with Christ in God.

4 When Christ, who is our life, shall appear, then shall ye also appear with him in glory.

5 Mortify therefore your members which are upon the earth; fornication, uncleanness, inordinate affection, evil concupiscence, and covetousness, which is idolatry:

6 For which things' sake the wrath of God cometh on the children of disobedience:

7 In the which ye also walked sometime, when ye lived in them.

8 But now ye also put off all these; anger, wrath, malice, blasphemy, filthy communication out of your mouth.

9 Lie not one to another, seeing that ye have put off the old man with his deeds;

10 And have put on the new man, which is renewed in knowledge after the image of him that created him:

11 Where there is neither Greek nor Jew, circumcision nor uncircumcision, Barbarian, Scythian, bond nor free: but Christ is all, and in all.

12 Put on therefore, as the elect of God, holy and beloved, bowels of mercies, kindness, humbleness of mind, meekness, longsuffering;

13 Forbearing one another, and forgiving one another, if any man have a quarrel against any: even as Christ forgave you, so also do ye.

14 And above all these things put on charity, which is the bond of perfectness.

15 And let the peace of God rule in your hearts, to the which also ye are called in one body; and be ye thankful.

16 Let the word of Christ dwell in you richly in all wisdom; teaching and admonishing one another in psalms and hymns and spiritual songs, singing with grace in your hearts to the Lord.

17 And whatsoever ye do in word or deed, do all in the name of the Lord Jesus, giving thanks to God and the Father by him.

GOLDEN TEXT: Put on the new man, which is renewed in knowledge after the image of him that created him.—Colossians 3:10.

Following God's Purpose

Unit 2: Christ Above All

(Lessons 5-8)

Lesson Aims

The study of this lesson is designed to help the student:

1. Identify essential characteristics of a life in Christ.
2. Evaluate his or her own life in the light of those characteristics.
3. Become more like Christ.

Lesson Outline

INTRODUCTION
- A. Living in Your Environment
- B. Lesson Background

I. A NEW WAY OF LIFE (Colossians 3:1-4)
- A. Higher Aims (vv. 1-3)
  - *Look Up!*
- B. Higher Hope (v. 4)

II. AVOID THE BAD (Colossians 3:5-9)
- A. Sexual Sins and Greed (vv. 5-7)
- B. Bad Attitudes and Evil Talk (v. 8)
- C. Dishonesty (v. 9)
  - *Life in Christ*

III. EMBRACE THE GOOD (Colossians 3:10-17)
- A. God's Image (v. 10)
- B. Christian Attitudes (vv. 11-14)
  - *A New Garb*
- C. Christian Living (vv. 15-17)

CONCLUSION
- A. The Father Is Not Blind
- B. Prayer
- C. Thought to Remember

Visual 7 of the visuals packet illustrates verse 17 of the text. The visual is shown on page 397.

Introduction

A. Living in Your Environment

Suddenly all heads turned toward one spot on the pier overlooking the Pacific Ocean. It was apparent that a man had a big one on his hook—a real fighter! The rod was bent, and the line was tight. After a lot of persistence, the fisherman finally brought the fish close enough to the surface for us to see it. What a catch! It must have been six feet long!

The fisherman walked slowly toward the shore to beach his catch, but the fish was not about to give up. It fought with unbelievable energy every inch of the way. Finally the fisherman was able to pull it out of the water.

Then something interesting happened. The fish quit fighting. The longer it was out of the water, the weaker it became. The fish needed to be in the water to survive.

As a fish cannot survive anywhere except in the water, a Christian cannot exist as a Christian except "in Christ." Christ is the proper environment for Christians. The devil wants to "beach" us. He wants to drag us to a way of life that is out of Christ. If he can do that, we rapidly grow weaker.

B. Lesson Background

In Colossians 2, Paul wrote that we who were dead in sins were buried with Christ in baptism and then raised in Christ, so that we were made alive again (Colossians 2:12, 13). Colossians 3 stresses our growth following this rebirth, our new character in our new condition, our new function following our forgiveness.

I. A New Way of Life (Colossians 3:1-4)

A. Higher Aims (vv. 1-3)

1. If ye then be risen with Christ, seek those things which are above, where Christ sitteth on the right hand of God.

Risen refers to our resurrection to a new life at baptism (Colossians 2:12). Since we are *risen with Christ,* we have new aims for our new life. Christ *sitteth on the right hand of God:* He is in the immediate and intimate presence of God. Our aim is to live in the same way we would live if we also were in the immediate and intimate presence of God—as indeed we are. We *seek those things which are above:* we try to copy the life-style of Heaven.

2. Set your affection on things above, not on things on the earth.

The Greek word for *affection* usually refers to thinking, and some versions have *mind* instead. But we are seeking the things above (v. 1) as well as thinking about them. They are in our affection as well as in our mind. The devil is after our minds and affections, but we give them rather to *things above.* We place them where our treasure is—with Christ in Heaven—there is where our affections and thinking should be focused. It is true that we will become whatever we set our minds to.

3. For ye are dead, and your life is hid with Christ in God.

Again we see the profound meaning of baptism. We were dead in our sins; we were buried in baptism; we were made alive again—but the sinners we used to be *are dead* still. Now we live a new kind of life, a life that *is hid with Christ in God.* This statement stresses at least two important truths: (1) We have security and safety with Christ. Have you ever hidden something to keep it safe? With Christ we are hidden from condemnation. (2) We have resources available to us. To be hidden with Christ does not mean isolation from the world, but involvement in the world in a different way. Having died to the world's way of life, we now draw inspiration and guidance and power from the Christ with whom we live.

The world cannot understand how Christ could love His enemies, not retaliate against violence, and forgive; and the world cannot understand the kind of life we live. Our deepest resources for living in a non-Christian society are hidden—they are with Christ in God.

LOOK UP!

The Center for European Renewal Ministries in the Selly Oak Colleges is carefully examining all facets of church life to find the key to restoration of Christian leadership in "post-Christian Europe." These studies seek to penetrate the apathy of secular society and call people once more to Christ and the church.

Dr. Dan Beebe, of Birmingham, England, is one of the leaders in rethinking how the church can once again reach the western world where Christian influence and the church are declining. In a talk at Selly Oak in 1990, Dr. Beebe made the remark that the hardest step in making a commitment to Biblical renewal is the reconversion of the mind. Having been schooled in liberal theology and Biblical criticism, theologians find it hard to accept the truth of the gospel and the historic reality of Jesus Christ. This acceptance, he intimated, is the first step towards reconversion and commitment to evangelism and remolding western secular society.

Besides accepting the Bible accounts of Jesus' life and teaching, theologians and all the rest of us need to follow Paul's direction: "Set your affection [or your mind, or your heart] on things above, not on things on the earth." Until we turn away from the non-Christian climate in our western world thought, we will not live the life or give the witness of Jesus that can change the world of which we are a part. —W. P.

B. Higher Hope (v. 4)

4. When Christ, who is our life, shall appear, then shall ye also appear with him in glory.

Our inner resource that now is hidden will become known to all: *Christ . . . shall appear.* All will see Him and honor Him. Paul has turned from the past ("ye are dead") to the present ("your life is hid") and to the future (then shall ye also appear with him). We were buried with Christ in baptism; we were raised with Christ through baptism; we will appear with Christ in glory. All the tribes of earth will see Him coming "with power and great glory" (Matthew 24:30). With Him in glory will be the Christians who have died and those still living at His coming (1 Thessalonians 4:16, 17).

Christians do not place their hope on things around them that they can see, but on what they cannot see—the future. They know the future belongs to Christ and the Heavenly Father. When Jesus comes, the resources that the world cannot understand will be made plain. We who now are growing into His likeness will find our growth complete. "We shall be like him" (1 John 3:1-3). But we cannot live without Him now and expect to become like Him then. If our hope is to become like Him, we are in a daily process of growing into His likeness now.

II. Avoid the Bad (Colossians 3:5-9)

A. Sexual Sins and Greed (vv. 5-7)

5. Mortify therefore your members which are upon the earth; fornication, uncleanness, inordinate affection, evil concupiscence, and covetousness, which is idolatry.

To have our aim, our emotions, thinking, and life focused on Him in Heaven with the anticipation that we will be transformed totally into His character means we will be in the process of being transformed in the here and now. To put our minds on heavenly things is to release our minds from the priority of earthly things.

The first century was saturated with sexual perversions, as is the twentieth century. The Christ-filled life cannot have any part with evil things, however pleasant they may be. We must *mortify*—put to death—the non-Christian lifestyle. We are to demonstrate outwardly the radical change that has taken place inwardly. Our new position in Christ is to be seen by our new practices on earth.

Putting on Christ is accompanied by putting off what is Christ-less. *Mortify . . . your members* means we will not allow the desires of our physical bodies to control us. We are to control them instead. We are to determine what our eyes will look at and what our hands will touch; and the decision is to be according to the inner resources of Christ, not according to the temporary desires of our bodies. While our physical bodies can make us vulnerable, the inner Christ can make us victorious.

Fornication and *uncleanness* are sexual sins. *Inordinate affection* and *evil concupiscence* are the passionate lust and evil desire that lead to such sins. *Covetousness* is a greedy desire for more, either of sensual pleasure or of money and property. It is *idolatry* because it puts something else above God, because it allows something else to control what one does.

6. For which things' sake the wrath of God cometh on the children of disobedience:

If we who become Christians are not motivated to change their practices because of his new position, there is another motivation to consider—*the wrath of God.* We will reap what we sow (Galatians 6:7-9). This does not mean we need to live our lives in fear of being lost, but it does mean there are serious consequences if the Christian repudiates his new position and new practice.

7. In the which ye also walked sometime, when ye lived in them.

The sins named in verse 5 are not condemned by heathen standards, and many of the Colossian Christians had once been heathen. The apostle Paul reminds them that they have made a reversal of life-style, and they should stay on the new pathway. We must not allow our past life-style outside of Christ to determine our present life-style in Christ. We have made a change; now we are to show it.

B. Bad Attitudes and Evil Talk (v. 8)

8. But now ye also put off all these; anger, wrath, malice, blasphemy, filthy communication out of your mouth.

But now we are not heathen. We have made a reversal, and we are to live changed lives. *Put off* is what we do to dirty clothes. One of the ancient baptismal rituals was to discard a person's old clothes and put on a new robe. Today we do not throw away the clothes, but often we do put on clean baptismal robes. Whether that happens or not, there is a taking off and putting on. We put off negative attitudes—*anger, wrath,* and *malice*—that cause the sins of speech—*blasphemy* and *filthy communication. Blasphemy* means slandering God and others. *Filthy communication* refers to abusive speech that hurts others. Words that wound people are flooding the world with a deluge of destruction.

C. Dishonesty (v. 9)

9. Lie not one to another, seeing that ye have put off the old man with his deeds.

In the fifties a popular song was entitled, "The Great Pretender." Sometimes that can describe us. Judas was a "great pretender" while staying in the fellowship of the apostles. To give up dishonesty is to admit our weaknesses instead of projecting a false image of being strong, to admit our sins instead of leading others to think we are pure, and to admit to others that their actions hurt us instead of pretending we aren't bothered. We are not to cover up our weaknesses or sins with our lies, but rather to depend on God to cover them with his love and power.

LIFE IN CHRIST

Fulton J. Sheen once said, "We want to be saved, but not from our sins. . . . We are willing to be saved from poverty, from war, from ignorance, from disease, from economic insecurity; such types of salvation leave our individual whims and passions and concupiscences untouched."

As Shakespeare wrote, "Aye, there's the rub!" We all want redemption, renewal, new life—but shun the responsibility such change carries along with its blessings.

Being a new person is the exciting result of coming to Jesus. However, being a new person also demands "putting off" the old one. This transformation of the outward way of life is based on a corresponding transformation of inner character.

When my son was just a boy objecting to baths, he made this classic observation: "Dad, you can make me bathe, but you can't keep me clean unless I decide I want to be." All of us are somewhat like that. Jesus does cleanse us from all sin, but He does not keep us clean unless we want to be. We must decide to be the "new man" He has made it possible for us to be. Paul said, "Lie not one to another, seeing that ye have put off the old man with his deeds; and have put on the new man, which is renewed in knowledge after the image of him that created him." He also lists some other things that are to be abandoned, along with lying, and some good things that are to be a part of our life. We need to exert ourselves to be what we have been made in Jesus.

—W. P.

III. Embrace the Good (Colossians 3:10-17)

A. God's Image (v. 10)

10. And have put on the new man, which is renewed in knowledge after the image of him that created him.

The *new man* is God's restoration of us to our original created nature—"in the image of God" (Genesis 1:27). God created us in His likeness, but sin shattered that likeness. When we are born again, God renews His divine nature in us and we are referred to as "new creatures" (2 Corinthians 5:17).

God is not finished with us yet. We continue to progress in our nature. One of the first steps is to increase *knowledge:* to know more of God's nature, so we can allow His nature to grow in us.

B. Christian Attitudes (vv. 11-14)

11. Where there is neither Greek nor Jew, circumcision nor uncircumcision, Barbarian, Scythian, bond nor free: but Christ is all, and in all.

Anyone who is in Christ and who has been restored to God's image is in the same fellowship as all others, regardless of the church he or she attends. In spite of our racial identity (*Greek nor Jew*), our religious past (*circumcision nor uncircumcision*), our economic status (*bond nor free*), we are kin to each other because *Christ* is in us all. We have been created to have fellowship not only with God, but also with one another (1 John 1:3). We should lay aside our prejudices and maintain our bond of unity in the spirit of peace and love.

12. Put on therefore, as the elect of God, holy and beloved, bowels of mercies, kindness, humbleness of mind, meekness, long-suffering.

The virtues in this verse are social lubricants that keep our unity functioning within the fellowship of God's family. *Bowels of mercies* means loving compassion or sympathy. We would say, "a heart of mercy"; but some of the ancients supposed that such a feeling came from the "insides" in general rather than from the heart. *Kindness* means being polite and considerate. *Humbleness of mind* emphasizes being a willing servant of others. *Meekness* means being gentle. *Long-suffering* refers to putting up with the oddities and differences that we find in other people. While these may sound simple, they are indispensable in Christian cooperation and fellowship. Each of these is a mark of strength, not weakness.

13. Forbearing one another, and forgiving one another, if any man have a quarrel against any: even as Christ forgave you, so also do ye.

Forbearing and *forgiving* come from a disposition toward reconciliation rather than revenge, toward friendship rather than factions, toward sweetness rather than schisms. We are to end a quarrel by forgiving another person, even though that person may have been wrong. *Even as Christ forgave you, so also do ye.* It is cruel and coldhearted to refuse forgiveness to someone who has repented of wrongdoing. To do so is to put that person out in the cold. It is as inhumane to do that in our attitude as it would be to do so in a literal sense.

14. And above all these things put on charity, which is the bond of perfectness.

visual 7

Charity is not just giving to the poor. It is Christ's kind of love in us and expressed through us. It keeps us bound together when the devil wants to divide us. It is *the bond of perfectness* or maturity because it holds us together and enables us to help each other mature properly, becoming more like Christ.

A NEW GARB

Dress appropriate to their style of living was a fetish of the flower people and street people of the late sixties and the seventies. Blue jeans, faded, worn, patched, and labeled were "in"; or a dress that did not fit would do. Poor-fitting shoes or none at all were in style, along with headbands, protest slogans, and slovenly personal care. If you were not so garbed, you were part of the establishment and foreign to the protest movement that swept America in those sad but exciting days.

Helen was a flower child with whom some Christian students shared Christ and their new life, hope, and future in Him. Jesus captured Helen's heart, and she turned to Him. After she was baptized, her old way of dress vanished.

When Helen was asked about the change, her answer was a joy to hear. "Since Jesus cleaned me up inside I felt I needed to clean up outside. Where I hated, protested, and lived on the lowest level, I now love, share Jesus, and have determined to be as near like my Lord as I can. Since I'm His new creation, I need a new garb so those around me can see as well as hear the change Jesus brought into my life."

Don't all our changed hearts need a new garb of Christian action that expresses love and honors Jesus in all we are, say, and do? —W. P.

C. Christian Living (vv. 15-17)

15. And let the peace of God rule in your hearts, to the which also ye are called in one body; and be ye thankful.

The *peace of God* is to fill our *hearts* and be the controlling motive for our actions and reactions with one another in the family of God. God has called us into *one body,* and He is not pleased when we split that body with our disagreements. The body of Christ has only one head, and the head should have only one body.

All of us should ask ourselves if peace is a motivating factor in our relationships. Would we rather fight than be flexible? Would we rather be obnoxious than be optimistic about another's ideas? Would we rather dictate to others than to accept the diversity that God has put within His body?

16. Let the word of Christ dwell in you richly in all wisdom; teaching and admonishing one another in psalms and hymns and spiritual songs, singing with grace in your hearts to the Lord.

The *word of Christ* is not just what He spoke with His own lips; it is also what He showed by His way of living, and what was taught by His inspired apostles and prophets when He was no longer teaching personally on earth. That word is to live in us. Jesus is the Word (John 1:1). That Word became flesh, and lived so nobly that people could see in Him the nature of the Father (John 14:9). God's nature should be reflected again in what we say and what we do. It is not enough just to put *the word of Christ* in our memory banks. *Wisdom* includes the moral discretion to use *the word of Christ* properly, both to guide our lives and to instruct one another. With wisdom we not only make the right kind of moral decisions, but we also are to be *teaching and admonishing one another.* One of the ways to do that is through our singing. We are not to sing just anything, but we are to lift up the majesty of God, the love of Christ, the fellowship of the Holy Spirit, and the encouragement of one another. By the time we finish singing, more grace should be in our hearts.

17. And whatsoever ye do in word or deed, do all in the name of the Lord Jesus, giving thanks to God and the Father by him.

To do something in the name of Jesus is to do it by His authority, because it is what He wants us to do, because it is the kind of thing He would do, because it brings honor to Him. As His people, we are to live in such a way that we do not embarrass Him, but exalt Him. To live in the name of Christ is to take John the Baptist's position: "He must increase, but I must decrease" (John 3:30). We put aside the way we would do things, and practice the way Jesus would do them.

This does not apply to what we do in church only, but to *whatsoever ye do.* That means at our work places, in our homes, in our leisure time, in our reading, in our purchases, in the payment of our debts, in our commitments, in our fellowship—in *whatsoever ye do.* If we are "in Christ," there is no corner of our lives that is outside of Him. Therefore, we need to manifest His style continually.

Conclusion

A. The Father Is Not Blind

A mediocre football player made his college team, but seldom had a chance to play. In midseason he was called home by the death of his father. When he came back, he begged the coach to put him in the game. Because the boy was so clumsy, the coach continued to refuse. During the last quarter, however, he finally gave in. That young player made two touchdowns in flawless plays.

After the football game, the coach asked him about his tremendous success. The boy responded, "Coach, my father has been blind all of my life. You know he died last week. Today is the first time he has ever been able to watch me play."

Our Father in Heaven takes a great deal of pride in watching us live out our Christianity on the field of life.

B. Prayer

Thank You, Heavenly Father, for not giving up on us. Thank You for Your compassion, kindness, gentleness, and patience. May You see yourself reflected in us. In the precious name of Jesus we pray. Amen.

C. Thought to Remember

Put off the old person with his deeds, and put on the new person, renewed after the image of God.

Home Daily Bible Readings

Monday, July 12—Put On the New Nature in Christ (Colossians 3:1-11)

Tuesday, July 13—Let Christ's Word Dwell in You (Colossians 3:12-17)

Wednesday, July 14—Serve the Lord Christ (Colossians 3:18-25)

Thursday, July 15—Be Steadfast in Prayer (Colossians 4:1-6)

Friday, July 16—Encourage One Another in Christ (Colossians 4:7-11)

Saturday, July 17—Know and Do God's Will (Colossians 4:12-18)

Sunday, July 18—A Great Variety, but One God (1 Corinthians 12:1-11)

Learning by Doing

This page contains an alternate lesson plan emphasizing learning activities. Classes desiring such student involvement will find these suggestions helpful.

Learning by Doing

As students participate in today's class session, they should:

1. Identify the practical commands of Paul in Colossians 3:1-17.
2. Summarize his teaching in verses 1-4, 5-9, and 10-17.
3. Choose at least one command they can obey more completely in the coming days.

Into the Lesson

Point students to the section of the student book titled, "What Is the Problem?" The following monologues are printed there for students to consider. For each one, they should decide what's wrong with the faith of the Christian who is speaking.

The distracted Christian. I'm glad my family is in the church. It's important to have a religious foundation. We get there often—whenever we're not traveling or busy. Yes, we do enjoy our cabin in the mountains many weekends. But when you're in a pressure cooker like my job, you have to get away now and then, don't you?

The sensual Christian. A gal from my office and I have been living together for three months. I feel guilty about not spending more time with the kids, but I think they realize I can't live with their mother. I've told her not to send any of our church friends over here to talk to me. Do I believe in God? Sure. Do I think I'm going to get to Heaven? I don't know, but I do know getting to Heaven later isn't worth living in Hell now, even if Heaven does exist.

The anti-social Christian. How about that Linda and Bill Mason! Getting to church late in their brand-new Cadillac. Wearing a new outfit every Sunday. Volunteering for every committee so they can run our little congregation. Who do they think they are, anyway? He is such a blowhard, always bragging about his promotions and commissions. And she has to have *the* most aggravating voice in the western hemisphere. Would I be sorry if they left our church? You've got to be kidding! Nothing could make me happier!

Into the Word

Ask class members to look again at today's text, this time with the above monologues in mind. Can students see how this text speaks to each of the problems these Christians are demonstrating?

Move on to a deeper look at today's text. Point students to the printed text in the student book, or duplicate Colossians 3:1-17 from a contemporary translation for them to read and mark.

Distribute the following instruction sheet, or point students to the student book where these guidelines are given:

Read through today's text silently. Note the meaning of the verses and your reaction to them by marking your copy of the passage as follows:

1. *Underline* negatives to avoid.
2. *Circle* positives to adopt.
3. *Asterisk* (*) sentences that explain the place of Christ in the Christian's life.
4. *Put a plus* (+) beside sentences that *encourage* you.
5. *Put a minus* (-) beside sentences that *discourage* you.
6. *Put a question mark* (?) beside sentences you *don't understand.*
7. *Put an exclamation mark* (!) beside sentences you need to *apply to your own life.*

Give students several minutes to do the study. Then, in an all-class discussion, list on your chalkboard all the negatives and positives class members found, followed by every reference they discovered to the place of Christ in the Christian's life.

Ask class members to share which verses encouraged or discouraged them. Ask them to tell why. Finally, ask if there are any question marks, and answer the questions if you can.

Ask the students to form themselves into groups of two or three. Write on your chalkboard the three headings from the lesson outline: New Way of Life (vv. 1-4), Avoid the Bad (vv. 5-9), and Embrace the Good (vv. 10-17). Ask the small groups to write one sentence for each heading to summarize each section of Scripture.

Into Life

Go around the room and read all the sentence summaries students have written. The cumulative effect of this should encourage and challenge class members as they share each other's insights.

Ask members to gather again into their groups of two or three to share with each other where they placed exclamation points in the margins of the text.

Close the class with a prayer time.

Let's Talk It Over

The questions on this page are designed to encourage review of the lesson Scriptures and to promote discussion of the lesson by the class. The answers provided are only discussion starters. Let your class talk it over from there.

1. How can we create an environment appropriate to our life as new creatures?

When we become Christians, we have to make adjustments—some in ourselves, and perhaps some in our surroundings. We do not want to forsake our old friends, but rather to win them to our new faith; but there may be some persons and some groups that may become so hostile to our Christian living that we will have to leave them behind along with some of our own habits. God has given us the church as an environment in which we will be helped to grow spiritually. If some of our old friends are left behind, they can be replaced by new friends, our brothers and sisters in Christ. It is very helpful when husband and wife make the decision to become Christians together. Then the home also becomes an environment that is conducive to right living and spiritual growth.

2. In describing the old man that is put off, Paul mentions several outward acts that are wrong: fornication, blasphemy, filthy talk, lying (vv. 5-9). Why do you suppose he calls attention to these rather than the motives from which the actions come?

Wrong actions do arise from impure hearts, but the hearts are not so easily seen and dealt with. We put off the old man by getting rid of the visible things—wrong actions and bad habits. In the process we conquer also the unseen motives such as covetousness, wrath, and malice. These cannot live if they are not allowed to express themselves.

3. In describing the new man we put on, Paul speaks not so much of outward actions as of unseen motives, qualities of heart and mind: mercy, humility, meekness, forbearance, charity (vv. 12-14). Why do you suppose he mentions these rather than visible acts that spring from them?

The change of heart is the vital part of conversion. We attack the bad actions of the bad heart because we can see them and stop them. But in putting on the new man we go straight to the heart of the matter. We make noble motives our own, and they naturally produce the good works of the Christian life. The transformation of the heart is the essence of conversion.

4. Why must the Christian be careful to put on the new man when the old man has been set aside?

A friend of mine quit smoking by putting something else in the place of the cigarettes he had been using. Each time he felt like reaching for a cigarette, he took a piece of a candy bar instead. He gained some weight (which he later lost) but he broke the habit by replacing his habitual action by another. It is a mistake to think we can put away wrong actions and motives without putting something else in their place. Our hearts and lives cannot be left empty. It is vital that we put on the new man to fill the place vacated when we drive the old man out.

5. What is the role of forgiveness in our new life as Christians?

One of the goals of the Christian life is to create an environment where a person's spiritual life may flourish. Enmity between two individuals is an obstacle to the inner peace of both. Hurt feelings and hatred stand between a person and true peace. Forgiveness may mean giving up what is rightfully ours or losing what is due us, but still it may be good for us because it opens the door to peace. In putting away animosity we set aside that which destroys our inner contentment. Forgiveness allows our hearts to come to rest.

6. How is our peace on earth related to our goal of eternal life?

Surveys show that the number-one desire of the American public is for inner peace. Such peace eludes many, but it comes to those who put their trust in Jesus Christ. Peace comes when we know that all is well in our relationship with God, and that we and our world are in His hand. Thus, even in times of stress and turmoil, the Christian can know inner peace. God is in control. From everything, He brings good to those who love Him (Romans 8:28). The peace that all people seek comes when we experience the salvation of God and are certain that our relationship with Him is right. Reconciliation with God is possible because the enmity caused by sin is removed by Christ's sacrifice, and we can be certain that our life is in God's hands. Thus we are assured not only of eternal life, but also of peace in our hearts and minds here and now.

Christ Unites

July 25
Lesson 8

DEVOTIONAL READING: 1 Peter 2:4-10.

LESSON SCRIPTURE: Philemon.

PRINTED TEXT: Philemon 4-21.

Philemon 4-21

4 I thank my God, making mention of thee
always in my prayers,
5 Hearing of thy love and faith, which thou
hast toward the Lord Jesus, and toward all
saints;
6 That the communication of thy faith may
become effectual by the acknowledging of
every good thing which is in you in Christ
Jesus.
7 For we have great joy and consolation in
thy love, because the bowels of the saints are
refreshed by thee, brother.
8 Wherefore, though I might be much bold
in Christ to enjoin thee that which is convenient,
9 Yet for love's sake I rather beseech thee,
being such a one as Paul the aged, and now
also a prisoner of Jesus Christ.
10 I beseech thee for my son Onesimus,
whom I have begotten in my bonds:
11 Which in time past was to thee unprofitable, but now profitable to thee and to me:
12 Whom I have sent again: thou therefore
receive him, that is, mine own bowels:
13 Whom I would have retained with me,
that in thy stead he might have ministered
unto me in the bonds of the gospel:
14 But without thy mind would I do nothing; that thy benefit should not be as it were
of necessity, but willingly.
15 For perhaps he therefore departed for a
season, that thou shouldest receive him for
ever;
16 Not now as a servant, but above a servant, a brother beloved, specially to me, but
how much more unto thee, both in the flesh,
and in the Lord?
17 If thou count me therefore a partner, receive him as myself.
18 If he hath wronged thee, or oweth thee
aught, put that on mine account;
19 I Paul have written it with mine own
hand, I will repay it: albeit I do not say to
thee how thou owest unto me even thine own
self besides.
20 Yea, brother, let me have joy of thee in
the Lord: refresh my bowels in the Lord.
21 Having confidence in thy obedience I
wrote unto thee, knowing that thou wilt also
do more than I say.

GOLDEN TEXT: If thou count me therefore a partner, receive him as myself.
—Philemon 17.

Following God's Purpose

Unit 2: Christ Above All

(Lesson 5-8)

Lesson Aims

This lesson is designed to help students:

1. Know how Paul pleaded for reconciliation between Philemon and Onesimus.
2. Become able ministers of reconciliation.

Lesson Outline

INTRODUCTION
- A. Reconciliation as Cancellation
- B. Lesson Background

I. PAUL'S RESPECT FOR PHILEMON (Philemon 4-9)
- A. A Prayer of Thanksgiving (vv. 4, 5)
- B. A Prayer for Effectiveness (vv. 6, 7)
- C. A Request, Not an Order (vv. 8, 9)
  Without Compulsion

II. PAUL'S REQUEST FOR ONESIMUS (Philemon 10-14)
- A. For a Son in the Faith (vv. 10-12)
- B. For a Good Helper (vv. 13, 14)
  Christ Unites

III. REASONS FOR A WELCOME (Philemon 15-21)
- A. For Philemon's Benefit (vv. 15-19)
- B. For Paul's Joy (vv. 20, 21)
  Encouraging the Saints

CONCLUSION
- A. The Government That Changes Things
- B. Prayer
- C. Thought to Remember

Display visual 8 of the visuals packet and let it remain before the class throughout the session. The visual is shown on page 405.

Introduction

A. Reconciliation as Cancellation

A married couple went to a counselor, saying, "We need some re-cancellation." That was their way of saying *reconciliation.* The mispronunciation suggests an excellent concept. Reconciliation does involve cancellation of what imprisons us in the past, for it frees us to a new relationship.

B. Lesson Background

Not everything powerful comes in large packages. The book of Philemon is an example.

A slave named Onesimus had run away from his master, Philemon. Somehow that slave came into contact with Paul while Paul was a prisoner in Rome. Converted to Christianity, the runaway became a friend of Paul and a helper to him. Paul wrote this letter to the slave's master, who happened to be one of Paul's friends.

This letter is meaningful to us in these ways:

1. *A model of reconciliation.* This letter calls for acceptance of another as a Christian brother, though class distinctions put a big gap between them.

2. *An intercessory letter.* This is a magnificent example of one Christian's intercession for another Christian, with no benefit coming to the intercessor.

3. *A counter-cultural letter.* There were millions of slaves in the Roman Empire. The usual punishment for a runaway slave was harsh. What Paul requested went against the grain of the times. There are occasions when we Christians must take a stand against the customs of our time.

4. *A revolutionary letter.* We discover in this letter one of the powerful ways to change a social system. It is not by picking up arms, but by encouraging the change to begin from the inside. Paul was asking Philemon to make some internal changes that would result in a different way of treating Onesimus. There are extraordinary possibilities in ordinary people. We are to encourage and utilize those potentialities. All people are created in the image of God, and that's how God expects us to treat them.

5. *A persuasive letter.* There are many principles of persuasiveness in this letter; but none call for being belligerent, mean, dictatorial, or inflexible. Any of us who seek to persuade others can learn lessons from the way Paul persuaded Philemon.

I. Paul's Respect for Philemon (Philemon 4-9)

A. A Prayer of Thanksgiving (vv. 4, 5)

4. I thank my God, making mention of thee always in my prayers.

Paul never allowed the circumstances of his life to interfere with his prayer time. In the four letters Paul wrote during this Roman imprisonment, not once did he complain about his situation. Instead, his prayers were punctuated by thankfulness to God.

It is notable also that Paul prayed specifically for individuals and for churches. Philemon was on his prayer list because he was on his heart.

5. Hearing of thy love and faith, which thou hast toward the Lord Jesus, and toward all saints.

Paul was thankful specifically for Philemon's *love and faith.* There is a connection between *love and faith . . . toward the Lord Jesus* and love and faith toward our brothers in Christ. God does not call us to have a relationship with Christ only, but also with all Christians. We contradict Christian teaching if we meet to express our faith in Christ while nursing animosity toward people sitting around us.

Notice that Philemon's love was not restricted to a few of the saints—his favorite ones—but was *toward all saints.* Later in the letter we will see that Paul depended on Philemon's broad love and called for it to be expressed to the runaway slave.

B. A Prayer for Effectiveness (vv. 6, 7)

6. That the communication of thy faith may become effectual by the acknowledging of every good thing which is in you in Christ Jesus.

Philemon would be able to communicate his faith by helping spread the gospel. He could do this more effectively if people could see and acknowledge *every good thing* in his Christian life. Among other good things, forgiveness and a cordial welcome to the runaway slave would show people that Christianity makes a difference, and so many of them would be more ready to accept it. Paul prayed that Philemon's sharing of the gospel would become more effective in this way.

7. For we have great joy and consolation in thy love, because the bowels of the saints are refreshed by thee, brother.

The ancients used *bowels* as we use *heart,* to mean the feelings and emotions. Philemon refreshed the hearts of fellow Christians by his love and helpfulness. Well knowing what good things were in the character and life of Philemon, Paul hoped he would make his witness even more effective by his kindness to the runaway slave.

C. A Request, Not an Order (vv. 8, 9)

8. Wherefore, though I might be much bold in Christ to enjoin thee that which is convenient.

Wherefore ties the following request to Philemon's kind character recognized in verse 7. The request would be in line with Philemon's well-known disposition.

As an apostle Paul had the right to issue an order, and no doubt Philemon would have carried it out. But as someone has observed, a person changed against his will is of the same opinion still. Paul hoped to persuade rather than command. *Convenient* means fitting and proper. What Paul was about to ask was the right thing for Philemon to do. Paul had no doubt about that. But it would not be so easy for Philemon to see how right it was. He was the one who had lost a slave. If he now would take that slave back without punishment, would other slaves be encouraged to run away? How often do one's selfish interests cloud one's perception of right and wrong!

Since Paul did not use his authority to make demands, isn't that a good model for leaders in the church today? Shouldn't we make requests and allow God's grace and Spirit to work on people? That calls for trust in God and in people; it also calls for patience. It means we do not insist on having our own way, but work to help others grow up in Christ's way. What would happen to the harmony in the church if more people would quit trying to be controllers and would become models of compassionate service?

9. Yet for love's sake I rather beseech thee, being such a one as Paul the aged, and now also a prisoner of Jesus Christ.

Paul wanted Philemon to make this decision on his own and on the basis of love—love for God, love for fellow Christians, and especially love for a senior saint—*Paul the aged*—and love for a person who is being persecuted for doing what is right—*a prisoner of Jesus Christ.* We who are enjoying the prime of life ought to be especially considerate of those who have grown old in the service of Christ, and doubly considerate if their service has brought them inconvenience and suffering. But notice that the apostle Paul's age did not give him the right to be cranky, bossy, grouchy, or hard to get along with. The older we are in Christ Jesus, the more we should become gracious, open, flexible, understanding, and forgiving.

How to Say It

ONESIMUS. O-*ness*-ih-muss.
PHILEMON. Fih-*lee*-mun or Fie-*lee*-mun.

WITHOUT COMPULSION

Doing what is right should be a free choice, and not a forced activity. The balance between free choice and compulsion is not easily maintained in creating good and equitable social order and relationships. God calls all people to choose to do the right, but He also ordains government to restrain those who choose to do the wrong (Romans 13:3, 4).

Jackie Robinson, an outstanding college athlete at U.C.L.A. in California, was carefully trained by men who knew racial equality needed to be achieved in professional sports. Because of his skill, the Brooklyn Dodgers dared to give him a place on their all-white team in an all-white league. As the first black major-league baseball player, he was jeered and taunted in every stadium.

One day, as he played at Ebbets Field, his home stadium in Brooklyn, he made an error. The fans booed and mocked Robinson. The shortstop, Pee Wee Reese, walked over, put his arm around the dejected man, and stood with him facing the hostile crowd. Seeing this voluntary act of acceptance and encouragement by their popular shortstop, the fans quieted and settled back in the stands. Robinson stayed and became a star player for the Brooklyn Dodgers. He later said Reese's arm around his shoulders that day saved his baseball career.

It was not an act of compulsion. It was the right deed, freely done, at the right time. It began to turn the tide of needed reform in baseball and in the minds and hearts of the American people.

It is amazing what one act, voluntarily done at the right moment, can do. Do what is right, freely and openly. The rewards are worth the risk! —W. P.

II. Paul's Request for Onesimus (Philemon 10-14)

A. For a Son in the Faith (vv. 10-12)

10. I beseech thee for my son Onesimus, whom I have begotten in my bonds.

It is clear from this verse that the runaway slave, *Onesimus*, became acquainted with Paul in his Roman imprisonment and was converted by Paul. Paul called him *my son*, meaning his son in the faith. Paul "fathered" Onesimus by leading him to Christ and teaching him the Christian way. Therefore Paul mentioned Onesimus' present situation, not his past crime. We may often follow his example. We need to let the past be the past and relate to people as they are now, for God does wonderful things in the lives of people—even those who have been wrong and have wronged others.

11. Which in time past was to thee unprofitable, but now profitable to thee and to me.

The name *Onesimus* literally means "profitable" or "useful." Onesimus was not living up to the meaning of his name when he ran away, but he changed when he became a Christian. Then he was useful to Paul, and he was ready to be useful to Philemon. However, his usefulness depended on Philemon's willingness to use him as much as on Onesimus' willingness to be used. A Christian slave, welcomed warmly and treated as a brother, would be much more useful than a slave treated cruelly because he once had run away.

12. Whom I have sent again: thou therefore receive him, that is, mine own bowels.

Paul could have turned Onesimus in to the Roman officials and had him sent back to Philemon in chains. Instead of wanting to send back a slave to his master, Paul wanted to send back a Christian brother to a Christian brother. Christianity must live above social barriers and cultural expectations, some of which leave gaps instead of building bridges. The culture of that day called for a runaway slave to be tortured, or beaten, or executed, or branded with a letter on the forehead that would identify him as a runaway. But Paul knew what it meant to be forgiven. He once had been the greatest of sinners, persecuting the church of Christ. But Jesus had forgiven him and had sent him to urge others to be cleansed. Onesimus also had come to Jesus and had been forgiven. Now Paul wanted Philemon also to forgive him and welcome him as a brother. The Greek word for *sent again* is a word used technically for sending someone to a higher court. Paul was turning the case over to Philemon for a verdict; but Paul was acting as Onesimus' advocate, asking Philemon to *receive him*, accept him as a Christian brother and as Paul's son in the faith. In so doing he would receive not only Onesimus, but also Paul's own heart—though Paul used the word *bowels* instead of heart. What Philemon would do for Onesimus, he would be doing for Paul. Isn't that what fellowship is all about?

B. For a Good Helper (vv. 13, 14)

13. Whom I would have retained with me, that in thy stead he might have ministered unto me in the bonds of the gospel.

Onesimus had been a very good helper, and the apostle Paul would have liked to keep him permanently in Rome. Since the slave belonged to Philemon, the service he gave to Paul was really Philemon's contribution. But Paul gave up the help he could get and sent the slave back to his Christian brother, Philemon. Shouldn't that be our mind-set? Shouldn't we be willing to give up what is a benefit to us in order to benefit someone else?

14. But without thy mind would I do nothing; that thy benefit should not be as it were of necessity, but willingly.

Paul might have kept Onesimus in Rome, reasoning that his good friend Philemon would gladly contribute the slave's service to the good work Paul was doing. But Paul rejected that thought. He did not want such a contribution without Philemon's knowledge and consent. He preferred to receive only what was given willingly. In his imprisonment Paul needed a helper, but his needs took second place to Philemon's rights. Every Christian should be likewise unselfish. That may call for an increase of love—love that is kind, doesn't behave in ugly ways, doesn't seek its own, rejoices in the truth (1 Corinthians 13:4-7).

CHRIST UNITES

An incident occurred at Exeter Hall in England that should teach us all. A prizefighter who was debauched, miserable, degraded, and ignorant signed a pledge never to use alcohol again. Beside him stood a gentleman who employed many men in the building trade. He had led the fighter to know Christ and had encouraged him to sign the temperance pledge.

He did not just advise the fighter to "stick with it." He did not say, "I hope you can keep your vow," or "You have made a good decision." His question was, "Where will you sleep tonight?"

The fighter's reply came easily. "I will sleep where I slept last night."

"And where was that?" asked the builder.

"I slept in the streets," the poor man confessed.

"Not tonight," the gentleman replied. "You made vows to the Lord and to yourself tonight, and you belong to this society committed to overcoming the use of alcohol. You are a member in full standing and you are going to come home with me."

Oneness in purpose united these men. The builder received the reformed alcoholic because in Christ they had now a common goal and relationship.

Isn't this what Paul was asking Philemon to do with Onesimus? Do we practice what Paul taught? Practical unity is a gem we desire but seldom own. —W. P.

III. Reasons for a Welcome (Philemon 15-21)

A. For Philemon's Benefit (vv. 15-19)

15. For perhaps he therefore departed for a season, that thou shouldest receive him for ever.

Sometimes it is hard to see anything good in a loss we have suffered; but Paul was looking at this situation through the eyes of Romans 8:28: "We know that in all things God works for the good of those who love him" (*New International Version*). He said perhaps Onesimus left *for a season* so Philemon could have him back *for ever.* In his absence this slave was so changed that he would not run away again; but would serve well and faithfully as long as he lived. Philemon had a better slave than he had had before.

16. Not now as a servant, but above a servant, a brother beloved, specially to me, but how much more unto thee, both in the flesh, and in the Lord?

visual 8

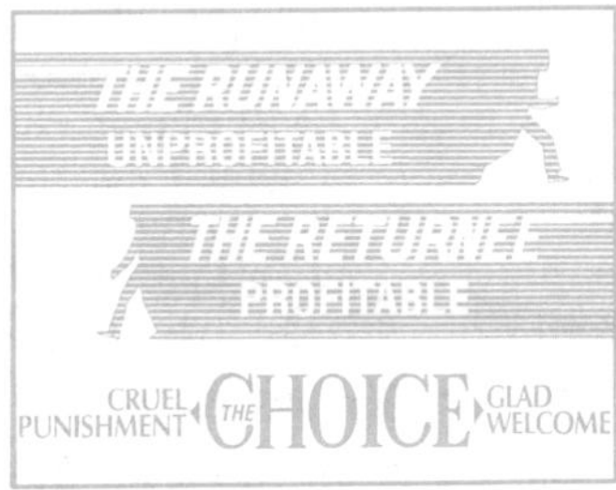

Philemon not only had a better slave; he also had *a brother beloved.* Paul did not ask the owner to free the slave, but to love him as a brother. Onesimus was *specially* beloved to Paul because of his helpfulness. He would be *much more* beloved to Philemon, for he would serve him equally well and for a longer time. Thus he would be dear to Philemon *in the flesh,* in a worldly, secular way. He would also be dear *in the Lord,* as a Christian brother. Our earthly relationships are heightened by our common sonship to the Heavenly Father through Jesus Christ. Our new relationship with one another cannot be restricted to just worshiping together on Sunday; it must flow into our work ethic with one another during the week. This does not mean there will no longer be employer or employee. Those distinctions will be there even between Christian brothers. But it means we are to use the principles of Christian ethics toward each other—fairness and kindness.

17. If thou count me therefore a partner, receive him as myself.

All the preceding led to Paul's request in this verse. Paul was so tuned to the tightened fellowship of God's people that he made it clear that whatever Philemon would do to Onesimus he would do to Paul himself. This is what it means to be members in the same body, the body of Christ. This is what it means to be members of the same family, the family of God.

18. If he hath wronged thee, or oweth thee aught, put that on mine account.

Paul was not only ready to go to bat for Onesimus; he was also ready to take responsibility for him. Perhaps Onesimus had stolen something when he ran away. At least he had robbed Philemon of his service for a time. Paul was willing to pay for whatever the loss to Philemon had been. That is real brotherhood.

19. I Paul have written it with mine own hand, I will repay it: albeit I do not say to thee how thou owest unto me even thine own self besides.

Perhaps Paul was dictating the letter and someone was writing it down; but at this point he took the pen and wrote with his own hand that he would pay whatever debt Onesimus owed to Philemon. At the same time, he reminded Philemon that he owed Paul something. Probably Paul had brought Philemon to Christ, and therefore Philemon was indebted to Paul for his *own self,* his eternal life. Philemon could never repay Paul for that, and so he could hardly accept the payment that Paul offered.

B. For Paul's Joy (vv. 20, 21)

20. Yea, brother, let me have joy of thee in the Lord: refresh my bowels in the Lord.

If Philemon would welcome Onesimus as a brother in Christ, it would bring *joy* to Paul, joy that would *refresh* Paul's *bowels*—or his heart, as we would say in modern language. And who knows how many other people in the church would be delighted with that evidence of a beautiful Christian spirit? The way we treat one person affects many people. There is a networking of relationships within the family of God. We need to accept some who once acted unacceptably, to forgive those who have hurt us. We must be willing to be reconciled to those who have rejected us—run away from us.

Paul was asking Philemon not to be embittered by what happened, but to be bettered by it. Isn't this a classic example? We should not lock people into their past, in the immaturity and insensitivity that they have left behind. We should be open to what the grace of God can do in and to persons, regardless of their past blunders.

21. Having confidence in thy obedience I wrote unto thee, knowing that thou wilt also do more than I say.

Paul said nothing about how bad it would be to greet Onesimus with cruelty. He merely expressed his confidence that Philemon would do all he asked and more. What an affirmation of encouragement! People are more likely to live up to our trust if we let them know we trust them.

Real social change must be effected from within. Brotherly love between a master and a slave will ultimately make slavery meaningless—and it did.

ENCOURAGING THE SAINTS

Goethe wrote, "Correction does much, but encouragement does more. Encouragement after censure is as the sun after a shower." Too much correction with no encouragement destroys the spirit.

W. L. Jessup, who founded San Jose Bible College, has always been an encourager. Honored at the North American Christian Convention in July of 1991 for over sixty years of ministry, Bill is best remembered for his confidence that students and senior saints could succeed in all the Lord wanted them to do.

As president of the college for twenty-one years he led the faculty and students in planting new congregations all over northern California. His selection as "King of the Seniors" in Santa Clara County, the world-famous Silicon Valley, was for Bill's enthusiastic leadership in organizing and maintaining seniors' groups and activities in church and community life.

Now in his later eighties, Bill still teaches a weekly Bible class in the mobile-home park where he lives and is an example of Christian life and concern in both church and city.

Paul set an example in life, word, correction, and encouragement in following Christ that Bill Jessup has emulated in his lifelong ministry. You too can be an encourager if you share with those around you the joy and encouragement that are yours in Jesus. It will bless their lives and give them hope in Him. —W. P.

Conclusion

A. The Government That Changes Things

Lasting social changes are not entirely due to the government outside of us. What brings about lasting social change is the government within us—the indwelling Spirit of God.

B. Prayer

Thank You, Father, for sending Jesus to be the bridge over our troubled waters. Help us to help others over troubled waters by laying ourselves down as a bridge of reconciliation. Amen.

C. Thought to Remember

"Now all these things are from God, who reconciled us to Himself through Christ, and gave us the ministry of reconciliation" (2 Corinthians 5:18, *New American Standard Bible*).

Home Daily Bible Readings

Monday, July 19—Christ Refreshes Others Through Faithful Servants (Philemon 1-7)
Tuesday, July 20—Christ Frees and Unites (Philemon 8-14)
Wednesday, July 21—Christ Transforms Relationships (Philemon 15-25)
Thursday, July 22—We Are One Fellowship in Christ (1 Corinthians 1:1-9)
Friday, July 23—Christ Above All (1 Corinthians 1:10-17)
Saturday, July 24—God's New People in Christ (1 Peter 2:4-10)
Sunday, July 25—Gladly Share Your Blessings (2 Corinthians 9)

Learning by Doing

This page contains an alternate lesson plan emphasizing learning activities. Classes desiring such student involvement will find these suggestions helpful.

Learning Goals

As students participate in today's class session, they should:

1. Decide how the story of Paul, Philemon, and Onesimus illustrates the need and the opportunity for reconciliation today.
2. Choose one situation where they can either act as intercessor, offer reconciliation, or pray to experience reconciliation.

Into the Lesson

Before class members arrive, scramble the word *reconciliation* on the chalkboard. To begin today's session, ask how many class members have noticed the scrambled word and how many have figured out what the letters spell.

Option: Instead of scrambling the word on the chalkboard, before class write each letter with a dark pen on a different index card. Give each letter to a different arriving student. To begin today's session, ask the class members with the cards to arrange themselves, in front of the class, in the correct order to spell the word.

If your class is large, make this a team exercise. Prepare two sets of the letters (maybe each with ink of a different color) to distribute to class members. See which team can spell the word first!

After any one of the above activities, ask the class, "What are some situations in our society where reconciliation is sometimes necessary?" List examples on the chalkboard as students think of them. Here are some possibilities: labor/management, police/citizens, teachers/parents, husband/wife, parent/child.

If students haven't already mentioned them, ask, "What are some situations in a church where reconciliation is sometimes necessary?"

Into the Word

Bridge to Bible study with two one-minute monologues. One begins, "I am Philemon." The other begins, "I am Onesimus." After studying the background to this lesson, you may deliver these monologues. Or contact two class members several days ahead of time to prepare these brief speeches that can explain the context for today's study.

Or you may prepare a brief lecture introduction to the book of Philemon, using the five points from the Lesson Background in this book.

Then involve students with one of the following Scripture-study ideas:

Another letter. Ask students, after studying the text, to write another letter based on the book of Philemon. They should use one of these ideas:

Paul writes to another Christian and explains, "Here's why I wrote to Philemon."

Onesimus writes to another slave in Philemon's household to say, "I've been changed, and I'm coming home with a letter from Paul. Here's what it says."

Philemon responds to Paul's letter: "I've received your letter, and here's my reply."

Q and A. Assign a different third of the class each of the main players in this drama, Paul or Onesimus or Philemon. As they study today's text they should decide, "What do we learn about his person?"

After about six minutes, each group should choose a spokesman to represent the person they've studied. Then the rest of the class asks that person questions, and he tries to answer based on his group's examination of the text.

Complete the outline. The "Lesson Background" lists five characteristics of this letter. Students should read the letter and decide how and why each of these characteristics is true. (The five characteristics are in the student book.)

After any of these, summarize by discussing, "What does this little letter teach about reconciliation?"

Into Life

Look again at the chalkboard list that you made at the beginning of the class time. Ask, "How could the lessons of this text make a difference in any one of these situations?"

Since Philemon is about and to Christians, you may want to concentrate on the need for reconciliation in church relationships or within Christian families.

Ask class members to think of a situation they're close to where reconciliation is needed. Whom are they most like in this situation:

Onesimus, who needs to be reconciled?

Philemon, who needs to express reconciliation?

Paul, who can act as intercessor to bring two Christians together?

End with guided prayer, asking God to help in each of these situations.

Let's Talk It Over

The questions on this page are designed to encourage review of the lesson Scriptures and to promote discussion of the lesson by the class. The answers provided are only discussion starters. Let your class talk it over from there.

1. How does Paul demonstrate "life-style evangelism"?

Though Paul was imprisoned, he did not allow his circumstances to turn him away from his major thrust in life. He led his guards to know Jesus Christ. We do not know how he began a relationship with Onesimus, but somehow it allowed him to share the message of the cross. The relationship continued after the act of conversion, so that Paul was able to guide the Christian growth of Onesimus. Paul was not stopped by circumstances, difference in age, or doubt that he would ever be free. We can only wonder how many others this prisoner brought to Christ.

2. When we become Christians, how does our new attitude change us?

Before a person becomes a Christian one lives largely for himself or herself. Onesimus lived for selfish concerns. He was an unprofitable slave: a runaway and an outlaw. After his conversion he learned that Christians live for God, and that our Heavenly Father will reward us for faithful service even if we serve another person. As Christians we learn to live for the good of others, and thus we become "profitable" servants. Onesimus' conversion made him a better slave. Christians ought to be better at what they do because they work to the glory of God.

3. In this lesson text, what suggestions do we see for our ministry to older people?

We see the role of good news, whereby "Paul the aged" gains encouragement of heart. Even though he cannot see Philemon, he is cheered by the news of his love and faith, and the refreshment he is providing for the saints.

We see an emphasis on fellowship between a younger person and an older one. Onesimus is attentive to Paul, giving him needed help. Older people with no family members near may often be in need of help. An attentive Christian can observe such needs and supply them.

We see "Paul the aged" eagerly continuing with such Christian work as was possible in the circumstances, and we see him in earnest prayer for a Christian brother. Many older people need to be encouraged to continue in some Christian work, especially in a ministry of prayer when other areas of service are closed to them.

4. How does Paul's practice stand as a model for us in intercessory prayer?

In each of his "prison epistles" Paul mentions his habit of prayer. He managed to keep himself informed so that he not only could pray for the needs of others, but also could thank God when such prayers were answered. He must have spent a good part of the day in prayer, for his prayers touch many people and churches. We busy and practical people too often neglect to pray. We need to learn the habit of prayer as we see this great apostle practice it.

5. What type of leadership shown by Paul can be effective in the church today?

In his dealings with Philemon, Paul could very well have asserted his apostolic authority and issued an order, and probably his order would have been obeyed. However, when a person in authority issues an order to someone, he or she may create such resentment that the order is obeyed grudgingly rather than enthusiastically. What is ordered then may be done, but the heart of the person doing it may not be in agreement. Paul chose to make a request rather than to issue an order. Philemon was free to refuse if he chose. If he would do as Paul asked, he would do it of his own free will, and his fellowship with both Paul and Onesimus would be more cordial. Many church leaders of today agree that a request works better than a demand—and especially when the leader does not have the authority of an inspired apostle.

6. How does reconciliation relate to fellowship?

Fellowship is a common bond of friendship and love between two persons that causes them to enjoy each other's presence. Fellowship is broken when either party feels that he or she has been mistreated or that the open relationship has been used unfairly for his or her disadvantage. The fellowship then needs to be restored. This restoration is what we call reconciliation. It requires forgiveness and whatever else is necessary to remove the barriers to the openness and expressions of love that produce true fellowship. Fellowship is so vital to the warmth of Christianity that it is necessary for us to be continually involved in ministries of reconciliation.

New Life

August 1
Lesson 9

DEVOTIONAL READING: Ephesians 1:3-14.

LESSON SCRIPTURE: Ephesians 1:15—2:10; 3:14-19.

PRINTED TEXT: Ephesians 2:1-10; 3:14-19.

Ephesians 2:1-10

**1 And you hath he quickened, who were
dead in trespasses and sins;
2 Wherein in time past ye walked according to the course of this world, according to
the prince of the power of the air, the spirit
that now worketh in the children of disobedience:
3 Among whom also we all had our conversation in times past in the lusts of our
flesh, fulfilling the desires of the flesh and of
the mind; and were by nature the children of
wrath, even as others.
4 But God, who is rich in mercy, for his
great love wherewith he loved us,
5 Even when we were dead in sins, hath
quickened us together with Christ, (by grace
ye are saved;)
6 And hath raised us up together, and
made us sit together in heavenly places in
Christ Jesus:
7 That in the ages to come he might show
the exceeding riches of his grace, in his kindness toward us, through Christ Jesus.
8 For by grace are ye saved through faith;
and that not of yourselves: it is the gift of
God:
9 Not of works, lest any man should boast.
10 For we are his workmanship, created in
Christ Jesus unto good works, which God
hath before ordained that we should walk in
them.**

Ephesians 3:14-19

**14 For this cause I bow my knees unto the
Father of our Lord Jesus Christ,
15 Of whom the whole family in heaven
and earth is named,
16 That he would grant you, according to
the riches of his glory, to be strengthened
with might by his Spirit in the inner man;
17 That Christ may dwell in your hearts by
faith; that ye, being rooted and grounded in
love,
18 May be able to comprehend with all
saints what is the breadth, and length, and
depth, and height;
19 And to know the love of Christ, which
passeth knowledge, that ye might be filled
with all the fulness of God.**

GOLDEN TEXT: By grace are ye saved through faith; and that not of yourselves: it is the gift of God.—Ephesians 2:8.

Following God's Purpose

Unit 3: Newness Through Christ

(Lessons 9-13)

Lesson Aims

This study should help students to:

1. Recall two ways to die and two ways to live.
2. Explain what is meant by **grace** in connection with salvation.
3. Find one way to follow God's leading better in their own lives.

Lesson Outline

INTRODUCTION
- A. Her Greatest Moment and Ours
- B. Lesson Background

I. THE DEAD AND THE LIVING (Ephesians 2:1-7)
- A. The Dead (vv. 1-3)
- B. The Living (vv. 4-7)
  Transformed!

II. THE CHANGE (Ephesians 2:8-10)
- A. By God's Grace (v. 8)
- B. Not by Man's Works (v. 9)
- C. Unto Good Works (v. 10)
  Accepting Help

III. PRAYER FOR CHRISTIANS (Ephesians 3:14-19)
- A. Prayer to the Father (vv. 14, 15)
- B. Prayer for Indwelling (vv. 16, 17)
- C. Prayer for Understanding (vv. 18, 19)
  New Life

CONCLUSION
- A. No Condemnation
- B. Prayer
- C. Thought to Remember

Display visual 9 of the visuals packet and let it remain before the class throughout the session. Refer to it when appropriate as you discuss today's text. The visual is shown on page 413.

Introduction

A. Her Greatest Moment and Ours

The marvelous singer, Marian Anderson, was once asked, "Miss Anderson, what has been the single greatest moment in your career? Was it the time you sang at Easter Sunrise Service at the Washington Monument in the presence of over seventy thousand people?"

Ms. Anderson replied, "That was a magnificent moment, but not my finest."

"Was it the time you sang at the White House for President Roosevelt and the Queen of England?" Though that was unforgettable, that was not her greatest moment.

She then replied that her greatest moment was when she went to Alabama, walked up the three steps to the shack, opened the screen door, walked in, and said, "Mama, you don't have to take in washing anymore." That must have been her mother's greatest moment too.

The greatest single moment in our lives is when we allow Jesus to walk up the steps of our hearts, when we open the door, and when He walks in and declares, "You are not condemned anymore. The grace of God has covered all your sins."

B. Lesson Background

In Ephesians 1:3-8, Paul mentions many of the blessings we have in Christ: all spiritual blessings (v. 3), chosen to be holy and without blame (v. 4), adopted by God (v. 5), accepted by God (v. 6), redeemed and forgiven (v. 7). In verses 9 and 10, Paul reveals that God's purpose is to unite us all in Christ.

While Ephesians 1 identifies God's purpose to unite us, Ephesians 2 identifies God's motivation: mercy, love, and grace (vv. 4, 5). It speaks also of God's method: the sacrifice of Jesus (vv. 13, 14) and the change to a new life that we see in our text.

I. The Dead and the Living (Ephesians 2:1-7)

A. The Dead (vv. 1-3)

1. And you hath he quickened, who were dead in trespasses and sins.

The phrase *hath he quickened* is not in the Greek; that's why it is in italics in our Bibles. It is stated in verse 5, and the translators inserted it here too so we would not miss its connection with the death mentioned here. Verse 1 literally says, "And you being dead in trespasses and sins." Paul was not writing to people who were physically dead; they were very much alive and able to read what he wrote.

There are two ways to die. We die physically when our breath and spirit leave our physical body. That will happen to all of us if Jesus delays His coming for another hundred years. We die in a different way when we sin and God's Spirit leaves us. That's the kind of death Adam and Eve experienced when they partook of the tree of the knowledge of good and evil (Genesis 2:17). They did not die physically that day, but did die spiritually. Their created nature (in the image of God) was shattered. The Spirit that united them to God and one another left them with just the human spirit. Consequently, the unity they had experienced in the garden was broken—a unity with God, with self, with one another, and with nature. The "community of unity" became a "chaos of disunity."

To be *dead in trespasses and sins* is to be separated from God. If one is thus separated when he or she dies physically, that person will spend eternity where God is totally absent—Hell.

The word *trespasses* refers to going where we should not go, doing what we should not do. The word for *sins* means missing the mark, failing to do what we ought to do. We have not kept ourselves in God's image. We have fallen short.

2. Wherein in time past ye walked according to the course of this world, according to the prince of the power of the air, the spirit that now worketh in the children of disobedience.

Paul expanded on why persons are "dead"—that is, separated from God. We are dead when we have not acted according to our created nature but according to the culture of our time—*the course of this world.* We sin when we do not submit to our Creator, but to the temptation of the devil—*the prince of the power of the air.* That results in disobedience. *Children of disobedience* is a first-century way of describing people who disobey. The phrase *children of* means *characterized by.* For example, Barnabas was called "son of consolation" or "son of encouragement" because his life was characterized by his encouragement of others (Acts 4:36). If the people who know you best were describing you, what would they say you are a son of or a daughter of?

3. Among whom also we all had our conversation in times past in the lusts of our flesh, fulfilling the desires of the flesh and of the mind; and were by nature the children of wrath, even as others.

None of us can escape the fact that we have disobeyed God—*we all had our conversation in times past.* The word *conversation* is an old word referring to the way we live. We would use the word "life-style" today. To some extent, all of us have lived among "the children of disobedience."

In the lusts of our flesh means we have allowed the feelings and desires of our physical bodies to carry us beyond the limits God has set. We have done that in our thinking as well. The desires *of the mind* have helped those *of the flesh.* The body must be kept under control, even if it takes a hard struggle (1 Corinthians 9:27). The mind also must be controlled: "Do not think about how to gratify the desires of the sinful nature" (Romans 13:14, *New International Version*).

Because we sinned in the past, we were then *children of wrath.* We deserved the wrath of God that falls on sinners (Romans 1:18). We could not undo what we had done. We were helpless, "dead" (v. 1). But God made a change.

B. The Living (vv. 4-7)

4. But God, who is rich in mercy, for his great love wherewith he loved us.

God has made a change in each of us who is a Christian. This verse speaks of God's motives. He is *rich in mercy,* pity, compassion. It isn't just pity for pity's sake; it is pity for our sake. God's mercy is linked up with *his great love.* The Greek word for *love* (*agape*) means a totally unselfish love. Here are some things such a love does and does not do: (1) It sees a need. (2) It moves to meet that need. (3) It does not count the cost. (4) It does not consider whether or not the person deserves to have that need met. (5) It does not calculate what the person who loves will get out of it for himself. (6) It makes decisions for the well-being of the other person. No wonder such love is called *great love.* It is great in the kind of love it is. It is great in the things it does. It is great in the results it brings.

5. Even when we were dead in sins, hath quickened us together with Christ, (by grace ye are saved).

Quickened us means *made us alive.* When we were dead in our sins (separated from God), He made it possible for us to be reunited with Him. *Quickened us together with Christ* has an exact parallel in Colossians 2:12, 13, which is speaking about what happens at our baptism. Our deadness is buried with Christ, and we are raised to a new life. But lest we think that it happens just because of baptism, Paul emphasizes that *by grace* we *are saved.* We must accept God's gift, but we must never forget that we are saved by God's grace, not by our gumption.

We were dead in sins. That means we were separated from God, "having no hope, and without God in the world" (v. 12). But God changed that. He made us alive *together with Christ.* Christ was raised from physical death; because of His sacrifice we have been raised from spiritual death.

6. And hath raised us up together, and made us sit together in heavenly places in Christ Jesus.

We have been reunited not only with God, but also with one another—we *sit together.* Our eternal fellowship is in Heaven; but even on earth our fellowship is *in heavenly places,* for it is *in Christ Jesus.*

7. That in the ages to come he might show the exceeding riches of his grace, in his kindness toward us, through Christ Jesus.

The greatness and power and goodness of God's grace are seen in the transformation of the Ephesians and us from sinners to saints, from dead to alive. Thus *the exceeding riches of his grace* will be shown through all the ages till Jesus comes again. And through all the endless ages after He comes, these riches will be even more evident. Joyously we will live in the presence of God. There will be no pain, no crime, no death, no hatred, no sins.

In Christ we are forgiven; out of Christ we are condemned. In Christ we are blessed; outside of Christ we are cursed. In Christ we will be blameless at His coming; outside of Christ we will be blamed. In Christ we are accepted; outside of Christ we are rejected.

TRANSFORMED!

Spiritual reality is hard to grasp when people live in a secular, materialistic, sinning society. Living in the flesh, we tend to ignore the fact that we are dead spiritually. The new life available in Jesus needs to be seen to be believed.

Uncle Dave was the town drunk. He lived for the flesh and proudly boasted that he could "drink any man under the table." He neglected his family, used his income on himself, bragged of the "wild women" who were part of his dissolute life, and seemed proud of his dissipation. But underneath it all he was miserable.

An evangelist came to town preaching repentance, new life in Jesus, and freedom from the tyranny of the sins of the flesh. Uncle Dave began to attend the meetings. He listened and hoped. He despaired and prayed. In tearful repentance he accepted Jesus as Lord and was baptized.

New life did begin that night for Uncle Dave. His sinful ways were gone! He was now alive in the spirit, where before he had only lived in the flesh. Uncle Dave was a new man. Years later he died a sober, loving, kind husband and father, whose change from death to life eventually made him an elder in the church where he had found Jesus as his Savior and Lord.

Don't give up. Transformation is possible. Come to the Lord. He specializes in giving new life to those once dead in trespasses and sins.

—W. P.

II. The Change (Ephesians 2:8-10)

A. By God's Grace (v. 8)

8. For by grace are ye saved through faith; and that not of yourselves: it is the gift of God.

There is a divine side and a human side to our salvation. The divine side is God's *grace;* the human side is our *faith.* That means we trust that God will do what He promised.

What is *grace? Grace* is God's favor that we receive but do not earn. Jesus earned it. He never sinned; He was obedient even unto death. He earned God's favor for us; we did not deserve it by anything we did. Jesus earned eternal life, but He received death. We sinned and earned death, but in Christ we receive eternal life.

Grace can be described in an acrostic:

God's
Redemption
At
Christ's
Expense

Lest we put too much emphasis on our faith and begin to think salvation is our doing, Paul says, *Not of yourselves: it is the gift of God.* The next verse makes that more emphatic.

B. Not by Man's Works (v. 9)

9. Not of works, lest any man should boast.

God's gift of salvation is not earned by our works. If it were, we could boast about it. As it is, we can boast only about God's greatness, God's strength, God's gift, God's work. This verse corrects some errors in the thinking of many:

1. "I don't need Christ or the church; I am good enough." This is the idea that salvation comes by stacking up our good deeds over against our pile of bad deeds—whichever pile is higher wins. That's salvation by works. But this thought is invalidated when we read that "the wages of sin is death" (Romans 6:23). *Sin* here is singular. Just one sin earns death.

2. "What I do has nothing to do with my salvation." But believing in Jesus Christ is something I do. Repenting of sin is something I do. Baptism is something done to me, but I do accept it. All of these have to do with forgiveness and salvation (Acts 2:38; 16:31; 22:16). Taking action to accept a gift is not the same as working to earn it.

C. Unto Good Works (v. 10)

10. For we are his workmanship, created in Christ Jesus unto good works, which God hath before ordained that we should walk in them.

In Christ Jesus we are new creatures (2 Corinthians 5:17), not self-made, but God's *workmanship.* He has taken away our sin and restored us to our created nature. We have received God's Spirit and have His divine nature living in us (Ephesians 2:22).

While good works do not earn salvation, salvation is *unto good works.* We are saved to do them—the works that *God hath before ordained that we should walk in them.* What works are those? They are works that reflect the character of our Heavenly Father—works of grace, forgiveness, benevolence, generosity, and holiness. The faith of the saved is always expressed in good works. If it isn't, that faith is dead (James 2:17)—as dead as we were in our sins.

ACCEPTING HELP

One of our spiritual problems is to understand the balance between grace and good works. We are saved by grace and "created in Christ Jesus unto good works." What is the proper relationship between the two?

On a beautiful spring day a father and his young son were busy working together planting their vegetable garden. The boy had the task of gathering up the loose stones and throwing them in a pile at the end of the garden plot. After a while the boy said, "Dad, here's one I can't lift. I've tried as hard as I can, but I can't pick it up."

"Son," his father replied, "I don't expect you to do more than you can. That one is for me to handle. All you have to do with it is to ask me to help." With a strenuous effort the father lifted the heavy stone and placed it on the growing pile of rocks at the edge of the garden.

We cannot save ourselves, even with our best efforts. Jesus must touch us with God's grace to lift sin's impossible burden. Without His help we will fail. Even our best morality falls short. Sin requires pardon from God, and that is not easy even for the Almighty. It cost the life of His only begotten Son.

However, each day our Lord gives us opportunities to do good deeds that are well within the strength He provides. These are our responsibilities. Let us do the "good works" that Jesus created us to perform, while we depend on His grace to lift the burdens that are impossible for us. He does not require us to do the impossible. That is the work of His grace, and nothing is impossible for Him. —W. P.

visual 9

III. Prayer for Christians (Ephesians 3:14-19)

A. Prayer to the Father (vv. 14, 15)

14. For this cause I bow my knees unto the Father of our Lord Jesus Christ.

This portion is a transition from the privileges we have received from God to the purposes we are to serve for God. (Paul covered these in chapter 4.) Bowing the knees is an expression of humility and gratitude before God. After we receive salvation, we should live in humble thankfulness.

15. Of whom the whole family in heaven and earth is named.

We are reminded that we are united to God and to each other. Whoever claims God as Father must also claim others as brothers and sisters. We are in the same family with Christians here on earth and with the saints in Heaven. We must treat each other here on earth as we will treat each other in Heaven.

B. Prayer for Indwelling (vv. 16, 17)

16. That he would grant you, according to the riches of his glory, to be strengthened with might by his Spirit in the inner man.

Paul began to get specific in his prayer. In Christ we are new creatures. Paul prays that the inner person—that new creature that began as a spiritual babe—will be strengthened by the Holy Spirit so each of us can grow into the likeness of Him who has created and recreated us. While our outer person is decaying each day, the inner person should be renewed day by day (2 Corinthians 4:16). We are to grow up, not just grow old. The Holy Spirit is in us to enable us to become more like Christ.

17. That Christ may dwell in your hearts by faith; that ye, being rooted and grounded in love.

In the person of the Holy Spirit, Christ himself is within us to govern our total lives. He is not only our indwelling resident, but also our indwelling president. Paul highlighted that thought when he said, "Not I, but Christ liveth in me" (Galatians 2:20). Paul gave up his way of doing things to do things Christ's way. Christ's way is *rooted and grounded in love.* We are to grow till we can love as Christ loved. It should come from the inside out. He loved both the rich and the poor, the well and the sick, the religious leaders and social outcasts, those who did not like Him and those who were His friends. It is hard to love so many, but it can be done when we are open to the Holy Spirit who strengthens us as we give up our ego to Christ's lordship.

C. Prayer for Understanding (vv. 18, 19)

18. May be able to comprehend with all saints what is the breadth, and length, and depth, and height.

Our love should be like Christ's love, which reaches out in all directions—to the highest (richest, most powerful, most influential) and to the lowest (the poor, the untouchables, the unwanted). It reaches as far above and as far around us as space goes. No one is exempt, and no one should be left out of our love. How wide and deep is the love of your congregation? Are any citizens or any sections of your town beyond its reach?

19. And to know the love of Christ, which passeth knowledge, that ye might be filled with all the fulness of God.

To know the love of Christ is not just to know He loves us. We do not just accept His love; we let it become our kind of love. His kind of love surpasses knowledge, but we understand it better as we copy it. People will not understand it when they see it in us, and we cannot fully explain it. It is a love that is limitless; it knows no barriers or prejudices.

Filled with all the fulness of God means God's character has filled ours completely. His nature is seen in our lives. God's kind of love has taken over our human kind of love. God's selflessness has taken over our selfishness. God's kindness has taken over our roughness. God's Spirit has taken over our human spirits. Paul prays for the three persons of God to have an impact in and through our lives—the Spirit (v. 16), Christ (v. 17), and God (v. 19). The Father, the Son, and the Holy Spirit, into whom we are baptized, are to live in us. It is only as we are open to allow them to control us and live through us, that we understand what it means to be re-created in His image.

NEW LIFE

A reporter was attempting to belittle Dwight L. Moody's tremendous evangelistic ministry and his powerful preaching that emphasized God's grace by which sinners are redeemed and given power to live new and better lives in Jesus. "Mr. Moody," the interviewer asked, "Do you have enough grace to be burned at the stake?"

After a moment Mr. Moody replied, "No, at this moment in my life I do not."

Thinking he could further challenge the evangelist's reliance on grace, his inquirer said, "Don't you wish you had?"

"No, sir," came Moody's answer. "I do not need that measure of grace today. What I need right now is grace enough to live three days in Milwaukee and hold a convention."

Here is a key to our living the new life in Christ. By faith He lives in our hearts, and His grace is sufficient for each day's need. As we come to trust Him and to know His love, we only ask for grace for today.

This is the life of faith. This is our new life as Christians. As we mature in our faith and grow in Christ, we will come to know and receive all He has for us now and forever. At this time, all we need is enough of grace to live today and do His work in Milwaukee, or wherever we are. In His time we will "be filled with all the fulness of God."

—W. P.

Conclusion

A. No Condemnation

Because of God's grace, "there is therefore now no condemnation to them which are in Christ Jesus, who walk not after the flesh, but after the Spirit" (Romans 8:1). Our new kind of living is not for the purpose of getting to Heaven. Jesus purchased that for us on the cross. It is for the purpose of channeling God's love to those around us through the way we live our daily lives.

B. Prayer

Thank You, our Heavenly Father, for touching our guilt with Your grace, for invading our separation with Your Spirit, for looking at us with the eyes of a Father, not a foe. In Jesus' name we pray, amen.

C. Thought to Remember

By grace are you saved through faith. It is not of yourselves. It is the gift of God.

Home Daily Bible Readings

Monday, July 26—Life Apart From Christ (Ephesians 2:1-5)

Tuesday, July 27—Saved by Grace (Ephesians 2:6-10)

Wednesday, July 28—The Source of New Life (John 15:1-9)

Thursday, July 29—Bear Fruit of the New Life (John 15:10-17)

Friday, July 30—Renewed by God's Power (Isaiah 40:28-31)

Saturday, July 31—The Blessings of Newness (Ephesians 3:13-19)

Sunday, Aug. 1—A New Me (Galatians 6:11-16)

Learning by Doing

This page contains an alternate lesson plan emphasizing learning activities. Classes desiring such student involvement will find these suggestions helpful.

Learning Goals

Students in today's class should:

1. Compare the teachings of Ephesians 2:1-10 with commonly-held misconceptions about man's sin, God's grace, and the Christian's life-style.
2. Verbalize responses to at least one of these misconceptions.
3. Examine their own lives to see if they are harboring any of these wrong ideas themselves.

Into the Lesson

Duplicate the following statements, or read them to class members. (Or use the student book where they are reproduced.) Ask students to decide whether they agree or disagree with each sentence.

1. Since sin is an expected part of the human experience, God doesn't fret over our transgressions.
2. People outside the church and people inside the church are exactly like each other.
3. Christians needn't take sin too seriously, since God has.
4. Our sin shows the goodness of God.
5. Because of our sin, we must pray, obey, and serve in order to make up for the great error of our ways.
6. It is natural for Christians to think less of non-Christians because Christians are naturally more righteous than others.
7. We are saved by grace, therefore we need not worry about good works.

After each class member has written "Agree" or "Disagree" beside each statement, read them again and poll the class to see how opinions are divided. Allow some discussion, especially of those points where there is disagreement. Then tell the class that today's Bible study should help to settle the disagreements.

Into the Word

Ask students to keep these agree/disagree statements before them while they listen to Ephesians 2:1-10 as it is read aloud by a volunteer.

Divide the class into groups of about four. They are to see how this passage sheds light on the agree/disagree sentences. (If time is short and your class is large enough, assign one or two of the sentences to each group of four.) After about six minutes, reassemble the class and allow them to share what they decided.

You may want to add some of the following insights (numbered here to correspond with the introductory statements):

1. This whole passage shows how seriously God looks at transgression. Indeed, He calls non-Christians "dead" in their sins—hardly a normal state!
2. In a sense this is true: both the saved and the lost have the same need for salvation. But the difference is that Christians have life from Christ and others do not.
3. Christians should adopt the "mind of Christ." Christians should also see in this passage the high hopes and purposes God has for those He has saved (vv. 7, 10).
4. In a sense this is true, in that God will show the magnitude of His grace by contrasting it with the awfulness of our sin (v. 7).
5. This is exactly the opposite of what this text teaches. Verses 8 and 9 point out that we cannot earn our salvation or make up for our sin with our goodness.
6. The difference between Christians and non-Christians is that Christians have been forgiven for their gross failures and non-Christians have not. But the failures among both groups are equally distasteful. Verse 9 affirms that Christians have no reason to boast, no justification for smugness.
7. None of this means that good works are not important. They are not to earn salvation, but to demonstrate it. Verse 10 makes clear that God expects good works from His new creatures.

Into Life

In their same groups of four, ask students to decide the message of this text for one of the following categories of people:

- *Christians who have some sinful habit.*
- *Christians who are not sure they have lived a holy enough life to get to Heaven.*
- *Non-Christians who believe (and perhaps rightly so) that they are already just as good as most of those already going to church.*
- *Non-Christians who believe that they are too hopelessly evil for God to ever redeem them.*

Allow time for the groups to share what they have written. Ask class members, "What does this passage teach you about your relationship to God? How can this passage affect your Christian life this week?"

Let's Talk It Over

The questions on this page are designed to encourage review of the lesson Scriptures and to promote discussion of the lesson by the class. The answers provided are only discussion starters. Let your class talk it over from there.

1. In this modern society many of us have become so addicted to nicotine, alcohol, or other substances that we seem hopelessly dependent on such things to satisfy the craving "of the flesh and of the mind." How did we get into such a desperate condition? What can we do to break with our past and start over?

Some of us take up harmful habits in our youth because others are doing it, or just to be daring and defy the conventional wisdom of our elders. Some of us are looking for relief from physical, mental, or emotional pain, or from the stress arising from the fears and frustrations of daily living. Fundamentally, we disobey God by failing to depend on Him for our every need and for our strength to overcome temptations. Depending on dangerous things instead, we become helplessly enslaved by our addictions.

Being freed from such dependency requires a humble confession that we are powerless to overcome it by ourselves, that we desperately need the help of our loving and compassionate God. Such a confession must be followed by a commitment to say "no" to our appetites and "yes" to self-control, righteousness, and godliness (Titus 2:12).

2. All of us must acknowledge that in the past we once disobeyed God (Ephesians 2:2). How have we changed since becoming Christians so that now our lives are characterized by obedience to Him?

As Christians, many of us are more aware of the limits that God has placed on our thoughts, desires, and behaviors. We discipline ourselves to remain within God's standards of conduct and attitude. We no longer live to please ourselves; we now live to please God.

Jesus is our example, and His Word our guide. We study and imitate His life; we read the Scriptures and apply them to our lives.

3. In Ephesians 2:8 Paul speaks of the unmerited grace of God by which we are saved. How may such undeserved love and acceptance from God affect the way we relate to others?

Grateful for God's love, we learn to love others as He loves us (John 13:34). We love and help people who do not love us, and we become more unselfish in our love for those who do.

4. What are some of the good works that God has prepared for us to do? Specifically, what can we do this week?

Good works we can do include showing patience, kindness, and love in our relationships, extending forgiveness for any offense, sharing compassionately and generously with others, living humbly and unpretentiously with our neighbors, practicing self-control, speaking with truthfulness and love. This week we can start by being more tolerant with spouse or children, by apologizing to someone we have wronged, by visiting someone who is ill or shut-in, by inviting a lonely neighbor to our home, by starting a Bible study with a non-Christian friend.

5. When Christ's presence lives in us, we are to be "rooted and grounded in love" (Ephesians 3:17). How can we live out Christ's presence in us and love the way He loves? To whom may we need to begin to show this love?

Often we place limits on our love: we allow barriers to keep us separate from people who are different from us in race, nationality, social status, education, age, life-style, or religious background. Overcoming barriers will free Christ to live in and through us. We may need to extend Christ's love to the elderly in our church, the minority people at work, the foreigner down the street, the handicapped in our community, the under-privileged in our city, and the unevangelized at home and abroad.

6. Most of us want our lives to have a positive impact on others for Christ, but we often wonder whether we have the ability to meet life's opportunities and make a worthwhile contribution. But God's power is at work in us (Ephesians 3:20). How does that help us face life's challenges?

When we reach the limit of our resources, we can be reassured by knowing that God is infinite in His ability and that we can draw on His limitless resources for strength to go on. Moreover, Christ has experienced the pains, weaknesses, and temptations that we face. He can empathize with our struggles; He is ready to give immediate and sympathetic help to us (Hebrews 4:15, 16). Such confident hope can renew our spirits and strengthen our resolve.

New Fellowship

August 8
Lesson 10

DEVOTIONAL READING: Hebrews 13:1-7.

LESSON SCRIPTURE: Ephesians 2:11—3:6.

PRINTED TEXT: Ephesians 2:11-22.

Ephesians 2:11-22

11 Wherefore remember, that ye being in
time past Gentiles in the flesh, who are called
Uncircumcision by that which is called the
Circumcision in the flesh made by hands;
12 That at that time ye were without Christ,
being aliens from the commonwealth of Israel, and strangers from the covenants of
promise, having no hope, and without God in
the world:
13 But now, in Christ Jesus, ye who sometime were far off are made nigh by the blood
of Christ.
14 For he is our peace, who hath made both
one, and hath broken down the middle wall
of partition between us;
15 Having abolished in his flesh the enmity, even the law of commandments contained in ordinances; for to make in himself
of twain one new man, so making peace;
16 And that he might reconcile both unto
God in one body by the cross, having slain
the enmity thereby:
17 And came and preached peace to you
which were afar off, and to them that were
nigh.
18 For through him we both have access by
one Spirit unto the Father.
19 Now therefore ye are no more strangers
and foreigners, but fellow citizens with the
saints, and of the household of God;
20 And are built upon the foundation of
the apostles and prophets, Jesus Christ himself being the chief corner stone;
21 In whom all the building fitly framed
together groweth unto a holy temple in the
Lord:
22 In whom ye also are builded together
for a habitation of God through the Spirit.

GOLDEN TEXT: Ye are no more strangers and foreigners, but fellow citizens with the saints, and of the household of God.—Ephesians 2:19.

Following God's Purpose

Unit 3: Newness Through Christ

(Lessons 9-13)

Lesson Aims

At the conclusion of this lesson, students should be able to:

1. Tell what God has done to build bridges between himself and humankind, and between persons.
2. Tell what people on earth can do to improve their relationship with God and with one another.
3. Tell one way in which they themselves will draw closer to God or closer to fellowmen this week.

Lesson Outline

INTRODUCTION
- A. Before and After
- B. Lesson Background

I. THE EXCLUDED (Ephesians 2:11, 12)
- A. The Identity of the Excluded (v. 11)
- B. The Scope of the Exclusion (v. 12)

II. THE BRIDGE-BUILDER (Ephesians 2:13-18)
- A. Who He Is (v. 13)
  From Alien to Citizen
- B. What He Eliminated (vv. 14, 15)
  The Broken Wall
- C. What He Established (vv. 16-18)

III. THE NEW FELLOWSHIP (Ephesians 2:19-22)
- A. In the Same Family (v. 19)
- B. On the Same Foundation (v. 20)
  A Solid Foundation
- C. Being the Same Temple (v. 21)
- D. With the Same Indwelling God (v. 22)

CONCLUSION
- A. A Friend Defined
- B. Prayer
- C. Thought to Remember

Refer to visual 10 of the visuals packet as you introduce this lesson and as you proceed through a study of the text. The visual is shown on page 421.

Introduction

A. Before and After

We've all seen those before and after pictures—the picture of a person before a special hairdo or diet and then the picture afterwards. In this lesson, Paul gives us before and after pictures to show what Christ has done to unify humankind. Paul's picturing is done with words. Here are some features of it. Figures refer to verses in Ephesians 2.

Before	**After**
Without Christ 12	In Christ Jesus 13
Aliens 12	Fellow citizens 19
Strangers 12	Made one 14
No hope 12	Access to God 18
Without God 12	Household of God 19
Far off 13	Nigh 13
Enmity 15	Peace 14, 15, 17

It will be important to see these contrasts throughout this lesson and note how we can move from the "before" to the "after."

B. Lesson Background

Paul has discussed the spiritual situation of those who are outside of Christ. They are dead in trespasses and sins (Ephesians 2:1). Death basically means separation. We die physically when our spirit leaves our body; we die spiritually when God's Spirit leaves us. Anyone who dies physically without God's life within will spend eternity at a place where God is totally absent—that's Hell.

However, spiritual death can be reversed. Because of God's love, mercy, and grace, He made a way for our transfer from being dead without Christ to being alive in Christ (Ephesians 2:4-8). We saw that in last week's lesson.

In this week's lesson, Paul discusses the sociological situation of being out of Christ and then being in Christ. The spiritual situation is that we were separate from God, and then joined to Him; the sociological situation is that we were separate from one another, and then joined together. Christ is the master bridge-builder. He bridges our separation in both directions—upward toward God and outward toward one another.

I. The Excluded (Ephesians 2:11, 12)

A. The Identity of the Excluded (v. 11)

11. Wherefore remember, that ye being in time past Gentiles in the flesh, who are called Uncircumcision by that which is called the Circumcision in the flesh made by hands.

To call someone "uncircumcised" was a Jewish way of saying, "You are not included among God's people." The name was given to all people who were not Jews.

Racial barriers are with us still. Some of us avoid people of other races even when we know they are among God's people. Then there are economic barriers. Some people are uncomfortable with the wealthy, while others do not want to mingle with the poor and needy. There are health barriers excluding those who are physically or mentally handicapped as well as those who are sick. Occupations also may appear as barriers. Some people are not comfortable with a scientist, college professor, or doctor; while others are no less uncomfortable with migrant workers, custodians, or garbage collectors. There may even be a whole section of town that is excluded from the calling program of the church.

Each of us needs to ask, "What kind of people am I uncomfortable with—and why?"

B. The Scope of the Exclusion (v. 12)

12. That at that time ye were without Christ, being aliens from the commonwealth of Israel, and strangers from the covenants of promise, having no hope, and without God in the world.

There is an exclusion far more meaningful than any of those mentioned above. It applies to the heathen Gentiles of Paul's time and to people who do not believe in Jesus in our time. (1) They are separated from the Savior (Christ). (2) They are separated from God's people (the commonwealth of Israel). (3) They are separated from God's promises (covenants). (4) They are separated from the future (having no hope). (5) They are separated from God's presence (without God in the world).

That is total exclusion. That is what it means to be lost. But that situation does not have to be terminal. It can be changed.

II. The Bridge-Builder (Ephesians 2:13-18)

A. Who He Is (v. 13)

13. But now, in Christ Jesus, ye who sometime were far off are made nigh by the blood of Christ.

Those who were *far off* were the heathen Gentiles, and those far off today are those who do not believe in God and Christ. They are *far off* from the five realities in the preceding verse—Christ, the people of God, God's promises, God's future, and God's presence. But the situation has changed for some. What they were—far off—they no longer are. Now they are *nigh.*

What caused the change? *The blood of Christ*—His sacrifice on the cross. He died for all of our sins. Without Him we are all in the same category—sinners who are lost. But on the cross Jesus took our separation from the Father for us. He took the wrath we deserved. Though He committed no sin, God "made him to be sin for us" (2 Corinthians 5:21). God poured all of our sins into His sinless body on that tree (1 Peter 2:24). Indeed "he was wounded for our transgressions" (Isaiah 53:5), "and the Lord hath laid on him the iniquity of us all" (Isaiah 53:6). The condemnation that was ours became His. He accepted death in our place, so we could be transferred from separation from God to unity with God.

FROM ALIEN TO CITIZEN

His was just one tiny name on the passenger list of a liner from Genoa, Italy, in 1912. Baby Panos was all that was written on that line. No birthplace, no parents, nothing else. Baby Panos was one of many children under one year of age brought to the United States by friends of their parents. The parents were hoping for better lives for their children in the New World.

Baby Panos was raised by a family in San Jose, California. They gave him the name James. When Jim was old enough to be out on his own, he developed a small business in the city by hard work and saving. Still he was an alien in a foreign land, but it was the only land he knew.

Jim entered adult education classes in San Jose and learned how he could become a citizen. He studied United States history. He took the class specially designed for eligible aliens desiring United States citizenship.

Finally the great day came. James Panos stood proudly with other aliens from many cultures, countries, and relationships. He raised his hand and took the oath of allegiance to the United States of America. He was declared a citizen. In that moment Baby James Panos changed from alien to citizen with all the rights of his new relationship fully assured. It was a time of joy, celebration, and thanksgiving.

Lost and separated from God, our Father, we are all aliens and foreigners, outside the kingdom of Heaven. In Jesus we can be made citizens. But to have this new relationship we must know Him. We must acknowledge Him as our Lord and king. We must pledge allegiance to Him, and we must live up to our pledge. —W. P.

B. What He Eliminated (vv. 14, 15)

14. For he is our peace, who hath made both one, and hath broken down the middle wall of partition between us.

The Jews had erected in the temple a *wall of partition* between the court of the Gentiles and the court of the Jews. On that wall was a sign warning that any Gentile on the wrong side of the wall would be endangering his own life. Christ did not take down that wall of stone, but He ended the separation that it symbolized. People outside of Christ are all in the same category—lost sinners. People in Christ are all in the same category—redeemed people of God. "There is neither Jew nor Greek, there is neither bond nor free, there is neither male nor female: for ye are all one in Christ Jesus" (Galatians 3:28). If the barriers of race and bondage and gender are gone, so are the barriers of wealth and health and occupation. That does not mean there are no differences among us; it means those differences make no difference in our fellowship, love, and care. We belong to the same family as brothers and sisters, because we are children of the same eternal Father.

15. Having abolished in his flesh the enmity, even the law of commandments contained in ordinances; for to make in himself of twain one new man, so making peace.

One thing that distinguished Jews from Gentiles was the *law of commandments* that God had given to the Jews. That law was given to prepare people for the coming of the Messiah (Galatians 3:24, 25). When Jesus came, He nailed its ordinances to the cross with Him (Colossians 2:14). Now our law is the law of love (James 2:8). "Love-ism" replaces "legalism"; for when we love God with all our being and love others as ourselves, we have fulfilled the intentions of the law (Matthew 22:36-40; Romans 13:8-10). When anyone is in Christ, that person is automatically united with anyone else who is in Christ. So *of twain,* Jew and Gentile, Christ made *one new man, so making peace.*

The Christian belongs to Christ and to all other Christians. The differences between us are to be ignored in the way we see and treat each other. Paul elsewhere writes, "So from now on we regard no one from a worldly point of view" (2 Corinthians 5:16, *New International Version*). The deeds of Christ for us are more important than the differences in people around us. He died for the whole world, not just for one brand of humanity.

THE BROKEN WALL

The day the iron curtain came down will be remembered as long as human beings cherish freedom and are willing to fight for liberty.

The telecasts zoomed in on Berlin, the location where the WALL first divided the city and made East and West from one metropolis. It seemed that every citizen on both sides of the barrier wanted to pound away at least a little of the steel and concrete that separated families, divided a nation, and created havoc over much of Europe. It was a day to cherish in memory, a symbol of the dissolution of the Soviet control of satellite states and an end of the oppression of their puppet regimes. Detente began to give way to peace, and an end to the cold war was promised. The broken wall spoke of new hope, new relationships, and reconciliation possibilities between different cultures and political systems.

The restructuring of Europe will take years to accomplish; but the wall is abolished, and the people can begin to create a new order by their own decisions and dreams for the future.

Paul wrote of an even greater day when he told of the creation of "one new man" as the wall between Jew and Gentile was abolished by Jesus Christ on the cross. As Christians we need to celebrate this victory with joy and thanksgiving. It reunited us with God and His eternal kingdom. But more than we need to celebrate, we need to be faithful to our pledge. We need to honor and obey our King. —W. P.

C. What He Established (vv. 16-18)

16. And that he might reconcile both unto God in one body by the cross, having slain the enmity thereby.

To *reconcile* is to bring together. Christ died on the cross to unite us with God and one another. Reconciliation with one another is emphasized by the words *one body.* Christ has only one continuing body on earth—the church. While there is only one church, there are many different congregations. It may be likened to a human family. Brothers and sisters may live in different homes after they grow up, but they still belong to the same family. It is one family made up of several different households.

Since each of us is a member of that family or body, the church, we should work in coordination with the Head and in cooperation with one another. When the members of our physical bodies do not work in cooperation, we are not at ease—we are dis-eased. We spend a lot of money on medical care to bring parts of our physical bodies back into harmony. Likewise we should exert all our efforts to bring the members of Christ's body into harmony with one another, for Christ died to reconcile them to one another as well as to God. If we destroy the harmony, we destroy what Christ sacrificed himself for. No wonder Paul wrote that we should "keep the unity of the Spirit in the bond of peace" (Ephesians 4:3).

17. And came and preached peace to you which were afar off, and to them that were nigh.

The heathen Gentiles were *afar off* from God; the pious Jews were *nigh.* Also, some Gentiles were much farther than others, and some Jews were much nearer than others. But those who came to Christ were all united in peace.

Jesus *preached peace* by His attitudes and actions as well as His words. He *preached peace* when He did not retaliate against those who crucified Him. He preached peace when He did not hurl back insults at those who were insulting Him. He preached peace when He befriended the rich and the poor, the Jew and the Greek, males and females, young and old, the well and the sick.

Christ's peace is preached today in attitudes and actions: by being humble, being merciful, being forgiving, accepting one another, praying for one another, building up one another, and being kind to one another. How well is His message of peace being communicated through us today?

18. For through him we both have access by one Spirit unto the Father.

Christ insured our access to the Father by giving each of us the Holy Spirit. Regardless of who we are, all of us have the same access to the Father. His Spirit is not only near us; He is in us (1 Corinthians 6:19). We can speak to Him at any time of the day or the night, and we can draw resources from Him in every time of need. He is accessible always, not just for the ordained, the mature Christian, the church leader, the rich, the educated, the healthy, the American, but to all of us who are in Christ. We all have equal access to our Heavenly Father. He is no respecter of persons. He is no more and no less a Father to one than to another.

III. The New Fellowship (Ephesians 2:19-22)

A. In the Same Family (v. 19)

19. Now therefore ye are no more strangers and foreigners, but fellow citizens with the saints, and of the household of God.

The before and after pictures are clear in this verse. We move from being strangers to being friends and from being *foreigners* to being *fellow citizens* and members of the family of God. Those in the same family not only belong to the same Father, but also belong to one another. We should live like loving members of the same family. The Father himself commands those who love Him to love their brothers too (1 John 4:21). If we say we love God when we don't love our brothers, we are lying (1 John 4:20).

Our love for one another is part of the lifestyle that marks us as Christians (John 13:35). Sometimes Christians humorously remark that we are commanded to *love* other Christians, but we don't have to *like* them. But look at Romans 12:10. The Greek word for *brotherly love* indicates the friendly kind of love rather than the charitable kind. We need to grow in real friendship as well as in mutual helpfulness. Not only should we recognize ourselves as children of the same Father and therefore members of the same

visual 10

family as brothers and sisters, but we need to grow to be better friends with our brothers and sisters. Isn't that what we want in our children? Wouldn't we be disappointed if our children grew to adulthood admitting that they were kin to each other, but not liking each other?

B. On the Same Foundation (v. 20)

20. And are built upon the foundation of the apostles and prophets, Jesus Christ himself being the chief corner stone.

There will always be differences in the family of God, as there are differences in our human families. But if we are in Christ, we have been built upon the very same *foundation.* The parts of a house are very different—floors and ceilings, walls and stairs, windows and doors—but they are all shaped to fit the foundation and to harmonize with one another in a strong and beautiful structure.

The *foundation* upon which we rest is that *of the apostles and prophets* who were inspired spokesmen of God. Every element of character and life and fellowship is shaped to fit their teaching. The *corner stone* is the beginning from which all the rest takes its direction—and that *corner stone* is *Jesus Christ. The foundation of the apostles and prophets* is in perfect accord with Him, and we are to be in perfect accord with both. This we do as we apply to our lives what we learn about Christ in the four Gospels.

A SOLID FOUNDATION

In A.D. 1174 the foundations were laid for what, in time, would become one of the world's most famous buildings. It was designed by Bonanno Pisano and built of white marble. The purpose of the structure was to house the bells that would peal out the religious intensity of the city in honoring Christ and in calling the faithful to worship.

This campanile or bell tower was a thing of beauty in its planning and progress toward completion. However, there was one fatal flaw in its engineering. The foundations were unsound. By the time of dedication in the fourteenth century, the edifice had already begun to lean. Today it tilts more than seventeen feet from perpendicular. The poor foundations have destroyed its perfection. It now attracts tourists as the Leaning Tower of Pisa, but it cannot fulfill the purpose for which it was constructed.

A solid foundation is essential for a lasting structure. The church, the household of God, is built on the foundation of the apostles and prophets, inspired spokesmen for our Lord. Jesus Christ is the chief cornerstone. This building will endure and fulfill the purpose of its creation. We have a sure foundation on which we can rely.

Be sure you are building your faith and your life on this solid rock that will outlast time and bring you safely into eternal glory. —W. P.

C. Being the Same Temple (v. 21)

21. In whom all the building fitly framed together groweth unto a holy temple in the Lord.

God does not live in a temple of stone, but in all the rooms of all our hearts. Both individually and together, we are the temple of our Lord. As the temple of old was a special place of God's presence, so we are the material for the presence of our Lord in this world today. If we are truly His, we bring His presence wherever we go.

D. With the Same Indwelling God (v. 22)

22. In whom ye also are builded together for a habitation of God through the Spirit.

Our unity is heightened when we read that we are *builded together for a habitation of God.* God indeed does dwell inside of us! The Holy Spirit is the presence of God on earth. If the same God who lives in me lives in you also, then we are united by His presence. If God lives in a person, what we do to that person is done to God. Jesus said to Saul (later known as Paul), "Why are you persecuting me?" when Saul had been persecuting Christians (Acts 9:4). In the Day of Judgment the same Jesus will say, "Inasmuch as ye have done it unto one of the least of these my brethren, ye have done it unto me" (Matthew 25:40).

Since God has chosen to live in every person who is in Christ, regardless of that person's education, intelligence quotient, occupation, bank balance, or political affiliation, we as Christians should be willing to live with and for one another. It is one thing to live *with* someone, but it is something else to live *for* someone. We and our fellow Christians are united because of Christ. We are in the same family; we are God's temple on earth; we share the same foundation. We should help one another, not hurt one another.

We should live to include, not exclude. We should build up each other, not tear down. We should forgive one another, not hold bitterness. We should educate one another, not eliminate one another. We should grow together, not apart. We should fellowship with, not feud with. We should be at peace with each other, not at war. We should be kind, not blind. We should pick up, not pull down. We should heal each other, not destroy.

Conclusion

A. A Friend Defined

Many years ago an English publication offered a prize for the best definition of a friend. People sent in thousands of definitions. Here are some of them:

1. A friend is one who multiplies joys and divides griefs.
2. A friend is one who understands our silence.
3. A friend is like a watch that beats true for all time and never runs down.

The definition that won the prize was this: "A friend—the one who comes in when the whole world has gone out." Christ is such a friend. That's the kind of friendship He wants us to have with one another.

B. Prayer

Father, thank You for seeing us on the outside and bringing us on the inside to Jesus Christ. Amen.

C. Thought to Remember

"Now therefore ye are no more strangers and foreigners, but fellow citizens with the saints, and of the household of God" (Ephesians 2:19).

Home Daily Bible Readings

Monday, Aug. 2—Man's Hopeless Condition (Ephesians 2:11-16)
Tuesday, Aug. 3—Together in the Household of God (Ephesians 2:17-22)
Wednesday, Aug. 4—Dead to Sin (Romans 6:1-14)
Thursday, Aug. 5—The Inward Struggle (Romans 7:14-25)
Friday, Aug. 6—Controlled by the Spirit (Romans 8:1-10)
Saturday, Aug. 7—Inseparable (Romans 8:35-39)
Sunday, Aug. 8—Justified by Faith (Galatians 2:16-21)

Learning by Doing

This page contains an alternate lesson plan emphasizing learning activities. Classes desiring such student involvement will find these suggestions helpful.

Learning Goals

Students in today's class should:

1. Discover how God has reconciled us to himself and to each other through Christ.

2. Decide how Christians can better experience this reconciliation to each other today.

3. Choose one fellow Christian with whom they can experience a greater measure of this reconciliation.

Into the Lesson

Use one of the following ideas to begin:

• *Role play.* Ask for four volunteers who will act out the following situation. Tell three of the four that they want to plan an activity together for that afternoon, but none of them wants to include the fourth person. Do not tell the fourth person that he or she is to be excluded. Tell that person only that the other three are planning something, and he or she would like to be included.

Allow about five minutes for the role play. Discuss it briefly with the class. Ask, "Have you ever felt excluded from an activity that others were planning? How did you react? How did you feel about those who excluded you?"

• *Share and brainstorm.* Before class write "Outsiders" in large letters on your chalkboard. Ask class members to find partners and tell each other about a time when they felt like an outsider. After five minutes, let a few tell their stories to the whole class. Ask class members to list adjectives to describe how they felt when they were excluded. List these on the chalkboard as they call them out.

After either activity, tell class members that today's Scripture describes God's actions to make sure that every person can be brought into a relationship with Him and His people.

Into the Word

Before reading today's text for the class, tell students that you will ask them to write down, in only one or two words, their answer to this question: "What is this Scripture about?"

Read the text, and then distribute small pieces of paper and pencils to class members. Have them jot down their answers. Collect the slips of paper and read them back in random order.

If you wish, you may make these responses your "outline" for discussing and explaining the passage. Add points students don't mention.

Or point students to the following list of words included in their student books. (If you wish, display a poster that lists these words.)

Peace. Fellowship with Christians. Fellowship with God. Hostility. Unity. Citizenship. Reconciliation.

Ask students, perhaps in pairs, to find what our text is saying about each of these things. After several minutes, ask volunteers to share with the whole class what they've decided.

A third possibility for Bible study is to challenge class members to show the meaning of this passage artistically. Distribute drawing paper and crayons or felt-tip markers, and give the following instructions (also included in the student book for this lesson):

Verses 11, 12—Use no more than three lines to show the situation of Gentiles without Christ.

Verses 13-18—Draw a picture, shape, or symbol to indicate what Christ accomplished for the Ephesians—and for us.

Verses 19-22—Draw a picture, shape, or symbol to show how Christ's work can affect our human relationships.

Into Life

Discuss with students: "What does each of these word pictures tell you about how Christians should relate to each other today?" List the following phrases (quoted here from the *New International Version*): "Access to the Father" (v. 18); "fellow citizens" (v. 19); "God's household" (v. 19); "the whole building is joined together" (v. 21). Ask, "What factors sometimes keep us from relating to other Christians as members of the same family? Have you ever felt separate from another Christian, instead of connected to that person like parts of the same building? What could you do to feel more a part of each other? What rights do citizens of the same country share? What responsibilities? How much independence, diversity, or disagreement among Christians is allowed by these word pictures? How much is forbidden?"

Challenge students to decide if some barrier in their hearts is separating them from another member of Christ's family. What can they do to remove it?

Close with guided prayers, allowing class members to silently commit to bridging the broken relationships they have thought about.

Let's Talk It Over

The questions on this page are designed to encourage review of the lesson Scriptures and to promote discussion of the lesson by the class. The answers provided are only discussion starters. Let your class talk it over from there.

1. Many of us have had the painful experience of being excluded as an outsider, and also the joyful feeling of being included as a member. How does being excluded affect our feelings about ourselves, others, and God? In what way does being included influence our thinking about ourselves, others, and God?

Being excluded can be quite damaging to our self-esteem and self-confidence. Because of rejection, we may doubt our own worth; and our relationship with others is hindered by our insecurity. Some of us may actually believe that God himself cannot love and accept "rejects" like us.

On the other hand, being accepted can encourage us greatly by giving us confidence in ourselves and security in our relationships. God's love for us moves us to a response of gratitude and love for God. It also enables us to risk loving others.

2. How might our congregation grow in willingness to accept people who are different? How might we overcome the barriers between us and other people?

Putting ourselves in contact with individuals who are different from us can help us break out of our comfortable situations and interact with other people. A humble acceptance of the customs, culture, language, and background of other people may end some of the divisions that hinder the message of the gospel. Real love for those who are not like us can tear down the walls that impede the spread of God's ideal love and compassion for all men and women.

3. A prideful attitude may cause us to think, "My way is right. You are different and so you are wrong." Such an attitude insists that other people become like us to be accepted. How does such pride affect our relationships with those who are different from us? How might those relationships be changed if we would become more humble and unpretentious toward them?

Often our preconceived attitudes, opinions, and beliefs lead us to pass judgment on other people in order to justify keeping separated from them. With prejudice we may rationalize behaviors and attitudes that are not Christlike. Such prejudice further divides people from one another. On the other hand, humbly accepting other people can open up a whole new world of friendship as we listen sensitively, relate lovingly, and learn unpretentiously from each other.

4. Families sooner or later are broken by divorce or death, but many of us find in our church a sense of belonging to a family. How can we contribute to and benefit from being a part of "the family of God"?

By sharing our gifts, abilities, and talents with one another, by serving the needs of others, by encouraging and comforting one another, and by caring for each other we can contribute to our church family. The joy and satisfaction of ministering to one another in Jesus' name is one of the greatest benefits; but we may also receive from others the same help and encouragement that we give to them.

5. Jesus, our peace, has made access to God available to all people. He has provided a chance for salvation to everyone. How should His act of reconciliation affect us, our relationships, and our outreach?

With deep gratitude we should praise God for providing our redemption, undeserving though we are. With overflowing thankfulness for His love we should share the good news with our neighbors, friends, and co-workers. We should reach out to people of every culture, language, and ethnic group here and around the world.

6. What can we do to "keep the unity of the Spirit in the bond of peace"? (Ephesians 4:3).

The unity of the Spirit necessitates a commitment to God and to the authority of His Word. It requires a willingness to differ in human opinions and yet to stand uncompromisingly on Scriptural essentials. It demands a love that is both gracious and just. We can help by cultivating such a love in ourselves. With such a love to motivate us, we can listen to others' opinions and respect them even when we do not agree. And we can help by remembering that any question is settled when there is a plain statement in God's Word. We can help also by reminding others that God's Word is the final authority, but by doing it in a kindly way.

New Behavior

August 15
Lesson 11

Devotional Reading: Ephesians 4:25-32.

Lesson Scripture: Ephesians 5:1-20.

Printed Text: Ephesians 5:1-20.

Ephesians 5:1-20

1 Be ye therefore followers of God, as dear children;

2 And walk in love, as Christ also hath loved us, and hath given himself for us an offering and a sacrifice to God for a sweet-smelling savor.

3 But fornication, and all uncleanness, or covetousness, let it not be once named among you, as becometh saints;

4 Neither filthiness, nor foolish talking, nor jesting, which are not convenient: but rather giving of thanks.

5 For this ye know, that no whoremonger, nor unclean person, nor covetous man, who is an idolater, hath any inheritance in the kingdom of Christ and of God.

6 Let no man deceive you with vain words: for because of these things cometh the wrath of God upon the children of disobedience.

7 Be not ye therefore partakers with them.

8 For ye were sometime darkness, but now are ye light in the Lord: walk as children of light;

9 (for the fruit of the Spirit is in all goodness and righteousness and truth;)

10 Proving what is acceptable unto the Lord.

11 And have no fellowship with the unfruitful works of darkness, but rather reprove them.

12 For it is a shame even to speak of those things which are done of them in secret.

13 But all things that are reproved are made manifest by the light: for whatsoever doth make manifest is light.

14 Wherefore he saith, Awake thou that sleepest, and arise from the dead, and Christ shall give thee light.

15 See then that ye walk circumspectly, not as fools, but as wise,

16 Redeeming the time, because the days are evil.

17 Wherefore be ye not unwise, but understanding what the will of the Lord is.

18 And be not drunk with wine, wherein is excess; but be filled with the Spirit;

19 Speaking to yourselves in psalms and hymns and spiritual songs, singing and making melody in your heart to the Lord;

20 Giving thanks always for all things unto God and the Father in the name of our Lord Jesus Christ.

Golden Text: Be ye therefore followers of God, as dear children; and walk in love, as Christ also hath loved us, and hath given himself for us.—Ephesians 5:1, 2.

Following God's Purpose

Unit 3: Newness Through Christ

(Lesson 9-13)

Lesson Aims

At the conclusion of this lesson, the students should be able to:

1. Tell why God has determined that certain actions are to be labeled as sin.
2. List ways to become a positive moral influence in the community.
3. Think of one way they themselves will improve their Christian influence.

Lesson Outline

INTRODUCTION
- A. Changing the Tags
- B. Lesson Background

I. KEEP IT CLEAN (Ephesians 5:1-7)
- A. Mimic the Father (vv. 1, 2)
  - *The Love Walk*
- B. Say No to Filth (vv. 3, 4)
- C. The End of Filth (vv. 5, 6)
- D. Just Say No (v. 7)
  - *Opt Out!*

II. DEMONSTRATE WHO YOU ARE (Ephesians 5:8-10)
- A. Projectors of Light (v. 8)
- B. Producers of Fruit (v. 9)
- C. Pleasers of God (v. 10)

III. DISPEL THE DARKNESS (Ephesians 5:11-20)
- A. Don't Share Darkness (vv. 11-13)
- B. Act Wisely (vv. 14-16)
  - *Redeem the Time*
- C. Keep in Touch With God (vv. 17-20)

CONCLUSION
- A. Internal and Eternal
- B. Prayer
- C. Thought to Remember

Display visual 11 of the visuals packet and let it remain before the class. It highlights Paul's teaching in verse 8. The visual is shown on page 429.

Introduction

A. Changing the Tags

Tony Campolo tells about some boys who did a very creative prank on Halloween. They sneaked into a department store and changed the price tags. The next morning very expensive items were marked at ridiculously low prices, while inexpensive items were tagged at outrageously high prices. The reversal of values created confusion.

Values have been switched all around us. We are being told that staying married until death is not "the" thing, while living together without marriage is "in."

Students in a high school were forbidden to wear T-shirts with the name of their organization, Fellowship of Christian Athletes; but Satanic T-shirts were permitted.

The switching of values is not new. Centuries ago God spoke of a nation whose leaders had switched the tags and were calling evil good and good evil. They were substituting darkness for light and light for darkness; bitter for sweet and sweet for bitter (Isaiah 5:20). God promised to bring that nation down (Isaiah 5:26-30).

B. Lesson Background

The first three chapters of Ephesians tell about God's privileges for us that result in our unity with God and with fellow Christians. Chapter 4 highlights several attitudes and activities that will maintain unity in the bond of peace—lowliness, meekness, patience (4:2), not letting the sun go down on our anger, using our speech to build people up, letting go of bitterness, being kind and forgiving (4:26-32).

In chapter 5, Paul continues discussing God's purpose of maintaining unity. Now he turns the spotlight on our moral responsibilities.

I. Keep It Clean (Ephesians 5:1-7)

A. Mimic the Father (vv. 1, 2)

1. Be ye therefore followers of God, as dear children.

We come into the family of God as "born again" children. One characteristic of children is their imitation of their parents.

The Greek word for *followers* is the one from which we get our word *mimics*. We are to be mimics of God—of His character and the way He acts and reacts. We can imitate God with integrity, not with hypocrisy, because He has chosen to live in us through His Spirit (Ephesians 2:22), and because in Christ we have been recreated in the likeness of God (Ephesians 4:24).

2. And walk in love, as Christ also hath loved us, and hath given himself for us an offering and a sacrifice to God for a sweet-smelling savor.

Our lives need to be characterized by *love*, but what kind of love? The Hollywood style? No, we are to love as Christ does—unselfishly, each giving self up for the benefit of others. Jesus sacrificed His life on the cross; but from us He wants a living sacrifice, our loving lives devoted to His service (Romans 12:1). To love the way Christ loved is to take up our cross daily, to be sacrificing ourselves continually, as we follow Him.

THE LOVE WALK

You have heard of Lover's Leap, Lover's Retreat, Lover's Hideaway, Lover's Beach, and many other names commemorating events or circumstances associated with certain places. Some of these names speak of tragedy; others speak of joy. What all such places have in common is not their scenery or the incidents that happened there. They share lovers, who are special people with a special commitment to each other or to a cause worthy of devotion and sacrifice.

Lover's Walk is a favorite place along the Oregon coast. The vista of ocean, towering fir trees, lofty mountains, and secluded glades gives space for holding hands, a tender embrace, a gentle touch, and intimate talk of memories and personal relationships. It is a place for walking, dreaming, and sharing together all that is best in life and love. It was given its name by a man of God who went there to be alone with His Lord for prayer and devotion. Each of us needs a lover's walk to sustain or renew vows once so solemnly and joyously made to God or to some other companion.

Paul calls us to "walk in love." He describes the love walk as following Christ's example in His sacrifice for us. This is the way those who love Jesus can share the "sweetsmelling savor" of their Lord with others. Christ's love walk to the cross can bring all people back to God. Any lover's walk of lasting worth must include sacrifice, or it is too shallow for such a name. —W. P.

B. Say No to Filth (vv. 3, 4)

3. But fornication, and all uncleanness, or covetousness, let it not be once named among you, as becometh saints.

Fornication is the Greek word *porneia,* from which comes *pornography.* The Greek word means any kind of sexual perversion. It is emphasized by the following words, *all uncleanness. Covetousness* means craving something that does not belong to you. It is connected with sexual immorality because one form of it is craving a neighbor's wife (Exodus 20:17). Regardless of what society allows, we Christians must live like who we are—*saints.* Saints are not persons who are perfect, but persons who have placed their faith and life in the perfect Jesus.

4. Neither filthiness, nor foolish talking, nor jesting, which are not convenient: but rather giving of thanks.

How to Say It

PORNEIA (Greek). por-*nye*-uh or por-*nay*-uh.

We are presently living in a time saturated by filthy talk and words—words that are crude, dirty, and barbaric. They blast us through songs, television, books, and movies. Our Constitution that allows freedom of speech is used to legalize all sorts of filthy talk. The writers of our Constitution did not have that kind of freedom in mind. Freedom of speech ought to be coupled with responsibility—responsibility for the wellbeing of others, not just for expression of self.

When Paul wrote about *foolish talking* or *jesting,* he was not condemning good humor or fun or joking; he was writing about the kind of talk that is not in good taste because it hurts others. Some people say, "Sticks and stones may break my bones, but words will never hurt me." That is as wrong as the devil's word to Eve, "Ye shall not surely die." Words hurt, and sometimes they hurt so deeply that the wounds stay sensitive for years.

Instead of using our voices to cut people down, we need to use them in being thankful—to God and to others.

C. The End of Filth (vv. 5, 6)

5. For this ye know, that no whoremonger, nor unclean person, nor covetous man, who is an idolater, hath any inheritance in the kingdom of Christ and of God.

The *whoremonger* comes from the same Greek word that is used for *fornication* in verse 3. It means one who engages in any kind of sexual perversion. Such a person is *unclean,* filthy. A *covetous man* is *an idolater,* whether he craves someone's wife or something else. He makes a god of his craving: he puts it above the real God who said, "Thou shalt not covet." The person described in these ways is an addict of immoral practices. That person will not inherit *the kingdom of Christ and of God*—an eternity in Heaven. First Corinthians 6:9-11 describes a similar lifestyle, but adds good news. A person can change through faith and repentance, be totally forgiven, washed, sanctified, and justified. Then that person can inherit the kingdom of God.

6. Let no man deceive you with vain words: for because of these things cometh the wrath of God upon the children of disobedience.

There are many non-Christian deceivers, and even some of our brothers and sisters in the church may try to tell us that adultery and covetousness are not so bad as our grandparents thought. Such words are *vain,* which means empty and unproductive. They lead to nothing but sin that demands the wrath of God. We are children of God; we should not act like *children of disobedience.* That does not mean we are so perfect that we can never mess up, slip, fall, or sin; but it does mean we don't make that life-style the dominant pattern of our lives. If we sin, it is a rare exception followed quickly by repentance.

D. Just Say No (v. 7)

7. Be not ye therefore partakers with them.

We are not to participate in the immorality about us. Why does God call some actions sin? Is it because He is an old fuddy-duddy way up there in Heaven? Is it because He likes to veto our fun? Of course not. Sin is sin because it hurts people. Romans 13:8-10 makes that clear: "Love worketh no ill to his neighbor: therefore love is the fulfilling of the law." If we do no harm to other people, we fulfill God's expectations for us in our relationships. God hates sin because it hurts people. God loves people so much that He sent His Son to die for them. If we hurt people, we also hurt God.

The antidote to sin is love. Sin is lovelessness and lawlessness. We don't have to memorize a list of sins. What we have to do is ask, "Will this hurt someone?" If it will, it will hurt God, and it is sin.

OPT OUT!

Needlework is a genteel art, but one that requires much patience, a good eye, concentration, and determination. A little girl just eight years old was beginning to learn the skills of sewing. At times nothing seemed to go right. As often as not, a seam needed to be ripped out and started over again. It was a tedious task, but she had decided she would not give up. After some months she was becoming proficient in her new skill and proud of her achievements. One day she completed the hemming of a skirt with no missewn stitches. Proudly she displayed her work to her mother. Her words announcing her success were beyond her years. She said, "The best thing about not putting in crooked stitches is you don't have to take them out again!"

Life is like that. We spend bitter, agonizing hours trying to mend or remove the crooked patterns we create by doing or saying things that never should be a part of our conversation, actions, or life-style.

Wrong associations and temptations all about us make it easy to insert "crooked stitches" into our life patterns. Paul tells us to OPT OUT! How we live is a matter of choice, not chance. Speaking of those whose way of life shuts them out of God's kingdom, the apostle says, "Be not ye therefore partakers with them." It is easier to do right the first time than to attempt corrections later. —W.P.

II. Demonstrate Who You Are (Ephesians 5:8-10)

A. Projectors of Light (v. 8)

8. For ye were sometime darkness, but now are ye light in the Lord: walk as children of light.

Some people think the way to stay out of sin is to stay out of society. That is not so. Jesus modeled what it means to be a mature child of God: He came into society and was very much involved. We are to be *light.* The purpose of light is to dispel darkness. It cannot dispel darkness unless it penetrates the darkness. The call to *walk as children of light* implies that we are to walk where there is darkness. Otherwise there is no use for the light. We don't turn on a flashlight in the sunlight; we use it in the dark.

We are light *in the Lord,* which means we must stay in contact with Him. He is our source. We must never become unplugged from that source, or our light will flicker and fade.

B. Producers of Fruit (v. 9)

9. (For the fruit of the Spirit is in all goodness and righteousness and truth.)

The fruit of the Spirit is outlined elsewhere: love, joy, peace, long-suffering, gentleness, goodness, faith, meekness, temperance (Galatians 5:22, 23). That fruit is summed up in this verse as *goodness and righteousness and truth.*

In order to bear fruit, we as branches must be connected with the vine, Jesus (John 15:1-5). We bear fruit for the purpose of helping others and causing them to be attracted to Jesus. Others should get a "good taste" of Him through our lives.

C. Pleasers of God (v. 10)

10. Proving what is acceptable unto the Lord.

What is acceptable literally means what is well-pleasing. Proving it is doing it—trying it and finding it good. One secret of Jesus' effectiveness was that He did everything to please God (John 8:29). God himself said He was pleased (Matthew 3:17; 17:5). Paul wrote that our goal is to be pleasing to God at all times (2 Corinthians 5:9).

Pleasing God is the opposite of hurting others. Christian ethics is not a matter of legalistic listings, but of a positive ambition to be pleasing to God. We do right out of respect to Him.

III. Dispel the Darkness (Ephesians 5:11-20)

A. Don't Share Darkness (vv. 11-13)

11. And have no fellowship with the unfruitful works of darkness, but rather reprove them.

Have no fellowship means not to participate in the negative life-style. We have a responsibility to *reprove* wrongdoing, to show up the fruitlessness and uselessness of the wrong way by living in the right way. Someone has said that if we don't stand for something, we will fall for anything. So take a stand!

Unfruitful works of darkness means immorality of all kinds. Doing wrong brings more wrong (darkness); it never brings goodness (light). It never shows us the proper way to live, or the way to live forever. It gradually changes our moral standards and liberalizes our laws.

Many of our inventions can be misused to threaten our welfare, and even our existence. We harnessed nuclear energy, and now we are terrified because it may destroy us all. We invented the camera and the printing press; and they are misused to produce pornography. We invented drugs for medical purposes; but when they are used in the works of darkness, we have an epidemic of addiction.

12. For it is a shame even to speak of those things which are done of them in secret.

The more we talk casually about the shameful immorality around us, the more we become accustomed to it. Gradually we cease to be ashamed of it. The mass media have done a marvelous job of introducing shoddy moral values and immoral practices into the movies and into print. More and more people are regarding those values and practices as acceptable. Evil that is tolerated becomes a way of life for many. If you speak of shameful things at all, reprove them (v. 11) by word of mouth and way of life.

13. But all things that are reproved are made manifest by the light: for whatsoever doth make manifest is light.

We do not reprove or expose things by being mean, vindictive, or violent. We expose things by the light. We expose wrong by being right. We expose the blighted by the brightness. Wrong is to be seen as wrong in comparison with our goodness.

Goodness speaks for itself. We don't have to blow up a run-down car to show that it is run down. All we have to do is park a new one beside it. The put-down of stale bread is the marvelous aroma of fresh bread. We must let our Christian life-style be more magnetic, joyful, wholesome, fulfilling, and beneficial than any allurement of immorality. But we need to supplement our life-style with lip service. We need to speak up against what is evil and even boycott some evildoers.

B. Act Wisely (vv. 14-16)

14. Wherefore he saith, Awake thou that sleepest, and arise from the dead, and Christ shall give thee light.

Some students take this as a sample of the way to reprove those who are doing wrong. They are dead in sin, as we once were (Ephesians 2:1). They need to be called to the light of Christ and to be raised from the dead as we have been (Ephesians 2:4-6).

If this verse is a call to Christians rather than a reproof to sinners, it indicates that we should not sleep through the changes in moral standards as if we were spiritual Rip Van Winkles. We have risen from the dead (Ephesians 2:4-6). We have the light of Christ, and we should be willing to share it.

15. See then that ye walk circumspectly, not as fools, but as wise.

To *walk circumspectly* is to live carefully—*as wise.* Wisdom is not knowing facts; it is using facts in a moral way, a way that will help people, not harm them. Wisdom from above is pure, peaceable, gentle, reasonable, full of mercy and good fruits, impartial, and sincere (James 3:17). Over against wisdom is the foolishness of the pagan environment around us. It is wise to please God. When we please Him, we add something positive to our environment.

16. Redeeming the time, because the days are evil.

Redeeming the time means grabbing all opportunities to "show and tell" the Christian way. Showing may be a small thing like declining too much change from a clerk who makes a mistake, or leaving a note when you scrape someone's fender. It may be reporting your income honestly, being faithful to your married partner, giving your employer a full day's work for a day's

NOW
YOU ARE
LIGHT
IN THE
LORD;
WALK
AS
CHILDREN
OF
LIGHT.

visual 11

pay, treating your employee with kindness, writing to a television station or your political representative, or refusing to purchase products that sponsor immoral programs on TV.

REDEEM THE TIME

Remorse is a cruel tyrant, robbing us of satisfaction, sleep, a clear conscience, and peace with God. "If only. . . ," are the words that begin remorse's sad stories.

"All we were doing was fooling around. We meant no harm. We never thought about what might happen." Such statements could be made at times by you, or me, or anyone; but the speaker was a boy of fifteen. With his school friend, he had been enjoying the afternoon pushing stones over the two-hundred-foot precipice of Table Rock, located along the Rogue River in southern Oregon.

Having nothing to do, the boys wanted to see how large a boulder they could send crashing to the river below. Trying to move a huge round stone, one of them pulled and the other pushed. The seemingly immovable object moved suddenly, and the youth pulling it plunged over the cliff with the falling stone.

Innocent play. No wrong intended. An accident. Yes, but more. "If only we had not gone to Table Rock." "If only we had not been so near the edge." "If only . . ." Remorse will bring these words to anyone involved in such tragedy.

We all have our own "If only. . ." memories. Sin is worse than any accident in causing remorse. Living in an evil age, we need to be "redeeming the time." We must not walk "as fools" or we may have all eternity to think ,"If only . . ."

—W. P.

C. Keep in Touch With God (vv. 17-20)

17. Wherefore be ye not unwise, but understanding what the will of the Lord is.

It is wise to understand God's will, and the most certain way to understand it is to read His revealed Word. He is not playing hide and seek with us.

18. And be not drunk with wine, wherein is excess; but be filled with the Spirit.

Wine takes over our minds and actions when we are drunk. What we do and say comes from its influence. To *be filled with the Spirit* is to let our minds and actions be dominated by the Holy Spirit who lives in us and who speaks to us through the inspired Scriptures.

19. Speaking to yourselves in psalms and hymns and spiritual songs, singing and making melody in your heart to the Lord.

Some versions have *speaking one to another* instead of *speaking to yourselves.* In some of our songs we say words of teaching or encouragement to ourselves and each other—"Stand Up for Jesus," for example. Other songs give praise or thanks or petitions *to the Lord.* "Holy, Holy, Holy" is a song of praise to Him. In any case, don't sing with your lips only, but *in your heart.*

20. Giving thanks always for all things unto God and the Father in the name of our Lord Jesus Christ.

God is always giving us good things, and we should be *giving thanks always.* His blessing is so constant that we may take it for granted. Our gratitude should be as constant as His blessing. Giving thanks *for all things* may seem like too much—till we remember that "all things work together for good to them that love God" (Romans 8:28). We can be thankful for that.

Conclusion

A. Internal and Eternal

A little girl once quoted John 3:16 this way: "God so loved the world that He gave His only begotten Son, that whosoever believeth in him should not perish, but have internal life." The quotation was not accurate, but what she said was true. The life God gives is both eternal and internal. God wants us to show externally what He has given us internally for eternity.

B. Prayer

Thank You, Father, for being all-righteous and all-holy. Help us to cause Your life-style to make sense to everyone around us. In Jesus' name, amen.

C. Thought to Remember

"Be ye therefore followers of God, as dear children; and walk in love" (Ephesians 5:1, 2).

Home Daily Bible Readings

Monday, Aug. 9—Servants of Righteousness (Romans 6:15-23)

Tuesday, Aug. 10—Obedience (1 John 2:3-11)

Wednesday, Aug. 11—You Cannot Serve God and Mammon (Luke 16:9-13)

Thursday, Aug. 12—Duties of the Christian Life (Ephesians 5:15-21)

Friday, Aug. 13—Integrity Marks the Christian (Luke 11:33-42)

Saturday, Aug. 14—Walk in New Life (Ephesians 5:4-11)

Sunday, Aug. 15—The Surrendered Life (Romans 12:1-8)

Learning by Doing

This page contains an alternate lesson plan emphasizing learning activities. Classes desiring such student involvement will find these suggestions helpful.

Learning Goals

As students participate in today's class session, they should:

1. List all the commands to obey and sins to avoid from today's passage of Scripture.
2. Choose one of these commands to obey and one of the sins to avoid during the upcoming week.

Into the Lesson

Begin by dividing the class into two groups: those "in the light" and those "in the dark." Those "in the light" should find partners and list "three activities that require bright light." Those "in the dark" should pair off and list "three activities that require darkness."

After three or four minutes, make a chalkboard list for each half of the class. Discuss with students, "How are light and dark used in drama and literature as symbols? What does each usually stand for or signify? Why?"

Today's lesson calls Christians children of light. Discuss with the class, "In what ways are Christians in the light while non-Christians are in the dark?"

Into the Word

Depending on time and the interests of your class, choose one or both of these Bible-study activities for today's session:

Make a Chart. Distribute sheets of paper to class members and instruct them to put three headings across the top: Do This, Avoid This, Here's Why. (Or point class members to the student book, where this chart is printed.) Ask them, perhaps in groups of four or six, to place each teaching from today's text under one of the headings.

Let the groups report to the whole class. You may want to use their reports to make a master chart on a large sheet of blank newsprint or on an overhead projector transparency.

Write a Want Ad. Ask students to work together, in groups of four or six, to prepare a classified ad that begins, "Wanted: Children of Light." After studying today's text, they should paraphrase its description of the Christian life, want-ad style, for this pretend classified ad. Give them large sheets of newsprint or poster paper. After they've written their ad, they should copy it as a poster and tape it to the wall of your classroom for all to see.

Give class members about ten minutes to work. Then let each group share its want ad with the whole class.

If you prefer, but time is short, you may suggest both options to the class and allow students, in groups of four or six, to decide which of these Bible-study activities they prefer. In this case, have copies of the blank chart available as well as poster paper, pencils, and markers for the want-ad activity. When it comes time to share, allow the ad writers to go first. Then summarize Bible content as the chart completers tell what they have written.

Into Life

Ask class members, "How do you feel after reading this passage? Encouraged or discouraged? Upbeat or depressed? Why?" (If class members are hesitant to respond, take a poll. Ask for a show of hands after each of the adjectives suggested above.)

Ask class members to turn to a partner and discuss, "Is it harder or easier for you to obey this passage today than it was ten years ago?" Give only five minutes for discussion, and then allow volunteers to answer. Ask class members to decide why they answered as they did. What do their answers say about their Christian life? About the society we live in?

Discuss: "Of all the items we are told to do, which do you think is most difficult?" List answers on the chalkboard and ask class members to tell why they chose these.

Then ask, "Of all the sins we are told to avoid, which is the most difficult?" Make a similar list and again ask class members to defend their choices.

Distribute index cards and pencils to class members. Ask them to choose, from all the commands in today's passage, one that they most need to obey this week. They should write it on one side of the index card.

On the other side they should write the one item they most need to avoid, from all those mentioned in this passage.

You may wish to share with the class which of the commands and sins you would list on your own card.

Encourage class members to keep the cards in their pockets or purses or Bibles as a prayer reminder and goal for the upcoming week.

Let's Talk It Over

The questions on this page are designed to encourage review of the lesson Scriptures and to promote discussion of the lesson by the class. The answers provided are only discussion starters. Let your class talk it over from there.

1. As followers of God (Ephesians 5:1), we are to act as Jesus did. Why? How may our following of God help non-Christians?

As Christians, we no longer belong to ourselves. We have been "bought with a price," and we should live to honor God (1 Corinthians 6:20). Cheap lip service is not enough (Matthew 7:21-23); we must follow Christ's example of wholehearted obedience (John 8:29).

When we imitate the example of Jesus, unbelievers can come to know God because His holiness, righteousness, kindness, compassion, and forgiveness are displayed through our lives.

2. What are some specific ways in which our actions can demonstrate a sacrificial love that is concerned for God and others?

Many people are motivated by a selfish "look out for number one" way of thinking that often grieves God and hurts others. In contrast, if we as Christians are living a life of love, we will search out what pleases the Lord (Ephesians 5:10) and will seek the welfare of others above our own interests (Philippians 2:4). Our sacrificial love will be shown by acting kindly toward our neighbors, by extending forgiveness to friends and enemies, by expressing compassion to the sick, needy, and hurting, and by conducting ourselves justly and honestly in all situations.

3. As God's children, we are not to have even a hint of sin contaminating our lives (Ephesians 5:3-7). What can we do to keep sin from polluting our lives? How can we benefit from resisting sin's poisonous effects in our lives?

Withstanding the onslaught of sin requires total commitment to God. We must say "no" to unholiness and worldliness, and "yes" to discipline, righteousness, and godliness (Titus 2:12). Daily reading and studying of God's Word will reveal to us what pleases God. Maintaining companionship with others who are devoted to God will give us a positive influence and will provide encouragement to do what is right.

Successfully overcoming the temptation to sin will build our faith, purify our character, and develop our Christlikeness. Victory over the cravings of our sinful nature saves us much grief and heartache and grants us the joy that comes from pleasing our Father.

4. Thanksgiving helps displace evil thoughts and words (Ephesians 5:4) with gratitude for God's graciousness in our lives (Ephesians 5:20). What can we do to learn to "give thanks" in all situations? (1 Thessalonians 5:18).

We can stop grumbling, complaining, and gossiping in our families, friendships, work situations, and churches. We can replace these with joyfulness, pleasantness, and encouragement. We can look for ways to honor others and to acknowledge our appreciation for them.

We can look for God's blessings and for opportunities to express our gratitude. By focusing on God's power to work all things for good (Romans 8:28), we can remain thankful even in the gloomiest of circumstances.

5. Living as "children of light" (Ephesians 5:8) requires concern with our ethical behavior at home, work, and play. It necessitates deliberate moral decisions in every area of our lives. How can each of us be a ray of light in our dark corner of the world?

When we refuse to participate in talk or action that does not please God, when we speak against ungodly influences and moral decay, when we demonstrate Christlike alternatives, our light is shining. As we refuse to conform to the world and as we redeem each opportunity to live for God (Ephesians 5:16), we live up to our calling as people of light.

6. To some people the Lord's will (Ephesians 5:17) is a mystery, but as Christians we realize that the Scripture is clear on many specific matters. How does understanding God's purposes for mankind help us make right choices? How can the Lord's will be accomplished in our lives?

As Christians, we understand that God's ultimate plan for us is the restoration of our relationships with Him and restoration of our natures to godliness and holiness. We choose a way of life that helps to accomplish those purposes. God's will is done in our lives when our choices show that we love God above all else, when we love our neighbors as ourselves, when we are Christlike in every word and deed, and when we share the message of reconciliation with the lost around us.

New Family Order

August 22
Lesson 12

DEVOTIONAL READING: Colossians 3:12-21.

LESSON SCRIPTURE: Ephesians 5:21—6:4.

PRINTED TEXT: Ephesians 5:21—6:4.

Ephesians 5:21-33

21 Submitting yourselves one to another in the fear of God.

22 Wives, submit yourselves unto your own husbands, as unto the Lord.

23 For the husband is the head of the wife, even as Christ is the head of the church: and he is the saviour of the body.

24 Therefore as the church is subject unto Christ, so let the wives be to their own husbands in every thing.

25 Husbands, love your wives, even as Christ also loved the church, and gave himself for it;

26 That he might sanctify and cleanse it with the washing of water by the word,

27 That he might present it to himself a glorious church, not having spot, or wrinkle, or any such thing; but that it should be holy and without blemish.

28 So ought men to love their wives as their own bodies. He that loveth his wife loveth himself.

29 For no man ever yet hated his own flesh; but nourisheth and cherisheth it, even as the Lord the church:

30 For we are members of his body, of his flesh, and of his bones.

31 For this cause shall a man leave his father and mother, and shall be joined unto his wife, and they two shall be one flesh.

32 This is a great mystery: but I speak concerning Christ and the church.

33 Nevertheless, let every one of you in particular so love his wife even as himself; and the wife see that she reverence her husband.

Ephesians 6:1-4

1 Children, obey your parents in the Lord: for this is right.

2 Honor thy father and mother; which is the first commandment with promise;

3 That it may be well with thee, and thou mayest live long on the earth.

4 And, ye fathers, provoke not your children to wrath: but bring them up in the nurture and admonition of the Lord.

GOLDEN TEXT: [Submit] yourselves one to another in the fear of God.—Ephesians 5:21.

Following God's Purpose

Unit 3: Newness Through Christ

(Lessons 9-13)

Lesson Aims

This lesson will enable students to:

1. Describe the general responsibilities of family members.
2. Explain the meaning of submission, headship, and love.
3. Define his or her own responsibility in the family, or in the church family.

Lesson Outline

INTRODUCTION
- A. Why a Home?
- B. Lesson Background

I. THE MUTUAL RELATIONSHIP (Ephesians 5:21)
- *A Parable of a Mill*

II. THE WIFE'S PLACE (Ephesians 5:22-24)
- A. What She Is to Do (v. 22)
- B. Why She Is to Do It (v. 23)
- C. How She Is to Do It (v. 24)

III. THE HUSBAND'S PLACE (Ephesians 5:25-33)
- A. The Model (vv. 25-27)
- B. The Love (vv. 28-30)
- C. The Union (vv. 31-33)
  - *Becoming One*

IV. CHILDREN AND PARENTS (Ephesians 6:1-4)
- A. What a Child Is to Do (vv. 1-3)
- B. What a Father Is to Do (v. 4)
  - *Godly Guidance*

CONCLUSION
- A. You Can Take It With You
- B. Prayer
- C. Thought to Remember

Display visual 12 of the visuals packet and refer to it as you discuss today's text. The visual is shown on page 437.

Introduction

A. Why a Home?

Dr. S. Parkes Cadman tells the response of a young woman when her fiance showed her a house he planned to buy. She responded, "A home? Why do I need a home? I was born in a hospital, educated in a college, courted in an automobile, and expect to be married in a church. We can eat at fast food places. I will spend my mornings on the golf course, my afternoons at the clubs, and my evenings at the movies. When I die, I will be buried in the cemetery. Why do I need a home?"

Life in the 1990s is lived in the fast lane. We have many choices pulling for our attention and time. Is it possible that the place where we live is just a place to change clothes—is it a house but not a home?

The home is the environment for developing proper relationships. The kind of relationships we develop in the home will eventually be the kind we have outside the home.

B. Lesson Background

Throughout Ephesians Paul discusses unity in the church. What do family relationships have to do with that? Everything. We will bring our family relational skills (attitudes, actions, and reactions) into the family of the church. The first place for us to apply the positive life-style of chapters 4 and 5 is within our own homes.

I. The Mutual Relationship (Ephesians 5:21)

21. Submitting yourselves one to another in the fear of God.

Submission is mutual. Husbands and wives are to submit to each other. Submission does not mean blind obedience. It means the voluntary giving up of self-centered interests and agendas for the well-being of another person.

Lest we believe that submission is only for the wife, we must not forget that no one lived a more submitted life than Jesus. Not only did He submit to the Father, but He also submitted to His bride—the church—by giving himself up for her.

Submission is a beautiful word that describes the central character of Jesus. Divine as He was, He consented to take a human form and even submitted to death (Philippians 2:5-8). Some of the aspects of our submission are found in Philippians 2:3-7: (1) Do nothing from selfishness or empty conceit. (2) Regard the other as more important than self. (3) Look out for the interests of the other. (4) Sacrifice self. (5) Become a servant.

Mutual submission is done in reverence for Christ. The *King James Version* says *in the fear of God*, but the word is *Christ* in more Greek texts and more English versions. The word *fear* does not mean terror; it means respect and reverence for Christ.

A PARABLE OF A MILL

The mill opened, as usual, at 7 A.M. The men stood around joking a little and waiting for the whirring of the machinery to tell them it was time to begin their tasks.

At about 7:30 A.M. the crew began to get nervous. Why was the mill like some dead thing? Why weren't the normal sounds of operation being heard? What was the matter? The foreman was missing. Something was very wrong.

Then the fight in the office burst out into the mill yard. "We're both owners and operators of this plant, and don't you ever forget it! I know you're the superintendent, but nothing moves until we both give the order!" The noisy confrontation of the bosses amused but then troubled the mill hands. If no one was running the mill, how could the work get done?

The need was evident, and the solution not too difficult. Each of the owners needed to submit to the other; but someone had to give an order or the mill would not operate. Having the role of superintendent did not make one partner superior; it was essential for harmony and fulfilling the task.

A mill, carrying out its purpose of production, is like a family fulfilling its role. Each member of either institution must know his or her own responsibility and fill his or her own place, or the harmony that benefits the whole is destroyed. Someone does have to be in charge.

—W. P.

II. The Wife's Place (Ephesians 5:22-24)

A. What She Is to Do (v. 22)

22. Wives, submit yourselves unto your own husbands, as unto the Lord.

This verse is explaining the application of verse 21. The words *submit yourselves* do not appear in the Greek. Literally it reads, *Wives to your own husbands as to the Lord.* The verb *submit* is correctly inferred from verse 21.

This is not the military kind of submission—"Theirs not to make reply, theirs not to reason why, theirs but to do and die." It's the Master's kind—looking out for another's good.

To submit *as unto the Lord* involves: (1) respect, (2) humility, (3) love, (4) a desire to please, (5) a wish to serve, (6) faithfulness, (7) joy, (8) generosity, (9) thanksgiving, (10) fulfillment by contributing something significant to another, (11) self-denial.

B. Why She Is to Do It (v. 23)

23. For the husband is the head of the wife, even as Christ is the head of the church: and he is the saviour of the body.

The way the church should submit to Christ is the way the wife should submit to her husband. That comparison is continued through the whole paragraph (verses 24, 25, 29, 32). The word *head* may seem to suggest dictatorship and superiority, but Paul links it to Jesus' compassionate caring. His headship is seen in His being *saviour.* If a wife sees her husband as head in the way Christ is head of the church, she sees him as someone who will put his own interests second and her interests first, as someone who will provide for her, protect her, care for her, and serve her.

C. How She Is to Do It (v. 24)

24. Therefore as the church is subject unto Christ, so let the wives be to their own husbands in every thing.

The wife is to submit with the same attitude and affection with which the church submits to Christ. This letter to the Ephesians has mentioned some attitudes and activities that are proper in the church's response to Christ. It will be good to review them now as parts of a wife's response to her husband. See Ephesians 4:1-3, 25-32; 5:1, 2. Service wrapped in that package is what submission is all about. The call is for submission without coercion.

III. The Husband's Place (Ephesians 5:25-33)

A. The Model (vv. 25-27)

25. Husbands, love your wives, even as Christ also loved the church, and gave himself for it.

The husband's attitude and activities are to mirror what Christ has done and will do for the church, His bride. How much did Christ love the church? He *gave himself for it.* Consequently the husband's headship comes in the package of love and sacrifice. Neither a career, leisure, hobbies, the dog, entertainment, or sports should come between the husband and his wife. Would Christ have given himself for the church if He had valued it less than an automobile, a ball game, or a lodge? Then the husband should not allow any of those things to take priority over his wife. He should love her *as Christ also loved the church.* That kind of love is described in 1 Corinthians 13:4-7.

The husband's love is the starting point, the wife's submission is her voluntary response to that kind of love. The wife should be able to see in her husband someone who is rich in mercy (not necessarily money), who has an abundance of love (not necessarily loot), and who has a storehouse of truth (not necessarily treasures).

26. That he might sanctify and cleanse it with the washing of water by the word.

The purpose of Christ's love for the church was to *sanctify* it—to set it apart, dedicate it—and to *cleanse it* from sin for the good of the church as well as for His own good. Most commentators believe that *the washing of water* is Christian baptism in which sins are washed away from a repentant sinner (Acts 22:16). This is done in connection with *the word,* either Christ's word commanding baptism (Matthew 28:19, 20) or the word of the gospel by which people are led to believe and be baptized (Acts 18:8).

A husband's loving relationship with his wife is for her good, not just for his pleasure or advantage. He cannot atone for her sins as Christ did, but his unselfish love and care can help to cleanse her from negative attitudes and feelings so that she is on the path of maturing and changing into Christlikeness—God's goal for us all.

27. That he might present it to himself a glorious church, not having spot, or wrinkle, or any such thing; but that it should be holy and without blemish.

The result of Christ's love is to present to himself *a glorious church*—a church cleansed from every *spot* of sin, every *wrinkle* of evil, a church that does not live for itself but for Him. To be *holy* is to be set apart for Christ—no "affairs" with other lovers. To be *without blemish* is to be forgiven and purified. A husband's Christlike love for his bride helps her to grow in Christlike character, so that she and he together lay aside selfish attitudes and activities and become mature and responsible mates participating in the attitudes and activities of oneness. Thus they will be faithful to each other, as there is faithfulness between Christ and the church.

B. The Love (vv. 28-30)

28. So ought men to love their wives as their own bodies. He that loveth his wife loveth himself.

The husband's treatment of his wife is like a boomerang. That's because there is such an intimate unity. A man's wife is his own body; they are "one flesh" (v. 31). One part of a body cannot mistreat any other part of the body without injury to itself. So it is in a marriage relationship. The golden rule may be slightly modified here: "Do unto your wife as you would like to do to yourself," for in a way you are doing it to yourself. If you give her pain, you will feel pain too, or you will enjoy her joy.

29. For no man ever yet hated his own flesh; but nourisheth and cherisheth it, even as the Lord the church.

This verse moves into the gentle and affectionate side of marriage. The word *hated* does not refer to despising, but to neglecting—the opposite of *nourish and cherish.* These words describe tender loving care and affection. The wife needs more than mere physical necessities. She needs a gentle hand, sweet talk, and loving looks. She needs more than someone who pays the bills, mows the lawn, and washes the car. She needs caring and tender compassion, not just a competent caretaker.

Even as the Lord the church reminds us again that the husband's love for the wife is to be as strong and tender, as self-sacrificing and helpful, as Christ's love for the church.

30. For we are members of his body, of his flesh, and of his bones.

Love has a boomerang effect in the church and in a marriage. We must never forget that how a husband treats his wife is how he is treating a member of the church, and how he treats a member of the church is how he is treating Christ, for the church is His body. Christ takes it personally when the husband does or does not love his wife. A person in the body cannot mistreat another part of the body without personal disadvantage to himself.

C. The Union (vv. 31-33)

31. For this cause shall a man leave his father and mother, and shall be joined unto his wife, and they two shall be one flesh.

Three factors are seen in the kind of caring, loving, upbuilding relationship that makes *one flesh* of two. The three factors are named in Genesis 2:24, which is quoted in the verse before us.

1. Leaving. A married man does not stop respecting his parents. He does not necessarily move to another town. But he must not let attachment to his parents mar in any way his close, intimate relationship with his wife. While father and mother are mentioned here, the principle applies also to other interests that might weaken the unity, interdependence, and companionship of a husband and wife.

2. Cleaving. Our text has *joined.* The Greek word here and the Hebrew words in Genesis 2:24 are strong words for uniting together—the "super-glue" of the Bible. They refer to commitment, not just togetherness. Husband and wife not only live with each other, but also live for each other. They stick with the other for better or for worse; not only in health but also in sickness; not only with riches but also in poverty.

3. Weaving. *They two shall be one flesh.* This refers both to physical intimacy and to relational interdependence. The first can happen during the honeymoon; the second takes time to develop, for it is the opposite of independence. Husband and wife depend on each other emotionally, mentally, socially, and financially. Neither is complete without the other.

32. This is a great mystery: but I speak concerning Christ and the church.

Again Paul reminds us that the husband/wife relationship is built on the model of Christ and the church. Anytime we question some specific thing in our relationships, we need to go back and ask, "Does this mirror Christ and the church?"

It is interesting that God has chosen to refer to the church with the very same terms that we use to refer to our families. He is the *Father;* we are His *children;* we are to one another *brothers* and *sisters;* we come into His family by *adoption* and being *born again* (which happen at the same time); and the church is referred to as Christ's *bride.* Elsewhere Paul said that when he brings people to conversion, he is the matchmaker who brings them together with the husband, Christ (2 Corinthians 11:2). The church is a family, and Christ is our example of family love.

33. Nevertheless, let every one of you in particular so love his wife even as himself; and the wife see that she reverence her husband.

Since Christ's love for the church family is our example, a husband's love should mirror His. The wife's reaction should mirror the church's expected reaction to Christ. The husband's love is the starting point; the wife's respect is the corresponding response. That is the formula for harmony in marriage.

BECOMING ONE

"The institution of marriage is as old as the family of man, and came into being because God said, 'It is not good that the man should be alone.'" This opening statement of a marriage ceremony gives divine sanction and practical reality to the unique relationship between a man and woman in which they take on their new roles of husband and wife and so become a family. Children are the normal completion of the family social unit, and they come as a result of a husband and wife coming together in the oneness God ordained. Marriage, at its ideal, is the most wonderful personal relationship known to human beings.

visual 12

In 1934 Louis Anspacher made this excellent comment on marriage in an address he delivered at that time. Listen to his words: "Marriage is that relationship between man and woman in which the independence is equal, the dependence mutual, and the obligations reciprocal." In that one sentence Mr. Anspacher outlined the way to maintain individual identity while fulfilling the new family order God ordained from Eden to eternity.

Our difficulty is not in his words, which we do understand. Our problem is our need to make in marriage a commitment to practice love as Paul describes it by comparing marriage to Christ's oneness with His church. "One flesh" can be attained only when we love as He loved. This is the Scriptural new family order. —W. P.

IV. Children and Parents (Ephesians 6:1-4)

A. What a Child Is to Do (vv. 1-3)

1. Children, obey your parents in the Lord: for this is right.

The children's role is summed up in one word—*obey. This is right* means it is in line with God's desire, will, and purpose for our lives. *In the Lord* has been understood in three different ways; (1) Obey parents who are *in the Lord:* that is, who are Christians. (2) Obey *in the Lord:* that is, as a part of your duty to the Lord. (3) Obey only such commands as you can obey *in the Lord:* that is, without violating the Lord's will. Whatever the meaning of this phrase, parents do not have the right to demand that their children do immoral things. In our day we hear often of immoral use of children—child pornography, incest, and other abuses. The Lord would not require children to obey in such things, but often the children have no choice.

2. Honor thy father and mother; which is the first commandment with promise.

There are different ways to obey. Children are to obey not with haughtiness, but with honor to the parents; not with rebellion, but with respect; not with anger, but with affection. If we do not learn to respect authority as children, it will be difficult to learn as adults. Among the Ten Commandments, this is the first one with a specific *promise* attached. The promise is quoted in the next verse.

3. That it may be well with thee, and thou mayest live long on the earth.

A positive relationship with a parent affects the spiritual, social, and physical health. Anger and temper tantrums increase the blood pressure, constrict the arteries, and cause an excessive flow of fluids to be dumped into the stomach. Want to feel better? Then relate better. And of course children who obey their parents are much less likely to die in accidents, by murder, and by overdose of drugs.

B. What a Father Is to Do (v. 4)

4. And, ye fathers, provoke not your children to wrath: but bring them up in the nurture and admonition of the Lord.

This is addressed to the father as the head of the home, but the mother should heed it too. The command for children to obey does not give parents the right to be mean, overbearing, and cruel. Parents are *not* to be provoking or irritating their children by constant nagging, by hostility, by verbal put-downs, by humiliating insults. Parents are not to yank them up, but to *bring them up*. That takes time, patience, and understanding. It is to be done *in the nurture and admonition of the Lord*. That is not just nurture and admonition *about* the Lord, but the kind of nurture and admonition that comes from the Lord. The Greek word for *nurture* is a general term for the rearing of children; sometimes it means chastening (Hebrews 12:5). The Greek word for *admonition* indicates instruction, often with warning. The phrase *of the Lord* leads us to ask, How does Jesus nurture or discipline His people? How does He instruct and warn? The "howness" is just as important as the "whatness." Does He yell? Is He Lord without love? Is He Head without humility? His nurture or chastening is painful at times, but never without love (Hebrews 12:5-11). Children are not to be objects on which we vent our frustrations and exasperation; they are people in development.

GODLY GUIDANCE

The family named him Amos. His ancestry was partly unknown, but as he grew it appeared that Amos was an unusual combination of Mastiff and Great Dane. His enormous size was both his greatest asset and his worst enemy.

Discipline was a task in which he chose noncooperation. Soon his loving and amiable but destructive ways won him the title, "Famous Amos." His size intimidated. His eager digging in search of nothing destroyed full-grown shrubs and decimated flower beds. His barking and pawing at fences challenged nearby dogs in pens, but disturbed sleep and friendly relationships. In short, Famous Amos was an undisciplined, overgrown monster whose friendly advances frightened all but the very brave and terrorized his neighborhood. He was loved by his young owners, who saw Amos as the perfect family pet and under excellent control. All others viewed him as a moving disaster.

Families need discipline too. It must be loving but firm training that preserves personality but guides children into personal and social responsibility and acceptance. Children who receive and accept "the nurture and admonition of the Lord" become well disciplined and receive God's blessing.

Please! No "Famous Amoses" in your family!

—W. P.

Conclusion

A. You Can Take It With You

We have all heard it said, "You can't take it with you" when you die. In one sense that is correct. There will be no U-Hauls or moving vans following the hearse to the cemetery. We will leave material possessions behind us. But there is something we have here that we can take to Heaven. We can take our families.

Not every day with the family is Heavenly. Some days are tough. On some days we just need to say, "This too will pass." But in the final analysis, the family is worth all it costs. We have nothing that is eternal except the people in our families. They will exist forever and ever. Only people are created in the image of God and can grow up into His likeness.

B. Prayer

Thank You, Father, for modeling for us the kind of relationships we are to have in our human families. Thank You for giving us two families—our family on earth and our eternal family, the church. In Jesus' name, amen.

C. Thought to Remember

Be subject to one another out of reverence for Christ.

Home Daily Bible Readings

Monday, Aug. 16—The Family Before the Curse (Genesis 2:18-25)

Tuesday, Aug. 17—The Duties of the Wife (1 Peter 3:1-6)

Wednesday, Aug. 18—Submission Exemplified (Philippians 2:1-8)

Thursday, Aug. 19—Marital Mutuality (1 Corinthians 7:1-8)

Friday, Aug. 20—The Duties of the Husband (Ephesians 5:25-33)

Saturday, Aug. 21—The Duties of Children (Proverbs 23:15-25)

Sunday, Aug. 22—The Duties of Parents (Deuteronomy 6:1-9)

Learning by Doing

This page contains an alternate lesson plan emphasizing learning activities. Classes desiring such student involvement will find these suggestions helpful.

Learning Goals

Students in today's class should:

1. List the thoughts on submission and authority contained in today's passage.

2. Choose one family member with whom they need a healthier and stronger relationship and pray for God to help that relationship to improve.

Into the Lesson

Try one of these two ideas to get today's class session started.

• *Newlywed Game.* Do your own take-off from this TV show. Choose three married couples from your class. The wives form a panel to answer three questions while their husbands are out of the room where they cannot hear. After the wives' answers are recorded, they sit down as their husbands are asked back into the room. Then the questions are presented to the husbands, who try to guess how their wives have answered. Give points to each couple who matches answers.

Then reverse the process: The wives step out of the room while the husbands answer three questions. Then the ladies come back and try to guess how their husbands have answered.

You may use your own questions, or try these:

Ask the wives:

1. If you had $5,000 that you had to spend on a vacation, where would you go?

2. If you had one more child, what would you name him or her?

3. What's your least favorite chore around the house?

Ask the husbands:

1. If you could be a star in any sport, what would it be?

2. If you could afford to quit your job and pursue another career, what would you choose?

3. Name a family member who's had a big influence on you.

After the "game" is finished, tell class members that today's lesson is about family relationships. Does our performance in such a game as this indicate anything about the quality of our family relationships?

• *Read and react.* Read (or ask a volunteer to read) "Why a Home?" from the lesson introduction in this book. Then discuss with class members: "Is home life today stronger or weaker than it was a generation or two ago? Why? Is your family life healthier or less healthy than that of the family you grew up in?"

Tell class members that today's Scripture lesson gives clues for improving the health of family life today.

Into the Word

Write the following two words on the chalkboard, or show them on pieces of poster board that you've prepared before class: *Submission, Authority.*

Assign each of the words to half of the class and ask class members to choose partners to discuss the words. First they should jot down negative words they associate with their assigned word. How many can they list in sixty seconds? Then they should jot down as many positive words as they can list in sixty seconds.

Ask to hear some of both. Which list was longer?

Tell class members that submission and authority are the subjects of our study. Although there are negative reactions to these ideas today, Ephesians 5 and 6 help us understand them.

To see how this is true, class members should read today's text to see everything it says about their assigned topic. Ask them to do this in groups of four. Give them ten minutes, and then allow them to share their discoveries. Add your own insights gained from studying the lesson.

Into Life

Discuss these questions with the class.

1. How does the comparison of Christ and the church with husbands and wives change your view of the marriage relationship?

2. How do you react to the fact that God has chosen family names and experiences (Father, brother and sister, adoption, born again, bride) to describe relationships in the church? What does this teach you about the family? About the church?

3. At what age does a child no longer need to obey his parents? How should adult children honor their parents?

Ask class members to choose one family relationship—with a spouse, with a child, or with a parent—that needs to improve. They may share this with their partners if they wish. In any case, partners can pray for each other and each other's families as you close today's class.

Let's Talk It Over

The questions on this page are designed to encourage review of the lesson Scriptures and to promote discussion of the lesson by the class. The answers provided are only discussion starters. Let your class talk it over from there.

1. God's purpose is to unite everything in Christ (Ephesians 1:10). How can we submit to one another (5:21), and how does mutual submission contribute to unity in the church, in friendships, in marriages, and in work relationships?

Submission to one another out of reverence for the Lord implies a sacrifice of self-interest for the good of the relationship. Honor and respect for one another are necessary (Romans 12:10; 1 Peter 2:17), and so is humility toward each other (Philippians 2:3) and toward God (James 4:10).

When we submit to one another, we do not demand our own way, be rude, act belligerently, nor be self-serving (1 Corinthians 13:4-7). We relate with kindness, patience, compassion, gentleness, and love (Colossians 3:12-14). Our primary concern is for the other person (Philippians 2:4), and such selfless love has a unifying effect in our relationships (Colossians 3:14).

2. How might our marriages be changed if we would try earnestly to follow the instructions in Ephesians 5:22-33?

Examining ourselves, we might find that we do not often give up our wishes for the good of our spouse. Seeing that, we might come to see our spouse, not as someone who satisfies our desires and wishes, but rather as one whom we assist in realizing the potential God gave to her or him. The result would be a growing harmony in our relationship and the better development of both of us for God's glory.

3. Why are sound, Biblical marriages so important in our homes and our society today? How might marriages in our congregation that truly reflect a Christlike bond affect our children, our friends and neighbors, and our community?

When people around us see how we relate in our marriages, they receive an impression of what Christ's love is like. If they see a marriage of disrespect and disharmony, their view of Christ and His church will be negative. Thus un-Christlike marriages contribute to rebellion toward God and rejection of the gospel by children and non-Christians alike.

On the other hand, marriages where love and unity are the norm attract others to God and the church. Moreover, Christlike marriages provide stability and security for children and continuity and strength for society.

4. Obedience is essential for an orderly society and for personal spiritual growth. As parents, what can we do to help our children learn to obey the proper authorities?

Successful training begins with us, the parents. We must model obedience toward God and the authorities that God has placed over us (Romans 13:1-7). We must expect obedience from our children because it is the right thing to do (Ephesians 6:1). We must resist the permissive theories of our day and nurture respect for authority. This will help prepare our children for life.

5. Most of us want to be good parents. How can we strike a balance in our disciplining, being neither too lenient nor too harsh? How can we provide the nurturing discipline and the encouraging instruction of the Lord that our children need?

As fathers and mothers, we set the emotional and spiritual tone of our households. Our attitudes and moods affect not only the way we discipline, but also the way in which the discipline is received. We need to communicate our love even when we must be stern.

We should avoid threatening, bribing, losing our temper, bullying, refusing to explain, and using sarcasm or embarrassment. But we should not look the other way when our children disobey or behave inappropriately. We should not allow overindulgence, laziness, or lack of self-control in our children. We should not permit wrong attitudes to develop.

6. God's command to honor father and mother (Ephesians 6:2, 3) is not limited to those who are young. How can we adults honor our parents? Why is honoring our parents important?

We honor our parents by treating them with respect and affection, by considering their wishes, by protecting them against loneliness and poverty. Such behavior is important because it benefits our parents, provides a good example for our children, and glorifies God.

New Strength

August 29
Lesson 13

DEVOTIONAL READING: 2 Timothy 2:1-13.

LESSON SCRIPTURE: Ephesians 6:10-20.

PRINTED TEXT: Ephesians 6:10-20.

Ephesians 6:10-20

10 Finally, my brethren, be strong in the Lord, and in the power of his might.

11 Put on the whole armor of God, that ye may be able to stand against the wiles of the devil.

12 For we wrestle not against flesh and blood, but against principalities, against powers, against the rulers of the darkness of this world, against spiritual wickedness in high places.

13 Wherefore take unto you the whole armor of God, that ye may be able to withstand in the evil day, and having done all, to stand.

14 Stand therefore, having your loins girt about with truth, and having on the breastplate of righteousness;

15 And your feet shod with the preparation of the gospel of peace;

16 Above all, taking the shield of faith, wherewith ye shall be able to quench all the fiery darts of the wicked.

17 And take the helmet of salvation, and the sword of the Spirit, which is the word of God:

18 Praying always with all prayer and supplication in the Spirit, and watching thereunto with all perseverance and supplication for all saints;

19 And for me, that utterance may be given unto me, that I may open my mouth boldly, to make known the mystery of the gospel,

20 For which I am an ambassador in bonds; that therein I may speak boldly, as I ought to speak.

GOLDEN TEXT: Be strong in the Lord, and in the power of his might.—Ephesians 6:10.

Following God's Purpose

Unit 3: Newness Through Christ

(Lessons 9-13)

Lesson Aims

At the conclusion of this lesson, a student should be able to:

1. Identify the enemy of the Christian.
2. Identify any weakness in his or her own equipment for the Christian life.
3. Be strong in the Lord.

Lesson Outline

INTRODUCTION
- A. "We're in the Army Now"
- B. Lesson Background

I. ORDERS FROM HEADQUARTERS (Ephesians 6:10-13)
- A. Tap the Right Power (v. 10)
  New Strength
- B. Take the Right Stand (v. 11)
- C. Know the Right Enemy (v. 12)
- D. Put On the Right Armor (v. 13)

II. ARMOR FROM HEADQUARTERS (Ephesians 6:14-17)
- A. Truth and Righteousness (v. 14)
- B. Readiness (v. 15)
- C. Faith (v. 16)
- D. Salvation and the Word (v. 17)
  Proper Equipment

III. APPEAL TO HEADQUARTERS (Ephesians 6:18-20)
- A. At All Times (v. 18)
- B. For Fellow Soldiers (v. 19)
- C. With Specific Requests (v. 20)
  Speaking Out

CONCLUSION
- A. A United Army
- B. Prayer
- C. Thought to Remember

Display visual 13 of the visuals packet and let it remain before the class throughout the session. The visual is shown on page 444.

Introduction

A. "We're in the Army Now"

One of the popular songs during World War II was "We're in the Army Now." It was sung with enthusiasm and pride. People were not embarrassed to be in the military service. We knew who our enemy was; we knew where the battle lines were; we knew what the issues were; we cooperated to win the victory.

When we become Christians, we enlist in God's army. Many New Testament terms describing the Christian life come from military life: soldier, armor, watch, stand fast, fight the good fight.

Each of us needs to ask some hard questions:

1. Are we living as if we were still in boot camp—always preparing, but never taking a stand against the enemy?
2. Are we A.W.O.L.—absent without leave?
3. Are we on the verge of being deserters and traitors?
4. Have we taken early retirement?
5. Are we wearing the uniform that plainly shows whose side we're on?
6. Are we following our commander-in-chief?
7. Have we received any battle scars?
8. Do we shoot our own wounded or desert them when they have fallen on the field?
9. Do we wear our Christian uniform proudly, salute our commander Jesus, and take a stand against our enemy, the devil?

Christianity will win. There's no doubt about that. God is awesome and almighty. There will be a time when we will hear the loud voices of Heaven shouting, "The kingdoms of this world are become the kingdoms of our Lord, and of his Christ; and he shall reign for ever and ever" (Revelation 11:15).

B. Lesson Background

The book of Ephesians says much about the unity of the church. In this last section, we see the unified church in conflict with the world. The language of our text describes the equipment worn by Roman soldiers ready for battle. Paul wrote this letter while chained to a soldier, so it was easy for him to see what the soldier was wearing and make the application to Christians in the church.

The battle we face is between good and evil, between light and darkness, between God and Satan. Everybody is in one army or the other. The conflict is serious. The result is not just a temporary victory, but our destiny for eternity.

I. Orders From Headquarters (Ephesians 6:10-13)

A. Tap the Right Power (v. 10)

10. Finally, my brethren, be strong in the Lord, and in the power of his might.

If an army is to be successful in battle, it must have supplies from headquarters. No army can be victorious when its ammunition or fuel is gone.

There is no excuse for the Christian to run out of fuel. God's supply line is unfailing. It never runs out or wears out. We are not to *be strong* in our own strength, but *in the Lord.* To be *in the Lord* is to have protection and power. He is our foxhole, our fortress. More than that, He is our tank with power to go forward.

Paul piles up three words for power in this verse, as he did in Ephesians 1:19. The word *strong* comes from the word from which we get our word *dynamite.* Then he adds *power* and *might.* There is no foe that can defeat God. His power is inexhaustible.

Ephesians 3:20 summarizes it. Does it say God is able to do all that we ask or think? No, that's too weak. He is able to do above all that we ask or think. No, that's still too weak. He is able to do abundantly above all that we ask or think. Even that is too weak to describe God's power. Paul wrote that God "is able to do exceeding abundantly above all that we ask or think." That's the power we have available to us in our Christian life.

NEW STRENGTH

John Jones was a self-made man. By hard work, enterprise, and favorable conditions he created a small business empire. Wealth, recognition, and honor were his, along with complete confidence in his own ability. One of his favorite sayings was, "I don't fear God, man, or the devil. I am the master of myself and create my own destiny." John was proud and boastful as well as successful.

Then disaster struck. His wife was killed in an accident. His son got "hooked" on drugs. His daughter ran away from home and defied attempts to bring her back. John, who feared nothing and believed he could handle anything, could not cope. A moderate social drinker, he soon became an alcoholic, trying to drown his troubles. His empire began to fall apart. He was thinking of suicide as the only way out.

A Christian friend took John to a men's dinner at his church. There he heard the good news that Jesus specializes in impossible situations. John completely surrendered his life to the Lord. He turned from self-reliance to being "strong in the Lord, and in the power of his might." It was a long battle, but John became whole for the first time. He learned that there are forces we cannot overcome, but God can. —W. P.

B. Take the Right Stand (v. 11)

11. Put on the whole armor of God, that ye may be able to stand against the wiles of the devil.

To rest idly in the Lord is not to tap His power. There is something we need to do. We need to *put on the whole armor of God.* When we do that, His power is available to us. We apply His presence to our practice.

Since He is "able to do exceeding abundantly above all that we ask or think," when we put on the armor we are able to *stand against the wiles of the devil. Wiles* are deceitful scheming. The word *devil,* meaning slanderer, highlights how evil the devil is.

The devil will do anything to bring us down. He has a lot of friends, plans, weapons, and time to do it. He knows he is helpless as long as we are wearing God's armor. His scheme is to get us to take it off. He wants us to distance ourselves from God, to neglect our prayer and worship, and not to equip one another.

We are to take the right stand in this life. The right stand is against the devil. To take that stand, we need to stand for God. If we do not stand for the right, we will fall for the wrong. One of the weaknesses of the church today is that individual Christians are not actively and obviously standing against the kinds of things God stands against. Some even seem to be embarrassed by a stand for the right.

C. Know the Right Enemy (v. 12)

12. For we wrestle not against flesh and blood, but against principalities, against powers, against the rulers of the darkness of this world, against spiritual wickedness in high places.

Our chief enemy is not *flesh and blood,* not other people. We may leap to the conclusion that someone who believes in Christ is the enemy because he or she has some mistaken ideas and practices. But anyone who is in Christ should be seen as our friend and is a brother or sister. Even a person who is not in Christ is not necessarily our enemy. That person may be a POW, a prisoner of war held by our real enemy, Satan. We should do for Satan's captives what we do for POWs in a physical war; we should use energy, plans, and money to rescue them from the prison camp of Satan. What Satan does to people in his imprisonment is worse than the atrocities of the holocaust. Hitler wiped out temporary life; Satan wipes out eternal life.

Our enemy is Satan's army—*principalities* and *powers* of *darkness,* Satan's demons or helpers. Satan has spiritual forces we cannot see, as God has spiritual forces we cannot see. He does have human beings in his army too—people who are willing and eager soldiers of Satan. We are locked into a cosmic battle. The power of Satan's forces produces the polluted practices on earth—*spiritual wickedness.* When we stand up against wickedness, we stand against the power that is behind that wickedness—Satan and his cohorts.

D. Put On the Right Armor (v. 13)

13. Wherefore take unto you the whole armor of God, that ye may be able to withstand in the evil day, and having done all, to stand.

To tap the right power, to take the right stand, to know the right enemy, and to take a stand against the enemy require that Christians wear *the whole armor of God.* We do not just pick and choose what we like to wear. We need all that God offers us. Only with all of it will we be able to stand *in the evil day.*

Not every soldier liked wearing the heavy helmet, but it was necessary when the shrapnel flew. Not every soldier liked carrying the cumbersome shovel, but it was necessary to dig foxholes. Not every Christian likes to wear the total armor of God, but it is necessary. If we don't have it all, Satan will find our weakness with one of his schemes.

II. Armor From Headquarters (Ephesians 6:14-17)

A. Truth and Righteousness (v. 14)

14. Stand therefore, having your loins girt about with truth, and having on the breastplate of righteousness.

None of the armor that Paul has discussed protects the Christian's back. That's because the Christian is not to turn his back on the enemy and run; instead we are to advance boldly. Oh, yes, there are times when we "get away from it all" with others in order to regroup and gain new insight and strength. Instead of calling those "retreats," perhaps we ought to call them "advances." By them we advance in wisdom and power for the battle.

Truth means not only that we say what is correctly aligned with reality, but also that we do what is correctly aligned with reality. The reality is that we have been made new creatures (2 Corinthians 5:17). We are the children of God, and we are to mimic our Father's way (Ephesians 5:1). We are not to camouflage the armor of truth that we wear, neither at the office, nor at school, nor on the golf course, nor anywhere. To do so is not to wear it at all.

Righteousness is doing right and having a right relationship with God, self, and others (Matthew 22:35-40; Romans 13:8-10). Good soldiers always have a proper relationship with their commander and their fellow soldiers. Those in God's army must do no less.

B. Readiness (v. 15)

15. And your feet shod with the preparation of the gospel of peace.

Someone has observed that an infantry is no better than its footwear. To have well-equipped feet is to have an army that is on the march and advancing toward the next battle.

The Christian's *feet* are to be *shod with the preparation of the gospel of peace.* We don't march to destroy people, but to make peace between people and God and between people and other people. We are God's peacemakers, not His warmongers.

We march with feet prepared with the good news that God has made it possible for alienation to be transformed into harmony, for sins to be forgiven, for separations to be bridged by reconciliation. The neglected in the war zone, the hungry, the poor, the wounded, the sick, the deserted can all be cared for by God's army of peacemakers as we march with His evangelism and with His care and love for all people.

C. Faith (v. 16)

16. Above all, taking the shield of faith, wherewith ye shall be able to quench all the fiery darts of the wicked.

We are Satan's targets, and whatever *darts* he has he aims directly at our hearts. The heart is protected by the *shield,* which is our faith. We have hope in what we do not see (Hebrews 11:1). While we don't see God, we are able to see evidences of Him all around us. While we don't actually see the victory, we anticipate it due to God's promises.

We believe in our Heavenly country, our Heavenly king, the Heavenly constitution, the Heavenly liberty, the Heavenly love—and we maintain our faith on the battlefield of life. Satan's spiritual bullets cannot penetrate faith; they only bounce off.

D. Salvation and the Word (v. 17)

17. And take the helmet of salvation, and the sword of the Spirit, which is the word of God.

Not only is Satan after our hearts, he is also after our heads. Not only must we protect both,

visual 13

we also must fill both—the heart with God's emotions and the head with God's truth.

If the enemy can wound the head, the rest of the body is out of the fight. Satan is after the minds of us all. From our thoughts come our deeds. Our battle is to capture the minds of others. We are to take captive the thoughts of everyone, bringing them to obey Christ (2 Corinthians 10:5).

To wear *salvation* as our headgear is to know that we have security in Jesus. One of Satan's major "darts" is doubt of our salvation—our relationship with God, our worth, our destiny. We are to live our Christian lives knowing that we are saved in Christ.

We are not to wear the helmet of doom—an inferiority complex, a doubt of our salvation, a fear of Hell. God has saved us by Christ's death on the cross and His resurrection from the grave. All that Christ's saving work on the cross provides is ours.

Not only are we to surround our minds with a sense of security in Christ, but we are to fill our hands with the sense of God's presence in the front lines. *The sword* we carry is not to destroy but to save. It is not a nuclear power that can annihilate cities, but a Heavenly power that can transform evil into goodness, wrong into right, perversion into purity, sins into forgiveness, and the lost (the damned, condemned) into the saved (the rescued, the rewarded).

The *sword* we carry is *the word of God.* The living Word is Christ who lives within us; the written Word is the Bible that carries God's offer of salvation to all the lost and dying.

PROPER EQUIPMENT

There was a slow buildup of military personnel and machines before the Western allies began the Middle East War to free Kuwait from the unwarranted invasion and conquest by Iraq. Many newsmen and citizens were critical. Most felt that the coming conflict was justifiable on moral grounds, but asked, "Why the delay? Why the restriction on news releases? Why not get it over with?"

Using care and confidence, the military commanders brought together the needed personnel and the newest equipment, some of it not yet battle tested. Each unit moved into its proper position. Then and only then did the war begin.

Air forces pounded Iraqi positions for days. Then it was time for the ground offensive. In a hundred hours it was over. Lives were lost, but with the proper equipment casualties were minimized and Kuwait was freed.

Winning the battle over sin and Satan is an even more difficult task. We must be certain we are fully equipped with "the whole armor of God" to be ready for the battles that must precede our final victory in Christ. "Above all" we need "the shield of faith." It can "quench all the fiery darts of the wicked." When it is in place we cannot lose. Without it we cannot win. —W. P.

III. Appeal to Headquarters (Ephesians 6:18-20)

A. At All Times (v. 18)

18. Praying always with all prayer and supplication in the Spirit, and watching thereunto with all perseverance and supplication for all saints.

Prayer is keeping in contact with the command post. Without that, the armor is inadequate. Let an army lose contact with its command post, and there will be confusion and chaos regardless of the equipment it has.

We are to pray *in the Spirit.* The Spirit is in us (1 Corinthians 6:19), and we are in Him if we accept His leading. We are to pray as Christians, as the Spirit would have us pray. The Spirit intercedes for us when we are at the end of our rope and do not know what to say or ask (Romans 8:26).

Prayer is not just an intellectual conversation, neither is it a fanatical outburst of emotion. It is communication between a human spirit and God, who is a Spirit. It is real talk from a real person to a real God, a God who hears and answers.

We are not to take a vacation from prayer. We should pray *always*—actually talking with God every day, and living in awareness of God throughout the day. To cut off our prayers is to cut off God's power. To cut off our supplications is to cut off our supply. To cut off our calls for help is to cut off His help. *Watching* means being awake, alert, perceptive. If we are not watchful, we may become so wrapped up in material and physical needs that we go to sleep spiritually, becoming unaware of our deeper needs. We should be aware, not of our needs only, but of the needs of others. We do not pray selfishly, but *for all saints,* all Christians.

B. For Fellow Soldiers (v. 19)

19. And for me, that utterance may be given unto me, that I may open my mouth boldly, to make known the mystery of the gospel.

There is to be no jealousy or competition within the ranks of God's people. We are not to be combatting one another, but encouraging one another. Paul asks the people to pray for him. We are to pray for our fellow soldiers. No Christian can win the war alone. We need one another. We must continually intercede for those soldiers around us, for our own sake as well as theirs. They provide us encouragement, supplies, protection, rest, and victory.

Our prayers are to be specific. Verse 18 calls us to pray "for all saints," but verse 19 is more specific: *And for me*. It is not enough to pray for "all our missionaries." We need to mention them by name. We live in too much of a hurry. We want to get even our prayers over quickly, as we want to get quickly through the line at the grocery store. We should pray for our church leaders—by name. We should pray for our Sunday-school teachers—by name. Wouldn't you like to know that someone is praying for you—by name?

C. With Specific Requests (v. 20)

20. For which I am an ambassador in bonds; that therein I may speak boldly, as I ought to speak.

Paul wants the Ephesians not only to pray for him specifically, but also to make a specific request for him: courage to *speak boldly* while he is chained to a guard. We also must be specific in our prayers about needs. We should name the needs and name the people who have them. If we ask only in a general way, how can we expect specific answers? If a missionary is facing expulsion from a country, we need to pray that God will change the hearts of the political leaders in that country. If someone needs a thousand dollars, we should ask God for the specific amount. Our kids know how to ask us specifically. They don't just ask for blessings; they ask for a bike—even a certain brand and color. Specific praying is a powerful force in winning the battle against Satan.

One of Satan's keenest schemes is to allow us to pray regularly but to pray so generally, it will not make much difference.

Home Daily Bible Readings

Monday, Aug. 23—Our Enemy (Matthew 4:1-11)
Tuesday, Aug. 24—Our Position (Ephesians 1:1-6)
Wednesday, Aug. 25—Our Power (Ephesians 1:9-23)
Thursday, Aug. 26—Our Weapon (2 Corinthians 10:1-6)
Friday, Aug. 27—Our Consecration (2 Timothy 2:1-5)
Saturday, Aug. 28—Our Security (Ephesians 6:13-17)
Sunday, Aug. 29—Our Victory (Hebrews 2:9-15)

SPEAKING OUT

In 1858 Abraham Lincoln accepted the Republican nomination for United States Senator from the state of Illinois. In his acceptance speech, Lincoln said, "A house divided against itself cannot stand! I believe this government cannot endure, permanently half slave and half free. I do not expect the union to be dissolved, I do not expect the house to fall, but I do expect it will cease to be divided."

This now famous "house-divided-against-itself-speech" stirred the nation, but in the ensuing campaign against Douglas, his Democratic party opponent, Lincoln was defeated. Lincoln received the most popular votes, but Douglas was elected by the Illinois State Legislature to the United States Senate.

While Lincoln lost the election, he was now a figure of national prominence for his stand against slavery and for preservation of the union. Two years later, in 1860 at Chicago, the Republican party nominated Abraham Lincoln for President of the United States of America. He was elected. His courage in speaking out on the issue that was dividing the nation moved Lincoln from a Springfield lawyer's office to the White House.

We need courage to stand for our Christian convictions and speak out against the evil in our world. Prayer, the Word of God, and confidence in the truth will enable us to speak boldly "the mystery of the gospel." —W. P.

Conclusion

A. A United Army

No army can be victorious unless it is unified. Living the Christian life on the battlefield is like formation flying. You must keep your eye on the leader—Jesus Christ—but you must also fly in formation with others. Your well-being depends on mutual respect and trust. Take your eyes off the leader or ignore those around you, and you are on the way to trouble. There will be undoubtedly a crash.

B. Prayer

Thank You, Father, for defeating Satan by the cross and announcing his total defeat by the triumphant return of Jesus. Help us to let You defeat Satan in and through our lives, individually and corporately in the power of the indwelling Spirit. In Jesus' name we pray. Amen.

C. Thought to Remember

"Be strong in the Lord, and in the power of his might" (Ephesians 6:10).

Learning by Doing

This page contains an alternate lesson plan emphasizing learning activities. Classes desiring such student involvement will find these suggestions helpful.

Learning Goals

Students in today's class should:

1. List the pieces of armor mentioned in this passage and decide what enemy each piece protects against.

2. Choose one of these qualities that is weak in their lives and decide how to make it stronger.

Into the Lesson

Choose one of the following activities to get today's class session started.

• *War Stories.* Invite a veteran of armed conflict to be interviewed by your class. Perhaps this person is a member of your class or your church, or a guest from your community. Let him briefly describe combat experiences in the Mideast, Vietnam, Korea, World War II, or some other conflict.

Allow class members to ask questions. Plan some of your own questions whose answers will point out the commitment required of the fighter, the craftiness of the enemy that must be constantly watched for, and the sacrifice and hardship that sometimes come with battle.

Tell class members that today's text is one of many in the Bible that depicts the Christian life as a battle. Are they ready for the conflict?

• *Ad Search.* Bring a large stack of newspapers and magazines to the class. You may ask a few class members to bring some also, especially if you choose to use them in the Bible study.

For now, distribute the publications among class members and ask them to look for advertisements that depict one of the following: our desire for *power,* our pursuit of *safety,* or our need for *protection.* (Write these three words on the chalkboard as a reminder of the assignment.)

Allow six or eight minutes for students to find and clip their ads. Then let several show and explain what they've found. Tell class members that today's text shows us how to find all three of these by rightly recognizing the enemy and by employing the proper defense.

• *When I Was a Kid* . . . Ask class members to find partners and share their completions to at least one of these sentences:

1. When I was a kid, the place I felt the safest was. . . .

2. When I was a kid, I once needed protection from. . . .

3. When I was a kid, I felt most powerless when. . . .

After a few minutes allow a few class members to share sentences they heard. Then tell class members that our needs for protection and our struggles for power don't end when we become adults. Today's text addresses these issues.

Into the Word

Ask a class member to read verses 10-13 while the rest of the class listens to see what this paragraph has to say about safety, about protection, and about power. Ask a few class members to share insights. Then ask what these verses teach about the devil. Do we tend to think of the devil in these terms? If not, why not?

Challenge students to complete a Bible-study chart (available in the student book) that will help them analyze verses 13-18. The chart should have four headings: Armor piece, What it protects, What it represents, and What enemy it defends against. Students will find answers for the first three columns in the text. Then they must decide for themselves the best answers for the fourth column. Allot ten minutes for this.

Then discuss as a whole class. You may want to make an all-class chart on an overhead projector transparency as students discuss.

If you have time, point students to a stack of newspapers and magazines you have brought to class. Ask them to find examples in them that show the need today for any one of the qualities associated with a piece of armor.

Into Life

Discuss the following questions as you seek to lead students to commitment:

1. What significance do you see to the parts of the body protected by the various pieces of armor?

2. Every soldier has a mission; that's why adequate armor is needed. What is the mission of the Christian? How do verses 19 and 20 lend insight here?

3. Which of these pieces of armor is weakest in your life? Which is strongest? What can you do to "repair" the armor piece that's not strong enough for you?

If you wish, you may use "We're in the Army Now," from the Introduction of this lesson, as an inspirational reading to close today's session.

Let's Talk It Over

The questions on this page are designed to encourage review of the lesson Scriptures and to promote discussion of the lesson by the class. The answers provided are only discussion starters. Let your class talk it over from there.

1. Christians are in a fierce spiritual battle (Ephesians 6:10, 11). Why should we be fearless before Satan's onslaught? What can we do to stand firmly against his great opposition?

We can be firm and unafraid because we are not sustained by our own resources alone, but are strengthened constantly by God's prevailing, triumphant power. (See Philippians 4:13.)

To help us stand firm against our spiritual foe we can remember that apart from Christ we can do nothing (John 15:1-5). With His help we can resist temptation and evil (James 4:7). We can hold fast to the inspired teaching of the Bible, refusing to compromise in our lives or in our message (Titus 1:9).

2. How do Satan's dangerous attacks touch our lives? What can we do to withstand our enemy's deadly assaults?

Wickedness is all around us. We see and hear about demonic powers in movies, television shows, games, and newspapers. Evil influences permeate our society and battle to control the thoughts and attitudes in our schools, homes, and work places.

To prevail against wickedness we must recognize that Satan's subtle influences in the world of thoughts and ideas are not harmless. We need to watch what the hearts and minds of ourselves and our children are exposed to. We need carefully to choose the television shows, movies, music, reading materials, etc. that we allow to touch our lives.

3. Some Christians have a gaping hole in their armor because they lack uprightness in character. How can we put on "the breastplate of righteousness" (Ephesians 6:14) and practice integrity in our lives?

As Christians of integrity, we will do what we know to be right, just, and true. We will carefully search the Scriptures to see how to live in a way that pleases God. We will diligently apply ourselves to godliness each day.

4. "The shield of faith" (Ephesians 6:16) protects us from the power of sin and helps us to withstand evil. Why do we find it hard to rely on God when we are tempted? How can we strengthen our faith in Him?

Sometimes we try to face life's temptations and trials in our own strength because we are proud, independent, and stubborn individuals. We look to God only as a final resort, when all of our efforts have failed.

Increasing our faith should start with a humble admission of our need for God (James 4:6, 7, 10). We should completely entrust ourselves to His care, knowing that He has our best interests in mind (1 Peter 5:7) and can work everything for good (Romans 8:28). Our faith and reliance on Him will grow and deepen as we read, study, memorize, and meditate upon His Word (Romans 10:17). Living by that Word will increase our faith and will develop our understanding of and confidence in the Scriptures (2 Timothy 3:14-17).

5. What can we do to preserve the integrity and authority of Scripture in our teaching and living, and to maintain an uncompromising stand on God's Word? How can the authoritative Word of God defend us from the power of Satan?

We need to resist the subtle pressures to bend Scripture's teaching to meet the current trends of our day, be accepted by others, win the praise of others, or avoid scorn or opposition (2 Timothy 4:3-5). We must not shrink from declaring the full message of the gospel (Acts 5:20). We need to publicly and privately read and study the Scriptures (1 Timothy 4:13; 2 Timothy 2:15).

Although Satan hurls temptation, false teaching, and persecution at us, the Word of God can defend us by distinguishing error from truth, pronouncing judgment on the disobedient, and promising salvation for us and for those who respond to the gospel (Hebrews 4:12, 13). Understanding of God's Word fortifies us from the enemy and his lies.

6. Prayer is an essential part of the Christian's life. How can we grow in our practice of prayer?

We can develop a habit of mingling prayer with every incident in our lives. Earnestly and continually we can take our needs to God first. We can develop a prayer list, prayer cycle, or prayer notebook to assist us in praying specifically and regularly for ourselves and others.